REEF FISH
Behavior

FLORIDA CARIBBEAN BAHAMAS

NED DELOACH

with photographer
PAUL HUMANN

NEW WORLD PUBLICATIONS, INC.

Printed by
ARTEGRAFICA
Verona, Italy

THE
DIMWIT'S
DICTIONARY

SECOND EDITION

More Than 5,000 Overused Words and Phrases and Alternatives to Them

CASTLE BOOKS

This edition published in 2008 by
CASTLE BOOKS ®
A division of Book Sales, Inc.
114 Northfield Avenue
Edison, NJ 08837

This edition published by arrangement with and permission of
Marion Street Press, Inc.
PO Box 2249
Oak Park, IL 60303

Cover design by Michelle Crisanti

Library of Congress Cataloging-in-Publication Data:

Fiske, Robert Hartwell.
        The dimwit's dictionary: 5,000 overused words and phrases and alternatives to
them / by Robert Hartwell Fiske.
                p.   cm.
        1.   English language—Synonyms and antonyms—Dictionaries.
        2.   English language—Usage—Dictionaries.
        3.   English language—Terms and phrases
        4.   Clichés—Dictionaries. I. Title

PE1591.F566 2002
423'.1—dc21

                                                                        2002008424

ISBN-13: 978-0-7858-2356-8
ISBN-10: 0-7858-2356-5

Printed in the United States of America

A Note on the Second Edition

Aside from new entries and commentary, throughout this second edition you will find quotations from classic and contemporary authors of fiction. These quotations, however well written they or their surrounding words may be, are marred, adulterated by dimwitticisms.

Each dimwitticism is a failure to write clearly and compellingly, an admission that the author could not manage an original thought or a better turn of phrase, or could not be bothered to think of one.

Dimwitticisms, as these examples make startlingly clear, yield only facile writing, only false sentiment.

About the Author

Robert Hartwell Fiske is the editor and publisher of The Vocabula Review (www.vocabula.com), a monthly online journal about the English language.

Other Books by Robert Hartwell Fiske

The Dictionary of Concise Writing (Marion Street Press, second edition, 2006)

The Dictionary of Disagreeable English Deluxe Edition (Writer's Digest Books, 2006)

101 Wordy Phrases (Vocabula Books, 2005)

101 Foolish Phrases (Vocabula Books, 2005)

101 Elegant Paragraphs (Vocabula Books, 2005)

Vocabula Bound: Outbursts, Insights, Explanations, and Oddities (editor) (Marion Street Press, 2004)

Apologia

The Dimwit's Dictionary will annoy some people and amuse others. People who feel as though I am referring to them in some of the commentary in this book may be annoyed by what I write; those who feel as though I am referring to others may be amused by it. This is an annoying, amusing book.

If the tone of my commentary is sometimes acerbic, it's because tempered persuasion is effete, and considered argument tiresome. Few of us are able to learn well by pedantic or rote methods. But if I disturb or annoy a person, is he not more likely to remember what bothered him; is he not more likely to retain what was said; is he not more likely to learn? This pedagogy may strike some as unworkable, and perhaps its efficacy is suspect, but we surely know that other methods of tutelage are largely unsuccessful.

Robert Hartwell Fiske
editor@vocabula.com

CONTENTS

To Laura
Virtual officemate (VOM); purveyor of recipes and reason; and my
good, lovely friend

The great enemy of clear language is insincerity. When there is a gap between one's real and one's declared aims, one turns as it were instinctively to long words and exhausted idioms, like a cuttlefish squirting out ink.

George Orwell, "Politics and the English Language"

Thoughts, that breathe, and words, that burn.

Thomas Gray, The Progress of Poesy

For I have neither wit, nor words, nor worth,
Action, nor utterance, nor the power of speech,
To stir men's blood

William Shakespeare, Julius Caesar, act 3, scene 2

Watch your thoughts; they become words.
Watch your words; they become actions.
Watch your actions; they become habits.
Watch your habits; they become character.
Watch your character; it becomes destiny.

Anonymous

Never do I ever want to hear another word. There isn't one I haven't heard.

Alan Jay Lerner and Frederick Loewe, My Fair Lady

121

Foreword

When Robert Hartwell Fiske confronts Saint Peter, I hope he remembers to tell the man that he is the founding editor of *The Vocabula Review*, the online magazine devoted to contemporary language, its delights and its disasters. Saint Peter will immediately understand that Mr. Fiske has been on the side of the angels and therefore been doing the Lord's work. My worry is that, in reply, Saint Peter will commit one or another of the solecisms, illogicalities, or barbarisms that Mr. Fiske spends his days excoriating and that he will feel the need to correct him, causing him to lose his place on the other side of the gates.

Meanwhile, on this side of the gates, to hew to this theological metaphor a bit longer, Robert Hartwell Fiske has been doing a hell of a job.

Mr. Fiske has signed on, evidently for life, for that best of all losing causes, the battle to keep language clear, fresh, free from the pollution of empty jargon, idiotic euphemism, self-serving imprecision, comic redundancy, nonsense generally. He has many famous comrades from among the dead in this battle: Jonathan Swift, H. L. Mencken, George Orwell, H. W. Fowler, Sir Ernest Gowers, and others. And, as I am sure he has discovered, many unknown, still living allies in unexpected places who get quite properly worked up over politicians, advertisers, social scientists, so-called educators, and others attempting to swindle the rest of us through nicely calculated verbal fog.

You are what you eat, the old food faddists used to say. As I read him, Robert Hartwell Fiske is saying that we are, or soon become, what we say and write. Use language slovenly, dully, dopily and we soon ourselves become sloppy, dull, dopey. In *The Dimwit's Dictionary*, he explains his reigning idea in the first paragraph of his first chapter, when he announces that "Dimwitticisms are worn-out words and phrases; they are expressions that dull our reason and dim our insight, formulas that we rely on when we are too lazy to express what we think or even to discover how we feel. The more we use them, the more we conform — in thought and feeling — to everyone else who uses them." We know soon enough what makes them "dim"; the witticism comes into play because most people who adopt such overworked words as

13

"scenario" or such cumbersome academic locutions as "in terms of" think they are being clever, if not highly sophisticated.

Language mavens come in various intensities of aggression. Some come as recent graduates of the Gestapo school of language correction; one has only to read them to feel the leather glove sting across one's cheeks, the word *schweinhund* ringing in one's ears. Some come on as school masters, simply unable to understand why anyone would wish to split an infinitive or end a sentence with a preposition. Some come on as pussycats passing along to us their amazement at the wild and wayward curiosities of language, but always attempting to avoid seeming either formidable or forbidding.

My own favorite among the great language mavens is H. W. Fowler, whose tone I should describe as superior commonsensical. Here, for example, is the great man on those damnable split infinitives: "The English-speaking world may be divided into (1) those who neither know nor care what a split infinitive is; (2) those who do not know but care very much; (3) those who know and condemn; (4) those who know and approve; and (5) those who know and distinguish." Such is Fowler's elevated superiority. Here is his commonsense: "We maintain, however, that a real split infinitive, though not desirable in itself, is preferable to either of two things, to real ambiguity and to patent artificiality." In other words, the Fowler line is, split away before writing anything stupid. But then he adds: "We will split infinitives sooner than be ambiguous or artificial; more than that, we will freely admit that sufficient recasting will get rid of any split infinitives without involving either of those faults, and yet reserve to ourselves the right of deciding in each case whether recasting is worthwhile." Superior, as I say, with a saving commonsense.

Robert Hartwell Fiske's desire — it informs his tone — is to bring us to our senses, to make us understand that "our knowledge of the world expands as our familiarity with words increases" and contracts when we fall back on the categories of ineptitude he has designated the Moribund Metaphor, the Overworked Word, the Plebeian Sentiment, all of which may be said — he, in fact, does say — "blunt our understanding and quash our creativity. They actually shield us from our thoughts and feelings, from any profound sense of ourselves." He is, *au fond*, a reformer who wants us to be the fully developed men and women we "were meant to be."

But Mr. Fiske's reforming impulse doesn't get in the way of his scorning clichés and trite sentiments. His lists of Overworked Words and of Torpid Terms — "off-putting," "operative," "prioritize," "pursuant to," qualify for the latter category — are there because they "keep us dumb and dispassionate. They elicit the least from us." He also suggests words that he thinks worthy of being revitalized — lovely words such as "bedizen," "bootless," "quondam" — while what he calls Withered Words ought, in the phrase of Paul Valery, the great French critic, to be turned over to the "numismaticians of language" to be put "away in their Cabinets, with many another verbal coin that has passed from circulation."

Robert Hartwell Fiske is a verbal trainer, the linguistic equivalent of the personal trainer one sees in gyms and health clubs. He wants us to trim the fat off our mental life; to knock off those Ineffectual Phrases, Inescapable Pairs, Infantile Phrases, and Wretched Redundancies. He has the relentlessness but none of the dogmatism of the drill sergeant.

Reformer, verbal trainer, drill sergeant, in the end Robert Hartwell Fiske is a fisher of souls, a catcher in the wry, a man who, through looking carefully at language, understands its potency and loathes its power, when misused, for making life more dreary than it ought to be. After noting the spread of flat and predictable language in the contemporary world, he exclaims: "No wonder so many of us feel barren or inconsolable: There are few words that inspire us, few words that move us, few words that thrill or overwhelm us. Persuasion has lost much of its sway, conviction, much of its claim."

Mr. Fiske is, in short, a fanatic, an extremist who apparently believes that clear language is our only hope for clear thought, that dull language deadens the mind and dampens the imagination, that a felicitous phrase is good news, that a strong prose style is a gift to be cultivated and cherished, that nothing, no, nothing in the world exceeds language in its significance to the human enterprise. As it happens, I believe in all this, too, which makes it an honor to salute a fellow fanatic and wish him and his book the great good fortune both deserve.

JOSEPH EPSTEIN

Joseph Epstein, former editor of *The American Scholar*, teaches writing and literature at Northwestern University and is the author of many books, including *Narcissus Leaves the Pool* and *Snobbery: The American Version*.

16.

PART 1

On Dimwitticisms

CHAPTER 1 gres to pg. 29 = 12 pgs

Expressions That Dull Our Reason and Dim Our Insight

Whereas a witticism is a clever remark or phrase — indeed, the height of expression — a "dimwitticism" is the converse; it is a commonplace remark or phrase. Dimwitticisms are worn-out words and phrases; they are expressions that dull our reason and dim our insight, formulas that we rely on when we are too lazy to express what we think or even to discover how we feel. The more we use them, the more we conform — in thought and feeling — to everyone else who uses them.

The Dimwit's Dictionary is a compilation of thousands of dimwitticisms (clichés, colloquialisms, idioms, and the like) that people speak and write excessively.*

The Dimwit's Dictionary categorizes dimwitticisms by the following types:†

> Foreign phrases
> Grammatical gimmicks
> Ineffectual phrases
> Inescapable pairs
> Infantile phrases

---

* Many of the entries in this book are followed by synonyms that may be used in place of the worn-out word or phrase; others are followed by commentary; and still others by both. But even the mere inclusion of an entry — one unaccompanied by synonyms or commentary — damns it as a dimwitticism.

All dimwitticisms can be defined, but not all can be translated into one- or two-word synonyms. When this is so, the best solution may be to rewrite the sentence entirely.

† Dimwitticisms, quite obviously, could be categorized by more than one of these fourteen types. Many wretched redundancies are also torpid terms, many moribund metaphors also infantile phrases, but I have sought to identify them by their principal type.

18

Moribund metaphors
Overworked words
Plebeian sentiments
Popular prescriptions
Quack equations
Suspect superlatives
Torpid terms
Withered words
Wretched redundancies

Foreign phrases

Expressions such as *ad infinitum, ad nauseam, c'est la vie, crème de la crème, fait accompli, in loco parentis, je ne sais quoi, joie de vivre, mea culpa, mirabile dictu, modus vivendi, ne plus ultra, non compos mentis, par excellence, persona non grata, quid pro quo, raison d'être, sine qua non, très, verboten,* and *vive la différence,* though perfectly good foreign words and phrases, are, when used by English-speaking people, simply wearisome.

Grammatical gimmicks

Quite simply, *and everything* is a babbler's way of describing what he was unable to. This phrase and so many others like it — *and everything like that; and stuff (things); and (or) stuff (things) like that; and this and that; anyway; I mean; (and that) kind of stuff (thing); or something or other; or whatever; this, that, and the other (thing); you had to be there* — are grammatical gimmicks that we use to make up for the misfashioned words that precede them.

These are devices that we resort to whenever we are unable to adequately explain our thoughts or feelings. Grammatical gimmicks attest to just how dull and dimwitted we have become.

Ineffectual phrases

Ineffectual phrases are the expressions people use to delay or obstruct, to bewilder or make weary. The intent of those who use ineffectual phrases is to make it appear as though their sentences are more substantial than they actually are, but not one sentence is made more meaningful by their inclusion: *(please) be advised that; I'll tell you (something); it has come to (my) attention; it is important to realize (that); it is interesting to note (that); make no mistake (about it); (to) take this opportunity (to); the fact of the matter is; the fact remains; the thing about it is; what happened (is).*

How a person speaks often reveals how he thinks. And how he thinks determines how he behaves. A person who speaks ineffectually may think ineffectually, and a person who thinks ineffectually may behave ineffectually — perhaps badly.

Ineffectual phrases add only to our being ineffectual people.

Inescapable pairs

In an inescapable pair, the first word means much the same as the second or so often accompanies the second that any distinction between them is, in effect, forfeited.

Only occasionally, that is, do we see the word *allied* without the word *closely; asset* without *valuable; baby* without *beautiful; balance* without *delicate; distinction* without *dubious; error* without *egregious; tied* without *inextricably; missed* without *sorely; poverty* without *abject; principle* without *basic.*

And only occasionally do we see the word *aid* without the word *abet; alive* without *well; effective* without *efficient; hope* without *pray; hue* without *cry; pure* without *simple.*

When two words are treated as though they were one — the plight of every inescapable pair — our keenness is compromised, our discernment endangered.

No longer does every word tell; the words themselves have become witless.

Infantile phrases

Any thought or feeling in which these expressions are found is likely to be made instantly laughable: *absolutely, positively; all of the above; because (that's why); because why?; (as) compared to what?; going on (19); I'll bet you any amount of money; in no way, shape, or form; intestinal fortitude; it takes one to know one; me, myself, and I; mission accomplished; mutual admiration society; never (not) in a million years; real, live; really and truly; (you) started it; (I) take it back; the feeling's mutual; the (L)-word; (my) whole, entire life; with a capital (A); without further ado; (62) years young; (a) zillion(s) (of).*

Also included among these phrases that strike all but the dimwitted as derisory are notorious advertising slogans (*inquiring minds want to know; where's the beef*), song and film titles (*a funny thing happened to me on the way to; I can't get no satisfaction*), and alliterative or rhymed phrases (*a bevy of beauties; chrome dome*).

Other infantile phrases are more disturbing, for they reveal an adolescent, unformed reasoning. Explanations like *in the wrong place at the wrong time, it just happened, it's a free country,* and *everything's (it's all) relative* are as farcical as they are possibly fallacious.

Moribund metaphors*

Metaphors, like similes, should have the briefest of lives. Their vitality depends on their evanescence.

Yet must we ever endure the dimwitted *(it's) a jungle (out there), an emotional roller coaster, a stroll (walk) in the park, (like) being run over (getting hit) by a (Mack) truck, (as) cool as a cucumber, everything but the kitchen sink, (as) hungry as a horse, leak like a sieve, light at the end of the tunnel, out to lunch, over the hill, pass like ships in the night, (as) phony as a three-dollar bill, (a) piece of cake, rule the roost, window of opportunity, (every parent's) worst nightmare*, and countless other metaphors that characterize people as dull, everyday speakers and writers, indeed, as platitudinarians? Nothing new do they tell us. Nothing more do they show us.

Moreover, if it weren't for our plethora of metaphors, especially, sports images — *above par, a new ballgame, batting a thousand, do (make) an end run around, down for the count, hit a home run, off base, pull no punches, stand on the sidelines, step up to the plate, took the ball and ran with it* — and war images — *a call to arms, an uphill battle, battle lines are drawn, draw fire, earn his stripes, first line of defense, in the trenches, on the firing line, take by storm* — men and, even, women would be far less able to articulate their thoughts. We would speak and write more haltingly than we already do; our thoughts and feelings more misshapen than they already are.

Moribund metaphors interfere with our understanding not only when we use them singly but also, and especially, when we use them simultaneously, that is, when we use them together, metaphor on metaphor. Frequently incongruous, these metaphors disfigure any sentence in which they are found.

■ Putting yourself under pressure to churn out work for the *cream of the crop* at the beginning of your writing career may *put the brakes on* your creativity.

■ They want to get *all their ducks in a row* and make sure they're all *singing from the same hymn sheet.*

■ And by last Christmas, for any defense contractor, the dwindling Soviet threat had evolved from *meal ticket* into *writing on the wall.*

■ Our restaurant *cost* me and my wife *an arm and a leg,* but we didn't build it without planning and we certainly wouldn't let it *go down the drain.*

■ Right now, USAir's problem is trying to determine whether this is *a soft*

---

*Rather than have a separate section on "insipid similes," I include them here. Since a metaphor can be thought of as a condensed simile (which often uses the word *as* or *like*) and a simile usually can be converted into a metaphor, this does not strike me as taking too much license.

landing for the economy or a recession, and *the jury is still out*.

■ For 20 years she was *a rising star* in the business, but by last year her success had *gone to the dogs*.

■ In the face of mounting pressure to gut or eliminate the IRS, it continues to *shoot itself in the foot* by *biting the hands that feed them*.

■ Looking at those things, *it didn't take a rocket scientist* to see there was *something rotten in Denmark*.

■ Thanks to Clinton, Lewinsky, & Co., I'm *off the hook* and it's *on the table*.

■ We expect them to *cast their net* as far and wide as possible because any *stone that's not unturned* will be questioned.

We rely on metaphors not because we feel they make our speech and writing more vivid and inviting but because we fail to learn how to express ourselves otherwise; we know not the words.

In truth, the more of these metaphors that we use, the less effective is our speech and writing. Neither interesting nor persuasive, their expression fatigues us where we thought it would inform us, annoys us where we believed it would amuse us, and benumbs us where we hoped it would inspire us.

Overworked words

The broader your knowledge of words, the greater your ability to express yourself precisely and persuasively. So many speakers and writers, however, rely on certain words — overworked words like *action, actively, amazing, appreciate, approach, attitude, awesome, basically, crisis, definitely, devastate, effect, excellence, great, impact, implement, incredible, interesting, lasting, major, meaningful, mindset, natural, nice, ongoing, parameter, pretty, really, scenario, significant, situation, strange, thing, unbelievable, very, weird.*

Words, when overworked, diminish the meaning of all that they are used to describe. Our remarks and questions both are enfeebled by these tired terms. Nothing that we express with these overworked words has the force or effectiveness of less habitually spoken, less repeatedly written words.

Moreover, since a person understands little more than what the words he is knowledgeable of convey — a word means *only* so much — to rely on so few words reveals just how limited a person's understanding of himself, and those about him, is.

Our knowledge of the world increases as our familiarity with words does.

Plebeian sentiments

Plebeian sentiments reflect the views and values of the least thoughtful among us: *be nice; (I) gave (him) the best years of (my) life; (it) gives (me) something to do; (these things) happen to other people, not to (me); I (just) don't think about it; I just work here; I'm bored (he's boring); (it) keeps (me) busy; (it's) something to look forward to; there are no words to describe (express); you think too much; what can you do; why me?*

What's more, these expressions, base as they are, blunt our understanding and quash our creativity. They actually shield us from our thoughts and feelings, from any profound sense of ourselves.

People who use these expressions have not become who they were meant to be.

✓ Popular prescriptions

Powerless to repeat an author's epigram, unfit to recite a poet's verse, more than many of us are utterly able to echo a society's slogans and clichés: *absence makes the heart grow fonder; actions speak louder than words; a picture is worth a thousand words; beauty is in the eye of the beholder; better late than never; do as I say, not as I do; forgive and forget; hope for the best but expect the worst; it takes two; keep (your) nose to the grindstone; live and learn; misery loves company; money isn't everything; neither a borrower nor a lender be; take it one day (step) at a time; the best things in life are free; the meek shall inherit the earth; the sooner the better; time flies when you're having fun; two wrongs don't make a right; what goes around, comes around; you can't be all things to all people; you can't have everything.*

Popular prescriptions are the platitudes and proverbs by which people live their lives. It is these dicta that determine who we are and how we act; they define our intellectual and moral makeup.

Dull-witted speakers and writers depend on prescriptions like these to guide them through life. For this poor populace, life is, we may surmise, laid out. From the popular or proper course, there is scant deviation; a stray thought is, for them, a gray thought.

Popular prescriptions endure not for their sincerity but for their simplicity. We embrace them because they make all they profess to explain and all they profess to prescribe seem plain and uncomplicated.

Inexorably, we become as simple as they — we people, we platitudes.

Quack equations

This is the sort of simplicity much favored by mountebanks and pretenders, by businesspeople and politicians: *a deal is a deal; a politician is a politician; a promise is a promise; a rule is a rule; bald is beautiful; bigger is better; enough is enough; ethics is ethics; fair is fair; God is love; it is what it is; less is more; more is better; perception is reality; (what's) right is right; seeing is believing; talk is cheap; the law is the law is the law; what happened happened; what's done is done.* Quack equations too readily explain behavior that the undiscerning may otherwise find inexplicable and justify attitudes otherwise unjustifiable. No remedies for shoddy reasoning, no restoratives for suspect thinking, these palliatives soothe only our simple-mindedness.

Equally distressing is that there is no end to these quack equations: *alcohol is alcohol; he is who he is; math is math; money is money is money; people are people; plastic is plastic; prejudice is prejudice; their reasoning is their reasoning; the past is the past; wrong is wrong.* Forever being fabricated and continually being merchandized, shoddy thinking is far more easily dispensed than sound thinking.

Suspect superlatives

In dimwitted usage, superlatives are suspect. That which seems most laudable is often least, that which seems topmost, bottommost, that which seems best, worst: *an amazing person; (I'm) a perfectionist; area of expertise; celebrity; class; gentleman; great; personal friend; pursuit of excellence; the best and (the) brightest; the rich and famous.*

Torpid terms

Torpid terms are vapid words and phrases that we use in place of vital ones: *a majority of; a moving experience; a number of; a step (forward) in the right direction; cautiously optimistic; (take) corrective action; degree; effectuate; extent; (a) factor; incumbent upon; indicate; input; leaves a little (a lot; much; something) to be desired; move forward; negative feelings; off-putting; operative; prioritize; proactive; pursuant to; remedy the situation; represent(s); send a message; shocked (surprised) and saddened (dismayed); significant other; subsequent to; utilize; weight in proportion (proportionate) to height.*

Formulas as flat as these keep us dumb and dispassionate. They elicit the least from us.

With these unsound formulas, little can be communicated and still less can be accomplished. Torpid terms interfere with our understanding and with our taking action; they thwart our thinking and frustrate our feeling.

Withered words

There are many rare and wonderful words that we would do well to become familiar with — words that would revitalize us for our revitalizing them — words like *bedizen; bootless; caliginous; compleat; cotquean; hebdomadal; helpmeet; logorrhea; quondam; wont.*

Withered words, however — words like *albeit; amidst; amongst;*

behoove; betwixt; ergo; forsooth; perchance; said; sans; save; thence; unbeknownst; verily; whence; wherein; whereon; wherewith; whilst — are archaic and deserve only to be forgotten. People who use them say little that is memorable.

Wretched redundancies*

Reckless writers and slipshod speakers use many words where few would do: *advance planning; at this time; consensus of opinion; dead body; due to the fact that; first and foremost; free gift; just recently; in advance of; in and of itself; in spite of the fact that; in terms of; make a determination; on a ... basis; on the part of; past experience; period of time; (the) reason (why) is because; refer back; the single best (most); until such time as.* Yet for all the words, their expression is but impoverished; more words do not necessarily signify more meaning.

Life is measured by its meaning, and a good deal of that meaning is inherent in the words we use. If so many of our words are superfluous — and thus do not signify — so much of our life is, ineluctably, meaningless.

In the end, we are no more superfluous than are the words we use.

In themselves, dimwitticisms are as innocuous as any other single word or phrase might be, but within sentences, among thoughts struggling to be expressed and ideas seeking to be understood, dimwitticisms ravage the writer's efforts as much as they do the reader's, the speaker's as much as the listener's.

Dimwitticisms give rise to ineloquence, and it is precisely this that marks so much of our speech and writing. Whatever the occasion, whether celebratory or funereal, quotidian or uncommon, people speak and write the same dimwitted words and phrases. No wonder so many of us feel barren or inconsolable: there are few words that inspire us, few words that move us, few words that thrill or overwhelm us. Persuasion has lost much of its sway, conviction, much of its claim.

Consider these further examples of dimwitted usage.

1. From a dialogue between a television correspondent and a school superintendent:

So you feel like you were *left holding the bag*?
Yes, it's fair to say we were *left out in the cold*.

---

*For a more complete listing of redundancies, see my *Dictionary of Concise Writing* (also published by Marion Street Press).

Left holding the bag and *left out in the cold* are both moribund metaphors. 2. From the spoken words of a high school "genius":

> It was *like her worst nightmare or something.*

Like is an infantile phrase, *her worst nightmare* is a moribund metaphor, and *or something* is a grammatical gimmick.

3. From the words of a computer scientist:

> The encryption technology used today is the same as that used twenty years ago by military establishments *and that type of stuff.*

And that type of stuff is a grammatical gimmick.

4. From a business consultant's economic forecast:

> *Basically,* it's a *pretty nice* forecast.

Basically, pretty, and *nice* are all overworked words.

5. From a political lobbyist's analysis:

> If we could *level the playing field,* it would be better than having them *stick out like a sore thumb.*

Level the playing field and *stick out like a sore thumb* are both moribund metaphors.

6. From the author of a college textbook:

> In the beginning, and certainly before democratic forms of government *arrived on the scene,* tribal chieftains used their armies to maintain order.

Arrive on the scene is an infantile phrase.

7. From a news program's report on the death of a woman:

> The company released a statement saying she was an outstanding employee and her colleagues are *shocked and saddened* by her death.

Shocked and saddened is a torpid term.

8. From an article by a health-care professional:

   It is interesting to note the impressive array of distinguished mental health professionals who have assumed a derogatory stance on prevention.

It is interesting to note is an ineffectual phrase.

9. From a meteorologist's weather forecast:

   Averagewise, around November 10, we see the first snowflakes of the season fall.

Averagewise is a grammatical gimmick.

10. From a police report on the death of a vagrant:

    This could have happened to anyone; he happened to be *in the wrong place at the wrong time.*

In the wrong place at the wrong time is an infantile phrase.

11. From a man speaking before a congressional committee:

    There are no words to describe how *devastating* this experience has been.

There are no words to describe is a plebeian sentiment, and *devastating* is an overworked word.

12. From a questionnaire soliciting opinions about a business service:

    Thank you in advance for your time and assistance; your answers can *make a difference.*

Thank you in advance is a plebeian sentiment, and *make a difference* is a suspect superlative.

13. From the CEO of a multimillion-dollar company:

    A mensch is a man *with a capital M.*

With a capital M is an infantile phrase.

14. From an elementary school principal's letter to parents:

Please be advised that Mr. Kline will no longer be your child's fifth-grade teacher as of Monday, November 22.

Please be advised that is an ineffectual phrase.

15. From an interview with a local government official:

The fact of the matter is these are tolls that should have been removed long ago.

The fact of the matter is is an ineffectual phrase.

16. From a newspaper article:

But few couples even bother to discuss the *"F" word* — finances — before they *tie the knot.*

The *"F" word* is an infantile phrase, and *tie the knot* is a moribund metaphor.

17. From a U.S. government official:

We will *take corrective action to the extent that* we can; we're not going to be *caught asleep at the switch.*

Both *take corrective action* and *to the extent that* are torpid terms, and *caught asleep at the switch* is a moribund metaphor.

18. From a television news correspondent:

At the end of the day, the bottom line is, no matter how powerful Karl Rove is, defending their guy here does mean protecting the president, *period.*

At the end of the day and *the bottom line* are moribund metaphors, and *period* is an infantile phrase.

19. From a high school counselor's letter of recommendation:

If he continues to get support in college, with his *incredible* effort to overcome his difficulties, he can *definitely* succeed.

Both *incredible* and *definitely* are overworked words.
20. From a letter written by a lawyer:

> The $325 is *an ounce of prevention* that will alleviate you having to *play* expensive *catch up later on down the road.*

An ounce of prevention is a moribund metaphor, *play catch up* is a moribund metaphor, and *later on down the road* is a wretched redundancy.

People who rely on dimwitticisms like these appear to express themselves more fluently and articulately than those few who do not. But this is a sham articulateness, for without the use of phrases like left holding the bag, left out in the cold, her worst nightmare, and that type of stuff, basically, level the playing field, stick out like a sore thumb, arrive on the scene, shocked and saddened, it is interesting to note, in the wrong place at the wrong time, with a capital M, a breath of fresh air, incredible, and definitely, most people would stammer helplessly.

As unsettling and dissatisfying as it can be to read a sentence in which a single dimwitticism occurs, more than one in a sentence heightens our perturbation. Moreover, to *mix* dimwitticisms, as in some of the preceding examples, compounds our distress. To mix metaphors, as in example 5 (and even example 1), has long been frowned upon by grammarians and careful users of the language. But equally disheartening is it to mix one of these categories with another. Joining a plebeian sentiment with an overworked word, as in example 11, or with a suspect superlative, as in example 12, makes a sentence, let us say, less convincing. Joining an infantile phrase with a moribund metaphor, as in example 18, surely makes a sentence less clever. What's more, to join not two but three or more categories, as in example 2, makes a sentence altogether comical and inconsiderable. No less than mixed metaphors are these combinations worthy of our derision.

Dimwitticisms are ubiquitous, and we cannot easily escape them. Few of us can express a thought without them. We learn them unknowingly; insidiously do they become part of our wording unless we recognize what they are and withstand their onslaught. Genuine articulateness is writing and speech that scarcely makes use of dimwitticisms, and it is achieved only with much effort.

Certainly, it is the least effective speakers and writers who use the most dimwitticisms. A person's ability to express himself well is inversely proportional to the number of dimwitticisms he uses.

A person who expresses himself with genuineness instead of in jargon, with feeling instead of in formulas is capable as few have been, as few are, and as few will be; this is a person to heed.

End of Chpt. 1

CHAPTER 2 *goes to pg. 45 = 16 pgs.*

Writing That Demands to Be Read Aloud, Speech That Calls to Be Captured in Print

he Dimwit's Dictionary would be incomplete without a brief discussion of what it means to express oneself well and *wittily*.

Though some dictionaries divide usage into standard English and nonstandard English — and others into standard, nonstandard, and substandard — today, our understanding of the English language would be best served if we were to recognize more exacting labels.

Let us then consider the adoption of four categories of usage.

Egregious English
Uneducated English
Everyday English
Elegant English

This scheme is largely an attempt to give recognition to speech and writing that is beyond standard, or everyday, English — to elegant English. Without such a listing, people may not understand that they *can* speak and write elegantly. Certainly, as the superfluity of dimwitticisms makes plain, elegant English is English rarely heard, English seldom seen.

Here, first, are some examples of egregious English, uneducated English, and everyday English.

Egregious English

About egregious English there is little to say — other than it is a lifeless, indeed, death-inducing, dialect that ought not to be said. Here, though, are a few examples.

■ He knew they *was* out there for 10 to 15 minutes before he *done* anything.

■ I *seen* things out there in the world that I never thought I would see.

■ My mom is the one that *brung* me up.

■ Don't you have family members that you could *of went* to?

■ Men have treated me *terrible.*

■ I took everything *literate.*

■ She wasn't being abused about *nothing.*

■ We don't go to parties *no* more; we don't go *no* where.

■ That *don't* matter, I'm still there with you, *ain't* I?

■ I shouldn't have *did* it.

■ I shot *me* a burglar.

■ Let's start over here with the two of *yous.*

■ I *gots* a lot of thinking to do.

Uneducated English

Abuses of language abound, especially among those who speak and write uneducated English.

Whereas people who aspire to write and speak the language well still maintain standards of speech and observe distinctions between words, the uneducated, like some juggernaut, massacre and obliterate. They slay nearly all that they say.

afeard (ascared). ■ He says he's *afeard* of being alone in the dark. Use *afraid* or *scared.*

alls. ■ *Alls* I can say is he was a good cop. Use *All.* ■ *Alls* you hear them talk about is their baby. Use *All.* ■ *Alls* I wanted to say is that I forgive him. Use *All.*

anyways. ■ *Anyways,* I have to go now. Use *Anyway* or Delete. ■ You shouldn't be sleeping around when you're married *anyways.* Use *anyway* or Delete.

anywheres. ■ He hasn't got *anywheres* to go. Use *anywhere.*

a (long) ways. ■ I think magazines can go *a long ways* to effecting that. Use *a long way.* ■ Is it *a long ways?* Use *a long way.*

being as. ■ *Being as* he's such a great dad, I thought he wouldn't mind. Use *Because, Considering (that), In that,* or *Since.*

being as how. ■ That's not so bad, *being as how* we didn't even know we would be on the ballot. Use *because, considering (that), in that,* or *since.*

being that. ■ *Being that* we seem to be getting along so well, I thought we might go to dinner. Use *Because, Considering (that), In that,* or *Since.*

better had. ■ You *better had* do as your father says. Use *had better, ought to,* or *should.*

complected. ■ I'm 5'2", 110 lbs., and very *light-complected.* Use *light-complexioned.*

could of. ■ I *could of* if I wanted to. Use *could have.*

don't let's (let's don't). ■ *Don't let's* get upset about it. Use *Let's not.*

drownded. ■ Two men *drownded* when their boat capsized. Use *drowned.*

drug. ■ He *drug* up the past and complained about the argument we had that time. Use *dragged.* ■ What I've done is *drug* all the chapters into one folder. Use *drag.*

good. ■ He did *good* last night. Use *well.* ■ He helps me to do *good* in school. Use *well.*

had(n't) ought. ■ I *had ought* to go. Use *ought* or *should.* ■ You *hadn't ought* tell him what she said. Use *ought not to* or *should not.*

heighth. ■ She's over 6 feet in *heighth.* Use *height.* ■ I am the same size as you in *heighth.* Use *height.*

hisself. ■ I heard it from Walter *hisself.* Use *himself.* ■ I was afraid he was going to hurt *hisself.* Use *himself.*

in regards to. ■ The system has failed me *in regards to* disciplining my kids. Use *in regard to.* ■ *In regards to* your question, the most important thing is that we don't have a father figure in our lives. Use *Concerning.*

irregardless (of). ■ Remember to treat all patients with respect and compassion *irregardless of* their health status. Use *despite, irrespective of, no matter what, regardless of,* or *whatever.*

irregardless of the fact that. ■ *Irregardless of the fact that* she was raised by someone else, she is still our daughter. Use *Although, Even though,* or *Though.*

leastways. ■ There's no sense of accomplishment, *leastways* not for me. Use *at least.*

leave us. ■ *Leave us* go now before it starts to pour. Use *Let us.*

like. ■ It's *like* déjà vu all over again. Delete *like.* ■ And she's *like,* "*Like,* he wasn't *like* anyone I've, *like,* ever met." Delete *like.* ■ And I'm *like* I just couldn't believe it. Delete *like.*

may of. ■ I *may of* met him once before. Use *may have.*

might of. ■ It *might of* been me; I *might of* been sitting in the back seat. Use *might have; might have.*

more -(i)er. ■ You're probably *more busier* than I am. Use *busier* or *more busy.* ■ I've gotten a lot *more braver.* Use *braver* or *more brave.* ■ At Christmas time, people are a little *more friendlier.* Use *friendlier* or *more friendly.*

most -(i)est. ■ We want to take this opportunity to humbly express to you our *most sincerest* appreciation for the many expressions of sympathy you have shown us. Use *most sincere* or *sincerest.* ■ The panel consisted of some of the town's *most lustiest* women. Use *most lusty* or *lustiest.*

muchly. ■ Thank you *muchly.* USE *very much.*

not hardly. ■ Is she plump? *Not hardly.* USE *Hardly.* ■ I *couldn't hardly* breathe because he had broken my ribs. USE *could hardly.*

not scarcely. ■ I *can't scarcely* hear you. USE *can scarcely.*

nowheres. ■ He was *nowheres* near their house. USE *nowhere.*

seeing as. ■ *Seeing as* you're a woman, does the audience respond to you differently? USE *Because, Considering (that), In that,* or *Since.*

seeing as how. ■ Quite possibly it is my fault *seeing as how* I did not respond the way I thought I would. USE *because, considering (that), in that,* or *since.*

seeing that. ■ *Seeing that* this isn't a programming book, you should have little trouble. USE *Because, Considering (that), In that,* or *Since.*

(my)self. ■ How about *yourself?* USE *you.* ■ She told my sister and *myself* that she was pregnant by him. USE *me.* ■ Richard and *myself* are going to lunch. USE *I.* ■ Very large people like *yourselves* can eat tiny amounts of food and not lose an ounce. USE *you.* ■ Let's hope someone comes along, like *myself,* to take his place. USE *me.* ■ We feel Mr. Roedler's comments do an injustice to collectors like *ourselves* who currently pay $1,500 to $2,000 for radios of this type. USE *us.*

should of. ■ I *should of* known. USE *should have.*

somewheres. ■ I left it *somewheres.* USE *somewhere.*

that there (those there). ■ *That there* man was the one who hit her. DELETE *there.* ■ *That* way *there,* I can get my degree a few months sooner. DELETE *there.*

theirself (theirselves). ■ Irish people I know don't think of *theirselves* as Irish. USE *themselves.*

this here (these here). ■ *This* is my little brother *here.* DELETE *here.* ■ *These* shirts *here* are lighter than those. DELETE *here.*

thusly. ■ *Thusly,* I feel he was irresponsible and I feel I should tell him.

USE *Thus.* ■ Because this was described as school shootings and *thusly* presented as gender neutral, the gendered nature of the killing and shooting was ignored. USE *thus.*

went and. ■ We *went and* called 911. DELETE *went and.* ■ He *went and* left me. DELETE *went and.*

what all. ■ She can't seem to find anyone who understands *what all* she has been through. DELETE *all.* ■ I don't know *what all* the deal was with her, but she rejected me. DELETE *all.*

where at. ■ Nobody knows *where* the $100 is *at.* DELETE *at.* ■ I know *where* she is *at.* DELETE *at.* ■ I know *where* he works *at.* DELETE *at.*

with regards to. ■ Customers are looking for standard-based applications *with regards to* networking. USE *with regard to.* ■ *With regards to* the paper you gave out recently, I don't want to read about what you have against your opponent but what you are going to do for the city. USE *With regard to.*

would have. ■ What I am sure of is if we *would have* never confronted them, these white kids would have never given in to us. USE *had.* ■ If I *would have* been Paula, I would not have started a sexual harassment lawsuit. USE *had.* ■ I wish none of this *would have* ever happened. USE *had.*

would of. ■ I asked myself what I *would of, could of,* and *should of* done. USE *would have, could have,* and *should have.*

Indeed, much uneducated English is everyday English. The language pullulates with people who hover between the uneducated and the everyday.

Everyday English

Though there are many gauges of it, everyday English is certainly marked, as well as marred, by an ignorance of the meanings of words and the distinctions between words.

Everyday speakers and writers are apt to confuse the meaning of one word for that of another. Half-conscious of the words they use and the meanings of them, these people speak and write words as if they scarcely mattered.

Everyday speakers and writers often confuse the first of the follow-

ing expressions (no more than a few of the many hundreds that are confused) with the second:

amount is confused with *number*. ■ Buy a qualifying *amount* of books and
save 10% on all your subsequent purchases of non-discounted books. Use
number. ■ All these methods will get you a minuscule *amount* of terrorists
and a maximum *amount* of drug dealers instead. Use *number*.

breech is confused with *broach*. ■ I really respect that kind of honesty, and
have *breeched* the subject at times to encourage fellow pioneers to bring
some integrity to the table in such matters. Use *broached*. ■ When dis-
cussing changes in the current severance package, *breech* the topic within
the context of changes of other benefit plans. Use *broach*. ■ Since we've
breeched the subject, I have to say the Associated Press poll shows John
Kerry doing better with women by 1 percentage point than Al Gore did
with women. Use *broached*.

collaborate is confused with *corroborate*. ■ As our feedback reflects, we
applaud some comments that *collaborate* our views on the proposals for
further enhancement of relay services across the nation. Use *corroborate*.
■ At this point, we really only have Daniel's word and to back it up, it
would be necessary to find Aerojet employees or White Sands people
who could *collaborate* his statement. Use *corroborate*.

flaunt is confused with *flout*. ■ Why is Ted Kennedy a "pseudo-Catholic"
— he claims to be a Catholic but *flaunts* the rules of the church he belongs
to. Use *flouts*. ■ Companies regularly *flaunt* the laws, collecting and disseminating personal information. Use *flout*. ■ North Korea continues to
flaunt international law by speeding ahead with their nuclear program
with no consequences whatsoever. Use *flout*.

irrelevant is confused with *irreverent*. ■ It was full of *irrelevant* fun almost
to the point of Marx Brothers-style of antics, with a small dose of the horrors of war thrown in. Use *irreverent*. ■ His *irrelevant* style of humour is
both witty and makes us think of how we see ourselves. Use *irreverent*.

it's is confused with *its*. ■ By now, even the most out of touch among you
must realize that the government of the United States is at war against *it's*
own people. Use *its*. ■ Freemasonry requires that *it's* members confess a
belief in a supreme being. Use *its*.

medias is confused with *media*. ■ When suicide bombers attack schools,
bus stations, marketplaces, or other highly populated civilian areas, the

biased liberal *medias* of the world all turn a blind eye. Use *media*. ■ Her art covers many aspects and *medias*, but today she is most widely noted for her sport action figures, portraits and pet portraits, but also does seascapes, landscapes, or still life should a client request them. Use *media*. ■ I want extra batteries for the remotes, an extra bulb for the projector, two backup copies of the presentation (naturally, in two different *medias*). Use *media*.

meretricious is confused with *meritorious*. ■ I informed her that that was a *meretricious* plan except for the fact that it involves lying. Use *meritorious*. ■ They serve the public interest by reminding readers not to believe a message simply because it is widely distributed, and carries the *meretricious* authority of the published word. Use *meritorious*.

palatable is confused with *palpable*. ■ If only we could only capture that *palatable* feeling in a bottle so that it can touch us on a more regular basis, it would do so much good. Use *palpable*. ■ About six months later I remember thinking that we were headed for a full-fledged recession, there was an almost *palatable* uneasiness in the air. Use *palpable*.

proscribe is confused with *prescribe*. ■ We are on record to abide by the 1949 Geneva Conventions and their relevant sections that *proscribe* the rules of war. Use *prescribe*. ■ They often *proscribe* rules of behavior which we must follow to attain rewards or avoid punishment in this or the after world. Use *prescribe*.

respectively is confused with *respectfully*. ■ Graduates of St. Clare School will act *respectively* towards self and others. Use *respectfully*. ■ Behave *respectively* to adults and each other. Use *respectfully*.

straight-laced is confused with *strait-laced*. ■ He's as healthy and *straight-laced* a guy as you'll meet, and in today's society, that is amazing. Use *strait-laced*. ■ Anyone who's worked in advertising knows it's not exactly a *straight-laced* environment. Use *strait-laced*.

vociferous is confused with *voracious*. ■ No, he wasn't a *vociferous* reader or running a recycling business. Use *voracious*. ■ At the age of 18 she opened her own studio and began to teach; a *vociferous* reader, she read everything she could about dance and took master classes from all the recognized leaders. Use *voracious*.

where is confused with *that*. ■ I saw on TV *where* he was awarded a prize. Use *that*. ■ I read *where* your neighbor was sentenced for soliciting sex.

Use *that.* ■ It is wonderful, although I can see *where* they might have thought it went on too long. Use *that.*

who is confused with *whom.* ■ You all know exactly *who* I am talking about — which is odd considering that we don't have princes. Use *whom.* ■ This is a man *who* even Republican cohorts sometimes find disturbing, for the way he uses almost anything to his advantage. Use *whom.*

Soon, it is clear, we will be a society unable to distinguish one word from another, sense from nonsense, truth from falsehood, good from evil. We will soon utter only mono- and disyllabic words, be entertained only by what pleases our peers, and adore whatever is easy or effortless. Unfamiliar wording and original phrasing will soon sound incoherent or cacophonic to us, while well-known inanities like *have a nice day, what goes around comes around,* and *hope for the best but expect the worst* will serve as our mantra, our maxim, our motto.

Elegant English

We all know far too well how to write everyday English, but few of us apparently know how to write elegant English — English that is expressed with music as well as meaning, style as well as substance. The point of this category is to show that the language can, indeed, be spoken or written with grace and polish — qualities that much contemporary English is bereft of and could benefit from.

So prevalent is everyday English that the person who speaks correctly and uses words deliberately is often thought less well of than the person who speaks solecistically and uses slang unreservedly. Today, fluency is in disfavor. Neither everyday nor even uneducated English seems to offend people quite as much as does elegant English. People neither fume nor flinch when they hear sentences like those illustrated earlier; but let them listen to someone who speaks, or read someone who writes, elegantly, and they may be instantly repelled. Doubtless, well-turned phrases and orotund tones suggest to them a soul unslain.

Even so, it is not classism but clarity, not snobbery but sensibility that users of elegant English prize and wish to promote. Nothing so patently accessible as usage could ever be justly called invidious. As long as we recognize the categories of usage available to us, we can decide whether to speak and write the language well or badly. And we might more readily decide that elegant English is indeed vital were it more widely spoken by our public figures and more often written in our better books. Countless occasions where elegant English might have been used — indeed, ought to have been used — by a president or politician, a luminary or other notable, have passed with uninspired, if not bumbling, speech or writing.

Further, elegant English needs to be reliably compiled in a new type of dictionary — one that does indeed pay more attention to the phrases and rhetorical figures we use or might use, one that can accommodate the category of elegant English. Such a dictionary would be as new as it is old, for it would also need to note and, more than that, endorse the distinctions between words. It would even prescribe distinctions between words where, perhaps, there have been none.

Here are some examples of elegant English.

The grammatically correct *It is I* is elegant, and the grammatically incorrect *It is me* is not. ■ *It was her* who spoke to me that way. Use *It was she*. ■ He knew it was *her*, but she didn't know it was *him*. Use *she; he*.

The ubiquitous *like* is everyday, whereas *as, as if*, and *as though* are elegant. ■ He felt *like* he had been cheated by the system. Use *as though*. ■ *Like* I was saying, he didn't know what the circumstances were. Use *As*.

Elegant is *graduated from* or *was graduated from*; everyday is *graduated*. ■ Even before *graduating* college, Hughes had published two books of poetry. Use *graduating from* or *he was graduated from*. ■ I *graduated* one of the finest medical schools in the country. Use *graduated from* or *was graduated from*.

How come is everyday English, and *how has it come about that* or *how is it that* is elegant. ■ *How come* everyone else is wrong and you are right? Use *How is it that*.
Me neither, that makes two of us, and *you're not the only one* are everyday; *neither do I, no more do I*, and *nor do I* elegant. ■ I no longer trust her. *You're not the only one*. Use *Neither do I, Nor do I*, or *No more do I*. ■ I myself know nothing about the subject. *Me neither*. Use *Neither do I, Nor do I*, or *No more do I*.

Likewise or *likewise, I'm sure* in the following examples is everyday, even uneducated; the alternatives are not. ■ I'm so happy to have met you. *Likewise, I'm sure*. Use *And I, to have met you*, or *And I, you*. ■ I enjoy meeting intelligent people. *Likewise*. Use *As I do*.

A lot, very, and *very much* are hopelessly everyday expressions; *enormously, hugely, immensely, mightily, monstrously*, and *prodigiously* are not. ■ We are *very* proud of her. Use *enormously*.

All right, O.K., and *whatever* are everyday, but *(just) as you like, (just) as you please*, and *very well* are elegant. ■ I think I'll stay here for the night. *O.K.*

USE *Just as you please.* ■ I'm supposed to say that, not you. *Whatever.* USE *Very well.*

Phrases like *aren't I? aren't you?* and *wasn't I?* are everyday, but *am I not? are you not?* and *was I not?* are elegant. ■ *Aren't I* going with you next week? USE *Am I not.* ■ He was right, *wasn't he?* USE *was he not.*

Everyday are words like *awful, bad, horrible,* and *terrible.* Elegant are words like *abominable, dreadful, frightful, ghastly, hideous, insufferable, intolerable, monstrous, unspeakable,* and *unutterable.* ■ What a *terrible* place this city of yours is. USE *monstrous.* ■ This peach pie looks *horrible.* USE *frightful.*

The fact that is everyday, and the largely forgotten *that* elegant. ■ *The fact that* they declared bankruptcy means little to me if not to you. USE *That.* ■ Yes, *the fact that* she behaved like an imbecile did influence any interest we might have had in befriending her. USE *that.*

Similarly, *in order that* and *so that* are everyday; *that* is elegant. ■ We spoke to her sternly *in order that* she might learn from her mistakes. USE *that.* ■ *In order that* we might profit from our experience, he had us write an essay on what we learned from it. USE *That.*

Words like *absolutely, definitely,* and *totally* are everyday; *itself* is elegant. ■ She is *definitely lovely.* USE *loveliness itself.* ■ Throughout the whole affair, he was *absolutely kind.* USE *kindness itself.*

Extremely, so, terribly, and *very* are everyday; *in the extreme* and *too* are not. ■ It's *very* lovely. USE *too.* ■ I found his book *extremely confusing.* USE *confusing in the extreme.*

I don't believe so, I don't think so, and *no (I don't)* are everyday; *I think not* is elegant. ■ Would you like to walk along with us? Thanks, but *I don't think so.* USE *I think not.* ■ Do you have any other questions for our guest? *No.* USE *I think not.*

Phrases such as *am I to* are elegant, but *shall I* or *will I* is everyday. ■ What *will I* do with her? USE *am I to.*

Everyday are *(that's) correct, (most) definitely, I agree, (you're) right, sure;* elegant are *exactly so, just so, precisely so, quite right, quite so,* and *yes.* ■ August is hardly the time to visit Paris. *That's right.* USE *Quite right.* ■ She is the wisest person I know. *Most definitely.* USE *Exactly so.*

Expressions like *that's correct, you're right,* and *yes, she has* are everyday. Expressions like *I am* and *she has* are elegant. ■ Is it really your birthday today? *That's right.* Use *It is.* ■ Are we there already? *Yes.* Use *We are.*

A phrase such as *do you have* is everyday next to the elegant *have you.* ■ *Do I have* time to take a shower? Use *Have I.* ■ *Do you have* anything to drink? Use *Have you.*

An understood *you* is decidedly everyday; the plainly stated *do* is not. ■ We had a little adventure last night. Oh, *tell* me all about it. Use *do tell.* ■ *Leave* me alone. Use *Do leave.*

Although the first three categories of usage, egregious, uneducated, and everyday English, comprise rudimentary structures — a single word, sometimes two or three words — elegant English, a more developed style, generally requires at least a few, and often many, words, as these further examples illustrate.

1. Those who profess to favor freedom, and yet deprecate agitation, are men who want crops without plowing up the ground. They want rain without thunder and lightning. They want the ocean without the awful roar of its waters.

Frederick Douglass, Speech

2. I confess I love littleness almost in all things. A little convenient estate, a little cheerful house, a little company, and a very little feast; and, if I were to fall in love again (which is a great passion, and therefore, I hope, I have done with it), it would be, I think, with prettiness, rather than with majestical beauty.

Abraham Cowley, *Of Greatness*

3. Take away but the pomps of death, the disguises and solemn bugbears, the tinsel, and the actings by candle-light, and proper and fantastic ceremonies, the ministrels and the noise-makers, the women and the weepers, the swoonings and the shriekings, the nurses and the physicians, the dark room and the ministers, the kindred and the watchers; and then to die is easy, ready, and quitted from its troublesome circumstances.

Jeremy Taylor, *The Rule and Exercises of Holy Dying*

4. Let me wither and wear out mine age in a discomfortable, in an unwholesome, in a penurious prison, and so pay my debts with my bones, and recompense the wastefulness of my youth, with the beggary of mine age; Let me wither in a spittle under sharp, and foul, and infa-

mous diseases, and so recompense the wantonness of my youth, with that loathsomeness in mine age.

JOHN DONNE, *Let Me Wither*

5. A poor relation — is the most irrelevant thing in nature, — a piece of impertinent correspondency, — an odious approximation, — a haunting conscience, — a preposterous shadow, lengthening in the noontide of your prosperity, — an unwelcome remembrancer, — a perpetually recurring mortification, — a drain on your purse, — a more intolerable dun upon your pride, — a drawback upon success, — a rebuke to your rising, — a stain in your blood, — a blot on your scutcheon, — a rent in your garment, — a death's head at your banquet, — Agathocles' pot, — a Mordecai in your gate, — a Lazarus at your door, — a lion in your path, — a frog in your chamber, — a fly in your ointment, — a mote in your eye, — a triumph to your enemy, an apology to your friends, — the one thing not needful, — the hail in harvest, — the ounce of sour in a pound of sweet.

CHARLES LAMB, *Poor Relations*

6. Somewhere, I knew not where — somehow, I knew not how — by some beings, I knew not whom — a battle, a strife, an agony, was conducting, — was evolving like a great drama, or piece of music; with which my sympathy was the more insupportable from my confusion as to its place, its cause, its nature, and its possible issue. I, as is usual in dreams (where, of necessity, we make ourselves central to every movement), had the power, and yet had not the power, to decide it. I had the power, if I could raise myself, to will it; and yet again had not the power, for the weight of twenty Atlantics was upon me, or the oppression of inexpiable guilt. "Deeper than ever plummet sounded," I lay inactive. Then, like a chorus, the passion deepened. Some greater interest was at stake; some mightier cause than ever yet the sword had pleaded, or trumpet had proclaimed. Then came sudden alarms; hurryings to and fro; trepidations of innumerable fugitives. I knew not whether from the good cause or the bad; darkness and lights; tempest and human faces; and at last, with the sense that all was lost, female forms, and the features that were worth all the world to me, and but a moment allowed — and clasped hands, and heart-breaking partings, and then — everlasting farewells! and, with a sigh, such as the caves of hell sighed when the incestuous mother uttered the abhorred name of death, the sound was reverberated — everlasting farewells! and again, and yet again reverberated — everlasting farewells!

THOMAS DE QUINCEY, *Confessions of an Opium Eater*

7. Great is all townsmen's dread of the Beduw, as if they were the demons of this wild waste earth, ever ready to assail the Haj passengers; and there is no Beduwy durst chop logic in the dark with these often ferocious shooters, that might answer him with lead and who are heard, from time to time, firing backward into the desert all night.

Charles M. Doughty, Travels in Arabia Deserta

8. Listen! for if you are not totally callous, if your consciences are not seared, I will speak daggers to your souls, and awake you to all the horrors of guilty recollection. I will follow you with whips and stings through every maze of your unexampled turpitude, and plant thorns under the rose of ministerial approbation.

Edmund Burke, Speech

9. As to my old opinions, I am heartily sick of them. I have reason, for they have deceived me sadly. I was taught to think, and I was willing to believe, that genius was not a bawd, that virtue was not a mask, that liberty was not a name, that love had its seat in the human heart. Now I would care little if these words were struck out of the dictionary, or if I had never heard them. They are become to my ears a mockery and a dream. Instead of patriots and friends of freedom, I see nothing but the tyrant and the slave, the people linked with kings to rivet on the chains of despotism and superstition. I see folly join with knavery, and together make up public spirit and public opinions. I see the insolent Tory, the blind Reformer, the coward Whig! If mankind had wished for what is right, they might have had it long ago.

William Hazlitt, On the Pleasure of Hating

10. Poor Cromwell, — great Cromwell! The inarticulate Prophet; Prophet who could not speak. Rude, confused, struggling to utter himself, with his savage depth, with his wild sincerity; and he looked so strange, among the elegant Euphemisms, dainty little Falklands, didactic Chillingworths, diplomatic Clarendons! Consider him. An outer hull of chaotic confusion, visions of the Devil, nervous dreams, almost semi-madness; and yet such a clear determinate man's-energy working in the heart of that. A kind of chaotic man. The ray as of pure starlight and fire, working in such an element of boundless hypochondria, unformed black of darkness! And yet withal this hypochondria, what was it but the very greatness of the man? The depth and tenderness of his wild affections: the quantity of sympathy he had with things, — the quantity of insight he would yet get into the heart of things, the mastery he would yet get over things: this was his hypochondria. The man's misery, as man's misery always does, came of his greatness. Samuel Johnson too is that kind of man. Sorrow-stricken, half-distracted; the wide element of mournful

black enveloping him, — wide as the world. It is the character of a prophetic man; a man with his whole soul seeing, and struggling to see.

THOMAS CARLYLE, *Heroes and Hero Worship*

11. The character of the Italian statesman seems, at first sight, a collection of contradictions, a phantom as monstrous as the portress of hell in Milton, half divinity, half snake, majestic and beautiful above, grovelling and poisonous below. We see a man whose thoughts and words have no connection with each other, who never hesitates at an oath when he wishes to seduce, who never wants a pretext when he is inclined to betray. His cruelties spring, not from the heat of blood, or the insanity of uncontrolled power, but from deep and cool meditation. His passions, like well-trained troops, are impetuous by rule, and in their most headstrong fury never forget the discipline to which they have been accustomed. His whole soul is occupied with vast and complicated schemes of ambition, yet his aspect and language exhibit nothing but philosophical moderation. Hatred and revenge eat into his heart; yet every look is a cordial smile, every gesture a familiar caress. He never excites the suspicion of his adversaries by petty provocations. His purpose is disclosed, only when it is accomplished. His face is unruffled, his speech is courteous, till vigilance is laid asleep, till a vital point is exposed, till a sure aim is taken; and then he strikes for the first and last time. Military courage, the boast of the sottish German, of the frivolous and prating Frenchman, of the romantic and arrogant Spaniard, he neither possesses nor values. He shuns danger, not because he is insensible to shame, but because, in the society in which he lives, timidity has ceased to be shameful. To do an injury openly is, in his estimation, as wicked as to do it secretly, and far less profitable. With him the most honorable means are those which are the surest, the speediest, and the darkest. He cannot comprehend how a man should scruple to deceive those whom he does not scruple to destroy. He would think it madness to declare open hostilities against rivals whom he might stab in a friendly embrace, or poison in a consecrated wafer.

THOMAS BABINGTON MACAULAY, *Machiavelli*

12. Animated by this important object, I shall disdain to cull my phrases or polish my style; — I aim at being useful, and sincerity will render me unaffected; for, wishing rather to persuade by the force of my arguments, than dazzle by the elegance of my language, I shall not waste my time in rounding periods, nor in fabricating the turgid bombast of artificial feelings, which, coming from the head, never reach the heart. — I shall be employed about things, not words! — and, anxious to render my sex more respectable members of society, I shall try to avoid that flowery diction which has slided from essays into novels, and from novels into famil-

iar letters and conversation.

These pretty nothings — these caricatures of the real beauty of sensibility, dropping glibly from the tongue, vitiate the taste, and create a kind of sickly delicacy that turns away from simple unadorned truth; and a deluge of false sentiments and overstretched feelings, stifling the natural emotions of the heart, render the domestic pleasures insipid, that ought to sweeten the exercise of those severe duties, which educate a rational and immortal being for a nobler field of action.

MARY WOLLSTONECRAFT, *A Vindication of the Rights of Woman*

Elegant English, as these examples show, is exhilarating; it stirs our thoughts and feelings as ably as dimwitted English blurs them.

The Dimwit's Dictionary will aid us in our quest for elegant, for *wittier*, speech and writing. The goal is to promote understanding and rouse people to action. The goal is to express ourselves as never before — in writing that demands to be read aloud, in speech that calls to be captured in print.

End of chpt. 2

46.

THE
DIMWIT'S
DICTIONARY

SECOND EDITION

A

abandon all hope, ye who enter here An infantile phrase (see page 20).

(the) ABCs of A moribund metaphor (see page 21). *basics; basis; elements; essentials; foundation; fundamentals; principles; rudiments.* ■ The program will discuss the *ABCs of* eating right. REPLACE WITH *fundamentals.*

abject poverty An inescapable pair (see page 20).

abortive attempt (effort) An inescapable pair (see page 20). *breakdown; failure; malfunction.*

above and beyond the call of duty A moribund metaphor (see page 21).

above par A moribund metaphor (see page 21). *excellent; exceptional; first-class; first-rate; outstanding; remarkable; superior; superlative.*

absence makes the heart grow fonder A popular prescription (see page 23).

absence of A torpid term (see page 24). SEE ALSO *lack of; less than (enthusiastic).*

absolutely An overworked word (see page 22). *altogether; categorically; completely; entirely; fully; perfectly; positively; quite; roundly; thoroughly; totally; unconditionally; unreservedly; utterly; wholly.* SEE ALSO *definitely; most assuredly; most (very) definitely.*

absolutely, positively An infantile phrase (see page 20). ■ A programmer must *absolutely, positively* keep a finger on the format's pulse. DELETE *absolutely, positively.* ■ On a wide range of topics, he is the go-to guy — when you *absolutely, positively* have to know what happened. DELETE *absolutely, positively.*

Here's a variation that the writer may have prided himself on: ■ But what you *positively, absolutely* do not want is to get hurt in a stupid exhibition game. DELETE *positively, absolutely.*

absurd An overworked word (see page 22). *comical; extravagant; farcical; foolhardy; foolish; idiotic; illogical; imbecilic; impractical; inane; incongruous; irrational; laughable; ludicrous; moronic; nonsensical; preposterous; ridiculous; senseless; silly; unreasonable.*

accentuate the positive An infantile phrase (see page 20). *be confident; be encouraged; be heartened; be hopeful; be optimistic; be positive; be rosy; be sanguine.*

(an) accident waiting to happen A moribund metaphor (see page 21). ■ Any network that does not have a standardized backup procedure in place is *an accident waiting to happen.* ■ The fire at the InterRoyal mill was a tragic *accident waiting to happen.*

An accident waiting to happen twists seriousness into silliness. The significance of what we say, the danger, perhaps, in what we do, we seldom see when we think with such frivolous phrases. Our understanding may be distorted, our responses dulled.

accidents will happen A popular prescription (see page 23).

according to Hoyle An infantile phrase (see page 20). *accurately; by the rules; conventionally; correctly; customarily; properly; regularly; rightly; traditionally.*

ace in the hole A moribund metaphor (see page 21).

Achilles' heel (tendon) A moribund metaphor (see page 21). *defect; deficiency; disadvantage; failing; fault; flaw; foible; fragility; frailness; frailty; handicap; imperfection; liability; limitation; shortcoming; susceptibility; susceptibleness; vulnerability; vulnerableness; weakness.* ■ If the Bruins had an *Achilles' heel* last season, it was that they were a tad oversized. REPLACE WITH *weakness.*

acid test A moribund metaphor (see page 21). *assay; crucible; ordeal; proof; test; trial.*

across the board A moribund metaphor (see page 21). *(for) all; all over; (for) everyone; everyplace; everywhere; throughout (the land); universally.* ■ There is increased consumer confidence — not just here but *across the board*. REPLACE WITH *everywhere.*

> The war was over, things looked robust across the board, and Big Don was living the charmed life at the age of thirty-three. — Kevin Brennan, *Parts Unknown*

action plan A torpid term (see page 24). *action; course; direction; intention; method; move; plan; policy; procedure; route; scheme; strategy.* ■ The UN is expected to produce a global *action plan* aimed at reducing demand and improving treatment, rehabilitation, and interdiction. REPLACE WITH *strategy.*

actions speak louder than words A popular prescription (see page 23).

active An overworked word (see page 22). Only thoughtless speakers and writers, apes and jackanapes, use the adjective *active* to modify a noun. In doing so, they emasculate the meaning of these words. So common is the adjectival *active*, we might easily wonder if anything is possible or achievable, serious or sincere that does not have this word preceding it. ■ Please believe me when I tell you that the only thing that stands between you and a better, more responsive government is your *active participation* in the process. DELETE *active*. ■ Nor did the president demonstrate *active interest* in the issue. DELETE *active*. ■ Some practitioners think that *active movement* might be the key to a cure. DELETE *active*. ■ An *active search* is on for the shooter. DELETE *active*. SEE ALSO *actively*.

actively An overworked word (see page 22). The popular use of *actively* suggests that any verb not affixed to it is feckless.

We cannot simply *consider* an idea lest we be accused of not thinking; we cannot simply *engage* in a pursuit lest we be accused of not trying; we cannot simply *participate* in a conversation lest we be accused of not speaking. ■ Another possibility is *actively being considered* by the administration: the use of force. DELETE *actively*. ■ The core group of ASC founders worried that the membership was restricted too narrowly to policing, so they *actively encouraged* others to participate. DELETE *actively*. ■ I have no intention of mailing a second letter to anyone who does not *actively show* an interest in becoming part of my collectors club. DELETE *actively*. ■ Police are *actively searching* for the killer, *actively looking* in all areas, and *actively examining* all the evidence. DELETE *actively*. ■ Not only do many people not enjoy speaking in public, they *actively dislike* and even fear it. DELETE *actively*. ■ Seek them out *actively*. DELETE *actively*. ■ Right now we're not *actively aware* of what her true motivation was. DELETE *actively*. ■ Reporters get mired in routine like everyone and need, from time to time, to *actively work* on expanding the number of places they go and the variety of people with whom they talk. DELETE *actively*.

Here is an example of just how absurd our fixation on *actively* has become: ■ Among the new features of WSF2 R3.3 that he is *actively looking forward to* is the statistical information that can be provided through SMF records. DELETE *actively*. SEE ALSO *active*.

acutely aware An inescapable pair (see page 20). ■ Fans have become *acutely aware* that player strikes and lockouts are battles over who gets the biggest piece of what the fan provides.

adamantly oppose An inescapable pair (see page 20).

add fuel to the fire A moribund metaphor (see page 21). *activate; aggravate; agitate; animate; arouse; awaken; encourage; enkindle; enliven; exacerbate; excite; feed; foment; heighten; ignite; impassion; incite; increase; inflame; intensify; invigorate; make worse; nourish; prod; provoke; rejuvenate; revitalize;* *revive; rouse; shake up; stimulate; stir up; vitalize; worsen.*

add insult to injury A moribund metaphor (see page 21). *aggravate; arouse; enkindle; enliven; exacerbate; excite; feed; foment; heighten; ignite; impassion; incite; increase; inflame; intensify; invigorate; make worse; nourish; prod; provoke; rouse; shake up; stimulate; stir up; what's worse; worsen.*

ad infinitum A foreign phrase (see page 19). *ceaselessly; endlessly; evermore; forever; forevermore; to infinity; without limit.*

ad nauseam A foreign phrase (see page 19).

advance planning A wretched redundancy (see page 25). *planning.* ■ This project will require a lot of *advance planning*. DELETE *advance*.

advance warning A wretched redundancy (see page 25). *warning.* ■ Although the bank's 17,000 employees have known for more than a month that the ax was about to fall, the *advance warning* did little to blunt the effect. DELETE *advance*. SEE ALSO *forewarn; warn in advance*.

advice is cheap A quack equation (see page 23).

afraid (frightened; scared) of (his) own shadow A moribund metaphor (see page 21). *afraid; alarmed; apprehensive; cowardly; craven; diffident; fainthearted; fearful; frightened; pavid; pusillanimous; recreant; scared; terror-striken; timid; timorous; tremulous.*

after (once; when) all is said and done
A wretched redundancy (see page 25).
all in all; all told; altogether; eventually; finally; in all; in the end; on the whole; overall; ultimately. ■ *After all is said and done*, it truly was an exceptional decade. REPLACE WITH *On the whole.* ■ *When all is said and done*, we humans are a curious species. REPLACE WITH *All told.*

> Inside the sack was a spool of twine, a sugar cane knife to sever the umbilical cord, and a garden spade to bury the creature once all was said and done. — Kathy Hepinstall, *The House of Gentle Men*

after the fact A torpid term (see page 24). *afterward; later.* ■ We don't have a choice, *after the fact*. REPLACE WITH *afterward.*

age before beauty A popular prescription (see page 23).

(the) agony and the ecstasy A moribund metaphor (see page 21).

agree to disagree An infantile phrase (see page 20).

ahead of the game A moribund metaphor (see page 21). *advantageous; auspicious; blessed; charmed; enchanted; favored; felicitous; flourishing; fortuitous; fortunate; golden; happy; in luck; lucky; propitious; prosperous; successful; thriving.*

ahead of (his) time A moribund metaphor (see page 21). *advanced; ground-breaking; innovative; inventive; new; original; pioneering; progressive; radical; revolutionary; unconventional.*

aid and abet An inescapable pair (see page 20). *abet; aid; assist; encourage; help; support.* ■ One of the best-known detectives comes from literature in the person of Sherlock Holmes, a private investigator *aided and abetted* by his friend Dr. Watson. REPLACE WITH *assisted.*

> The two women were simply aiding and abetting each other to disband the Seraglio. — Penelope Fitzgerald, *Human Voices*

airtight alibi An inescapable pair (see page 20).

à la A foreign phrase (see page 19) (see page 19). *according to; in the manner of; like.* ■ I don't want to put myself in a bad position and get beat *à la* this man. REPLACE WITH *like.* ■ The media may be engaged in a witch hunt *a la* the late U.S. Senator Joe McCarthy and perhaps should cut back on their coverage. REPLACE WITH *in the manner of.*

alas A withered word (see page 24). *regrettably; sadly; sorrowfully; unfortunately; unhappily.* ■ *Alas*, the program checks only the first two directory entries. REPLACE WITH *Unfortunately.*

alas and alack An infantile phrase (see page 20). *regrettably; sadly; sorrowfully; unfortunately; unhappily.*

albatross around (my) neck A moribund metaphor (see page 21). *affliction;*

burden; charge; cross; difficulty; encumbrance; hardship; hindrance; impediment; load; obstacle; obstruction; onus; oppression; ordeal; problem; trial; trouble; weight. ■ Then came that unspeakable song, "Begin the Beguine," which is still *an albatross around my neck*. REPLACE WITH *a burden*.

albeit A withered word (see page 24). *although; even if; even though; though.* Like other withered words, *albeit* strikes some people as more exquisite sounding — and therefore, apparently, more intellectual sounding — than any of its synonyms. But this is perceived by only the deaf and the dimwitted. ■ *Albeit* somewhat dated, a study performed eight years ago is attracting attention once again. REPLACE WITH *Although*.

alive and kicking A moribund metaphor (see page 21). *alive; blooming; doing well; energetic; existent; existing; extant; fit; flourishing; growing; hale; hardy; healthful; healthy; hearty; live; lively; living; prospering; robust; sound; still exists; strong; surviving; thriving; vigorous; vital; well; well-off.* One of the consequences of endlessly saying and hearing and writing and reading formulaic phrases is that, eventually, people *do* become weary of them.

But instead of expressing themselves differently — more eloquently or more inventively, perhaps — people will simply substitute one word in these selfsame formulas for another.

Thus, along with *alive and kicking*, there is, for instance, *alive and well* (SEE) and even *alive and thriving*; along with *a thing of the past*, there is *a phenomenon of the past*; along with *business as usual*, there is *politics as usual* (SEE) and *life as usual*; along with *mover and shaker*,

there is *mover and shaper*; along with *neck of the woods*, there is the noisome *portion of the earth*; along with *needs and wants*, there is *needs and desires*; along with *in no way*, there is *in no way, shape, or form* and the preposterous *in no way, shape, form, or fashion*; along with *remedy the situation*, there is *rectify the situation*; along with *out the window*, there is *out the door*; and along with *nothing could be further from the truth*, there is, incomprehensibly, *nothing could be further from the actual facts*.

Would that it ended here, but there are also far too many people who begin with a hackneyed phrase and then transmogrify it into an ever-so-silly, garish one.

Thus, *between a rock and a hard place* (SEE) becomes: ■ In the past decade, newspaper publishers have been squeezed *between the Net and a hard place*. ■ The Al Queda fighters are *between an anvil and a hammer*.

A needle in a haystack (SEE) becomes: ■ Her friend wrote back and said this was impossible, like looking for *a needle on the bottom of the ocean*.

From bad to worse (SEE) becomes: ■ Moscow now has about 90 days to try to keep a *bad situation from collapsing into something infinitely worse*.

Doesn't have a snowball's chance in hell (SEE) becomes: ■ There is nobody on Russia's political horizon who embraces Mr. Yeltsin's westernized brand of economic policy and *has a Siberian snowball's chance of winning a presidential election*.

An accident waiting to happen (SEE) becomes: ■ The holidays are *a cornucopia of awkward moments waiting to happen*. ■ Expectations are resentments *waiting to happen*.

Not with a bang but with a whimper

(SEE) becomes: ■ This week *started out with a bang and ended with a whimper* for bank stocks. ■ Hurricane Bonnie hit New England *with a whimper, not a bang.* ■ After *beginning my career there with a bang, I cannot end with a whimper.* ■ It could *end with a whimper or a wallop.*

Walk softly and carry a big stick (SEE) becomes: ■ The guiding principle in foreign policy of this administration seems to be *speak loudly and carry a twig.*

Snatch victory from the jaws of defeat (SEE) becomes: ■ In the end, Republicans will simply *snatch defeat from the jaws of victory* if they successfully oust a president they loathe but lose their majorities in both houses of Congress as a result.

Light at the end of the tunnel (SEE) becomes: ■ Is it possible that we're actually seeing a *light at the end of* Star Trek's *TV continuum?*

Not worth the paper it's written (printed) on (SEE) becomes: ■ Consumers can put their trust in a few of these Web site seals, but in many cases they *aren't worth the pixels that they're painted with.*

Going to hell in a hand basket (SEE) becomes: ■ The good news, culturally speaking, is that if we're *going to Hell in a Saks shopping bag,* at least we are going there slowly.

People propagate these monstrosities. Equally distressing is that, in doing so, they think they *are* being clever and inventive. Among pedestrian people, this is what it means to be thoughtful, this is what it means to be creative.

Is it any wonder that speech is so often soporific, writing so often wearisome?

alive and well An infantile phrase (see page 20). *alive; blooming; doing well;* *energetic; existent; existing; extant; fit; flourishing; growing; hale; hardy; healthful; healthy; hearty; live; lively; living; prospering; robust; sound; still exists; strong; surviving; thriving; vigorous; vital; well; well-off.* ■ Scholarship and readership are *alive and well* and will outlast the publishing binge of the commercial houses. REPLACE WITH *flourishing.* ■ The work ethic of American workers is unquestionably *alive and well.* REPLACE WITH *sound.*

all and sundry A wretched redundancy (see page 25). *all; everybody; everyone; everything.* SEE ALSO *various and sundry.*

> From morning till night you saw her sitting on a low chair in the kitchen, surrounded by a Chinese cook and two or three native girls, giving her orders, chatting sociably with all and sundry, and tasting the savoury messes she devised. — W. Somerset Maugham, *The Moon and Sixpence*

all dressed up and no place to go An infantile phrase (see page 20).

all ears A moribund metaphor (see page 21). *attentive; heedful; listening; paying attention; paying heed.*

(as) all get-out A moribund metaphor (see page 21). *acutely; awfully; consumedly; exceedingly; extraordinarily; extremely; greatly; hugely; immensely; intensely; mightily; prodigiously; severely; terribly; very.* ■ He was *funny as all get-out.* REPLACE WITH *extremely funny.*

all hell broke loose A moribund metaphor (see page 21).

all mouth A moribund metaphor (see page 21). *boastful; vainglorious.*

all of the above An infantile phrase (see page 20). ■ Are you just looking for a companion or are you looking for a sexual partner? *All of the above.* SEE ALSO *none of the above.*

all over the lot (map) A moribund metaphor (see page 21). *diffuse; dispersed; disseminated; scattered; strewn; unfocused.*

all roads lead to Rome A moribund metaphor (see page 21).

all rolled into one A moribund metaphor (see page 21). *admixture; amalgam; blend; combination; mix; mixture.*

all's fair in love and war A popular prescription (see page 23).

all's well that ends well A popular prescription (see page 23).

all systems (are) go A moribund metaphor (see page 21).

all that glitters isn't gold A popular prescription (see page 23).

(and) all that jazz A grammatical gimmick (see page 19) (see page 19). ■ He tells me what to do *and all that jazz.* DELETE *and all that jazz.*

all the world's a stage A moribund metaphor (see page 21).

all things considered A wretched redundancy (see page 25). *all in all; all told; altogether; in all; on the whole; overall.*

all (good) things must end A popular prescription (see page 23).

all thumbs A moribund metaphor (see page 21). *ambisinister; awkward; blundering; bumbling; bungling; clumsy; gawky; gauche; ham-handed; heavy-handed; inapt; inept; lubberly; lumbering; maladroit; uncoordinated; uncouth; ungainly; ungraceful; unhandy; unskillful; unwieldy.*

all-time record A wretched redundancy (see page 25). *record.* ■ If anyone spent time skiing here this past winter, they'd be happy to find the boycott has resulted in an *all-time record* number of skiers. DELETE *all-time.* SEE ALSO *record-breaking; record-high.*

all to the good A moribund metaphor (see page 21). *adequate; advantageous; beneficial; satisfactory; sufficient.*

(from) all walks of life A moribund metaphor (see page 21).

all wet A moribund metaphor (see page 21). *amiss; astray; deceived; deluded; erring; erroneous; fallacious; false; faulty; inaccurate; incorrect; in error; misguided; misinformed; mislead; mistaken; not correct; not right; wrong.* ■ Whoever told you that alcohol is less of a problem than drugs is *all wet.* REPLACE WITH *mistaken.*

all wool and a yard wide A moribund metaphor (see page 21). *actual; authentic; earnest; genuine; heartfelt; honest; legitimate; pure; real; sincere; sterling; true; unadulterated; unalloyed; veritable.*

all work and no play makes Jack a dull boy A popular prescription (see page 23).

(the) almighty dollar A moribund metaphor (see page 21).

along the lines of A wretched redundancy (see page 25). *akin to; close to; like; resembling; similar to; such as.* ■ It's generally safe to ask people in the field if they've ever heard of anything *along the lines of* your idea. REPLACE WITH *similar to.*

It turned out that Agent Samson was something along the lines of a circuit-court speech therapist. — David Sedaris, *Me Talk Pretty One Day*

(the) alpha and omega of A moribund metaphor (see page 21).

amazing An overworked word (see page 22). *astonishing; astounding; extraordinary; marvelous; outstanding; remarkable; spectacular; startling; stunning; wonderful; wondrous.*

(an) amazing person A suspect superlative (see page 24). *An amazing person* is so only in the eyes of another who, we can be confident, is not.

(as) American as apple pie An insipid simile. *all-American; decent; good; honorable; moral; proper; pure; right; straight; upright; virtuous; wholesome.*

(the) American dream A suspect superlative (see page 24). ■ *The American dream* has become a nightmare.

amidst A withered word (see page 24). *amid; among.* ■ *Amidst* all of life's distractions, what is it that keeps us going? REPLACE WITH *Amid.*

(9:00) a.m. ... (in the) morning A wretched redundancy (see page 25). *(9:00) a.m.; (in the) morning.* ■ Monday's events can be defined to occur from *8 a.m.* Monday *morning* to *8 a.m.* Tuesday *morning.* DELETE *morning.* ■ This *morning* at 9:35 *a.m.* a violent clash took place between prisoners. DELETE *a.m..*

amongst A withered word (see page 24). *among. Amongst,* among the potentially bright, is preferable to *among,* but only because their potential has yet to be realized. ■ If there is a lack of confidence *amongst* those concerned, the strictly political element will be more obvious. REPLACE WITH *among.* ■ Someday, perhaps, you'll be able to find it *amongst* the software programs at the store, next to SimCity: the ultimate Language Architect simulator game. REPLACE WITH *among.* ■ I'm sorry to say that after passing this *amongst* some colleagues, we've agreed that it is not thorough enough to be a reference book. REPLACE WITH *among.*

a (absolute) must An infantile phrase (see page 20). *compulsory; critical; essential; imperative; important; indispensable; mandatory; necessary; needed; obligatory; required; requisite; vital.* ■ Prior experience writing user and technical documentation in the computer field is *a must.* REPLACE WITH *necessary.* ■ It is not *an absolute must* to read this part in order to use the second half of the book. REPLACE WITH *essential.* SEE ALSO *(a) must have; (a) must see; a (definite) plus.*

analyze to death A moribund metaphor (see page 21). *analyze; anatomize; dissect; examine; inspect; investigate; scrutinize; study.* SEE ALSO *to death.*

(that's) ancient history A moribund metaphor (see page 21). *aged; ancient; antediluvian; antique; archaic; elderly; history; hoary; old; past; prehistoric; seasoned; superannuated.*

> He knew that it had something to do with the scandal, but that was ancient history. — Frederick Buechner, *The Storm*

and all A grammatical gimmick (see page 19) (see page 19). — We're going to look at all these nice buildings *and all*. DELETE *and all*. SEE ALSO *and all like that; and everything (else); and everything like that; and stuff (things); and (or) stuff (things) like that.*

and all like that A grammatical gimmick (see page 19). ■ We went to different agencies for help *and all like that*. DELETE *and all like that*. ■ He caught me off guard by asking for my name and address *and all like that*. DELETE *and all like that*. SEE ALSO *and all; and everything (else); and everything like that; and stuff (things); and (or) stuff (things) like that.*

and etc. (et cetera) A wretched redundancy (see page 25). *and so forth; and so on; and the like; etc.* ■ We bought the generic-brand products *and et cetera*. REPLACE WITH *and the like*.

and everything (else) A grammatical gimmick (see page 19). ■ We're responsible for this baby *and everything else*. DELETE *and everything else*. ■ You guys fight *and everything*, but she really does love you. DELETE *and everything*. SEE ALSO *and all; and all like that; and everything like that; and stuff (things); and (or) stuff (things) like that.*

and everything like that A grammatical gimmick (see page 19). ■ They adopted that way of speaking *and everything like that*. DELETE *and everything like that*. ■ Don't you feel cheap and used *and everything like that*? DELETE *and everything like that*. SEE ALSO *and all; and all like that; and everything (else); and stuff (things); and (or) stuff (things) like that.*

and/or A wretched redundancy (see page 25). *and; or.* ■ Implant dentistry can be an effective alternative to dentures *and/or* missing teeth. REPLACE WITH *or*. ■ But computers may make both more attractive than the alternatives adopted by those who have abandoned wives *and/or* children by failing to meet their financial obligations. REPLACE WITH *and*.

and so on, and so forth A grammatical gimmick (see page 19). *and so forth; and so on; and the like; etc.* ■ I'm more interested in films about human relationships *and so on, and so forth*. DELETE *and so on, and so forth*. SEE ALSO *blah, blah, blah; et cetera, et cetera.*

and stuff (things) A grammatical gimmick (see page 19). ■ His legs had black bruises on them *and stuff*. DELETE *and stuff*. ■ The customers are really nice people; they're friends *and stuff*. DELETE *and stuff*. ■ They wanted him to go for a bike ride *and things*. DELETE *and things*. ■ We got invited to a lot of Hollywood parties *and things*. DELETE *and things*. SEE ALSO *and all; and all like that; and everything (else); and everything like that; and (or) stuff (things) like that.*

and (or) stuff (things) like that A grammatical gimmick (see page 19). ■ I love women — the way they look *and stuff like that.* DELETE *and stuff like that.* ■ People shouldn't shoot others over money *or things like that.* ■ I was upset because my mother went through two divorces *and stuff like that.* DELETE *and stuff like that.* ■ As a big man, they look at you as big and healthy *and things like that.* DELETE *and things like that.* SEE ALSO *and all; and all like that; and everything (else); and everything like that; and stuff (things); and (or) stuff (things) like that.*

and that kind of stuff (thing) A grammatical gimmick (see page 19). ■ He's a changed man; he's learned to read and write *and that kind of thing.* DELETE *and that kind of thing.* ■ I was working on getting the house settled *and that kind of stuff.* DELETE *and that kind of stuff.* SEE ALSO *(and that) sort of stuff (thing); (and that) type of stuff (thing).*

and that sort of stuff (thing) A grammatical gimmick (see page 19). ■ I enjoy walking in the park *and that sort of thing.* DELETE *and that sort of thing.* SEE ALSO *(and that) kind of stuff (thing); (and that) type of stuff (thing).*

and that type of stuff (thing) A grammatical gimmick (see page 19). ■ I like interesting conversation and interacting *and that type of thing.* DELETE *and that type of thing.* SEE ALSO *(and that) kind of stuff (thing); (and that) sort of stuff (thing).*

and this and that A grammatical gimmick (see page 19). ■ He told me how much he cared for me *and this and that.* DELETE *and this and that.* SEE ALSO *and this, that, and the other (thing).*

and this, that, and the other (thing) A grammatical gimmick (see page 19). ■ She would say to me, you've got the best of both worlds, you're special, you're loved, *and this, that, and the other thing.* DELETE *and this, that, and the other thing.* SEE ALSO *and this and that.*

an embarrassment of riches A moribund metaphor (see page 21). ■ It's a city with *an embarrassment of riches.*

anent A withered word (see page 24). *about; concerning.*

angel of mercy A suspect superlative (see page 24). *liberator; redeemer; rescuer; savior.*

anon A withered word (see page 24). 1. *at another time; later.* 2. *shortly; soon.* 3. *at once; immediately.*

another day, another dollar A popular prescription (see page 23).

ants in (his) pants A moribund metaphor (see page 21). *aflame; agitated; animated; anxious; eager; ebullient; effervescent; enthusiastic; excitable; excited; fervent; fervid; fidgety; frantic; frenzied; impassioned; impatient; jittery; jumpy; lively; nervous; restive; restless; skittish; spirited.*

a ... number (of) A torpid term (see page 24). ■ You can use the computer to discover students who are making *a large number of* mistakes. REPLACE WITH *many.* ■ *A good number* of troops have arrived in Moscow. REPLACE WITH *Hundreds.* ■ *An overwhelming number of* the participatory lenders have now joined the major banks in supporting our plan. REPLACE WITH *Almost all.* ■

They are dependent upon the teacher's pension, which is fully given at the age of 62 after *a large number of teaching years*. REPLACE WITH *years of teaching*. SEE ALSO *a (the) ... majority (of); a sufficient number (of)*.

any and all A wretched redundancy (see page 25). *all; any.* ■ *Any and all* accidental needle sticks must be reported to the physician at once. REPLACE WITH *All*. ■ We welcome *any and all* comments and suggestions regarding this project. REPLACE WITH *any*.

anyhow A grammatical gimmick (see page 19). ■ *Anyhow*, we got the divorce in 1992. DELETE *Anyhow*. SEE ALSO *anyway*.

any port in a storm A moribund metaphor (see page 21).

anything and everything A wretched redundancy (see page 25). *anything; everything.* ■ A deadbeat is generally defined as a person dedicated to getting *anything and everything* possible for nothing. REPLACE WITH *anything* or *everything*.

anything (everything) is possible A popular prescription (see page 23).

any (every) (reason) under the sun A moribund metaphor (see page 21). *any; anything; every; everything.* ■ Americans sue each other for almost *every reason under the sun*. REPLACE WITH *every reason*. ■ Our catering staff has designed a menu and planned a party for almost *every reason under the sun*. REPLACE WITH *every reason*. ■ Capricorns have the ability to write about *any subject under the sun*. REPLACE WITH *anything*.

> Maybe from the old habit of doing everything as one man; maybe when you have lived for four years in a world ordered completely by men's doings, even when it is danger and fighting, you don't want to quit that world: maybe the danger and the fighting are the reasons, because men have been pacifists for every reason under the sun except to avoid danger and fighting. — William Faulkner, *The Unvanquished*

anyway A grammatical gimmick (see page 19). ■ But *anyway*, I'll talk to you later in the week. DELETE *anyway*. ■ So *anyway*, I just wanted to verify that with you. DELETE *anyway*. SEE ALSO *anyhow*.

appearances can be deceiving A popular prescription (see page 23).

(first) appear (arrive; come) on the horizon (scene) An infantile phrase (see page 20). *appear; arise; become available; begin; be introduced; come forth; develop; emerge; occur; originate; present itself; rise; spring; start; surface; turn up.* ■ TTAPS first *appeared on the scene* in 1983 with a paper in *Science* on the global atmospheric consequences of nuclear war. REPLACE WITH *emerged*. ■ It is at the time of William the Conqueror and the Norman conquest of England that the office of shire reeve first *appears on the scene*. REPLACE WITH *appears*. ■ Clearly, oil used in the internal combustion engine presented such a change when it *came on the scene* in the early part of the twentieth century. REPLACE WITH *became available*. ■ The Component Object Model (COM) has caused more confusion since its inception than any other programming technology that has ever *appeared on the horizon.* REPLACE WITH *been introduced.*

(an) apple a day keeps the doctor away A popular prescription (see page 23).

(the) apple doesn't fall far from the tree A popular prescription (see page 23).

(the) apple of (my) eye A moribund metaphor (see page 21). *hero; idol; star.*

apple polisher A moribund metaphor (see page 21). *apparatchik; bootlicker; fawner; flatterer; flunky; follower; lackey; minion; stooge; sycophant; toady; yes-man.*

(like comparing) apples and oranges A moribund metaphor (see page 21). *different; discordant; discrepant; dissimilar; dissonant; divergent; incommensurable; incommensurate; incomparable; incompatible; incongruent; incongruous; inconsistent; inconsonant; inharmonious; unlike.*

(I) appreciate (it) An overworked word (see page 22). 1. *grateful for; thankful for; thank you.* 2. *admire; cherish; esteem; prize; relish; treasure; value; welcome.* ■ We *appreciate* your help. REPLACE WITH *are grateful for.* ■ We *appreciate you* being here. REPLACE WITH *thank you for.* ■ I *appreciate* every letter that I have received. REPLACE WITH *treasure.* SEE ALSO *common courtesy.*

(take) appropriate (corrective) action A torpid term (see page 24). This ponderous phrase will stem one person's drive while it saps another's desire. From such a phrase, only dull-minded deeds

and uninspired acts may result, which is quite likely all that the user of it, bureaucrat he routinely is, either wishes for or can imagine. ■ If there's enough public pressure, they may rethink their defensiveness and begin to *take corrective action.* REPLACE WITH *behave differently.* ■ The bus driver was not exercising caution in this instance, and *corrective action has been taken.* REPLACE WITH *he was fired.* ■ By the time someone decides to *take corrective action,* the customer may be in too deep. REPLACE WITH *act.* ■ The district will *take appropriate action* to ensure such occurrences do not continue. REPLACE WITH *do what it must.*

April showers bring May flowers A popular prescription (see page 23).

area of expertise A suspect superlative (see page 24). *area; business; calling; craft; field; forte; job; line; métier; occupation; profession; specialty; strength; trade; vocation.*

(we) aren't going to take it anymore A popular prescription (see page 23).

(cost an) arm and a leg A moribund metaphor (see page 21). 1. *a big (brobdingnagian; colossal; enormous; gargantuan; giant; gigantic; grand; great; huge; immense; large; massive; monstrous; prodigious; tremendous; vast) amount; a great deal; a lot.* 2. *costly; dear; expensive; high-priced; precious; priceless; valuable.*

armed and dangerous An inescapable pair (see page 20).

armed (themselves) to the teeth A moribund metaphor (see page 21).

(an) army of A moribund metaphor (see page 21). SEE ALSO *a barrage of.*

paround about A wretched redundancy (see page 25). *about; around.* ■ Let's meet *around about* noon. REPLACE WITH *about* or *around.*

(work) around the clock A moribund metaphor (see page 21). *always; ceaselessly; constantly; continually; continuously; endlessly; eternally; everlastingly; evermore; forever; forevermore; frequently; interminably; nonstop; permanently; perpetually; persistently; recurrently; regularly; repeatedly; unceasingly; unremittingly.*

(just; right) around the corner A moribund metaphor (see page 21). *approaching; at hand; close; close by; coming; forthcoming; imminent; impending; near; nearby; nearing; pending; vicinal.* ■ Deregulation of the utility industry was *just around the corner,* and several other companies were prepared to enter the market. REPLACE WITH *at hand.*

arrow in the heart A moribund metaphor (see page 21). *injury; wound.*

(another) arrow in the quiver A moribund metaphor (see page 21). *device; gambit; maneuver; means; plan; ploy; ruse; scheme; stratagem; strategy; tactic; tool; trick.*

art is long, and life is short A popular prescription (see page 23).

as a man sows so shall he reap A popular prescription (see page 23).

as a matter of fact A wretched redundancy (see page 25). *actually; indeed; in fact; in faith; in reality; in truth; truly.* ■

As a matter of fact, children get disappointed when they grow up to find the adult's prescription didn't match the real world. REPLACE WITH *In truth.*

as a result of A wretched redundancy (see page 25). *after; because of; by; due to; following; for; from; in; out of; owing to; through; with.* ■ *As a result of* this letter, ten of us did not attend the wedding. REPLACE WITH *Because of.*

as defined in (the dictionary) An infantile phrase (see page 20). This is a device that only abecedarian writers would ever use; even so, it should always be x'd. ■ *As defined in the dictionary,* "Health is the absence of disease." ■ Creationism, *as defined in Webster's New Universal Dictionary,* is the doctrine that matter and all things were created, substantially as they now exist, by an omnipotent creator, and not gradually evolved or developed. SEE ALSO *(the) dictionary defines.*

as far as ... (goes; is concerned) A wretched redundancy (see page 25). *about; as for; as to; concerning; for; in; of; on; over; regarding; respecting; to; toward; with.* ■ *As far as* improvements *go,* you'd have a battle. REPLACE WITH *As for.* ■ *As far as* those bargains *are concerned,* attempts to place measures on the table would be regressive and an illegal act. REPLACE WITH *Concerning.* SEE ALSO *where ... is concerned.*

as far as the eye can see An insipid simile. *all around; all over; all through; broadly; everyplace; everywhere; extensively; panoramically; panoptically; throughout; ubiquitously; universally; widely.*

> The room was enormous, like something in a nightmare, one could hardly see from one end of it to the other, and as far as the eye could see was dotted with tables which were all full. — Barbara Pym, *Excellent Women*

ashes to ashes (dust to dust) A moribund metaphor (see page 21).

(like) asking for the moon An insipid simile.

ask me no questions and I'll tell you no lies A popular prescription (see page 23).

asleep at the switch (wheel) A moribund metaphor (see page 21). 1. *forgetful; careless; heedless; inattentive; lethean; neglectful; negligent; oblivious; remiss; slack; thoughtless; unmindful; unthinking.* 2. *asleep; daydreaming.*

(as) (wholesome) as mom and apple pie An insipid simile. *decent; ethical; exemplary; good; honest; honorable; just; moral; pure; righteous; straight; upright; virtuous; wholesome.*

as (you) sow, so shall (you) reap A popular prescription (see page 23).

as the crow flies A moribund metaphor (see page 21). *by air; directly; lineally; linearly; straight.*

(as) (vain) as the day is long An insipid simile. *acutely; awfully; consumedly; enormously; exceedingly; extraordinarily; extremely; greatly; hugely; immensely; intensely; mightily; prodigiously; severely; terribly; very.* ■ She's *as neurotic as the day is long.* REPLACE WITH *prodigiously neurotic.* ■ Celeste is *as bright as the day is long.* REPLACE WITH *enormously bright.*

as the saying goes (is) An infantile phrase (see page 20). This phrase reminds us of our ordinariness. *As the saying goes (is)* announces our having spoken, and thought, words that countless others have spoken and thought. What thoughts are we missing, what images are unavailable to us because we use the same damn words and phrases again and again? Let us strive for better than banality.

as to A torpid term (see page 24). *about; for; from; in; of; on; to; with.* Except when used to begin a sentence, *as to* is if not solecistic then certainly sloppy for a more precise *about* or *of, for* or *with, from* or *to, on* or *in.* This phrase, midsentence, identifies a philistine, a person who, though he writes, doesn't much care to. ■ One hint *as to* his possibly altered standing comes from the latest version of the *Encyclopaedia Britannica,* which, although Roget was an editor of the seventh edition and a contributor of more than 300,000 words to it, gives him somewhat short shrift today, with an entry of a mere twenty lines. REPLACE WITH *of.* ■ Suddenly expectations and preconceptions *as to* how things should be done and what steps could be taken disappear, often leaving the displaced family members feeling confused, resentful and, perhaps most

(stand) at the crossroads of history A moribund metaphor (see page 21).

at the drop of a hat A moribund metaphor (see page 21). *at once; directly; fast; forthwith; hurriedly; immediately; instantly; momentarily; promptly; quickly; rapidly; right away; speedily; straightaway; summarily; swiftly; without delay.* ■ You can get additional information to reporters *at the drop of a hat* if you make up a press kit in advance. REPLACE WITH *speedily.*

> She also said there was a community of radicals who considered her a heroine and would help her at the drop of a hat. — Danzy Senna, *Caucasia*

at the eleventh hour A moribund metaphor (see page 21). *belatedly; late.*

at the end of (my) rope (tether) A moribund metaphor (see page 21). *dejected; despairing; desperate; despondent; disconsolate; distressed; forlorn; frantic; frenetic; frenzied; hopeless; in despair; woebegone; woeful; wretched.*

at the end of the day A moribund metaphor (see page 21). 1. *eventually; finally; in the end; in time; ultimately.* 2. *all in all; all told; altogether; in all; on the whole; overall.*

The popular phrase was once the equally silly *in the final* (or *last*) *analysis.* More sensible phrases include *eventually, finally, in the end, in time, ultimately* (or, perhaps, *all in all, all told, overall*), but people, unsure of who they are, imitate one another; people today say *at the end of the day.* If we were less inclined to say what others say (and do what others do), the world might be a wholly differ-

ent place. Reason might even prevail.

In most instances, *at the end of the day* is unnecessary and can, without forfeiting any meaning, be deleted from a sentence. ■ We simply have to acknowledge the fact that the better side won *at the end of the day.* DELETE *at the end of the day.* ■ He wants each library, old or new, to be a place people want to come to, think is enjoyable, get a lot out of and have fun at, because *at the end of the day,* it'll just make their lives better. DELETE *at the end of the day.* ■ Like every other relationship you have personally or professionally you don't always agree on things, but *at the end of the day* he was the manager so even if I didn't like something what could I do about it? DELETE *at the end of the day.* ■ That is a step in the right direction; I just do hope that the alliance will work *at the end of the day.* DELETE *at the end of the day.*

at the helm A moribund metaphor (see page 21). *in charge; in control.*

at the top of (his) game A moribund metaphor (see page 21).

at the top of (my) lungs A moribund metaphor (see page 21). *blaringly; boisterously; boomingly; deafeningly; earsplittingly; loudly; noisily; obstreperously; resoundingly; roaringly; stentorianly; thunderingly; thunderously; tumultuously; vociferously.*

at (behind) the wheel A moribund metaphor (see page 21). *in charge; in control.*

at this time A wretched redundancy (see page 25). This phrase and several others like it, including *at the present* *time, at this juncture in life, at this moment in our national life, at this point in time, at this point in time right now, at this stage in the history of my life, at this time in our history,* mean no more than *at present, now, today,* or *yet.* ■ We don't see any significant breakthroughs *at this juncture.* REPLACE WITH *now.* ■ What can she do to help you *at this stage of the game?* REPLACE WITH *now.* ■ *At this point in time,* the conditions for an agreement have not been met. REPLACE WITH *The conditions for an agreement have not yet been met.* SEE ALSO *at that time.*

attitude An overworked word (see page 22). For example: *attitude problem; holier-than-thou attitude; patronizing attitude; superior attitude; wait-and-see attitude.*

attributable to the fact that A wretched redundancy (see page 25). *because; considering; for; in that; since.* ■ This is *attributable to the fact that* people at Pan Am have done such a good job. REPLACE WITH *because.* SEE ALSO *due to the fact that; owing to the fact that.*

at (his) wit's end A moribund metaphor (see page 21). *baffled; befuddled; bewildered; confounded; confused; disconcerted; flummoxed; mixed up; muddled; nonplused; perplexed; puzzled.*

audible (inaudible) to the ear A wretched redundancy (see page 25). *audible (inaudible).* SEE ALSO *visible (invisible) to the eye.*

au naturel A foreign phrase (see page 19). *bare; disrobed; naked; nude; stripped; unclothed; uncovered; undressed.*

(an) avalanche of A moribund metaphor (see page 21). ■ His antics on the court spawned *an avalanche of* imitators. SEE ALSO *a barrage of.*

(your) average Joe A moribund metaphor (see page 21). *average; common; commonplace; conventional; customary; everyday; familiar; mediocre; middling; normal; ordinary; quotidian; regular; standard; typical; unexceptional; unremarkable; usual.*

avid reader A suspect superlative (see page 24). An *avid reader* suggests someone who reads little more than mysteries, gothic novels, and self-help books.

These are people whose avidity is more for how many books they read than it is for any meaning in books — people, that is, who prefer counting to reading. ■ I am an *avid reader* and my advanced education includes writing courses and an intensive two-year writing course.

avoid (it) like the plague An insipid simile. 1. *abhor; abominate; detest; hate; loathe.* 2. *avoid; dodge; elude; eschew; evade; recoil from; shirk; shrink from; shun; spurn.* ■ Your clients will probably either love Los Angeles or *avoid it like the plague.* REPLACE WITH *loathe it.*

> The clientele were mostly businessmen in three-piece suits laughing boisterously and blowing cigarette smoke in each other's faces, or talking earnestly and confidently to well-dressed young women who were more probably their secretaries than their wives. In short, it was the kind of establishment that Robyn would normally have avoided like the plague. — David Lodge, *Nice Work*

awesome An overworked word (see page 22). Like *awful* and *terrific*, the word *awesome* has been made ridiculous by those who are bent on using it solely in its most popular sense.

Awesome means *awe-inspiring, majestic*, or *terrifying*, but of late, it most often merely means *fantastic* or *terrific* or *great*, worn words all. SEE ALSO *awful; terrific*.

awful An overworked word (see page 22). *Awful* means *awe-inspiring* or *terrifying*, but of late, it means no more than *very bad* or *unpleasant*. SEE ALSO *awesome; terrific*.

(the) ax fell A moribund metaphor (see page 21).

ax (axe) to grind A moribund metaphor (see page 21). *animosity; bitterness; enmity; grievance; grudge; hostility; indignation; ill will; offense; rancor; resentment; spite; umbrage.*

B

babe in the woods A moribund metaphor (see page 21). *amateur; apprentice; beginner; greenhorn; neophyte; newcomer; novice; novitiate; tyro.* ■ He's a *babe in the woods* compared to Clinton and the Democrats. REPLACE WITH *neophyte*.

back (up) against the wall A moribund metaphor (see page 21). 1. *catch; corner;*

enmesh; ensnare; entangle; entrap; net; snare; trap. 2. *at risk; endangered; imperiled; in danger; in jeopardy; threatened.* ■ People will do amazing things when *their backs are against the wall*. REPLACE WITH *they're endangered.*

(meanwhile) back at the ranch A moribund metaphor (see page 21).

back in the saddle (again) A moribund metaphor (see page 21).

> Maybe the convertible was not an attempt to get a concert pianist back in the saddle — back, as it were, on the horse that had thrown him — but an invitation to the mindless, happy, noisy, unambitious life that till then had been denied him. — Christopher Miller, *Sudden Noises from Inanimate Objects: A Novel in Liner Notes*

back into a corner A moribund metaphor (see page 21). *catch; corner; enmesh; ensnare; entangle; entrap; net; snare; trap.*

(get) back on (his) feet A moribund metaphor (see page 21). *ameliorate; amend; come round; convalesce; gain strength; get better; heal; improve; look up; meliorate; mend; rally; recover; recuperate; refresh; regain strength; renew; revive; strengthen.* ■ Even the construction industry is starting to *get back on its feet*. REPLACE WITH *recover*.

back on track A moribund metaphor (see page 21).

back to basics A torpid term (see page 24). ■ Banks and savings and loans are getting *back to basics* and concentrating on home mortgages.

back to square one A moribund metaphor (see page 21).

(go) back to the drawing board A moribund metaphor (see page 21). ■ Beware of protracted and angry discussions; they are usually a sign that there is not enough support for the idea, and you should go *back to the drawing board*.

back to the salt mines A moribund metaphor (see page 21).

back to the wall A moribund metaphor (see page 21). 1. *at risk; endangered; hard-pressed; imperiled; in a bind; in a fix; in a jam; in a predicament; in a quandary; in danger; in difficulty; in jeopardy; in peril; in trouble; jeopardized.* 2. *at bay; caught; cornered; enmeshed; ensnared; entangled; entrapped; netted; snared; trapped.*

bad apple A moribund metaphor (see page 21). *brute; degenerate; fiend; knave; lout; rake; rascal; rogue; ruffian; scamp; scoundrel; villain.*

bad blood (between them) A moribund metaphor (see page 21). *abhorrence; anger; animosity; antipathy; aversion; detestation; enmity; hate; hatred; hostility; ill will; loathing; malice; malignity; rancor; repugnance; revulsion; venom; virulence.*

bad egg A moribund metaphor (see page 21). *brute; degenerate; fiend; knave; lout; rake; rascal; rogue; ruffian; scamp; scoundrel; villain.*

badge of courage (honor) A moribund metaphor (see page 21).

(a) bad penny A moribund metaphor (see page 21). *bastard; blackguard; cad; charlatan; cheat; cheater; fake; fraud; impostor; knave; mountebank; phony; pretender; quack; rascal; rogue; scoundrel; swindler; undesirable; villain; wretch.*

(a) bad penny always turns up A popular prescription (see page 23).

bag and baggage An inescapable pair (see page 20). 1. *accouterments; baggage; bags; belongings; cases; effects; encumbrances; equipment; gear; impedimenta; luggage; portmanteaus; possessions; property; sacks; satchels; stuff; suitcases; supplies; things.* 2. *altogether; completely; entirely; fully; roundly; thoroughly; totally; utterly; wholly.*

bag of bones A moribund metaphor (see page 21). *asthenic; attenuated; bony; cachectic; emaciated; gaunt; lank; lanky; lean; narrow; rail-thin; scraggy; scrawny; skeletal; skinny; slender; slight; slim; spare; spindly; svelte; sylphid; thin; trim; wispy.*

bag (bagful) of tricks A moribund metaphor (see page 21). *accouterment; equipage; equipment; gear; paraphernalia; resources; supplies; things; tools.*

baker's dozen A moribund metaphor (see page 21). *thirteen.*

(as) bald as a baby's backside An insipid simile. *alopecic; bald; baldheaded; baldpated; glabrous; hairless; depilated; pilgarlic; smooth; tonsured.*

(as) bald as a billiard ball An insipid simile. *alopecic; bald; baldheaded; bald-*

pated; glabrous; hairless; depilated; pilgarlic; smooth; tonsured.

bald is beautiful A quack equation (see page 23).

ball of fire A moribund metaphor (see page 21). *active; animated; ardent; dynamic; emotional; energetic; impassioned; intense; lively; passionate; spirited; sprightly; vigorous; vital; vivacious.*

ballpark figure A moribund metaphor (see page 21). *appraisal; assessment; estimate; estimation; guess; idea; impression; opinion; sense.* ■ Can you give me a *ballpark figure* of how much you made last year? REPLACE WITH *idea.*

(the) ball's in (your) court A moribund metaphor (see page 21). ■ I think, nationally, *the ball is* definitely *in our court* now.

bang for (your) buck An infantile phrase (see page 20). *quality; value; worth.*

banging (my) head against the wall A moribund metaphor (see page 21).

baptism of fire A moribund metaphor (see page 21).

bare-bones (budget) A moribund metaphor (see page 21).

bare essentials (necessities) An inescapable pair (see page 20).

barefaced (bold-faced) lie An inescapable pair (see page 20).

bargaining chip A moribund metaphor (see page 21).

bark at the moon A moribund metaphor (see page 21).

(her) bark is worse than (her) bite A moribund metaphor (see page 21).

bark up the wrong tree A moribund metaphor (see page 21). *amiss; astray; deceived; deluded; erring; erroneous; fallacious; false; faulty; inaccurate; incorrect; in error; misguided; misinformed; mislead; mistaken; not correct; not right; wrong.*

> Ray had neither encouraged nor discouraged her over Minkie — he hadn't seemed at all interested in the party — although he said something about her barking up the wrong tree with John Lenier. — Tessa Hadley, *Everything Will Be All Right*

(a) barking dog never bites A popular prescription (see page 23).

(a) barrage of A moribund metaphor (see page 21). If our language seems languid, it's partly because our metaphors are moribund.

This, *a barrage of,* is one of a certain kind of moribund metaphor that is especially irksome to come upon; *a bastion of, a chorus of, a cloud of, a deluge of, a firestorm of, a flood of, a flurry of, a hailstorm of, a mountain of, an army of, an avalanche of, an explosion of, an ocean of, an orgy of, a rising tide of, a sea of, a small army of, a spate of, a storm of, a symphony of, a torrent of, a world of* are all shabby, unimaginative expressions.

These are the least evocative, the least metaphorical, of metaphors. ■ He says *the barrage of marketing* has made teens tougher to teach.

barrel of laughs A moribund metaphor (see page 21). *hilarious; hysterical; side-splitting; uproarious.*

basically An overworked word (see page 22). People often use *basically* thinking it lends an intellectual air to the meaning of their words. *Basically*, in truth, only steals the sense from whatever words accompany it, for it proclaims their uncertainty and inexactitude as loudly as it does the speaker's or writer's pomposity.

Of course, there are also people, with few pretensions, who use *basically* either because they do not know what they say or because they do not know what to say. ■ *Basically*, the program is designed to operate with the same skills used when doing the exercise with a pencil and paper. ■ If the man wants custody, he must prove the woman to be *basically* unfit. ■ The rest of the day will be *basically* partly cloudy. ■ What *basically* began as an experiment to determine whether a family-type YMCA would survive quickly evolved into a challenge to serve a very enthusiastic community. ■ *Basically*, the next step is adding the molasses.

basic (and) fundamental A wretched redundancy (see page 25). *basal; basic; elementary; essential; fundamental; primary; rudimentary.*

basic principle An inescapable pair (see page 20). Seldom do we find *principle* without the word *basic* preceding it. A principle, however, is a basic truth or assumption. ■ Whether or not you are aware of it, there are *basic principles* of human interaction. DELETE *basic*. ■ The *basic principle* of laser protection is the same as for any direct fire weapon. DELETE *basic*.

basis in fact (reality) A wretched redundancy (see page 25). *basis; fact; reality; truth; veracity.* ■ The June 2 editorial that describes the final, wheezy stages of the movement to eliminate cigarettes has no *basis in fact.* REPLACE WITH *basis.* ■ To see whether such beliefs have any *basis in fact,* five different brands of fruit cocktail were chosen. REPLACE WITH *veracity.*

(a) bastion of A moribund metaphor (see page 21). SEE ALSO *a barrage of.*

bathed in tears A moribund metaphor (see page 21).

(like) a bat out of hell An insipid simile. *abruptly; apace; at once; briskly; directly; expeditiously; fast; forthwith; hastily; hurriedly; immediately; instantaneously; instantly; posthaste; promptly; quickly; rapidly; rashly; right away; speedily; straightaway; suddenly; swiftly; wingedly.*

The word saved me, as words always have, and I could stir again, and stir I did, charging up the eastern loop of the trail back like a bat out of hell. — Jincy Willett, *Winner of the National Book Award: A Novel of Fame, Honor, and Really Bad Weather*

(has) bats in (his) belfry A moribund metaphor (see page 21). *batty; cracked; crazy; daft; demented; deranged; fey; foolish; goofy; insane; lunatic; mad; maniacal; neurotic; nuts; nutty; psychotic; raving; silly; squirrelly; touched; unbalanced; unhinged; unsound; wacky; zany.*

batten down the hatches A moribund metaphor (see page 21).

batting a thousand A moribund metaphor (see page 21).

> I was batting a thousand on predicting human behavior. Maybe *I* should become a psychologist. — Jane Mendle, *Kissing in Technicolor*

(good) batting average A moribund metaphor (see page 21).

battle lines are drawn A moribund metaphor (see page 21).

(a) beacon (ray) of hope A moribund metaphor (see page 21). *anticipation; expectancy; expectation; hope; hopefulness; optimism; possibility; promise; prospect; sanguinity.*

(please) be advised that An ineffectual phrase (see page 19) (see page 19). This phrase is designed to make the reader pay attention to whatever follows it. The effect it has on anyone with sensibility, however, is quite the opposite: *(please) be advised that* stupefies the attentive reader thereby ensuring that whatever follows it is hardly attended to and, even, roundly ridiculed. ■ *Please be advised that* some of the ads in this category may require a fee for services or processing. DELETE *Please be advised that.* ■ *Please be advised that* the valuation below is proposed and not final. DELETE *Please be advised that.* ■ *Please be advised that* this office has been retained by North American Mortgage Company to conduct real estate closing for the above-referenced property. DELETE *Please be advised that.* ■ *Please be advised that* it takes seven to ten days to process any request for medical records information. DELETE *Please be advised that.* ■ *Please be advised that* the

Norfolk County Mosquito Control Project is now accepting applications for the position of Assistant Superintendent. DELETE *Please be advised that.* ■ *Please be advised that* I will be on vacation from June 26 to July 10. DELETE *Please be advised that.* SEE ALSO *(please) be informed that; this is to inform you that.*

be-all and end-all A moribund metaphor (see page 21). *acme; ideal; perfection; quintessence; ultimate.*

(catch a) bear by the tail A moribund metaphor (see page 21).

beat about (around) the bush A moribund metaphor (see page 21). *avoid; be equivocal; be evasive; dissemble; dodge; doubletalk; equivocate; evade; fence; hedge; palter; prevaricate; quibble; shuffle; sidestep; stall; tergiversate; waffle.*

beat a path to (your door) A moribund metaphor (see page 21). *dash; hasten; hurry; hustle; make haste; race; run; rush; scamper; scurry; sprint.*

beat a (hasty) retreat A moribund metaphor (see page 21). *abscond; clear out; decamp; depart; desert; disappear; escape; exit; flee; fly; go; go away; leave; move on; part; pull out; quit; retire; retreat; run away; take flight; take off; vacate; vanish; withdraw.*

beat (his) brains out A moribund metaphor (see page 21). 1. *assail; assault; attack; batter; beat; cudgel; flagellate; flog; hit; lambaste; lash; lick; mangle; pound; pummel; strike; thrash; trounce.* 2. *annihilate; assassinate; butcher; destroy; exterminate; kill; massacre; murder; slaughter; slay.* 3. *beat; conquer; crush; defeat;*

outdo; overcome; overpower; overwhelm; prevail; quell; rout; succeed; triumph; trounce; vanquish; win. 4. attempt; drudge; endeavor; essay; exert; grind; grub; labor; moil; slave; strain; strive; struggle; sweat; toil; travail; try; work.

beat (them) hands down A moribund metaphor (see page 21). beat; conquer; crush; defeat; outdo; overcome; overpower; overwhelm; prevail; quell; rout; succeed; triumph; trounce; vanquish; win.

(like) beating (flogging) a dead horse An insipid simile. barren; bootless; effete; feckless; feeble; fruitless; futile; impotent; inadequate; inconsequential; inconsiderable; ineffective; ineffectual; infertile; insignificant; inutile; meaningless; meritless; nugatory; null; of no value; pointless; powerless; profitless; purposeless; redundant; sterile; superfluous; trifling; trivial; unavailing; unimportant; unnecessary; unproductive; unprofitable; unserviceable; unworthy; useless; vain; valueless; weak; worthless.

beat (smashed) into (to) a pulp A moribund metaphor (see page 21). 1. assail; assault; attack; batter; beat; cudgel; flagellate; flog; hit; lambaste; lash; lick; mangle; pound; pummel; strike; thrash; trounce. 2. beat; conquer; crush; defeat; outdo; overcome; overpower; overwhelm; prevail; quell; rout; succeed; triumph; trounce; vanquish; win. 3. crush; flatten; macerate; mash; pound; pulp; pulverize; squash.

> He knew that the baby was going to hit first, and he would see it, would know it for a whole fraction of a second before he was smashed into a pulp himself. — Katherine Dunn, *Geek Love*

beat (it) into the ground A moribund metaphor (see page 21). debilitate; deplete; drain; empty; enervate; exhaust; fatigue; overdo; overwork; sap; tire; wear out; weary.

beat the bushes A moribund metaphor (see page 21). hunt; look for; quest; ransack; rummage; scour; search; seek.

beat the (living) daylights out of A moribund metaphor (see page 21). 1. assail; assault; attack; batter; beat; cudgel; flagellate; flog; hit; lambaste; lash; lick; mangle; pound; pummel; strike; thrash; trounce. 2. beat; conquer; crush; defeat; outdo; overcome; overpower; overwhelm; prevail; quell; rout; succeed; triumph; trounce; vanquish; win. 3. castigate; chastise; discipline; penalize; punish.

beat the drum A moribund metaphor (see page 21). advertise; announce; broadcast; cry out; declaim; disseminate; exclaim; proclaim; promulgate; publicize; publish; shout; trumpet; yell.

beat the stuffing out of A moribund metaphor (see page 21). 1. assail; assault; attack; batter; beat; cudgel; flagellate; flog; hit; lambaste; lash; lick; mangle; pound; pummel; strike; thrash; trounce. 2. beat; conquer; crush; defeat; outdo; overcome; overpower; overwhelm; prevail; quell; rout; succeed; triumph; trounce; vanquish; win.

beat to death A moribund metaphor (see page 21). 1. annihilate; assassinate; butcher; destroy; exterminate; kill; massacre; murder; slaughter; slay. 2. debilitate; deplete; drain; empty; enervate; exhaust; fatigue; overdo; overwork; sap; tire; wear out; weary. SEE ALSO to death.

beat (him) to the punch A moribund metaphor (see page 21).

beat up on (each other) A moribund metaphor (see page 21). *assail; assault; attack; batter; beat; cudgel; flagellate; flog; hit; lambaste; lash; lick; mangle; pound; pummel; strike; thrash; trounce.*

beauteous A withered word (see page 24). *beautiful.* ■ Saturday should be a *beauteous* day. REPLACE WITH *beautiful.*

beautiful baby An inescapable pair (see page 20).

beauty and the beast A moribund metaphor (see page 21).

beauty is in the eye of the beholder A popular prescription (see page 23).

because (that's why) An infantile phrase (see page 20). ■ Why did you hit him? *Because.* SEE ALSO *it just happened.*

because of the fact that A wretched redundancy (see page 25). *because; considering; for; given; in that; since.* ■ I married him only *because of the fact that* his family has money. REPLACE WITH *because.* ■ Many people told me I had to break off my relationship with her *because of the fact that* I was being unfair to her. REPLACE WITH *because.* SEE ALSO *by virtue of the fact that; considering the fact that; given the fact that; in consideration of the fact that; in view of the fact that; on account of the fact that.*

because why? An infantile phrase (see page 20). ■ They were afraid of him, too. *Because why?* DELETE *Because.*

(no) bed of roses A moribund metaphor (see page 21). *agreeable; ambrosial; beguiling; celestial; charming; delectable; delicious; delightful; divine; enchanting; engaging; enjoyable; fun; heavenly; glorious; gratifying; inviting; joyful; joyous; luscious; pleasant; pleasing; pleasurable.*

(a) beehive of activity A moribund metaphor (see page 21). *active; astir; bustling; busy; buzzing; energetic; humming; hopping; hustling; lively; vigorous.*

(a) bee in (her) bonnet A moribund metaphor (see page 21). 1. *caprice; crotchet; fancy; humor; impulse; maggot; notion; quirk; urge; vagary; whim.* 2. *craze; enthusiasm; fixation; infatuation; mania; obsession; passion; preoccupation.*

> Poor Nelson. He has this bee in his bonnet — doing something for this girl nobody knows. — John Updike, *Rabbit Remembered*

(she's) been around the block (and back) A moribund metaphor (see page 21). 1. *adult; aged; aging; elderly; full-grown; hoary; hoary-headed; mature; old; worn.* 2. *able; adept; apt; capable; competent; deft; dexterous; experienced; expert; practiced; proficient; seasoned; skilled; skillful; veteran.*

before (you) can say (Jack Robinson) A moribund metaphor (see page 21). *abruptly; apace; at once; briskly; directly; expeditiously; fast; forthwith; hastily; hurriedly; immediately; instantaneously; instantly; posthaste; promptly; quickly; rapidly; rashly; right away; speedily; straightaway; suddenly; swiftly; unexpectedly; wingedly.*

beg, borrow, or steal A moribund metaphor (see page 21).

beggars can't be choosers A popular prescription (see page 23).

begin (start) a new chapter (in my life) A moribund metaphor (see page 21).

behind closed doors A moribund metaphor (see page 21). *clandestinely; confidentially; covertly; furtively; mysteriously; in private; in secret; privately; quietly; secludedly; secretly; slyly; stealthily; surreptitiously; undercover.*

behind every successful man stands a woman A popular prescription (see page 23).

behind the eight ball A moribund metaphor (see page 21). *at risk; endangered; hard-pressed; imperiled; in a bind; in a fix; in a jam; in a predicament; in a quandary; in danger; in difficulty; in jeopardy; in peril; in trouble; jeopardized.*

(work) behind the scenes A moribund metaphor (see page 21). *clandestinely; confidentially; covertly; furtively; mysteriously; in private; in secret; privately; quietly; secludedly; secretly; slyly; stealthily; surreptitiously; undercover.*

behind the times A moribund metaphor (see page 21). *antediluvian; antiquated; archaic; dead; obsolescent; obsolete; old; old-fashioned; outdated; outmoded; out of date; out of fashion; passé; superannuated.*

(I'll) be honest with you A plebeian sentiment (see page 23).

behoove A withered word (see page 24). 1. *be advantageous for; benefit; be worthwhile to.* 2. *be necessary for; be proper for.*

(please) be informed that An ineffectual phrase (see page 19) (see page 19). ■ *Please be informed that* your wife has retained my office in the matter of her petition for a divorce. DELETE *Please be informed that.* ■ If you are running a version of Almanac earlier than 3.0, *please be informed that* the format of the desktop data files has been changed. DELETE *please be informed that.* SEE ALSO *(please) be advised that; this is to inform you that.*

(like) being run over (getting hit) by a (Mack) truck An insipid simile. *atomized; crushed; dashed; demolished; depleted; depressed; destroyed; devastated; distraught; distressed; exhausted; obliterated; overcome; overpowered; overwhelmed; prostrate; ravaged; ruined; shattered; undone; upset.* ■ I feel *like I've been run over by a Mac truck.* REPLACE WITH *obliterated.*

bells and whistles A moribund metaphor (see page 21). *adornments; attributes; characteristics; decorations; embellishments; features; flourishes; frills; highlights; innovations; novelties; ornaments; properties; qualities; specialties; traits.* ■ They sport few of the *bells and whistles* found in programs like Netscape and Mosaic. REPLACE WITH *features.*

bell the cat A moribund metaphor (see page 21).

> It was time to bell the cat, or at least inquire about its alibi. — Joan Hess, *The Murder at the Mimosa Inn*

below par A moribund metaphor (see page 21). *inferior; poor; second-class; second-rate; shoddy; subordinate; substandard.*

(hit) below the belt A moribund metaphor (see page 21). *dishonorable; foul; inequit-able; unconscientious; underhanded; unethical; unfair; unjust; unprincipled; unscrupulous; unsportsmanlike.*

below (under) the radar (of) (screen) A moribund metaphor (see page 21). 1. *disregarded; hidden; ignored; imperceptible; indiscernible; invisible; overlooked; undetectable; undetected; unheard of; unknown; unnoticeable; unnoticed; unobserved; unperceived; unrevealed; unseen.* 2. *discreet; inconspicuous; self-effacing; unassuming; understated; unobtrusive.* ■ The underreported remain *below the radars of* most news organizations. REPLACE WITH *imperceptible to.* ■ We don't need to be *under the radar* anymore, we need to be out there. REPLACE WITH *unobtrusive.*

belt-tightening (measures) A moribund metaphor (see page 21).

bend (my) ear A moribund metaphor (see page 21).

bend over backward(s) A moribund metaphor (see page 21). *aim; attempt; endeavor; essay; exert; labor; moil; strain; strive; struggle; toil; try hard; undertake; work at.* ■ If anything, he will have to *bend over backward* to not appear to be showing favoritism. REPLACE WITH *struggle.*

be nice A plebeian sentiment (see page 23). *"Be nice,"* we often are admonished. There can be no complaint with being agreeable when agreeability is warranted, but to soporiferously accept niceness as a virtue, untarnished and true, is utterly benighted.

To be capable of expressing anger and indignation is thwarted by our society's placing a premium on politeness.

Let us not, of course, be rude gratuitously, nor seek to be singular for its own sake, nor foolish or fantastic for the quick cachet. Do, however, let us become more concerned with giving fuller expression to ourselves.

We do possibly irreparable harm to ourselves when we, to avoid unpleasantness, fail to show another how we truly feel. Unknown to ourselves and unknowable to others we homunculi are, for anonymity is won when anger is lost. SEE ALSO *if you can't say something nice, don't say anything; I'm sorry.*

bent out of shape A moribund metaphor (see page 21). 1. *agitated; anxious; aroused; displeased; disquieted; excited; flustered; perturbed; troubled; upset; worried.* 2. *acerbated; angered; annoyed; bothered; disturbed; exasperated; galled; irked; irritated; miffed; nettled; provoked; rankled; riled; roiled; upset; vexed.*

(the) best and (the) brightest A suspect superlative (see page 24). *best; brightest; choice; choicest; elite; excellent; finest; first-class; first-rate; foremost; greatest; highest; matchless; nonpareil; optimal; optimum; outstanding; paramount; peerless; preeminent; premium; prominent; select; superior; superlative; top; unequaled; unexcelled; unmatched; unrivaled; unsurpassed.* ■ He decried the "cult of efficiency" into which have fallen so many of *the best and brightest* of the conservative young. REPLACE WITH *the brightest.* ■ Bandied about were the names of several of *the best and brightest* of the next generation. REPLACE WITH *the elite.*

(the) best defense is a good offense A popular prescription (see page 23).

(the) best (that) money can buy A suspect superlative (see page 24).

(in) (the) best of all (possible) worlds A suspect superlative (see page 24). *best; choice; elite; excellent; finest; first-class; first-rate; foremost; greatest; highest; ideal; matchless; nonpareil; optimal; optimum; outstanding; paramount; peerless; preeminent; premium; prominent; select; superior; superlative; supreme; top; unequaled; unexcelled; unmatched; unrivaled; unsurpassed.* ■ *In the best of all possible worlds,* test procedures for which neither type of error is possible could be developed. REPLACE WITH *ideally.*

best of the bunch (lot) A suspect superlative (see page 24). *best; brightest; choice; choicest; elite; excellent; finest; first-class; first-rate; foremost; greatest; highest; matchless; nonpareil; optimal; optimum; outstanding; paramount; peerless; preeminent; premium; prominent; select; superior; superlative; top; unequaled; unexcelled; unmatched; unrivaled; unsurpassed.*

best-selling author A suspect superlative (see page 24). *Best-selling authors,* of course, are often responsible for the worst written books. SEE ALSO *a good read; a (must) read.*

(the) best (greatest) thing since sliced bread A moribund metaphor (see page 21).

(the) best things in life are free A popular prescription (see page 23).

(she's) (the) best thing that ever happened to (me) A plebeian sentiment (see page 23).

bet (your) bottom dollar (life) A moribund metaphor (see page 21). ■ I would have *bet my bottom dollar* that this would not have happened.

(my) better half An infantile phrase (see page 20). *consort; helpmate; helpmeet; husband; mate; spouse; wife.*

better late than never A popular prescription (see page 23).

better safe than sorry A popular prescription (see page 23).

(it's) better than nothing A popular prescription (see page 23).

bet the farm (ranch) (on) A moribund metaphor (see page 21).

between a rock and a hard place A moribund metaphor (see page 21). *at risk; endangered; hard-pressed; imperiled; in a bind; in a dilemma; in a fix; in a jam; in a predicament; in a quandary; in danger; in difficulty; in jeopardy; in peril; in trouble; jeopardized.* ■ When you need to regenerate a degraded stripe set with parity, you will be faced with a *rock and a hard place* dilemma. DELETE *rock and a hard place.*

> But now my father's advice and my sister's counsel war in my head. Between a rock and a hard place, I must find a middle ground. — Donna Hill, *An Ordinary Woman*

between Scylla and Charybdis A moribund metaphor (see page 21). *at risk; endangered; hard-pressed; imperiled; in a bind; in a dilemma; in a fix; in a jam; in a predicament; in a quandary; in danger; in difficulty; in jeopardy; in peril; in trouble; jeopardized.*

between the devil and the deep blue sea A moribund metaphor (see page 21). *at risk; endangered; hard-pressed; imperiled; in a bind; in a dilemma; in a fix; in a jam; in a predicament; in a quandary; in danger; in difficulty; in jeopardy; in peril; in trouble; jeopardized.*

between you and me (and the four walls) A moribund metaphor (see page 21). *classified; confidential; personal; private; privy; restricted; secret.*

betwixt A withered word (see page 24). *between.*

betwixt and between An inescapable pair (see page 20). *divided; drifting; faltering; in between; irresolute; loose; shaky; swaying; torn; tottering; uncertain; undecided; unfixed; unresolved; unsettled; unsteady; unsure; vacillating; wavering; wobbly.*

(a) bevy of beauties An infantile phrase (see page 20).

beware of Greeks bearing gifts A popular prescription (see page 23).

beyond (without) a shadow of a doubt A moribund metaphor (see page 21). *absolutely; conclusively; decidedly; definitely; incontrovertibly; indisputably; indubitably; irrefragably; irrefutably; positively; unconditionally; uncontestably; undeniably; undoubtedly; unequivocally; unmistakably; unquestionably.*

beyond the pale A moribund metaphor (see page 21). *improper; inappropriate; unacceptable; unreasonable; unseemly; unsuitable; unthinkable.*

beyond (my) wildest dreams A moribund metaphor (see page 21). *astonishing; astounding; beyond belief; beyond comprehension; breathtaking; extraordinary; fabulous; fantastic; implausible; imponderable; inconceivable; incredible; marvelous; miraculous; outlandish; overwhelming; prodigious; sensational; spectacular; unbelievable; unimaginable; unthinkable; wonderful.*

> I was incredulous because this was so far beyond my wildest hopes. — Chris Stewart, *Driving Over Lemons*

(as) big as a house An insipid simile. *big; brobdingnagian; colossal; enormous; gargantuan; giant; gigantic; grand; great; huge; immense; large; massive; monstrous; prodigious; tremendous; vast.*

(as) big as life An insipid simile.

big cheese A moribund metaphor (see page 21).
1. *administrator; boss; brass; chief; commander; director; executive; foreman; head; headman; leader; manager; master; (high) muckamuck; officer; official; overseer; president; principal; superintendent;*

supervisor. 2. *aristocrat; dignitary; eminence; lord; luminary; magnate; mogul; notable; patrician; personage; ruler; sovereign; worthy.*

big deal An infantile phrase (see page 20). *appreciable; central; climacteric; consequential; considerable; critical; crucial; essential; grave; major; material; important; meaningful; momentous; pivotal; pregnant; principal; serious; significant; substantial; vital; weighty.*

big fish in a small pond A moribund metaphor (see page 21).

bigger is better A quack equation (see page 23).

bigger isn't necessarily better A popular prescription (see page 23).

(the) bigger the better A quack equation (see page 23).

(the) bigger they are, the harder they fall A popular prescription (see page 23).

big gun A moribund metaphor (see page 21). 1. *administrator; boss; brass; chief; commander; director; executive; foreman; head; headman; leader; manager; master; (high) muckamuck; officer; official; overseer; president; principal; superintendent; supervisor.* 2. *aristocrat; dignitary; eminence; lord; luminary; magnate; mogul; notable; patrician; personage; ruler; sovereign; worthy.*

(the) big picture A moribund metaphor (see page 21). ■ Let's not make decisions without looking at *the big picture.*

big shot A moribund metaphor (see page 21). 1. *administrator; boss; brass; chief; commander; director; executive; foreman; head; headman; leader; manager; master; (high) muckamuck; officer; official; overseer; president; principal; superintendent; supervisor.* 2. *aristocrat; dignitary; eminence; lord; luminary; magnate; mogul; notable; patrician; personage; ruler; sovereign; worthy.*

big-ticket (item) A moribund metaphor (see page 21). 1. *costly; expensive; high-priced.* 2. *all-important; central; chief; imperative; important; key; main; significant; vital.* ■ We can market these *big-ticket* items, which have a large profit margin. REPLACE WITH *expensive.*

In the many months it had taken me to retrieve the box from the closet, I discovered that I had forgiven her for a number of things, although for none of the big-ticket items — like having existed at all, for instance, and then having lived so long. — Anne Lamott, *Plan B: Further Thoughts on Faith*

(like a) big weight has been lifted from (my) shoulders An insipid simile. 1. *allay; alleviate; assuage; lighten; mitigate; relieve; soothe.* 2. *deliver; disburden; disencumber; disentangle; emancipate; extricate; free; liberate; manumit; release; relieve; save; set free; unburden; unchain; unencumber; unfetter; unshackle.*

big wheel A moribund metaphor (see page 21). 1. *administrator; boss; brass; chief; commander; director; executive; foreman; head; headman; leader; manager; master; (high) muckamuck; officer; official; overseer; president; principal; superintendent; supervisor.* 2. *aristocrat;*

dignitary; eminence; lord; luminary; magnate; mogul; notable; patrician; personage; ruler; sovereign; worthy.

(a) bird in the hand (is worth two in the bush) A popular prescription (see page 23).

bird's-eye view A moribund metaphor (see page 21). *outline; overview; profile; review; sketch; summary; survey.*

birds of a feather (flock together) A moribund metaphor (see page 21). *akin; alike; commensurate; comparable; consonant; duplicate; equal; equivalent; identical; indistinguishable; interchangeable; like; same; similar; undifferentiated.* ■ Politically, they are *birds of a feather.* REPLACE WITH *indistinguishable.*

bite (his) head (nose) off A moribund metaphor (see page 21). *admonish; animadvert; berate; castigate; censure; chasten; chastise; chide; condemn; criticize; denounce; denunciate; discipline; excoriate; fulminate against; imprecate; impugn; inveigh against; objurgate; punish; rebuke; remonstrate; reprehend; reprimand; reproach; reprobate; reprove; revile; scold; swear at; upbraid; vituperate.*

bite off more than (he) can chew A moribund metaphor (see page 21). 1. *overcommit; overpledge.* 2. *arrogant; brazen; cocksure; overconfident.* ■ Even in private circles, there is concern that the government has *bitten off more than it can chew.*

> The truth was that Joe was a talented but careless performer, liable to bite off more than he could chew. — Michael Chabon, *The Amazing Adventures of Kavalier & Clay*

bite the bullet A moribund metaphor (see page 21). *bear; endure; put up with; stand; suffer; tolerate.*

bite the dust A moribund metaphor (see page 21). 1. *decease; depart; die; expire; extinguish; pass away; pass on; perish; terminate.* 2. *be beaten; be conquered; be crushed; be defeated; be outdone; be overcome; be overpowered; be overwhelmed; be quelled; be routed; be trounced; be vanquished.* 3. *cease; close; complete; conclude; derail; desist; discontinue; end; finish; halt; quit; settle; stop; terminate.* 4. *be unsuccessful; bomb; break down; collapse; fail; fall short; falter; fizzle; flop; fold; founder; mess up; miscarry; not succeed; stumble; topple.*

(they) bite the hand that feeds (them) A moribund metaphor (see page 21). *unappreciative; ungrateful; unthankful.*

bite your tongue A moribund metaphor (see page 21).

bits and pieces An inescapable pair (see page 20). *bits; chunks; components; crumbs; elements; factors; fragments; ingredients; modicums; morsels; nuggets; parts; particles; pieces; scraps; segments; shreds; snips; snippets; specks.* ■ All the *bits and pieces* that make up the whole must be carefully and objectively examined. REPLACE WITH *elements.*

> The ancestors of the place hovered over the bits and pieces of their finished lives. — Annie Proulx, *That Old Ace in the Hole*

bitter acrimony An inescapable pair (see page 20).

(a) bitter (tough) pill to swallow A moribund metaphor (see page 21).

(as) black as coal An insipid simile. *black; blackish; caliginous; dark; ebony; ecchymotic; fuliginous; inky; jet; nigrescent; nigritudinous; raven; sable; swarthy; tenebrific; tenebrous.*

(as) black as night An insipid simile. *black; blackish; caliginous; dark; ebony; ecchymotic; fuliginous; inky; jet; nigrescent; nigritudinous; raven; sable; swarthy; tenebrific; tenebrous.*

After that speech he glared at me in silence, then flung down the spear he had snatched up in his sudden rage and stalked out of the house and into the wood, but before long he was back again seated in his old place, brooding on my words with a face as black as night. — W. H. Hudson, *Green Mansions*

(as) black as pitch An insipid simile. *black; blackish; caliginous; dark; ebony; ecchymotic; fuliginous; inky; jet; nigrescent; nigritudinous; raven; sable; swarthy; tenebrific; tenebrous.*

(as) black as the ace of spades An insipid simile. *black; blackish; caliginous; dark; ebony; ecchymotic; fuliginous; inky; jet; nigrescent; nigritudinous; raven; sable; swarthy; tenebrific; tenebrous.*

black sheep (of the family) A moribund metaphor (see page 21). *curiosity; deviant; eccentric; extremist; iconoclast; individual; individualist; maverick; misfit; nonconformist; oddball; oddity; renegade; undesirable.*

Nate had been labeled the black sheep of the family years ago. — Robin Jones Gunn, *Gardenias for Breakfast*

blah, blah, blah A grammatical gimmick (see page 19). ■ He told me, I want you to come out here; I miss you; *blah, blah, blah.* DELETE *blah, blah, blah.* SEE ALSO *and so on, and so forth; et cetera, et cetera.*

blast from the past An infantile phrase (see page 20).

blatant lie An inescapable pair (see page 20).

blessed event An infantile phrase (see page 20). 1. *baby; infant; newborn.* 2. *birth; childbearing; childbirth; parturition.*

blessed with (has) the gift of gab An infantile phrase (see page 20). *babbling; blathering; chatty; facile; fluent; garrulous; glib; jabbering; logorrheic; longwinded; loquacious; prolix; talkative; verbose; voluble; windy.*

(a) blessing in disguise A moribund metaphor (see page 21).

(as) blind as a bat An insipid simile. 1. *blind; eyeless; purblind; sightless; unseeing; unsighted; visionless.* 2. *addleheaded; bovine; cretinous; decerebrate; dense; dull; dull-witted; fatuous; fat-witted; half-witted; harebrained; hebetudinous; idiotic; ignorant; imbecilic; incogitant; insensate; mindless; moronic; muddled; nescient; obtuse; phlegmatic; slow; slow-witted; sluggish; thick; torpid; undiscerning; unintelligent; vacuous; witless.*

blind faith An inescapable pair (see page 20).

(the) blind leading the blind A moribund metaphor (see page 21).

(a) blip on the (radar) screen A moribund metaphor (see page 21). *frivolous; inappreciable; immaterial; inconsequential; inconsiderable; insignificant; meager; meaningless; minor; negligible; next to nothing; nugatory; paltry; petty; scant; scanty; scarcely anything; slight; trifling; trivial; unimportant; unsubstantial; worthless.*

As laughable as it is moribund, *a blip on the (radar) screen* belies the writing ability of whoever uses it. ■ War and peace abroad was *barely a blip on the screen* compared with gun control at home. REPLACE WITH *inconsiderable*.

blondes have more fun An infantile phrase (see page 20).

bloodcurdling scream (yell) An inescapable pair (see page 20).

blood is thicker than water A popular prescription (see page 23).

blood, sweat, and tears A moribund metaphor (see page 21). *assiduity; diligence; discipline; drudgery; effort; endeavor; exertion; grind; hard work; industry; labor; moil; persistence; slavery; strain; struggle; sweat; toil; travail; work.* ■ However unautobiographical or fictional a book is, it still comes out by *blood, sweat, and tears*. REPLACE WITH *toil*.

(the) bloom is off the rose A moribund metaphor (see page 21).

blow a fuse A moribund metaphor (see page 21). *bellow; bluster; clamor; explode; fulminate; fume; holler; howl; rage; rant; rave; roar; scream; shout; storm; thunder; vociferate; yell.*

blow a gasket A moribund metaphor (see page 21). *bellow; bluster; clamor; explode; fulminate; fume; holler; howl; rage; rant; rave; roar; scream; shout; storm; thunder; vociferate; yell.*

blow away A moribund metaphor (see page 21). 1. *annihilate; assassinate; butcher; destroy; exterminate; kill; massacre; murder; slaughter; slay.* 2. *amaze; astonish; astound; awe; dazzle; dumbfound; flabbergast; overpower; overwhelm; shock; startle; stun; stupefy; surprise.*

blow by blow A moribund metaphor (see page 21).

blow (his) cover A moribund metaphor (see page 21). *ascertain; discover; expose; find out; learn.*

blow (run) hot and cold A moribund metaphor (see page 21). 1. *ambivalent; divided; indecisive; irresolute; torn; uncertain; uncommitted; undecided; unsure.* 2. *capricious; changeable; erratic; fickle; fitful; flighty; fluctuating; haphazard; inconsistent; inconstant; intermittent; irregular; mercurial; occasional; random; sometime; spasmodic; sporadic; unpredictable; unsettled; unstable; unsteady; vacillating; volatile; wavering; wayward.*

blow (my) mind A moribund metaphor (see page 21). *amaze; astonish; astound; awe; dazzle; dumbfound; flabbergast; overpower; overwhelm; shock; startle; stun; stupefy; surprise.*

> And Elizabeth said one thing at the very end that really blew Rosie's mind, about how when she first got sober, she felt as if the mosaic she had been assembling out of life's little shards got dumped to the ground, and there was no way to put it back together. — Anne Lamott, *Crooked Little Heart*

blow off steam A moribund metaphor (see page 21). 1. *bellow; bluster; clamor; complain; explode; fulminate; fume; holler; howl; object; protest; rage; rant; rave; roar; scream; shout; storm; thunder; vociferate; yell.* 2. *be merry; carouse; carry on; celebrate; debauch; disport; frolic; party; play; revel; riot; roister; rollick; romp; skylark.*

blow on the cue ball A moribund metaphor (see page 21).

blow (things) out of proportion A moribund metaphor (see page 21). *elaborate; embellish; embroider; enhance; enlarge; exaggerate; hyperbolize; inflate; magnify; overdo; overreact; overstress; overstate; strain; stretch.* ■ It was not the sort of event that has now been exaggerated and *blown out of proportion*. DELETE *and blown out of proportion*.

blow (them) out of the water A moribund metaphor (see page 21). 1. *annihilate; assassinate; butcher; destroy; exterminate; kill; massacre; murder; slaughter; slay.* 2. *beat; conquer; crush; defeat;*

outdo; overcome; overpower; overwhelm; prevail; quell; rout; succeed; triumph; trounce; vanquish; win. 3. *amaze; astonish; astound; awe; dazzle; dumbfound; flabbergast; overpower; overwhelm; shock; startle; stun; stupefy; surprise.*

blow (your) own horn A moribund metaphor (see page 21). *acclaim; applaud; bluster; boast; brag; celebrate; cheer; commend; compliment; congratulate; crow; extol; flatter; gloat; hail; honor; laud; praise; puff; salute; self-congratulate; strut; swagger.*

blow smoke A moribund metaphor (see page 21). *adumbrate; becloud; befog; camouflage; cloak; cloud; conceal; cover; disguise; dissemble; enshroud; harbor; hide; keep secret; mask; obfuscate; obscure; overshadow; screen; shroud; suppress; veil; withhold.*

blow (his) stack A moribund metaphor (see page 21). *bellow; bluster; clamor; explode; fulminate; fume; holler; howl; rage; rant; rave; roar; scream; shout; storm; thunder; vociferate; yell.*

blow the whistle (on) A moribund metaphor (see page 21). 1. *bare; betray; disclose; divulge; expose; give away; reveal; show; tell; uncover; unveil.* 2. *betray; deliver up; inform on; report; turn in.* ■ Fear of reprisal arises when people consider whether or not to *blow the whistle on* someone who violates ethical standards. REPLACE WITH *report*. ■ He *blew the whistle on* company corruption. REPLACE WITH *exposed*.

blow to bits A moribund metaphor (see page 21). *annihilate; assassinate; butcher; demolish; destroy; devastate; eradicate; exterminate; kill; massacre; murder; oblit-*

erate; pulverize; rack; ravage; raze; ruin; shatter; slaughter; slay; smash; undo; wrack; wreck.

blow (my) top A moribund metaphor (see page 21). *bellow; bluster; clamor; explode; fulminate; fume; holler; howl; rage; rant; rave; roar; scream; shout; storm; thunder; vociferate; yell.*

blow to smithereens A moribund metaphor (see page 21). *annihilate; assassinate; butcher; demolish; destroy; devastate; eradicate; exterminate; kill; massacre; murder; obliterate; pulverize; rack; ravage; raze; ruin; shatter; slaughter; slay; smash; undo; wrack; wreck.*

(until) (I'm) blue in the face A moribund metaphor (see page 21). 1. *angry; annoyed; enraged; exasperated; furious; incensed; infuriated; irate; irked; irritated; mad; raging; wrathful.* 2. *beat; bushed; debilitated; depleted; exhausted; fatigued; fed up; spent; tired; wearied; weary; worn out.*

blue-ribbon commission (committee; panel) A suspect superlative (see page 24).

boggle (my) mind An infantile phrase (see page 20). *baffle; befuddle; bemuse; bewilder; confound; confuse; disconcert; flummox; muddle; mystify; nonplus; perplex; puzzle.*

> They had been friends forever, sitting in this room for longer than Amy had been alive, although it boggled Amy's mind to think that.
> — Elizabeth Strout, *Amy and Isabelle*

(as) bold as brass An insipid simile. *audacious; bold; brash; brass; brassy; brazen; cheeky; forward; impertinent; impudent; insolent; outrageous; saucy; shameless; unabashed.*

a bolt from (out of) the blue A moribund metaphor (see page 21). *bombshell; shock; surprise; thunderbolt; thunderclap.*

bone of contention A moribund metaphor (see page 21).

bone to pick A moribund metaphor (see page 21). *animosity; bitterness; enmity; grievance; grudge; hostility; indignation; ill will; offense; rancor; resentment; spite; umbrage.*

(cite) book, chapter, and verse A moribund metaphor (see page 21). *explain; expound; lecture.* ■ She will *give me chapter and verse* about the merits of XYZ Chemical and why it should be a glorious investment. REPLACE WITH *lecture me.*

book of woes A moribund metaphor (see page 21).

bore the pants off (me) A moribund metaphor (see page 21). *annoy; bore; discourage; disgust; exasperate; exhaust; fatigue; irk; irritate; sicken; tire; wear out; weary.*

bore to death (extinction) A moribund metaphor (see page 21). *annoy; bore; discourage; disgust; exasperate; exhaust; fatigue; irk; irritate; sicken; tire; wear out; weary.* SEE ALSO *to death.*

bore to tears A moribund metaphor (see page 21). *annoy; bore; discourage; disgust; exasperate; exhaust; fatigue; irk; irritate; sicken; tire; wear out; weary.*

born to the purple A moribund metaphor (see page 21).

born under a lucky star A moribund metaphor (see page 21). *advantageous; auspicious; blessed; charmed; enchanted; favored; felicitous; flourishing; fortuitous; fortunate; golden; happy; in luck; lucky; propitious; prosperous; successful; thriving.*

born with a silver spoon in (his) mouth A moribund metaphor (see page 21). *advantageous; auspicious; blessed; charmed; enchanted; favored; felicitous; flourishing; fortuitous; fortunate; golden; happy; in luck; lucky; propitious; prosperous; successful; thriving.*

bottle up (inside) A moribund metaphor (see page 21). *block; check; contain; control; curb; hide; hold back; repress; restrain; smother; stem; stifle; suppress.*

> I became more guilty and more frightened, and kept all this bottled up inside me, and naturally, inescapably, one night, when this woman had finished preaching, everything came roaring, screaming, crying out, and I fell to the ground before the altar. — James Baldwin, *The Fire Next Time*

(the) bottom fell out A moribund metaphor (see page 21). *break down; break up; collapse; crash; crumple; disintegrate; end; fail; fall apart; fold; stop.* ■ He elected to stop financing condominium projects nearly two years before *the bot-*

tom fell out of that business.

bottomless pit A moribund metaphor (see page 21). *abyss; hades; hell; inferno; netherworld; perdition.*

(the) bottom line A moribund metaphor (see page 21). This is a bottomlessly ordinary term. People bewitched by words that have a trace of technicality to them are inclined to use it. In striving to sound technical, they manage to sound only typical. 1. *conclusion; consequence; culmination; decision; denouement; effect; end; outcome; result; upshot.* 2. *crux; essence; key; keynote; main point; salient point.* ■ The *bottom line* is that America can compete if the politicians are kept out of the picture. REPLACE WITH *upshot.* ■ The *bottom line* is that both kinds of water are generally safe. REPLACE WITH *conclusion.* ■ The *bottom line* is you get what you pay for. REPLACE WITH *main point.* ■ The *bottom line* for parents: choose gifts carefully. REPLACE WITH *keynote.* SEE ALSO *feedback; input; interface; output; parameters.*

bottom of the barrel A moribund metaphor (see page 21). 1. *alluvium; debris; deposit; detritus; dregs; grounds; lees; precipitate; remains; residue; residuum; sediment; settlings; silt; wash.* 2. *close; completion; conclusion; end; ending; finale; finish; termination.* 3. *bums; deadbeats; derelicts; duds; failures; flobs; hobos; losers; pariahs; rabble; renegades; riffraff; scum; tramps; vagabonds; vagrants; washouts.*

bottom of the heap A moribund metaphor (see page 21). *bottom; depths; nadir; pits; rock bottom.*

> You slip around the truth once, and then again, and one more time, and there you are, feeling, for a moment, that it was sudden, your arrival at the bottom of the heap. — Jane Hamilton, *A Map of the World*

bound and determined An inescapable pair (see page 20). *bent on; determined; resolute; resolved.*

> While I'm not vain enough to buy a new winter coat — I will not spend hundreds of dollars on a piece of clothing I am bound and determined not to need a month from now — I am sufficiently self-conscious to leave the coat open, counting on a thick scarf to keep out the bitter damp. — Ayelet Waldman, *Love and Other Impossible Pursuits*

bow and scrape A moribund metaphor (see page 21). *bootlick; bow; crawl; cringe; crouch; fawn; grovel; kowtow; slaver; stoop; toady; truckle.*

bowled over A moribund metaphor (see page 21). *amazed; astonished; astounded; flabbergasted; shocked; staggered; stunned; surprised.*

(like a) bowl of cherries An insipid simile. *agreeable; ambrosial; beguiling; celestial; charming; delectable; delicious; delightful; divine; enchanting; engaging; enjoyable; fun; heavenly; glorious; gratifying; inviting; joyful; joyous; luscious; pleasant; pleasing; pleasurable.*

brain drain An infantile phrase (see page 20).

brand new An inescapable pair (see page 20). ■ Did you forget he got himself a *brand new* car to drive around in? DELETE *brand*.

(the) bread always falls on the buttered side A moribund metaphor (see page 21).

bread and butter A moribund metaphor (see page 21). 1. *food; keep; livelihood; living; subsistence; support; sustenance.* 2. *basis; center; core; essence; foundation; heart; hub; mainstay; nucleus; root; soul; spirit.* ■ Interfaces are the *bread and butter* of component technology. REPLACE WITH *core*.

breadth and depth An inescapable pair (see page 20). *ambit; area; breadth; compass; degree; extent; field; magnitude; range; reach; scope; sphere; sweep.*

break (his) back A moribund metaphor (see page 21). *attempt; drudge; endeavor; essay; exert; grind; grub; labor; moil; slave; strain; strive; struggle; sweat; toil; travail; try; work.*

break down (the) barriers A moribund metaphor (see page 21).

break (my) neck A moribund metaphor (see page 21). *attempt; drudge; endeavor; essay; exert; grind; grub; labor; moil; slave; strain; strive; struggle; sweat; toil; travail; try; work.*

break out of the mold A moribund metaphor (see page 21).

(it) breaks (my) heart A moribund metaphor (see page 21). *desolate; disappoint; discourage; dishearten; dispirit; distress; sadden.*

break the bank A moribund metaphor (see page 21). *bankrupt; deplete; drain; exhaust; impoverish; pauperize; ruin.*

break the ice A moribund metaphor (see page 21).

breathe (new) life into A moribund metaphor (see page 21). *animate; arouse; enliven; exhilarate; inspire; inspirit; invigorate; revivify; spur; stimulate; vitalize; vivify.* ■ The Citizens for Limited Taxation petition would block school reform at the very time it is needed most to *breathe life into* our public schools. REPLACE WITH *invigorate.*

breathless anticipation An inescapable pair (see page 20).

(a welcome) breath of fresh air A moribund metaphor (see page 21). *animating; arousing; bracing; enlivening; exciting; exhilarating; inspiring; inspiriting; invigorating; provoking; refreshing; rousing; stimulating; vivifying.*

Of what it purports to describe, *a (welcome) breath of fresh air* offers the opposite. If intelligent or heartfelt sentences are invigorating, this dimwitticism should make us gasp as though we've been throttled by foul-smelling thoughtlessness. ■ A toy industry analyst called the news *a breath of fresh air.* REPLACE WITH *exciting.* ■ Ordinarily, I find Friedman *a welcome breath of fresh air* — he has little patience for fools and plagiarists. REPLACE WITH *refreshing.*

(a) breed apart (unto itself) A moribund metaphor (see page 21). *aberrant; abnormal; anomalistic; anomalous; atypical; bizarre; curious; deviant; different; distinct; distinctive; eccentric; exceptional; extraordinary; fantastic; foreign;* *grotesque; idiosyncratic; independent; individual; individualistic; irregular; novel; odd; offbeat; original; peculiar; puzzling; quaint; queer; rare; remarkable; separate; singular; uncommon; unconventional; unexampled; unique; unnatural; unorthodox; unparalleled; unprecedented; unusual; weird.*

(it's) a breeze A moribund metaphor (see page 21). *apparent; basic; clear; clear-cut; conspicuous; distinct; easily done; easy; effortless; elementary; evident; explicit; facile; limpid; lucid; manifest; obvious; patent; pellucid; plain; simple; simplicity itself; straightforward; translucent; transparent; unambiguous; uncomplex; uncomplicated; understandable; unequivocal; unmistakable.*

bright and early An inescapable pair (see page 20).

(as) bright as a (new) button An insipid simile. 1. *beaming; bright; brilliant; burnished; dazzling; effulgent; gleaming; glistening; glittering; glossy; incandescent; luminous; lustrous; radiant; resplendent; shiny; sparkling.* 2. *able; adroit; alert; apt; astute; bright; brilliant; capable; clever; competent; discerning; enlightened; insightful; intelligent; judicious; keen; knowledgeable; learned; logical; luminous; perceptive; perspicacious; quick; quick-witted; rational; reasonable; sagacious; sage; sapient; sensible; sharp; shrewd; smart; sound; understanding; wise.*

(as) bright as a new penny An insipid simile. 1. *beaming; bright; brilliant; burnished; dazzling; effulgent; gleaming; glistening; glittering; glossy; incandescent; luminous; lustrous; radiant; resplendent; shiny; sparkling.* 2. *able; adroit; alert; apt;*

astute; bright; brilliant; capable; clever; competent; discerning; enlightened; insightful; intelligent; judicious; keen; knowledgeable; learned; logical; luminous; perceptive; perspicacious; quick; quick-witted; rational; reasonable; sagacious; sage; sapient; sensible; sharp; shrewd; smart; sound; understanding; wise.

(as) bright as a new pin An insipid simile. 1. *beaming; bright; brilliant; burnished; dazzling; effulgent; gleaming; glistening; glittering; glossy; incandescent; luminous; lustrous; radiant; resplendent; shiny; sparkling.* 2. *able; adroit; alert; apt; astute; bright; brilliant; capable; clever; competent; discerning; enlightened; insightful; intelligent; judicious; keen; knowledgeable; learned; logical; luminous; perceptive; perspicacious; quick; quick-witted; rational; reasonable; sagacious; sage; sapient; sensible; sharp; shrewd; smart; sound; understanding; wise.*

(she) brightens up a room A moribund metaphor (see page 21). *is beaming; is brilliant; is dazzling; is gleaming; is glowing; is incandescent; is luminescent; is luminous; is radiant; is resplendent; is shimmering; is sunny.* ■ When she walks into a room, she *brightens up the room.* REPLACE WITH *is incandescent.*

bright-eyed and bushy tailed A moribund metaphor (see page 21). *active; adroit; alert; alive; animated; dynamic; eager; energetic; frisky; hearty; lively; nimble; peppy; perky; quick; ready; spirited; sprightly; spry; vibrant; vigorous; vivacious.*

bring (take) (her) down a notch (peg) A moribund metaphor (see page 21). *abase; chasten; debase; decrease; deflate; degrade; demean; depreciate; depress;* *diminish; disgrace; dishonor; embarrass; humble; humiliate; lower; mortify; puncture; shame.*

bring (her) down from (her) high horse A moribund metaphor (see page 21). *abase; chasten; debase; decrease; deflate; degrade; demean; depreciate; depress; diminish; disgrace; dishonor; embarrass; humble; humiliate; lower; mortify; puncture; shame.*

bring down the house A moribund metaphor (see page 21). *acclaim; applaud; bellow; cheer; clamor; holler; howl; roar; scream; shout; vociferate; yell.*

bring home the bacon A moribund metaphor (see page 21). *earn a living; earn money; prosper; succeed.*

bring to a close (a halt; an end; a stop) A wretched redundancy (see page 25). *cease; close; complete; conclude; derail; discontinue; end; finish; halt; settle; stop; terminate.* ■ We are pleased to be able to *bring* this longstanding litigation *to a close.* REPLACE WITH *conclude.* ■ You might be contributing to *bringing* the nation's longest peacetime economic expansion *to a grinding halt.* REPLACE WITH *halting.* SEE ALSO *come to a close (a halt; an end; a stop); grind to a halt.*

bring to a head A moribund metaphor (see page 21). *cap; climax; conclude; consummate; crest; crown; culminate; peak.*

bring (come) to closure A torpid term (see page 24). 1. *cease; close; complete; conclude; discontinue; end; finish; halt; stop.* 2. *conclude; decide; determine; establish; resolve; settle.*

bring (them) to (their) knees A moribund metaphor (see page 21). *beat; conquer; cow; cripple; crush; defeat; disable; dispirit; enervate; enfeeble; humble; incapacitate; lame; make helpless; neutralize; oppress; overcome; overpower; overrun; overthrow; overwhelm; repress; subdue; subjugate; suppress; vanquish.* ■ A network of computers was *brought to its knees* by something out of our control that seemed to live in and even infect the system. REPLACE WITH *vanquished.*

bring to the table A moribund metaphor (see page 21). *advance; bring up; broach; contribute; give; introduce; offer; present; proffer; propose; provide; raise; submit; suggest; tender.* ■ As a company that knows education, we thought we had something to *bring to the table.* REPLACE WITH *offer.*

brought it home to (me) A moribund metaphor (see page 21).

(as) brown as a berry An insipid simile. *beige; bronze; bronzed; brown; burnished; chestnut; copper; coppery; ecru; fawn; mahogany; ocherous; russet; sienna; sun-tanned; tan; tanned; tawny.*

(win) brownie points A moribund metaphor (see page 21).

brutally honest An inescapable pair (see page 20).

brute force An inescapable pair (see page 20).

bucket of bolts A moribund metaphor (see page 21).

(won't) budge an inch A moribund metaphor (see page 21). 1. *be influenced; be persuaded; be swayed; be won over.* 2. *budge; move; nudge; shift.*

build a better mousetrap (and the world will beat a path to your door) A popular prescription (see page 23).

build bridges A moribund metaphor (see page 21).

build bridges where there are walls A moribund metaphor (see page 21).

build castles in Spain (the air) A moribund metaphor (see page 21). *brood; daydream; dream; fantasize; imagine; meditate; muse; reflect.*

building blocks of A moribund metaphor (see page 21).

(like a) bull in a china closet (shop) An insipid simile. *awkward; blundering; bumbling; bungling; clumsy; gawky; gauche; ham-handed; heavy-handed; inapt; inept; lubberly; lumbering; maladroit; uncoordinated; uncouth; ungainly; ungraceful; unhandy; unskillful; unwieldy.*

bump in the road A moribund metaphor (see page 21). *bar; barrier; block; blockage; check; deterrent; difficulty; encumbrance; handicap; hindrance; hurdle; impediment; interference; obstacle; obstruction.*

(like a) bump on a log An insipid simile. *dead; dormant; dull; immobile; immovable; inactive; inanimate; indolent; inert; inoperative; languid; latent; lethargic; lifeless; listless; motionless; phlegmatic; quiescent; quiet; sluggish; stagnant; static; stationary; still; stock-still; torpid; unresponsive.*

bumpy road (ahead) A moribund metaphor (see page 21). *complication; difficulty; dilemma; mess; muddle; ordeal; pickle; plight; predicament; problem; quandary; trial; trouble.*

bunch of baloney A moribund metaphor (see page 21). *balderdash; baloney; nonsense; rubbish.*

bundle of joy A moribund metaphor (see page 21). *babe; baby; child; infant; neonate; newborn; nursling; suckling; toddler; tot; weanling.*

bundle of nerves A moribund metaphor (see page 21). *agitated; anxious; eager; edgy; excitable; excited; fidgety; frantic; jittery; jumpy; nervous; ill at ease; on edge; restive; restless; skittish; uncomfortable; uneasy.*

burn a hole in (my) pocket A moribund metaphor (see page 21).

burn (your) bridges (behind) (you) A moribund metaphor (see page 21).

burning desire An inescapable pair (see page 20). *ardor; eagerness; fervor; passion; vehemence; zeal.* ■ Suppose you sell group insurance to employers, and your prospect has ten employees and a *burning desire* to expand the business. REPLACE WITH *zeal.*

(it) burns (me) up A moribund metaphor (see page 21). *acerbate; anger; annoy; bother; bristle; chafe; enrage; incense; inflame; infuriate; irk; irritate; madden; miff; provoke; rile; roil; vex.*

burn the candle at both ends A moribund metaphor (see page 21). 1. *drudge; grind; grub; labor; moil; slave; strain;*

strive; struggle; sweat; toil; travail; work hard. 2. *debilitate; deplete; drain; empty; enervate; exhaust; fatigue; overdo; overwork; sap; tire; wear out; weary.* 3. *be merry; carouse; carry on; celebrate; debauch; disport; frolic; party; play; revel; riot; roister; rollick; romp; skylark.*

burn the midnight oil A moribund metaphor (see page 21). *drudge; grind; grub; labor; moil; slave; strain; strive; struggle; sweat; toil; travail; work hard; work long hours.* ■ We are indebted to our wives and families for their patience while we *burned the midnight oil.* REPLACE WITH *worked long hours.*

bursting at the seams A moribund metaphor (see page 21). 1. *aflame; agitated; animated; anxious; eager; ebullient; effervescent; enthusiastic; excitable; excited; fervent; fervid; frantic; frenzied; impassioned; impatient; lively; restless; spirited.* 2. *abounding; brimful; brimming; bursting; chock-full; congested; crammed; crowded; dense; filled; full; gorged; jammed; jam-packed; overcrowded; overfilled; overflowing; packed; replete; saturated; stuffed; swarming; teeming.*

burst on (onto) the scene A moribund metaphor (see page 21). *appear; arise; come forth; emerge; occur; originate; present itself; rise; surface; turn up.*

bur under (his) saddle A moribund metaphor (see page 21). *affliction; annoyance; bane; bother; burden; curse; difficulty; inconvenience; irritant; irritation; load; nuisance; ordeal; pain; pest; plague; problem; torment; tribulation; trouble; vexation; weight; worry.*

bury (her) head in the sand A moribund metaphor (see page 21). *cower;*

cringe; grovel; quail; recoil; shrink. ■ When confronted with negative press, school officials ought not to *bury their heads in the sand.* REPLACE WITH *cower.*

bury the hatchet A moribund metaphor (see page 21). *make peace.*

business as usual A torpid term (see page 24). ■ All too many male-dominated workplaces still are doing *business as usual* and denying women equal pay and benefits. ■ In simple terms, it means *business as usual;* specifically, all business will be conducted today as it was yesterday. SEE ALSO *politics as usual.*

> The tile floor smelled strongly of antiseptic and faintly of cat pee: Business as usual. — Jo-Ann Mapson, *The Wilder Sisters*

business is business A quack equation (see page 23).

bust (my) ass A moribund metaphor (see page 21). *attempt; drudge; endeavor; essay; exert; grind; grub; labor; moil; slave; strain; strive; struggle; sweat; toil; travail; try; work.*

(as) busy as a beaver An insipid simile. *assiduous; busy; diligent; grinding; hardworking; indefatigable; industrious; inexhaustible; sedulous; slaving; tireless; toiling; unflagging; unrelenting; untiring.*

(as) busy as a bee An insipid simile. *assiduous; busy; diligent; grinding; hardworking; indefatigable; industrious; inexhaustible; sedulous; slaving; tireless; toiling; unflagging; unrelenting; untiring.*

butterflies in (her) stomach A moribund metaphor (see page 21). 1. *agitat-*

ed; anxious; eager; edgy; excitable; excited; fidgety; frantic; jittery; jumpy; nervous; ill at ease; on edge; restive; restless; skittish; uncomfortable; uneasy. 2. *nauseated; nauseous; queasy; sick; squeamish.*

butter (them) up A moribund metaphor (see page 21). *acclaim; applaud; celebrate; commend; compliment; extol; flatter; laud; praise.*

butter wouldn't melt in (her) mouth A moribund metaphor (see page 21). *affected; artful; artificial; coy; crafty; cunning; deceitful; dishonest; demure; dissembling; dissimulating; duplicitous; fake; false; false-hearted; feigned; foxy; guileful; insincere; lying; mannered; mendacious; phony; plastic; sly; sneaky; tricky; two-faced; uncandid; underhanded; unfrank; unnatural; untrue; untruthful; wily.*

button (zip) your lip A moribund metaphor (see page 21). 1. *be silent; be still; hush; keep quiet; quiet; silence.* 2. *be closed-mouthed; be quiet; be reticent; be silent; be speechless; be taciturn; be uncommunicative.*

buy a pig in a poke A moribund metaphor (see page 21).

buy into A moribund metaphor (see page 21). *accept; adopt; advocate; affirm; agree to; assent to; back; believe in; endorse; espouse; favor; further; hold; sanction; side with; support.* ■ When others witness your confidence in an activity, they are more likely to *buy into* your plans of action. REPLACE WITH *back.*

buy the farm A moribund metaphor (see page 21). *cease to exist; depart; die; expire; pass away; pass on; perish.*

buy time A moribund metaphor (see page 21). *defer; delay; hold off; hold up; postpone; put aside; put off; set aside; shelve; suspend; table; waive.*

by a hair's breadth A moribund metaphor (see page 21). *barely; by a little; hardly; just; merely; narrowly; only just; scarcely.*

(won) by a landslide A moribund metaphor (see page 21).

by a whisker A moribund metaphor (see page 21). *barely; by a little; hardly; just; merely; narrowly; only just; scarcely.*

by fits and starts A moribund metaphor (see page 21). *convulsively; erratically; fitfully; intermittently; irregularly; paroxysmally; randomly; spasmodically; sporadically; unevenly.*

by hook or (by) crook A moribund metaphor (see page 21). *somehow; someway.*

(growing) by leaps and bounds A moribund metaphor (see page 21). *abruptly; apace; briskly; fast; hastily; hurriedly; posthaste; promptly; quickly; rapidly; rashly; speedily; straightaway; swiftly; wingedly.*

by no (not by any) stretch of the imagination A moribund metaphor (see page 21). *at no time; by no means; in no way; never; no; not; not at all; not ever; not in any way; not in the least.*

> Rubashov found that by no stretch of his imagination could he picture his neighbor's state of mind, in spite of all his practice in the art of 'thinking through others' minds'. — Arthur Koestler, *Darkness at Noon*

(go; pass) by the board A moribund metaphor (see page 21). *abandoned; completed; concluded; disappeared; discarded; done; ended; finished; forfeited; gone (by); lost; over; passed; vanished.* ■ There was a little rain, sleet, and snow, but all that has *gone by the board*. REPLACE WITH *passed*.

(go) by the book A moribund metaphor (see page 21). 1. *correctly; properly; rightly.* 2. *according to the rules.* ■ She's done everything *by the book*. REPLACE WITH *correctly*.

by the same token A wretched redundancy (see page 25). *also; and; as well; besides; beyond that (this); even; further; furthermore; in addition; likewise; moreover; more than that (this); similarly; still more; too; what is more.*

by the seat of (his) pants A moribund metaphor (see page 21). *automatically; by impulse; by instinct; by intuition; by reflex; impulsively; instinctively; intuitively; reflexively; spontaneously; unthinkingly; viscerally.*

by the skin of (his) teeth A moribund metaphor (see page 21). *barely; by a little; hardly; just; merely; narrowly; only just; scarcely.*

by the sweat of (his) brow A moribund metaphor (see page 21). *arduously; backbreakingly; burdensomely; exhaustingly;*

fatiguingly; gruelingly; laboriously; onerously; strenuously; toilfully; toilsomely; toughly; wearisomely; with difficulty.

by virtue of the fact that A wretched redundancy (see page 25). *because; considering; for; in that; since.* ■ There are a lot of people who expect too little *by virtue of the fact that* that's all they've known. REPLACE WITH *because.* SEE ALSO *because of the fact that; considering the fact that; given the fact that; in consideration of the fact that; in view of the fact that; on account of the fact that.*

C

call a halt (an end; a stop) to A wretched redundancy (see page 25). *cease; close; complete; conclude; derail; discontinue; end; finish; halt; settle; stop.* ■ Let's *call a halt to* this insanity. REPLACE WITH *end.* SEE ALSO *put a halt (an end; a stop) to.*

call a spade a spade A moribund metaphor (see page 21). 1. *be aboveboard; be artless; be candid; be forthright; be frank; be genuine; be guileless; be honest; be ingenuous; be naive; be sincere; be straightforward; be truthful; be veracious; be veridical.* 2. *be blunt; clear; be direct; be explicit; be plain; be specific.*

call into question A wretched redundancy (see page 25). *challenge; contradict; dispute; doubt; question.*

call off the dogs A moribund metaphor (see page 21).

call (out) on the carpet A moribund metaphor (see page 21). *admonish; animadvert; berate; castigate; censure; chasten; chastise; chide; condemn; criticize; denounce; denunciate; discipline; excoriate; fulminate against; imprecate; impugn; inveigh against; objurgate; punish; rebuke; remonstrate; reprehend; reprimand; reproach; reprobate; reprove; revile; scold; swear at; upbraid; vituperate.* ■ Popular sentiment indicates that *calling the president on the carpet* is not a labor the people wish to bear. REPLACE WITH *rebuking the president.* ■ She *called Starr on the carpet* as well, notably for alleged leaks to the press. REPLACE WITH *upbraided Starr.*

callow youth An inescapable pair (see page 20). *adolescent; artless; callow; green; guileless; immature; inexperienced; inexpert; ingenuous; innocent; juvenile; naive; raw; simple; undeveloped; unfledged; unskilled; unskillful; unsophisticated; untaught; untrained; unworldly; young; youthful.*

call the plays A moribund metaphor (see page 21). *administer; boss; choose; command; control; decide; determine; dictate; direct; dominate; govern; in charge; in command; in control; manage; manipulate; master; order; overpower; oversee; predominate; prevail; reign over; rule; superintend.*

call the shots A moribund metaphor (see page 21). *administer; boss; choose; command; control; decide; determine; dictate; direct; dominate; govern; in charge; in command; in control; manage; manipulate; master; order; overpower; oversee;*

predominate; prevail; reign over; rule; superintend.

> It's neither true nor fair to say I'm to blame for her predicament, but I have a long history of letting Sylvia call the shots. — Dave King, *The Ha-Ha*

(the) calm before the storm A moribund metaphor (see page 21).

calm, cool, and collected An infantile phrase (see page 20). *at ease; calm; collected; composed; controlled; cool; imperturbable; insouciant; nonchalant; placid; poised; relaxed; sedate; self-possessed; serene; tranquil; unemotional; unperturbed; unruffled.* ■ She seemed so *calm, cool, and collected* in the interview. REPLACE WITH *calm.*

(we) came, (we) saw, (we) conquered An infantile phrase (see page 20).

can chew gum and think (walk) at the same time A moribund metaphor (see page 21). *be able; be adept; be adroit; be ambidextrous; be capable; be competent; be deft; be dexterous; be nimble; be proficient; be skilled; be skillful.*

candor and frankness An inescapable pair (see page 20). *candor; frankness; honesty; openness; sincerity; truth; truthfulness; veracity.*

(you) can (can't) have your cake and eat it too A popular prescription (see page 23).

can I ask (tell) you something? A plebeian sentiment (see page 23). This is a question asked by the ignorant, by the ill-bred, not the well mannered. ■ *Can I*

tell you something? I don't really like to go out. DELETE *Can I tell you something?* ■ *Can I ask you something?* Do you want me to give you a check so you can take care of that? DELETE *Can I ask you something?* SEE ALSO *let me ask you something.*

(open up a) can of worms A moribund metaphor (see page 21). *complication; difficulty; dilemma; mess; muddle; ordeal; pickle; plight; predicament; problem; quandary; trial; trouble.*

(I) can take it or leave it An infantile phrase (see page 20). *apathetic; cool; halfhearted; indifferent; insouciant; languid; laodicean; lukewarm; nonchalant; tepid; unenthusiastic.*

(I) can't complain An infantile phrase (see page 20). *all right; average; fair; fine; good; mediocre; not bad; passable; pretty good; tolerable; well.*

(we) can't help you if you don't want to be helped A popular prescription (see page 23).

(he) can't see beyond (the end of) (his) nose A moribund metaphor (see page 21). 1. *blind; eyeless; purblind; shortsighted; sightless; unseeing; unsighted; visionless.* 2. *addleheaded; bovine; cretinous; decerebrate; dense; dull; dull-witted; fatuous; fat-witted; half-witted; harebrained; hebetudinous; idiotic; ignorant; imbecilic; incogitant; insensate; mindless; moronic; muddled; nescient; obtuse; phlegmatic; slow; slow-witted; sluggish; thick; torpid; undiscerning; unintelligent; vacuous; witless.*

can't see the forest (woods) for the trees A moribund metaphor (see page 21). *nearsighted; myopic; purblind; shortsighted.*

(with) cap (hat) in hand A moribund metaphor (see page 21). *deferentially; diffidently; humbly; modestly; respectfully; sheepishly; unassumingly; unpretentiously.*

captain of industry A moribund metaphor (see page 21). *administrator; boss; brass; chief; commander; director; executive; foreman; head; headman; leader; manager; master; (high) mucka-muck; officer; official; overseer; owner; president; principal; proprietor; superin-tendent; supervisor.*

capture the attention of A torpid term (see page 24). *absorb; attract; beguile; bewitch; captivate; charm; enamor; engage; engross; enrapture; enthrall; entice; entrance; fascinate; mesmerize; occupy.* ■ The civil rights struggle *captured the attention of* the entire nation. REPLACE WITH *captivated.*

(the) cards (deck) are stacked against (him) A moribund metaphor (see page 21).

card up (his) sleeve A moribund metaphor (see page 21).

(like) carrying coals to Newcastle An insipid simile. *barren; bootless; effete; feckless; feeble; fruitless; futile; impotent; inadequate; inconsequential; inconsider-able; ineffective; ineffectual; infertile; insignificant; inutile; meaningless; merit-less; nugatory; null; of no value; pointless; powerless; profitless; purposeless; redun-dant; sterile; superfluous; trifling; trivial; unavailing; unimportant; unnecessary; unproductive; unprofitable; unserviceable; unworthy; useless; vain; valueless; weak; worthless.*

carry (his) own weight A moribund metaphor (see page 21).

carry the ball A moribund metaphor (see page 21).

carry the weight of the world on (my) shoulders A moribund metaphor (see page 21).

(it's a) catch-22 A moribund metaphor (see page 21). 1. *contradiction; dilemma; impasse; incongruity; paradox; plight; predicament; quandary; situation.* 2. *conundrum; enigma; puzzle; riddle.*

carte blanche A foreign phrase (see page 19).

carved (cast; fixed) in stone A mori-bund metaphor (see page 21). 1. *decid-ed; determined; established; firm; fixed; resolved; set; settled.* 2. *changeless; con-stant; eternal; everlasting; firm; fixed; immutable; invariable; irreversible; irrev-ocable; permanent; rigid; stable; unalter-able; unchangeable; unchanging; unend-ing.* ■ The state's census count is not yet *fixed in stone.* REPLACE WITH *immutable.* ■ Your choice of per-server or per-seat licensing is not *cast in stone.* REPLACE WITH *unalterable.*

cash in (their) chips A moribund metaphor (see page 21). *cease to exist; decease; depart; die; expire; pass away; pass on; perish.*

cash on the barrel A moribund metaphor (see page 21).

cast a shadow over A moribund metaphor (see page 21). 1. *becloud; cloak; darken; eclipse; mask; obscure; shroud; veil.* 2. *belittle; confound;*

degrade; demean; embarrass; humiliate; lower; shame. SEE ALSO *hang like a cloud (over).*

cast in (our) lot with A moribund metaphor (see page 21). *ally; collaborate; comply; concur; conspire; cooperate; join; unite; work together.*

cast into the pot A moribund metaphor (see page 21).

castles in Spain (the air) A moribund metaphor (see page 21). *apparition; caprice; chimera; delusion; dream; fanciful idea; fancy; fantasty; fluff; frivolity; hallucination; illusion; imagination; maggot; mirage; phantasm; vagary; vision; whim; whimsy.*

cast (his) net A moribund metaphor (see page 21).

cast (your) pearls before swine A moribund metaphor (see page 21).

cast the first stone A moribund metaphor (see page 21).

catalyst for change A moribund metaphor (see page 21). ■ These are the young people who will be the *catalysts for change* in their own communities in the coming decades.

catch as catch can A moribund metaphor (see page 21). 1. *aimless; free; irregular; uncontrolled; unplanned.* 2. *by any means; however possible.*

catch forty winks A moribund metaphor (see page 21). *doze; go to bed; nap; rest; retire; sleep; slumber.*

catch in the act A moribund metaphor (see page 21). *catch; decoy; ensnare; entrap; net; trap.*

catch the wave A moribund metaphor (see page 21).

catch (him) with (his) pants down A moribund metaphor (see page 21). *catch unawares; surprise.* ■ He isn't the first president to be *caught with his pants down,* nor will he be the last. REPLACE WITH *caught unawares.*

(like a) cat on a hot tin roof An insipid simile. *agitated; anxious; eager; edgy; excitable; excited; fidgety; frantic; jittery; jumpy; nervous; ill at ease; on edge; restive; restless; skittish; uncomfortable; uneasy.*

cat's got (your) tongue A moribund metaphor (see page 21). *be closed-mouthed; be quiet; be reticent; be silent; be speechless; be taciturn; be uncommunicative.*

(the) cat's out of the bag A moribund metaphor (see page 21).

(look) (like) (the) cat that (ate) swallowed the canary An insipid simile. *complacent; gleeful; pleased; self-satisfied; smug; thrilled.* ■ On the day after an election in which President Clinton was supposed to have been chastened, many of the faces at the White House looked *like the cat that swallowed the canary.* REPLACE WITH *complacent.*

caught in the crossfire A moribund metaphor (see page 21).

> He paused from this pattern only to whisper, when an innocent — and I must admit, quite plump — regular Joe got caught in the crossfire, "That should've been me!" — Marian Keyes, *Angels*

caught red-handed A moribund metaphor (see page 21).

caught with (her) hand in the cookie jar A moribund metaphor (see page 21).

cautiously optimistic A torpid term (see page 24). *confident; encouraged; heartened; hopeful; optimistic; rosy; sanguine*. *Optimistic* is a perfectly vigorous word, but modified by *cautiously* or *guardedly*, as it so often is, it becomes valueless. *Cautiously optimistic* is a phrase favored by poltroons and politicians, most of whom make a point of devaluing the meaning of their words. ■ The retailer was *cautiously optimistic* about its latest report. DELETE *cautiously*. ■ When I realized that CBS was interested, I became *cautiously optimistic*. REPLACE WITH *hopeful*. ■ On the Rhode Island waterfront, the fishermen are *cautious but optimistic*. DELETE *but optimistic*. SEE ALSO *guardedly optimistic*.

cease and desist An inescapable pair (see page 20). *cease; desist; end; halt; stop*.

celebrity A suspect superlative (see page 24). As the most popular books are sometimes the least worthy of being read, so the most public people are sometimes the least worthy of being known.

If we must acknowledge these crea-tures — these *celebrities* — let us better understand them for who they are. All dictionary definitions of *celebrity* should include 1. a mediocrity; a vulgarian; a coxcomb. 2. a scantly talented person who through shameless self-aggrandizement and utter inanity becomes widely known. 3. a repellent person. SEE ALSO *the rich and famous*.

center around A wretched redundancy (see page 25). *center on*. ■ Concern will *center around* military governments. REPLACE WITH *center on*.

center of attention A suspect superlative (see page 24). *cynosure*. People who seek to be the *center of attention* are forever peripheral to themselves.

(take) center stage A moribund metaphor (see page 21).

c'est la vie A foreign phrase (see page 19). To this popular French expression of resignation, there are more than a few English-language equivalents. SEE ALSO *such is life; that's how (the way) it goes; that's how (the way) the ball bounces; that's how (the way) the cookie crumbles; that's life; that's life in the big city; that's show biz; what are you going to do; what can you do*.

chalk it up to experience A popular prescription (see page 23).

champing (chomping) at the bit A moribund metaphor (see page 21). *anxious; ardent; avid; craving; desiring; desirous; eager; enthusiastic; fervent; fervid; frantic; frenzied; impassioned; impatient; intent; itching; keen; longing; pining; ready; vehement; yearning; zealous*. ■ State corrections officials were *chomping* *at the bit* to show not only that the program was tightly managed but also that it was benefiting offenders and citizens alike. REPLACE WITH *eager*. ■ It leaves me *chomping at the bit* to be able to do something with these tapes. REPLACE WITH *longing*.

change (shift; switch) gear A moribund metaphor (see page 21). *alter; change; convert; metamorphose; modify; transform; transmute.*

> But the very thing I became aware of first was that time had shifted gear and was vibrating differently, and it was this that was the first assault on my own habitual pattern of substance. — Doris Lessing, *Briefing for a Descent Into Hell*

change on a dime A moribund metaphor (see page 21). *be adaptable; be flexible; be malleable; be versatile.* ■ He sees AmEx's program as an example of what the smartest marketers will be doing: creating rewards programs that can *change on a dime* based on what consumers tell them. REPLACE WITH *be flexible*.

changing of the guard A moribund metaphor (see page 21).

charity begins at home A popular prescription (see page 23).

chart a new course A moribund metaphor (see page 21).

cheap shot A moribund metaphor (see page 21).

cheek by jowl A moribund metaphor (see page 21). *attached; close; inseparable; intimate; side by side.*

chew (her) out A moribund metaphor (see page 21). *admonish; animadvert; belittle; berate; castigate; censure; chasten; chastise; chide; condemn; criticize; denounce; denunciate; discipline; excoriate; fulminate against; imprecate; impugn; inveigh against; objurgate; punish; rebuke; remonstrate; reprehend; reprimand; reproach; reprobate; reprove; revile; scold; swear at; upbraid; vituperate.*

chew the cud A moribund metaphor (see page 21). *brood; cerebrate; cogitate; consider; contemplate; deliberate; excogitate; meditate; ponder; reflect; ruminate; think.*

chew the fat (rag) A moribund metaphor (see page 21). *babble; blab; cackle; chaffer; chat; chitchat; chatter; confabulate; converse; gossip; jabber; palaver; prate; prattle; rattle; talk.*

(that's) chicken feed A moribund metaphor (see page 21). *frivolous; immaterial; inconsequential; inconsiderable; inferior; insignificant; minor; negligible; niggling; nugatory; petty; secondary; trifling; trivial; unimportant; worthless.*

chicken-or-egg (question) A moribund metaphor (see page 21).

(like a) chicken with its head cut off An insipid simile. *agitated; crazed; crazy; demented; deranged; distraught; frantic; frenetic; frenzied; insane; mad; raging; wild.*

(the) child is father of the man A popular prescription (see page 23).

children should be seen and not heard
A popular prescription (see page 23).

(that's) child's play A moribund
metaphor (see page 21). *apparent; basic;
clear; clear-cut; conspicuous; distinct; easily done; easy; effortless; elementary; evident; explicit; facile; limpid; lucid; manifest; obvious; patent; pellucid; plain; simple; simplicity itself; straightforward;
translucent; transparent; unambiguous;
uncomplex; uncomplicated; understandable; unequivocal; unmistakable.*

> This was child's play for him, and
> he got a dollar and seventy-five
> cents a day for it .... — Upton
> Sinclair, *The Jungle*

chill to the bone (marrow) A moribund metaphor (see page 21). 1. *chill;
cool; freeze; ice; refrigerate.* 2. *alarm;
appall; benumb; daunt; frighten; horrify;
intimidate; panic; paralyze; petrify; scare;
shock; startle; terrify; terrorize.*

> The mere sight of that medley of
> wet nakedness chilled him to the
> bone. — James Joyce, *A Portrait of
> the Artist as a Young Man*

chink in (his) armor A moribund
metaphor (see page 21). *defect; deficiency; disadvantage; failing; fault; flaw;
foible; fragility; frailness; frailty; handicap; limitation; shortcoming; susceptibility; susceptibleness; vulnerability; vulnerableness; weakness.*

(a) chip off the old block A moribund
metaphor (see page 21). *carbon copy;
clone; double; duplicate; mirror image;
replica; twin.*

chip on (her) shoulder A moribund
metaphor (see page 21). *animosity; bitterness; enmity; grievance; grudge; hostility; indignation; ill will; offense; rancor;
resentment; spite; umbrage.*

chock full (of) A torpid term (see page
24). *abounding; brimful; brimming;
bursting; congested; crammed; crowded;
dense; filled; full; gorged; jammed; jam-
packed; overcrowded; overfilled; packed;
replete; saturated; stuffed; swarming;
teeming.*

(a) chorus of A moribund metaphor
(see page 21). SEE ALSO *a barrage of.*

chrome dome An infantile phrase (see
page 20). *alopecic; bald; baldheaded;
baldpated; glabrous; hairless; depilated;
pilgarlic; smooth; tonsured.*

Cinderella story A moribund
metaphor (see page 21). *dream; fantasy.*

class A suspect superlative (see page 24).
The antithesis of culture, *class* is a quality possessed by those who have neither
elegance nor grace nor poise nor polish.
■ This always hurts me because I know
who he is: a very intelligent, sensitive,
classy human being. REPLACE WITH
admirable.

Here's a description of a woman that
no discerning man would ever wish to
meet: ■ I am a shapely and petite, 31-
year-old, exquisitely feminine, *classy*
lady. REPLACE WITH *elegant.* SEE ALSO
gentleman; lady.

(as) clean as a hound's tooth An
insipid simile. *antiseptic; clean; cleansed;
disinfected; germ-free; hygienic; immaculate; sanitary; sanitized; scoured;
scrubbed; spotless; stainless; sterile;*

unblemished; unsoiled; unspotted; unsullied; untarnished; washed.

(as) clean as a whistle An insipid simile. *antiseptic; clean; cleansed; disinfected; germ-free; hygienic; immaculate; sanitary; sanitized; scoured; scrubbed; spotless; stainless; sterile; unblemished; unsoiled; unspotted; unsullied; untarnished; washed.*

clean bill of health A moribund metaphor (see page 21). *blooming; doing well; energetic; fit; flourishing; good; hale; hardy; healthful; healthy; hearty; robust; sound; strong; vigorous; well; well-off.*

clean (his) clock A moribund metaphor (see page 21). 1. *assail; assault; attack; batter; beat; cudgel; flagellate; flog; hit; lambaste; lash; lick; mangle; pound; pummel; strike; thrash; trounce.* 2. *beat; conquer; crush; defeat; outdo; overcome; overpower; overwhelm; prevail; quell; rout; succeed; triumph; trounce; vanquish; win.*

cleanliness is next to godliness A popular prescription (see page 23).

clear a (major) hurdle A moribund metaphor (see page 21). ■ The proposed sale and redevelopment of Lafayette Place *cleared a final hurdle* yesterday.

(a) clear and present danger An infantile phrase (see page 20). *danger; hazard; menace; peril; threat; troublemaker.* ■ He is *a clear and present danger.* REPLACE WITH *a menace.*

(as) clear as a bell An insipid simile. *audible; clarion; clear; distinct; plain; pure; sharp.*

(as) clear as crystal An insipid simile. *apparent; basic; clear; clear-cut; conspicuous; crystalline; distinct; easily done; easy; effortless; elementary; evident; explicit; facile; limpid; lucid; manifest; obvious; patent; pellucid; plain; simple; simplicity itself; straightforward; translucent; transparent; unambiguous; uncomplex; uncomplicated; understandable; unequivocal; unmistakable.*

(as) clear as day An insipid simile. *apparent; basic; clear; clear-cut; conspicuous; crystalline; distinct; easily done; easy; effortless; elementary; evident; explicit; facile; limpid; lucid; manifest; obvious; patent; pellucid; plain; simple; simplicity itself; straightforward; translucent; transparent; unambiguous; uncomplex; uncomplicated; understandable; unequivocal; unmistakable.*

(as) clear as mud An insipid simile. *ambiguous; blurred; blurry; cloudy; dim; fuzzy; hazy; indistinct; muddy; murky; nebulous; obfuscatory; obscure; opaque; unclear; vague.*

clear sailing A moribund metaphor (see page 21). *apparent; basic; clear; clear-cut; conspicuous; distinct; easily done; easy; effortless; elementary; evident; explicit; facile; limpid; lucid; manifest; obvious; patent; pellucid; plain; simple; simplicity itself; straightforward; translucent; transparent; unambiguous; uncomplex; uncomplicated; understandable; unequivocal; unmistakable.*

clear the air A moribund metaphor (see page 21).

clear the decks A moribund metaphor (see page 21).

climbing the walls A moribund metaphor (see page 21). *agitated; anxious; eager; edgy; excitable; excited; fidgety; frantic; jittery; jumpy; nervous; ill at ease; on edge; restive; restless; skittish; uncomfortable; uneasy.*

climb (move up) the ladder (of success) A moribund metaphor (see page 21). *advance; flourish; progress; prosper; rise; succeed.*

clinging vine A moribund metaphor (see page 21). *clinging; dependent; subject; subordinate; subservient.*

cling like a limpet An insipid simile. *adhere; affix; attach; bind; cleave; cling; cohere; connect; fasten; fuse; hitch; hold; join; stick.*

clip (her) wings A moribund metaphor (see page 21). *abase; chasten; debase; decrease; deflate; degrade; demean; depreciate; depress; diminish; disgrace; dishonor; embarrass; humble; humiliate; lower; mortify; puncture; shame.*

(the) clock is ticking A moribund metaphor (see page 21).

(a) cloud of A moribund metaphor (see page 21). ■ But he did so under *a cloud of* uncertainty over whether what he said could be used against him later by law enforcement officials.

close (near) at hand A moribund metaphor (see page 21). *accessible; at hand; close; close by; handy; near; nearby; neighboring; vicinal.*

close but no cigar An infantile phrase (see page 20). *almost; just about; nearly.*

closely allied An inescapable pair (see page 20).

closely guarded secret A torpid term (see page 24).

> Each year He returned and incarnated Himself in a different leading citizen whose identity was always a closely guarded secret, and with His nondenominational mysteries He brought a playful glamour to the city. — Jonathan Franzen, *The Twenty-Seventh City*

close scrutiny An inescapable pair (see page 20).

close (shut) the door on (to) A moribund metaphor (see page 21). *ban; banish; bar; block; disallow; dismiss; eliminate; exclude; hinder; ignore; impede; obstruct; preclude; prevent; prohibit; proscribe; reject; rule out.*

(hold cards) close to the chest (vest) A moribund metaphor (see page 21). *clandestine; cloaked; closed; concealed; confidential; covert; furtive; hidden; masked; mysterious; private; secretive; secret; shrouded; sly; stealthy; surreptitious; veiled.* ■ If police have any leads, they are keeping them *close to the vest.* REPLACE WITH *secret.*

clothes make the man A popular prescription (see page 23).

clutch (grasp) at straws A moribund metaphor (see page 21).

(the) coast is clear A moribund metaphor (see page 21).

cock of the walk A moribund metaphor (see page 21). *administrator; boss; brass; chief; commander; director; executive; foreman; head; headman; leader; magnate; manager; master; mogul; (high) muckamuck; notable; officer; official; overseer; patrician; personage; president; principal; ruler; superintendent; supervisor.*

cog in the wheel A moribund metaphor (see page 21). *aide; apparatchik; assistant; cog; dependent; drudge; flunky; helper; hireling; inferior; junior; minion; secondary; servant; slave; subaltern; subordinate; underling; vassal.*

cold and calculating An inescapable pair (see page 20).

> There was something cold and calculating about Elizabeth, small as she was. — Muriel Maddox, *Llantarnam*

(as) cold as a witch's tit An insipid simile. *algid; arctic; brumal; chilly; cold; cool; freezing; frigid; frosty; frozen; gelid; glacial; hibernal; hyperborean; ice-cold; icy; nippy; polar; rimy; wintry.*

(as) cold as ice An insipid simile. *algid; arctic; brumal; chilly; cold; cool; freezing; frigid; frosty; frozen; gelid; glacial; hibernal; hyperborean; ice-cold; icy; nippy; polar; rimy; wintry.*

(as) cold as marble An insipid simile. *algid; arctic; brumal; chilly; cold; cool; freezing; frigid; frosty; frozen; gelid; glacial; hibernal; hyperborean; ice-cold; icy; nippy; polar; rimy; wintry.*

cold enough to freeze the balls off a brass monkey A moribund metaphor (see page 21). *algid; arctic; brumal; chilly; cold; cool; freezing; frigid; frosty; frozen; gelid; glacial; hibernal; hyperborean; ice-cold; icy; nippy; polar; rimy; wintry.*

(get) cold feet A moribund metaphor (see page 21). *afraid; alarmed; apprehensive; cowardly; craven; diffident; fearful; frightened; pavid; pusillanimous; recreant; scared; timid; timorous; tremulous.* ■ When the woman heard that the story opened with the theft of the godparents' guns, she *got cold feet*. DELETE *became apprehensive.*

cold fish A moribund metaphor (see page 21). *apathetic; callous; chilly; cold; cool; detached; dispassionate; distant; emotionless; frigid; glacial; hard; hardhearted; harsh; heartless; hostile; icy; impassive; indifferent; passionless; pitiless; reserved; unconcerned; unemotional; unfeeling; unfriendly; unresponsive.*

cold turkey A moribund metaphor (see page 21).

collaborate together A wretched redundancy (see page 25). *collaborate.* ■ Staff from the American and European sides *collaborate together* to make the journey and the home stay a rewarding experience. DELETE *together.*

collect (gather) dust A moribund metaphor (see page 21). *fallow; idle; in abeyance; inactive; inoperative; set aside; unoccupied; unused.*

combine together A wretched redundancy (see page 25). *combine.* ■ Look at each reviewer's comments separately or *combine* them *together* for a consolidated view. DELETE *together*.

come around A moribund metaphor (see page 21). *agree; consent; feel as (we) do; support (us); think as (I) think.* ■ We believe that in the end the public is going to *come around.* REPLACE WITH *support us.*

come back to haunt A moribund metaphor (see page 21). *haunt; recoil on; redound on; return to; revisit.*

> If Maggie Feller had learned one thing in her fourteen years of dealing with members of the opposite sex, it was this: your bad hookups will always come back to haunt you. — Jennifer Weiner, *In Her Shoes*

come clean A moribund metaphor (see page 21). *acknowledge; admit; affirm; allow; avow; be forthright; be frank; be honest; be sincere; be straightforward; be truthful; be veracious; concede; confess; disclose; divulge; expose; grant; own; reveal; tell; uncover; unveil.* ■ It is time for the president to *come clean.* REPLACE WITH *be forthright.*

come forward (with) A moribund metaphor (see page 21). *advance; broach; introduce; offer; present; propose; propound; submit; suggest; tender.* ■ Nobody has *come forward with* a good argument for any way to create more jobs and raise the incomes of working people without expanding trade. REPLACE WITH *proposed.* SEE ALSO *put forward.*

come full circle A moribund metaphor (see page 21).

come hell or high water A moribund metaphor (see page 21). *no matter what; regardless.*

(chickens) come home to roost A moribund metaphor (see page 21).

come in from the cold A moribund metaphor (see page 21). ■ Alternative medicine is *coming in from the cold.* REPLACE WITH *gaining respectability.*

come in through the back door A moribund metaphor (see page 21).

come knocking (on my door) A moribund metaphor (see page 21).

come on like gangbusters An insipid simile. 1. *assertive; commanding; dynamic; emphatic; energetic; forceful; intense; mighty; potent; powerful; strong; vehement; vigorous; virile.* 2. *authoritarian; authoritative; autocratic; bossy; despotic; dictatorial; dogmatic; domineering; imperious; iron-handed; lordly; overbearing; peremptory; tyrannical.*

come on strong A moribund metaphor (see page 21). 1. *assertive; commanding; dynamic; emphatic; energetic; forceful; intense; mighty; potent; powerful; strong; vehement; vigorous; virile.* 2. *authoritarian; authoritative; autocratic; bossy; despotic; dictatorial; dogmatic; domineering; imperious; iron-handed; lordly; overbearing; peremptory; tyrannical.*

come out in the wash A moribund metaphor (see page 21).

come out of left field A moribund metaphor (see page 21).

come out of the closet A moribund metaphor (see page 21).

come (crawl) out of the woodwork A moribund metaphor (see page 21).

come out (up) smelling like a rose An insipid simile.

come out swinging A moribund metaphor (see page 21). *aggressive; antagonistic; battling; bellicose; belligerent; combative; fighting; militant; pugnacious; truculent; warlike.*

comes (goes) with the territory (turf) A moribund metaphor (see page 21). *is expected; is inescapable; is inevitable; is necessary; is unavoidable.* ■ He's got to understand that these questions *go with the territory.* REPLACE WITH *are inevitable.*

come to a boil A moribund metaphor (see page 21). *cap; climax; conclude; consummate; crest; crown; culminate; peak.*

come to a close (a halt; an end; a stop) A wretched redundancy (see page 25). *cease; close; complete; conclude; derail; discontinue; end; finish; halt; settle; stop; terminate.* ■ The days of easy credit, strong liquidity, and speculation are *coming to a close.* REPLACE WITH *ending.* SEE ALSO *bring to a close (a halt; an end; a stop); grind to a halt.*

come to (find) a happy medium A moribund metaphor (see page 21). *compromise.*

come to a head A moribund metaphor (see page 21). *cap; climax; conclude; consummate; crest; crown; culminate; peak.*

come to blows A moribund metaphor (see page 21). *battle; brawl; clash; fight; grapple; jostle; make war; scuffle; skirmish; tussle; war; wrestle; wrangle.*

> Winnie said she believed at that moment it would come to blows, though she had never seen a man strike a woman, nor a woman strike a man for that matter. — Beth Gutcheon, *More Than You Know*

come to find out An infantile phrase (see page 20). *ascertain; determine; discern; discover; find out; learn; realize.*

come to grips with A moribund metaphor (see page 21). *accept; comprehend; cope with; deal with; face; handle; struggle with; understand.*

come to pass A moribund metaphor (see page 21). *befall; come about; happen; occur; result; take place.*

come to terms with A torpid term (see page 24). *accept; comprehend; cope with; deal with; face; handle; struggle with; understand.*

come to the end of the line (road) A moribund metaphor (see page 21).

come up empty (handed) A moribund metaphor (see page 21). *find nothing.*

come up roses A moribund metaphor (see page 21).

(as) comfortable as an old shoe An insipid simile. *comfortable; cosy; habitable; homey; inhabitable; livable; safe; snug.*

coming (falling) apart at the seams A moribund metaphor (see page 21). *breaking down; collapsing; crumbling; decaying; decomposing; degenerating; deteriorating; disintegrating; dissipating; dissolving; dying; ending; fading; failing; unraveling.* ■ How do you hold it together at work when your life is *coming apart at the seams*? REPLACE WITH *disintegrating.* ■ For the last year and a half it seems the world economy has been *coming apart at the seams.* REPLACE WITH *unraveling.*

(as) common as dirt An insipid simile. *average; basic; common; commonplace; customary; everyday; normal; omnipresent; ordinary; prevalent; quotidian; regular; standard; typical; ubiquitous; unexceptional; universal; unremarkable; usual; widespread; workaday.*

common courtesy A suspect superlative (see page 24). If this expression is not heard as often as it once was, it's because courtesy is today not so common.

Genuine expressions of courtesy such as *please* and *thank you* (SEE) and *you're welcome* have been usurped by glib ones such as *have a nice day* and *I appreciate it* and *no problem.*

What's more, a vapid phrase like *how goes it* (SEE), or a vulgar one like *hey* (SEE), is more popular than an authentic *hello.*

The worsening of our speech accompanies the withering of our souls. SEE ALSO *(I) appreciate (it); have a good (nice) day (evening).*

compare and contrast A wretched redundancy (see page 25). *compare; contrast.* ■ Competition is essential to enable consumers to *compare and contrast* alternatives. REPLACE WITH *compare* or *contrast.*

(as) compared to what? An infantile phrase (see page 20). SEE ALSO *everything's (it's all) relative; (as) opposed to what?.*

complete and utter A wretched redundancy (see page 25). *absolute; compleat; complete; consummate; deadly; outright; perfect; thorough; thoroughgoing; total; unmitigated; unqualified; utter.* ■ She may be my boss, but she is also a *complete and utter* fool. REPLACE WITH *complete.*

component part A wretched redundancy (see page 25). *component; part.* ■ Denial is a *component part* of dying. REPLACE WITH *component* or *part.*

comrades in arms A moribund metaphor (see page 21).

concerted effort An inescapable pair (see page 20).

conflicted A torpid term (see page 24). *Conflicted* is a perfectly silly choice of words. It's as if to say having conflicting feelings about something — as common as that is — is more than that, more complicated or less explicable, and only a psychological-sounding term might adequately convey this.

People indefatigably mimic one another; *conflicted,* like so many other ridiculously popular terms, would have less appeal if people were more confident and inclined to think for themselves. ■ Many such parents *feel conflicted* about segregating their children in special classes but think they have no alternative. REPLACE WITH *have conflicting feelings.* ■ The single most important element to a successful production of *Julius Caesar* is to see Brutus as a truly honorable, yet *conflicted* soul whose actions belie his intentions. REPLACE WITH *torn*. ■ My guess is that you have underlying and perhaps, *conflicted* feelings about the way this change occurred. REPLACE WITH *conflicting*.

And some people use *conflicted* to mean war-torn or embattled. ■ RONCO involvement in humanitarian demining in *conflicted* countries evolves from 20 years experience with worldwide development and humanitarian assistance contracts. REPLACE WITH *embattled*. ■ The war on drugs cannot alone explain why the U.S. is sending 60 Black Hawk and Huey helicopters to this *conflicted* nation. REPLACE WITH *war-torn*.

connect together A wretched redundancy (see page 25). *connect*. ■ The next step was to *connect* these systems *together* into a system called APRS. DELETE *together*.

consensus of opinion A wretched redundancy (see page 25). *consensus*. ■ The *consensus of opinion* is that newspaper endorsements are momentum builders. REPLACE WITH *consensus*.

considering the fact that A wretched redundancy (see page 25). *because; considering; for; in that; since; when*. ■ I don't see how you can say you're not a prostitute *considering the fact that* you are paid for your time. REPLACE WITH *when*. SEE ALSO *because of the fact that; by virtue of the fact that; given the fact that; in consideration of the fact that; in view of the fact that; on account of the fact that*.

conspicuous by (his) absence A torpid term (see page 24). ■ If I didn't sing about what I was going through, it would have been *conspicuous by its absence*.

contact An overworked word (see page 22). *ask; call; inform; phone; query; question; reach; speak to; talk to; tell; write to*.

continue on A wretched redundancy (see page 25). *continue*. ■ We're going to *continue on* with more of this. DELETE *on*.

continuing refrain An inescapable pair (see page 20).

contrary to popular belief (opinion) A torpid term (see page 24). ■ *Contrary to popular opinion*, a strong dollar does not attract foreign investment to U.S. stocks but to U.S. bonds.

conventional wisdom A suspect superlative (see page 24). ■ Washington is in thrall at the moment to two competing *conventional wisdoms*.

conversation piece A plebeian sentiment (see page 23). This is an annoying little term. That people might need an object whose purpose is mainly to stimulate conversation reveals just how infertile, just how fallow, our minds are.

convicted felon A wretched redundancy (see page 25). *felon*. ■ You were a deputy sheriff and now you're a *convicted felon*? DELETE *convicted*.

cook (his) goose A moribund metaphor (see page 21).

(the) cook's tour A moribund metaphor (see page 21).

cook the books A moribund metaphor (see page 21).

(as) cool as a cucumber An insipid simile. *at ease; calm; collected; composed; controlled; cool; imperturbable; insouciant; nonchalant; placid; poised; relaxed; sedate; self-possessed; serene; tranquil; unemotional; unperturbed; unruffled.*

cool customer A moribund metaphor (see page 21). *at ease; calm; collected; composed; controlled; cool; imperturbable; insouciant; nonchalant; placid; poised; relaxed; sedate; self-possessed; serene; tranquil; unemotional; unperturbed; unruffled.*

cool (your) heels A moribund metaphor (see page 21). *be patient; hold on; relax; wait.*

cooperate together A wretched redundancy (see page 25). *cooperate.* ■ It's important that we *cooperate together* in order to resolve our problems. DELETE *together.*

cost a pretty penny A moribund metaphor (see page 21). *costly; dear; expensive; high-priced; precious; priceless; valuable.*

(I) could (should) write a book A plebeian sentiment (see page 23). If all those who proclaim *I could write a book* — or all those who are advised *You should write a book* — were to do so, we would be immersed (more than we already are) in the vengeful, petty, or everyday lamentations of hollow-headed homemakers, shameless celebrities, and failed or forgotten businesspeople. ■ *I could write a book* about the way parents pay high prices in raising a disabled child.

count (pinch) (my) pennies A moribund metaphor (see page 21). *be cheap; be economical; be frugal; be miserly; be niggardly; be parsimonious; be stingy; be thrifty.*

course of action A wretched redundancy (see page 25). *action; course; direction; intention; method; move; plan; policy; procedure; route; scheme; strategy.*

cover all the bases A moribund metaphor (see page 21).

cover a lot of ground A moribund metaphor (see page 21).

cover (his) tracks A moribund metaphor (see page 21).

crack the whip A moribund metaphor (see page 21). 1. *bully; coerce; intimidate; menace; terrorize; threaten.* 2. *castigate; chastise; discipline; penalize; punish.*

crap shoot A moribund metaphor (see page 21).

(as) crazy as a coot An insipid simile. *batty; cracked; crazy; daft; demented; deranged; fey; foolish; goofy; insane; lunatic; mad; maniacal; neurotic; nuts; nutty; psychotic; raving; silly; squirrelly; touched; unbalanced; unhinged; unsound; wacky; zany.*

(as) crazy as a loon An insipid simile. *batty; cracked; crazy; daft; demented; deranged; fey; foolish; goofy; insane; lunatic; mad; maniacal; neurotic; nuts;*

nutty; psychotic; raving; silly; squirrelly; touched; unbalanced; unhinged; unsound; wacky; zany.

> She was quite put out with him, it seemed, or else she was making her mind up that he was crazy as a loon — one of the two. — Barbara Kingsolver, *Prodigal Summer*

crazy like a fox An insipid simile. *artful; cagey; clever; conniving; crafty; cunning; foxy; guileful; shifty; shrewd; sly; smart; subtle; tricky; wily.*

(the) cream of the crop A moribund metaphor (see page 21). *best; brightest; choice; choicest; elite; excellent; finest; first-class; first-rate; foremost; greatest; highest; matchless; nonpareil; optimal; optimum; outstanding; paramount; peerless; preeminent; premium; prominent; select; superior; superlative; top; unequaled; unexcelled; unmatched; unrivaled; unsurpassed.*

crème de la crème A foreign phrase (see page 19). *best; brightest; choice; choicest; elite; excellent; finest; first-class; first-rate; foremost; greatest; highest; matchless; nonpareil; optimal; optimum; outstanding; paramount; peerless; preeminent; premium; prominent; select; superior; superlative; top; unequaled; unexcelled; unmatched; unrivaled; unsurpassed.* ■ But I have the *crème de la crème* of celebrity users. REPLACE WITH *foremost.* ■ The following list contains the *crème de la crème* of online record retailers. REPLACE WITH *best.*

crisis An overworked word (see page 22). We have a "crisis" for all occurrences. For example: *career crisis; crisis in* the making; crisis in values; crisis of confidence; crisis proportions; crisis situation; crisis stage; current crisis; economic crisis; educational crisis; energy crisis; extinction crisis; family crisis; financial crisis; fiscal crisis; identity crisis; mid-life crisis; moral crisis; mounting crisis; national crisis; political crisis;* and even, incomprehensibly, *severe crisis.*

Surely, some of these crises are less than that. The terms we use to characterize events and emotions largely decide how we react to them. SEE ALSO *devastate.*

(shed) crocodile tears A moribund metaphor (see page 21).

(as) crooked as a dog's hind legs An insipid simile.

(as) cross as a bear An insipid simile. *angry; bad-tempered; bilious; cantankerous; choleric; churlish; crabby; cranky; cross; curmudgeonly; disagreeable; dyspeptic; grouchy; gruff; grumpy; ill-humored; ill-tempered; irascible; irritable; mad; peevish; petulant; quarrelsome; short-tempered; splenetic; surly; testy; vexed.*

cross (my) fingers A moribund metaphor (see page 21). *hope for; pray for; think positively; wish.*

cross (my) heart and hope to die A moribund metaphor (see page 21). *affirm; asseverate; assert; attest; aver; avow; declare; pledge; promise; swear; testify; vow; warrant.*

cross swords A moribund metaphor (see page 21). 1. *altercate; argue; disagree; dispute; feud; fight; quarrel; spat; squabble; wrangle.* 2. *battle; brawl; clash; fight; grapple; jostle; make war; scuffle; skirmish; tussle; war; wrestle.*

(we'll) cross that bridge when (we) come to it A moribund metaphor (see page 21).

cross the line A moribund metaphor (see page 21).

cross the Rubicon A moribund metaphor (see page 21).

cross to bear A moribund metaphor (see page 21). *affliction; burden; charge; cross; difficulty; encumbrance; hardship; hindrance; impediment; load; obstacle; obstruction; onus; oppression; ordeal; problem; trial; trouble; weight.*

crush like a bug An insipid simile. 1. *annihilate; assassinate; butcher; destroy; exterminate; kill; massacre; murder; slaughter; slay.* 2. *beat; conquer; crush; defeat; outdo; overcome; overpower; overwhelm; prevail; quell; rout; succeed; triumph; trounce; vanquish; win.*

> It was entirely possible that one song could destroy your life. Yes, musical doom could fall on a lone human form and crush it like a bug. — Jonathan Lethem, *The Fortress of Solitude*

cry (weep) like a baby An insipid simile. *cry; howl; shriek; sob; ululate; wail; weep; whimper; whine.*

> The next morning she found him gathering eggs in the henhouse, weeping like a baby. — Jennifer Haigh, *Baker Towers*

cry over spilt milk A moribund metaphor (see page 21). *lament; mourn; sulk.*

crystal clear A moribund metaphor (see page 21). *apparent; basic; clear; clear-cut; conspicuous; crystalline; distinct; easily done; easy; effortless; elementary; evident; explicit; facile; limpid; lucid; manifest; obvious; patent; pellucid; plain; simple; simplicity itself; straightforward; translucent; transparent; unambiguous; uncomplex; uncomplicated; understandable; unequivocal; unmistakable.* ■ What seems *crystal clear* to you, and perhaps to others, is not all that obvious to me. REPLACE WITH *obvious*.

cry (say) uncle A moribund metaphor (see page 21). *abdicate; accede; acquiesce; bow; capitulate; cede; concede; give in; give up; quit; relinquish; retreat; submit; succumb; surrender; yield.*

cry wolf A moribund metaphor (see page 21).

(see) (the) cup (glass) half empty A moribund metaphor (see page 21). *despairing; hopeless; pessimistic.*

(see) (the) cup (glass) half full A moribund metaphor (see page 21). *cheerful; hopeful; optimistic; pollyanna; pollyannaish; positive; roseate; sanguine; upbeat.*

(not) (her) cup of tea A moribund metaphor (see page 21). *bent; choice; leaning; pick; inclination; predilection; preference; propensity; tendency.* ■ Choosing a logo and letterhead design from a catalog may not be everyone's *cup of tea*. REPLACE WITH *preference*.

> In any case, Edwin always felt that Norman was more Marcia's friend than he was, more her cup of tea if anyone was. — Barbara Pym, *Quartet in Autumn*

curiosity killed the cat A popular prescription (see page 23).

curse a blue streak A moribund metaphor (see page 21). *anathematize; blaspheme; condemn; curse; cuss; damn; defile; desecrate; excoriate; execrate; fulminate; imprecate; swear at.*

cushion the blow A moribund metaphor (see page 21). ■ We think that will help *cushion the blow* for some people.

(a) cut above (the rest) A moribund metaphor (see page 21). *abler; better; exceptional; greater; higher; more able (accomplished; adept; capable; competent; qualified; skilled; talented); outstanding; standout; superior; superlative.*

cut and dried (dry) A moribund metaphor (see page 21). 1. *common; commonplace; customary; everyday; normal; ordinary; quotidian; regular; routine; standard; typical; usual.* 2. *anodyne; banal; bland; boring; deadly; dry; dull; everyday; flat; humdrum; insipid; jejune; lifeless; lusterless; mediocre; monotonous; prosaic; stale; tedious; tiresome; unexciting; uninteresting; vapid; watered-down.*

cut a rug A moribund metaphor (see page 21). *dance.*

(as) cute as a button An insipid simile. *appealing; attractive; beautiful; becoming; captivating; comely; cute; dazzling; exquisite; fair; fetching; good-looking; gorgeous; handsome; lovely; nice-looking; pleasing; pretty; pulchritudinous; radiant; ravishing; seemly; stunning.*

cut (them) off at the pass A moribund metaphor (see page 21).

cut off (my) nose to spite (my) face A moribund metaphor (see page 21).

cut (its) own throat A moribund metaphor (see page 21).

cut (her) teeth (on) A moribund metaphor (see page 21). ■ Case majored in political science at Williams College and *cut his teeth* as a marketing executive at PepsiCo Inc. and Procter & Gamble.

cut the legs out from under A moribund metaphor (see page 21).

cut the mustard A moribund metaphor (see page 21). *fare well; flourish; meet expectations; prevail; progress; prosper; succeed; thrive; triumph; win.*

cutthroat competition An inescapable pair (see page 20).

cut through red tape A moribund metaphor (see page 21).

(the) cutting edge A moribund metaphor (see page 21). *advanced; ground-breaking; innovative; inventive; new; original; pioneering; progressive; radical; revolutionary; unconventional.*

cut to pieces A moribund metaphor (see page 21).1. *annihilate; assassinate; butcher; destroy; exterminate; kill; massacre; murder; slaughter; slay.* 2. *beat; conquer; crush; defeat; outdo; overcome; overpower; overwhelm; prevail; quell; rout; succeed; triumph; trounce; vanquish; win.*

cut (costs) to the bone A moribund metaphor (see page 21).

cut (stung) to the quick A moribund metaphor (see page 21). *affront; crush;*

dash; devastate; hurt; injure; insult; offend; outrage; shatter; slap; slight; upset; wound.

(could) cut (it) with a knife A moribund metaphor (see page 21).

> Amid Grandfather and I was a silence you could cut with a scimitar. — Jonathan Safran Foer, *Everything Is Illuminated*

D

damaged goods A moribund metaphor (see page 21).

dancing in the aisles (streets) A moribund metaphor (see page 21). *be merry; carouse; carry on; celebrate; debauch; disport; frolic; party; play; revel; riot; roister; rollick; romp; skylark.*

(a) dark day A moribund metaphor (see page 21).

(a) day at the beach A moribund metaphor (see page 21). 1. *easily done; easy; effortless; elementary; facile; simple; simplicity itself; straightforward; uncomplex; uncomplicated.* 2. *agreeable; beguiling; charming; delightful; enchanting; engaging; enjoyable; fun; glorious; gratifying; inviting; joyful; joyous; pleasant; pleasing; pleasurable.*

(her) day in court A moribund metaphor (see page 21).

day in (and) day out A moribund metaphor (see page 21). *ceaseless; constant; continual; continuous; daily; diurnal; endless; eternal; everlasting; evermore; every day; frequent; interminable; nonstop; permanent; perpetual; persistent; recurrent; regular; repeated; unceasing; unremitting.*

> And the day in, day out routine of school — was that a sham, too, a cunning deception perpetrated to soften us up with rational expectations and foster nonsensical feelings of trust? — Philip Roth, *The Plot Against America*

day (moment) in the sun A moribund metaphor (see page 21).

> I guess maybe my brother had his moment in the sun for the four years he was alive before Kate got diagnosed, but ever since then, we've been too busy looking over our shoulders to run headlong into growing up. — Jodi Picoult, *My Sister's Keeper*

days of wine and roses An infantile phrase (see page 20).

dead and buried An inescapable pair (see page 20). *ceased; completed; concluded; dead; deceased; defunct; departed; done; ended; exanimate; expired; extinct; extinguished; finished; gone; inanimate; lifeless; no more; over; past; perished; stopped; terminated.*

dead and gone A wretched redundancy (see page 25). *ceased; completed; concluded; dead; deceased; defunct; departed; done; ended; exanimate; expired; extinct; extinguished; finished; gone; inanimate;*

lifeless; no more; over; past; perished; stopped; terminated.

> Instead, they returned to Ireland when I was four, my brother, Malachy, three, the twins, Oliver and Eugene, barely one, and my sister, Margaret, dead and gone.
> — Frank McCourt, *Angela's Ashes*

(as) dead as a dodo An insipid simile. 1. *ceased; completed; concluded; dead; deceased; defunct; departed; done; ended; exanimate; expired; extinct; extinguished; finished; gone; inanimate; lifeless; no more; over; perished; stopped; terminated.* 2. *antediluvian; antiquated; archaic; dead; obsolescent; obsolete; old; old-fashioned; outdated; outmoded; out of date; out of fashion; passé; superannuated.* 3. *beat; bushed; debilitated; depleted; drained; drowsy; enervated; exhausted; fatigued; groggy; sapped; sleepy; sluggish; slumberous; somnolent; soporific; spent; tired; weary; worn out.*

(as) dead as a doornail An insipid simile. 1. *ceased; completed; concluded; dead; deceased; defunct; departed; done; ended; exanimate; expired; extinct; extinguished; finished; gone; inanimate; lifeless; no more; over; perished; stopped; terminated.* 2. *antediluvian; antiquated; archaic; dead; obsolescent; obsolete; old; old-fashioned; outdated; outmoded; out of date; out of fashion; passé; superannuated.* 3. *beat; bushed; debilitated; depleted; drained; drowsy; enervated; exhausted; fatigued; groggy; sapped; sleepy; sluggish; slumberous; somnolent; soporific; spent; tired; weary; worn out.*

> I settled on getting raised from the dead, since a big part of me still felt dead as a doornail. — Sue Monk Kidd, *The Secret Life of Bees*

dead body A wretched redundancy (see page 25). *body.* ■ Their car was abandoned on a bridge, and *dead bodies* were nowhere to be found. DELETE *dead.*

dead duck A moribund metaphor (see page 21).

deader than a doornail A moribund metaphor (see page 21). 1. *ceased; completed; concluded; dead; deceased; defunct; departed; done; ended; exanimate; expired; extinct; extinguished; finished; gone; inanimate; lifeless; no more; over; perished; stopped; terminated.* 2. *antediluvian; antiquated; archaic; dead; obsolescent; obsolete; old; old-fashioned; outdated; outmoded; out of date; out of fashion; passé; superannuated.* 3. *beat; bushed; debilitated; depleted; drained; drowsy; enervated; exhausted; fatigued; groggy; sapped; sleepy; sluggish; slumberous; somnolent; soporific; spent; tired; weary; worn out.*

dead in the water A moribund metaphor (see page 21). *dead; dormant; dull; inactive; inanimate; indolent; inert; inoperative; languid; latent; lethargic; lifeless; listless; motionless; phlegmatic; quiescent; quiet; sluggish; stagnant; static; stationary; still; stock-still; torpid.* ■ The civil rights impulse from the 1960s is *dead in the water.* REPLACE WITH *listless.*

dead on arrival A moribund metaphor (see page 21).

dead on (her) feet A moribund metaphor (see page 21). *beat; bushed; debilitated; depleted; drained; drowsy; enervated; exhausted; fatigued; groggy; sapped; sleepy; sluggish; slumberous; somnolent; soporific; spent; tired; weary; worn out.*

dead ringer A moribund metaphor (see page 21).

dead serious An inescapable pair (see page 20).

dead to the world A moribund metaphor (see page 21). 1. *asleep; dozing; napping; sleeping.* 2. *anesthetized; benumbed; comatose; insensate; insensible; insentient; oblivious; senseless; soporiferous; soporific; stuporous; unconscious.*

(as) deaf as a post An insipid simile. 1. *deaf; unhearing.* 2. *heedless; inattentive; oblivious; unmindful.*

deaf, dumb, and blind A moribund metaphor (see page 21). *anesthesized; cataleptic; comatose; insensate; insensible; insentient; numb; sensationless; unconscious; unfeeling.*

deal a (crushing; devastating; major; serious) blow to A moribund metaphor (see page 21). 1. *annihilate; assassinate; butcher; demolish; destroy; devastate; eradicate; exterminate; kill; massacre; murder; obliterate; pulverize; rack; ravage; raze; ruin; shatter; slaughter; slay; smash; undo; wrack; wreck.* 2. *beat; conquer; crush; defeat; outdo; overcome; overpower; overwhelm; prevail; quell; rout; succeed; triumph; trounce; vanquish; win.*
   Still another phrase favored by journalists *deal a (crushing; devastating; major; serious) blow to,* though it tries mightily to move us, leaves us unimpressed. Drained of any force it might once have had, this dimwitticism exhausts us precisely as much as it is exhausted. ■ Falling real estate values, the stock market crash, and changes in the rules under which S&Ls operate *dealt crushing blows to* the bank's success.

REPLACE WITH *vanquished.* ■ Most recently, it was Bennett who *dealt the most devastating blow* to Clinton's leadership. REPLACE WITH *most wracked.*

a deal is a deal A quack equation (see page 23).

(like) death warmed over An insipid simile. *anemic; ashen; blanched; bloodless; cadaverous; colorless; deathlike; doughy; haggard; lusterless; pale; pallid; pasty; peaked; sallow; sickly; wan; whitish.*

declare war (on) A moribund metaphor (see page 21).

deepen the wound A moribund metaphor (see page 21).

deeper in (into) the hole A moribund metaphor (see page 21).

(has) deep pockets A moribund metaphor (see page 21). *affluent; moneyed; opulent; prosperous; rich; wealthy; well-off; well-to-do.*

deep six (*v*) A moribund metaphor (see page 21). *discard; eliminate; get rid of; jettison; reject; throw away; toss out.*

definitely An overworked word (see page 22). So popular is this word that we might well marvel at the assuredness of those who use it. But, of course, the overuse of *definitely* bespeaks carelessness more than it does confidence. SEE ALSO *absolutely; most assuredly; most (very) definitely.*

degree A torpid term (see page 24). *Degree* — and the superfluity of phrases in which it is found — should be excised from almost all of our speech and writing. No sentence is made more compelling by the use of this word and its diffuse phrases. ■ I believe he has *a very high degree* of integrity and takes extreme pride in his workmanship. REPLACE WITH *a good deal.* ■ Increased employee morale would require *a lesser degree of* accuracy. REPLACE WITH *less.* ■ Their hopes are based, *to a large degree,* on signs that business activity is pulling out of its recent slowdown. REPLACE WITH *largely.* ■ *To a larger degree* than was expected, these economically stunted nations can count on help from the 12-nation organization. REPLACE WITH *More.* ■ Another realm in which schools of choice can and do differ is *the degree to which* the staff and parents are involved in the day-to-day operations of the school. REPLACE WITH *how much.* SEE ALSO *extent.*

> She knew she was sick but she didn't know the degree to which it was commonplace, a matter of spring flu, the usual malaise, passed from student to student and among faculty members. — Joyce Carol Oates, *Solstice*

déjà vu A foreign phrase (see page 19).

déjà vu all over again An infantile phrase (see page 20). ■ The police served him with a restraining order; it was *déjà vu all over again.*

delicate balance An inescapable pair (see page 20).

(a) deluge of A moribund metaphor (see page 21). SEE ALSO *a barrage of.*

den of iniquity A moribund metaphor (see page 21).

den of thieves A moribund metaphor (see page 21).

desperately seeking An infantile phrase (see page 20).

despite (in spite of) or (maybe; perhaps) because of (the fact that) An ineffectual phrase (see page 19). These phrases sound as though they have the ring of respectability to them — that is, they sound intelligent — but since the phrases are formulaic (a staple among journalists and those who write like them) and the contribution they make to a sentence uncertain (*despite* virtually nullifies *because of*), they are actually disreputable — that is, they are dimwitted. ■ *Despite* his old-fashioned style, *or perhaps because of* it, Mansfield remains an extremely popular lecturer. ■ *In spite of or, perhaps, because of the fact that* we humans are normally vision experts at a very young age, we have little intuition about how vision develops or how we accomplish seeing. ■ Excessive weight gain occurred during periods of this pregnancy *despite, or because of,* the mother's emotional problems. ■ Lately, she finds herself having a hard time falling asleep, *despite — or perhaps because of* — her exhaustion. ■ But this is what the harvest is all about, and *despite* the hard work, *or actually,* precisely *because of* it, a harvest wants to be celebrated. ■ They sustain a high level of motivation and achieve performance peak after performance peak *in spite of* (*or perhaps because of*) the lack of traditional supervision and rewards.

> Despite or perhaps because of the fact that he left us, he knows it's vital that he does nothing to undermine my self-confidence. — William Nicholson, *The Society of Others*

despite the fact that A wretched redundancy (see page 25). *although; but; even if; even though; still; though; yet.* ■ Long a critic of exorbitant executive salaries, he agreed to a 4.7 percent raise, *despite the fact that* his company's profits doubled. REPLACE WITH *even though.* ■ *Despite the fact that* no serious adverse effects have been found, there are still risks. REPLACE WITH *Although.* SEE ALSO *in spite of the fact that; regardless of the fact that.*

devastate An overworked word (see page 22). We can hardly wonder why so many of us are so easily *devastated*. This word is pervasive. Rarely are we *disconsolate*, rarely are we *flustered*. If only we would use more measured terms, we might feel less weak and woundable.

Consider these terms, all more moderate: *agitated; bothered; crestfallen; despondent; disappointed; discomposed; disconsolate; distressed; disturbed; downcast; downhearted; flustered; heartbroken; heartsick; perturbed; ruffled; unsettled; upset.* ■ When Glen was transferred to a city 100 miles away, I was *devastated*. REPLACE WITH *heartbroken*.

But if devastation it is, here are other terms that might relieve us of our reliance on this one: *atomized; crushed; demolished; desolate; destroyed; distraught; obliterated; overcome; overpowered; overwhelmed; prostrate; ravaged; ruined; shattered; undone.* ■ Dean and Jenna were *devastated* when she lost their baby. REPLACE WITH *shattered*. SEE ALSO *crisis*.

(the) devil finds work for idle hands to do A popular prescription (see page 23).

devil's disciple A moribund metaphor (see page 21).

(the) devil take the hindmost A moribund metaphor (see page 21).

devil to pay A moribund metaphor (see page 21).

develop steam A moribund metaphor (see page 21).

diametrically opposed An inescapable pair (see page 20).

(a) diamond in the rough A moribund metaphor (see page 21). *bad-mannered; coarse; common; crass; crude; ill-bred; ill-mannered; impolite; rough; rude; uncivilized; uncouth; uncultured; unrefined; unsophisticated; vulgar.*

(the) dictionary defines An infantile phrase (see page 20). ■ *Webster's New World Dictionary defines* investigate as "to search into; examine in detail; inquire into systematically." ■ *The dictionary defines* gratitude as "a feeling of thankful appreciation for favors or benefits received." SEE ALSO *as defined in (the dictionary).*

didn't miss a beat A moribund metaphor (see page 21).

Bess didn't miss a beat. She looked up, looked Christine straight in the eye and said, "Chris, don't go cutting the fool." — Nancy Bartholomew, *Stand by Your Man*

die laughing A moribund metaphor (see page 21).

(the) die is cast A moribund metaphor (see page 21).

die (wither) on the vine A moribund metaphor (see page 21). *atrophy; be unsuccessful; bomb; break down; collapse; decay; fail; fall short; falter; fizzle; flop; flounder; fold; founder; languish; mess up; miscarry; miss; not succeed; shrivel; stumble; topple; wilt; wither.* ■ We believe Medicare is going to *wither on the vine* because we think people are going to voluntarily leave it. REPLACE WITH *founder.* ■ The history of computing is littered with great products that *withered on the vine.* REPLACE WITH *failed.*

different strokes for different folks A popular prescription (see page 23).

difficult task An inescapable pair (see page 20).

digging (your) own grave A moribund metaphor (see page 21).

dig in (his) heels A moribund metaphor (see page 21). *be adamant; be balky; be bullheaded; be cantankerous; be contrary; be contumacious; be determined; be dogged; be firm; be headstrong; be inflexible; be intractable; be mulish; be obdurate; be obstinate; be ornery; be perverse; be refractory; be resistant; be resolute; be resolved; be rigid; be stubborn; be unyielding; be willful.* ■ By then, the auto industry was *digging in its heels,* and almost as soon as the law was approved, its provisions were called too stringent. REPLACE WITH *becoming resolute.*

(a) dime a dozen A moribund metaphor (see page 21). *average; basic; common; commonplace; customary; everyday; normal; omnipresent; ordinary; prevalent; quotidian; regular; standard; typical; ubiquitous; unexceptional; universal; unremarkable; usual; widespread.* ■ Sikhs in Kenya are *a dime a dozen.* REPLACE WITH *ubiquitous.*

> What you find out in your thirties is that clever children are a dime a dozen. It's what you do later that counts, and so far I had done nothing. — Christina Schwarz, *All Is Vanity*

(a) direct line to God An infantile phrase (see page 20). ■ A pair of men spotted outside the Marshalls' house leads Dunning to the Preacher, a bookseller with questionable intentions and *a direct line to God.* ■ These nontraditionalist Christians frequently assert *a direct line to God,* purporting to know details about the consummation of the world.

> When she pictures *shefa,* she thinks of the red phone on the President's desk that is supposed to be a direct line to the Soviet Union. *Shefa* will be her red telephone, a direct line to God. — Myla Goldberg, *Bee Season*

dirt cheap A moribund metaphor (see page 21). *cheap; economical; inexpensive; low-cost; low-priced; not costly.*

dirty pool A moribund metaphor (see page 21).

(a) dirty word A moribund metaphor (see page 21). *abhorrent; abominable; a curse; an abomination; anathema; antipathetic; detestable; execrable; hateful; loathsome; monstrous; offensive; repugnant.* ■ Some in the academic community may disagree, but to working families corporate takeovers are still *a dirty word*. REPLACE WITH *anathema*.

dis An infantile phrase (see page 20). *Dis* is a prefix aspiring to be a word. Are we to allow *un* and *anti, non* and *pre* to follow? People are increasingly mono- and disyllabic as it is; let's rail against this foolishness, this affront, this dimwitted *dis*. ■ And not only does the little *dissing* contest draw the battle lines in today's best-selling music world, but it serves as a reminder of the way *Rolling Stone* manages to embody two sides without appearing totally ridiculous. REPLACE WITH *disparaging*. ■ This issue addresses five other means of *dissing* employees: buck passing, procrastination, inattentiveness, impatience and public reprimands. REPLACE WITH *disrespecting*. ■ More bad news for Leonardo DiCaprio: ABC News is *dissing* him big-time. REPLACE WITH *dismissing*. ■ Gov. Bill Owens made a media splash Monday, playing TV critic and *dissing* first lady of TV news Barbara Walters on national television. REPLACE WITH *disparaging*. ■ Watch Letterman stir up trouble with a Top 10 list or by *dissing* the soft drink Dr. Pepper as "liquid manure." REPLACE WITH *denigrating*. ■ Franzen, despised and envied by all writers for his talent, his luck, his good looks, and his marketing acumen, essentially *dissed* the Oprah award for being ... lowbrow. REPLACE WITH *dismissed*.

disappear (vanish) into thin air A moribund metaphor (see page 21). *disappear; disperse; dissolve; evaporate; fade; vanish; vaporize; volatilize.*

disappear (vanish) without a trace A moribund metaphor (see page 21). *dis-*

appear; disperse; dissolve; evaporate; fade; vanish; vaporize; volatilize.

discretion is the better part of valor A popular prescription (see page 23).

dismal failure An inescapable pair (see page 20). ■ The mayor's attempt at improving the quality of life on Boston Common at night was a *dismal failure*.

divine intervention An inescapable pair (see page 20).

do a disappearing act A moribund metaphor (see page 21). *abscond; clear out; decamp; depart; desert; disappear; escape; exit; flee; fly; go; go away; leave; move on; part; pull out; quit; retire; retreat; run away; take flight; take off; vacate; vanish; withdraw.*

do a hatchet job on A moribund metaphor (see page 21). *asperse; badmouth; belittle; besmirch; bespatter; blacken; calumniate; defame; defile; denigrate; denounce; depreciate; deride; disparage; impugn; insult; libel; malign; profane; revile; scandalize; slander; slap; slur; smear; sully; taint; traduce; vilify; vitiate.*

do a job on A moribund metaphor (see page 21). 1. *blight; cripple; damage; deface; disable; disfigure; harm; hurt; impair; incapacitate; injure; lame; maim; mar; mess up; rack; ruin; sabotage; spoil; subvert; undermine; vitiate; wrack; wreck.* 2. *agitate; bother; disquiet; distress; disturb; fluster; jar; jolt; pain; perturb; ruffle; shake; trouble; unsettle; upset; wound.* SEE ALSO *do a number on.*

do all (everything) in (my) power A torpid term (see page 24). ■ I believe that Cashbuild has *done everything in its* *power* to cope with the changing South American environment.

do an about-face A moribund metaphor (see page 21). *apostatize; backtrack; flip-flop; recidivate; renege; reverse; tergiversate.* SEE ALSO *do a 180.*

do (make) an end run around A moribund metaphor (see page 21). *avoid; bypass; circumvent; dodge; duck; elude; evade; go around; parry; sidestep; skirt.* ■ Trying to *do an end run around* the person responsible for making purchasing decisions isn't advisable. REPLACE WITH *sidestep.*

do a number on A moribund metaphor (see page 21). 1. *blight; cripple; damage; deface; disable; disfigure; harm; hurt; impair; incapacitate; injure; lame; maim; mar; mess up; rack; ruin; sabotage; spoil; subvert; undermine; vitiate; wrack; wreck.* 2. *agitate; bother; disquiet; distress; disturb; fluster; jar; jolt; pain; perturb; ruffle; shake; trouble; unsettle; upset; wound.* SEE ALSO *do a job on.*

do a 180 A moribund metaphor (see page 21). *apostatize; backtrack; flip-flop; recidivate; renege; reverse; tergiversate.* SEE ALSO *do an about face.*

do as I say, not as I do A popular prescription (see page 23).

doctor, lawyer, Indian chief A moribund metaphor (see page 21).

dodge the bullet A moribund metaphor (see page 21).

(it) doesn't amount to a hill of beans A moribund metaphor (see page 21). *barren; bootless; effete; feckless; feeble;* *fruitless; futile; impotent; inadequate; inconsequential; inconsiderable; ineffective; ineffectual; infertile; insignificant; inutile; meaningless; meritless; nugatory; null; of no value; pointless; powerless; profitless; purposeless; sterile; trifling; trivial; unavailing; unimportant; unproductive; unprofitable; unserviceable; unworthy; useless; vain; valueless; weak; worthless.*

> I had too much to do, I told myself, to worry with last-minute, undoubtedly invalid last wills and testaments that probably wouldn't amount to a hill of beans. — Ann B. Ross, *Miss Julia Speaks Her Mind*

doesn't have a clue A moribund metaphor (see page 21). *addlebrained; addleheaded; addlepated; Boeotian; bovine; brainless; clueless; cretinous; decerebrate; dense; dim-witted; doltish; dull; dumb; dunderheaded; empty-headed; fatuous; fat-witted; harebrained; hebetudinous; ignorant; imbecilic; incogitant; insensate; ludicrous; mindless; moronic; muddled; nescient; obtuse; oxlike; phlegmatic; slow-witted; sluggish; stupid; torpid; unaware; unintelligent; unknowing; vacuous; witless.*

doesn't have a snowball's chance in hell A moribund metaphor (see page 21). *impossible; unachievable; unattainable; unfeasible.*

doesn't have both oars in the water A moribund metaphor (see page 21). *batty; cracked; crazy; daft; demented; deranged; fey; foolish; goofy; insane; lunatic; mad; maniacal; neurotic; nuts; nutty; psychotic; raving; silly; squirrelly; strange; touched; unbalanced; unhinged; unsound; wacky; zany.*

doesn't have two nickels to rub together A moribund metaphor (see page 21). *bankrupt; broke; destitute; distressed; impecunious; impoverished; indigent; insolvent; needy; penniless; poor; poverty- stricken; underprivileged.*

doesn't hold water A moribund metaphor (see page 21). *baseless; captious; casuistic; casuistical; erroneous; fallacious; false; faulty; flawed; groundless; illogical; inaccurate; incorrect; invalid; irrational; jesuitical; mistaken; nonsensical; non sequitur; paralogistic; senseless; sophistic; sophistical; specious; spurious; unfounded; unreasonable; unsound; untenable; untrue; unveracious; wrong.*

doesn't know (her) ass from a hole in the wall A moribund metaphor (see page 21). 1. *addlebrained; addleheaded; addlepated; Boeotian; bovine; brainless; clueless; cretinous; decerebrate; dense; dimwitted; doltish; dull; dumb; dunderheaded; empty-headed; fatuous; fat-witted; harebrained; hebetudinous; ignorant; imbecilic; incogitant; insensate; ludicrous; mindless; moronic; muddled; nescient; obtuse; oxlike; phlegmatic; slow-witted; sluggish; stupid; torpid; unaware; unintelligent; unknowing; vacuous; witless.* 2. *deficient; inadequate; inapt; incapable; incompetent; ineffective; inefficacious; inept; lacking; not able; unable; unfit; unqualified; unsatisfactory; unskilled; wanting.*

doesn't know (his) ass from (his) elbow A moribund metaphor (see page 21). 1. *addlebrained; addleheaded; addlepated; Boeotian; bovine; brainless; clueless; cretinous; decerebrate; dense; dimwitted; doltish; dull; dumb; dunderheaded; empty-headed; fatuous; fat-witted; harebrained; hebetudinous; ignorant;* *imbecilic; incogitant; insensate; ludicrous; mindless; moronic; muddled; nescient; obtuse; oxlike; phlegmatic; slow-witted; sluggish; stupid; torpid; unaware; unintelligent; unknowing; vacuous; witless.* 2. *deficient; inadequate; inapt; incapable; incompetent; ineffective; inefficacious; inept; lacking; not able; unable; unfit; unqualified; unsatisfactory; unskilled; wanting.*

doesn't know enough to come in out of the rain A moribund metaphor (see page 21). 1. *addlebrained; addleheaded; addlepated; Boeotian; bovine; brainless; clueless; cretinous; decerebrate; dense; dimwitted; doltish; dull; dumb; dunderheaded; empty-headed; fatuous; fat-witted; harebrained; hebetudinous; ignorant; imbecilic; incogitant; insensate; ludicrous; mindless; moronic; muddled; nescient; obtuse; oxlike; phlegmatic; slow-witted; sluggish; stupid; torpid; unaware; unintelligent; unknowing; vacuous; witless.* 2. *adolescent; artless; callow; green; guileless; immature; inexperienced; inexpert; ingenuous; innocent; juvenile; naive; raw; simple; undeveloped; unfledged; unskilled; unskillful; unsophisticated; untaught; untrained; unworldly; young; youthful.*

dog and pony show A moribund metaphor (see page 21).

(the) dog days of summer A moribund metaphor (see page 21). *boiling; hot; humid; scorching; sizzling; sweltering.*

dog-eat-dog A moribund metaphor (see page 21). *barbarous; bloodthirsty; brutal; cold-blooded; compassionless; cruel; cutthroat; feral; ferocious; fierce; hard; hard-hearted; harsh; heartless; implacable; inexorable; inhuman; merciless; murderous; rancorous; relentless;*

ruthless; savage; uncompassionate; unmerciful; unrelenting; vicious; virulent; wild.

(a) dog's age A moribund metaphor (see page 21). *ages; a long time; a long while; an age; an eternity; decades; eons; forever; months; years.*

(lead a) dog's life A moribund metaphor (see page 21). *misery; unhappiness; wretchedness.*

dollars and sense An infantile phrase (see page 20).

dollars to doughnuts A moribund metaphor (see page 21). *be certain; be sure.*

> I had no place to stay, and dollars to doughnuts, sitting in front of me was a building with a vacant apartment. — Janet Evanovich, *Ten Big Ones*

(a) done deal A infantile phrase. *absolute; completed; concluded; conclusive; consummated; definitive; final; finished.* ■ There seems to be a misconception that this is *a done deal*. REPLACE WITH *consummated.*

don't count your chickens before they're hatched A popular prescription (see page 23).

don't cry over spilled milk A popular prescription (see page 23).

don't do anything I wouldn't do An infantile phrase (see page 20).

don't get mad, get even A popular prescription (see page 23). ■ Hillary, *don't get mad, get even* — write a book.

don't get me wrong An infantile phrase (see page 20). ■ I'm not trying to condone what I've done. *Don't get me wrong.* REPLACE WITH *Don't misunderstand me.* SEE ALSO *I hear you.*

don't give up the ship A popular prescription (see page 23). *carry on; continue; ensue; go on; keep up; persevere; persist; press on; proceed.*

don't hold (your) breath A moribund metaphor (see page 21).

don't knock it until you try it A popular prescription (see page 23).

don't rock the boat A moribund metaphor (see page 21).

don't see eye to eye A moribund metaphor (see page 21). *clash; conflict; differ; disagree; think differently.*

don't start anything you can't finish A popular prescription (see page 23).

doom and gloom An inescapable pair (see page 20).

doomed to failure A torpid term (see page 24). *damned; doomed; hopeless; ill-fated.*

do or die A popular prescription (see page 23).

do's and don'ts *canon; codes; conventions; conventionality; customs; decorum; directives; etiquette; formula; formulary; guidelines; law; manners; policy; precepts; protocol; proprieties; regulations; rules; standards.*

dot the i's and cross the t's A moribund metaphor (see page 21). *careful; conscientious; exact; exacting; fastidious; finical; finicky; fussy; meticulous; nice; painstaking; particular; picky; precise; punctilious; scrupulous; thorough.*

double-edge sword A moribund metaphor (see page 21).

doubting Thomas A moribund metaphor (see page 21). *cynic; disbeliever; doubter; skeptic.*

down and out A moribund metaphor (see page 21). *bankrupt; broke; destitute; distressed; impecunious; impoverished; indigent; insolvent; needy; penniless; poor; poverty- stricken; underprivileged.*

down at the heels A moribund metaphor (see page 21). 1. *dowdy; frowzy; messy; ragged; run-down; seedy; shabby; slipshod; sloppy; slovenly; tattered; threadbare; unkempt; untidy; worn.* 2. *bankrupt; broke; destitute; distressed; impecunious; impoverished; indigent; insolvent; needy; penniless; poor; poverty-stricken; underprivileged.*

down (out) for the count A moribund metaphor (see page 21). 1. *asleep; napping; sleeping; slumbering; snoozing.* 2. *cataleptic; comatose; dormant; inactive; insensible; lifeless; out cold; passed out; unconscious; unresponsive.*

down in the dumps A moribund metaphor (see page 21). *aggrieved; blue; cheerless; dejected; demoralized; depressed; despondent; disconsolate; discouraged; disheartened; dismal; dispirited; doleful; downcast; downhearted; dreary; forlorn; funereal; gloomy; glum; grieved; low; melancholy; miserable; morose; mournful; plaintive; sad; sorrowful; unhappy; woebegone; woeful.*

down in the mouth A moribund metaphor (see page 21). *aggrieved; blue; cheerless; dejected; demoralized; depressed; despondent; disconsolate; discouraged; disheartened; dismal; dispirited; doleful; downcast; downhearted; dreary; forlorn; funereal; gloomy; glum; grieved; low; melancholy; miserable; morose; mournful; plaintive; sad; sorrowful; unhappy; woebegone; woeful.*

Thought it was Nora, but when I opened the door, Lewis was standing there in his rumpled linen suit, looking a bit down in the mouth, not a trace of the bulldog in his face. — Richard B. Wright, *Clara Callan*

(go) down the drain A moribund metaphor (see page 21). 1. *be misused; be squandered; be thrown way; be wasted.* 2. *break down; collapse; deteriorate; die; disappear; disintegrate; disperse; dissipate; dissolve; evaporate; fade; fail; finish; forfeit; go; lose; pass; scatter; vanish; vaporize; volatilize; waste.* 3. *annihilated; crushed; demolished; destroyed; obliterated; overturned; ravaged; ruined; scuttled; shattered; smashed; undone; wrecked.* ■ One major mistake and your career is *down the drain*. REPLACE WITH *ruined.* ■ Without new revenue, our schools will *go down the drain*. REPLACE WITH *collapse.*

down the hatch A moribund metaphor (see page 21). *drink; gulp; guzzle; imbibe; quaff; swallow.*

(later on) down the line (path; pike; road) A wretched redundancy (see page

25). *at length; before long; eventually; from now; in time; later; ultimately.* ■ Even though this knowledge might not seem essential right now, it just might prove invaluable *down the line*. REPLACE WITH *later*. ■ Two players will be added to the team *later, some months down the road*. REPLACE WITH *some months later*. ■ *Later on down the line*, we did in fact marry. REPLACE WITH *At length*.

(go) down the tubes A moribund metaphor (see page 21). 1. *be despoiled; be destroyed; be devastated; be dissipated; be pillaged; be plundered; be ravaged; be ruined; break down; collapse; disintegrate; fail; fall short; flop; founder; miscarry; topple.* 2. *be misused; be squandered; be thrown way; be wasted.* ■ Her article points out a major reason why our country is *going down the tubes*. REPLACE WITH *foundering*. ■ All the money my parents spent on my braces *went down the tubes*. REPLACE WITH *was wasted*.

down to earth A moribund metaphor (see page 21). *artless; common; earthly; everyday; genuine; guileless; mortal; mundane; natural; normal; plain; secular; staid; temporal; unaffected; unassuming; unpretentious; worldly.*

(come) down to the wire A moribund metaphor (see page 21).

drag (their) feet A moribund metaphor (see page 21). *arrest; balk; block; bridle; check; dawdle; defer; delay; detain; encumber; hamper; hesitate; hinder; hold up; impede; inhibit; obstruct; pause; postpone; put off; retard; stall; stay; stonewall; suspend.* ■ The regional Bells have *dragged their feet* in rolling out DSL services. REPLACE WITH *dawdled*.

drag into (through) the mud A moribund metaphor (see page 21). *asperse; badmouth; belittle; besmirch; bespatter; blacken; calumniate; defame; defile; denigrate; denounce; depreciate; deride; disparage; impugn; insult; libel; malign; profane; revile; scandalize; slander; slap; slur; smear; sully; taint; traduce; vilify; vitiate.* ■ His name was *dragged through the mud* last week thanks to a Harvard Law School professor. REPLACE WITH *defamed*.

> He sat down again, trembling with rage; person after person was being dragged into the mud. — E. M. Forster, *A Passage to India*

drag kicking and screaming A moribund metaphor (see page 21).

draw a bead on A moribund metaphor (see page 21). 1. *aim at; focus on; sight; train on.* 2. *admonish; animadvert; berate; castigate; censure; chasten; chastise; chide; condemn; criticize; denounce; denunciate; discipline; impugn; objurgate; punish; rebuke; remonstrate; reprehend; reprimand; reproach; reprobate; reprove; revile; scold; upbraid; vituperate.*

draw a blank A moribund metaphor (see page 21). 1. *be addleheaded; be bovine; be cretinous; be decerebrated; be dense; be dull; be dull-witted; be fatuous; be fat-witted; be half-witted; be harebrained; be hebetudinous; be idiotic; be ignorant; be imbecilic; be incogitant; be insensate; be mindless; be moronic; be muddled; be nescient; be obtuse; be phlegmatic; be slow; be slow-witted; be sluggish; be thick; be torpid; be undiscerning; be unintelligent; be vacuous; be witless.* 2. *be absent-minded; be forgetful; be lethean; be oblivious.* ■ A successful attorney,

Caroline *draws a blank* when it comes to men. REPLACE WITH *is witless.*

draw a veil over A moribund metaphor (see page 21). *adumbrate; becloud; befog; camouflage; cloak; cloud; conceal; cover; disguise; dissemble; enshroud; harbor; hide; keep secret; mask; obfuscate; obscure; overshadow; screen; shroud; suppress; veil; withhold.*

draw fire (from) A moribund metaphor (see page 21).

draw in (his) horns A moribund metaphor (see page 21). *back away; back down; back off; disengage; evacuate; fall back; recede; regress; retire; retreat; withdraw.*

draw in the reins A moribund metaphor (see page 21). *bridle; check; curb; curtail; halt; restrain; stall; stay; stop.*

draw the line (at) A moribund metaphor (see page 21).

draw the long bow A moribund metaphor (see page 21). *elaborate; embellish; embroider; enhance; enlarge; exaggerate; hyperbolize; inflate; magnify; overdo; overreact; overstress; overstate; strain; stretch.*

(a) dream (fairy tale) come true A plebeian sentiment (see page 23).

dredge up dirt A moribund metaphor (see page 21).

dressed to kill A moribund metaphor (see page 21). *elaborately; elegantly; extravagantly; fashionably; flamboyantly; flashily; gaudily; lavishly; ostentatiously; profusely; richly; showily; smartly; stylishly.*

dribs and drabs An inescapable pair (see page 20). *bits; chunks; crumbs; fragments; modicums; morsels; nuggets; particles; pieces; scraps; segments; shreds; snips; snippets; specks.*

drink like a fish An insipid simile. *alcoholic; bibulous.*

drive a stake through the heart (of) A moribund metaphor (see page 21). 1. *execute; kill; massacre; murder; slaughter; slay.* 2. *annihilate; demolish; destroy; eliminate; eradicate; exterminate; liquidate; obliterate; ravage; ruin; sack; wreck.* ■ The IRB's decision *drives a stake through the heart of* the myth peddled by Carey sympathizers inside and outside the Teamsters. REPLACE WITH *slays.*

drive a wedge between A moribund metaphor (see page 21).

drive (me) bananas (crazy; nuts) A moribund metaphor (see page 21). *annoy; badger; bedevil; bother; chafe; distress; disturb; exasperate; gall; grate; harass; harry; hassle; heckle; hector; hound; irk; irritate; nag; nettle; persecute; pester; plague; provoke; rankle; rile; roil; tease; torment; vex.*

drive (me) to drink A moribund metaphor (see page 21). *annoy; badger; bedevil; bother; chafe; distress; disturb; exasperate; gall; grate; harass; harry; hassle; heckle; hector; hound; irk; irritate; nag; nettle; persecute; pester; plague; provoke; rankle; rile; roil; tease; torment; vex.*

drive (me) up the wall A moribund metaphor (see page 21). *annoy; badger; bedevil; bother; chafe; distress; disturb; exasperate; gall; grate; harass; harry; hassle; heckle; hector; hound; irk; irritate;*

nag; nettle; persecute; pester; plague; provoke; rankle; rile; roil; tease; torment; vex.

driving force A wretched redundancy (see page 25). *drive; energy; force; impetus; motivation; power.*

drop (fall) by the wayside A moribund metaphor (see page 21). 1. *abate; cease to be; diminish; disappear; dissolve; dwindle; fade; go away; recede; vanish.* 2. *be unsuccessful; fail; fall short; founder.* 3. *give in; give way; submit; succumb; surrender; yield.* ■ Social class distinctions have mostly *fallen by the wayside*, and scientists are now more likely to admit the collective nature of research. REPLACE WITH *disappeared.*

> Believe me in those days the girls were dropping by the wayside like seeds off a poppyseed bun and you learned to look at every day as a prize. — Barbara Kingsolver, *The Bean Trees*

drop-dead gorgeous A moribund metaphor (see page 21). *attractive; beautiful; comely; exquisite; fair; fetching; good looking; gorgeous; handsome; lovely; pretty; pulchritudinous; ravishing.*

(a) drop in the bucket (ocean) A moribund metaphor (see page 21). *frivolous; inappreciable; immaterial; inconsequential; inconsiderable; insignificant; meager; meaningless; negligible; next to nothing; nugatory; paltry; petty; scant; scanty; scarcely anything; slight; trifling; trivial; unimportant; unsubstantial; worthless.* ■ Relative to need, it's *a drop in the bucket.* REPLACE WITH *next to nothing.* ■ When art is part of a larger construction budget, the money is usually *a drop in the bucket* compared with overall costs. REPLACE WITH *inconsiderable.*

drop like a hot potato An insipid simile. *abandon; abdicate; desert; discard; ditch; drop; forgo; forsake; get rid of; give up; jettison; leave; quit; reject; relinquish; renounce; surrender; throw away; toss out; yield.*

drop like flies An insipid simile. *annihilate; decimate; demolish; slaughter.*

drop off the face of the earth A moribund metaphor (see page 21). *disappear; vanish.*

drop the ball A moribund metaphor (see page 21). *be unsuccessful; bomb; break down; collapse; fail; fall short; falter; fizzle; flop; fold; founder; mess up; miscarry; not succeed; stumble; topple.*

(a) drowning man will clutch at a straw A popular prescription (see page 23).

(as) drunk as a lord An insipid simile. *besotted; crapulous; drunk; inebriated; intoxicated; sodden; stupefied; tipsy.*

(as) drunk as a skunk An insipid simile. *besotted; crapulous; drunk; inebriated; intoxicated; sodden; stupefied; tipsy.*

(as) dry as a bone An insipid simile. *arid; dehydrated; desiccated; droughty; dry; exsiccated; parched; sear; shriveled; thirsty; wilted; withered.*

(as) dry as dust An insipid simile. *anodyne; banal; barren; bland; boring; deadly; dreary; dry; dull; everyday; flat; humdrum; inanimate; insipid; jejune; lifeless; lusterless; mediocre; monotonous; prosaic; routine; spiritless; stale; tedious; tiresome; unexciting; uninteresting; vapid; wearisome.*

dubious distinction An inescapable pair (see page 20). ■ Now the Cowboys are coming off a 34-0 shutout in Philadelphia while the Giants have the *dubious distinction* of being the first team to lose to Washington this season.

duck soup A moribund metaphor (see page 21). *easily done; easy; effortless; elementary; facile; simple; simplicity itself; straightforward; uncomplex; uncomplicated.*

due to circumstances beyond (our) control An ineffectual phrase (see page 19). Of those who use this phrase, we may remark that their speech is no more grammatical than their actions are genuine.

Due to, as often as not, should be *because of* or *owing to*, and only the similarly disingenuous would believe that *circumstances beyond our control* is an explanation rather than an evasion.

In the end, those who express themselves badly are less credible than those who express themselves well. ■ *Due to circumstances beyond our control*, no motel rooms are available in the area on June 25th, 26th, and 27th. ■ *Due to circumstances beyond our control*, the following items may not be available as advertised. SEE ALSO *due to popular demand.*

due to popular demand An ineffectual phrase (see page 19). There is with this phrase the same solecism and a similar suspicion as with *due to circumstances beyond (our) control* (SEE). ■ *Due to popular demand*, The Magic Show will be held over another two weeks.

due to the fact that A wretched redundancy (see page 25). *because; considering; for; in that; since.* ■ Requirements continue to decrease slowly *due to the fact that* activity generally decreases with age. REPLACE WITH *since.* ■ Could this be *due to the fact that* it is undecidable? REPLACE WITH *because.* SEE ALSO *attributable to the fact that; owing to the fact that.*

(as) dull as dishwater An insipid simile. 1. *addleheaded; bovine; cretinous; decerebrate; dense; dull; dull-witted; fatuous; fat-witted; half-witted; harebrained; hebetudinous; idiotic; ignorant; imbecilic; incogitant; insensate; mindless; moronic; muddled; nescient; obtuse; phlegmatic; slow; slow-witted; sluggish; thick; torpid; undiscerning; unintelligent; vacuous; witless.* 2. *anodyne; banal; barren; bland; boring; deadly; dreary; dry; dull; everyday; flat; humdrum; inanimate; insipid; jejune; lifeless; lusterless; mediocre; monotonous; prosaic; routine; spiritless; stale; tedious; tiresome; unexciting; uninteresting; vapid; wearisome.*

(as) dumb as a stone An insipid simile. *addlebrained; addleheaded; addlepated; Boeotian; bovine; brainless; clueless; cretinous; decerebrate; dense; dim-witted; doltish; dull; dumb; dunderheaded; empty-headed; fatuous; fat-witted; harebrained; hebetudinous; ignorant; imbecilic; incogitant; insensate; ludicrous; mindless; moronic; muddled; nescient; obtuse; oxlike; phlegmatic; slow-witted; sluggish; stupid; torpid; unaware; unintelligent; unknowing; vacuous; witless.*

(as) dumb as dirt An insipid simile. *addlebrained; addleheaded; addlepated; Boeotian; bovine; brainless; clueless; cretinous; decerebrate; dense; dim-witted; doltish; dull; dumb; dunderheaded; empty-headed; fatuous; fat-witted; hare-*

brained; hebetudinous; ignorant; imbecilic; incogitant; insensate; ludicrous; mindless; moronic; muddled; nescient; obtuse;
oxlike; phlegmatic; slow-witted; sluggish;
stupid; torpid; unaware; unintelligent;
unknowing; vacuous; witless. ■ Frankly, I
think these allegations are simply *dumb
as dirt*. REPLACE WITH *Boeotian*.

during (in; over) the course of A
wretched redundancy (see page 25).
during; in; over; throughout. ■ *In the
course of* a 30 minute conversation, she
spoke about her married life and her
plans for the future. REPLACE WITH
During. ■ *Over the course of* a woman's
life, she may experience a kaleidoscope
of health concerns. REPLACE WITH
Throughout.

> She had drunk a quantity of
> champagne, and during the course
> of her song she had decided,
> ineptly, that everything was very,
> very sad — she was not only
> singing, she was weeping too. —
> F. Scott Fitzgerald, *The Great
> Gatsby*

during the period (time) that A
wretched redundancy (see page 25).
while. ■ *During the time that* we were
with him, he called her several uncom-
plimentary names. REPLACE WITH
While.

(when) (the) dust settles A moribund
metaphor (see page 21).

(like a) Dutch uncle An insipid simile.

dyed-in-the-wool A moribund
metaphor (see page 21). *ardent; constant; devoted; faithful; inflexible;
intractable; loyal; refractory; resolute;*
rigid; staunch; steadfast; unbending;
unwavering; unyielding.

(a) dying breed A moribund metaphor
(see page 21). *declining; dying; moribund; waning*.

dynamic duo An infantile phrase (see
page 20).

E

each and every (one) A wretched
redundancy (see page 25). *all; each;
everybody; everyone*. ■ Software develop-
ers have changed the way *each and every
one* of us does business. REPLACE WITH
each.

each one A wretched redundancy (see
page 25). *each*. ■ The fact that these
companies do have to compete for business gives *each one* an incentive to work
harder and to lower prices. DELETE *one*.
SEE ALSO *either one; neither one*.

each to his own A popular prescription
(see page 23).

eagle eyed A moribund metaphor (see
page 21). *alert; attentive; observant; vigilant; watchful*.

(the) early bird catches the worm A
popular prescription (see page 23).

(the) end justifies the means A popular prescription (see page 23).

(the) exception, not (rather than) the rule A torpid term (see page 24). *aberrant; abnormal; anomalistic; anomalous; atypical; bizarre; curious; deviant; different; distinct; distinctive; eccentric; exceptional; extraordinary; fantastic; foreign; grotesque; idiosyncratic; independent; individual; individualistic; irregular; notable; noteworthy; novel; odd; offbeat; original; peculiar; puzzling; quaint; queer; rare; remarkable; separate; singular; strange; uncommon; unconventional; unexampled; unique; unnatural; unorthodox; unparalleled; unprecedented; unusual; weird.*

Most people find it easier to mimic a repeatedly used phrase like this — however wordy and inexact, however obtuse and tedious — than to remember a rarely used word like *aberrant* or *anomalous*. ■ Today, in region after region, single-town school districts are *the exception, not the rule.* REPLACE WITH *exceptional.* ■ Arrest or issuing a citation is *the exception, not the rule.* REPLACE WITH *atypical.*

(the) exception that proves the rule An infantile phrase (see page 20).

(the) exception to the rule A torpid term (see page 24). *aberrant; abnormal; anomalistic; anomalous; atypical; bizarre; curious; deviant; different; distinct; distinctive; eccentric; exceptional; extraordinary; fantastic; foreign; grotesque; idiosyncratic; independent; individual; individualistic; irregular; notable; noteworthy; novel; odd; offbeat; original; peculiar; puzzling; quaint; queer; rare; remarkable; separate; singular; strange; uncommon; unconventional; unexampled; unique; unnatural; unorthodox; unparalleled; unprecedented; unusual; weird.*

earn (his) stripes A moribund metaphor (see page 21).

(as) easy as A B C An insipid simile. *apparent; basic; clear; clear-cut; conspicuous; distinct; easily done; easy; effortless; elementary; evident; explicit; facile; limpid; lucid; manifest; obvious; patent; pellucid; plain; simple; simplicity itself; straightforward; translucent; transparent; unambiguous; uncomplex; uncomplicated; understandable; unequivocal; unmistakable.*

(as) easy as 1 2 3 An insipid simile. *apparent; basic; clear; clear-cut; conspicuous; distinct; easily done; easy; effortless; elementary; evident; explicit; facile; limpid; lucid; manifest; obvious; patent; pellucid; plain; simple; simplicity itself; straightforward; translucent; transparent; unambiguous; uncomplex; uncomplicated; understandable; unequivocal; unmistakable.*

(as) easy as pie An insipid simile. *apparent; basic; clear; clear-cut; conspicuous; distinct; easily done; easy; effortless; elementary; evident; explicit; facile; limpid; lucid; manifest; obvious; patent; pellucid; plain; simple; simplicity itself; straightforward; translucent; transparent; unambiguous; uncomplex; uncomplicated; understandable; unequivocal; unmistakable.* ■ It's *easy as pie* to strike up a conversation with the person sitting next to you. REPLACE WITH *easy.*

It was easy as pie to slip back into my old self. — Laurie Colwin, *Goodbye Without Leaving*

easy on the eyes A moribund metaphor (see page 21). *attractive; beautiful; comely; exquisite; fair; fetching; good looking;*

gorgeous; handsome; lovely; pretty; pulchritudinous; ravishing.

> One of the four girls, the one in red, asked, "Will you be going, Michael?" An outsider, she was, but very easy on the eyes. — Anne Tyler, *The Amateur Marriage*

easy on the pocket(book) A moribund metaphor (see page 21). *affordable; cheap; economical; inexpensive; low-cost; low-priced; reasonable.*

an easy (simple) task A torpid term (see page 24). *apparent; basic; clear; clear-cut; conspicuous; distinct; easily done; easy; effortless; elementary; evident; explicit; facile; limpid; lucid; manifest; obvious; patent; pellucid; plain; simple; simplicity itself; straightforward; translucent; transparent; unambiguous; uncomplex; uncomplicated; understandable; unequivocal; unmistakable.* ■ Identifying opinion leaders is not *a simple task* since they tend to be product specific and differ over time. REPLACE WITH *easy.*

eat crow A moribund metaphor (see page 21). *be abased; be chastened; be debased; be degraded; be demeaned; be disgraced; be dishonored; be embarrassed; be humbled; be humiliated; be lowered; be mortified; be shamed.*

eat dirt A moribund metaphor (see page 21). *be abased; be chastened; be debased; be degraded; be demeaned; be disgraced; be dishonored; be embarrassed; be humbled; be humiliated; be lowered; be mortified; be shamed.*

eat, drink, and be merry A popular prescription (see page 23). *be merry; carouse; carry on; celebrate; debauch; dis-*

port; frolic; party; play; revel; riot; roister; rollick; romp; skylark.

eat, drink, and be merry, for tomorrow we die A popular prescription (see page 23).

eat (your) heart out A moribund metaphor (see page 21). *ache; agonize; grieve; hurt; lament; mourn; pine; sorrow; suffer; worry.*

eat (live) high off (on) the hog A moribund metaphor (see page 21). *epicureanly; extravagantly; lavishly; lushly; luxuriantly; opulently; prodigally; profusely; sumptuously; very well.*

eat humble pie A moribund metaphor (see page 21). *be abased; be chastened; be debased; be degraded; be demeaned; be disgraced; be dishonored; be embarrassed; be humbled; be humiliated; be lowered; be mortified; be shamed.*

> But telling my editors they were about to be fined several thousand dollars was not a prospect I relished. So I took a deep breath and ate humble pie. — Neely Tucker, *Love in the Driest Season*

eat like a bird An insipid simile. *be abstemious.; be ascetic.*

eat like a horse An insipid simile. 1. *be esurient; be famished; be gluttonous; be greedy; be hungry; be insatiable; be omnivorous; be rapacious; be ravenous; be starved; be starving; be voracious.* 2. *glut; gorge; overdo; overeat; overfeed; overindulge; sate; satiate; stuff; surfeit.*

eat like a pig An insipid simile. 1. *be esurient; be famished; be gluttonous; be* greedy; be hungry; be insatiable; be omnivorous; be rapacious; be ravenous; be starved; be starving; be voracious. 2. glut; gorge; overdo; overeat; overfeed; overindulge; sate; satiate; stuff; surfeit.

eat out of (the palm of) (her) hand A moribund metaphor (see page 21). abide by; acquiesce; comply with; conform; follow; obey; yield.

eat (me) out of house and home A moribund metaphor (see page 21). 1. be esurient; be famished; be gluttonous; be greedy; be hungry; be insatiable; be omnivorous; be rapacious; be ravenous; be starved; be starving; be voracious. 2. glut; gorge; overdo; overeat; overfeed; overindulge; sate; satiate; stuff; surfeit.

eat (him) (up) alive A moribund metaphor (see page 21). 1. consume; enclose; envelop; surround. 2. exploit; use.

We might had charged the stage to eat him up alive if he had been any more sly and enchanting and wise. — Philip Roth, *The Ghost Writer*

eat (her) words A moribund metaphor (see page 21). disavow; recant; repudiate; retract; take back; withdraw.

ebb and flow A moribund metaphor (see page 21). ■ Optimists try to attribute a linear progression to the *ebb and flow* of history.

effect An overworked word (see page 22). For example: *chilling effect; cumulative effect; domino effect; dramatic effect; negative effect; snowball effect; sobering effect; trickle-down effect*. ■ LeBlanc's lawyers say that would *have a chilling effect on* fraud lawsuits brought by gov-

ernment employees. REPLACE WITH *discourage*. ■ You can learn how to free yourself from the *destructive effects* of negative people in your workplace. REPLACE WITH *detriment*. SEE ALSO *has an effect on*.

effective and efficient An inescapable pair (see page 20). Businesspeople, in particular, seem unable to use the word *effective* without also using *efficient*. And though businesses endlessly plume themselves on how *effective and efficient* they are (and how *excellent* their products and services are), this is rarely true. In the end, the dimwitted *effective and efficient* may mean to us all what it has come to mean to businesses: 1. shoddy and inept, 2. uncaring and purblind, 3. money-grubbing and malevolent. ■ For these methods, more *effective and efficient* methods are available. REPLACE WITH *effective* or *efficient*. ■ More than an audit, the study should evaluate the *efficiency and effectiveness* of social services and public works. REPLACE WITH *efficiency* or *effectiveness*. ■ The work place should be a safe environment where one can *effectively and efficiently* perform required duties. REPLACE WITH *effectively* or *efficiently*.

effectuate A torpid term (see page 24). bring about; carry out; cause; do; effect; execute; occasion. SEE ALSO *eventuate*.

(with) egg on (my) face A moribund metaphor (see page 21). abashed; ashamed; chagrined; confused; discomfited; discomposed; disconcerted; embarrassed; flustered; humbled; humiliated; mortified; nonplused; perplexed; red-faced; shamed; shamefaced; sheepish; upset. ■ Everybody likes to see Harvard *with egg on its face*. REPLACE WITH *embarrassed*.

egregious error An inescapable pair (see page 20).

either one A wretched redundancy (see page 25). *either.* ■ He doesn't care about *either one* of you. DELETE *one.* SEE ALSO *each one; neither one.*

(an) element A torpid term (see page 24). ■ Proper validation is *an* essential *element.* DELETE *an element.* ■ Black turnout was especially low, and that was *a* key *element* to her victory. DELETE *a element.* SEE ALSO *(a) factor.*

elevate to an art form A moribund metaphor (see page 21). ■ He would add to the gridlock, then compound the people's frustrations by *elevating* the blame game *to an art form.*

empty void A wretched redundancy (see page 25). *emptiness; void.* ■ I know that without me around my mother got lonely and just needed someone to fill the *empty void.* REPLACE WITH *emptiness* or *void.*

enclosed herein (herewith) A wretched redundancy (see page 25). *enclosed; here.* ■ *Enclosed herein* is the complete manuscript. REPLACE WITH *Here* or *Enclosed.*

enclosed please find A wretched redundancy (see page 25). *enclosed is; here is.* ■ *Enclosed please find* materials that you might find useful prior to your arrival. REPLACE WITH *Enclosed are.* ■ *Enclosed please find* a listing of single family properties that are available for purchase by eligible buyers. REPLACE WITH *Here is.*

endangered species A moribund metaphor (see page 21). ■ We all recog-nize that the nuclear family is an *endangered species.*

end of the line A moribund metaphor (see page 21). *close; completion; conclusion; culmination; consummation; end; ending; finale; finish; fulfillment; termination.*

end on a high note A moribund metaphor (see page 21).

end result A wretched redundancy (see page 25). *result.* ■ The *end result* should be that all mothers and fathers would pay what they can afford. DELETE *end.*

enjoy it while (you) can A popular prescription (see page 23).

enough is enough A quack equation (see page 23). Though often used to conclude an argument, *enough is enough* is the least compelling of summations. No one can argue *enough is enough* and expect to be persuasive. The phrase convinces us only that its user reasons ineffectually and unremarkably.

equally as A wretched redundancy (see page 25). *as; equally.* ■ *Equally as* important, this program provides comprehensive preventive coverage. REPLACE WITH *As* or *Equally.*

ere A withered word (see page 24). *before.* ■ So I avoided the hole and assumed it might likely be June *ere* it was patched. REPLACE WITH *before.*

ergo A withered word (see page 24). *consequently; hence; therefore.*

establishment A torpid term (see page 24). *business; club; company; firm; outlet; shop; store.* ■ You should park close to the entrance of the *establishment* you are shopping at. REPLACE WITH *store.*

et cetera (etc., etc.; et cetera, et cetera) A grammatical gimmick (see page 19). ■ I'm very outgoing and adaptable, *et cetera, et cetera.* DELETE *et cetera, et cetera.* ■ She told me he was everything she was looking for, *et cetera, et cetera.* DELETE *et cetera, et cetera.* ■ Dr. Holmes was a man of brilliant conversational gifts — one of the most notable of that noted circle which composed the "Saturday Club" in Boston — Longfellow, Emerson, Lowell, Whittier, Thoreau, Bayard Taylor, *etc., etc.* DELETE *etc., etc.*

When thoughts stumble and then stop, words, or at least intelligible words, do as well. As often as not, *et cetera* is a means of expressing, without having to admit to its meaning, all those words only dimly thought. SEE ALSO *blah, blah, blah; and so on, and so forth.*

et tu, Brute A foreign phrase (see page 19).

even Steven An infantile phrase (see page 20).

even the score A moribund metaphor (see page 21).

eventuate A torpid term (see page 24). *befall; come about; end; happen; occur; result; take place.* SEE ALSO *effectuate.*

ever and anon A withered word (see page 24). *now and then; occasionally.*

everybody and (his) brother (mother) An infantile phrase (see page 20). *all; everybody; everyone.* ■ *Everybody and their mother* is on line today. REPLACE WITH *Everybody.* ■ It's like *everybody and their brother* is having a hearing on Enron.

everybody talks about the weather, but nobody does anything about it An infantile phrase (see page 20).

every cloud has a silver lining A popular prescription (see page 23).

every effort is being made A suspect superlative (see page 24). This phrase, disembodied though it is, serves to disarm people as it dismisses them. ■ *Every effort is being made* to find the perpetrators of this heinous crime. ■ *Every effort has been made* to make this verification as simple and painless as possible. ■ During this time, please be patient as *every effort is being made* to process your order in a timely manner. ■ First, we want to be sure that *every effort is being made* to spot, recover, preserve, identify and deliver any human remains to the families of the victims. SEE ALSO *that's interesting; that's nice.*

every nook and cranny A moribund metaphor (see page 21). *all around; all over; all through; everyplace; everywhere; throughout.*

every single (solitary) A wretched redundancy (see page 25). *every.* ■ *Every single solitary* night we see people dying. REPLACE WITH *Every.*

every step of the way A moribund metaphor (see page 21). 1. *always; ceaselessly; constantly; continually; continuous-*

ly; endlessly; eternally; everlastingly; ever-more; forever; forevermore; frequently; interminably; nonstop; permanently; perpetually; persistently; recurrently; regularly; repeatedly; unceasingly; unremittingly. 2. *all during; all over; all through; everywhere; throughout.*

everything but the kitchen sink A moribund metaphor (see page 21). *aggregate; all; all things; entirety; everything; gross; lot; sum; total; totality; whole.*

everything happens for a reason A popular prescription (see page 23).

everything's coming up roses An infantile phrase (see page 20). *be auspicious; be encouraging; be good; be hopeful; be optimistic; be promising; be propitious; be rosy.*

everything's (it's all) relative An infantile phrase (see page 20). SEE ALSO *(as) compared to what? (as) opposed to what?*

everything under the sun A moribund metaphor (see page 21). *all; all things; everything.* ■ I tried *everything under the sun* to get her to shape up. REPLACE WITH *everything.*

everything (it) will turn out for the best A popular prescription (see page 23).

everything you always wanted to know about ... but were afraid to ask An infantile phrase (see page 20).

every time (you) turn around A moribund metaphor (see page 21). *always; ceaselessly; constantly; continually; continuously; endlessly; eternally; everlastingly; evermore; forever; forevermore; frequently;*

interminably; often; permanently; perpetually; persistently; recurrently; regularly; repeatedly; unceasingly; unremittingly.

every Tom, Dick, and Harry A moribund metaphor (see page 21). *all; citizenry; commonage; commonalty; common people; crowd; everybody; everyone; herd; hoi polloi; masses; mob; multitude; plebeians; populace; proletariat; public; rabble.* ■ I am not advocating that you tip *every Tom, Dick, and Harry.* REPLACE WITH *everyone.*

every trick in the book A moribund metaphor (see page 21). ■ They're pulling *every trick in the book* to keep this amendment off the 1992 ballot.

excellence An overworked word (see page 22). The word is overworked, and the concept undervalued. Too much, today, passes for *excellence.* Too much of our work is shoddy, too much of our wisdom, suspect, too much of our worth, unsure. ■ With your help, we will continue that tradition of *excellence.* SEE ALSO *pursue (strive for) excellence.*

excess verbiage A wretched redundancy (see page 25). *verbiage.*

excruciating pain An inescapable pair (see page 20). ■ This medication was initially prescribed to soothe the *excruciating pain* that I was suffering.

excuse me? An infantile phrase (see page 20). No longer exclusively a polite way of signifying that you did not hear what a person has said, *excuse me* is also — especially among the young and stupidly egoistic — an impolite way of signifying that you did not like what a person has said. With an autocratic intonation, the person expresses hostility to what he hears. This phrase is particularly loathsome, for those who use it dare not be openly angry or upset; they try to disguise their anger and arrogance behind a mantle of mannerliness. SEE ALSO *I'm sorry; thank you; whatever.*

expert opinion A suspect superlative (see page 24).

expletive deleted An infantile phrase (see page 20).

explore every avenue A moribund metaphor (see page 21).

(an) explosion of A moribund metaphor (see page 21). SEE ALSO *a barrage of.*

express (concern) A torpid term (see page 24). Phrases like *express concern, express doubt, express opposition, express thanks* make any sentence instantly sodden. ■ Officials *express concern* about the slow pace of economic growth. REPLACE WITH *worry.* ■ House Democrats continue to *express anger* about the state's ethics and campaign finance laws. REPLACE WITH *fume.* ■ I want to *express my appreciation to* all of you who have lent us a hand in this endeavor. REPLACE WITH *thank.*

extend (hold out) the olive branch A moribund metaphor (see page 21). *be accommodating; be agreeable; be conciliatory; be obliging; be peaceable; be propitiatory.*

extent A torpid term (see page 24). Like *degree*, the word *extent*, along with the phrases in which it is found, is best avoided.

These are lifeless expressions, and it is listless people who use them. ■ In some cases, they've been transformed *to such an extent* that you can no longer recognize them. REPLACE WITH *so much.* ■ The study said that women, *to a greater extent* than men, manage by personal interactions with their subordinates. REPLACE WITH *more.* ■ Resources are always used *to the optimum extent.* REPLACE WITH *optimally.* ■ Sooner or later, we will see *to what extent* the central banks are prepared to back up words with actions. REPLACE WITH *how far.* ■ *The extent to which* these practices are seen as flowing in one direction, down from headquarters to subsidiaries, may influence *the extent to which* these practices are adopted and *to what extent* the behavior, beliefs, and values of the corporate culture are incorporated or even complied with. REPLACE WITH *How much, how much,* and *how much.* SEE ALSO *degree.*

extenuating circumstances A torpid term (see page 24).

> It was a lovely apology for missing drinks the previous evening due to extenuating circumstances, you know, my job. — Michele Mitchell, *The Latest Bombshell*

(an) eye for an eye (and a tooth for a tooth) A popular prescription (see page 23).

(his) eyes are bigger than (his) stomach A moribund metaphor (see page 21).

eyes are the windows of the soul A moribund metaphor (see page 21).

(has) eyes in the back of (his) head A moribund metaphor (see page 21). *alert; attentive; aware; eagle-eyed; heedful; keen; observant; perceptive; vigilant; wakeful; watchful.*

eyes (are) wide open A moribund metaphor (see page 21). *alert; attentive; aware; cognizant; conscious; eagle-eyed; heedful; keen; observant; perceptive; vigilant; wakeful; watchful.*

F

fabulous An overworked word (see page 22). As still another synonym for *very good* or *extremely pleasing, fabulous* is indeed overused. In its sense of *hard to believe* or *astounding*, it is now and again used, and in its sense of *like a fable* or *legendary*, it is woefully unused.

(the) face that launched a thousand ships A moribund metaphor (see page 21).

face the music A moribund metaphor (see page 21). *pay; suffer.*

Not to be a member of the communion of saints or gods or demigods or fathers or mothers or grandfathers or grandmothers or brothers or sisters or brethren of any kind, germane to me through consanguinity, affinity, or any other kind of linear or genitive or collateral bond. To face the music at last. — Edna O'Brien, *Night*

(the) (plain; simple) fact is (that) An ineffectual phrase (see page 19). ■ *The fact is* at least the govenor is trying. DELETE *The fact is.* ■ *The simple fact is* we are now spending nearly $1 trillion on health care. DELETE *The simple fact is.* ■ *The plain fact is* American women are buying guns like they've never bought them before. DELETE *The plain fact is.*

(the) (simple) fact of the matter is An ineffectual phrase (see page 19). ■ *The fact of the matter is* the police took the children from you. DELETE *The fact of the matter is.* ■ Despite her behavior, *the simple fact of the matter is* I still love her. DELETE *the simple fact of the matter is.* SEE ALSO *the truth of the matter is.*

(the) fact remains (that) An ineffectual phrase (see page 19). ■ We call this campaign a "snoozer," but *the fact remains* both candidates did behave responsibly. DELETE *the fact remains.* ■ Whether one prefers the proverb's optimism or Euripides' pessimism, *the fact remains that* the way in which investigations are conducted can have a significant impact on the outcome of any case. DELETE *the fact remains that.*

(the) fact that An ineffectual phrase (see page 19). ■ *The fact that* many more computers are in communication with one another increases concern that users' privacy will be violated. REPLACE WITH *That.* ■ *The fact that* she was rather attractive did not escape their notice. REPLACE WITH *That.*

In other rooms, in other houses, all over the world, other bodies devoted to sex, or compost, or holism, or Marxism, are forming

> thousands of similar wheels: but what makes these wheels so fatally different from the one now running at Hyde's Mortimer is the fact that all the others are running in wrong directions. — Nigel Dennis, *Cards of Identity*

(a) factor A torpid term (see page 24). ■ I think the TV show was *a* contributing *factor* to this tragedy. REPLACE WITH *contributed*. ■ They thought the biggest problem we were dealing with was *a* jealousy *factor*. REPLACE WITH *jealousy*. ■ The key *factor* in the decline appears to be the Irish-American voter's willingness to vote for candidates from other ethnic groups. REPLACE WITH *key to*. SEE ALSO *(an) element*. ■ The presence of a long umbilical cord is *a* contributory *factor* to the occurrence of nuchal cord. REPLACE WITH *contributes*.

facts and figures An inescapable pair (see page 20).

facts and information A wretched redundancy (see page 25). *data; facts; information.*

fade into the sunset A moribund metaphor (see page 21). *disappear; disperse; dissolve; evaporate; fade; vanish; vaporize; volatilize.*

fade into the woodwork A moribund metaphor (see page 21). *depart; disappear; disperse; dissolve; evaporate; fade; vacate; vanish; vaporize; volatilize; withdraw.* ■ It is easy to *fade into the woodwork* and never have to deal with those problems. REPLACE WITH *disappear*.

fading fast A moribund metaphor (see page 21). *beat; bushed; debilitated; depleted; drained; drowsy; enervated; exhausted; fatigued; groggy; sapped; sleepy; sluggish; slumberous; somnolent; soporific; spent; tired; weary; worn out.*

fair and equitable An inescapable pair (see page 20). *equitable; fair; just.* ■ The key to maintaining that system is ensuring that you are treated *fairly and equitably*. REPLACE WITH *equitably* or *fairly*.

fair and square An inescapable pair (see page 20). *aboveboard; creditable; equitable; fair; honest; honorable; just; lawful; legitimate; open; proper; reputable; respectable; right; square; straightforward; upright; veracious; veridical.*

fair game A moribund metaphor (see page 21).

fair is fair A quack equation (see page 23).

fair share A torpid term (see page 24). *allocation; allotment; allowance; amount; apportionment; dole; lot; measure; part; piece; portion; quota; ration; share.* ■ We are setting out to get our *fair share* of the residential real estate mortgage business.

fair to middling A wretched redundancy (see page 25). *average; common; fair; mediocre; middling; moderate; ordinary; passable; tolerable.*

fait accompli A foreign phrase (see page 19).

fall between (through) the cracks A moribund metaphor (see page 21). *be discounted; be disregarded; be elided; be forgotten; be ignored; be left out; be missed; be neglected; be omitted; be overlooked; be skipped; be slighted; be* *snubbed; elapse; end; fail; go by; lapse; slid; slip.* ■ Such a caring environment is particularly important for students who have few other sources of support and who might well *fall through the cracks* in a less personalized school setting. REPLACE WITH *be forgotten.* ■ Between groping for meaningful full-time employment and anguishing over the political state of our country, I've allowed some things to *fall between the cracks.* REPLACE WITH *lapse.*

fall flat on (its) face A moribund metaphor (see page 21). *be unsuccessful; blunder; bomb; break down; bungle; collapse; fail; fall short; falter; fizzle; flop; fold; founder; mess up; miscarry; not succeed; stumble; topple.* ■ Some professional investors are betting the company will *fall flat on its face.* REPLACE WITH *fail.*

fall from grace A moribund metaphor (see page 21). *collapse; decline; downfall; failure; fall; misadventure; misfortune; offense; peccadillo; ruin; sin; transgression; wrongdoing.*

fall in (into) line (place) A moribund metaphor (see page 21). *abide by; accede; accommodate; accord; acquiesce; adapt; adhere to; agree; behave; comply; concur; conform; correspond; follow; harmonize; heed; mind; obey; observe; submit; yield.*

fall into (my) lap A moribund metaphor (see page 21). ■ It just kind of *fell into my lap.*

fall on deaf ears A moribund metaphor (see page 21). *disregard; ignore.*

fall through the floor A moribund metaphor (see page 21). *collapse; crash; decline; decrease; descend; dip; drop; ebb;*

fall; plummet; plunge; recede; sink; slide; slip; subside; topple; tumble. ■ But Cellucci said the bond rating *fell through the floor* in the late 1980s during the fiscal crisis. REPLACE WITH *collapsed.*

fame and fortune A suspect superlative (see page 24). SEE ALSO *the rich and famous.*

familiarity breeds contempt A popular prescription (see page 23).

> When we first discussed my working on the books' pages, Nathan argued that, if I ever achieved my ambition to become the books editor, I would end up hating books. Familiarity bred contempt.
> — Elizabeth Buchan, *Revenge Of The Middle-Aged Woman*

(the) family that prays together stays together A popular prescription (see page 23).

fan (fuel) the fire (flames) A moribund metaphor (see page 21). *activate; agitate; animate; arouse; awaken; encourage; enkindle; enliven; exacerbate; excite; feed; foment; ignite; impassion; incite; inflame; intensify; invigorate; make worse; nourish; prod; provoke; rejuvenate; revitalize; revive; rouse; shake up; stimulate; stir up; vitalize; worsen.*

far and away A wretched redundancy (see page 25). *by far; much.*

far and wide An inescapable pair (see page 20). *all around; all over; all through; broadly; everyplace; everywhere; extensively; throughout; ubiquitously; universally; widely.* SEE ALSO *high and wide; left and right.*

far-reaching consequences (implications) An inescapable pair (see page 20).

fashion statement A plebeian sentiment (see page 23). Making a *fashion statement* is the concern of adolescents and addle-brained adults who have yet to fashion for themselves a sense of identity. Their habiliments interest them more than does their humanity.

People so intent on being fashionable make only misstatements. They but blither.

fast and furious An inescapable pair (see page 20).

(as) fast as (her) legs can carry (her) An insipid simile. *abruptly; apace; at once; briskly; directly; expeditiously; fast; forthwith; hastily; hurriedly; immediately; instantaneously; instantly; posthaste; promptly; quickly; rapidly; rashly; right away; speedily; straightaway; swiftly; wingedly.*

fasten your seat belts A moribund metaphor (see page 21).

faster than a speeding bullet (more powerful than a locomotive, able to leap small buildings at a single bound) An infantile phrase (see page 20).

fast track A moribund metaphor (see page 21).

fast trigger finger A moribund metaphor (see page 21).

(as) fat as a cow An insipid simile. *ample; big; bulky; chubby; chunky; colossal; corpulent; dumpy; enormous; fat; flabby; fleshy; gigantic; heavy; hefty; huge; immense; large; mammoth; massive; obese; plump; portly; pudgy; rotund; round; squat; stocky; stout.*

(as) fat as a pig An insipid simile. *ample; big; bulky; chubby; chunky; colossal; corpulent; dumpy; enormous; fat; flabby; fleshy; gigantic; heavy; hefty; huge; immense; large; mammoth; massive; obese; plump; portly; pudgy; rotund; round; squat; stocky; stout.*

fat cat A moribund metaphor (see page 21). *billionaire; capitalist; financier; magnate; materialist; millionaire; mogul; multimillionaire; nabob; plutocrat; tycoon.*

(the) fat's in the fire A moribund metaphor (see page 21).

fear and trembling An inescapable pair (see page 20). *alarm; anxiety; apprehension; consternation; dismay; dread; fear; foreboding; fright; horror; panic; terror; trembling; trepidation.*

feast or famine An inescapable pair (see page 20).

(a) feather in (his) cap A moribund metaphor (see page 21). *accomplishment; achievement; feat; success; triumph; victory.*

> But I can remember that from quite early on, for some reason, Isabel decided that Edith was rather a feather in her cap, someone that little bit special to be fed to her country neighbours in rationed morsels. — Julian Fellowes, *Snobs*

feather (their) nest A moribund metaphor (see page 21). ■ He repeatedly denied allegations that he used his three years at the Denver-based thrift to *feather his* own *nest*.

feed (you) a line A moribund metaphor (see page 21). *deceive; dissemble; distort; equivocate; falsify; fib; lie; misconstrue; mislead; misrepresent; pervert; prevaricate.*

feedback A torpid term (see page 24). *answers; data; feelings; ideas; information; recommendations; replies; responses; suggestions; thoughts; views.* ■ Your *feedback* helps us continually improve. REPLACE WITH *suggestions.* ■ And as *feedback* is obtained, it is the duty of the firm's leaders to convey it to all members of the firm. REPLACE WITH *ideas.* SEE ALSO *(the) bottom line; input; interface; output; parameters.*

feeling no pain A moribund metaphor (see page 21). *besotted; crapulous; drunk; inebriated; intoxicated; sodden; stupefied; tipsy.*

feeling (his) oats A moribund metaphor (see page 21). *active; alive; animated; dynamic; energetic; exuberant; frisky; indefatigable; inexhaustible; invigorated; lively; peppy; spirited; sprightly; spry; tireless; unflagging; vibrant; vigorous; vivacious; zestful; zesty.*

(the) feeling's mutual An infantile phrase (see page 20).

feel the pinch A moribund metaphor (see page 21).

feel the heat A moribund metaphor (see page 21).

fertile ground A moribund metaphor (see page 21).

few and far between A wretched redundancy (see page 25). *exiguous; limited; inadequate; infrequent; meager; rare; scant; scanty; scarce; sparse; uncommon; unusual.* ■ Role models are *few and far between* in those groups. REPLACE WITH *scarce.*

(has a) few screws loose A moribund metaphor (see page 21). *batty; cracked; crazy; daft; demented; deranged; fey; foolish; goofy; insane; lunatic; mad; maniacal; neurotic; nuts; nutty; psychotic; raving; silly; squirrelly; strange; touched; unbalanced; unhinged; unsound; wacky; zany.*

(the) first step is always the hardest A popular prescription (see page 23).

(bid) a fond farewell An infantile phrase (see page 20).

(a) fool and his money are soon parted A popular prescription (see page 23).

(a) force to be reckoned with An infantile phrase (see page 20). *adversary; antagonist; challenger; competitor; contender; contestant; force; opponent; rival.* ■ The combination of Walsh, the broadcast of Celtics games this season, and hot Fox network programming will make WFXT *a force to be reckoned with.* REPLACE WITH *a contender.*

(the) four corners of the earth (world) A moribund metaphor (see page 21). *all over; everyplace; everywhere; the world over; throughout (the land); universally; worldwide.* ■ These changes will affect our American patients as well as those who come to the clinic from the *four* *corners of the world.* REPLACE WITH *the world over.*

fiddle while Rome burns A moribund metaphor (see page 21).

(a) fifth wheel A moribund metaphor (see page 21). *excessive; extra; extraneous; immaterial; incidental; inconsequential; insignificant; irrelevant; needless; nonessential; superabundant; superfluous; unimportant; unnecessary.* ■ With his mother doing the cooking and other household chores, I would feel like *a fifth wheel.* REPLACE WITH *superfluous.*

fight a losing battle A moribund metaphor (see page 21).

fight fire with fire A moribund metaphor (see page 21).

fight like cats and dogs An insipid simile 1. *altercate; argue; disagree; dispute; feud; fight; quarrel; spat; squabble; wrangle.* 2. *battle; brawl; clash; fight; grapple; jostle; make war; scuffle; skirmish; tussle; war; wrestle.*

filled to bursting (overflowing) A moribund metaphor (see page 21). *abounding; brimful; brimming; bursting; chock-full; congested; crammed; crowded; dense; filled; full; gorged; jammed; jampacked; overcrowded; overfilled; overflowing; packed; replete; saturated; stuffed; swarming; teeming.*

filled to the brim A moribund metaphor (see page 21). *abounding; brimful; brimming; bursting; chock-full; congested; crammed; crowded; dense; filled; full; gorged; jammed; jam-packed; overcrowded; overfilled; packed; replete; saturated; stuffed; swarming; teeming.*

> I recall the scent of some kind of toilet powder — I believe she stole it from her mother's Spanish maid — a sweetish, lowly, musky perfume. It mingled with her own biscuity odor, and my senses were suddenly filled to the brim; a sudden commotion in a nearby bush prevented them from overflowing .... — Vladimir Nabokov, *Lolita*

fill in the blanks An infantile phrase (see page 20).

fill (his) shoes A moribund metaphor (see page 21).

fill the bill A moribund metaphor (see page 21). 1. *be appropriate; be apt; be befitting; be felicitous; be fit; be fitting; be happy; be meet; be proper; be right; be seemly; be suitable; be suited.* 2. *be acceptable; be adequate; be qualified; be satisfactory; be sufficient.*

fill to capacity A wretched redundancy (see page 25). *fill.* ■ Our free public facilities are *filled to capacity*, and there are long waiting lists for some programs. REPLACE WITH *filled.*

filthy lucre A moribund metaphor (see page 21). *money; riches; wealth.*

final and irrevocable An inescapable pair (see page 20). *final; firm; irrevocable; unalterable.*

final chapter A moribund metaphor (see page 21). *close; completion; conclusion; consummation; culmination; denouement; end; ending; finale; finish; termination.*

final conclusion A wretched redundancy (see page 25). ■ We have made no *final conclusions* on responsibility for the attacks in Kenya and Tanzania. DELETE *final.*

final culmination A wretched redundancy (see page 25). culmination. ■ Owning a farm was the *final culmination* of all our efforts. DELETE *final.*

final decision A wretched redundancy (see page 25). decision. ■ That's one of the things we have under consideration, but no final *decision* has been made. DELETE *final.*

(the) final (last) frontier A moribund metaphor (see page 21).

(that's) the final (last) straw A moribund metaphor (see page 21).

finalize A torpid term (see page 24). *complete; conclude; consummate; end; execute; finish; fulfill; made final; terminate.* ■ Delays in *finalizing* the state budget and its allocations to cities and towns make a special town meeting necessary. REPLACE WITH *completing.* SEE ALSO utilize.

finder's keepers, loser's weepers An infantile phrase (see page 20).

find (some) middle ground A moribund metaphor (see page 21). *compromise.*

fine and dandy An inescapable pair (see page 20). *all right; excellent; fine; good; O.K.; well.* SEE ALSO *well and good.*

(a) fine (pretty) kettle of fish A moribund metaphor (see page 21). *complica-*

tion; difficulty; dilemma; mess; muddle; ordeal; pickle; plight; predicament; problem; quandary; trial; trouble.

fine line A moribund metaphor (see page 21). ■ There is a very *fine line* between vision and delusion.

fingers on the pulse of A moribund metaphor (see page 21).

fire (launch) a salvo A moribund metaphor (see page 21).

(all) fired (hopped, psyched) up A moribund metaphor (see page 21). *afire; aflame; anxious; ardent; burning; eager; enthusiastic; excited; fanatic; fanatical; fervent; fervid; fiery; impassioned; inflamed; intense; perfervid; keen; passionate; vehement; zealous.*

fire in (his) belly A moribund metaphor (see page 21). *ambitious; ardent; determined; dogged; driven; eager; enthusiastic; fervent; impassioned; motivated; passionate; persistent; pushy; resolute; strong-willed.*

(a) firestorm of A moribund metaphor (see page 21). ■ That decision unleashed *a firestorm of* protest in the Capitol. SEE ALSO *a barrage of.*

firmly establish An inescapable pair (see page 20). Adverbs often modify other words needlessly. Here, firmly is superfluous, for establish means "to make firm." ■ The play *firmly established* him as a dramatist. DELETE *firmly.*

first and foremost A wretched redundancy (see page 25). *chief; chiefly; first; foremost; initial; initially; main; mainly;*

most important; mostly; primarily; primary; principal; principally. ■ *First and foremost* these people must have a commitment to public service. REPLACE WITH *Most important.* SEE ALSO *first and most important.*

first and most important A wretched redundancy (see page 25). *chief; chiefly; first; foremost; initial; initially; main; mainly; most important; mostly; primarily; primary; principal; principally.* SEE ALSO *first and foremost.*

first begin (start) A wretched redundancy (see page 25). *begin; start.* ■ When we *first started* exploring the idea, we didn't even know if it was possible to do. DELETE *first.*

first line of defense A moribund metaphor (see page 21).

first of all A wretched redundancy (see page 25). *first.* ■ *First of all,* I am delighted about our progress in that area. REPLACE WITH *First.* SEE ALSO *second of all.*

first (highest; number-one; top) priority A torpid term (see page 24). Nothing soulful can be said using these expressions, so when a U.S. cardinal drearily sermonizes "The protection of children must be our number-one priority," we are hardly convinced that this is his or the church's principal concern. When we read, in some corporate promotional piece, "Your satisfaction is our number-one priority," we are likewise, and for good reason, suspicious. Mechanical expressions like *first (highest; number-one; top) priority* defy tenderness, resist compassion, and counter concern. SEE ALSO *reach epidemic proportions.*

fish or cut bait A moribund metaphor (see page 21).

(like a) fish out of water An insipid simile. *awkward; blundering; bumbling; bungling; clumsy; gawky; gauche; ham-handed; heavy-handed; inapt; inept; lubberly; lumbering; maladroit; uncoordinated; uncouth; ungainly; ungraceful; unhandy; unskillful; unwieldy.*

(bigger; other) fish to fry A moribund metaphor (see page 21).

Now, I wish I could remember Daddy's reply to all her nagging, but I had bigger fish to fry that weekend and didn't much care that Missy had inexplicably fallen in love with her own uncle .... — Janis Owens, *The Schooling of Claybird Catts*

(as) fit as a fiddle An insipid simile. *athletic; beefy; brawny; energetic; fit; good; hale; hardy; healthful; healthy; hearty; husky; lanky; lean; manly; muscular; powerful; robust; shapely; sinewy; slender; solid; sound; stalwart; stout; strong; sturdy; thin; trim; vigorous; virile; well; well-built.*

fit for a king A moribund metaphor (see page 21). *august; awe-inspiring; distinguished; elegant; eminent; exalted; exquisite; extraordinary; extravagant; glorious; grand; great; impressive; kingly; luxurious; magnificent; majestic; monarchical; nobel; opulent; princely; regal; royal; sovereign; splendid; stately; sumptuous.*

fitting and proper An inescapable pair (see page 20). *appropriate; apt; befitting; felicitous; fit; fitting; happy; meet; proper; right; seemly; suitable; suited.* ■ And it is generally regarded as *fitting and proper* for women to do this. REPLACE WITH *fitting*.

fit to be tied A moribund metaphor (see page 21). *angry; cross; enraged; fuming; furious; incensed; indignant; infuriated; irate; mad; outraged; raging; wrathful.*

fix (her) wagon A moribund metaphor (see page 21). 1. *castigate; censure; chasten; chastise; chide; criticize; discipline; penalize; punish; rebuke; reprove; scold.* 2. *spank.*

flaming inferno An infantile phrase (see page 20). *blaze; conflagration; fire; inferno.*

flash in the pan A moribund metaphor (see page 21). *brief; ephemeral; evanescent; fleeting; momentary; short; short-lived; short-term; temporary; transient; transitory.*

(as) flat as a board An insipid simile. *even; flat; flush; horizontal; level; plane; smooth.*

(as) flat as a pancake An insipid simile. *even; flat; flush; horizontal; level; plane; smooth.*

flat on (his) back A moribund metaphor (see page 21). *afflicted; ailing; crippled; debilitated; defenseless; disabled; diseased; feeble; fragile; helpless; ill; incapacitated; indisposed; infirm; not (feeling) well; sick; sickly; unhealthy; unwell; valetudinarian; weak.*

(my) (own) flesh and blood A moribund metaphor (see page 21). 1. *brother; child; daughter; father; kin; mother;* parent; relative; sibling; sister; son. 2. *depth; reality; substance.*

flight of fancy A moribund metaphor (see page 21). *caprice; chimera; crotchet; daydream; delusion; dream; fancy; fantasy; hallucination; humor; illusion; imagination; notion; phantasm; vagary; whim; whimsy.*

flip (her) lid A moribund metaphor (see page 21). *bellow; bluster; clamor; explode; fulminate; fume; holler; howl; rage; rant; rave; roar; scream; shout; storm; thunder; vociferate; yell.*

(on the) flip side (of the coin) A moribund metaphor (see page 21). 1. *antithesis; contrary; converse; opposite; reverse.* 2. *but; in contrast; conversely; however; inversely; whereas; yet.*

(whatever) floats your boat A moribund metaphor (see page 21).

(a) flood of A moribund metaphor (see page 21). ■ The evidence indicates NAFTA will lead to *a flood of* auto exports from the United States to Mexico. ■ Should the doctors win, labor leaders predict *a flood of* physicians signing up with unions. SEE ALSO *a barrage of.*

flotsam and jetsam An inescapable pair (see page 20). 1. *debris; litter; rack; refuse; rubbish; rubble; wrack; wreckage.* 2. *bits; fragments; modicums; odds and ends; particles; pieces; remnants; scraps; shreds; snippets; trifles.* 3. *itinerants; rovers; tramps; vagabonds; vagrants; wanderers.*

flowing with milk and honey A moribund metaphor (see page 21).

fly (ride) below (under) the radar (of) A moribund metaphor (see page 21). 1. *disregarded; hidden; ignored; imperceptible; indiscernible; invisible; overlooked; undetectable; undetected; unheard of; unknown; unnoticeable; unnoticed; unobserved; unperceived; unrevealed; unseen.* 2. *discreet; inconspicuous; self-effacing; unassuming; understated; unobtrusive.* ■ The sport isn't exactly *riding under the radar* in the United States anymore, thanks in large part to Lance Armstrong's dominant reign in the Tour de France. REPLACE WITH *unnoticed.* ■ *Flying under the radar* are the Russians, who may just be warming up for the medal round. REPLACE WITH *Unassuming.*

fly-by-night A moribund metaphor (see page 21). *irresponsible; undependable; unreliable; untrustworthy.*

fly by the seat of (his) pants A moribund metaphor (see page 21). *be extemporaneous; be instinctive; be spontaneous; impromptu; improvise.* ■ Administrators who *fly by the seat of their pants* typically rely on trial and error because there are no overarching objectives and guidelines. REPLACE WITH *are instinctive.*

flying high A moribund metaphor (see page 21). 1. *advantageous; auspicious; blessed; charmed; enchanted; favored; felicitous; flourishing; fortuitous; fortunate; golden; happy; in luck; lucky; propitious; prosperous; successful; thriving.* 2. *blissful; blithe; buoyant; cheerful; delighted; ecstatic; elated; enraptured; euphoric; exalted; excited; exhilarated; exultant; gay; glad; gleeful; good-humored; happy; intoxicated; jolly; jovial; joyful; joyous; jubilant; merry; mirthful; overjoyed; pleased; rapturous; thrilled.*

fly in the face of A moribund metaphor (see page 21). *buck; challenge; contradict; defy; disobey; dispute; disregard; flout; go against; ignore; militate against; neglect; oppose; overlook; resist; violate.* ■ This is nonsensical and *flies in the face of* history and basic economic principles. REPLACE WITH *contradicts.*

fly in the ointment A moribund metaphor (see page 21). *bar; barrier; block; blockage; catch; check; deterrent; difficulty; encumbrance; handicap; hindrance; hitch; hurdle; impediment; interference; obstacle; obstruction; rub; snag.*

fly off the handle A moribund metaphor (see page 21). *bellow; blow up; bluster; clamor; explode; fulminate; fume; holler; howl; rage; rant; rave; roar; scream; shout; storm; thunder; vociferate; yell.* ■ To tell the truth, investors are *flying off the handle* everywhere you look. REPLACE WITH *howling.* ■ Meditation makes me a much calmer person; I don't *fly off the handle* so much. REPLACE WITH *rant.*

fly the coop A moribund metaphor (see page 21). *abscond; clear out; decamp; depart; desert; disappear; escape; exit; flee; fly; go; go away; leave; move on; part; pull out; quit; retire; retreat; run away; take flight; take off; vacate; vanish; withdraw.*

fly (too) close to the sun A moribund metaphor (see page 21). *chance; dare; endanger; gamble; hazard; imperil; jeopardize; make bold; peril; risk; venture.*

(a) flurry of A moribund metaphor (see page 21). ■ The U.S. stock market's strong recovery in the last months of 1998 prompted *a flurry of* charitable giving in December. SEE ALSO *a barrage of.*

(a) fly on the wall A moribund metaphor (see page 21).

foaming (frothing) at the mouth A moribund metaphor (see page 21). *angry; berserk; convulsive; crazed; delirious; demented; demoniac; deranged; enraged; feral; ferocious; fierce; frantic; frenzied; fuming; furious; hysterical; infuriated; in hysterics; insane; incensed; irate; mad; maddened; maniacal; murderous; possessed; rabid; raging; ranting; raving; savage; seething; wild; wrathful.*

focus attention (concentration) on A wretched redundancy (see page 25). *concentrate on; focus on.* ■ Microsoft has always *focused its attention on* software products and software standards. REPLACE WITH *focused on.* ■ It is hardly magic to *focus concentration on* success instead of failure. REPLACE WITH *concentrate on.* SEE ALSO *focus effort (energy) on.*

focus effort (energy) on A wretched redundancy (see page 25). *concentrate on; focus on.* ■ This downsizing will cut our expenses and allow us to *focus our efforts on* serving our customers. REPLACE WITH *focus on.* ■ Owners can *focus their energy on* expanding the business to a point where it can function outside of a "nurtured" environment. REPLACE WITH *focus on.* SEE ALSO *focus attention (concentration) on.*

focus in on A wretched redundancy (see page 25). *focus on.* ■ I have to *focus in on* what I want to accomplish. DELETE *in.*

fold (their) tent A moribund metaphor (see page 21). *abscond; clear out; decamp; depart; desert; disappear; escape; exit; flee; fly; go; go away; leave; move on; part; pull out; quit; retire; retreat; run away; take flight; take off; vacate; vanish; withdraw.*

follow in (her) footsteps A moribund metaphor (see page 21).

follow suit A moribund metaphor (see page 21). *copy; do as much; follow; imitate; mimic.* ■ NYNEX is expected to *follow suit* in the near future. REPLACE WITH *do as much.* ■ When American Airlines slashed fares, TWA *followed suit.* REPLACE WITH *did as much.*

follow the crowd A moribund metaphor (see page 21). *abide by; accede; accommodate; accord; acquiesce; adapt; adhere to; agree; behave; comply; concur; conform; correspond; follow; harmonize; heed; mind; obey; observe; submit; yield.*

follow your instincts A popular prescription (see page 23).

food for thought A moribund metaphor (see page 21). SEE ALSO *(it's) something to think about.*

food for worms A moribund metaphor (see page 21). *dead; deceased; defunct; departed; exanimate; expired; extinct; extinguished; finished; gone; inanimate; lifeless; no more; perished; terminated.*

fools rush in where angels fear to tread A popular prescription (see page 23).

footloose and fancy free A moribund metaphor (see page 21). *at liberty; autonomous; free; independent; self-reliant; unattached; unbound; unconfined; unconstrained; unencumbered; unentangled; unfettered; uninhibited; unrestrained; unrestricted; unshackled; untied.*

footprints in the sands of time A moribund metaphor (see page 21).

foot the bill A moribund metaphor (see page 21). *pay (for)*.

> To argue would mean she was offering to foot the bill, something she had done so often over their years of living together that it had become expected of her. — Amy Tan, *The Bonesetter's Daughter*

for all intents and purposes A wretched redundancy (see page 25). *effectively; essentially; in effect; in essence; practically; virtually.* ■ *For all intents and purposes*, the civil rights acts of 1964 and 1965 signified the demise of official segregation in the United States. REPLACE WITH *In effect*. SEE ALSO *for all practical purposes; to all intents and purposes; to all practical purposes.*

for all practical purposes A wretched redundancy (see page 25). *effectively; essentially; in effect; in essence; practically; virtually.* ■ Services are, *for all practical purposes*, sold as products to end users, so the distinction between services and goods is artificial at best. REPLACE WITH *essentially*. SEE ALSO *for all intents and purposes; to all intents and purposes; to all practical purposes.*

for all (he was) worth A moribund metaphor (see page 21).

for a song A moribund metaphor (see page 21). *cheaply; economically; inexpensively.*

> A real beauty, with wood-spoke wheels and navy mohair upholstery. He was getting it for a song, from a widow who'd never learned to drive her husband's car. — Anita Shreve, *Sea Glass*

for better or for worse A torpid term (see page 24).

> But the family room, the only room where any of us has ever spent any time, has always been, for better or for worse, the ultimate reflection of our true inclinations. — Dave Eggers, *A Heartbreaking Work of Staggering Genius*

forever and a day A moribund metaphor (see page 21). *always; ceaselessly; constantly; continually; continuously; endlessly; eternally; everlastingly; evermore; forever; forevermore; immortally; indefinitely; interminably; permanently; perpetually; persistently; unceasingly; unremittingly.*

for every action there's an equal and opposite reaction A popular prescription (see page 23).

for every negative there is a positive A popular prescription (see page 23).

for everything there is a season A popular prescription (see page 23).

forewarn A wretched redundancy (see page 25). *warn.* ■ *Forewarn* your clients that they might be stared at by locals. REPLACE WITH *Warn*. SEE ALSO *advance warning; warn in advance.*

forewarned is forearmed A quack equation (see page 23).

for free A wretched redundancy (see page 25). *free.*

forgive and forget A popular prescription (see page 23).

fork in the road A moribund metaphor (see page 21).

formative years A torpid term (see page 24). *adolescence; childhood; immaturity; juvenility.*

forsooth A withered word (see page 24). *actually; indeed; in fact; in faith; in reality; in truth; truly.*

(it's) for the birds A moribund metaphor (see page 21). 1. *absurd; asinine; childish; comical; farcical; fatuous; flighty; foolhardy; foolish; frivolous; giddy; idiotic; immature; inane; laughable; ludicrous; nonsensical; preposterous; ridiculous; senseless; silly.* 2. *barren; bootless; effete; feckless; feeble; fruitless; futile; impotent; inadequate; inconsequential; inconsiderable; ineffective; ineffectual; infertile; insignificant; inutile; meaningless; meritless; nugatory; null; of no value; pointless; powerless; profitless; purposeless; sterile; trifling; trivial; unavailing; unimportant; unproductive; unprofitable; unserviceable; unworthy; useless; vain; valueless; weak; worthless.*

for the (simple) fact that A wretched redundancy (see page 25). *because; considering; for; in that; since.* ■ Women received some assistance in the colonial period *for the simple fact that* American Protestants strongly favored "peaceable" and intact families. REPLACE WITH *because.* SEE ALSO *for the (simple) reason that.*

for the most part A wretched redundancy (see page 25). *almost all; chiefly; commonly; generally; greatly; in general; largely; mainly; most; mostly; most often; much; nearly all; overall; normally; typically; usually.* ■ The search for solutions to these crises has focused *for the most part* on the legal system. REPLACE WITH *largely.*

for (with) the purpose of -ing A wretched redundancy (see page 25). *for (-ing); so as to; to.* ■ These analyses have been used *for the purpose of criticizing* the shortcomings of Western management. REPLACE WITH *for criticizing* or *to criticize.* ■ The other was the development in 1923 of a comparison microscope that could be used *for the purpose of determining* whether or not a bullet found at the scene of a crime was fired by a particular gun. REPLACE WITH *for determining* or *to determine.*

for the (simple) reason that A wretched redundancy (see page 25). *because; considering; for; in that; since.* ■ Polls dominate political discourse *for the simple reason that* "Everyone else has an opinion; the pollster has a fact." REPLACE WITH *because.* SEE ALSO *for the (simple) fact that.*

for your information An ineffectual phrase (see page 19). ■ *For your information,* he loves me, and I love him. DELETE *For your information.*

foul up (gum up; screw up) the works A moribund metaphor (see page 21). 1. *agitate; confuse; disorder; disorganize; disquiet; disrupt; disturb; fluster; jar; jinx;*

jolt; jumble; mix up; muddle; perturb; rattle; ruffle; shake up; stir up; unnerve; unsettle; upset. 2. blight; cripple; damage; disable; harm; hurt; impair; incapacitate; lame; mar; mess up; rack; ruin; sabotage; spoil; subvert; undermine; vitiate; wrack; wreck.

free and easy An inescapable pair (see page 20). casual; carefree; easygoing; informal; insouciant; lighthearted; nonchalant; relaxed; untroubled.

free and gratis An infantile phrase (see page 20). free.

(as) free as a bird An insipid simile. autonomous; free; independent; self-reliant; unattached; unbound; unconfined; unconstrained; unencumbered; unentangled; unfettered; uninhibited; unrestrained; unrestricted; unshackled; untied.

(as) free as the wind An insipid simile. autonomous; free; independent; self-reliant; unattached; unbound; unconfined; unconstrained; unencumbered; unentangled; unfettered; uninhibited; unrestrained; unrestricted; unshackled; untied.

free gift A wretched redundancy (see page 25). gift. ■ With every renewal, you will receive a *free gift*. DELETE *free*.

(no) free lunch A moribund metaphor (see page 21).

free ride A moribund metaphor (see page 21).

freezing cold An inescapable pair (see page 20). algid; arctic; brumal; chilly; cold; cool; freezing; frigid; frosty; frozen;

gelid; glacial; hibernal; hyperborean; ice-cold; icy; nippy; polar; rimy; wintry.

(as) fresh as a daisy An insipid simile. active; alive; animated; blooming; dynamic; energetic; fresh; healthy; hearty; lively; peppy; refreshed; rested; rosy; ruddy; spirited; sprightly; spry; vibrant; vigorous; vivacious.

fret and fume An inescapable pair (see page 20).

a friend in need (is a friend indeed) A popular prescription (see page 23).

frighten by (his) own shadow A moribund metaphor (see page 21). alarm; appall; benumb; daunt; frighten; horrify; intimidate; panic; paralyze; petrify; scare; shock; startle; terrify; terrorize; unnerve.

frighten (scare) out of (her) wits A moribund metaphor (see page 21). alarm; appall; benumb; daunt; frighten; horrify; intimidate; panic; paralyze; petrify; scare; shock; startle; terrify; terrorize; unnerve.

frighten the life out of A moribund metaphor (see page 21). alarm; appall; benumb; daunt; frighten; horrify; intimidate; panic; paralyze; petrify; scare; shock; startle; terrify; terrorize; unnerve.

(go) from a simmer to a hard boil A moribund metaphor (see page 21).

from A to Z A moribund metaphor (see page 21). 1. all during; all over; all through; throughout. 2. altogether; completely; entirely; fully; perfectly; quite; roundly; thoroughly; totally; unreservedly; utterly; wholly.

from beginning to end A moribund metaphor (see page 21). 1. *always; ceaselessly; constantly; continually; continuously; endlessly; eternally; everlastingly; evermore; forever; forevermore; frequently; interminably; nonstop; permanently; perpetually; persistently; recurrently; regularly; repeatedly; unceasingly; unremittingly.* 2. *all during; all over; all through; throughout.* 3. *altogether; completely; entirely; fully; perfectly; quite; roundly; thoroughly; totally; unreservedly; utterly; wholly.*

from (the) cradle to (the) grave A moribund metaphor (see page 21). 1. *always; ceaselessly; constantly; continually; continuously; endlessly; eternally; everlastingly; evermore; forever; forevermore; frequently; interminably; nonstop; permanently; perpetually; persistently; recurrently; regularly; repeatedly; unceasingly; unremittingly.* 2. *all during; all over; all through; throughout.*

from darkness to light A moribund metaphor (see page 21).

No longer a pariah, you were now a desired guest at parties, where you were supposed to speak eloquently about the struggle, to tear up and talk about the walk from the darkness into the light. — Lisa Fugard, *Skinner's Drift*

from dawn to (until) dusk A moribund metaphor (see page 21). *all day; all the time; always; ceaselessly; constantly; continually; continuously; endlessly; eternally; everlastingly; evermore; forever; forevermore; frequently; interminably; nonstop; permanently; perpetually; persistently; recurrently; regularly; repeatedly; unceasingly; unremittingly.* ■ She has to put up with this kind of stuff *from dawn to dusk.* REPLACE WITH *endlessly.*

(the) (date) from hell A moribund metaphor (see page 21).

from hence A wretched redundancy (see page 25). *hence.*

from pillar to post A moribund metaphor (see page 21). ■ You can't let your convictions be shaken, or you'll jump *from pillar to post* the moment times become difficult.

from rags to riches A moribund metaphor (see page 21).

from soup to nuts A moribund metaphor (see page 21). *all; all things; everything.*

from start to finish A moribund metaphor (see page 21). 1. *always; ceaselessly; constantly; continually; continuously; endlessly; eternally; everlastingly; evermore; forever; forevermore; frequently; interminably; nonstop; permanently; perpetually; persistently; recurrently; regularly; repeatedly; unceasingly; unremittingly.* 2. *all during; all over; all through; throughout.*

from stem to stern A moribund metaphor (see page 21). 1. *all during; all over; all through; throughout.* 2. *altogether; completely; entirely; fully; perfectly; quite; roundly; thoroughly; totally; unreservedly; utterly; wholly.*

from the bottom (depths) of (my) heart A moribund metaphor (see page 21). *earnestly; fervently; genuinely; heartily; honestly; sincerely; unreservedly; wholeheartedly.*

from the frying pan into the fire A moribund metaphor (see page 21).

(straight) from the horse's mouth A moribund metaphor (see page 21).

from the word *go* An infantile phrase (see page 20).

> Even my life so far has been plain. More Daisy than Elizabeth from the word go. — Meg Rosoff, *How I Live Now*

from tip to toe A moribund metaphor (see page 21). 1. *all during; all over; all through; throughout.* 2. *altogether; completely; entirely; fully; perfectly; quite; roundly; thoroughly; totally; unreservedly; utterly; wholly.*

from top to bottom A moribund metaphor (see page 21). 1. *all during; all over; all through; throughout.* 2. *altogether; completely; entirely; fully; perfectly; quite; roundly; thoroughly; totally; unreservedly; utterly; wholly.*

from whence A wretched redundancy (see page 25). *whence.* ■ The dolphins were judged sufficiently healthy to be taken back to the sea *from whence* they came. DELETE *from.* ■ And it all boiled over on talk radio — *from whence* it moved into the nation's high schools and junior highs and into late-night television. DELETE *from.*

front and center An inescapable pair (see page 20). *foremost; high; leading; main; major; prominent; salient; top.*

> John and I used to talk about how the current phase of the moon as well as the names of trees and flowers and birds — at least the local ones! — should be front and center in people's brains; maybe such a connection to nature would help to make us more civilized. — Elizabeth Berg, *The Year of Pleasures*

(on the) front burner A moribund metaphor (see page 21). *cardinal; chief; foremost; head; important; leading; main; paramount; predominant; primary; principal; prominent; topmost; uppermost.* ■ Preserving Yellowstone is probably a priority for most Americans, but at the moment it's not *on anyone's front burner.* REPLACE WITH *paramount.* ■ Procter & Gamble was faced with a *front-burner* actor suffering from a mysterious ailment. REPLACE WITH *leading.*

fuel the fire of A moribund metaphor (see page 21). 1. *fire; ignite; inflame; kindle.* 2. *galvanize; goad; incite; induce; needle; poke; prod; prompt; provoke; spur; stimulate; urge.* 3. *activate; animate; arouse; electrify; energize; enliven; excite; inspirit; invigorate; motivate; quicken; stimulate; stir; vitalize; vivify.*

full capacity A wretched redundancy (see page 25). *capacity.* ■ Buses are running closer to *full capacity* than at any time since the strike began. DELETE *full.*

full frontal assault A moribund metaphor (see page 21).

full of (herself) A moribund metaphor (see page 21). *egocentric; egoistic; egotistic; egotistical; narcissistic; self-absorbed; selfish; solipsistic.*

full of beans A moribund metaphor (see page 21). 1. *active; alive; animated; dynamic; energetic; exuberant; frisky; indefatigable; inexhaustible; invigorated; lively; peppy; spirited; sprightly; spry; tireless; unflagging; vibrant; vigorous; vivacious; zestful; zesty.* 2. *amiss; astray; deceived; deluded; erring; erroneous; fallacious; false; faulty; inaccurate; incorrect; in error; misguided; misinformed; mislead; mistaken; not correct; not right; wrong.*

full of holes A moribund metaphor (see page 21). 1. *defective; faulty; flawed; impaired; imperfect; marred; tainted.* 2. *baseless; captious; casuistic; casuistical; erroneous; fallacious; false; faulty; flawed; groundless; illogical; inaccurate; incorrect; invalid; irrational; jesuitic; jesuitical; mistaken; nonsensical; non sequitur; paralogistic; senseless; sophistic; sophistical; specious; spurious; unfounded; unreasonable; unsound; untenable; untrue; unveracious; wrong.*

full of hot air A moribund metaphor (see page 21). 1. *aggrandizing; blustering; boasting; bragging; coloring; crowing; elaborating; embellishing; embroidering; exaggerating; fanfaronading; gloating; hyperbolizing; magnifying; overstating; swaggering.* 2. *amiss; astray; deceived; deluded; erring; erroneous; fallacious; false; faulty; inaccurate; incorrect; in error; misguided; misinformed; mislead; mistaken; not correct; not right; wrong.*

full of piss and vinegar A moribund metaphor (see page 21). *active; alive; animated; dynamic; energetic; hearty; indefatigable; inexhaustible; lively; peppy; spirited; sprightly; spry; tireless; unflagging; vibrant; vigorous; vivacious.*

full of vim and vigor A moribund metaphor (see page 21). *active; alive; animated; dynamic; energetic; hearty; indefatigable; inexhaustible; lively; peppy; spirited; sprightly; spry; tireless; unflagging; vibrant; vigorous; vivacious.*

full plate A moribund metaphor (see page 21). *booked; busy; employed; engaged; involved; obligated; occupied.*

full potential A wretched redundancy (see page 25). *potential.* ■ Youngsters with talents that range from mathematical to musical are not challenged to work to their *full potential.* DELETE *full.*

(at) full speed (ahead) A moribund metaphor (see page 21). *abruptly; apace; at once; briskly; directly; expeditiously; fast; forthwith; hastily; hurriedly; immediately; instantaneously; instantly; posthaste; promptly; quickly; rapidly; rashly; right away; speedily; straightaway; swiftly; wingedly.*

(at) full steam (ahead) A moribund metaphor (see page 21). *abruptly; apace; at once; briskly; directly; expeditiously; fast; forthwith; hastily; hurriedly; immediately; instantaneously; instantly; posthaste; promptly; quickly; rapidly; rashly; right away; speedily; straightaway; swiftly; wingedly.*

a funny thing happened to me on the way to An infantile phrase (see page 20). ■ But *a funny thing happened on the way to* the Memorial Plaza.

149

G

gain a foothold A moribund metaphor (see page 21).

gain an advantage over A torpid term (see page 24). *beat; conquer; crush; defeat; outdo; overcome; overpower; overwhelm; prevail; quell; rout; succeed; triumph; trounce; vanquish; win.*

gain steam A moribund metaphor (see page 21).

game plan A moribund metaphor (see page 21). *action; course; direction; intention; method; move; plan; policy; procedure; route; scheme; strategy.*

game, set, and match A moribund metaphor (see page 21).

garden variety A moribund metaphor (see page 21). *average; common; commonplace; customary; everyday; fair; mediocre; middling; normal; ordinary; passable; plain; quotidian; regular; routine; simple; standard; tolerable; typical; uneventful; unexceptional; unremarkable; usual; workaday.*

gather together A wretched redundancy (see page 25). *gather.* ■ This summer's training provided all 1,500 youth an opportunity to *gather together* from around the country and to develop their skills and knowledge. DELETE *together.*

(I) gave (him) the best years of (my) life A plebeian sentiment (see page 23).

gaze into a crystal ball A moribund metaphor (see page 21). *anticipate; augur; divine; envision; forebode; forecast; foreknow; foresee; foretell; predict; prognosticate; prophesy; vaticinate.*

general consensus A wretched redundancy (see page 25). *consensus.* ■ The *general consensus* is that house prices have hit bottom. DELETE *general.*

(the) genie is out of the bottle A moribund metaphor (see page 21).

(as) gentle as a lamb An insipid simile. *affable; agreeable; amiable; amicable; compassionate; friendly; gentle; goodhearted; good-natured; humane; kind; kind-hearted; kindly; personable; pleasant; tender; tolerant.*

gentleman A suspect superlative (see page 24). Slipshod usage has reduced *gentleman* to a vulgarism. Common or crude people say *gentleman* when *man* would serve; though *gentleman* may sound dignified, it is actually dimwitted. Moreover, any man who doesn't, in revulsion, quiver at being called a *gentleman* is likely in jeopardy of becoming as vulgar as the word. ■ I am seeking a professional *gentleman* with diversified interests. REPLACE WITH *man.* ■ One *gentleman* told me it is a fantasy world and not to believe everything I hear. REPLACE WITH *man.* SEE ALSO *lady.*

(the) genuine article A moribund metaphor (see page 21). *actual; authentic; genuine; legitimate; pure; real; sterling; true; unadulterated; unalloyed; veritable.*

> He had constantly to be reassured. *Was* this the genuine article? *Was* this the real guaranteed height of a Good Time? — Christopher Isherwood, *Goodbye to Berlin*

get (our) act together An infantile phrase (see page 20). ■ They don't have the luxury of five years to *get their act together*.

get (has) a fix on A moribund metaphor (see page 21). *ascertain; assess; comprehend; determine; evaluate; learn; understand.*

get (has) a handle on A moribund metaphor (see page 21). 1. *cope with; deal with.* 2. *ascertain; assess; comprehend; determine; evaluate; learn; understand.*

get a life An infantile phrase (see page 20).

get away with murder A moribund metaphor (see page 21).

get (my) back up A moribund metaphor (see page 21). *acerbate; anger; annoy; bother; bristle; chafe; enrage; exasperate; gall; incense; inflame; infuriate; irk; irritate; madden; miff; pique; provoke; rile; roil; vex.*

get (his) dander up A moribund metaphor (see page 21). *acerbate; anger; annoy; bother; bristle; chafe; enrage; exasperate; gall; incense; inflame; infuriate; irk; irritate; madden; miff; pique; provoke; rile; roil; vex.*

get down to brass tacks A moribund metaphor (see page 21).

get (put) (all) (your) ducks in a row A moribund metaphor (see page 21). *arrange; categorize; classify; order; organize; prepare; ready; sort.*

> Everywhere they're smoothing down imperfections, putting hairs in place, putting ducks in a row, replacing divots. — Jonathan Lethem, *Motherless Brooklyn*

get (their) feet wet A moribund metaphor (see page 21).

get (your) foot in the door A moribund metaphor (see page 21).

get (my) goat A moribund metaphor (see page 21). *acerbate; anger; annoy; bother; bristle; chafe; enrage; incense; inflame; infuriate; irk; irritate; madden; miff; provoke; rile; roil; vex.* ■ "In denial" is one of those politically correct terms that *gets my goat*. REPLACE WITH *infuriates me*.

get (her) hackles up A moribund metaphor (see page 21). *acerbate; anger; annoy; bother; bristle; chafe; enrage; incense; inflame; infuriate; insult; irk; irritate; madden; miff; offend; provoke; rile; roil; vex.*

get (your) house in order A moribund metaphor (see page 21).

get in (my) hair A moribund metaphor (see page 21). *annoy; badger; bedevil; bother; chafe; distress; disturb; gall; grate; harass; harry; hassle; heckle; hector; hound; irk; irritate; nag; nettle; persecute; pester; plague; provoke; rankle; rile; roil; tease; torment; vex.*

get into the act A moribund metaphor (see page 21).

get in touch with (your) feelings A popular prescription (see page 23). *be aware; be cognizant; be conscious; be insightful; be mindful; be perceptive; be sensitive.*

get off (my) back A moribund metaphor (see page 21).

get (it) off (your) chest A moribund metaphor (see page 21). *acknowledge; admit; affirm; allow; avow; concede; confess; disclose; divulge; expose; grant; own; reveal; tell; uncover; unveil.*

get off on the wrong foot A moribund metaphor (see page 21).

get off the dime A moribund metaphor (see page 21). 1. *be certain; be decided; be decisive; be determined; be positive; be resolute; be sure.* 2. *budge; move; stir.*

get off the ground A moribund metaphor (see page 21). *begin; commence; embark on; inaugurate; initiate; introduce; launch; originate; start.* ■ Like all true entrepreneurs, they were eager to *get* another project *off the ground.* REPLACE WITH *launch.*

get on (my) nerves A moribund metaphor (see page 21). *annoy; badger; bedevil; bother; chafe; distress; disturb; gall; grate; harass; harry; hassle; heckle; hector; hound; irk; irritate; nag; nettle; persecute; pester; plague; provoke; rankle; rile; roil; tease; torment; vex.*

get on the stick A moribund metaphor (see page 21). *be active; be lively; move; stir.*

get (go) on with (my) life A popular prescription (see page 23). SEE ALSO *put (it) behind (us).*

get out of Dodge A moribund metaphor (see page 21). *abscond; clear out; decamp; depart; desert; disappear; escape; exit; flee; fly; go; go away; leave; move on; part; pull out; quit; retire; retreat; run away; take flight; take off; vacate; vanish; withdraw.* ■ The most sensible thing to do was *get out of Dodge.* REPLACE WITH *leave.*

get (it) out of (your) system A moribund metaphor (see page 21). *acknowledge; admit; affirm; allow; avow; concede; confess; disclose; divulge; expose; grant; own; reveal; tell; uncover; unveil.*

(don't) get (your) panties in a bunch A moribund metaphor (see page 21). 1. *agitated; anxious; aroused; displeased; disquieted; excited; flustered; perturbed; troubled; upset; worried.* 2. *acerbated; angered; annoyed; bothered; disturbed; exasperated; galled; irked; irritated; miffed; nettled; provoked; rankled; riled; roiled; upset; vexed.*

get (your) skates on A moribund metaphor (see page 21). *accelerate; advance; bestir; bustle; charge; dash; go faster; hasten; hurry; quicken; run; rush; speed up; sprint.*

get the ax A moribund metaphor (see page 21). *canned; discharged; dismissed; fired; let go; ousted; released; sacked; terminated.*

get (start) the ball rolling A moribund metaphor (see page 21). *begin; commence; embark on; inaugurate; initiate; introduce; launch; originate; start.*

get the better of A moribund metaphor (see page 21). 1. *beat; conquer; crush; defeat; outdo; overcome; overpower; overwhelm; prevail; quell; rout; succeed; triumph; trounce; vanquish; win.* 2. *outmaneuver; outsmart; outwit.*

> My body had got the better of me and could no longer be trusted. — Christina Schwarz, *Drowning Ruth*

get (give) the bum's rush A moribund metaphor (see page 21). *chuck; eject; expel; fling; throw out.*

(I) get the picture A moribund metaphor (see page 21). *appreciate; apprehend; comprehend; discern; fathom; grasp; know; perceive; realize; recognize; see; understand.*

get the word out A moribund metaphor (see page 21). *advertise; announce; broadcast; disseminate; proclaim; promote; promulgate; publicize; publish; trumpet.*

(let's) get this show on the road A moribund metaphor (see page 21). *begin; commence; embark; inaugurate; initiate; launch; originate; start.*

get to the bottom of (this) A moribund metaphor (see page 21). *appreciate; apprehend; comprehend; discern; fathom; grasp; know; perceive; realize; recognize; see; understand.*

get under (my) skin A moribund metaphor (see page 21). *acerbate; anger; annoy; bother; bristle; chafe; disturb; exasperate; gall; grate; irk; irritate; miff; nettle; provoke; rankle; rile; roil; upset; vex.*

get-up-and-go A moribund metaphor (see page 21). *ambition; bounce; dash; drive; dynamism; élan; energy; enthusiasm; initiative; liveliness; motivation; spirit; verve; vigor; vim; vitality; vivacity; zeal.*

(full of) get up and go A moribund metaphor (see page 21). 1. *active; alive; animated; dynamic; energetic; exuberant; frisky; indefatigable; inexhaustible; invigorated; lively; peppy; spirited; sprightly; spry; tireless; unflagging; vibrant; vigorous; vivacious; zestful; zesty.* 2. *ambitious; assiduous; busy; determined; diligent; hard-working; industrious; motivated; perseverant; persevering; persistent; sedulous.*

get up on the wrong side of the bed A moribund metaphor (see page 21). *bad-tempered; cantankerous; crabby; cranky; cross; disagreeable; grouchy; ill-humored; ill-natured; ill-tempered; irascible; irritable; quarrelsome; peevish; petulant; splenetic; sullen; surly; testy.*

get (her) walking papers A moribund metaphor (see page 21). *canned; discharged; dismissed; fired; let go; ousted; released; sacked; terminated.*

get wind of A moribund metaphor (see page 21). *ascertain; become aware of; discover; find out; hear about; learn.*

get (our) wires crossed A moribund metaphor (see page 21). *baffle; befuddle; bewilder; confound; confuse; disconcert; flummox; mix up; muddle; nonplus; perplex; puzzle.*

(it'll) get worse before it gets better A plebeian sentiment (see page 23). ■ Things will *get worse* at the bank *before they get better.*

gild (paint) the lily A moribund metaphor (see page 21). *overdo; overstate.*

give (her) a bum steer A moribund metaphor (see page 21). *bamboozle; befool; beguile; betray; bilk; bluff; cheat; con; deceive; defraud; delude; dupe; feint; fool; gyp; hoodwink; lead astray; misdirect; misguide; misinform; mislead; spoof; swindle; trick.*

give (her) a dose (taste) of (her) own medicine A moribund metaphor (see page 21).

give and take An inescapable pair (see page 20). *collaboration; cooperation; exchange; reciprocity.*

give (them) an inch and (they'll) take a mile A moribund metaphor (see page 21).

give (them) a piece of (his) mind A moribund metaphor (see page 21). *admonish; animadvert; berate; castigate; censure; chasten; chastise; chide; condemn; criticize; denounce; denunciate; discipline; impugn; objurgate; punish; rebuke; remonstrate; reprehend; reprimand; reproach; reprobate; reprove; revile; scold; upbraid; vituperate.*

> She didn't come down to give them a piece of her mind because it was no use fighting; they were sometimes able to get me some small job or other, through the influence of Jimmy's uncle Tambow, who delivered the vote of his relatives in the ward and was a pretty big wheel in Republican ward politics. — Saul Bellow, *The Adventures of Augie March*

give (him) a run for (his) money A moribund metaphor (see page 21).

give away the store A moribund metaphor (see page 21).

give (her) a wide berth (to) A moribund metaphor (see page 21). *avoid; bypass; circumvent; dodge; elude; evade; shun; sidestep; skirt.*

give birth (to) A moribund metaphor (see page 21). *bring about; cause; effect; generate; give rise to; inaugurate; initiate; introduce; occasion; produce; provoke; result in.*

give credit where credit is due A popular prescription (see page 23).

give (my) eyeteeth (right arm) for A moribund metaphor (see page 21).

give it a rest A moribund metaphor (see page 21). 1. *be silent; be still; hush; keep quiet; quiet; silence.* 2. *cease; close; complete; conclude; derail; desist; discontinue; end; finish; halt; quit; settle; stop; terminate.*

give it a shot (whirl) A moribund metaphor (see page 21). *aim; attempt; endeavor; essay; exert; labor; moil; strain; strive; struggle; toil; try hard; undertake; work at.*

give it (take) (your) best shot A moribund metaphor (see page 21). *aim; attempt; endeavor; essay; exert; labor; moil; strain; strive; struggle; toil; try; try hard; undertake; work at; work hard.*

> It was all very well to tell yourself, as he had been doing for years, that all you could do was give it your best shot. — Jane Smiley, *Moo*

given the fact that A wretched redundancy (see page 25). *because; considering; for; in that; since; when.* ■ *Given the fact that* all kibbutz youth were inducted into the army and commingled with tens of thousands of potential mates from outside their kibbutz before they got married, the rate of 200 marriages from within the same kibbutz is far more than could be expected by chance. REPLACE WITH *Since.* ■ I'd be interested in being a guest, but I gather you can't even consider it *given the fact that* I live in Cancun. REPLACE WITH *since.* SEE ALSO *because of the fact that; by virtue of the fact that; considering the fact that; in consideration of the fact that; in view of the fact that; on account of the fact that.*

(it) gives (me) something to do A plebeian sentiment (see page 23). SEE ALSO *(it) keeps (me) busy; (it) keeps (me) out of trouble; (it's) something to do.*

give (him) the back of (my) hand A moribund metaphor (see page 21). *abuse; affront; disdain; insult; offend; outrage; scorn; slap.*

give (her) the brush (brush-off) A moribund metaphor (see page 21). *abuse; affront; avoid; disdain; disregard; ignore; insult; neglect; offend; outrage; overlook; rebuff; reject; scorn; shun; sidestep; slap; slight; slur; skirt; sneer; snub; spurn.*

give (him) the business A moribund metaphor (see page 21). *admonish; animadvert; berate; castigate; censure; chasten; chastise; chide; condemn; criticize; denounce; denunciate; discipline; impugn; objurgate; punish; rebuke; remonstrate; reprehend; reprimand; reproach; reprobate; reprove; revile; scold; upbraid; vituperate.*

give (him) the cold shoulder A moribund metaphor (see page 21). *abuse; affront; avoid; disdain; disregard; ignore; insult; neglect; offend; outrage; overlook; rebuff; reject; scorn; shun; sidestep; slap; slight; slur; skirt; sneer; snub; spurn.*

give the devil his due A moribund metaphor (see page 21).

give (her) the pink slip A moribund metaphor (see page 21). *discharge; dismiss; fire; lay off; sack; suspend; terminate; throw out.*

give (him) the runaround A moribund metaphor (see page 21). *avoid; dodge; doubletalk; equivocate; evade; fence; hedge; palter; prevaricate; quibble; shuffle; sidestep; tergiversate; waffle.*

give (him) the third degree A moribund metaphor (see page 21). *catechize; cross-examine; examine; grill; inquire; interrogate; pump; question; quiz; test.*

give the thumbs down (sign) A moribund metaphor (see page 21). *decline; deny; disallow; disapprove; forbid; nix; prohibit; proscribe; refuse; reject; rule out; say no; turn down; veto.*

give the thumbs up (sign) A moribund metaphor (see page 21). *accredit; affirm; allow; approve; authorize; back; bless; certify; countenance; endorse; favor; permit; ratify; sanction; support.*

give (me) the time of day A moribund metaphor (see page 21). *be affable; be approachable; be cordial; be friendly; be genial; be pleasant; be polite; be receptive; be responsive; be sociable.*

> In about an hour, I would be sitting across the table from the most attractive woman who had ever stooped so low as to give me the time of day. — Don Keith, *The Forever Season*

give up the ghost A moribund metaphor (see page 21). *cease to exist; decease; depart; die; expire; pass away; pass on; perish.*

(a) glimmer of hope A moribund metaphor (see page 21). *anticipation; expectancy; expectation; hope; hopefulness; optimism; possibility; promise; prospect; sanguinity.*

gloom and doom An inescapable pair (see page 20).

go against the grain (of) A moribund metaphor (see page 21). *buck; challenge; contradict; defy; disobey; dispute; disregard; flout; go against; ignore; neglect; oppose; overlook; resist; violate.* ■ Does the message *go against the grain of* corporate philosophy? REPLACE WITH *flout.*

> It is not in our makeup to intervene. This goes against the grain, is entirely out of our character. — Kate Walbert, *Our Kind*

go ahead, make my day An infantile phrase (see page 20).

go belly up A moribund metaphor (see page 21). *break down; collapse; disinte-grate; fail; fall short; flop; founder; miscarry; topple.* ■ All the biotech start-ups in the Bioventures portfolio would likely *go belly up* if the veterinary school is shut down. REPLACE WITH *fail.*

God is love A quack equation (see page 23).

go downhill A moribund metaphor (see page 21). *decay; decline; degenerate; destroy; deteriorate; disintegrate; ebb; erode; fade; fall off; languish; lessen; plummet; ruin; wane; weaken; wither; worsen.* ■ The bad news is that during the second night, everybody's performance *went downhill.* REPLACE WITH *deteriorated.*

(he) goes An infantile phrase (see page 20). Only the adolescent or the addle-brained prefer this gruesome *goes* to *acknowledge; admit; announce; assert; asseverate; aver; avow; comment; confess; cry; declare; disclose; divulge; exclaim; mention; note; observe; proclaim; pronounce; remark; reveal; say; state; utter.* ■ They say they don't know anything, and then they *go,* "if we hear anything, we'll call you." REPLACE WITH *say.* ■ He walked into the room, and she *goes,* "Guess what?" REPLACE WITH *exclaims.* ■ I asked what do you like about her, and he *went,* "I don't know." REPLACE WITH *confessed.* ■ And then he *goes,* "I don't want to see you any more." REPLACE WITH *announces.*

go for the gold An infantile phrase (see page 20).

go for the gusto An infantile phrase (see page 20).

go forward A torpid term (see page 24). 1. *advance; continue; develop; go on; grow; happen; improve; increase; make headway; make progress; move on; occur; proceed; progress; take place.* 2. *shall; will;* delete.

■ The way in which this is drafted will allow those takeovers to *go forward,* which would allow for a greater efficiency and productivity. REPLACE WITH *proceed.* ■ It is still our expectation that the summit will *go forward* and be productive. REPLACE WITH *occur.* ■ We look forward to *going forward.* REPLACE WITH proceeding. SEE ALSO *a step forward; a step (forward) in the right direction; move forward; move (forward) in the right direction; proceed forward.*

Going forward is replacing auxiliary verbs like *will* and *shall,* which to the politicians and businesspeople who now rely on *going forward,* do not convey futurity as effectively. *Going forward,* to these dimwitted thinkers, seems to reveal the future more forcefully; yet distinctions in tense, mood, and voice may be forfeited along with a subtle, yet indispensable, sense of what it means to be human.

■ This highlights perhaps the greatest risk to the economy *going forward.* DELETE *going forward.* ■ We need to train more Iraqi troops *going forward.* DELETE *going forward.* ■ I can't wait to share ideas about what we can do *going forward.* DELETE *going forward.* ■ *Going forward,* as the company has more mature branches, its profit margins should benefit and widen a bit more. DELETE *going forward.* ■ The company will continue to face challenges *going forward.* DELETE *going forward.* ■ This is an excellent opportunity for both companies and we look forward to maintaining positive momentum *going forward.* DELETE *going forward.*

going, going, gone An infantile phrase (see page 20).

going great guns A moribund metaphor (see page 21).

going on (19) An infantile phrase (see page 20). ■ I'm 69 *going on 70.* ■ I've been there 5 years, *going on 6 years.*

> Elizabeth Costello is a writer, born in 1928, which makes her sixty-six years old, going on sixty-seven. — J. M. Coetzee, *Elizabeth Costello*

going to hell in a handbasket A moribund metaphor (see page 21). *collapse; corrode; crumble; decay; decline; degenerate; destroy; deteriorate; disintegrate; ebb; erode; fade; fail; fall off; fester; flag; languish; lessen; plummet; putrefy; regress; rot; ruin; stagnate; ulcerate; wane; weaken; wither; worsen.* ■ The typical reaction people seem to have is that public education is *going to hell in a handbasket.* REPLACE WITH *deteriorating.*

going (have) to live with that for the rest of my life A plebeian sentiment (see page 23).

go (send) into a tailspin A moribund metaphor (see page 21). 1. *be unsuccessful; bomb; break down; collapse; fail; fall short; falter; fizzle; flop; fold; founder; mess up; miscarry; not succeed; stumble; topple.* 2. *be ailing; be anxious; be unhealthy; be ill; be sick; be sickly; be unwell.*

go into orbit A moribund metaphor (see page 21). 1. *be delighted; be ecstatic; be elated; be enraptured; be euphoric; be exalted; be excited; be exhilarated; be exultant; be gay; be glad; be gleeful; be good-*

humored; be happy; be intoxicated; be jolly; be jovial; be joyful; be joyous; be jubilant; be merry; be mirthful; be overjoyed; be pleased; be rapturous; be thrilled. 2. *be angry; be annoyed; be enraged; be exasperated; be furious; be incensed; be infuriated; be irate; be irked; be irritated; be mad; be raging; be wrathful.*

go kicking and screaming A moribund metaphor (see page 21). *antagonistically; defiantly; disagreeably; grudgingly; recalcitrantly; reluctantly; renitently; resistantly; resistingly; unconsentingly; unwillingly.*

golden opportunity An inescapable pair (see page 20). ■ We have a *golden opportunity* to prevent this cycle from continuing.

(a) goldmine of (information) A moribund metaphor (see page 21). SEE ALSO *a barrage of.* ■ His diary is nonetheless *a goldmine of information* about earlier American gay social life.

go (run) like the wind An insipid simile. *abruptly; apace; at once; briskly; directly; expeditiously; fast; forthwith; hastily; hurriedly; immediately; instantaneously; instantly; posthaste; promptly; quickly; rapidly; rashly; right away; speedily; straightaway; swiftly; wingedly.*

(has) gone with the wind A moribund metaphor (see page 21). 1. *be forgotten; dead; disappeared; dissolved; evaporated; past; vanished.* 2. *ephemeral; evanescent; fleeting; flitting; fugacious; fugitive; short-lived; transient; transitory; volatile.* ■ I would retain some of what I read, and then it would very likely *be gone with the wind.* REPLACE WITH *vanish.*

good and sufficient An inescapable pair (see page 20). *adequate; good; satisfactory; sufficient.*

(as) good as gold An insipid simile. *best; excellent; exceptional; fine; finest; first-class; first-rate; good; great; optimal; optimum; superior; superlative.*

good, bad, and (or) indifferent A torpid term (see page 24). ■ We really don't know what the effect will be; it could be *good, bad, or indifferent.*

(the) good, (the) bad, and (the) ugly An infantile phrase (see page 20). ■ Teach yourself to open up more and share with your readership by forcing yourself to look at *the good, bad, and ugly* of your life.

(the) good doctor An infantile phrase (see page 20). ■ I think everything *the good doctor* has said is hogwash.

good egg A moribund metaphor (see page 21). *agreeable; decent; ethical; forthright; honest; just; moral; righteous; straight; trustworthy; upright; virtuous.*

(a) good man is hard to find A popular prescription (see page 23).

(the) good news is (that) An infantile phrase (see page 20). ■ *The good news is that* most students report that speaking gets easier as the term progresses.

(the) good old days A suspect superlative (see page 24). *antiquity; history; the past; yesterday.* ■ We're going back to *the good old days* on gas prices.

(a) good read An infantile phrase (see page 20). This is a hideous expression that only the very badly read — those, that is, who read merely to be entertained — could possibly verbalize. The people who use this phrase are the people who read *best-selling authors* (SEE) ■ This bookstore caters to those looking for *a good read in paperback.* REPLACE WITH *a readable paperback.* ■ While Foley's piece on football stadiums was *a good read*, it is entirely off the mark in terms of the proposed megaplex. REPLACE WITH *entertaining.* ■ It is hard to make air-conditioning repair *a good read.* REPLACE WITH *captivating.* SEE ALSO *a (must) read.*

good riddance to bad rubbish An infantile phrase (see page 20).

good (great) stuff When we need to use the word *stuff* to describe something we like, something we also call *good* or *great*, we might wonder if we have lost all sense of what is likable and what not.

Stuff best describes the nondescript and uneventful, the poor, the ordinary, and the pathetic.

good things come in small packages A popular prescription (see page 23).

(and a) good time was had by all An infantile phrase (see page 20).

go off half-cocked A moribund metaphor (see page 21). *careless; emotional; foolhardy; hasty; headlong; heedless; impulsive; incautious; indiscreet; precipitate; rash; reckless; thoughtless; unmindful; unthinking.*

go off the deep end A moribund metaphor (see page 21). 1. *be careless; be emotional; be foolhardy; be hasty; be headlong; be heedless; be impulsive; be incautious; be indiscreet; be precipitate; be rash;* *be reckless; be thoughtless; be unmindful; be unthinking.* 2. *acerbate; anger; annoy; bother; bristle; chafe; enrage; incense; inflame; infuriate; irk; irritate; madden; miff; provoke; rile; roil; vex.*

go (her) one better A moribund metaphor (see page 21). *beat; best; better; defeat; eclipse; exceed; excel; outclass; outdo; outflank; outmaneuver; outpace; outperform; outplay; outrank; outrival; outsmart; outstrip; outthink; outwit; overcome; overpower; overshadow; prevail; rout; surpass; top; triumph; trounce; vanquish; whip; win.*

goose egg A moribund metaphor (see page 21). *cipher; naught; zero.*

(his) goose is cooked A moribund metaphor (see page 21).

(kill) (the) goose that lays the golden egg A moribund metaphor (see page 21).

go overboard A moribund metaphor (see page 21). *exaggerate; hyperbolize; overdo; overreact; overstress; overstate.*

go (send) over the edge A moribund metaphor (see page 21). 1. *be unsuccessful; bomb; break down; collapse; fail; fall short; falter; fizzle; flop; fold; founder; mess up; miscarry; not succeed; stumble; topple.* 2. *be ailing; be anxious; be unhealthy; be ill; be sick; be sickly; be unwell.* 3. *acerbate; anger; annoy; bother; bristle; chafe; enrage; incense; inflame; infuriate; irk; irritate; madden; miff; provoke; rile; roil; vex.*

> Jack is their guide: young and irreverent, thank God. Reverence would send Paul over the edge. — Julia Glass, *Three Junes*

go (head) south A moribund metaphor (see page 21). *collapse; crash; decline; decrease; descend; dip; drop; ebb; fail; fall; plummet; plunge; recede; regress; retire; sink; slide; slip; subside; topple; tumble.* ■ And it is possible that the market may *go south* before the shares can be offered. REPLACE WITH *fall*. ■ Obviously, any of these could cause your spirits to *go south* temporarily. REPLACE WITH *ebb*. ■ He expressed some concern for her job if the relationship should *go south*. REPLACE WITH *fail*.

go the extra mile A moribund metaphor (see page 21). ■ Average citizens who regularly *go the extra mile* to make this a better world are everywhere.

go their separate ways A moribund metaphor (see page 21). *break up; divorce; part; separate; split up.*

go the way of all flesh A moribund metaphor (see page 21). *cease to exist; decease; depart; die; end; expire; pass away; pass on; perish.*

go the way of the dinosaur A moribund metaphor (see page 21). *become extinct; cease to exist; disappear; vanish.*

go the whole hog An infantile phrase (see page 20). *do completely; do entirely; do fully; do thoroughly; do totally; do utterly; do wholly; do wholeheartedly.*

Perhaps it was that if I was going to have a predawn wedding in a crimson dress, I might as well go the whole hog and be hovering at an unsuspecting witness's bedside as he woke. — Suzannah Dunn, *The Queen of Subtleties*

go through the ceiling (roof) A moribund metaphor (see page 21). *bellow; bluster; clamor; explode; fulminate; fume; holler; howl; rage; rant; rave; roar; scream; shout; storm; thunder; vociferate; yell.*

go through the mill A moribund metaphor (see page 21).

go (shoot) through the roof A moribund metaphor (see page 21). *ascend; balloon; billow; bulge; climb; escalate; expand; go up; grow; improve; increase; inflate; mount; multiply; rise; skyrocket; soar; surge; swell.* ■ Some people thought it was an extravagance at a time when billings aren't exactly *going through the roof*. REPLACE WITH *soaring*. ■ My quality of life has *gone through the roof* since he quit his job. REPLACE WITH *improved immeasurably*.

go to bat for A moribund metaphor (see page 21). *abet; advance; advocate; aid; assist; back; bolster; champion; defend; espouse; fight for; further; help; support; uphold.* ■ All I want to say is that it is easier to *go to bat for* people when they recognize they're wrong. REPLACE WITH *defend*.

go toe to toe with A moribund metaphor (see page 21). *battle; compete; contend; fight; struggle; vie.*

(we) got off on the wrong foot A moribund metaphor (see page 21).

go to pieces A moribund metaphor (see page 21). *decay; decline; degenerate; destroy; deteriorate; disintegrate; ebb; erode; fade; fall off; languish; lessen; ruin; wane; weaken; wither; worsen.*

go to pot A moribund metaphor (see page 21). *decay; decline; degenerate; destroy; deteriorate; disintegrate; ebb; erode; fade; fall off; languish; lessen; ruin; wane; weaken; wither; worsen.*

go to (her) reward A moribund metaphor (see page 21). *cease to exist; decease; depart; die; expire; pass away; pass on; perish.*

go (run) to seed A moribund metaphor (see page 21). *decay; decline; degenerate; deteriorate; devitalize; disintegrate; ebb; erode; fade; fall off; languish; lessen; ruin; wane; weaken; wither; worsen.*

go to the dogs A moribund metaphor (see page 21). *decay; decline; degenerate; destroy; deteriorate; disintegrate; ebb; erode; fade; fall off; languish; lessen; ruin; wane; weaken; wither; worsen.*

go to the mat (for) A moribund metaphor (see page 21). 1. *battle; brawl; clash; fight; grapple; jostle; scuffle; skirmish; tussle; war; wrestle.* 2. *advocate; aid; assist; back; champion; defend; espouse; help; protect; shield; support; uphold.* 3. *argue; dispute; fight; quarrel; wrangle.*

go up in flames A moribund metaphor (see page 21). *annihilate; break down; crumble; demolish; destroy; deteriorate; die; disintegrate; dissolve; end; eradicate; exterminate; obliterate; pulverize; rack; ravage; raze; ruin; shatter; smash; undo; wrack; wreck.*

go up (the chimney) in smoke A moribund metaphor (see page 21). *annihilate; break down; crumble; demolish; destroy; deteriorate; die; disappear; disintegrate; dissipate; dissolve; end; eradicate;* *evaporate; exterminate; fade; obliterate; pulverize; rack; ravage; raze; ruin; shatter; smash; undo; vanish; vaporize; volatilize; wrack; wreck.* ■ Everything I worked for over the last ten years is *going up in smoke.* REPLACE WITH *evaporating.*

go with the flow A moribund metaphor (see page 21). *abide by; accede to; accept; accommodate; acquiesce; adapt to; adhere to; adjust to; agree to; assent; be agreeable; be complacent; bend; be resigned; bow; comply with; concede to; concur; conform; consent to; fit; follow; reconcile; submit; succumb; yield.* ■ We have to *go with the flow.* REPLACE WITH *acquiesce.*

(as) graceful as a swan An insipid simile. *agile; graceful; limber; lissome; lithe; lithesome; nimble; supple.*

grace (us) with (his) presence A torpid term (see page 24). ■ Most of these essays first appeared in *The New Yorker,* which Liebling *graced with his presence* between 1935 and 1963.

(like) Grand Central Station An insipid simile. 1. *abounding; brimful; brimming; bursting; chock-full; congested; crammed; crowded; dense; filled; full; gorged; jammed; jam-packed; overcrowded; overfilled; overflowing; packed; replete; saturated; stuffed; swarming; teeming.* 2. *busy; hectic.*

(the) grass is (always) greener (on the other side of) A popular prescription (see page 23).

(pure) gravy A moribund metaphor (see page 21). 1. *benefit; earnings; gain; money; proceeds; profit.* 2. *a benefit; a bonus; a dividend; a gift; a gratuity; a* *lagniappe; an extra; a perk; a perquisite; a pourboire; a premium; a tip.*

> And he'd like being told the good news. He'd smile, maybe. Anything you win for nothing, anything that falls into your lap, it's all gravy, right? — Joyce Carol Oates, *Blonde*

gravy train A moribund metaphor (see page 21).

grease (her) palm with silver A moribund metaphor (see page 21). 1. *bribe; induce; pay; suborn.* 2. *compensate; pay; recompense; tip.*

grease the skids A moribund metaphor (see page 21). *arrange; get ready; organize; prepare; set up.*

great A suspect superlative (see page 24). That which is called *great* is seldom more than *good*, and that which is *good* is scarcely mentionable. *Great expectations* often turn out to be slight realizations, and *great stuff* is seldom more than stuff.

Great is also, of course, a hugely overworked word. Consider this laughable sentence: ■ When I think of their golf course, the first word that comes to mind is *great*.

Alternatives to the quotidian *great* include *consequential; considerable; consummate; distinguished; eminent; excellent; exceptional; exemplary; exquisite; extraordinary; fine; flawless; grand; ideal; illustrious; impeccable; imposing; impressive; magnificent; marvelous; matchless; momentous; nonpareil; notable; noteworthy; perfect; preeminent; remarkable; select; splendid; superb; superior; superlative; supreme; transcendent; weighty; wonderful.*

(the) great American novel A suspect superlative (see page 24).

(the) great beyond A moribund metaphor (see page 21). *afterlife; eternity; everlastingness.*

(go) great guns A moribund metaphor (see page 21). *abruptly; briskly; expeditiously; fast; hastily; hurriedly; posthaste; promptly; quickly; rapidly; speedily; straightaway; swiftly; wingedly.*

green around the gills A moribund metaphor (see page 21). 1. *afflicted; ailing; diseased; ill; indisposed; infirm; not (feeling) well; sick; sickly; suffering; unhealthy; unsound; unwell; valetudinarian.* 2. *nauseated; nauseous; queasy; sick; squeamish; vomiting.*

(as) green as grass An insipid simile. 1. *aquamarine; emerald; green; greenish; teal; verdant; virescent.* 2. *adolescent; artless; awkward; callow; green; guileless; immature; inexperienced; inexpert; ingenuous; innocent; juvenile; naive; raw; simple; undeveloped; unfledged; unseasoned; unskilled; unskillful; unsophisticated; untaught; untrained; unworldly; young; youthful.*

green-eyed monster A moribund metaphor (see page 21). *envy; jealousy.*

green light A moribund metaphor (see page 21). *allowance; approval; assent; authority; authorization; blessing; consent; freedom; leave; liberty; license; permission; permit; power; sanction; warrant.*

Like *red light*, the expression *green light* appeals to people who grasp the meaning of colorful visuals and expressive pictures more easily than they do polysyllabic words and complicated thoughts. Some people upgrade simple or straightforward ideas to unintelligible ones; others degrade substantive or nuanced ideas to unsophisticated ones. *Green light* is an example of the latter, but both tactics suggest an insincere mind, an unknowable heart.

■ The Baby Bells — which already have *the green light* to go into just about any other venture — have railed against the remaining restrictions since they were imposed. REPLACE WITH *permission*. ■ The FBI was given *the green light* by the Justice Department to continue its investigation. REPLACE WITH *authorization*. ■ Why would we be surprised when others take that message as a *green light* to lie, cheat, steal, and do whatever will benefit them? REPLACE WITH *license*. SEE ALSO *red light*.

green with envy A moribund metaphor (see page 21). *covetous; desirous; envious; grudging; jealous; resentful.*

grim reaper A moribund metaphor (see page 21). *death.*

grin and bear it A popular prescription (see page 23).

grind to a halt A moribund metaphor (see page 21). *cease; close; complete; conclude; end; finish; halt; settle; stop; terminate.* ■ Once it becomes apparent that no payment is forthcoming, construction activity can quickly *grind to a halt*. REPLACE WITH *halt*.

grist for the mill A moribund metaphor (see page 21).

gross exaggeration An inescapable pair (see page 20). *embellishment; exaggeration; hyperbole; overstatement.*

(get in on the) ground floor A moribund metaphor (see page 21).

ground zero A moribund metaphor (see page 21).

grow (spread) like a cancer An insipid simile. *augment; breed; duplicate; grow; increase; metastasize; multiply; mushroom; procreate; proliferate; propagate; reproduce; snowball; spread; swell.*

(doesn't) grow on trees A moribund metaphor (see page 21). *exiguous; limited; inadequate; infrequent; meager; rare; scant; scanty; scarce; sparse; uncommon; unusual.*

gruesome twosome An infantile phrase (see page 20).

guardedly optimistic A torpid term (see page 24). *confident; encouraged; heartened; hopeful; optimistic; rosy; sanguine.* ■ Firefighters are *guardedly optimistic* that they have the blaze under control. DELETE *guardedly*. ■ We're *guardedly optimistic* that this synthetic compound may work. DELETE *guardedly*. SEE ALSO *cautiously optimistic*.

guardian angel A suspect superlative (see page 24). *liberator; redeemer; rescuer; savior.*

guesstimate An infantile phrase (see page 20). *appraisal; assessment; estimate; estimation; guess; impression; opinion.* ■ If you would like a *guesstimate* of time required for your site, we would be happy to give you one. REPLACE WITH *estimate*. ■ Yet with just a few moments of thought you can make a surprisingly good *guesstimate*. REPLACE WITH *guess*. ■ They were asked to guess what the contents were and *guesstimate* how many objects were in the envelope. REPLACE WITH *guess*.

Guesstimate is a perfectly ridiculous merger that people who are uncomfortable with using *guess* will turn to. Most of us prefer knowing to not knowing, or at least we prefer letting others believe we are knowledgeable. *Guesstimate*, these people reason, adds intelligence and respectability to their wild *guess*, their unsubstantiated *estimate*.

(as) guilty as sin An insipid simile. *at fault; blamable; blameful; blameworthy; censurable; condemnable; culpable; guilty; in error; reprehensible.*

(a) guilty conscience needs no accuser A popular prescription (see page 23).

H

(a) hailstorm of A moribund metaphor (see page 21). ■ Thus, President Gerald R. Ford's 1974 pardon of former President Richard M. Nixon provoked *a hailstorm of* criticism and may have contributed to Mr. Ford's defeat two years later by Jimmy Carter. SEE ALSO *a barrage of.*

hale and hearty An inescapable pair (see page 20). *energetic; fine; fit; good; hale; healthful; healthy; hearty; robust; sound; strong; vigorous; well.*

(anyone with) half a brain A moribund metaphor (see page 21).

half a loaf is better than none A moribund metaphor (see page 21).

half-baked (idea) A moribund metaphor (see page 21). *bad; blemished; defective; deficient; faulty; flawed; ill-conceived; imperfect; inadequate; incomplete; inferior; malformed; poor; unsound.*

(go at it) hammer and tongs A moribund metaphor (see page 21). *actively; aggressively; dynamically; emphatically; energetically; fast; ferociously; fervently; fiercely; forcefully; frantically; frenziedly; furiously; hard; intensely; intently; mightily; passionately; powerfully; robustly; savagely; spiritedly; strenuously; strongly; vehemently; viciously; vigorously; violently; wildly; with vigor.*

> He'd always been of the hammer-and-tongs school. She taught him sexual stealth, the occasional necessity of stillness. — Ian McEwan, *Amsterdam*.

handed to (her) on a silver platter A moribund metaphor (see page 21).

hand and (in) glove A moribund metaphor (see page 21). *amiable; amicable; attached; brotherly; chummy; close; confidential; devoted; familiar; friendly; inseparable; intimate; loving; thick.*

(goes) hand in hand A moribund metaphor (see page 21). *be indissoluble; be indivisible; be inseparable; be together.*

> New churches were established in the surrounding villages and a few schools with them. From the very

beginning religion and education went hand in hand. — Chinua Achebe, *Things Fall Apart*

hand over fist A moribund metaphor (see page 21). *apace; briskly; expeditiously; fast; hastily; hurriedly; posthaste; quickly; rapidly; speedily; swiftly; wingedly.*

(my) hands are tied A moribund metaphor (see page 21).

(the) hand that rocks the cradle (rules the world) A popular prescription (see page 23).

handwriting (is) on the wall A moribund metaphor (see page 21). *divination; foreboding; forewarning; indication; omen; portent; prediction; premonition; presage; presentiment; sign; signal; warning.*

hang (hold) (on) by a thread A moribund metaphor (see page 21). ■ The small towns in western Massachusetts are *holding on by a thread.*

hang fire A moribund metaphor (see page 21). 1. *be delayed; be slow.* 2. *be undecided; be unsettled.*

hang (your) hat on A moribund metaphor (see page 21).

hang (our) hats A moribund metaphor (see page 21). *dwell; inhabit; live; reside; stay.*

It is not the same as Hoving Road where we all once hung our hats, but things change in ways none of us can expect, no matter how damn much we know or how

smart and good-intentioned each of us is or thinks he is. — Richard Ford, *The Sportswriter*

hang in there A moribund metaphor (see page 21). *carry on; get along; manage; succeed.* ■ Even though profits remain down, most firms are still *hanging in there.* REPLACE WITH *succeeding.* ■ I'm *hanging in there.* REPLACE WITH *managing.*

hang like a cloud (over) An insipid simile. 1. *becloud; cloak; darken; eclipse; mask; obscure; shroud; veil.* 2. *belittle; confound; degrade; demean; embarrass; humiliate; lower; shame.* ■ Their parents' divorce *hangs like a cloud over* their lives. REPLACE WITH *beclouds.* ■ There is nothing that Jesus does not understand about the heartache that *hangs like a cloud over* the history of our lives. REPLACE WITH *darkens.* ■ The aftermath of the bitter July incident *hangs like a cloud over* professors, students, and administrators alike. REPLACE WITH *embarrasses.* SEE ALSO *cast a shadow (over).*

hang on every word A moribund metaphor (see page 21). *attend to; hark; hear; hearken; heed; listen; pay attention; pay heed.*

hang over (our) heads A moribund metaphor (see page 21). *hang over; impend; loom; menace; overhang; overshadow; threaten; tower over.*

(these things) happen to other people, not to (me) A plebeian sentiment (see page 23).

(as) happy as a clam (at high tide) An insipid simile. *blissful; blithe; buoyant;*

cheerful; delighted; ecstatic; elated; enraptured; euphoric; exalted; excited; exhilarated; exultant; gay; glad; gleeful; good-humored; happy; intoxicated; jolly; jovial; joyful; joyous; jubilant; merry; mirthful; overjoyed; pleased; rapturous; thrilled.

(as) happy as a lark An insipid simile. *blissful; blithe; buoyant; cheerful; delighted; ecstatic; elated; enraptured; euphoric; exalted; excited; exhilarated; exultant; gay; glad; gleeful; good-humored; happy; intoxicated; jolly; jovial; joyful; joyous; jubilant; merry; mirthful; overjoyed; pleased; rapturous; thrilled.*

> They are happy as larks, they shine with their luck, their joy. — Audrey Niffenegger, *The Time Traveler's Wife*

(as) happy as Larry An insipid simile. *blissful; blithe; buoyant; cheerful; delighted; ecstatic; elated; enraptured; euphoric; exalted; excited; exhilarated; exultant; gay; glad; gleeful; good-humored; happy; intoxicated; jolly; jovial; joyful; joyous; jubilant; merry; mirthful; overjoyed; pleased; rapturous; thrilled.*

happy camper An infantile phrase (see page 20). *blissful; blithe; buoyant; cheerful; delighted; ecstatic; elated; enraptured; euphoric; exalted; excited; exhilarated; exultant; gay; glad; gleeful; good-humored; happy; intoxicated; jolly; jovial; joyful; joyous; jubilant; merry; mirthful; overjoyed; pleased; rapturous; thrilled.* ■ The six families who bought in to the project, all at full price, are not *happy campers* these days. REPLACE WITH *pleased.*

(a) hard (tough) act to follow A moribund metaphor (see page 21).

hard and fast (rule) A moribund metaphor (see page 21). *absolute; binding; certain; defined; dogmatic; entrenched; established; exact; exacting; fast; firm; fixed; hard; immutable; inflexible; invariable; permanent; resolute; rigid; set; severe; solid; steadfast; strict; stringent; unalterable; unbending; uncompromising; unyielding.* ■ Events are happening too quickly in Eastern Europe to make *hard and fast* plans at this point. REPLACE WITH *firm.*

(as) hard as a rock An insipid simile. 1. *adamantine; firm; granitelike; hard; petrified; rock-hard; rocklike; rocky; solid; steellike; steely; stonelike; stony.* 2. *athletic; beefy; brawny; burly; firm; fit; hale; hardy; hearty; husky; manly; mighty; muscular; powerful; puissant; robust; rugged; sinewy; solid; stalwart; stout; strapping; strong; sturdy; tough; vigorous; virile; well-built.* 3. *constant; dependable; determined; faithful; fast; firm; fixed; inexorable; inflexible; loyal; obdurate; resolute; resolved; rigid; solid; stable; staunch; steadfast; steady; stern; tenacious; unflinching; unwavering; unyielding.*

(as) hard as nails An insipid simile. 1. *athletic; beefy; brawny; burly; firm; fit; hale; hardy; hearty; husky; manly; mighty; muscular; powerful; puissant; robust; rugged; sinewy; solid; stalwart; stout; strapping; strong; sturdy; tough; vigorous; virile; well-built.* 2. *constant; dependable; determined; faithful; fast; firm; fixed; inexorable; inflexible; loyal; obdurate; resolute; resolved; rigid; solid; stable; staunch; steadfast; steady; stern; tenacious; unflinching; unwavering; unyielding.*

hard (tough) nut to crack A moribund metaphor (see page 21). 1. *arduous; backbreaking; burdensome; difficult;*

exhausting; fatiguing; hard; herculean; laborious; not easy; onerous; severe; strenuous; toilful; toilsome; tough; troublesome; trying; wearisome. 2. *impenetrable; incomprehensible; inexplicable; inscrutable; mysterious; obscure; unexplainable; unfathomable; ungraspable; unintelligible; unknowable.*

hard (rough) on the eyes A moribund metaphor (see page 21). *coarse; homely; ill-favored; plain; ugly; unattractive; unbeautiful; uncomely; unsightly.*

hard (tough) row to hoe A moribund metaphor (see page 21). *arduous; backbreaking; burdensome; difficult; exhausting; fatiguing; hard; herculean; laborious; not easy; onerous; severe; strenuous; toilful; toilsome; tough; troublesome; trying; wearisome.*

hard to believe A torpid term (see page 24). *beyond belief; beyond comprehension; doubtful; dubious; farfetched; implausible; improbable; incomprehensible; inconceivable; incredible; inexplicable; questionable; remote; unbelievable; unimaginable; unlikely; unrealistic.*

hard (tough) to swallow A moribund metaphor (see page 21). 1. *beyond belief; beyond comprehension; doubtful; dubious; farfetched; implausible; improbable; incomprehensible; inconceivable; incredible; inexplicable; questionable; remote; unbelievable; unimaginable; unlikely; unrealistic.* 2. *disagreeable; distasteful; indigestible; unpalatable; unpleasant.*

has a finger in every pie A moribund metaphor (see page 21).

has a heart as big as all outdoors An insipid simile. *beneficent; benevolent;* *compassionate; big-hearted; generous; good-hearted; humane; kind; kind-hearted; kindly; sensitive; sympathetic; understanding.*

has a heart of gold A moribund metaphor (see page 21). *beneficent; benevolent; compassionate; big-hearted; generous; good-hearted; good-natured; humane; kind; kind-hearted; kindly; sensitive; sympathetic; understanding.*

has a heart of stone A moribund metaphor (see page 21). *apathetic; callous; chilly; cold; cool; detached; dispassionate; distant; emotionless; frigid; glacial; hard; hardhearted; harsh; heartless; hostile; icy; impassive; indifferent; passionless; pitiless; reserved; unconcerned; unemotional; unfeeling; unfriendly; unresponsive.*

has an effect on A wretched redundancy (see page 25). *acts on; affects; bears on; influences; sways; works on.* ■ That's one of the problems that *has an effect on* everyone's quality of life. REPLACE WITH *affects.* SEE ALSO *effect.*

has an impact on A wretched redundancy (see page 25). *acts on; affects; bears on; influences; sways; works on.* ■ That too *had an impact on* the jury. REPLACE WITH *swayed.* SEE ALSO *impact.*

has a swelled head A moribund metaphor (see page 21). *arrogant; cavalier; conceited; disdainful; egocentric; egotistic; egotistical; haughty; lofty; pompous; pretentious; proud; narcissistic; self-centered; self-important; self-satisfied; supercilious; superior; vain.*

has both feet on the ground A moribund metaphor (see page 21). *busi-*

nesslike; careful; cautious; circumspect; expedient; judicious; politic; practical; pragmatic; prudent; realistic; reasonable; sensible; utilitarian.

has (his) hands full A moribund metaphor (see page 21). *booked; busy; employed; engaged; involved; obligated; occupied.*

has (him) in the palm of (my) hand A moribund metaphor (see page 21). *be in charge; be in command; be in control.*

has the patience of Job A moribund metaphor (see page 21). *accepting; accommodating; acquiescent; complacent; complaisant; compliant; cowed; deferential; docile; dutiful; easy; forbearing; gentle; humble; long-suffering; meek; mild; obedient; passive; patient; prostrate; quiet; reserved; resigned; stoical; submissive; subservient; timid; tolerant; tractable; unassuming; uncomplaining; yielding.*

has to do with A wretched redundancy (see page 25). *concerns; deals with; is about; pertains to; regards; relates to.* ■ The most recent academy committee mission *has to do with* climate-monitoring satellites. REPLACE WITH *concerns.*

has two left feet A moribund metaphor (see page 21). *awkward; blundering; bumbling; bungling; clumsy; gawky; gauche; ham-handed; heavy-handed; inapt; inept; lubberly; lumbering; maladroit; uncoordinated; uncouth; ungainly; ungraceful; unhandy; unskillful; unwieldy.*

has (him) under (her) thumb A moribund metaphor (see page 21). *administer; boss; command; control; dictate; direct; dominate; domineer; govern; in*

charge; in command; in control; manage; manipulate; master; misuse; order; overpower; oversee; predominate; prevail; reign over; rule; superintend; tyrannize; use.

hat in hand A moribund metaphor (see page 21). *diffidently; humbly; meekly; modestly; respectfully; unassumingly.*

haul (rake) over the coals A moribund metaphor (see page 21). *admonish; animadvert; berate; castigate; censure; chasten; chastise; chide; condemn; criticize; denounce; denunciate; discipline; excoriate; fulminate against; imprecate; impugn; inveigh against; objurgate; punish; rebuke; remonstrate; reprehend; reprimand; reproach; reprobate; reprove; revile; scold; swear at; upbraid; vituperate.*

have a conniption (fit) A moribund metaphor (see page 21). *bellow; bluster; clamor; explode; fulminate; fume; holler; howl; rage; rant; rave; roar; scream; shout; storm; thunder; vociferate; yell.*

have a good (nice) day (evening) A plebeian sentiment (see page 23). We are bovine creatures who find that formulas rather than feelings suit us well enough; indeed, they suit us mightily. How pleasant it is not to have to think of a valid sentiment when a vapid one does so nicely; how effortless to rely on triteness rather than on truth.

Dimwitticisms veil our true feelings and avert our real thoughts. SEE ALSO *common courtesy.*

have a hemorrhage A moribund metaphor (see page 21). *bellow; bluster; clamor; explode; fulminate; fume; holler; howl; rage; rant; rave; roar; scream; shout; storm; thunder; vociferate; yell.*

have (take) a listen An infantile phrase (see page 20). *listen.* As inane as it is insulting, *have (take) a listen* obviously says nothing that *listen* alone does not. Journalists and media personalities who use this offensive phrase ought to be silenced; businesspeople, dismissed; public officials, pilloried.

■ But some fans will take a walk and *take a listen* to the sales pitch, intrigued by such generous offers and possibility of making such a huge profit. REPLACE WITH *listen.* ■ It has been far too long since I have had the opportunity to hear the Seneca Chamber Orchestra, so I went over to Christ Church United Methodist to *have a listen,* and boy, has it grown. REPLACE WITH *listen.* ■ *Take a listen* and decide for yourself. REPLACE WITH *Listen.* ■ But first we will *take a listen* to attorney Frederic Woocher arguing against the law. REPLACE WITH *listen.*

have (me) by the ears A moribund metaphor (see page 21). *clasp; cleave (to); clench; clutch; grab; grasp; grip; hold; secure; seize.*

> In spite of the recent falls in the value of the Nasdaq index and the value of Amazon stock, the new technology had the city by the ears .... — Salman Rushdie, *Fury*

(the) have-nots A moribund metaphor (see page 21). *bankrupt; broke; destitute; distressed; impecunious; impoverished; indigent; insolvent; needy; penniless; poor; poverty- stricken; underprivileged.* ■ You, me, and many others can afford to pay a little more for health insurance if it gives some to the *have-nots.* REPLACE WITH *indigent.*

(the) haves A moribund metaphor (see page 21). *affluent; comfortable; moneyed; opulent; privileged; prosperous; rich; wealthy; well-off; well-to-do.*

(you) have to learn to walk before (you) can run A popular prescription (see page 23).

(you) have to love (yourself) before (you) can love another A popular prescription (see page 23).

(you) have (your) whole life ahead of (you) A popular prescription (see page 23).

(stand) head and shoulders above (the rest) A moribund metaphor (see page 21). *abler; better; exceptional; greater; higher; more able (accomplished; adept; capable; competent; qualified; skilled; talented); outstanding; standout; superior; superlative.* ■ By now, a few names should clearly be *heads and shoulders above* all others. REPLACE WITH *better than.*

head for the hills A moribund metaphor (see page 21). *abscond; clear out; decamp; depart; desert; disappear; escape; exit; flee; fly; go; go away; leave; move on; part; pull out; quit; retire; retreat; run away; take flight; take off; vacate; vanish; withdraw.*

head in the clouds and feet on the ground A moribund metaphor (see page 21).

head into the home stretch A moribund metaphor (see page 21).

(has a good) head on (his) shoulders A moribund metaphor (see page 21).

able; adroit; apt; astute; bright; brilliant; capable; clever; competent; discerning; effective; effectual; efficient; enlightened; insightful; intelligent; judicious; keen; knowledgeable; learned; logical; luminous; perceptive; perspicacious; quick; rational; reasonable; sagacious; sage; sapient; sensible; sharp; shrewd; smart; sound; understanding; wise.

head on the block A moribund metaphor (see page 21).

head over heels A moribund metaphor (see page 21). altogether; ardently; completely; deeply; earnestly; entirely; fervently; fully; intensely; passionately; perfectly; quite; roundly; thoroughly; totally; unreservedly; utterly; wholly; zealously.

head over heels (in love) A moribund metaphor (see page 21). besotted; crazed; haunted; infatuated; lovesick; mad; obsessed; possessed; smitten.

> Even in his Mammon days, he always leaned to the general while I tumbled head over heels into the particular; he loved ideas and I personalities; he was all for argument and I yearned for gossip. — Louis Auchincloss, *The Rector of Justin*

(as) healthy as a horse An insipid simile. athletic; beefy; brawny; energetic; fine; fit; good; hale; hardy; hearty; healthful; healthy; husky; lanky; lean; manly; muscular; powerful; robust; shapely; sinewy; slender; solid; sound; stalwart; strong; sturdy; thin; trim; vigorous; virile; well; well-built.

heap dirt (scorn) on A moribund metaphor (see page 21). asperse; bad-mouth; belittle; besmirch; bespatter; blacken; calumniate; defame; defile; denigrate; denounce; depreciate; deride; disparage; impugn; insult; libel; malign; profane; revile; scandalize; slander; slap; slur; smear; sully; taint; traduce; vilify; vitiate.

hear by (via) the grapevine A moribund metaphor (see page 21).

heart and soul A moribund metaphor (see page 21). 1. altogether; completely; entirely; fully; perfectly; quite; roundly; thoroughly; totally; unreservedly; utterly; wholly. 2. earnestly; fervently; genuinely; heartily; honestly; sincerely; unreservedly; wholeheartedly.

(a) heartbeat away A moribund metaphor (see page 21).

(my) heart bleeds for (you) A moribund metaphor (see page 21). commiserate; empathize; feel bad; feel sorry; pity; sympathize.

(his) heart is in the right place A moribund metaphor (see page 21). be well-intentioned.

(you) hear what I'm saying? An ineffectual phrase (see page 19). ■ She's the one who did it, not me. You hear what I'm saying? DELETE You hear what I'm saying? SEE ALSO (you) know what I mean? (you) know what I'm saying; (you) know what I'm telling you? (do) you know?.

(I) hear you An infantile phrase (see page 20). appreciate; apprehend; comprehend; grasp; see; understand.

(the) heat is on A moribund metaphor (see page 21). be coerced; be compelled; be forced; be pressured.

heaven on earth A moribund metaphor (see page 21). *ambrosial; angelic; beatific; blissful; delightful; divine; enchanting; glorious; godlike; godly; heavenly; joyful; magnificent; resplendent; splendid; sublime.*

(as) heavy as lead An insipid simile. *bulky; heavy; hefty; weighty.*

(through) hell and high water A moribund metaphor (see page 21). *adversity; affliction; calamity; catastrophe; difficulty; distress; hardship; misadventure; misfortune; ordeal; trial; tribulation; trouble; woe.*

hell (hellbent) for leather A moribund metaphor (see page 21). *breakneck; brisk; fast; hasty; hurried; immediate; madcap; prompt; quick; rapid; rash; speedy; swift; wild; winged.* ■ Connors clearly thought that he had more to gain by pursuing his *hell-for-leather* expansion in the region.

hell has no fury like (a woman scorned) An insipid simile.

hell on earth A moribund metaphor (see page 21). *chthonian; chthonic; hellish; impossible; infernal; insufferable; insupportable; intolerable; painful; plutonic; sulfurous; unbearable; uncomfortable; unendurable; unpleasant; stygian; tartarean.* ■ Being a stepmother is *hell on earth*. REPLACE WITH *hellish*. SEE ALSO *a living hell*.

hell on wheels A moribund metaphor (see page 21). 1. *boisterous; disorderly; feral; obstreperous; rambunctious; riotous; roistering; rowdy; uncontrolled; undisciplined; unrestrained; unruly; untamed; wild.* 2. *angry; bad-tempered; bilious;*

cantankerous; choleric; churlish; crabby; cranky; cross; curmudgeonly; disagreeable; dyspeptic; grouchy; gruff; grumpy; ill-humored; ill-tempered; irascible; irritable; mad; peevish; petulant; quarrelsome; short-tempered; splenetic; surly; testy; vexed.

hem and haw An inescapable pair (see page 20).
dally; dawdle; hesitate; vacillate; waver.

hemorrhage red ink A moribund metaphor (see page 21).

(like a) herd of elephants An insipid simile.

(right) here and now An inescapable pair (see page 20). *currently; now; nowadays; presently; the present; today.*

here's the thing An ineffectual phrase (see page 19). ■ *Here's the thing*, whoever is mayor must be able to work with the community. DELETE *Here's the thing*. ■ *Here's the thing*, men don't even know that we're different. DELETE *Here's the thing*. SEE ALSO *that's the thing; the thing about (of) it is; the thing is.*

here, there, and everywhere A wretched redundancy (see page 25). *all over; everywhere; omnipresent; ubiquitous.*

here today, gone tomorrow An infantile phrase (see page 20). *brief; ephemeral; evanescent; fleeting; flitting; fugacious; fugitive; impermanent; momentary; passing; short; short-lived; temporary; transient; transitory; volatile.* ■ I still love it even though nothing is as *here today, gone tomorrow* as a job in TV. REPLACE WITH *fleeting*. ■ In politics, issues *that* *are here today are gone tomorrow.* REPLACE WITH *are ephemeral.*

here to stay An infantile phrase (see page 20). *constant; deep-rooted; enduring; entrenched; established; everlasting; fixed; lasting; long-lived; permanent; secure; stable; unending.* ■ They questioned whether ability grouping is *here to stay.* REPLACE WITH *permanent.*

hero A suspect superlative (see page 24). Seldom someone who strives valorously to achieve a noble goal, *hero* has come to mean anyone who simply does his job or, perhaps, doing it, dies. As often, *hero* is used to describe a person who behaves ethically or suitably — merely, as he was told or taught.

Only comic book characters and cartoon creatures, today, define the word well.

■ The brother of former POW Jessica Lynch is calling his sister a *hero.* ■ A two-year-old boy who dialed 999 after his mother suffered an epileptic fit was today hailed a "little *hero*" by police in England. ■ Juventus goal *hero* David Trezeguet says his teammates are confident they can reach the Champions League final after last night's 2-1 defeat by Real Madrid. ■ A Brazilian bulldozer driver has become a national *hero* after refusing to knock down a house shared by a single mother and her seven children. ■ A male nurse who died of SARS was yesterday given a *hero's* funeral attended by Chief Executive Tung Chee-hwa.

hey An infantile phrase (see page 20). As a substitute for *hello* or *hi, hey* is a cheerless one. Perhaps the best way to discourage people from using *hey* is to respond with a hearty *diddle, diddle?*

■ You have a sharp mind for business and know how to relate to those who are self-employed or who work in unconventional careers (because, *hey,* you're part of the group!).

hide (their) heads in the sand A moribund metaphor (see page 21). *brush aside; avoid; discount; disregard; dodge; duck; ignore; neglect; omit; pass over; recoil from; shrink from; shun; shy away from; turn away from; withdraw from.* ■ Even when informed of the problem, some denominations are continuing to *hide their heads in the sand.*

(neither) hide nor (or) hair A moribund metaphor (see page 21). *nothing; sign; soupçon; trace; vestige.*

(left) high and dry An inescapable pair (see page 20). *abandoned; alone; deserted; forgotten; helpless; left; powerless; stranded.*

> His voice trailed off, he didn't know where; it left him high and dry, just staring at Ikmen like a fool. — Barbara Nadel, *Belshazzar's Daughter*

high and low An inescapable pair (see page 20). *all around; all over; all through; broadly; everyplace; everywhere; extensively; throughout; ubiquitously; universally; widely.* SEE ALSO *far and wide; left and right.*

high and mighty An inescapable pair (see page 20). *arrogant; cavalier; conceited; condescending; contemptuous; despotic; dictatorial; disdainful; dogmatic; domineering; haughty; imperious; insolent; lofty; overbearing; overweening; patronizing; pompous; pretentious; scornful; self-*

important; supercilious; superior; vainglo-rious.

(as) high as a kite An insipid simile. 1. *agitated; aroused; ebullient; effusive; enthused; elated; excitable; excited; exhila-rated; expansive; impassioned; inflamed; overwrought; stimulated.* 2. *besotted; cra-pulous; drunk; inebriated; intoxicated; sodden; stupefied; tipsy.*

high (top) man on the totem pole A moribund metaphor (see page 21). *administrator; boss; brass; chief; com-mander; director; executive; foreman; head; headman; leader; manager; master; (high) muckamuck; officer; official; over-seer; president; principal; superintendent; supervisor.*

(give) high marks A moribund metaphor (see page 21).

high on the hog A moribund metaphor (see page 21). *extravagantly; lavishly; luxuriantly.* ■ It's the state officials who are living *high on the hog*. REPLACE WITH *extravagantly*.

high-water mark A moribund metaphor (see page 21).

highway robbery A moribund metaphor (see page 21).

hindsight is 20/20 A quack equation (see page 23).

hired gun A moribund metaphor (see page 21). 1. *assassin; killer; mercenary; murderer.* 2. *adviser; authority; consult-ant; counselor; expert; guru; specialist.*

hit a home run A moribund metaphor (see page 21). *advance; fare well; flourish;* *prevail; progress; prosper; succeed; thrive; triumph; win.*

hit (strike; touch) a nerve A moribund metaphor (see page 21).

hit (him) (straight) between the eyes A moribund metaphor (see page 21). *amaze; astonish; astound; awe; dazzle; dumbfound; flabbergast; overpower; over-whelm; shock; startle; stun; stupefy; sur-prise.*

hit (rock) bottom A moribund metaphor (see page 21). *bankrupt; broke; destitute; distressed; impecunious; impoverished; indigent; insolvent; penni-less; poor; poverty-stricken.*

hitch (your) wagon to a star A mori-bund metaphor (see page 21). *be ambi-tious; be determined; be motivated; be striving.*

hit (close to) home A moribund metaphor (see page 21).

hit (me) like a ton of bricks An insipid simile. *amaze; astonish; astound; awe; confound; daze; dazzle; dumbfound; flab-bergast; overpower; overwhelm; shock; stagger; startle; stun; stupefy; surprise.* ■ The report *hit Congress like a ton of bricks*. REPLACE WITH *overwhelmed Congress*.

hit or miss A moribund metaphor (see page 21). *aimless; arbitrary; capricious; casual; erratic; haphazard; incidental; inconsistent; infrequent; irregular; lax; loose; occasional; odd; offhand; random; sporadic; uncontrolled; unplanned.*

hit over the head A moribund metaphor (see page 21).

hit pay dirt A moribund metaphor (see page 21). *flourish; get rich; prevail; prosper; succeed; thrive; triumph; win.*

hit the ceiling A moribund metaphor (see page 21). *bellow; bluster; clamor; explode; fulminate; fume; holler; howl; rage; rant; rave; roar; scream; shout; storm; thunder; vociferate; yell.*

hit the ground running A moribund metaphor (see page 21). ■ I get up in the morning and *hit the ground running.*

hit the hay A moribund metaphor (see page 21). *doze; go to bed; nap; rest; retire; sleep; slumber.*

hit the jackpot A moribund metaphor (see page 21). *flourish; get rich; prevail; prosper; succeed; thrive; triumph; win.*

hit the nail (squarely) on the head A moribund metaphor (see page 21). *be correct; be right.*

hit the road A moribund metaphor (see page 21). *abscond; clear out; decamp; depart; desert; disappear; escape; exit; flee; fly; go; go away; leave; move on; part; pull out; quit; retire; retreat; run away; take flight; take off; vacate; vanish; withdraw.*

hit the roof A moribund metaphor (see page 21).1. *be angry; be annoyed; be enraged; be exasperated; be furious; be incensed; be infuriated; be irate; be irked; be irritated; be mad; be raging; be wrathful.* 2. *bellow; bluster; clamor; explode; fulminate; fume; holler; howl; rage; rant; rave; roar; scream; shout; storm; thunder; vociferate; yell.* ■ He *hit the roof.* REPLACE WITH *became enraged.*

hit the sack A moribund metaphor (see page 21). *doze; go to bed; nap; rest; retire; sleep; slumber.*

hit the skids A moribund metaphor (see page 21). *decay; decline; degenerate; destroy; deteriorate; disintegrate; ebb; erode; fade; fall off; languish; lessen; ruin; wane; weaken; wither; worsen.*

hit (him) while (he's) down A moribund metaphor (see page 21).

(as) hoarse as a crow An insipid simile. *grating; gravelly; gruff; guttural; harsh; hoarse; rasping; raspy; throaty.*

hoist with (his) own petard A moribund metaphor (see page 21).

(can't) hold a candle (to) A moribund metaphor (see page 21). 1. *compare; equal; equate; liken; match; measure up; meet; rival.* 2. *be inferior.* ■ Various third-party utilities are available to improve this situation, but only one of them *holds a candle to* the NetWare SALVAGE utility. REPLACE WITH *rivals.* ■ When it comes to hosting wackos, the oft-maligned Web can't *hold a candle to* AM radio. REPLACE WITH *compare to.*

hold a gun to A moribund metaphor (see page 21). *coerce; command; compel; constrain; demand; dictate; force; insist; make; order; pressure; require.*

hold all the cards A moribund metaphor (see page 21). *administer; boss; command; control; dictate; direct; dominate; govern; in charge; in command; in control; manage; manipulate; master; order; overpower; oversee; predominate; prevail; reign over; rule; superintend.*

hold (their) feet to the fire A moribund metaphor (see page 21). *coerce; command; compel; constrain; demand; enforce; force; goad; impel; importune; incite; induce; insist; instigate; make; oblige; press; pressure; prod; push; require; spur; urge.* ■ The task now for those senators who truly support reform is to *hold their colleagues' feet to the fire* and bring this bill up again and again. REPLACE WITH *pressure their colleagues.* ■ He campaigns by movement-building: helping candidates, running ads to promote tax cuts, and *holding congressional Republicans' feet to the fire.* REPLACE WITH *prodding congressional Republicans.*

hold (your) fire A moribund metaphor (see page 21). 1. *be silent; be still; hush; keep quiet; quiet; silence.* 2. *be closed-mouthed; be quiet; be reticent; be silent; be speechless; be taciturn; be uncommunicative.*

hold (their) ground A moribund metaphor (see page 21). 1. *hold fast; stand firm.* 2. *assert; command; decree; dictate; insist; order; require.*

hold (my) hand A moribund metaphor (see page 21). *accompany; escort; guide.* ■ The intent of this text is to *hold your hand* through the learning process. REPLACE WITH *guide you.*

hold (her) head up (high) A moribund metaphor (see page 21). *be proud; show self-respect.*

hold on for dear life A torpid term (see page 24). *clutch; grab; grasp; hold; seize.*

hang (hold) on to your hat A moribund metaphor (see page 21). *be careful; be cautious; be prepared; be wary; look out; take heed; watch out.*

hold the fort A moribund metaphor (see page 21). 1. *defend; guard; protect.* 2. *look after.*

hold the phone A moribund metaphor (see page 21). *be patient; hold on; pause; slow down; wait.*

hold the purse strings A moribund metaphor (see page 21). *administer; boss; command; control; dictate; direct; dominate; govern; in charge; in command; in control; manage; manipulate; master; order; overpower; oversee; predominate; prevail; reign over; rule; superintend.*

hold (my) breath A moribund metaphor (see page 21). *agitated; anxious; eager; edgy; excitable; excited; fidgety; frantic; jittery; jumpy; nervous; ill at ease; on edge; restive; restless; skittish; uncomfortable; uneasy.*

Still, though I'd already unlatched the door for her, I felt unprepared for her arrival, needing to back away and sit again in my leather chair. I was holding my breath, waiting for her to go away. — Elizabeth Rosner, *The Speed of Light*

hold (your) tongue A moribund metaphor (see page 21). 1. *be silent; be still; hush; keep quiet; quiet; silence.* 2. *be closed-mouthed; be quiet; be reticent; be silent; be speechless; be taciturn; be uncommunicative.*

hold true A wretched redundancy (see page 25). *hold.* ■ What *holds true* for them may not *hold true* for others. DELETE *true.*

hold water A moribund metaphor (see page 21). *hold; is true; is valid.* ■ We have to ask if the ancient ideas of the roles of bonds still *hold water.* REPLACE WITH *hold.*

hold your horses A moribund metaphor (see page 21). *be patient; calm down; hang on; hold on; pause; slow down; wait.*

home free A moribund metaphor (see page 21). *guarded; protected; safe; secure; sheltered; shielded; undamaged; unharmed; unhurt; unscathed.*

home is where the heart is A popular prescription (see page 23).

homely as a mud fence An insipid simile. *coarse; homely; ill-favored; plain; ugly; unattractive; unbeautiful; uncomely; unsightly.*

(down) (the) home stretch A moribund metaphor (see page 21).

(as) honest as the day is long An insipid simile. *aboveboard; blunt; candid; direct; earnest; faithful; forthright; frank; genuine; honest; reliable; sincere; straightforward; trustworthy; truthful; upright; veracious; veridical.*

honest truth A wretched redundancy (see page 25). *honesty; truth.* ■ If you want the *honest truth,* I am in love with him. REPLACE WITH *truth.*

honestly and truly An inescapable pair (see page 20). ■ I *honestly and truly* believed he was the best I could hope for. REPLACE WITH *honestly* or *truly.*

honesty is the best policy A popular prescription (see page 23).

(the) honeymoon is over A moribund metaphor (see page 21).

hook, line, and sinker A moribund metaphor (see page 21). *altogether; completely; entirely; fully; perfectly; roundly; quite; thoroughly; totally; unreservedly; utterly; wholly.*

hoot and holler An inescapable pair (see page 20). *bay; bawl; bellow; blare; caterwaul; clamor; cry; holler; hoot; howl; roar; screak; scream; screech; shout; shriek; shrill; squawk; squeal; vociferate; wail; whoop; yell; yelp; yowl.*

hope and expect (expectation) A wretched redundancy (see page 25). *hope; expect (expectation); trust.* ■ I *hope and expect* you'll be seeing a lot more of this. REPLACE WITH *expect* or *hope.*

hope and pray An inescapable pair (see page 20). ■ I *hope and pray* that in future features of this sort, the *Globe* puts the emphasis where it belongs.

hope for the best A popular prescription (see page 23). *be confident; be encouraged; be heartened; be hopeful; be optimistic; be positive; be rosy; be sanguine.*

hope for the best but expect the worst A popular prescription (see page 23). ■ Since governments can never know how stable the oil-exporting countries are, governments of importing countries should *hope for the best but prepare for the worst.*

(just) hope (it'll) go away A popular prescription (see page 23).

hopeless romantic An inescapable pair (see page 20).

hopes and dreams An inescapable pair (see page 20).

hope springs eternal A popular prescription (see page 23). *confident; encouraged; heartened; hopeful; optimistic; rosy; sanguine.*

hopping mad An inescapable pair (see page 20). *agitated; alarmed; angry; annoyed; aroused; choleric; enraged; fierce; fuming; furious; incensed; inflamed; infuriated; irate; irritable; mad; maddened; raging; splenetic.*

(a) hop, skip, and a jump A moribund metaphor (see page 21).

hornet's nest A moribund metaphor (see page 21). *complexity; complication; difficulty; dilemma; entanglement; imbroglio; labyrinth; maze; muddle; perplexity; plight; predicament; problem; puzzle; quagmire; tangle.* ■ Senator Dodd called the jurisdictional issue a *hornet's nest* but said he was ready to tackle it. REPLACE WITH *imbroglio.*

horse of a different (another) color A moribund metaphor (see page 21). *aberrant; abnormal; anomalistic; anomalous; atypical; bizarre; curious; deviant; different; distinct; distinctive; eccentric; exceptional; extraordinary; fantastic; foreign; grotesque; idiosyncratic; independent; individual; individualistic; irregular; novel; odd; offbeat; original; peculiar; puzzling; quaint; queer; rare; remarkable; separate; singular; uncommon; unconven-tional; unexampled; unique; unnatural; unorthodox; unparalleled; unprecedented; unusual; weird.*

(the) hostess with the mostess An infantile phrase (see page 20).

hot air A moribund metaphor (see page 21). *aggrandizement; bluster; boasting; braggadocio; bragging; bravado; crowing; elaboration; embellishment; embroidery; exaggeration; fanfaronade; gasconade; gloating; hyperbole; overstatement; rodomontade; swaggering.*

hot and bothered An inescapable pair (see page 20). *agitated; anxious; aroused; bothered; displeased; disquieted; disturbed; excited; flustered; perturbed; troubled; upset; worried.*

hot and heavy An inescapable pair (see page 20). *aggressive; dynamic; emphatic; energetic; ferocious; fervent; fierce; forceful; frantic; frenzied; furious; intense; mighty; passionate; powerful; robust; savage; spirited; strenuous; strong; vehement; vicious; vigorous; violent.*

(as) hot as fire An insipid simile. *aflame; blazing; blistering; boiling; burning; fiery; flaming; heated; hot; ovenlike; roasting; scalding; scorching; searing; simmering; sizzling; steaming; sweltering; torrid; tropical; warm.*

(as) hot as hades (hell) An insipid simile. *aflame; blazing; blistering; boiling; burning; fiery; flaming; heated; hot; ovenlike; roasting; scalding; scorching; searing; simmering; sizzling; steaming; sweltering; torrid; tropical; warm.*

hot little hands A moribund metaphor (see page 21).

hotly contested An inescapable pair (see page 20).

hot potato A moribund metaphor (see page 21). *card; character; eccentric; exception; original.*

hot ticket A moribund metaphor (see page 21). *card; character; eccentric; exception; original.*

hot to trot A moribund metaphor (see page 21). 1. *concupiscent; horny; lascivious; lecherous; lewd; libidinous; licentious; lustful; prurient.* 2. *anxious; eager; impatient; ready; willing.*

hot under the collar A moribund metaphor (see page 21). *agitated; alarmed; angry; annoyed; aroused; choleric; enraged; fierce; fuming; furious; incensed; inflamed; infuriated; irate; irritable; mad; maddened; raging; splenetic.*

(a) house divided against itself cannot stand A popular prescription (see page 23).

(like a) house of cards An insipid simile. *breakable; broken-down; crumbly; decrepit; dilapidated; flimsy; fragile; frangible; friable; precarious; ramshackle; rickety; shabby; shaky; tottering; unsound; unstable; unsteady; unsure; wobbly.* ■ He argued that the government's case against them is *a house of cards.* REPLACE WITH *rickety.*

how could this have happened? A plebeian sentiment (see page 23).

how did (I) get into this? A plebeian sentiment (see page 23).

how goes it? (how's it going? how you doing?) An ineffectual phrase (see page 19). These phrases are uttered by the unalert and inert. *How goes it? how's it going?* and *how you doing?* are gratuitous substitutes for a gracious *hello.*

how much (do) you want to bet? An infantile phrase (see page 20).

hue and cry An inescapable pair (see page 20). *clamor; commotion; din; hubbub; noise; outcry; protest; racket; shout; tumult; uproar.*

huff and puff An inescapable pair (see page 20). 1. *blow; breathe heavily; gasp; huff; pant; puff; wheeze.* 2. *bellow; bluster; clamor; explode; fulminate; fume; holler; howl; rage; rant; rave; roar; scream; shout; storm; thunder; vent; vociferate; yell.*

Finally as she stood there huffing and puffing, while he was near apoplectic, she would agree to a compromise. — J. P. Donleavy, *The Saddest Summer of Samuel S*

huge throng A wretched redundancy (see page 25). *throng.* ■ A *huge throng* of young people attended the concert. DELETE *huge.*

hugs and kisses An inescapable pair (see page 20).

human nature being what it is An ineffectual phrase (see page 19) ■ *Human nature being what it is,* most of us would rather speak our own mind than listen to what someone else says. DELETE *Human nature being what it is.* ■ *Human nature being what it is,* when people place demands on others, their initial reaction is to rebel. DELETE *Human nature being what it is.* ■ *Human nature being what it is,* getting an extra day made everybody slow down. DELETE *Human nature being what it is.*

(my) humble abode An infantile phrase (see page 20). ■ I recently had the opportunity to visit CMD's headquarters in Boulder, Colorado, not far from my *humble abode.* REPLACE WITH *home.*

humongous An infantile phrase (see page 20). *big; brobdingnagian; colossal; elephantine; enormous; gargantuan; giant; gigantic; grand; great; huge; immense; large; mammoth; massive; monstrous; prodigious; stupendous; titanic; tremendous; vast.*

Not quite a misusage, *humongous* is altogether a monstrosity. And though it's not fair to say that people who use the word are monstrous as well, at some point we come to be — or at the least are known by — what we say, what we write.

■ My appetite was *humongous.* REPLACE WITH *enormous.* ■ We were up against a *humongous* insurance company. REPLACE WITH *colossal.* ■ My feeling is that there is a *humongous* gap between justice for the rich and the poor and working class. REPLACE WITH *huge.* ■ The players should recognize the exception for what it is: a *humongous* bargaining chip. REPLACE WITH *titanic.*

Before you know it you are paying a humongous divorce settlement to a woman who had more than once declared that she was an innocent who had no understanding of money matters. — Saul Bellow, *Ravelstein*

(as) hungry as a bear An insipid simile. *esurient; famished; gluttonous; greedy; hungry; insatiable; omnivorous; rapacious; ravenous; starved; starving; voracious.*

(as) hungry as a horse An insipid simile. *esurient; famished; gluttonous; greedy; hungry; insatiable; omnivorous; rapacious; ravenous; starved; starving; voracious.*

hunt with the hounds and run with the hares A moribund metaphor (see page 21).

hurdle to clear A moribund metaphor (see page 21). *bar; barrier; block; blockage; check; deterrent; difficulty; encumbrance; handicap; hindrance; hurdle; impediment; interference; obstacle; obstruction.*

hurl insults A moribund metaphor (see page 21).

hustle and bustle An inescapable pair (see page 20). *bustle; commotion; hustle; stir.* ■ Macau presents a restful alternative to the *hustle and bustle* of Hong Kong. REPLACE WITH *bustle* or *hustle.*

I

I can't believe I'm telling you this A plebeian sentiment (see page 23). Only the foolish or the unconscious, unaware of or ambivalent about the words they use or why they use them, can exclaim *I can't believe I'm telling you this*. Language use, the essence of being human, entails certain responsibilities — care and consciousness among them; otherwise, it's all dimwitted. SEE ALSO *I don't know why I'm telling you this*.

I can't get no satisfaction An infantile phrase (see page 20).

icing on the cake A moribund metaphor (see page 21). *a benefit; a bonus; a dividend; a gift; a gratuity; a lagniappe; an extra; a perk; a perquisite; a pourboire; a premium; a tip*. ■ Accreditation is still only *icing on the cake* and does not guarantee a department any rewards beyond the recognition of peers. REPLACE WITH *a perquisite*.

Dr. Pierce and Deena had returned to our Sunday school class, buoying my spirits. And several of the alumni from the Live Free or Die class had stopped attending, which was icing on the cake. — Philip Gulley, *Life Goes On: A Harmony Novel*

(an) idea whose time has come An infantile phrase (see page 20). ■ The good-news section is *an idea whose time has come*.

idle rich An inescapable pair (see page 20).

I don't know A plebeian sentiment (see page 23). ■ New passion is sweet, but after you know someone for a while, it fades. *I don't know*. ■ I know who I am — I have a good sense of that — but I will never know you, or anyone else, as

well. *I don't know*.

For a person to conclude his expressed thoughts and views with *I don't know* would nullify all he seemed to know if it weren't that *I don't know* is less an admission of not knowing than it is an apology for presuming to.

I don't know if (whether) I'm coming or going A moribund metaphor (see page 21). *baffled; befuddled; bewildered; confounded; confused; disconcerted; flummoxed; mixed up; muddled; perplexed; puzzled*.

I don't know, what do you want to do? An infantile phrase (see page 20).

I don't know why I'm telling you this A plebeian sentiment (see page 23). SEE ALSO *I can't believe I'm telling you this*.

I (just) don't think about it A plebeian sentiment (see page 23). SEE ALSO *you think too much*.

if and when A wretched redundancy (see page 25). *if; when*. ■ *If and when* a conflict should arise, it should be taken care of as soon as possible to protect the harmonious environment. REPLACE WITH *If* or *when*. SEE ALSO *if, as, and when; when and if; when and whether; when, as, and if; whether and when*.

if, as, and when A wretched redundancy (see page 25). *if; when*. SEE ALSO *if and when; when and if; when, as, and if; when and whether; whether and when*.

if at first you don't succeed (try, try again) A popular prescription (see page 23).

I feel (understand) your pain The people who spout about how empathic they are (*I feel your pain; I know how you feel*) are often the same people who have scant notion of what it is to be sensitive, kindhearted, even responsive. The emphasis is on showing empathy, which we do more for our own welfare than for others'; it's socially obligatory to be, or pretend to be, empathic. Ultimately, empathy will be thought no more highly of than sympathy now is. SEE ALSO *I'm sorry.*

if it ain't broke, don't fix it A popular prescription (see page 23).

if it feels good, it can't be bad A popular prescription (see page 23).

if it isn't one thing, it's another A plebeian sentiment (see page 23). SEE ALSO *it's one thing after another.*

if it's (not) meant to be, it's (not) meant to be A popular prescription (see page 23).

if it sounds too good to be true, it (probably) is A popular prescription (see page 23).

if the shoe fits (wear it) A moribund metaphor (see page 21).

if the truth be (were) known (told) An ineffectual phrase (see page 19).

if you can't beat them, join them A popular prescription (see page 23).

if you can't say something nice, don't say anything A plebeian sentiment (see page 23). SEE ALSO *be nice.*

if you can't stand the heat, stay out of the kitchen A popular prescription (see page 23).

if you don't know, I'm not going to tell you An infantile phrase (see page 20).

ignorance is bliss A plebeian sentiment (see page 23).

I (I've) got to (have to) tell you (something) An ineffectual phrase (see page 19). Like *I'll tell you (something), I'll tell you what, I'm telling you,* and *let me tell you (something), I (I've) got to (have to) tell you (something)* is a mind-numbing expression spoken only by people who are unaware of how foolish they sound — and of how foolish they are. These are the same people who are wont to begin other sentences with *Look* or *Listen, Hey* or *Okay.* ■ *I got to tell you,* he was the only person I could discuss my frustrations with. DELETE *I got to tell you.* ■ *I've got to tell you something,* I'm so proud of you. DELETE *I've got to tell you something.* ■ *I have to tell you,* the emerging country rates are up 21 percent. DELETE *I have to tell you.*

I just work here A plebeian sentiment (see page 23).

I'll bet you any amount of money An infantile phrase (see page 20).

ill-gotten gains An inescapable pair (see page 20).

I'll tell you (something) An ineffectual phrase (see page 19). This phrase — like *I got to (have to) tell you (something); I'll tell you what; I'm telling you; let me tell you (something)* — is mouthed by unimpressive men and irritating women, the one no more able, no more elegant than the other. ■ You got off easy, *I'll tell you.* DELETE *I'll tell you.* ■ *I'll tell you something*, they look like the greatest team ever. DELETE *I'll tell you something.* ■ *I'll tell you something, if it doesn't work out, you've always got a job here.* DELETE *I'll tell you something.* ■ The publisher got a sharp letter from me, *I'll tell you.* DELETE *I'll tell you.* SEE ALSO *I got to (have to) tell you (something); I'll tell you what; I'm telling you; let me tell you (something).*

I'll tell you what An ineffectual phrase (see page 19). ■ *I'll tell you what*, let's pause for a commercial and then you can tell us your story. DELETE *I'll tell you what.* ■ *I'll tell you what*, I'm not bitter against women, but I sure judge them quicker now. DELETE *I'll tell you what.* SEE ALSO *I got to (have to) tell you (something); I'll tell you (something); I'm telling you; let me tell you (something).*

I love (him) but I'm not in love with (him) A popular prescription (see page 23). The need to distinguish between loving someone and being *in* love with someone is fundamentally false. That there are different kinds of love is nothing that any discerning person has to be reminded of.

Some who make such a distinction may do so to ease their conscience, to absolve themselves for not loving someone who likely loves them and whom they surely feel gratitude or obligation to. In these instances, saying *I love (him) but I'm not in love with (him)* is simply a way of feeling good about having made someone feel bad.

Love, like few other words, ought not to be trifled with. ■ *I love him but I'm not in love with him.* REPLACE WITH *I love him.* SEE ALSO *be nice; excuse me?*

I'm bored (he's boring) A plebeian sentiment (see page 23). Being boring is preferable to being bored. The boring are often thoughtful and imaginative; the bored, thoughtless and unimaginative.

We would do well to shun those who whine about how bored they are or how boring another is. It's they, these bored ones, who in their eternal quest for entertainment and self-oblivion are most suited to causing trouble, courting turmoil, and coercing talk. SEE ALSO *(it) keeps (me) busy.*

I mean A grammatical gimmick (see page 19). Elliptical for "what I mean to say," *I mean* is said by those who do not altogether know what they mean to say. ■ Nobody deserves to die like that. *I mean*, he didn't stand a chance. DELETE *I mean.* ■ *I mean*, being in the entertainment field is not easy; *I mean*, I work hard at my job and still have performances to give. DELETE *I mean.* ■ I enjoy the outdoors; *I mean*, how can you live here and not enjoy it? DELETE *I mean.* ■ *I mean*, if you were in the movies or on TV, *I mean*, many more people would be interested. DELETE *I mean.*

imitation is the sincerest form of flattery A popular prescription (see page 23).

I'm not perfect (you know) A plebeian sentiment (see page 23). Even though *(I'm) a perfectionist* (SEE) is A suspect superlative (see page 24) — meaning that people who proclaim this do not easily disabuse themselves of the notion of being perfect — *I'm not perfect (you know)* is A plebeian sentiment (see page 23) — meaning that people who proclaim this all too easily excuse themselves for being imperfect. ■ I have some deep-seated anger. Hey, *I'm not perfect, you know.* SEE ALSO *(I'm) a perfectionist; nobody's perfect.*

I'm not stupid (you know) A plebeian sentiment (see page 23). ■ *I'm not stupid, you know;* I'm 24 years old, and I've been around.

impact (on) (*v*) An overworked word (see page 22). *act on; affect; bear on; influence; sway; work on.* ■ Let's look at two important trends that may *impact* the future of those languages. REPLACE WITH *influence.* ■ Everybody's district is *impacted* in a different way. REPLACE WITH *affected.* SEE ALSO *has an impact on.*

implement An overworked word (see page 22). *accomplish; achieve; carry out; complete; execute; fulfill; realize.*

I'm sorry A plebeian sentiment (see page 23). No simple apology, the plebeian *I'm sorry* pretends to soothe while it actually scolds. Even though it may seem like an apology — often for something that requires nothing of the sort — *I'm sorry* is said, unapologetically, in a tone of resentment.

Traditionally, a woman's emotion — for women have been, more than men, reluctant to express anger, bare and unbounded — resentment more and more of late finds favor with men and women alike.

■ Nine years old is too young to be left alone, *I'm sorry.* ■ I have to disagree. *I'm sorry.* ■ I know you guys are going to blow up after I'm done talking, but *I'm sorry.* SEE ALSO *excuse me?; nice; thank you.*

Another common usage of *I'm sorry* is when people hear another speak of some difficulty. This is the height of dimwitted English, for the people who say *I'm sorry* — an expression precisely as untrue as it is trite — likely have no more empathy in their hearts than there are syllables in the sentence. SEE ALSO *I feel (understand) your pain.*

I'm telling you An ineffectual phrase (see page 19). ■ It has more twists and turns than Route 66, *I'm telling you.* DELETE *I'm telling you.* ■ *I'm telling you,* there are people who take this seriously. DELETE *I'm telling you.* SEE ALSO *I got to (have to) tell you (something); I'll tell you (something); I'll tell you what; let me tell you (something).*

in a big (major) way A torpid term (see page 24). *acutely; a great deal; badly; consumedly; enormously; exceedingly; extremely; greatly; hugely; immensely; intensely; largely; mightily; prodigiously; seriously; strongly; very much.* ■ He wants to meet me *in a big way.* REPLACE WITH *very much.* ■ It hurt me *in a big way.* REPLACE WITH *badly.* SEE ALSO *in the worst way.*

> The photographer had barked "Smile!" I'd overcompensated in a big way. — Susan Isaacs, *After All These Years*

in a bind A moribund metaphor (see page 21). *at risk; endangered; hard-pressed; imperiled; in a bind; in a dilemma; in a fix; in a jam; in a predicament; in a quandary; in danger; in difficulty; in jeopardy; in peril; in trouble; jeopardized.*

in (the) absence of A wretched redundancy (see page 25). *absent; having no; lacking; minus; missing; not having; with no; without.* ∎ *In the absence of* these articulated linkages, changes introduced will be difficult to monitor. REPLACE WITH *Absent.*

in a class by (itself) A moribund metaphor (see page 21). *different; exceptional; extraordinary; incomparable; inimitable; matchless; nonpareil; notable; noteworthy; novel; odd; original; peculiar; peerless; remarkable; singular; special; strange; uncommon; unequaled; unexampled; unique; unmatched; unparalleled; unrivaled; unusual; without equal.*

(head) in a (the) cloud(s) A moribund metaphor (see page 21). *absent; absentminded; absorbed; abstracted; bemused; captivated; daydreaming; detached; distracted; distrait; dreamy; engrossed; enraptured; faraway; fascinated; immersed; inattentive; in thought; lost; mesmerized; oblivious; preoccupied; rapt; spellbound.*

> It brought it all back to me. Celia Langley. Celia Langley standing in front of me, her hands on her hips and her head in a cloud. — Andrea Levy, *Small Island*

in a delicate condition A moribund metaphor (see page 21). *anticipating; enceinte; expectant; expecting; gravid; parturient; pregnant; with child.*

in a dog's age A moribund metaphor (see page 21).

in advance of A wretched redundancy (see page 25). *ahead of; before.* ∎ *In advance of* introducing our guest, let me tell you why he's here. REPLACE WITH

Before. SEE ALSO *in advance of; previous to; subsequent to.*

in a (the) family way A moribund metaphor (see page 21). *anticipating; enceinte; expectant; expecting; gravid; parturient; pregnant; with child.*

in a (blue) funk A moribund metaphor (see page 21). *aggrieved; blue; cheerless; dejected; demoralized; depressed; despondent; disconsolate; discouraged; disheartened; dismal; dispirited; doleful; downcast; downhearted; dreary; forlorn; funereal; gloomy; glum; grieved; low; melancholy; miserable; morose; mournful; plaintive; sad; sorrowful; unhappy; woebegone; woeful.*

in a good mood A torpid term (see page 24). *blissful; blithe; buoyant; cheerful; cheery; content; contented; delighted; elated; excited; gay; glad; gleeful; happy; jolly; joyful; joyous; merry; pleased; sanguine; satisfied.* SEE ALSO *positive feelings.*

in a heartbeat A moribund metaphor (see page 21). *abruptly; apace; at once; briskly; directly; expeditiously; fast; forthwith; hastily; hurriedly; immediately; instantaneously; instantly; posthaste; promptly; quickly; rapidly; rashly; right away; speedily; straightaway; swiftly; wingedly.*

> Bless me, father, for I have sinned, I have lied to my husband, left him never knowing he will have a child, and would do it all again in a heartbeat. — Ann Patchett, *Patron Saint of Liars*

in a jam A moribund metaphor (see page 21). *at risk; endangered; hardpressed; imperiled; in a bind; in a dilem-*

ma; *in a fix; in a jam; in a predicament; in a quandary; in danger; in difficulty; in jeopardy; in peril; in trouble; jeopardized.*

in a lather A moribund metaphor (see page 21). *agitated; distraught; disturbed; excited; nervous; shaken; uneasy; upset.*

in a manner of speaking A wretched redundancy (see page 25). *as it were; in a sense; in a way; so to speak.* ■ Your contractor is correct *in a manner of speaking.* REPLACE WITH *in a sense.*

in and of itself (themselves) A wretched redundancy (see page 25). *as such; in itself (in themselves).* ■ This trend is interesting *in and of itself* but is also quite instructive. REPLACE WITH *in itself.* ■ All the benefits are worthwhile *in and of themselves,* but they have the additional benefit of translating into improved cost efficiency. REPLACE WITH *in themselves.*

in a nutshell A moribund metaphor (see page 21). *briefly; concisely; in brief; in short; in sum; succinctly; tersely.*

> One thing leads to another; that is, houses lead to commodes, and then commodes lead to houses, which lead to land, which leads to dairy cattle, which lead to cheese, which leads to pizza pies, which lead to manicotti and veal Parmesan, which lead to wine, which leads to love, which leads to babies, houses, and commodes. That was Gordon Baldwin in a nutshell. — Jane Smiley, *Good Faith*

in any way, shape, form, or fashion An infantile phrase (see page 20). *at all;*

in any way; in some way; in the least; somehow; someway. That anyone uses this expression is wondrous. To discerning listeners and readers, *in any way, shape, form, or fashion,* as well as similar assemblages, is as rickety as it is ridiculous.

■ If students are asked to leave the University, their return certainly should not be celebrated *in any way, shape, form, or fashion.* DELETE *in any way, shape, form, or fashion.* ■ Do you feel being on television will help you *in any way, shape, or form?* REPLACE WITH *somehow.* ■ That control is no longer there, not *in any way, shape, or form.* REPLACE WITH *at all.* ■ He wants something that doesn't resemble the landmark *in any way, shape, or fashion.* REPLACE WITH *in the least.* SEE ALSO *in every way, shape, and (or) form; in no way, shape, form, or fashion.*

in a pickle A moribund metaphor (see page 21). *at risk; endangered; hardpressed; imperiled; in a bind; in a dilemma; in a fix; in a jam; in a predicament; in a quandary; in danger; in difficulty; in jeopardy; in peril; in trouble; jeopardized.*

> Well, if he was in a pickle in regard to his followers, why the hell should she make it easy for him? — Susan Isaacs, *Red, White and Blue*

in a pig's eye A moribund metaphor (see page 21). *at no time; by no means; hardly; in no way; never; no; not at all; not ever; not in any way; not in the least; scarcely; unlikely.*

(stuck) in a rut A moribund metaphor (see page 21). *bogged down; caught; cornered; enmeshed; ensnared; entangled;*

entrapped; netted; mired; snared; stuck; trapped.

in a (constant) state of flux A torpid term (see page 24). *capricious; changeable; erratic; ever-changing; fluid; variable.*

in a timely fashion (manner; way) A wretched redundancy (see page 25). *in time; promptly; quickly; rapidly; right away; shortly; soon; speedily; swiftly; timely.* ■ He believes in getting the job done *in a timely fashion* and is very committed to achieving that goal.

(off) in a world of (his) own A moribund metaphor (see page 21). *absent; absent-minded; absorbed; abstracted; bemused; captivated; daydreaming; detached; distracted; distrait; dreamy; engrossed; enraptured; faraway; fascinated; immersed; inattentive; lost; mesmerized; oblivious; preoccupied; rapt; spellbound.*

in (her) birthday suit A moribund metaphor (see page 21). *bare; disrobed; naked; nude; stripped; unclothed; uncovered; undressed.*

in close (near) proximity to A wretched redundancy (see page 25). *close by; close to; in proximity; near; nearby.* ■ Cities were born out of the desire and necessity of human beings to live and work *in close proximity to* each other. REPLACE WITH *close to.* ■ In those cases, the verb will be in agreement with the subject that is *closest in proximity to* the verb. REPLACE WITH *closest to.*

in (the) clover A moribund metaphor (see page 21). *affluent; moneyed; opulent; prosperous; rich; successful; wealthy; well-off; well-to-do.*

in cold blood A moribund metaphor (see page 21). *deliberately; intentionally; knowingly; mindfully; on purpose; premeditatively; willfully.*

in connection with A wretched redundancy (see page 25). *about; as for; as to; concerning; for; in; of; on; over; regarding; respecting; to; toward; with.* ■ The police wanted to talk to him *in connection with* a fur store robbery. REPLACE WITH *about.* ■ *In connection with* the hiring incidents, this was the first time he denied any wrongdoing. REPLACE WITH *Concerning.*

in consideration of the fact that A wretched redundancy (see page 25). *because; considering; for; in that; since.* ■ *In consideration of the fact that* we have to have something submitted by January 15, we have get to started on this. REPLACE WITH *Since.* SEE ALSO *because of the fact that; considering the fact that; by virtue of the fact that; given the fact that; in view of the fact that; on account of the fact that.*

in (my) corner A moribund metaphor (see page 21).

incredible An overworked word (see page 22). 1. *beyond belief; beyond comprehension; doubtful; dubious; implausible; imponderable; improbable; incomprehensible; inconceivable; inexplicable; questionable; unfathomable; unimaginable; unthinkable.* 2. *astonishing; astounding; breathtaking; extraordinary; fabulous; fantastic; marvelous; miraculous; overwhelming; prodigious; sensational; spectacular; wonderful; wondrous.*

Like the platitudinous *unbelievable* (SEE), this word is very much overused. One of the hallmarks of dimwitted language is the unimaginativeness of those who use it. We would do well to try to distinguish ourselves through our speech and writing rather than rely on the words and phrases that so many others are wont to use. Those who speak as others speak, inescapably, think as others think. ■ But that someone would shoot a two-year-old child is *incredible*. REPLACE WITH *unimaginable*. ■ All these people are *incredibly* brave. REPLACE WITH *astonishingly*.

incumbent upon A torpid term (see page 24). *binding; compelling; compulsory; essential; imperative; mandatory; necessary; obligatory; required; requisite; urgent.*

in (his) cups A moribund metaphor (see page 21). *besotted; crapulous; drunk; inebriated; intoxicated; sodden; stupefied; tipsy.*

indebtedness A torpid term (see page 24). *debt.*

indelible impression An inescapable pair (see page 20). To describe something considered unforgettable with a cliché — an unoriginal, a forgettable, phrase — is indeed dimwitted. ■ The tundra will make an *indelible impression* on you. ■ War has made an *indelible impression* on international art movements, as well as on Australian art.

It was never published, but I saw it once and it made an indelible impression on my mind. — Sherwood Anderson, *Winesburg, Ohio*

in-depth analysis An inescapable pair (see page 20).

indicate A torpid term (see page 24). *Indicate* has virtually devoured every word that might be used instead of it.

More designative words include *acknowledge; admit; affirm; allow; announce; argue; assert; avow; bespeak; betoken; claim; confess; comment; concede; contend; declare; disclose; divulge; expose; feel; hint; hold; imply; insinuate; intimate; maintain; make known; mention; note; point out; profess; remark; reveal; say; show; signal; signify; state; suggest; tell; uncover; unveil.* ■ He *indicated* that he would be fine. REPLACE WITH *said*. ■ People have provided us with documents that *indicate* that veterans were exposed. REPLACE WITH *reveal*. ■ They have *indicated* that they do not understand the managed competition proposals and don't want to. REPLACE WITH *confessed*. ■ Last week's decision of the Federal Reserve Board *indicated* that minority-lending records will be an issue for many years to come. REPLACE WITH *signaled*.

individual(s) (*n*) A torpid term (see page 24). *anybody; anyone; everybody; everyone; man; men; people; person; somebody; someone; those; woman; women; you.* ■ This *individual* needs to be stopped. REPLACE WITH *woman*. ■ He seemed like a friendly enough *individual*. REPLACE WITH *person*.

in due course (time) A torpid term (see page 24). *at length; eventually; in time; ultimately; yet.*

in each others' pocket A moribund metaphor (see page 21). 1. *indissoluble; indivisible; inseparable; involved; together.* 2. *dependent; reliant.*

in every way, shape, form, or fashion An infantile phrase (see page 20). *altogether; completely; entirely; fully; quite; roundly; thoroughly; in all ways; in every way; perfectly; totally; unreservedly; utterly; wholly.* ■ For centuries, since the first African ancestors were brought here, whites have tried to imitate blacks *in every way, shape, form, or fashion* and I'm tired of it. REPLACE WITH *in all ways.* ■ He supports her *in every way, shape, and form.* REPLACE WITH *thoroughly.* SEE ALSO *in any way, shape, form, or fashion; in no way, shape, form, or fashion.*

in excess of A wretched redundancy (see page 25). *above; better than; beyond; faster than; greater than; larger than; more than; over; stronger than.* ■ *In excess of* 10 candidates wanted to make the town of Andover both their profession and their home. REPLACE WITH *More than.* ■ Police said Mr. Howard was driving *in excess of* 90 miles per hour. REPLACE WITH *faster than.*

in extremis A foreign phrase (see page 19). *decaying; declining; deteriorating; disintegrating; dying; ebbing; expiring; fading; failing; near death; sinking; waning.*

inextricably tied An inescapable pair (see page 20). ■ In good times and in bad, our future and our fortunes are *inextricably tied* together.

in fine fettle A moribund metaphor (see page 21). *energetic; fine; fit; good; hale; hardy; healthful; healthy; hearty; robust; sound; strong; trim; vigorous; well.*

in for a rude awakening (shock) A torpid term (see page 24). ■ The companies that still think the only ones who

are going to make it are Caucasian males are *in for a rude awakening.*

in for a (pleasant) surprise A torpid term (see page 24). ■ If she had set out to write a story about a spoiled brat, she was *in for a surprise.*

in full swing A moribund metaphor (see page 21).

in harm's way A moribund metaphor (see page 21). *exposed; insecure; obnoxious; unguarded; unprotected; unsafe; unsheltered; unshielded; vulnerable.*

in high gear A moribund metaphor (see page 21). *abruptly; apace; briskly; directly; expeditiously; fast; hastily; hurriedly; immediately; instantaneously; instantly; posthaste; promptly; quickly; rapidly; rashly; speedily; swiftly; wingedly.*

> Rosemary was in high gear. She was mounting a campaign to woo the chairman of the committee that would vote the bill out to the full Senate or decide to let it die ignominiously. — Marge Piercy, *The Third Child*

in hot water A moribund metaphor (see page 21). *at risk; endangered; hardpressed; imperiled; in danger; in difficulty; in jeopardy; in peril; in trouble; jeopardized.*

in its (their) entirety A wretched redundancy (see page 25). *all; complete; completely; entire; entirely; every; full; fully; roundly; whole; wholly.* ■ This would leave Wednesday, either partially or *in its entirety*, for coordination. REPLACE WITH *entirely.*

inject (new) life into A moribund metaphor (see page 21). *animate; energize; enliven; inspirit; invigorate; vitalize.*

in less than no time A moribund metaphor (see page 21). *abruptly; apace; at once; briskly; directly; expeditiously; fast; forthwith; hastily; hurriedly; immediately; instantaneously; instantly; posthaste; promptly; quickly; rapidly; rashly; right away; speedily; straightaway; suddenly; swiftly; unexpectedly; wingedly.*

(keep) (us) in line A moribund metaphor (see page 21). *acquiescent; amenable; behaving; biddable; compliant; docile; dutiful; in conformity; law abiding; obedient; pliant; submissive; tame; tractable; yielding.*

in loco parentis A foreign phrase (see page 19).

in (our) midst A wretched redundancy (see page 25). *amid; among.* ■ There are growing numbers of crazy people *in our midst.* REPLACE WITH *among us.*

in nature A wretched redundancy (see page 25). ■ He said the diaries are personal *in nature.* DELETE *in nature.* ■ Laws governing freedom to protest politically obviously are political *in nature.* DELETE *in nature.*

(as) innocent as a newborn babe (child) An insipid simile. *artless; guileless; ingenuous; innocent; naïve; simple.*

in nothing (no time) flat A torpid term (see page 24). *abruptly; apace; at once; briskly; directly; expeditiously; fast; forthwith; hastily; hurriedly; immediately; instantaneously; instantly; posthaste; promptly; quickly; rapidly; rashly; right*

away; speedily; straightaway; suddenly; swiftly; unexpectedly; wingedly.

in no way, shape, form, or fashion An infantile phrase (see page 20). *at no time; by no means; in no way; never; no; not; not at all; not ever; not in any way; not in the least.* ■ The gas contributed *in no way, shape, or form* to the fire. REPLACE WITH *not at all.* ■ *In no way, shape, or form* did she resemble a 63-year-old woman. REPLACE WITH *In no way.* ■ *In no way, shape, form, or fashion* was there any wrongdoing or misappropriation of funds. REPLACE WITH *Never.* SEE ALSO *in any way, shape, form, or fashion; in every way, shape, and (or) form.*

in one ear and out the other A moribund metaphor (see page 21). *forgetful; heedless; inattentive; lethean; neglectful; negligent; oblivious; remiss; thoughtless; unmindful; unthinking.*

> I hand them over, glad to be relieved of them. Maybe she'll understand them better than I. Anchee's explanations, I'm afraid, went in one ear and out the other.
> — Dennis Danvers, *The Watch*

(get) in on the ground floor A moribund metaphor (see page 21).

in over (my) head A moribund metaphor (see page 21). 1. *overburdened; overextended; overloaded; overwhelmed.* 2. *in arrears; in debt.*

(he's) in (his) own world A moribund metaphor (see page 21). *self-absorbed; self-involved; solipsistic.*

in point of fact A wretched redundancy (see page 25). *actually; indeed; in fact;*

in faith; in reality; in truth; truly. ■ *In point of fact,* we do all the wrong things, and we have for years. REPLACE WITH *In fact.* ■ *In point of fact,* Krakatoa is west of Java, but east apparently sounded better to Hollywood. REPLACE WITH *Actually.* ■ There aren't, *in point of fact,* one or two buildings; there are two exactly. DELETE *in point of fact.*

input A torpid term (see page 24). *data; feelings; ideas; information; recommendations; suggestions; thoughts; views.* ■ We would appreciate *input* from anyone who has knowledge in the above areas. REPLACE WITH *information.* ■ Of course, discretion must be used in evaluating their *inputs* since sales reps are biased toward lowering prices and pushing volume. REPLACE WITH *suggestions.* SEE ALSO *(the) bottom line; feedback; interface; output; parameters.*

inquiring minds (want to know) An infantile phrase (see page 20).

in (with) reference to A wretched redundancy (see page 25). *about; as for; as to; concerning; for; in; of; on; over; regarding; respecting; to; toward; with.* ■ *With reference to* the latest attempt to forge statehood for the District of Columbia, I favor our ancestors' concept that the District ought to be an entity unto itself. REPLACE WITH *As for.*

in (with) regard to A wretched redundancy (see page 25). *about; as for; as to; concerning; for; in; of; on; over; regarding; respecting; to; toward; with.* ■ *With regard to* the *StataQuest,* I am expecting the first six chapters sometime this week. REPLACE WITH *Regarding.*

in (high) relief A moribund metaphor (see page 21). *clearly; conspicuously; distinctly; manifestly; markedly; noticeably; obviously; perceptibly; plainly; prominently; unmistakably; visibly.*

in (with) respect to A wretched redundancy (see page 25). *about; as for; as to; concerning; for; in; of; on; over; regarding; respecting; to; toward; with.* ■ Some history *with respect to* the origins and evolution of the AS/400 will then be discussed. REPLACE WITH *on.*

in seventh heaven A moribund metaphor (see page 21). *blissful; blithe; buoyant; cheerful; delighted; ecstatic; elated; enraptured; euphoric; exalted; excited; exhilarated; exultant; gay; glad; gleeful; good-humored; happy; intoxicated; jolly; jovial; joyful; joyous; jubilant; merry; mirthful; overjoyed; pleased; rapturous; thrilled.*

in short order A torpid term (see page 24). *abruptly; apace; at once; briskly; directly; expeditiously; fast; forthwith; hastily; hurriedly; immediately; instantaneously; instantly; posthaste; promptly; quickly; rapidly; rashly; right away; speedily; straightaway; swiftly; wingedly.*

in short supply A torpid term (see page 24). *exiguous; inadequate; meager; rare; scant; scanty; scarce; sparse; uncommon; unusual.*

inside (and) out A moribund metaphor (see page 21). *altogether; completely; entirely; fully; perfectly; quite; roundly; thoroughly; totally; unreservedly; utterly; wholly.*

(an) inspiration to us all A suspect superlative (see page 24). How inspirational could anyone be when he is described with such an uninspired expression? ■ He's been *an inspiration to us all.*

in spite of the fact that A wretched redundancy (see page 25). *although; but; even if; even though; still; though; yet.* ■ This is true *in spite of the fact that* a separate symbol has been designated for input and output operations. REPLACE WITH *even though.* SEE ALSO *despite the fact that; regardless of the fact that.*

> Right away after the move I longed for it, in spite of the fact that I'd been in a conspicuous position, the kid of a proselytizing socialist schoolteacher and a city-slicker piano-playing mother. — Jane Hamilton, *Disobedience*

in (within) striking distance A moribund metaphor (see page 21).

integral part An inescapable pair (see page 20). This is another example of one word modifying another to little or no purpose.

integrate together A wretched redundancy (see page 25). *integrate.* ■ The cost of the transmitters can be significantly reduced if all the lasers can be *integrated together* on a single substrate. DELETE *together.*

interesting An overworked word (see page 22). *absorbing; alluring; amusing; arresting; bewitching; captivating; charming; curious; diverting; enchanting; engaging; engrossing; entertaining; enthralling; enticing; exciting; fascinating; gripping; intriguing; invigorating; inviting; pleasing; provocative; refreshing; riveting; spell-*

binding; stimulating; taking; tantalizing.

Not only An overworked word (see page 22), *interesting* is also a worsened one, for it connotes uninteresting as often as it denotes interesting. SEE ALSO *that's interesting.*

interface A torpid term (see page 24). SEE ALSO *(the) bottom line; feedback; input; output; parameters.*

in terms of A wretched redundancy (see page 25). This phrase is most often a plodding replacement for words like *about; as for; as to; concerning; for; in; of; on; regarding; respecting; through; with.* And with some slight thought, the phrase frequently can be pared from a sentence. ■ *In terms of* what women need to know about men, I have learned a lot. REPLACE WITH *Regarding.* ■ A key element *in terms of* quality health care is going to be having the best *in terms of the* education and continuing educational abilities to train the best in this country. REPLACE WITH *of;* DELETE *in terms of the.* ■ For further information, you would want to read outside sources that analyze *your competitors in terms of their products.* REPLACE WITH *your competitors' products.*

intestinal fortitude An infantile phrase (see page 20). *boldness; bravery; courage; daring; determination; endurance; fearlessness; firmness; fortitude; grit; guts; hardihood; hardiness; intrepidity; mettle; nerve; perseverance; resolution; resolve; spirit; spunk; stamina; steadfastness; tenacity.* ■ It takes a little luck and a lot of *intestinal fortitude* to break into a game. REPLACE WITH *daring.* ■ Voters will need *intestinal fortitude* to make it to election day. REPLACE WITH *fortitude.*

in the affirmative A wretched redundancy (see page 25). *affirmatively; favorably; positively; yes.* ■ The answer is *in the affirmative.* REPLACE WITH *yes.*

in the altogether A moribund metaphor (see page 21). *bare; disrobed; naked; nude; stripped; unclothed; uncovered; undressed.*

in the arms of Morpheus A moribund metaphor (see page 21). *asleep; dozing; dreaming; napping; sleeping; slumbering; unconscious.*

in the back of (my) mind A moribund metaphor (see page 21). *subconsciously; subliminally.* ■ I always knew, *in the back of my mind,* that something was bothering him. REPLACE WITH *subconsciously.*

(it's) in the bag A moribund metaphor (see page 21). *assured; certain; definite; guaranteed; incontestable; incontrovertible; indisputable; indubitable; positive; secure; sure; unquestionable.*

in the ballpark of A moribund metaphor (see page 21). *about; around; close to; more or less; near; nearly; or so; roughly; some.* ■ Estimates put the cost of each TAO work time gained or lost *in the ballpark of* $3 million per year. REPLACE WITH *around.* SEE ALSO *in the neighborhood of; in the vicinity of.*

in the black A moribund metaphor (see page 21). *debt-free; debtless.*

in the blink of an eye A moribund metaphor (see page 21). *abruptly; apace; at once; briskly; directly; expeditiously; fast; forthwith; hastily; hurriedly; immediately; instantaneously; instantly;* *posthaste; promptly; quickly; rapidly; rashly; right away; speedily; straightaway; suddenly; swiftly; unexpectedly; wingedly.* ■ Self-indulgent, run-on sentences will *earn you a rejection slip in the blink of an eye.* REPLACE WITH *quickly earn you a rejection slip.*

in the buff A moribund metaphor (see page 21). *bare; disrobed; naked; nude; stripped; unclothed; uncovered; undressed.*

in (on) the cards A moribund metaphor (see page 21). *certain; destined; expected; fated; foreordained; foreseeable; imminent; impending; liable; likely; possible; probable; ordained; prearranged; predestined; predetermined; predictable; sure.* ■ I think that kind of complexity is not *in the cards.* REPLACE WITH *likely.*

in the chips A moribund metaphor (see page 21). *affluent; moneyed; opulent; prosperous; rich; wealthy; well-off; well-to-do.*

in the clear A moribund metaphor (see page 21). 1. *absolved; acquitted; blameless; clear; excused; exonerated; faultless; guiltless; inculpable; innocent; irreproachable; unblamable; unblameworthy; vindicated.* 2. *guarded; protected; safe; secure; sheltered; shielded.* 3. *debt-free; debtless.*

in the closet A moribund metaphor (see page 21). *clandestine; concealed; confidential; covert; hidden; private; secret; secluded; shrouded; surreptitious; undercover; unspoken; veiled.*

in the cold light of reason A moribund metaphor (see page 21).

(keep) in the dark A moribund metaphor (see page 21). *ignorant; incognizant; insensible; mystified; nescient; unacquainted; unadvised; unapprised; unaware; unenlightened; unfamiliar; uninformed; uninitiated; uninstructed; unintelligent; unknowing; unschooled; untaught; unversed.* ■ They told me everything; I was never *kept in the dark.* REPLACE WITH *uninformed.*

in the dead of night A moribund metaphor (see page 21).

> Some of it she told him anyway, that it was extremely urgent she communicate with a friend in Tijuana, that quite possibly it was a matter of life and death, which is why she had taken it upon herself to wake him in the dead of night and for that, together with the breaking of his window, she had apologized profusely. — Kem Nunn, *Tijuana Straits*

in the depths of depression (despair) A moribund metaphor (see page 21). *aggrieved; blue; cheerless; dejected; demoralized; depressed; despondent; disconsolate; discouraged; disheartened; dismal; dispirited; doleful; downcast; downhearted; dreary; forlorn; funereal; gloomy; glum; grieved; low; melancholy; miserable; morose; mournful; plaintive; sad; sorrowful; unhappy; woebegone; woeful.*

in the distant future A wretched redundancy (see page 25). *at length; eventually; finally; in the end; in time; later; one day; over the (months); over time; someday; sometime; ultimately; with time.* ■ A similar agreement with Mexico could result in a true North American common market *in the distant future.* REPLACE WITH *one day.* SEE ALSO *in the immediate future; in the near future; in the not-too-distant future.*

in the doghouse A moribund metaphor (see page 21). *in disfavor; in disgrace.*

in the doldrums A moribund metaphor (see page 21). 1. *dead; dormant; dull; immobile; immovable; inactive; inanimate; indolent; inert; inoperative; languid; latent; lethargic; lifeless; listless; motionless; phlegmatic; quiescent; quiet; sluggish; stagnant; static; stationary; still; stock-still; torpid; unresponsive.* 2. *aggrieved; blue; cheerless; dejected; demoralized; depressed; despondent; disconsolate; discouraged; disheartened; dismal; dispirited; doleful; downcast; downhearted; dreary; forlorn; funereal; gloomy; glum; grieved; low; melancholy; miserable; morose; mournful; plaintive; sad; sorrowful; unhappy; woebegone; woeful.*

in the driver's seat A moribund metaphor (see page 21). *administer; boss; command; control; dictate; direct; dominate; govern; in charge; in command; in control; manage; manipulate; master; order; overpower; oversee; predominate; prevail; reign over; rule; superintend.* ■ Buyers are most definitely *in the driver's seat.* REPLACE WITH *in charge.* ■ Unlike traditional pension plans, which your employer controls, 401(k) plans put you *in the driver's seat.* REPLACE WITH *in control.*

(down) in the dumps A moribund metaphor (see page 21). *aggrieved; blue; cheerless; dejected; demoralized; depressed; despondent; disconsolate; discouraged; disheartened; dismal; dispirited; doleful; downcast; downhearted; dreary; forlorn; funereal; gloomy; glum; grieved; low;*

melancholy; miserable; morose; mournful; plaintive; sad; sorrowful; unhappy; woebegone; woeful.

in the event (that) A wretched redundancy (see page 25). *if; should.* ■ *In the event* you think I am overreacting, let me call attention to the realities of the contemporary workplace. REPLACE WITH *If* or *Should.*

in the final (last) analysis A wretched redundancy (see page 25). *in the end; ultimately.*

in the first place A wretched redundancy (see page 25). *first.* ■ *In the first place,* I don't want to, and *in the second place,* I can't afford to. REPLACE WITH *First; second.* SEE ALSO *in the second place.*

in the flesh A moribund metaphor (see page 21). 1. *alive.* 2. *in person; present.*

in the fullness of time A moribund metaphor (see page 21). *at length; eventually; in time; ultimately; yet.*

Here in the fullness of time would lie Kaiser himself. — Evelyn Waugh, *The Loved One*

in the heat of battle A moribund metaphor (see page 21).

in the heat of the moment A moribund metaphor (see page 21).

in the immediate future A wretched redundancy (see page 25). *at once; at present; before long; currently; directly; immediately; in a (week); next (month); now; presently; quickly; shortly; soon; straightaway; this (month).* ■ I will, *in the immediate future,* contact my fellow mayor in New York and ask him to make a decision. REPLACE WITH *this week.* SEE ALSO *in the distant future; in the near future; in the not-too-distant future.*

in (on) the issue (matter; subject) of A wretched redundancy (see page 25). *about; as for; as to; concerning; for; in; of; on; over; regarding; respecting; to; toward; with.* ■ This state used to be a leader *on the issue of* health reform. REPLACE WITH *in.* ■ *On the matter of* quality in teaching, he proposed a more symbiotic relationship between classroom time and research. REPLACE WITH *As for.*

in the know A moribund metaphor (see page 21). 1. *able; adept; apt; capable; competent; conversant; deft; dexterous; experienced; expert; familiar; practiced; proficient; seasoned; skilled; skillful; veteran.* 2. *adroit; astute; bright; brilliant; clever; discerning; effective; effectual; efficient; enlightened; insightful; intelligent; judicious; keen; knowledgeable; learned; logical; luminous; perceptive; perspicacious; quick; rational; reasonable; sagacious; sage; sapient; sensible; sharp; shrewd; smart; sound; understanding; wise.*

(live) in the lap of luxury A moribund metaphor (see page 21). *affluent; moneyed; opulent; prosperous; rich; wealthy; well-off; well-to-do.*

in (over) the long run (term) A wretched redundancy (see page 25). *at length; eventually; finally; in the end; in time; later; long-term; one day; over the (months); over time; someday; sometime; ultimately; with time.* ■ *In the long run,* that may be the most important thing. REPLACE WITH *Over time.* SEE ALSO *in (over) the short run (term).*

in the market for A moribund metaphor (see page 21). *able to afford; desire; looking for; need; ready to buy; require; seeking; want; wish for.*

in the midst of A wretched redundancy (see page 25). *amid; among; between; encircled by; encompassed by; in; inside; in the middle of; surrounded by.* ■ The United States, *in the midst of* increasing tension over Korea, is softening its tone on China. REPLACE WITH *amid.* ■ My profound conviction is that anytime we are together, Christ is *in the midst of* us. REPLACE WITH *among.*

in the money A moribund metaphor (see page 21). *affluent; moneyed; opulent; prosperous; rich; wealthy; well-off; well-to-do.*

in the near future A wretched redundancy (see page 25). *before long; directly; eventually; in time; later; one day; presently; quickly; shortly; sometime; soon.* ■ I'm looking forward to the possibility that you might review my work *in the near future.* REPLACE WITH *soon.* SEE ALSO *in the distant future; in the immediate future; in the not-too-distant future.*

in the neighborhood of A wretched redundancy (see page 25). *about; around; close to; more or less; near; nearly; or so; roughly; some.* ■ The rebels may have killed *in the neighborhood of* ten people. REPLACE WITH *close to.* SEE ALSO *in the ballpark of; in the vicinity of.*

in the not-too-distant future A wretched redundancy (see page 25). *before long; directly; eventually; in time; later; one day; presently; quickly; shortly; sometime; soon.* ■ *In the not-too-distant future,* Americans will have the tele-phone equivalent of a superhighway to every home and business. REPLACE WITH *Before long.* SEE ALSO *in the distant future; in the immediate future; in the near future.*

in the not-too-distant past A wretched redundancy (see page 25). *before; earlier; formerly; not long ago; once; recently.* ■ *In the not-too-distant past,* women were expected to be home, be nice, be sexy, and be quiet. REPLACE WITH *Not long ago.* SEE ALSO *in the past; in the recent past.*

in the offing A moribund metaphor (see page 21). *approaching; at hand; close; coming; expected; forthcoming; imminent; impending; looming; near; nearby.*

in the past A wretched redundancy (see page 25). ■ I'm just saying what we did do *in the past.* DELETE *in the past.* ■ We can remember *in the past* when we sometimes had two or three representa-tives. DELETE *in the past.* SEE ALSO *in the not-too-distant past; in the recent past.*

in the picture A moribund metaphor (see page 21). SEE ALSO *not in the picture.*

in the pink A moribund metaphor (see page 21). *energetic; fine; fit; good; hale; hardy; healthful; healthy; hearty; robust; sound; strong; vigorous; well.*

in the pipeline A moribund metaphor (see page 21).

in the process of -ing A wretched redundancy (see page 25). *as; while;* delete. Even though *in the process of* seems to add significance to what is being said — and to who is saying it — it plainly subtracts from both. ■ The hurricane is *in the process of* making a slow turn to the northeast. DELETE *in the process of.* ■ I'm *in the process of* going on a lot of interviews. DELETE *in the process of.* ■ The office is still *in the process of* collecting facts. DELETE *in the process of.*

> In the process of taking his jacket off, the Artiste thrust his thick chest forward. — Tom Wolfe, *A Man in Full*

in (within) the realm of possibility A wretched redundancy (see page 25). *believable; conceivable; conjecturable; doable; feasible; imaginable; likely; plausible; possible; practicable; supposable; thinkable; workable.* ■ Appointment of a "civilian" generalist public administrator possessing some public safety background is also *within the realm of possibility.* REPLACE WITH *possible.* ■ I'm afraid it is *within the realm of possibility* that that many warheads may be missing. REPLACE WITH *conceivable.*

in the recent past A wretched redundancy (see page 25). *before; earlier; formerly; lately; not long ago; of late; once; recent; recently.* ■ *In the recent past,* such performers were on the fringes of American culture. REPLACE WITH *Recently.* SEE ALSO *in the not-too-distant past; in the past.*

in the red A moribund metaphor (see page 21). *in arrears; in debt.*

in the right direction A torpid term (see page 24). ■ Furthermore, when onerous regulations are brought to the attention of senior officials, the govern-

ment has taken steps *in the right direction.* REPLACE WITH *to make them less unwieldy.*

in the right place at the right time An infantile phrase (see page 20). SEE ALSO *in the wrong place at the wrong time.*

in the saddle A moribund metaphor (see page 21). *administer; boss; command; control; dictate; direct; dominate; govern; in charge; in command; in control; manage; manipulate; master; order; overpower; oversee; predominate; prevail; reign over; rule; superintend.*

in the same boat A moribund metaphor (see page 21).

> They might all be in the same boat — sharing a comparatively small plot of land — but that didn't mean it was necessary to socialize. — Katie Fforde, *Wild Designs*

in the second place A wretched redundancy (see page 25). *second.* ■ *In the second place,* I sincerely believe that the merger has given it another chance to become the quality institution these students deserve. REPLACE WITH *Second.* SEE ALSO *in the first place.*

in (over) the short run (term) A wretched redundancy (see page 25). *at present; before long; currently; directly; eventually; in time; later; next (month); now; one day; presently; quickly; shortly; short-term; sometime; soon; this (month).* ■ I hope we're able to do something about this *in the short term.* REPLACE WITH *soon.* SEE ALSO *in (over) the long run (term).*

in the soup A moribund metaphor (see page 21). *at risk; endangered; hardpressed; imperiled; in a bind; in a dilemma; in a fix; in a jam; in a predicament; in a quandary; in danger; in difficulty; in jeopardy; in peril; in trouble; jeopardized.*

in the spotlight A moribund metaphor (see page 21).

in the swim A moribund metaphor (see page 21). *absorbed; active; busy; employed; engaged; engrossed; immersed; involved; occupied; preoccupied; wrapped up in.*

in the swing of things A moribund metaphor (see page 21). *in step; in sync; in tune.*

in the thick of (it) A moribund metaphor (see page 21). 1. *amid; among; encircled; encompassed; in the middle; surrounded.* 2. *absorbed; active; busy; employed; engaged; engrossed; immersed; involved; occupied; preoccupied; wrapped up in.*

in the trenches A moribund metaphor (see page 21).

in the twinkling (wink) of an eye A moribund metaphor (see page 21). *abruptly; apace; at once; briskly; directly; expeditiously; fast; forthwith; hastily; hurriedly; immediately; instantaneously; instantly; posthaste; promptly; quickly; rapidly; rashly; right away; speedily; straightaway; suddenly; swiftly; unexpectedly; wingedly.*

It actually struck the Minister-President on the shoulder as he stooped over his dying servant, then falling between his feet exploded with a terrific concentrated violence, striking him dead to the ground, finishing the wounded man and practically annihilating the empty sledge in the twinkling of an eye. — Joseph Conrad, *Under Western Eyes*

in the vicinity of A wretched redundancy (see page 25). *about; around; close to; more or less; near; nearly; or so; roughly; some.* ■ The final phase prohibits smoking anywhere *in the vicinity of* the main building's entrance. REPLACE WITH *near.* ■ The public puts its approval of Clinton's conduct *in the vicinity of* 70 percent. REPLACE WITH *around.* SEE ALSO *in the ballpark of; in the neighborhood of.*

in the wake of A moribund metaphor (see page 21). *after; behind; ensuing; following; succeeding.* SEE ALSO *(hot) on the heels of; reach epidemic proportions.*

in the wastebasket A moribund metaphor (see page 21). *abandoned; discarded; dismissed; jettisoned; rejected; repudiated; thrown out; tossed out.*

in the way of A wretched redundancy (see page 25). ■ They don't think they'll meet much *in the way of* resistance. DELETE *in the way of.* ■ The result is a staggering investment in foreign-oriented training with little *in the way of* return on investment. DELETE *in the way of.* ■ They didn't have much *in the way of* money. DELETE *in the way of.* ■ The result is that this disorganized interview usually provides little *in the way of* valuable information. DELETE *in the way of.*

in the worst (possible) way A torpid term (see page 24). *acutely; a great deal; badly; consumedly; exceedingly; extremely; greatly; hugely; immensely; intensely; mightily; prodigiously; seriously; very much.* ■ The Eagles want to win *in the worst way.* REPLACE WITH *very much.* SEE ALSO *in a big way.*

in the wrong place at the wrong time An infantile phrase (see page 20). An ascription of meaningfulness for those who unhappily speak it, it is an accedence to meaninglessness for those who sadly hear it. Along with *in the right place at the right time* (SEE), this phrase is evidence of what reason has been reduced to. ■ That little girl was just *in the wrong place at the wrong time.*

in this day and age A moribund metaphor (see page 21). *at present; currently; now; presently; these days; today.* ■ *In this day and age*, we need to train medical students to see beyond the front door of the hospital and to see the broader issues. REPLACE WITH *Today.*

in (their) time of need A torpid term (see page 24). ■ The ultimate beneficiaries are those who turn to the Clinic *in their time of need.*

in two shakes (of a lamb's tail) A moribund metaphor (see page 21). *abruptly; apace; at once; briskly; directly; expeditiously; fast; forthwith; hastily; hurriedly; immediately; instantaneously; instantly; posthaste; promptly; quickly; rapidly; rashly; right away; speedily; straightaway; suddenly; swiftly; unexpectedly; wingedly.*

in view of the fact that A wretched redundancy (see page 25). *because; considering; for; in that; since.* ■ *In view of*

the fact that you couldn't pay your bills, you became a prostitute? REPLACE WITH *Because.* SEE ALSO *because of the fact that; considering the fact that; by virtue of the fact that; given the fact that; in consideration of the fact that; on account of the fact that.*

(a lot of) irons in the fire A moribund metaphor (see page 21). 1. *assignments; chores; duties; involvements; jobs; projects; responsibilities; tasks.* 2. *possibilities; potentialities; prospects.*

I second that emotion An infantile phrase (see page 20).

I shall return An infantile phrase (see page 20).

(money) isn't everything A popular prescription (see page 23). ■ Price is important, but *price isn't everything.*

it doesn't take (you don't have to be) a rocket scientist (an Einstein; a PhD) to (know) An infantile phrase (see page 20). We can be reasonably certain that the people who use this expression are not rocket scientists, not Einsteins, not PhDs. We can be less certain that the people who use this phrase are not dullwitted, not obtuse, not brainless. ■ *It doesn't take a rocket scientist to* see that a brutal police attack on a peaceful march is unacceptable and outrageous. ■ *It doesn't take a rocket scientist to* understand that high standards and a quality education should rank over diversity. ■ *It doesn't take an Einstein to* know that when kids see Mark McGwire they're going to head to the mall and buy the supplements. ■ *It doesn't take a rocket scientist to* figure out what's going on here. ■ *It doesn't take a PhD to* realize that the problem with the lagoon is what it contains — trash and polluted water. SEE ALSO *alive and kicking.*

it felt (seemed) like a lifetime An insipid simile. SEE ALSO *it felt (seemed) like an eternity.*

it felt (seemed) like an eternity An insipid simile. ■ Although it took 10 hours to convince the man to come down, *it felt like an eternity.* SEE ALSO *it felt (seemed) like a lifetime.*

it has been brought to (my) attention An ineffectual phrase (see page 19). ■ *It has been brought to my attention* that we have no record of your order. REPLACE WITH *I have been told.* SEE ALSO *it has come to (my) attention.*

it has come to (my) attention An ineffectual phrase (see page 19). ■ *It has come to our attention* that the number 3 is very popular. REPLACE WITH *We have learned.* ■ *It has come to my attention that* your deposit was received too late to be disbursed to your creditors this month. DELETE *It has come to my attention that.* SEE ALSO *it has been brought to (my) attention.*

it is important to note (that) An ineffectual phrase (see page 19). Attachments like *it is important to note (that)* and *it is interesting to note (that)* suggest that whatever follows them is probably not so important or interesting. Only people who mistrust the import or interest of their own statements use phrases like these — clear signals that their meaning is likely without merit, their message likely without allure. ■ *It is important to note that* you can change these settings for any docu-

ment. DELETE *It is important to note that.* SEE ALSO *it is interesting to note (that); it is significant to note (that).*

it is important to realize (that) An ineffectual phrase (see page 19). ■ *It is important to realize that* analogical reasoning is used to explain and clarify, whereas causal reasoning is used to prove. DELETE *It is important to realize that.*

it is important to remember (that) An ineffectual phrase (see page 19). ■ *It is important to remember that* all three phases are important to your success. DELETE *It is important to remember that.*

it is important to understand (that) An ineffectual phrase (see page 19). ■ *It is important to understand that* turning the grid lines on and off changes only the display on the monitor and not the printout. DELETE *It is important to understand that.* SEE ALSO *you have to understand (that).*

it is interesting to note (that) An ineffectual phrase (see page 19). ■ *It is interesting to note that* although the sex hormone makes men more subject to baldness than women, it is more acceptable for women to wear wigs. DELETE *It is interesting to note that.* ■ *It is interesting to note that* in America bylines were largely an outcome of false reporting in another war, the Civil War. DELETE *It is interesting to note that.* SEE ALSO *it is important to note (that); it is significant to note (that).*

(so) ... it isn't (even) funny An infantile phrase (see page 20). ■ We've got so much overcapacity in the securities business *it isn't funny.* ■ I'm so sick of her *it isn't funny.*

it isn't over till it's over A popular prescription (see page 23).

it is significant to note (that) An ineffectual phrase (see page 19). ■ *It is significant to note that* the original database has not been altered. DELETE *It is significant to note that.* SEE ALSO *it is important to note (that); it is interesting to note (that).*

it is what it is A quack equation (see page 23).

it is worth noting (that) An ineffectual phrase (see page 19). ■ *It is worth noting that* he regarded her as "one of the finest writers of fiction." DELETE *It is worth noting that.*

it just happened An infantile phrase (see page 20). As an explanation for how circumstances or incidents unfold, none is more puerile. And though we might excuse children such a sentiment, it is rarely they who express it.

It just happened is a phrase used by those too slothful or too fearful to know what has happened. ■ It wasn't something I planned; *it just happened.* ■ What can I say? *It just happened.* SEE ALSO *because (that's why); whatever happens happens.*

it makes you (stop and) think A plebeian sentiment (see page 23).

it must (should) be mentioned (that) An ineffectual phrase (see page 19). ■ *It should be mentioned that* hiperspace is used by authorized programs only. DELETE *It should be mentioned that.*

it must (should) be noted (that) An ineffectual phrase (see page 19). ■ *It*

should be noted that not all parents require an extensive interview. DELETE *It should be noted that.* ■ In terms of who conducts investigations, *it should be noted that* patrol personnel also may be used as investigators. DELETE *it should be noted that.*

it must (should) be pointed out (that) An ineffectual phrase (see page 19). ■ *It should be pointed out that* when you send this type of letter you must follow through with the filing in the court, or it can be looked on as a threat. DELETE *It should be pointed out that.*

it must (should) be realized (that) An ineffectual phrase (see page 19). ■ *It should be realized that* uncoupling is complete when the partners have defined themselves and are defined by others as separate and independent of each other. DELETE *It should be realized that.*

it must (should) be understood (that) An ineffectual phrase (see page 19). ■ *It should be understood that* a quitting concern assumption would be clearly disclosed on the financial statement. DELETE *It should be understood that.*

it never ends A plebeian sentiment (see page 23).

it never rains, but it pours A moribund metaphor (see page 21).

I told you (so) An infantile phrase (see page 20).

it's a bird, it's a plane, (it's Superman) An infantile phrase (see page 20).

it's a dirty job, but someone's got to do it A popular prescription (see page 23).

it's a dream come true A moribund metaphor (see page 21). ■ To be mentioned in the same sentence as Bette Davis — *it's a dream come true.*

it's a free country An infantile phrase (see page 20). This expression is one that only fettered thinkers could possibly use. One of the difficulties with dimwitticisms is that, because they are so familiar, people will most often use them thoughtlessly. Manacled as people are to these well-worn phrases, original thoughts and fresh words are often unreachable. ■ If owners of eating establishments want to allow smoking, let them do so — *it's a free country.* ■ *It's a free country.* It's what makes America great. ■ *It's a free country*, and no one tells me what to say!

it's a jungle (out there) A moribund metaphor (see page 21).

it's all Greek to me An infantile phrase (see page 20). *abstract; abstruse; ambiguous; arcane; blurred; blurry; cloudy; confusing; cryptic; deep; dim; esoteric; impenetrable; inaccessible; incoherent; incomprehensible; indecipherable; indistinct; muddy; murky; nebulous; obscure; puzzling; recondite; unclear; unfathomable; unintelligible; vague.*

it's a long story A torpid term (see page 24). *It's a long story* — cipher for *I don't want to tell you* — is a mannerly expression that we use to thwart the interest of a person in whom we are not much interested. SEE ALSO *that's for me to know and you to find out.*

it's always darkest just before dawn A popular prescription (see page 23).

it's always something A plebeian sentiment (see page 23).

it's an art A suspect superlative (see page 24). ■ Parallel parking is not easy; *it's an art.* ■ Creating a seamless event involves skill and experience; *it's an art.* ■ Congress is involved with changing the bankruptcy system; *it's an art* with no exact formula. ■ Admissions is not a precise science, *it's an art.*

it's a nice place to visit but I wouldn't want to live there A popular prescription (see page 23).

it's a two-way street A moribund metaphor (see page 21).

it's a whole different ballgame A moribund metaphor (see page 21).

it's better than nothing A popular prescription (see page 23).

it's better to have loved and lost than never to have loved at all A popular prescription (see page 23).

it's like a death in the family An insipid simile.

it's like losing a member of the family An insipid simile.

it's more fun than a barrel of monkeys A moribund metaphor (see page 21). *amusing; comical; entertaining; funny; hilarious; humorous; hysterical; riotous; risible; side-splitting.*

it's not over till (until) it's over A quack equation (see page 23). People say *it's not over till (until) it's over* in earnest, as if it were a weighty remark, a solemn truth when, of course, it's nothing but dimwitted. We might have an occasional insight, even a revelation, if we didn't persistently speak, and think in terms of, this kind of rubbish. ■ But *it isn't over till it's over*, and right now we have a statement from Dubai Ports World and little else.

it's not over till (until) the fat lady sings An infantile phrase (see page 20).

it's (been) one of those days A plebeian sentiment (see page 23).

it's one thing after another A plebeian sentiment (see page 23). SEE ALSO *if it isn't one thing, it's another*.

it's the same old story A torpid term (see page 24).

it's what's inside that counts A popular prescription (see page 23).

it takes all kinds A popular prescription (see page 23).

it takes one to know one An infantile phrase (see page 20).

it takes two A popular prescription (see page 23).

it takes two to tango A popular prescription (see page 23).

it was a dark and stormy night An infantile phrase (see page 20).

it will all come out in the wash A moribund metaphor (see page 21).

it works both ways A popular prescription (see page 23).

J

(made) (her) jaw drop A moribund metaphor (see page 21). *amaze; astonish; astound; awe; confound; dumbfound; flabbergast; jar; jolt; overwhelm; shock; start; startle; stun; stupefy; surprise.* ■ There are a couple levels that are truly inspired, though there's nothing that will *make your jaw drop*. REPLACE WITH *astound you.* ■ But Jabra, a company that usually doesn't let us down with its Bluetooth headsets, has rolled out a model that *made our jaw drop*. REPLACE WITH *stunned us.*

> She found herself living again a moment at her mother's funeral, which at the time had made her jaw drop with amazement. — Rebecca West, *Sunflower*

(has) (his) jaw set A moribund metaphor (see page 21). *be determined; be firm; be fixed; be inexorable; be inflexible; be obdurate; be resolute; be resolved; be rigid; be tenacious; be unflinching; be unwavering; be unyielding.* ■ Both Frist and DeLay seem to *have their jaws set* on this one. REPLACE WITH *be firm.*

(Dr.) Jekyll-(Mr.) Hyde (personality) A moribund metaphor (see page 21). *capricious; changeable; erratic; fickle; fitful; flighty; fluctuating; haphazard; inconsistent; inconstant; intermittent; irregular; mercurial; occasional; random; sometime; spasmodic; sporadic; unpredictable; unsettled; unstable; unsteady; vacillating; volatile; wavering; wayward.*

je ne sais quoi A foreign phrase (see page 19).

John Hancock A moribund metaphor (see page 21). *signature.*

Johnny-come-lately A moribund metaphor (see page 21). *climber; latecomer; newcomer; parvenu; upstart.*

joie de vivre A foreign phrase (see page 19).

join at the hip A moribund metaphor (see page 21). *indissoluble; indivisible; inseparable; together.*

join forces A moribund metaphor (see page 21). *ally; collaborate; comply; concur; conspire; cooperate; join; unite; work together.*

join together A wretched redundancy (see page 25). *join.* ■ ASA *joins* a powerful job scheduler *together* with select elements of automated operations to create a unique software system. DELETE *together.*

judge not, lest you be judged A popular prescription (see page 23).

juggling act A moribund metaphor (see page 21).

jump all over A moribund metaphor (see page 21). *admonish; anathematize; berate; blame; castigate; censure; chastise; chide; condemn; criticize; curse; decry; denounce; execrate; imprecate; inculpate; indict; rebuke; reprimand; reproach; reprove; scold; upbraid.*

jump down (her) throat A moribund metaphor (see page 21). *admonish; animadvert; berate; castigate; censure; chasten; chastise; chide; condemn; criticize; denounce; denunciate; discipline; excoriate; fulminate against; imprecate; impugn; inveigh against; objurgate; punish; rebuke; remonstrate; reprehend; reprimand; reproach; reprobate; reprove; revile; scold; swear at; upbraid; vituperate.*

jump for joy A moribund metaphor (see page 21). *be blissful; be blithe; be buoyant; be cheerful; be delighted; be ecstatic; be elated; be enraptured; be euphoric; be exalted; be excited; be exhilarated; be exultant; be gay; be glad; be gleeful; be good-humored; be happy; be intoxicated; be jolly; be jovial; be joyful; be joyous; be jubilant; be merry; be mirthful; be overjoyed; be pleased; be rapturous; be thrilled.*

jump from the frying pan into the fire A moribund metaphor (see page 21).

jump in with both feet A moribund metaphor (see page 21).

I wanted to jump in with both feet, but something stopped me. — Jessica Speart, *Coastal Disturbance*

jumping-off point A moribund metaphor (see page 21).

jump on the bandwagon A moribund metaphor (see page 21). *be included; be involved; enlist; enroll; join; sign up; take part.* ■ Once everyone in an industry has learned about something that works, there's a tendency to *jump on the bandwagon.*

jump out of (her) skin A moribund metaphor (see page 21). *be amazed; be astonished; be astounded; be awed; be flabbergasted; be jarred; be jolted; be overwhelmed; be shocked; be started; be startled; be stunned; be stupefied; be surprised.*

jump ship A moribund metaphor (see page 21). *abandon; desert; forsake; leave; quit.*

jump the gun A moribund metaphor (see page 21).

jump through hoops A moribund metaphor (see page 21).

(the) jury is still out A moribund metaphor (see page 21). *be arguable; be debatable; be disputable; be doubtful; be dubious; be in doubt; be moot; be open; be questionable; be uncertain; be unclear; be undecided; be undetermined; be unknown; be unresolved; be unsettled; be unsolved; be unsure.*

Still another way to express not knowing or being undecided, *the jury is still out,* used figuratively, is as foolish a phrase as it is a meaning. Any sentence in which this dimwitticism is used is sentenced to being forgettable.

just exactly A wretched redundancy (see page 25). *exactly; just.* ■ *Just exactly* what do you mean? REPLACE WITH *Just* or *Exactly.*

just recently A wretched redundancy (see page 25). *just; recently.* ■ I *just recently* completed my bachelor's degree. REPLACE WITH *just* or *recently.*

just what the doctor ordered A moribund metaphor (see page 21).

just when you thought it was safe to An infantile phrase (see page 20).

K

keep a (the) lid on A moribund metaphor (see page 21). *bridle; check; constrain; control; curb; govern; harness; hold back; inhibit; muzzle; repress; restrain; stifle; suppress.* ■ Its leaders have said they cannot *keep a lid on* popular anger if the government does not begin to respond to citizens' demands. REPLACE WITH *restrain.*

> Buster had declined, of course, but there was talk that he got some of his employees to join and keep the lid on things. — Loraine Despres, *The Scandalous Summer of Sissy LeBlanc*

keep a low profile A moribund metaphor (see page 21).

keep an ear to the ground A moribund metaphor (see page 21). *be alert; be attentive; be awake; be aware; be eagle-eyed; be heedful; be informed; be keen; be* *observant; be vigilant; be wakeful; be watchful.*

keep an eye out for A moribund metaphor (see page 21). *be alert; be attentive; be awake; be aware; be eagle-eyed; be heedful; be informed; be keen; be observant; be vigilant; be wakeful; be watchful; hunt; look for; search.*

keep a stiff upper lip A moribund metaphor (see page 21). *be brave; be courageous; be determined; be resolute.*

keep (them) at arm's length A moribund metaphor (see page 21). ■ In some cases, you need to *keep hurtful people at arm's length* so they can't continue hurting you.

keep a watchful eye on A moribund metaphor (see page 21). *be alert; be attentive; be awake; be aware; be eagle-eyed; be heedful; be informed; be keen; be observant; be vigilant; be wakeful; be watchful.*

keep body and soul together A moribund metaphor (see page 21). *endure; exist; keep alive; live; manage; subsist; survive.*

keep (your) chin up A moribund metaphor (see page 21). *be brave; be courageous; be determined; be resolute.*

keep (his) cool A moribund metaphor (see page 21). *be calm; be composed; be patient; be self-possessed; be tranquil.*

keep (our) distance A moribund metaphor (see page 21). *be aloof; be chilly; be cool; be reserved; be standoffish; be unamiable; be unamicable; be uncompanionable; be uncongenial; be unfriendly; be unsociable; be unsocial.*

keep (his) eye on the ball A moribund metaphor (see page 21). 1. *be alert; be attentive; be awake; be aware; be eagle-eyed; be heedful; be observant; be vigilant; be wakeful; be watchful.* 2. *be able; be adroit; be apt; be astute; be bright; be brilliant; be capable; be clever; be competent; be discerning; be effective; be effectual; be efficient; be enlightened; be insightful; be intelligent; be judicious; be keen; be knowledgeable; be learned; be logical; be luminous; be perceptive; be perspicacious; be quick; be rational; be reasonable; be sagacious; be sage; be sapient; be sensible; be sharp; be shrewd; be smart; be sound; be understanding; be wise.*

keep (your) eyes (open) peeled A moribund metaphor (see page 21). *be alert; be attentive; be awake; be aware; be eagle-eyed; be heedful; be observant; be vigilant; be wakeful; be watchful.*

keep (its) finger on the pulse of A moribund metaphor (see page 21). ■ The Chinese government has been able to *keep its finger on the pulse of* technology acquisition activities.

keep (your) fingers crossed A moribund metaphor (see page 21). *hope for; pray for; think positively; wish.*

keep (me) glued to (my) seat A moribund metaphor (see page 21).

keep (my) head above water A moribund metaphor (see page 21). *be solvent; exist; live; subsist; survive.*

keep (your) head on (your) shoulders A moribund metaphor (see page 21). *be calm; be composed; be patient; be self-possessed; be tranquil.*

keep (your) nose clean A moribund metaphor (see page 21). *behave.*

keep (your) nose to the grindstone A popular prescription (see page 23). *drudge; grind; grub; labor; moil; slave; strain; strive; struggle; sweat; toil; travail; work hard.*

keep on a short leash A moribund metaphor (see page 21).

keep (your) pants (shirt) on A moribund metaphor (see page 21). *be calm; be composed; be patient; be self-possessed; be tranquil; calm down; hold on; wait.*

(it) keeps (me) busy A plebeian sentiment (see page 23). SEE ALSO *(he's) boring; (it) gives (me) something to do; (it) keeps (me) out of trouble; (it's) something to do.*

(it) keeps (me) going A plebeian sentiment (see page 23).

keep smiling A plebeian sentiment (see page 23). *Keep smiling* is insisted on by ghoulish brutes who would rob us of our gravity, indeed, steal us from ourselves.

(it) keeps (me) out of trouble A plebeian sentiment (see page 23). SEE ALSO *(it) gives (me) something to do; (it) keeps (me) busy; (it's) something to do.*

keep the ball rolling A moribund metaphor (see page 21). *continue; go on; keep on; move on; persevere; persist; proceed.*

keep the faith A popular prescription (see page 23). *be confident; be encouraged; be heartened; be hopeful; be optimistic; be positive; be sanguine.*

keep the home fires burning A moribund metaphor (see page 21).

keep the wolves at bay A moribund metaphor (see page 21).

keep under (his) hat A moribund metaphor (see page 21). *camouflage; cloak; conceal; cover; disguise; enshroud; harbor; hide; keep secret; mask; screen; shroud; suppress; veil; withhold.*

keep under lock and key A moribund metaphor (see page 21). 1. *confine; detain; hold; imprison; intern; jail; lock up; restrain.* 2. *lock up; protect; secure.*

keep up appearances A plebeian sentiment (see page 23).

> She desired children, decorum, an establishment; she desired to avoid waste, she desired to keep up appearances. — Ford Madox Ford, *The Good Soldier*

keep up with the Joneses A plebeian sentiment (see page 23).

(a) kick in the pants A moribund metaphor (see page 21). 1. *encouragement; fillip; goad; impetus; impulse; incentive; incitation; incitement; inducement; jolt; motivation; motive; prod; provocation; push; shove; spur; stimulation; stimulus; thrust; urge.* 2. *animation; ebullience; elation; enthusiasm; excitement; exhilaration; exultation; jubilance; jubilation; liveliness; rapture; stimulation; vivacity.* 3. *admonishment; castigation; censure; chastisement; disapprobation; disapproval; rebuke; remonstrance; reprimand; reproof; scolding; upbraiding.*

(a) kick in the teeth A moribund metaphor (see page 21). *abuse; affront; contempt; contumely; derision; disappointment; disdain; impertinence; indignity; insult; offense; outrage; rebuff; rebuke; rejection; scorn; slap; slight; slur; sneer; snub.* ■ We have received a judgment that has been *a kick in the teeth.* REPLACE WITH *an insult.*

kick the bucket A moribund metaphor (see page 21). *cease to exist; decease; depart; die; expire; pass away; pass on; perish.*

> So when I put my phone to my ear and heard her choke out "He's gone" who could blame me for thinking that Dad had kicked the bucket and that now it was only her and me. — Marian Keyes, *The Other Side of the Story*

kick up (our) heels A moribund metaphor (see page 21). *be merry; carouse; carry on; cavort; celebrate; debauch; disport; frolic; gambol; party; play; revel; riot; roister; rollick; romp; skylark.*

(like a) kid in a candy shop (store) An insipid simile.

kill (them) by inches A moribund metaphor (see page 21). *afflict; agonize; crucify; excruciate; harrow; martyr; persecute; rack; torment; torture.*

kill the goose that lays the golden egg A moribund metaphor (see page 21).

kill two birds with one stone A moribund metaphor (see page 21).

kill (her) with kindness A moribund metaphor (see page 21).

kind (and) gentle An inescapable pair (see page 20). *affable; agreeable; amiable; amicable; compassionate; friendly; gentle; good-hearted; good-natured; humane; kind; kind-hearted; personable; pleasant; tender; tolerant.*

(a) ... kind (sort; type) of thing A grammatical gimmick (see page 19). ■ It was *a spur-of-the-moment kind of thing.* DELETE *a ... kind of thing.* ■ It's *a very upsetting sort of thing.* DELETE *a ... sort of thing.* ■ It's difficult to find a person to commit to in terms of a long-term relationship *type of thing.* DELETE *type of thing.*

kiss and make up A moribund metaphor (see page 21).

> You have to be careful when criticizing a friend's partner because the second they kiss and make up, *you* are the baddie who slagged off the love of her life. — Anna Maxted, *Running in Heels*

kiss and tell A moribund metaphor (see page 21).

kiss (him) goodbye A moribund metaphor (see page 21). *abandon; abdicate; cede; desert; forfeit; forgo; give up; lose (out on); relinquish; renounce; sacrifice; surrender; waive; yield.* ■ Without a new government-funded convention center, Boston will *kiss major gatherings and tourist events goodbye.* REPLACE WITH *forfeit major gatherings and tourist events.*

kiss of death A moribund metaphor (see page 21).

(the) (whole) kit and caboodle A moribund metaphor (see page 21). *aggregate; all; all things; entirety; everything; gross; lot; sum; total; totality; whole.*

kith and kin An inescapable pair (see page 20).
acquaintances; family; friends; kin; kindred; kinfolk; kinsman; kith; relatives.

knee-high to a grasshopper A moribund metaphor (see page 21). 1. *diminutive; dwarfish; elfin; elfish; lilliputian; little; miniature; minikin; petite; pygmy; short; small; teeny; tiny.* 2. *young; youthful.*

knee-jerk reaction A moribund metaphor (see page 21). *automatic; habitual; instinctive; inveterate; mechanical; perfunctory; reflex; spontaneous; unconscious; unthinking.*

knight in shining armor A moribund metaphor (see page 21).

knock-down, drag-out fight A moribund metaphor (see page 21). 1. *altercation; argument; disagreement; discord; disputation; dispute; feud; fight; misunderstanding; quarrel; rift; row; spat; squabble.* 2. *battle; brawl; clash; fight; grapple; jostle; make war; scuffle; skirmish; tussle; war; wrestle.*

knock (me) down with a feather A moribund metaphor (see page 21). *amaze; astonish; astound; awe; dazzle; dumbfound; flabbergast; overpower; overwhelm; shock; startle; stun; stupefy; surprise.*

knock (throw) for a loop A moribund metaphor (see page 21). *amaze; astonish; astound; awe; dazzle; dumbfound; flabbergast; overpower; overwhelm; shock; startle; stun; stupefy; surprise.*

knock off (his) feet A moribund metaphor (see page 21). *amaze; astonish; astound; awe; dazzle; dumbfound; flabbergast; overpower; overwhelm; shock; startle; stun; stupefy; surprise.*

knock on wood A moribund metaphor (see page 21). *hope for; pray for; think positively; wish.*

knock (himself) out A moribund metaphor (see page 21). *aim; attempt; endeavor; essay; exert; exhaust; labor; moil; strain; strive; struggle; toil; try hard; undertake; work at.*

knock-out punch A moribund metaphor (see page 21).

knock (her) socks off A moribund metaphor (see page 21). 1. *amaze; astonish; astound; awe; dazzle; dumbfound; flabbergast; overpower; overwhelm; shock; startle; stun; stupefy; surprise.* 2. *beat; better; conquer; defeat; exceed; excel; outclass; outdo; outflank; outmaneuver; outperform; outplay; overcome; overpower; prevail; rout; succeed; surpass; top; triumph; trounce; vanquish; whip; win.*

knock the bottom out of A moribund metaphor (see page 21). *belie; confute; contradict; controvert; counter; debunk; deny; disprove; discredit; dispute; expose; invalidate; negate; rebut; refute; repudiate.*

knock the spots off A moribund metaphor (see page 21). *beat; better;*

conquer; defeat; exceed; excel; outclass; outdo; outflank; outmaneuver; outperform; outplay; overcome; overpower; prevail; rout; succeed; surpass; top; triumph; trounce; vanquish; whip; win.

know for a fact An infantile phrase (see page 20). ▪ I *know for a fact* that he was there with her. DELETE *for a fact.* ▪ I'm sure they do; I *know for a fact* they do. DELETE *for a fact.*

(don't) know ... from Adam A moribund metaphor (see page 21). *unacquainted; unconversant; unfamiliar; unknown.*

(know) ... inside (and) out A moribund metaphor (see page 21). *completely; comprehensively; deeply; exhaustively; expertly; fully; in depth; in detail; profoundly; thoroughly; well.*

> They came here because they *knew* this place. They knew it inside and out. — Zadie Smith, *White Teeth*

knowledge is power A quack equation (see page 23).

know all the angles A moribund metaphor (see page 21). 1. *able; adept; apt; capable; competent; deft; dexterous; experienced; expert; practiced; proficient; seasoned; skilled; skillful; veteran.* 2. *adroit; astute; bright; brilliant; clever; discerning; effective; effectual; efficient; enlightened; insightful; intelligent; judicious; keen; knowledgeable; learned; logical; luminous; perceptive; perspicacious; quick; rational; reasonable; sagacious; sage; sapient; sensible; sharp; shrewd; smart; sound; understanding; wise.*

(a man is) known by the company (he) keeps A popular prescription (see page 23).

(you) know something? An ineffectual phrase (see page 19). ▪ *You know something?* I'm going to do whatever is in my power to end this relationship. DELETE *You know something?* ▪ *You know something?* I never loved you either. DELETE *You know something?* SEE ALSO *(you) know what?*

know what's what An infantile phrase (see page 20). 1. *able; adept; apt; capable; competent; deft; dexterous; experienced; expert; practiced; proficient; seasoned; skilled; skillful; veteran.* 2. *adroit; astute; bright; brilliant; clever; discerning; effective; effectual; efficient; enlightened; insightful; intelligent; judicious; keen; knowledgeable; learned; logical; luminous; perceptive; perspicacious; quick; rational; reasonable; sagacious; sage; sapient; sensible; sharp; shrewd; smart; sound; understanding; wise.*

know which side (her) bread is buttered on A moribund metaphor (see page 21).

know thyself A popular prescription (see page 23).

(you) know what? An ineffectual phrase (see page 19). ▪ *You know what?* When we return, you'll meet her mother. DELETE *You know what?* ▪ She broke up with me, and *you know what?*, I've got a career now, which is good. DELETE *you know what?* SEE ALSO *(you) know something?*

(you) know what I mean? An ineffectual phrase (see page 19). ▪ Some people have to work at it more than others. *Know what I mean?* DELETE *Know what I mean?* ■ How can you not be depressed if you don't remember things. *You know what I mean?* DELETE *You know what I mean?* SEE ALSO *(you) hear what I'm saying? (you) know what I'm saying? (you) know what I'm telling you? (do) you know?*

(you) know what I'm saying? An ineffectual phrase (see page 19). ■ It was an association that wasn't based on any fact. *You know what I'm saying?* DELETE *You know what I'm saying?* ■ I want a girl that's real. *You know what I'm saying?* DELETE *You know what I'm saying?* SEE ALSO *(you) hear what I'm saying? (you) know what I mean? (you) know what I'm telling you? (do) you know?*

(you) know what I'm telling you? An ineffectual phrase (see page 19). ■ I don't know; I can't think of the words. *You know what I'm telling you?* DELETE *You know what I'm telling you?* ■ I like to be with a woman who has the same mindset as I do. *You know what I'm telling you?* DELETE *You know what I'm telling you?* SEE ALSO *(you) hear what I'm saying? (you) know what I mean? (you) know what I'm saying? (do) you know?*

knuckle under A moribund metaphor (see page 21). *abdicate; accede; acquiesce; bow; capitulate; cede; concede; give in; give up; quit; relinquish; retreat; submit; succumb; surrender; yield.*

kudos A foreign phrase (see page 19).

L

(a) labor of love A moribund metaphor (see page 21).

> It has been a true labor of love, and something more — the only thing that has kept her calm during the long winter months of waiting for the hearing to begin.
> — Anita Shreve, *Fortune's Rocks*

lack of A torpid term (see page 24). Whatever happened to our negative words, to the prefixes *dis-, il-, im-, in-, ir-, mis-, non-,* and *un-?* No doubt many people say *absence of* or *lack of* because they know so few negative forms of the words that follow these phrases. These people will say *lack of moderation* instead of *immoderation* and *absence of pleasure* instead of *displeasure.*

Others subscribe to society's oral imperative that all things negative be left unsaid. To these people, *lack of respect* is somehow preferable to, and more positive than, *disrespect.* ■ These reports by the media reflect a *lack of sensitivity* to basic human decency. REPLACE WITH *insensitivity.* ■ It was her *lack of judgment* that lost us the sale. REPLACE WITH *misjudgment.* SEE ALSO *absence of; less than (enthusiastic).*

lady A suspect superlative (see page 24). *Lady* has become a pejorative term. No longer does it suggest a cultured, sophisticated woman; rather, it suggests a woman hopelessly common, forever coarse. ■ If you wanted to sweep one of these *ladies* off her feet, what would you do? REPLACE WITH *women*. ■ I am a *lady*, and I like to be treated as such. REPLACE WITH *well-bred woman*. ■ I have a question for both of you *ladies*. DELETE *ladies*. SEE ALSO *class; gentleman*.

(the) land of milk and honey A moribund metaphor (see page 21).

(the) land of nod A moribund metaphor (see page 21). *sleep; slumber.*

land on (her) feet A moribund metaphor (see page 21). *come through; continue; endure; hold on; persevere; persist; remain; survive.*

landslide victory A moribund metaphor (see page 21).

last but (by) no means least An infantile phrase (see page 20). This term, like *last but not least*, needs to be retired. It's a drab, depressing formula used by forlorn people, by *team players* (SEE) and troglodytes alike, by hacks and hirelings all.

last but not least An infantile phrase (see page 20).

> They were concerned for the newcomer, and they were concerned for themselves; midwives, barber-surgeons, nannies, priest and, last but not least, solicitors crowded around the event in droves. — Peter Esterhazy, *Celestial Harmonies*

lasting An overworked word (see page 22). For example: *lasting consequence; lasting contribution; lasting impact; lasting impression; lasting lesson; lasting peace.*

last nail in (his) coffin A moribund metaphor (see page 21).

last of the Mohicans An infantile phrase (see page 20).

(for a) laugh A plebeian sentiment (see page 23). This expression is spoken by people who tally their giggles and count their guffaws, people who value numbers and sums more than they do words and concepts, people who consider laughter a commodity and life a comedy. ■ I need *a laugh*. ■ Sue and I want to do these silly things to you *for a laugh*. ■ I'm always looking *for a laugh*. SEE ALSO *avid reader; on a scale of 1 to 10*.

laughing (my) head off A moribund metaphor (see page 21). *cachinnate; cackle; chortle; chuckle; convulse; guffaw; hoot; howl; laugh; roar; shriek.*

laughing on the outside and crying on the inside A moribund metaphor (see page 21).

laughter is the best medicine A popular prescription (see page 23).

launching pad (for) A moribund metaphor (see page 21). *base; beginning; foundation; springboard; start*

laundry list A moribund metaphor (see page 21).

lavishly illustrated An inescapable pair (see page 20).

(the) law is the law A quack equation (see page 23).

law of the jungle A moribund metaphor (see page 21).

(don't) lay a finger (hand) on A moribund metaphor (see page 21). *caress; feel; finger; fondle; handle; pat; paw; pet; rub; stroke; touch.*

lay an egg A moribund metaphor (see page 21). *abort; blunder; bomb; fail; fall short; falter; flop; flounder; go wrong; miscarry; not succeed; slip; stumble; trip.*

lay at (their) door A moribund metaphor (see page 21). *accredit to; ascribe to; assign to; associate to; attribute to; blame on; charge to; connect with; correlate to; credit to; equate to; impute to; link to; relate to; trace to.*

lay a trap for A moribund metaphor (see page 21). *catch; decoy; ensnare; entrap; net; trap.*

lay at the door (feet) of A moribund metaphor (see page 21). *accredit to; ascribe to; assign to; associate to; attribute to; blame on; charge to; connect with; correlate to; credit to; equate to; impute to; link to; relate to; trace to.* ■ It doesn't seem that all this volatility can be *laid at the feet of* foreigners. REPLACE WITH *blamed on.*

lay (put) (your) cards on the table A moribund metaphor (see page 21). *be aboveboard; be candid; be forthright; be frank; be honest; be open; be straightforward; be truthful.*

lay down the law A moribund metaphor (see page 21). 1. *assert; command; decree; dictate; insist; order; require.* 2. *admonish; berate; castigate; censure; chastise; chide; condemn; criti-* *cize; decry; rebuke; reprimand; reproach; reprove; scold; upbraid.*

lay (spread) it on thick A moribund metaphor (see page 21). 1. *elaborate; embellish; embroider; enhance; enlarge; exaggerate; hyperbolize; inflate; magnify; overdo; overreact; overstress; overstate; strain; stretch.* 2. *acclaim; applaud; celebrate; commend; compliment; congratulate; eulogize; extol; flatter; hail; laud; panegyrize; praise; puff; salute.*

lay (it) on the line A moribund metaphor (see page 21). *be aboveboard; be candid; be forthright; be frank; be honest; be open; be straightforward; be truthful.*

lay (her) out in lavendar A moribund metaphor (see page 21). *admonish; animadvert; berate; castigate; censure; chasten; chastise; chide; condemn; criticize; denounce; denunciate; discipline; excoriate; fulminate against; imprecate; impugn; inveigh against; lecture; objurgate; punish; rebuke; remonstrate; reprehend; reprimand; reproach; reprobate; reprove; revile; scold; swear at; upbraid; vituperate.*

lay the groundwork (for) A moribund metaphor (see page 21). *arrange; groom; make ready; plan; prepare; prime; ready.*

lead (her) by the nose A moribund metaphor (see page 21). *administer; boss; command; control; dictate; direct; dominate; domineer; govern; in charge; in command; in control; manage; manipulate; master; misuse; order; overpower; oversee; predominate; prevail; reign over; rule; superintend; tyrannize; use.*

lead down the garden path A moribund metaphor (see page 21). *bamboozle; befool; beguile; bilk; bluff; cheat; con; deceive; defraud; delude; dupe; feint; fool; gyp; hoodwink; lead astray; misdirect; misguide; misinform; mislead; spoof; swindle; trick; victimize.*

leader of the pack A moribund metaphor (see page 21). 1. *administrator; boss; brass; chief; commander; director; executive; foreman; head; headman; leader; manager; master; (high) muckamuck; officer; official; overseer; president; principal; superintendent; supervisor.* 2. *aristocrat; dignitary; eminence; lord; luminary; magnate; mogul; notable; patrician; personage; ruler; sovereign; worthy.*

(put) lead in your pencil A moribund metaphor (see page 21). *energy; force; life; power; punch; spirit; strength; verve; vigor; vim; vitality; zest.*

leak like a sieve An insipid simile. 1. *leaky; permeable.* 2. *forgetful; heedless; inattentive; lethean; neglectful; negligent; oblivious; remiss; thoughtless; unmindful; unthinking.*

lean and hungry (look) A moribund metaphor (see page 21).

lean and mean An inescapable pair (see page 20).

leaps off the page A moribund metaphor (see page 21).

learn the ropes A moribund metaphor (see page 21).

> She was left sitting until a slight, sparrow-like woman, with bright fringed hair and round blue eyes, came past and remarked warningly that she should keep her eyes open and learn the ropes. — Doris M. Lessing, *Martha Quest*

leave a bad taste in (my) mouth A moribund metaphor (see page 21).

leave a little (a lot; much; something) to be desired A torpid term (see page 24). *be deficient; be inadequate; be insufficient; be lacking; be substandard; be wanting.* ■ In the area of health, the U.S. position *leaves much to be desired.* REPLACE WITH *is sickly.* ■ The plan was great; it was the execution that *left a little to be desired.* REPLACE WITH *was not.* ■ Sorry about that, my handwriting *leaves something to be desired.* REPLACE WITH *is scarcely legible.*

leave holding the bag A moribund metaphor (see page 21). *abandon; depart from; desert; exclude; forsake; leave; quit; withdraw from.*

leave (out) in the cold A moribund metaphor (see page 21). *abandon; ban; banish; bar; desert; exclude; exile; forsake; ostracize; shut out.*

leave (him) in the dust A moribund metaphor (see page 21). *beat; best; better; defeat; eclipse; exceed; excel; outclass; outdo; outflank; outmaneuver; outpace; outperform; outplay; outrank; outrival; outsmart; outstrip; outthink; outwit; overcome; overpower; overshadow; prevail; rout; surpass; top; triumph; trounce; van-*

quish; whip; win. ■ It is here where Homo sapiens *leaves* other species *in the dust*, and the hands usually make it possible. REPLACE WITH *surpasses.*

leave (hanging) in the lurch A moribund metaphor (see page 21). *abandon; depart from; desert; exclude; forsake; leave; quit; withdraw from.* ■ We don't want to *leave* parents *hanging in the lurch.* REPLACE WITH *abandon.*

> Today, Jorie has once again left her poor friend Charlotte in the lurch, with no explanations or apologies.
> — Alice Hoffman, *Blue Diary*

leave no stone unturned A moribund metaphor (see page 21). *analyze; canvass; comb; examine; explore; filter; forage; hunt; inspect; investigate; look for; probe; quest; ransack; rummage; scour; scrutinize; search; seek; sieve; sift; winnow.*

leave the door (wide) open (for) A moribund metaphor (see page 21). ■ The remainder of the majority *left the door open for* a return to capital punishment.

leave well enough alone A popular prescription (see page 23).

left and right An inescapable pair (see page 20). *all around; all over; all through; broadly; everyplace; everywhere; extensively; throughout; ubiquitously; universally; widely.* SEE ALSO *far and wide; high and low.*

(a) legend in (his) own mind An infantile phrase (see page 20).

leg to stand on A moribund metaphor (see page 21).

(has a) leg up on A moribund metaphor (see page 21). *advantage (over); predominance over; superiority to; supremacy over.* ■ This is expected to give auto makers *a natural leg up.* REPLACE WITH *a natural advantage.* ■ Even I have *a leg up on* him in that department. REPLACE WITH *an advantage over.*

lend a (helping) hand (to) A moribund metaphor (see page 21). *aid; assist; benefit; favor; help; oblige; succor.* ■ During this holiday season, it is fitting for all of us to be thinking of *lending a helping hand to* those in need. REPLACE WITH *aiding.* ■ These writers believe it's their mission to *lend a hand* wherever there is a need. REPLACE WITH *help.*

lend an ear A moribund metaphor (see page 21). *attend to; heed; listen; note.*

(a) leopard cannot change his spots A popular prescription (see page 23).

leopards don't lose their spots A moribund metaphor (see page 21).

(the) lesser of two evils A torpid term (see page 24).

less is more A quack equation (see page 23).

(the) less said, the better A popular prescription (see page 23).

less than (enthusiastic) A torpid term (see page 24). ■ When Fred told his wife about the unbelievable opportunity, he was shocked at her *less than enthusiastic* response. REPLACE WITH *unenthusiastic.* ■ The response from their neighbors has been *less than hospitable.*

REPLACE WITH *inhospitable*. SEE ALSO *absence of; lack of*.

let bygones be bygones A popular prescription (see page 23).

let go of the past A popular prescription (see page 23).

let grass grow under (your) feet A moribund metaphor (see page 21). *be idle; be inactive; be lazy; be unemployed; be unoccupied; dally; dawdle; delay; hesitate; linger; loaf; loiter; loll; lounge; pause; relax; repose; rest; tarry; unwind; wait; waste time.*

let (take) (her) hair down A moribund metaphor (see page 21). *be casual; be free; be informal; be loose; be natural; be open; be relaxed; be unbound; be unconfined; be unrestrained; be unrestricted.*

let (him) have it with both barrels A moribund metaphor (see page 21). *admonish; animadvert; berate; castigate; censure; chasten; chastise; chide; condemn; criticize; denounce; denunciate; discipline; excoriate; fulminate against; imprecate; impugn; inveigh against; objurgate; punish; rebuke; remonstrate; reprehend; reprimand; reproach; reprobate; reprove; revile; scold; swear at; upbraid; vituperate.*

let it all hang out A moribund metaphor (see page 21). *acknowledge; admit; affirm; allow; avow; concede; confess; disclose; divulge; expose; grant; own; reveal; tell; uncover; unveil.*

let it be A popular prescription (see page 23).

let me ask you something An ineffectual phrase (see page 19). ■ *Let me ask you something*, is there anything about school that you like? DELETE *Let me ask you something*. ■ *Let me ask you something*: What would you think if I met three women tonight? DELETE *Let me ask you something*. SEE ALSO *can I ask (tell) you something?*

let me tell you (something) An ineffectual phrase (see page 19). Of course the people who use this phrase seldom enunciate *let me*; they mutter *lemme*, an inauspicious sign, we might reasonably believe, of what is to come. *Let me tell you (something)* is a vulgarity, very nearly an insult. It unveils a person, only crudely conscious of what he utters, who has as much respect for the language as he does for his listeners.
■ This is really class, *let me tell you*. DELETE *let me tell you*. ■ It's been one of those days, *let me tell you*. DELETE *let me tell you*. ■ *Let me tell you*, there is nothing scarier than being in hurricane force winds and hearing huge clangs and thumps and shattering of glass or metal. DELETE *Let me tell you*. SEE ALSO *I got to (have to) tell you (something); I'll tell you (something); I'll tell you what; I'm telling you*.

let nature take its course A popular prescription (see page 23).

let sleeping dogs lie A popular prescription (see page 23). *avoid; discount; disregard; dodge; duck; ignore; neglect; omit; pass over; shun; shy away from; turn away from; withdraw from.*

let the cat out of the bag A moribund metaphor (see page 21). *reveal secrets.*

let the chips fall where they may A moribund metaphor (see page 21).

let there be no mistake A torpid term (see page 24). SEE ALSO *make no mistake (about it)*.

let your fingers do the walking An infantile phrase (see page 20).

let your mind run wild A moribund metaphor (see page 21).

(a) level playing field A moribund metaphor (see page 21). *equality; equitableness; equity; fairness; impartiality; justice; justness.* ■ If you live in a democracy, there has to be *a level playing field*. REPLACE WITH *equality*. ■ Many people of goodwill sincerely, but mistakenly, believe that today we have achieved *a level playing field*. REPLACE WITH *fairness*.

level the playing field A moribund metaphor (see page 21). *balance; equalize; even out; level; make equal; make level.* ■ The chief aim of the bill is to *level the playing field* so that challengers and incumbents will have an equal opportunity to get their message across. ■ We're not out to hurt anybody, we're just out to *level the playing field*. SEE ALSO *a level playing field*.

lick (his) chops A moribund metaphor (see page 21).

lick into shape A moribund metaphor (see page 21). *drill; instruct; perfect; train.*

lick (your) wounds A moribund metaphor (see page 21).

lie down on the job A moribund metaphor (see page 21). *be idle; be inactive; be lazy; be unemployed; be unoccu-* *pied; dally; dawdle; linger; loaf; loiter; loll; lounge; malinger; tarry.*

lie like a rug An insipid simile. *deceive; dissemble; distort; equivocate; falsify; fib; lie; misconstrue; mislead; misrepresent; pervert; prevaricate.*

> He had the press, he had the money, and he would lie like a rug in order to manipulate people into helping him. — Diane Jessup, *The Dog Who Spoke With Gods*

lie low A moribund metaphor (see page 21). 1. *be closed-mouthed; be quiet; be reticent; be silent; be speechless; be still; be taciturn; be uncommunicative; keep quiet.* 2. *disappear; hide; hole up.*

lie through (his) teeth A moribund metaphor (see page 21). *deceive; dissemble; distort; equivocate; falsify; fib; lie; misconstrue; mislead; misrepresent; pervert; prevaricate.*

life begins at forty A popular prescription (see page 23).

life goes on A popular prescription (see page 23).

life in a fishbowl A moribund metaphor (see page 21).

life in the fast lane A moribund metaphor (see page 21).

life is a cabaret A moribund metaphor (see page 21).

life is for the living A popular prescription (see page 23).

life isn't (always) fair A popular prescription (see page 23).

life is short A quack equation (see page 23).

(live a) life of luxury A moribund metaphor (see page 21). *affluent; moneyed; opulent; prosperous; rich; wealthy; well-off; well-to-do.*

(live) (the) life of Reilly A moribund metaphor (see page 21). 1. *be affluent; be moneyed; be opulent; be prosperous; be rich; be wealthy; be well-off; be well-to-do.* 2. *be extravagant; be lavish; be lush; be luxuriant; be sumptuous; be very well.* ■ It was *the life of Reilly*, but something was missing.

lift a finger A moribund metaphor (see page 21). *aid; assist; benefit; favor; help; oblige; succor.*

light a fire under A moribund metaphor (see page 21). *arouse; awaken; excite; galvanize; goad; impel; incite; induce; motivate; prompt; provoke; push; rouse; spur; stimulate; stir; urge.* ■ May the bishops' counsel encourage those husbands already living their words and *light a fire under* those dozing. REPLACE WITH *rouse.*

(as) light as a feather An insipid simile. *airy; buoyant; delicate; ethereal; feathery; gaseous; gauzy; gossamer; light; lightweight; slender; slight; sylphid; thin; vaporous; weightless.*

(as) light as air An insipid simile. *airy; buoyant; delicate; ethereal; feathery; gaseous; gauzy; gossamer; light; lightweight; slender; slight; sylphid; thin; vaporous; weightless.*

light at the end of the tunnel A moribund metaphor (see page 21). *anticipation; expectancy; expectation; hope; hopefulness; optimism; possibility; promise; prospect; sanguinity.* ■ When the opportunity arose that he could work for the government, we saw *light at the end of the tunnel.* REPLACE WITH *possibility.*

(a) light went off (in my head) A moribund metaphor (see page 21). *afflatus; brainwave; breakthrough; flash; idea; insight; inspiration; revelation.*

like An infantile phrase (see page 20). A cachet of all who are grievously adolescent, *like* mars the meaning of every sentence in which it is used. ■ Our family is *like* very open. DELETE *like.* ■ They lived together for *like* twelve years. DELETE *like.* ■ I should, *like*, get up and do something. DELETE *like.* ■ It's *like* just a habit. DELETE *like.* ■ *Like*, you can't really overuse words. DELETE *Like.* ■ My mom said, "Why not circulate a petition and see what happens," which is what I did, but, *like*, I still can't believe it worked. DELETE *like.*

(know) (her) like a book An insipid simile. *altogether; completely; entirely; fully; perfectly; quite; roundly; thoroughly; totally; unreservedly; utterly; wholly.*

(works) like a charm An insipid simile. *accurately; easily; exactly; excellently; faultlessly; flawlessly; flowingly; impeccably; indefectibly; methodically; perfectly; precisely; regularly; smoothly; systematically; well.*

like a deer caught in the headlights An insipid simile. *afraid; alarmed; anxious; apprehensive; fearful; frightened; panicky; scared; terrified; timid; timorous.*

■ Tom looked *like a deer caught in the headlights.* REPLACE WITH *terrified.*

> Mark was fiddling with a brightly colored train, but, every so often, he glanced up at the television with the fascination of a rabbit caught in the headlights. — Elizabeth Buchan, *Revenge of the Middle-Aged Woman*

(take to it) like a duck to water An insipid simile. *easily; effortlessly; fluently; naturally; smoothly; with ease.*

(fits) like a glove An insipid simile. *accurately; easily; exactly; excellently; faultlessly; flawlessly; flowingly; impeccably; indefectibly; methodically; perfectly; precisely; regularly; smoothly; systematically; well.* ■ By having a single, reliable technology solution that fits all of our companies *like a glove,* we are delivering the best technology at the best price to our associates. REPLACE WITH *faultlessly.*

like a hole in the head An insipid simile. *by no means; hardly; in no way; not at all; not in any way; not in the least; scarcely.*

> Kate needed water like a hole in the head. Whisky: that might just help. — Judith Cutler, *Power on Her Own*

(go over) like a lead balloon An insipid simile. *badly; poorly; unsatisfactorily; unsuccessfully.*

like clockwork An insipid simile. *accurately; easily; exactly; excellently; faultlessly; flawlessly; flowingly; impeccably; indefectibly; methodically; perfectly; precisely; regularly; smoothly; systematically; well.*

like comparing dollars to doughnuts A moribund metaphor (see page 21). *different; discordant; discrepant; dissimilar; dissonant; divergent; incommensurable; incommensurate; incomparable; incompatible; incongruent; incongruous; inconsistent; inconsonant; inharmonious; unlike.*

like crazy (mad) An insipid simile. 1. *actively; aggressively; dynamically; emphatically; energetically; ferociously; fervently; fiercely; forcefully; frantically; frenziedly; furiously; hard; intensely; intently; mightily; passionately; powerfully; robustly; savagely; spiritedly; strenuously; strongly; vehemently; viciously; vigorously; violently; wildly; with vigor;* 2. *ardently; devotedly; eagerly; enthusiastically; fervently; fervidly; passionately; spiritedly; zealously.* 3. *hastily; hurriedly; posthaste; promptly; quickly; rapidly; speedily; swiftly; very fast; wingedly.* ■ He is also eating *like crazy.* REPLACE WITH *zealously.*

like hell An insipid simile. 1. *actively; aggressively; dynamically; emphatically; energetically; ferociously; fervently; fiercely; forcefully; frantically; frenziedly; furiously; hard; intensely; intently; mightily; passionately; powerfully; robustly; savagely; spiritedly; strenuously; strongly; vehemently; viciously; vigorously; violently; wildly; with vigor.* 2. *ardently; devotedly; eagerly; enthusiastically; fervently; fervidly; passionately; spiritedly; zealously.* 3. *hastily; hurriedly; posthaste; promptly; quickly; rapidly; speedily; swiftly; very fast; wingedly.*

(selling) like hotcakes An insipid simile. *briskly; fast; quickly; rapidly; speedily; swiftly; very well; wingedly.* ■ Their current album is selling *like hotcakes.* REPLACE WITH *swiftly.*

like it's going out of style An insipid simile. 1. *actively; aggressively; dynamically; emphatically; energetically; ferociously; fervently; fiercely; forcefully; frantically; frenziedly; furiously; hard; intensely; intently; mightily; passionately; powerfully; robustly; savagely; spiritedly; strenuously; strongly; vehemently; viciously; vigorously; violently; wildly; with vigor.* 2. *hastily; hurriedly; posthaste; promptly; quickly; rapidly; speedily; swiftly; very fast; wingedly.* ■ I've been taking aspirin *like it's going out of style.* REPLACE WITH *aggressively.* SEE ALSO *like there's no tomorrow.*

like (a streak of; greased) lightning An insipid simile. *abruptly; apace; at once; briskly; directly; expeditiously; fast; forthwith; hastily; hurriedly; immediately; instantaneously; instantly; posthaste; promptly; quickly; rapidly; rashly; right away; speedily; straightaway; swiftly; wingedly.*

(works) like magic An insipid simile. *amazingly; astonishingly; astoundingly; extraordinarily; inexplicably; magically; miraculously; mysteriously; phenomenally; remarkably; wondrously.*

like nobody's business An insipid simile. 1. *beautifully; brilliantly; consummately; dazzlingly; excellently; exceptionally; expertly; exquisitely; extraordinarily; fabulously; flawlessly; grandly; magnificently; marvelously; perfectly; remarkably; splendidly; superbly; superlatively; supremely; transcendently; very well; wonderfully; wondrously.* 2. *actively; aggressively; dynamically; emphatically; energetically; ferociously; fervently; fiercely; forcefully; frantically; frenziedly; furiously; hard; intensely; intently; mightily; passionately; powerfully; robustly; savagely;*

spiritedly; strenuously; strongly; vehemently; viciously; vigorously; violently; wildly; with vigor. ■ Here was the one and only Kronos Quartet in town again, playing — as always — *like nobody's business.* REPLACE WITH *superbly.* ■ He can play the piano *like nobody's business.* REPLACE WITH *beautifully.*

like seeing (looking) … through rose-colored glasses A moribund metaphor (see page 21). *hopeful; optimistic; pollyanna; pollyannaish; positive; roseate; sanguine; upbeat.* ■ Life then becomes *like seeing the world through rose-colored glasses:* beautiful and warm. REPLACE WITH *pollyannish.*

(sounds) like something out of a novel An insipid simile.

> Bluey had started by thinking they were like something out of a novel herself, the sort of novel set in another, intriguing age and society. — Joanna Trollope, *The Men and the Girls*

like the back of (my) hand An insipid simile. *altogether; completely; entirely; fully; perfectly; quite; roundly; thoroughly; totally; unreservedly; utterly; wholly.*

like there's no tomorrow An insipid simile. 1. *actively; aggressively; dynamically; emphatically; energetically; ferociously; fervently; fiercely; forcefully; frantically; frenziedly; furiously; hard; intensely; intently; mightily; passionately; powerfully; robustly; savagely; spiritedly; strenuously; strongly; vehemently; viciously; vigorously; violently; wildly; with vigor.* 2. *hastily; hurriedly; posthaste; promptly; quickly; rapidly; speedily; swiftly; very fast; wingedly.* SEE ALSO *like it's going out of style.*

like the shifting sands An insipid simile. *brief; ephemeral; evanescent; fleeting; flitting; fugacious; fugitive; impermanent; momentary; passing; short; short-lived; temporary; transient; transitory; volatile.*

like watching paint dry An insipid simile. *anodyne; banal; barren; bland; boring; deadly; dreary; dry; dull; everyday; flat; humdrum; inanimate; insipid; jejune; lifeless; lusterless; mediocre; monotonous; prosaic; routine; spiritless; stale; tedious; tiresome; unexciting; uninteresting; vapid; wearisome.*

like watching the grass grow An insipid simile. 1. *anodyne; banal; barren; bland; boring; deadly; dreary; dry; dull; everyday; flat; humdrum; inanimate; insipid; jejune; lifeless; lusterless; mediocre; monotonous; prosaic; routine; spiritless; stale; tedious; tiresome; unexciting; uninteresting; vapid; wearisome.* 2. *crawling; dallying; dawdling; deliberate; dilatory; faltering; hesitant; laggardly; lagging; leisurely; methodical; plodding; procrastinating; slothful; slow; slow-paced; sluggardly; sluggish; snaillike; systematic; tardy; tortoiselike; unhurried.*

like water An insipid simile. *abundantly; copiously; freely; generously; liberally; profusely; unreservedly.*

It might seem strange that a successful Hollywood lady would go for a nomadic gent who ran through passports like water, could spout off funny if lewd phrases in thirty languages, and never would be financially secure. — David Baldacci, *The Christmas Train*

like water (rolling) off a duck's back An insipid simile. *to no avail; with no result; without effect.*

like wildfire An insipid simile. 1. *briskly; fast; hastily; hurriedly; quickly; promptly; rapidly; speedily; swiftly.* 2. *actively; aggressively; dynamically; emphatically; energetically; ferociously; fervently; fiercely; forcefully; frantically; frenziedly; furiously; hard; intensely; intently; mightily; passionately; powerfully; robustly; savagely; spiritedly; strenuously; strongly; vehemently; viciously; vigorously; violently; wildly; with vigor.*

(draw [a] the) line in the sand A moribund metaphor (see page 21). *border; bound; boundary; frontier; limit; perimeter.*

For the time being he could see the line in the sand: on one side of it, all he had; on the other, all he'd lose. — Martin Amis, *Yellow Dog*

line of fire A moribund metaphor (see page 21).

lines are drawn A moribund metaphor (see page 21).

lining (his) pockets A moribund metaphor (see page 21).

link together A wretched redundancy (see page 25). *link.* ■ This business will *link together* the telephone, the television, and the computer. DELETE *together*.

(the) lion's share A moribund metaphor (see page 21). *almost all; most; much; nearly all.* ■ The company was late to develop HMOs, and it let competitors grab *the lion's share* of the market. REPLACE WITH *most*.

(my) lips are sealed A moribund metaphor (see page 21).

liquid refreshment An infantile phrase (see page 20). *beverage; drink; refreshment.*

litany of complaints A moribund metaphor (see page 21).

literary event A suspect superlative (see page 24).

(a) little bird told me An infantile phrase (see page 20).

(the) little boy's (girl's) room An infantile phrase (see page 20). *bathroom; lavatory; restroom; toilet.*

(like) (the) little engine (that could) An insipid simile.

(a) little (honesty) goes a long way A popular prescription (see page 23).

(a) little knowledge is a dangerous thing A popular prescription (see page 23).

little old lady from Dubuque A moribund metaphor (see page 21). *boor; bumpkin; commoner; common man; common person; conventional person; peasant; philistine; pleb; plebeian; vulgarian; yokel.* ■ By the time the contest was over, *little old ladies in Dubuque* could probably discourse on the subject.

(the) little woman An infantile phrase (see page 20). *consort; helpmate; helpmeet; mate; spouse; wife.*

lit to the gills A moribund metaphor (see page 21). *besotted; crapulous; drunk; inebriated; intoxicated; sodden; stupefied; tipsy.*

lit up like a Christmas tree An insipid simile.

live and learn A popular prescription (see page 23).

live and let live A popular prescription (see page 23).

live as though each day were your last A popular prescription (see page 23).

live dangerously A popular prescription (see page 23).

live each day to the fullest A popular prescription (see page 23).

live for the moment A popular prescription (see page 23).

live happily ever after A suspect superlative (see page 24).

live high off (on) the hog A moribund metaphor (see page 21).

live in a pigsty A moribund metaphor (see page 21).

live one day at a time A popular prescription (see page 23).

live wire A moribund metaphor (see page 21). *card; character; eccentric; exception; original.*

(learn to) live with it A popular prescription (see page 23).

(a) living hell A moribund metaphor (see page 21). *chthonian; chthonic; hellish; impossible; infernal; insufferable; insupportable; intolerable; painful; plutonic; sulfurous; unbearable; uncomfortable; unendurable; unpleasant; stygian; tartarean.*

The force and colorfulness of this metaphor is no longer evident. An uncommonly used word — such as *chthonic, insupportable, plutonic, sulfurous, stygian,* or *tartarean* — is often more potent and captivating than a commonly used metaphor. SEE ALSO *hell on earth.*

(a) living legend A suspect superlative (see page 24).

loaded for bear A moribund metaphor (see page 21). 1. *eager; prepared; primed; ready; set.* 2. *angry; bad-tempered; bilious; cantankerous; choleric; churlish; crabby; cranky; cross; curmudgeonly; disagreeable; dyspeptic; grouchy; gruff; grumpy; ill-humored; ill-tempered; irascible; irritable; mad; peevish; petulant; quarrelsome; riled; roiled; short-tempered; splenetic; surly; testy; vexed.*

lo and behold A withered word (see page 24).

location, location, location An infantile phrase (see page 20).

lock horns with A moribund metaphor (see page 21). *battle; brawl; clash; fight; grapple; jostle; make war; scuffle; skirmish; tussle; war; wrestle.*

lock, stock, and barrel A moribund metaphor (see page 21). *aggregate; all; all things; entirety; everything; gross; lot; sum; total; totality; whole.*

long and hard A torpid term (see page 24). *aggressively; dynamically; emphatically; energetically; ferociously; fervently; fiercely; forcefully; frantically; frenziedly; furiously; hard; intensely; intently; mightily; passionately; powerfully; robustly; savagely; spiritedly; strenuously; strongly; vehemently; viciously; vigorously; violently; wildly; with vigor.* ■ The compromise would be a partial victory for Baybanks, which has fought *long and hard* against the legislation. REPLACE WITH *mightily.*

(the) long and (the) short of (it) A wretched redundancy (see page 25). *basis; center; core; crux; essence; gist; heart; kernel; pith; substance.*

long in the tooth A moribund metaphor (see page 21). *aged; aging; ancient; antediluvian; antique; archaic; elderly; hoary; hoary-headed; old; patriarchal; prehistoric; seasoned; superannuated.*

> Notice these are all attractive, smart, funny women who happen to be a little long in the tooth. — Patricia Gaffney, *The Saving Graces*

long overdue An inescapable pair (see page 20). ■ This legislation is *long overdue.*

long road ahead A moribund metaphor (see page 21).

(a) long shot A moribund metaphor (see page 21). *doubtful; dubious; far-fetched; implausible; improbable; remote; unlikely; unrealistic.* ■ Something that might happen is *a longer shot* than something that may happen. REPLACE WITH *less likely.*

long time no see An infantile phrase (see page 20).

look a fright A moribund metaphor (see page 21). *disheveled; dowdy; frowzy; messy; ragged; run-down; scruffy; seedy; shabby; sloppy; slovenly; tattered; tousled; unkempt; untidy.*

(don't) look a gift horse in the mouth A popular prescription (see page 23).

look before you leap A popular prescription (see page 23). *be careful; be cautious; be circumspect; be prudent; be safe; be wary.*

look down (her) nose (at) A moribund metaphor (see page 21). *contemn; deride; despise; detest; disdain; jeer at; laugh at; mock; ridicule; scoff at; scorn; shun; slight; sneer; snub; spurn.*

look into a crystal ball A moribund metaphor (see page 21). *forecast; foreshadow; foretell; portend; predict; prefigure; presage; prognosticate; prophesy.*

look like a drowned rat An insipid simile. *bedraggled; drenched; dripping; saturated; soaked; sopping; wet.*

look over (our) shoulders A moribund metaphor (see page 21). *be anxious; be apprehensive; be fearful; be frightened; be insecure; be nervous; be panicky; be scared; be timid; be timorous; be uneasy.*

looks aren't everything A popular prescription (see page 23).

(take a) look see A infantile phrase. This phrase is one of the new illiteracies. Expressions like *a good read, a must have,* and *a look see* are favored today by

the "illiterati" — smart, articulate people who find it fashionable to speak unintelligibly. SEE ALSO *a good read; (a) must have; (a) must see; a (must) read.*

(she) looks like a million bucks (dollars) An insipid simile. 1. *appealing; attractive; beautiful; becoming; captivating; comely; cute; dazzling; exquisite; fair; fetching; good-looking; gorgeous; handsome; lovely; nice-looking; pleasing; pretty; pulchritudinous; radiant; ravishing; seemly; stunning.* 2. *energetic; fine; fit; good; hale; hardy; healthful; healthy; hearty; robust; sound; strong; vigorous; well.* 3. *affluent; moneyed; opulent; prosperous; rich; successful; wealthy; well-off; well-to-do.*

look the other way A moribund metaphor (see page 21). *brush aside; avoid; discount; disregard; dodge; duck; ignore; neglect; omit; pass over; recoil from; shrink from; shun; shy away from; turn away from; withdraw from.*

look what the tide brought in A moribund metaphor (see page 21).

look who's talking An infantile phrase (see page 20).

look what (who) the cat dragged in A moribund metaphor (see page 21).

loose cannon A moribund metaphor (see page 21). *capricious; changeable; erratic; fickle; fluctuating; inconsistent; inconstant; mercurial; unpredictable; unstable; unsteady; variable; volatile; wavering.*

lose (her) head (over) A moribund metaphor (see page 21). 1. *alarm; appall; benumb; daunt; frighten; horrify;*

intimidate; panic; paralyze; petrify; scare; shock; startle; terrify; terrorize. 2. *infatuated.*

lose (his) marbles (mind) A moribund metaphor (see page 21). *batty; cracked; crazy; daft; demented; deranged; fey; foolish; goofy; insane; lunatic; mad; maniacal; neurotic; nuts; nutty; psychotic; raving; silly; squirrelly; touched; unbalanced; unhinged; unsound; wacky; zany.*

> I'd had older men look at me that way since I'd lost my baby fat, but they usually didn't lose their marbles over me when I was wearing my royal blue parka and yellow elephant bell-bottoms — Alice Sebold, *The Lovely Bones*

lose steam A moribund metaphor (see page 21).

(a) losing battle A moribund metaphor (see page 21). *hopeless; impossible; incurable; irreclaimable; irredeemable; irremediable; irreparable; irretrievable; remediless.*

> And now the dog was dead, and Morris was saying that, as the dog should have known, his was a losing battle, and that that not given in love would be redressed in blood. — David Mamet, *The Old Religion*

lost in the shuffle A moribund metaphor (see page 21). *be discounted; be disregarded; be forgotten; be ignored; be neglected; be omitted; be passed over; be shunned.* ■ There is so much to teach that is writing related, that sometimes the writing itself can *get lost in the shuffle*. REPLACE WITH *be neglected*.

(a) lot of times A wretched redundancy (see page 25). *frequently; often.* ■ *A lot of times* people have a tendency to think that others are controlling their destiny. REPLACE WITH *Often*.

loud and clear An inescapable pair (see page 20). *apparent; audible; clear; conspicuous; definite; distinct; emphatic; evident; explicit; graphic; lucid; manifest; obvious; patent; pellucid; plain; sharp; translucent; transparent; unambiguous; uncomplex; uncomplicated; understandable; unequivocal; unmistakable; vivid.*

love and cherish An inescapable pair (see page 20).

love conquers all A popular prescription (see page 23).

love is blind A quack equation (see page 23).

love it or leave it An infantile phrase (see page 20).

love moves mountains A moribund metaphor (see page 21).

low blow A moribund metaphor (see page 21). *dishonorable; foul; inequitable; unconscientious; underhanded; unethical; unfair; unjust; unprincipled; unscrupulous; unsportsmanlike.*

lower the boom A moribund metaphor (see page 21). 1. *admonish; animadvert; berate; castigate; censure; chasten; chastise; chide; condemn; criticize; denounce; denunciate; discipline; excoriate; fulminate against; imprecate; impugn; inveigh against; objurgate; punish; rebuke; remonstrate; reprehend; reprimand; reproach; reprobate; reprove; revile; scold; swear at;*

upbraid; vituperate. 2. *abort; annul; arrest; cancel; cease; check; conclude; derail; discontinue; end; halt; nullify; quash; quell; revoke; squelch; stop; suspend; terminate.*

lowest common denominator A torpid term (see page 24). For some — copycat journalists, delicate marketing people, and feeble-minded social scientists perhaps — *lowest common denominator* is a long-winded, short-sighted way of avoiding more telling words.
■ Instead of disseminating the best in our culture, television too often panders to the *lowest common denominator.* REPLACE WITH *worst.* ■ If you fear making anyone mad, then you ultimately probe for the *lowest common denominator* of human achievement. REPLACE WITH *nadir.* ■ In that environment, each show tried to appeal to the *lowest common denominator.* REPLACE WITH *masses.* ■ The J.D. InterPrizes' *lowest common denominator* design concept allows for the widest possible viewing audience. REPLACE WITH *readily accessible.* ■ So movies must imitate the familiar and be pitched to the *lowest common denominator,* causing most of them to be flat, stale and familiar. REPLACE WITH *dull-minded.*

low (man) on the totem pole A moribund metaphor (see page 21). *inferior; junior; lesser; low ranking; minor; second rate; secondary; subordinate.* ■ If you're a freshman member, regardless of what party you're in, you're *low on the totem pole* to be sure. REPLACE WITH *low ranking.*

(a) lump in (her) throat A moribund metaphor (see page 21).

M

(as) mad as a hatter An insipid simile. *batty; cracked; crazy; daft; demented; deranged; fey; foolish; goofy; insane; lunatic; mad; maniacal; neurotic; nuts; nutty; psychotic; raving; silly; squirrelly; touched; unbalanced; unhinged; unsound; wacky; zany.*

(as) mad as a hornet An insipid simile. *angry; berserk; convulsive; crazed; delirious; demented; demoniac; deranged; enraged; feral; ferocious; fierce; frantic; frenzied; fuming; furious; hysterical; infuriated; in hysterics; insane; incensed; irate; mad; maddened; maniacal; murderous; possessed; rabid; raging; ranting; raving; savage; seething; wild; wrathful.*

(as) mad as a March hare An insipid simile. *batty; cracked; crazy; daft; demented; deranged; fey; foolish; goofy; insane; lunatic; mad; maniacal; neurotic; nuts; nutty; psychotic; raving; silly; squirrelly; touched; unbalanced; unhinged; unsound; wacky; zany.*

(as) mad as a wet hen An insipid simile. *angry; berserk; convulsive; crazed; delirious; demented; demoniac; deranged; enraged; feral; ferocious; fierce; frantic; frenzied; fuming; furious; hysterical; infuriated; in hysterics; insane; incensed; irate; mad; maddened; maniacal; murderous; possessed; rabid; raging; ranting; raving; savage; seething; wild; wrathful.*

(he) made (me) an offer (I) couldn't refuse An infantile phrase (see page 20). ■ We'd still be here today if Bally's hadn't *made us an offer we couldn't refuse.*

(you) made my day A plebeian sentiment (see page 23). Often a response to being complimented, *you made my day* appeals to the mass of people who rely on others for their opinion of themselves.

And if they embrace others' approval, so they bow to their criticism.

made of money A moribund metaphor (see page 21). *affluent; moneyed; opulent; prosperous; rich; successful; wealthy; well-off; well-to-do.*

magic bullet A moribund metaphor (see page 21). *answer; solution.*

(the) main event A moribund metaphor (see page 21).

major An overworked word (see page 22). For example: *major blow; major breakthrough; major commitment; major concern; major consideration; major defeat; major disaster; major new writer; major opportunity; major player; major ramifications; major road block; major setback; major thrust.*

(a) (the) … majority (of) A torpid term (see page 24). This phrase and others like it — *a large majority; an overwhelming majority; the vast majority* — are indispensable to those who luxuriate in circumlocutory language. They seldom mean more than an unpretentious *almost all, most,* or *nearly all.* ■ *The vast majority* of those people don't receive death sentences. REPLACE WITH *Most.* ■ Within two years, *the overwhelming majority of* Americans will have health coverage. REPLACE WITH *nearly all.* ■ *A large majority of* the participatory lenders have now joined the major banks in supporting our plan. REPLACE WITH *Almost all.* SEE ALSO *a … number (of).*

make a clean breast of A moribund metaphor (see page 21). *acknowledge; admit; affirm; allow; avow; concede; confess; disclose; divulge; expose; grant; own; reveal; tell; uncover; unveil.*

make a concerted effort A wretched redundancy (see page 25). *aim; attempt; endeavor; essay; labor; moil; seek; strive; toil; try; undertake; venture; work.* ■ True change will come only when those in power *make a concerted effort* to promote large numbers of women and blacks to high-status jobs. REPLACE WITH *try.*

make a conscious attempt (effort) A wretched redundancy (see page 25). *aim; attempt; endeavor; essay; labor; moil;*

seek; strive; toil; try; undertake; venture; work. ■ We *made a conscious effort* not to do what most companies do. REPLACE WITH *strived*. ■ Wash your hands and *make conscious attempts* not to touch your face, nose, and eyes. REPLACE WITH *try*.

make a conscious choice (decision) A wretched redundancy (see page 25). *Make a conscious choice* means no more than *choose*, and *make a conscious decision* no more than *decide*. Of course, this phrase suggests that those who use it may not otherwise be conscious of what they choose or decide, or even, it could be, do or say. ■ We *made a conscious decision* that this sort of legal terrorism would not affect the way we operate. REPLACE WITH *decided*. ■ They *made a conscious choice* not to have any bedroom scenes in this movie. REPLACE WITH *chose*. SEE ALSO *make an informed choice (decision)*.

make a decision A wretched redundancy (see page 25). *conclude; decide; determine; resolve.* ■ It's difficult to *make a decision* at this time. REPLACE WITH *decide*. ■ If he *made a decision* not to use protection, he should *make a decision* to support the child. REPLACE WITH *resolved* and *resolve*.

make a determination A wretched redundancy (see page 25). *conclude; decide; determine; resolve.* ■ We want the SJC to look at it and *make a determination* to clearly state what is permissible and impermissible. REPLACE WITH *determine*.

make a difference (about; on) A suspect superlative (see page 24). Many of us speak of making a difference, some of us strive to make a difference, and few of us succeed in making a difference. 1. *be climacteric; be consequential; be considerable; be critical; be crucial; be effective; be effectual; be helpful; be important; be significant; be useful; be vital; count; matter.* 2. *act on; affect; bear on; influence; sway; work on.* 3. *aid; assist; help.* ■ She is part of a great tradition in U.S. society, in which ordinary individuals voice their concerns in order to *make a difference about* issues that matter to them. REPLACE WITH *influence*. ■ You need to have a sense of humor and to recognize that there's hope, not only despair, in the world — and you need to know that you can *make a difference*. REPLACE WITH *be helpful*. ■ Your answers are important, and they do *make a difference*. REPLACE WITH *matter*.

make a federal case out of A moribund metaphor (see page 21). *elaborate; embellish; embroider; enhance; enlarge; exaggerate; hyperbolize; inflate; magnify; overdo; overreact; overstress; overstate; strain; stretch.*

make a getaway A moribund metaphor (see page 21). *abscond; clear out; decamp; depart; desert; disappear; escape; exit; flee; fly; go; go away; leave; move on; part; pull out; quit; retire; retreat; run away; take flight; take off; vacate; vanish; withdraw.*

make a monkey out of A moribund metaphor (see page 21). *abase; chasten; debase; degrade; demean; deride; disgrace; dishonor; dupe; embarrass; humble; humiliate; mock; mortify; ridicule; shame.*

> You make a money out of one of them and he jumps on your back and stays there for life, but let one make a money out of you and all

227

you can do is kill him or disappear. — Flannery O'Connor, *Everything That Rises Must Converge*

make a mountain out of a molehill A moribund metaphor (see page 21). *elaborate; embellish; embroider; enhance; enlarge; exaggerate; hyperbolize; inflate; magnify; overdo; overreact; overstress; overstate; strain; stretch.*

make an informed choice (decision) A wretched redundancy (see page 25). *choose; decide.* SEE ALSO *make a conscious choice (decision).*

make a pig of (myself) A moribund metaphor (see page 21). *cloy; cram; glut; gorge; overdo; overeat; overfeed; overindulge; sate; satiate; stuff; surfeit.*

make a quick exit A moribund metaphor (see page 21). *abscond; clear out; decamp; depart; desert; disappear; escape; exit; flee; fly; go; go away; leave; move on; part; pull out; quit; retire; retreat; run away; take flight; take off; vacate; vanish; withdraw.*

make a silk purse out of a sow's ear A moribund metaphor (see page 21).

make (my) blood boil A moribund metaphor (see page 21). *acerbate; anger; annoy; bother; bristle; chafe; enrage; incense; inflame; infuriate; irk; irritate; madden; miff; provoke; rile; roil; vex.*

make (both) ends meet A moribund metaphor (see page 21). *economize; endure; exist; live; manage; subsist; survive.* ■ Older people are having a tough enough time trying to *make ends meet.* REPLACE WITH *survive.*

make eyes at A moribund metaphor (see page 21). *flirt.*

make false statements A wretched redundancy (see page 25). *lie.* ■ The indictment alleges that he *made false statements* to the FEC and obstructed proceedings. REPLACE WITH *lied.*

make (my) flesh creep (crawl) A moribund metaphor (see page 21). *alarm; appall; disgust; frighten; horrify; nauseate; panic; repel; repulse; revolt; scare; shock; sicken; startle; terrify.*

make (my) hair stand on end A moribund metaphor (see page 21). *alarm; appall; disgust; frighten; horrify; nauseate; panic; repel; repulse; revolt; scare; shock; sicken; startle; terrify.*

make hay while the sun shines A moribund metaphor (see page 21). *capitalize on; exploit; take advantage.*

make heads or tails of A moribund metaphor (see page 21). *appreciate; apprehend; comprehend; discern; fathom; grasp; know; make sense of; perceive; realize; recognize; see; understand.* ■ His failures in punctuation make it almost impossible to *make heads or tails of* his convoluted sentences. REPLACE WITH *understand.*

make it big A moribund metaphor (see page 21). *prevail; succeed; triumph; win.*

make mincemeat (out) of A moribund metaphor (see page 21). *crush; defeat; demolish; destroy; devastate; hammer; obliterate; overpower; overwhelm; rack; ravage; rout; ruin; shatter; slaughter; smash; thrash; undo; wrack; wreck.*

make no bones (about it) A moribund metaphor (see page 21). *avidly; eagerly; enthusiastically; heartily; promptly; readily; unconditionally; unhesitatingly; unreservedly; unwaveringly; wholeheartedly.*

> She made no bones about accepting her client's invitation to dine, and showed no surprise when he confidentially murmured that he had a little proposition to put before her. — Dorothy L. Sayers, *Strong Poison*

make no mistake (about it) An ineffectual phrase (see page 19). ■ *Make no mistake about it*, if we were to leave, other nations would leave, too, and chaos would resume. ■ *Make no mistake*, Jacksonville is not a bad team. ■ *Make no mistake about it*, this impeachment issue has become a battle for who controls the Republican party. SEE ALSO *let there be no mistake.*

make (yourself) scarce An infantile phrase (see page 20). *abscond; clear out; decamp; depart; desert; disappear; escape; exit; flee; fly; go; go away; leave; move on; part; pull out; quit; retire; retreat; run away; take flight; take off; vacate; vanish; withdraw.*

make (me) see red A moribund metaphor (see page 21). *acerbate; anger; annoy; bother; bristle; chafe; enrage; incense; inflame; infuriate; irk; irritate; madden; miff; provoke; rile; roil; vex.*

(try to) make the best (most) of it A popular prescription (see page 23).

make the feathers (fur) fly A moribund metaphor (see page 21). *battle; brawl; clash; fight; grapple; jostle; make war; scuffle; skirmish; tussle; war; wrestle; wrangle.*

> When the flying fur from the divorce settled, I found myself with a grown daughter, a full-time university job (after years of part-time teaching), a modest securities portfolio, and an entire future to invent. — Frances Mayes, *Under the Tuscan Sun*

make the grade A moribund metaphor (see page 21). 1. *accomplish; achieve; make good; succeed.* 2. *be able; be accomplished; be adept; be adequate; be capable; be competent; be deft; be equal to; be equipped; be fitted; be proficient; be qualified; be skilled; be skillful; be suited; measure up.*

make up (his) mind A wretched redundancy (see page 25). *choose; conclude; decide; determine; pick; resolve; select; settle.*

make tracks A moribund metaphor (see page 21). *abscond; clear out; decamp; depart; desert; disappear; escape; exit; flee; fly; go; go away; leave; move on; part; pull out; quit; retire; retreat; run away; take flight; take off; vacate; vanish; withdraw.*

make waves A moribund metaphor (see page 21). *agitate; disrupt; disturb; perturb; rattle; ruffle; shake up; stir up; unsettle.*

(a) man's home is his castle A popular prescription (see page 23).

(the) man in the street A moribund metaphor (see page 21). *citizen; commoner; everyman; pleb; plebeian; vulgarian.*

(the) manner (means; mechanism; method; procedure; process) by (in) which A wretched redundancy (see page 25). These magisterial-sounding phrases should be replaced by one of the least stately of words: *how.* ■ I'm not going to discuss *the methods by which* we achieved that. REPLACE WITH *how.* ■ The philosophical methodology specifies *the procedure by which* concepts will be used to construct a theory. REPLACE WITH *how.* ■ It does less well in explaining *the process by which* a particular firm decides to implement a price change. REPLACE WITH *how.* ■ Virtually all of them have been critical of *the manner in which* the administration dealt with the situation. REPLACE WITH *how.*

(the) man who came to dinner An infantile phrase (see page 20).

many of my closest friends (are) A plebeian sentiment (see page 23). ■ *Many of my closest friends* are Italian.

marching orders A moribund metaphor (see page 21).

(a) marriage made in heaven A suspect superlative (see page 24). *ideal; model; perfect; wonderful.*

mass exodus A wretched redundancy (see page 25). *exodus.*

(it's a) matter of life and death A moribund metaphor (see page 21). *critical; crucial; essential; imperative; important; necessary; pressing; urgent; vital.*

maybe, maybe not An infantile phrase (see page 20).

maybe yes, maybe no An infantile phrase (see page 20).

may (might) possibly A wretched redundancy (see page 25). *may (might).* ■ I *might possibly* be there when you are. DELETE *possibly.*

mea culpa A foreign phrase (see page 19).

meal ticket A moribund metaphor (see page 21).

meaningful An overworked word (see page 22). So elusive is meaning in our lives that we think we must modify scores of words with the word *meaningful.* Though we may struggle not to believe that emptiness is all, attaching *meaningful* to words like *action, change, dialogue, discussion, experience* is no sound solution. *Meaningful* describes that which has meaning, and derides that which has none. SEE ALSO *significant.*

(...) means never having to say you're sorry An infantile phrase (see page 20).

meat and potatoes A moribund metaphor (see page 21). *basal; basic; elementary; essential; fundamental; primary; rudimentary.*

(the) medium is the message A quack equation (see page 23).

(as) meek as a lamb An insipid simile. *accepting; accommodating; acquiescent; complacent; complaisant; compliant; cowed; deferential; docile; dutiful; easy; forbearing; gentle; humble; long-suffering; meek; mild; obedient; passive; patient; prostrate; quiet; reserved; resigned; stoical;*

submissive; subservient; timid; tolerant; tractable; unassuming; uncomplaining; yielding.

(as) meek as Moses An insipid simile. accepting; accommodating; acquiescent; complacent; complaisant; compliant; cowed; deferential; docile; dutiful; easy; forbearing; gentle; humble; long-suffering; meek; mild; obedient; passive; patient; prostrate; quiet; reserved; resigned; stoical; submissive; subservient; timid; tolerant; tractable; unassuming; uncomplaining; yielding.

> Having embarrassed himself, he went in, meek as Moses, to the Judge. — Carson McCullers, *Clock Without Hands*

(the) meek shall inherit the earth A popular prescription (see page 23).

meeting of (the) minds A moribund metaphor (see page 21). accord; accordance; agreement; common view; compatibility; concord; concordance; concurrence; consensus; harmony; unanimity; understanding; unison; unity. ■ We're talking to him to see if we can have a *meeting of minds*. REPLACE WITH *agreement*.

meet (his) Waterloo A moribund metaphor (see page 21).

meet your maker A moribund metaphor (see page 21). *die.*

me, myself, and I An infantile phrase (see page 20).

mend fences A moribund metaphor (see page 21). *reconcile.* ■ Please continue to tell your readers it's never too late to try to *mend those fences*. REPLACE WITH *reconcile*.

(the) men in white coats A moribund metaphor (see page 21).

meteoric rise An inescapable pair (see page 20). ■ His approach has struck a chord with the American people — hence his unprecedented and *meteoric rise* to prominence.

methodology A torpid term (see page 24). A favorite among dimwitted academicians, this polysyllabic word means no more than *method*. ■ How did research *methodologies* change over time in the articles of the *American Journal of Psychology* between 1887 and 1930? REPLACE WITH *methods*.

Mickey-Mouse An infantile phrase (see page 20). *inferior; poor; second-class; second-rate; shoddy; subordinate; substandard.*

(the) Midas touch A moribund metaphor (see page 21).

middle-of-the-road A moribund metaphor (see page 21). 1. *average; common; conservative; conventional; everyday; mediocre; middling; normal; ordinary; quotidian; second-rate; standard; traditional; typical; uneventful; unexceptional; unremarkable; usual.* 2. *careful; cautious; circumspect; prudent; safe; wary.*

might makes right A popular prescription (see page 23).

(a) mile a minute A moribund metaphor (see page 21). *apace; briskly; expeditiously; fast; hastily; hurriedly; posthaste; quickly; rapidly; speedily; swiftly; wingedly.*

(a) mile wide and an inch deep A moribund metaphor (see page 21). 1. *blowhard; boaster; braggadocio; braggart; know-it-all; showoff; swaggerer; trumpeter; windbag.* 2. *glib; silver-tongued; slick; smooth-tongued.*

(the) milk of human kindness A moribund metaphor (see page 21). *commiseration; compassion; sympathy; understanding.*

milk the last drop out of A moribund metaphor (see page 21).

(a) million miles away A moribund metaphor (see page 21). *absent; absentminded; absorbed; abstracted; bemused; captivated; daydreaming; detached; distracted; distrait; dreamy; engrossed; enraptured; faraway; fascinated; immersed; inattentive; lost; mesmerized; oblivious; preoccupied; rapt; spellbound.*

millstone around (my) neck A moribund metaphor (see page 21). *burden; duty; encumbrance; hardship; hindrance; impediment; obligation; obstacle; obstruction; onus; responsibility.*

(has a) mind like a sieve An insipid simile. *forgetful; heedless; inattentive; lethean; neglectful; negligent; oblivious; remiss; thoughtless; unmindful; unthinking.*

mind like a steel trap An insipid simile. *adroit; astute; bright; brilliant; clever; discerning; enlightened; insightful; intelligent; judicious; keen; knowledgeable; learned; logical; luminous; perceptive; perspicacious; quick; rational; reasonable; sagacious; sage; sapient; sensible; sharp; shrewd; smart; sound; understanding; wise.*

mind (your) P's and Q's A moribund metaphor (see page 21). *be accurate; be careful; be exact; be meticulous; be particular; be precise.*

mindset An overworked word (see page 22). *attitude; bent; bias; cast; disposition; habit; inclination; leaning; outlook; penchant; perspective; point of view; position; predilection; predisposition; prejudice; proclivity; slant; stand; standpoint; temperament; tendency; view; viewpoint; way of thinking.* ■ You don't have these huge organizations built on patronage anymore, but the *mindset* is still there. REPLACE WITH *predisposition.* ■ What we are doing is changing people's *mindset*. REPLACE WITH *views.* ■ The report is critical of the *mindset* of those in charge of the pipeline. REPLACE WITH *attitude.*

mind the store A moribund metaphor (see page 21).

mirabile dictu A foreign phrase (see page 19).

miracle of miracles An infantile phrase (see page 20). *astonishingly; astoundingly; breathtakingly; extraordinarily; fabulously; fantastically; marvelously; miraculously; overwhelmingly; prodigiously; sensationally; spectacularly; wonderfully; wondrously.*
   ■ *Miracle of miracles*, it works because of two things: Keanu Reeves and theology. REPLACE WITH *Miraculously.* ■ *Miracle of miracles*, in our second at-bat, with the brace strapped on tight, we homered against the Mets. REPLACE WITH *Amazingly.* ■ I was cleaning the house the other day, and, *miracle of miracles*, my kids were actually helping. REPLACE WITH *astonishingly.*

And maybe if she closed her eyes she could see a time — miracle of miracles — when Helen Bober was enrolled here, not just a stranger on the run, pecking at a course or two at night, and tomorrow morning back at Levenspiel's Louisville Panties and Bras. — Bernard Malamud, *The Assistant*

misery loves company A popular prescription (see page 23).

mission accomplished An infantile phrase (see page 20).

a miss is as good as a mile A popular prescription (see page 23).

miss the boat A moribund metaphor (see page 21). *be deprived of; forego; forfeit; give up; lose out; miss out; sacrifice; surrender.* ■ If we define success in terms of material things, we *miss the boat.* REPLACE WITH *lose out.*

mix and mingle An inescapable pair (see page 20). *associate; consort; hobnob; fraternize; keep company; mingle; mix; socialize.*

mixed bag A moribund metaphor (see page 21).

Usually he was entertained by Tokyo Station, the mixed bag of commuters in three-piece suits and farmers in cone-shaped hats of straw. — Martin Cruz Smith, *December 6*

moan and groan An inescapable pair (see page 20). *bawl; bemoan; bewail; blubber; cry; groan; moan; snivel; sob; wail; weep; whimper; whine.*

modus operandi A foreign phrase (see page 19).

modus vivendi A foreign phrase (see page 19).

Monday morning quarterback(ing) A moribund metaphor (see page 21).

money can't buy everything A popular prescription (see page 23).

(like) money in the bank An insipid simile. *absolute; assured; certain; definite; guaranteed; sure; sure-fire.*

money is the root of all evil A popular prescription (see page 23).

money (making) machine A moribund metaphor (see page 21).

money talks A moribund metaphor (see page 21).

money to burn A moribund metaphor (see page 21).

monkey on (my) back A moribund metaphor (see page 21). 1. *addiction; fixation; habit; obsession.* 2. *complication; difficulty; dilemma; mess; muddle; ordeal; pickle; plight; predicament; problem; quandary; trial; trouble.*

monkey see, monkey do An infantile phrase (see page 20).

(a) month of Sundays A moribund metaphor (see page 21). *ages; a long time; a long while; an age; an eternity; decades; eons; forever; months; years.*

mop (wipe) the floor with A moribund metaphor (see page 21). 1. *assail;*

assault; attack; batter; beat; cudgel; flagel-late; flog; hit; lambaste; lash; lick; mangle; pound; pummel; strike; thrash; trample; trounce. 2. *beat; conquer; crush; defeat; outdo; overcome; overpower; overwhelm; prevail; quell; rout; subdue; succeed; triumph; trounce; vanquish; win.* ■ Amazon.com has *mopped the floor with* barnesandnoble.com. REPLACE WITH *routed.*

more is better A quack equation (see page 23).

more preferable A wretched redundancy (see page 25). *preferable.* ■ While the patient is still at risk to hemorrhage during that time, waiting may be *more preferable* to surgery. DELETE *more.*

more than (I) bargained for A torpid term (see page 24).

more ... than you could shake a stick at A moribund metaphor (see page 21). *countless; dozens of; hundreds of; incalculable; inestimable; innumerable; many; numerous; scores of; thousands of; untold.* ■ He had *more* women in his life *than you could shake a stick at.* REPLACE WITH *untold.*

(the) more the merrier A quack equation (see page 23).

(the) more things change, the more they stay the same A popular prescription (see page 23).

more times than I care to admit A torpid term (see page 24).

> I've been married twice, done in more times than I care to admit.
> — Sue Grafton, *E Is for Evidence*

most assuredly An infantile phrase (see page 20). *assuredly; certainly; decidedly; definitely; positively; surely; undoubtedly; unequivocally; unhesitatingly; unquestionably.* ■ The customer will *most assuredly* notify the maitre d' if he or she is expecting someone else. REPLACE WITH *certainly.* SEE ALSO *absolutely; definitely; most (very) definitely.*

most (very) definitely An infantile phrase (see page 20). It is irredeemably dimwitted to say *most definitely* when the more moderate, indeed, the more civilized *certainly, I (am), indeed; just so, quite right, surely, that's right,* or *yes* will do. ■ And you feel your daughter was unjustly treated? *Most definitely.* REPLACE WITH *I do.* ■ So whoever you meet has to accommodate your needs? *Very definitely.* REPLACE WITH *Yes.* ■ So when you're sitting around, you are the only white person there? *Most definitely.* REPLACE WITH *Just so.*

As a synonym for words like *assuredly; certainly; decidedly; definitely; positively; surely; undoubtedly; unequivocally; unhesitatingly; unquestionably;* the phrase *most definitely* is ridiculously redundant. ■ Getting this magazine out is a labor of love, but it is *most definitely* labor. REPLACE WITH *decidedly.* ■ Colder weather is *most definitely* on the way. REPLACE WITH *unquestionably.* ■ Would you do it again? *Most definitely.* REPLACE WITH *Unhesitatingly.* SEE ALSO *absolutely; definitely; most assuredly.*

motivating force A wretched redundancy (see page 25). *drive; energy; force; impetus; motivation; power.*

motley crew An inescapable pair (see page 20).

a mountain of A moribund metaphor (see page 21). SEE ALSO *a barrage of.* ■ Since January, Starr has assembled *a mountain of* evidence.

move forward A torpid term (see page 24). *advance; continue; develop; go on; grow; happen; improve; increase; make headway; make progress; move on; occur; proceed; progress; take place.* Politicos and spokespeople endlessly spout fuzzy phrases like *move forward* and *go forward* and *proceed forward* and even *move forward in the right direction.* Pellucid words like *advance, further, improve, proceed,* and *progress* seem to completely elude their intellects. ■ I believe that it was contact with the United States that has *moved* the process of economic reform *forward,* and hopefully some day will *move* the process of political reform *forward.* REPLACE WITH *advanced* and *advance.* ■ What we need is to empower the city in order to *move* it *forward.* REPLACE WITH *improve.* ■ As the company *moves forward,* it's very important that we hold on to those values. REPLACE WITH *grows.* ■ Serious hurdles remain to make this workable and complete, but this agreement today gives us a way to *move forward.* REPLACE WITH *proceed.* ■ Even if Congress decides they want to play politics this year, we can *move forward and* make progress. DELETE *move forward and.* ■ Using these components as our groundwork, we can now *move forward and* examine how to apply them in your web application. DELETE *move forward and.*

And here is a truly ludicrous example: ■ As the year *moves forward,* we will see more *forward movement* in global and domestic environmental issues. REPLACE WITH *advances* and *progress.* SEE ALSO *a step forward; a step (forward)*

in the right direction; go forward; move (forward) in the right direction; proceed forward.

move heaven and earth A moribund metaphor (see page 21). *aim; attempt; endeavor; essay; exert; exhaust; labor; moil; strain; strive; struggle; toil; try hard; undertake; work at.*

Even then I begged my grandfather to see that my testimony was published; but the Michaelises also belong to those old families that move heaven and earth to keep their names out of the papers. — Thornton Wilder, *Theophilus North*

move (forward) in the direction (of) -ing A torpid term (see page 24). *advance; continue; develop; go on; grow; happen; improve; increase; make headway; make progress; move on; occur; proceed; progress; take place.* ■ We've decided to *move in the direction of helping* the claimants make an educated choice. REPLACE WITH *help.*

move (forward) in the right direction A torpid term (see page 24). *advance; continue; develop; go on; grow; happen; improve; increase; make headway; make progress; move on; occur; proceed; progress; take place.*

Only the least eloquent speakers use *move forward* or *move forward in the right direction.* These expressions are wholly unable to move us. They dull our minds and immobilize our actions.

■ I know the company will resolve its problems and *move forward in the right direction.* REPLACE WITH *grow.* ■ All the numbers are looking pretty good and *moving in the right direction.*

REPLACE WITH *increasing*. ■ We are *moving in the right direction*, and I want to keep *moving in the right direction*. REPLACE WITH *making progress* and *making progress*.

Often, formulaic phrases like *move in the right direction* are simply bluster, as in this nearly nonsensical sentence: ■ I'm ready, willing, and able to bring people together and get everybody *moving in the right direction forward*.

Like slander and excessive swearing, *move (forward) in the right direction* exposes a person of questionable character and certain inarticulacy. SEE ALSO *a step forward; a step (forward) in the right direction; go forward; move forward; proceed forward*.

move it or lose it An infantile phrase (see page 20).

move mountains A moribund metaphor (see page 21). *aim; attempt; endeavor; essay; exert; exhaust; labor; moil; strain; strive; struggle; toil; try hard; undertake; work at*.

mover and shaker A moribund metaphor (see page 21). 1. *administrator; boss; brass; chief; commander; director; executive; foreman; head; headman; leader; manager; master; (high) muckamuck; officer; official; overseer; president; principal; superintendent; supervisor*. 2. *aristocrat; dignitary; eminence; lord; luminary; magnate; mogul; notable; patrician; personage; ruler; sovereign; worthy*.

moving target A moribund metaphor (see page 21).

(make) much ado about nothing An infantile phrase (see page 20). *elaborate;*

embellish; embroider; enhance; enlarge; exaggerate; hyperbolize; inflate; magnify; overdo; overestimate; overrate; overreact; overstress; overstate; strain; stretch. ■ If you think this discussion about apostrophes is *much ado about nothing*, tell that to the Apostrophe Protection Society. REPLACE WITH *overstated*.

muck and mire An inescapable pair (see page 20).

muddy the waters A moribund metaphor (see page 21). *becloud; blur; complicate; confuse; muddy; obscure*.

Still, Swenson can't muddy the waters by asking him to look at two books. — Francine Prose, *Blue Angel*

muscle in on A moribund metaphor (see page 21). *break in; encroach; infiltrate; intrude; penetrate; pierce*.

music to (my) ears A moribund metaphor (see page 21).

(a) must (miss) An infantile phrase (see page 20). Like all badly made terms, *(a) must (miss)* is no sooner said than it sounds stale, no sooner read than it sours. In all its variations — *a must have; a must read; a must see*; and so on — this phrase is altogether too *musty*. ■ A good soundtrack, but a dull story, bad acting and weak special effects make this *a must-miss*. ■ Phone interviewing skills are *a must* for most human resource professionals spend a good portion of their day on the phone. ■ Is that business trip *a must*? ■ It is a *must-stop* location for portfolio-toting high school and college students from across the country. ■ Over 200 *must-do* summer events are listed. ■ Aux Delices is *a must stop* for chowhounds. ■ If ever the Lightning faced *a must-win* game, this was it.

(a) must have An infantile phrase (see page 20). *compulsory; critical; essential; imperative; important; indispensable; mandatory; necessary; needed; obligatory; required; requisite; vital.* ■ His book is a student's friend, a professional's ally, a *must-have* reference. REPLACE WITH *indispensable.* ■ No application has yet emerged to make a miniaturized computer *a must-have.* REPLACE WITH *essential.* ■ Microsoft Services for NetWare is *a must-have* for any administrator who is managing a network that includes both types of users. REPLACE WITH *vital.* ■ This software is *a must have* in any web marketing company's toolbox. REPLACE WITH *mandatory.* SEE ALSO *(take) a look see; a (absolute) must; (a) must (miss); (a) must see; a (definite) plus.*

(a) must read An infantile phrase (see page 20). Colloquial usage such as this leads only to everyday thoughts and commonplace actions; few insights, fewer epiphanies, can be had with mediocre language. In essence, *a (must) read* is an expression that secures the banality of what it describes. ■ Tom Wolfe's *Bonfire of the Vanities* is *an enormously entertaining read.* REPLACE WITH *enormously entertaining.* ■ This book is *a tough read* but one of the most important recent accounts of personal identity. REPLACE WITH *tough to understand.* ■ There are a few books on the list that I feel are clearly *easy reads.* REPLACE WITH *easy to read.* ■ There are thousands of great books out there, but how many are *must reads?* REPLACE WITH *compelling.* ■ It's a very challenging *read.* REPLACE

WITH *book.* ■ Is it Tolstoy? is it Dostoyevsky? no, but it is a wonderfully satisfying *read.* REPLACE WITH *story.* ■ The manuscript is 312 pages long and *a pretty easy read.* REPLACE WITH *easily readable.* ■ But the problem with the "ho-hum" approach to a life story is that it makes for *a tiresome read.* REPLACE WITH *tiresome reading.* ■ I'm having a *quiet read.* REPLACE WITH *I'm reading quietly.* SEE ALSO *a good read; (take) a look see; (a) must (miss); (a) must have; (a) must see.*

(a) must see An infantile phrase (see page 20). 1. *compulsory; critical; essential; imperative; important; indispensable; mandatory; necessary; needed; obligatory; required; requisite; vital.* 2. *compelling; powerful.* ■ This is *must-see* TV. REPLACE WITH *compelling.* ■ It is the *must-see* event of the season. REPLACE WITH *obligatory.* SEE ALSO *(take) a look see; a (absolute) must; (a) must (miss); (a) must have; a (definite) plus.*

mutual admiration society An infantile phrase (see page 20). *affinity with.*

mutually exclusive An inescapable pair (see page 20). A phrase from the thoughtless person's formulary, *mutually exclusive* reduces the readability of any sentence in which it is used. *Mutually exclusive* screams a fallow imagination, a barren intellect, a cowering spirit.

■ It has managed to prove that Islam and democracy are not *mutually exclusive.* ■ Being selective and being aggressive are not *mutually exclusive.* ■ The two wildly different stories that jurors will be presented with in some ways are not *mutually exclusive.* ■ As Ferrari, Pegoretti and Cipollini all prove, a powerful engine and a sexy profile are not *mutually exclusive.*

N

nagging doubts An inescapable pair (see page 20).

nail (their) colors (flag) to the mast A moribund metaphor (see page 21).

(like) nailing jelly to a tree (the wall) An insipid simile. *barren; bootless; effete; feckless; feeble; fruitless; futile; impotent; inadequate; inconsequential; inconsiderable; ineffective; ineffectual; infertile; insignificant; inutile; meaningless; meritless; nugatory; null; of no value; pointless; powerless; profitless; sterile; trifling; trivial; unavailing; unimportant; unproductive; unprofitable; unserviceable; unworthy; useless; vain; valueless; weak; worthless.*

nail (him) to the wall A moribund metaphor (see page 21). 1. *admonish; anathematize; berate; blame; castigate; censure; chastise; chide; condemn; criticize; curse; decry; denounce; execrate; imprecate; inculpate; indict; rebuke; reprimand; reproach; reprove; scold; upbraid.* 2. *beat; better; conquer; defeat; exceed; excel; outclass; outdo; outflank; outmaneuver; outperform; outplay; overcome; overpower; prevail; rout; succeed; surpass; top; triumph; trounce; vanquish; whip; win.*

> But if he was a bad guy, I'd nail him to the wall. — Jane Heller, *Lucky Stars*

(as) naked as a jaybird An insipid simile. *bare; disrobed; naked; nude; stripped; unclothed; uncovered; undressed.*

(my) name is mud A moribund metaphor (see page 21).

name of the game A moribund metaphor (see page 21). *basis; center; core; crux; essence; gist; heart; kernel; pith; substance.*

(as) narrow as an arrow An insipid simile. *asthenic; attenuated; bony; cachectic; emaciated; gaunt; lank; lanky; lean; narrow; rail-thin; scraggy; scrawny; skeletal; skinny; slender; slight; slim; spare; spindly; svelte; sylphid; thin; trim; wispy.*

national pastime A moribund metaphor (see page 21). *baseball.*

neat and tidy An inescapable pair (see page 20). *neat; orderly; tidy.*

(as) neat as a pin An insipid simile. *methodical; neat; ordered; orderly; organized; systematic; tidy; trim; well-organized.*

necessary evil A torpid term (see page 24). ■ Their staunch refusal to concede that new taxes are, at the least, a *necessary evil*, could shut them out of the budget process altogether.

(a) necessary prerequisite A wretched redundancy (see page 25). *necessary; prerequisite.* ■ An understanding of expressions is *a necessary prerequisite* to learning any command language. DELETE *necessary.* ■ The transfer of information is *a necessary prerequisite* for the effective transfer of technology. DELETE *a prerequisite.*

necessary requirement A wretched redundancy (see page 25). *necessary; requirement.* ■ Because of the labor problems that we have been having with the police patrolmen's union, we will be unable to meet the *necessary requirements* by the deadline. DELETE *necessary.*

necessity is the mother of invention A popular prescription (see page 23).

neck and neck A moribund metaphor (see page 21). *abreast; close; equal; tied.*

> Up till a moment ago we were neck and neck but then my peel broke and I had to refind my purchase. — Janni Visman, *Yellow*

(our) neck of the woods A moribund metaphor (see page 21). *area; community; country; county; district; domain; environment; environs; locale; locality; milieu; neighborhood; part; region; section; sector; surroundings; territory; vicinity; zone.*

> Now, they don't read a lot of books in this neck of the woods. — Will Ferguson, *Happiness*

need(s) and want(s) An inescapable pair (see page 20).

(like) (finding; looking for a) needle in a haystack A moribund metaphor (see page 21).

negative (*n*) A torpid term (see page 24). *burden; deterrence; deterrent; disadvantage; drawback; encumbrance; frailty; hardship; hindrance; liability; limitation; obstacle; onus; shortcoming; weakness.* ■ I don't see how it's a *negative* to the United States to be supporting a democratic government. REPLACE WITH *disadvantage.* SEE ALSO *positive.*

negative effect (impact) A torpid term (see page 24). SEE ALSO *positive effect (impact).* ■ The committee is concerned with both short-term and long-term *negative effects.* REPLACE WITH *disruptions.* ■ Imaging helps to overcome the *negative effects* produced by generalizations. REPLACE WITH *inaccuracies.*

negative feelings A torpid term (see page 24). This expression tells us how little we listen to how we feel. In our quest for speed and efficiency, we have forfeited our feelings. The niceties of emotion — *anger, animosity, anxiety, depression, despair, displeasure, disquiet, distrust, fear, frustration, fury, gloom, grief, guilt, hatred, hopelessness, hostility, ill will, insecurity, jealousy, malice, melancholy, rage, resentment, sadness, shame, sorrow, stress,* and so on — have been sacrificed to a pointless proficiency. ■ It was reported that IAM headquarters failed to renew a $1 million bond that matured in June, due to their *negative feelings* toward El Al's actions. REPLACE WITH *displeasure.* ■ *Negative feelings* can trigger a cascade of stress hormones that accelerate the heart rate, shut down the immune system, and encourage blood clotting. REPLACE WITH *Resentment or anger.* ■ But *those negative feelings* can work against you if they render you unwilling or unable to act the next time you face a major decision. REPLACE WITH *anger and embarrassment.* ■ Though little is known about the effects of negative emotions on your heart, there are a few theories about why *negative feelings* can do so much damage. REPLACE WITH *stress and depression.* SEE ALSO *positive feelings.*

neither a borrower nor a lender be A popular prescription (see page 23).

neither fish nor fowl A moribund metaphor (see page 21). *indefinite; indeterminate; indistinct; undefined; undetermined.*

neither here nor there A moribund metaphor (see page 21). *extraneous; immaterial; impertinent; inapplicable; irrelevant.*

neither one A wretched redundancy (see page 25). *neither.* ■ *Neither one* of these choices is exclusive of the other. DELETE *one.* SEE ALSO *each one; either one.*

ne plus ultra A foreign phrase (see page 19).

nerves of steel A moribund metaphor (see page 21). *bold; brave; courageous; dauntless; fearless; intrepid; stouthearted; unafraid.*

nest egg A moribund metaphor (see page 21). *assets; finances; funds; resources; savings.*

never (not) in a million years An infantile phrase (see page 20). *at no time; by no means; in no way; never; no; not; not at all; not ever; not in any way; not in the least.* ■ I would never have imagined — *not in a million years* — feeling compelled to come to the defense of that grande dame of the administration, the president's wife. DELETE *not in a million years.*

never in my wildest dreams An infantile phrase (see page 20). *at no time; by no means; in no way; never; no; not; not at all; not ever; not in any way; not in the least.* ■ *Never in my wildest dreams* did I imagine that Pinochet would be arrested

here in London. DELETE *in my wildest dreams.*

never say die A popular prescription (see page 23).

never say never A popular prescription (see page 23).

new and improved A suspect superlative (see page 24).

new and innovative An inescapable pair (see page 20). *innovative; new.* ■ We used some *new and innovative* manufacturing techniques. REPLACE WITH *innovative* or *new.*

(a) (whole) new (different) ballgame A moribund metaphor (see page 21). ■ Although the procedure is basically the same, recording a macro is slightly different in Word and PowerPoint than in Excel, and creating a macro in Access is *a whole different ballgame.* REPLACE WITH *wholly different.*

new deck (pack) of cards A moribund metaphor (see page 21).

(the) new kid on the block A moribund metaphor (see page 21). ■ Being *the new kid on the block* does not excuse them from their responsibilities.

(a) new lease on life A moribund metaphor (see page 21). *animated; energized; enlivened; inspired; inspirited; invigorated; refreshed; reinvigorated; rejuvenated; revitalized; revived; roused; stimulated; stired; vitalized.*

(like) new wine in old bottles An insipid simile.

nice An overworked word (see page 22). *affable; agreeable; amiable; amicable; companionable; compassionate; congenial; cordial; delightful; friendly; genial; good; good-hearted; good-natured; humane; kind; kind-hearted; likable; neighborly; personable; pleasant; pleasing; sociable; tender; tolerant.*

The word *nice* we might reserve for its less well-known definitions of *fastidious* and *subtle.*

(as) nice as pie An insipid simile. *affable; agreeable; amiable; amicable; companionable; compassionate; congenial; cordial; delightful; friendly; genial; good; good-hearted; good-natured; humane; kind; kind-hearted; likable; neighborly; personable; pleasant; pleasing; sociable; tender; tolerant.*

And then once more her eyes glaze, her body deadens, and she cries out again and again, 'Who are you? Who are you? Who are you?' and she is crying and this time I simply want to escape this strange circle, and I get up and hastily pull on my clothes, and the Conga all the time saying, as nice as pie, genuinely upset, 'But why? Why are you going?' — Richard Flanagan, *Gould's Book of Fish*

nice work if you can get it A plebeian sentiment (see page 23).

nickel-and-dime A moribund metaphor (see page 21). 1. *cheap; economical; inexpensive; low-cost; low-priced.* 2. *cheap; frugal; miserly; niggardly; parsimonious; stingy; thrifty.* 3. *inconsequential; insignificant; minor; negligible; paltry; petty; small; small-time; trifling; trivial; unimportant.* ■ The banks were shoveling money into every *nickel-and-dime* developer that walked in. REPLACE WITH *insignificant.*

nickel-and-dime (him) to death A moribund metaphor (see page 21). ■ Many governors have begun to *nickel-and-dime taxpayers to death* with fees, fines, tolls, and excise taxes. SEE ALSO *to death.*

(like) night and day An insipid simile. *antipodal; antipodean; antithetical; contrary; converse; diametric; diametrical; different; inverse; opposite; reverse.*

(it's a) nightmare A moribund metaphor (see page 21). How impoverished our imaginations are. Nightmares ought to be terrifying, but this metaphor — so popular has it become — is hopelessly tame. *It was a nightmare* instills in us as little compassion as it does interest; it makes us yawn rather than yell. No longer is there terror to it.

Though an incident might well be *agonizing, alarming, appalling, awful, disgusting, disquieting, distressing, disturbing, dreadful, excruciating, frightening, frightful, ghastly, grisly, gruesome, harrowing, hideous, horrendous, horrible, horrid, horrific, horrifying, monstrous, nauseating, nightmarish, petrifying, repellent, repulsive, revolting, shocking, sickening, terrifying, tormenting, traumatic,* saying *it was a nightmare* makes it sound as though it were no more than an annoyance, no more than a mere inconvenience.

It was a nightmare, the metaphor, has hardly the force of a sweet dream. ■ It was *a nightmare.* REPLACE WITH *ghastly.* ■ If the birth mother shows up, it's *a nightmare* for the adopting mother. REPLACE WITH *disquieting.*

Altogether remarkable about this expression is that people use it to describe something that tormented or terrified them. They describe an extraordinary event with an ordinary phrase. How can we not doubt the sincerity of their words, the terror of their experience? Is this then what it is to be human, to be able to use language, expressing ourselves in platitudes to illustrate what affects us most deeply? Are so many of us still scribblers? SEE ALSO *(every person's) worst nightmare*.

nip and tuck A moribund metaphor (see page 21).

nip (it) in the bud A moribund metaphor (see page 21). *abort; annul; arrest; balk; block; cancel; check; contain; crush; derail; detain; end; extinguish; foil; frustrate; halt; hinder; impede; neutralize; nullify; obstruct; prevent; quash; quell; repress; restrain; retard; squash; squelch; squish; stall; stay; stifle; stop; subdue; suppress; terminate; thwart.* ■ Another reader in California has found a sure-fire method for *nipping travel stress in the bud*. REPLACE WITH *squelching travel stress*.

nipping at (your) heels A moribund metaphor (see page 21).

> Then he ran off behind his brother, as if embarrassment were nipping at his heels. — Patricia Jones, *Red on a Rose*

no big deal An infantile phrase (see page 20). *inappreciable; inconsequential; inconsiderable; insignificant; minor; negligible; niggling; nugatory; petty; trifling; trivial; unimportant; unsubstantial.*

nobody but nobody An infantile phrase (see page 20). *nobody; nobody at all; none; no one; no one at all.*

nobody's perfect A popular prescription (see page 23). SEE ALSO *(I'm) a perfectionist; I'm not perfect (you know).*

no easy task A torpid term (see page 24). *arduous; backbreaking; burdensome; difficult; exhausting; fatiguing; hard; herculean; laborious; not easy; onerous; severe; strenuous; toilful; toilsome; tough; troublesome; trying; wearisome.* ■ Getting this place ready has been *no easy task*. REPLACE WITH *backbreaking*.

no great shakes A moribund metaphor (see page 21). 1. *average; common; commonplace; customary; everyday; fair; mediocre; middling; normal; ordinary; passable; quotidian; regular; routine; standard; tolerable; typical; uneventful; unexceptional; unremarkable; usual.* 2. *inappreciable; inconsequential; inconsiderable; insignificant; minor; negligible; niggling; nugatory; petty; trifling; trivial; unimportant; unsubstantial.*

no guts, no glory A popular prescription (see page 23).

no holds barred A moribund metaphor (see page 21). *candidly; explicitly; openly; overtly; without restraint.*

no ifs, ands, ors, or buts An infantile phrase (see page 20). SEE ALSO *period*.

no man is an island A popular prescription (see page 23).

non compos mentis A foreign phrase (see page 19). *batty; cracked; crazy; cretinous; daft; demented; deranged;*

insane; lunatic; mad; maniacal; neurotic; nuts; nutty; psychotic; raving; squirrelly; touched; unbalanced; unhinged; unsound.

none of the above An infantile phrase (see page 20). ■ Do you want to talk to me or argue with me? *None of the above.* REPLACE WITH *Neither.* SEE ALSO *all of the above.*

no news is good news A quack equation (see page 23). ■ There is a new breed of progressive administrators who do not believe that *no news is good news.*

no offense (intended) An infantile phrase (see page 20).

> And I say that with no offence to the good people of Sydney intended. — Nick Hornby, *A Long Way Down*

(every) nook and cranny A moribund metaphor (see page 21). *complexities; details; fine points; intricacies; minutiae; niceties; particulars.* ■ There is lots of time in which to explore the *nooks and crannies* of virtually any topic on AM radio. REPLACE WITH *intricacies.*

no pain, no gain A popular prescription (see page 23).

no problem An infantile phrase (see page 20). 1. *you're welcome.* 2. *not at all; not in the least.* 3. *I'd be glad to; I'd be happy to.* 4. *it's O.K.; that's all right.* 5. *easy; easily; effortlessly; readily.* ■ Thanks very much. *No problem.* REPLACE WITH *You're welcome.* ■ Can you do it? *No problem.* REPLACE WITH *Easily.* SEE ALSO *common courtesy.*

no pun intended An infantile phrase (see page 20).

nose out of joint A moribund metaphor (see page 21). 1. *acerbated; angry; annoyed; bothered; cross; displeased; enraged; furious; grouchy; incensed; inflamed; infuriated; irate; irked; irritated; mad; miffed; peeved; provoked; riled; roiled; testy; upset; vexed.* 2. *covetous; desirous; envious; grudging; jealous; resentful.*

(it's) no skin off (my) nose A moribund metaphor (see page 21).

no small feat (task) A torpid term (see page 24). *arduous; backbreaking; burdensome; difficult; exhausting; fatiguing; hard; herculean; laborious; not easy; onerous; severe; strenuous; toilful; toilsome; tough; troublesome; trying; wearisome.*

(I'm) no spring chicken A moribund metaphor (see page 21). *aged; aging; ancient; antediluvian; antique; archaic; elderly; hoary; hoary-headed; old; patriarchal; prehistoric; seasoned; superannuated.*

no strings attached A moribund metaphor (see page 21). *unconditionally; unreservedly.*

no sweat A moribund metaphor (see page 21). *easily done; easy; effortless; elementary; facile; simple; simplicity itself; straightforward; uncomplex; uncomplicated.*

not a Chinaman's chance A moribund metaphor (see page 21). 1. *doubtful; dubious; farfetched; implausible; improbable; remote; unlikely; unrealistic.* 2. *hopeless; impossible; impracticable; impractical; infeasible; unrealizable; unworkable.*

not a ghost of a chance A moribund metaphor (see page 21). 1. *doubtful; dubious; farfetched; implausible; improbable; remote; unlikely; unrealistic.* 2. *hopeless; impossible; impracticable; impractical; infeasible; unrealizable; unworkable.*

not a hope in hell A moribund metaphor (see page 21). 1. *doubtful; dubious; farfetched; implausible; improbable; remote; unlikely; unrealistic.* 2. *hopeless; impossible; impracticable; impractical; infeasible; unrealizable; unworkable.*

not all (what) (it's) cracked up to be A torpid term (see page 24). *deficient; disappointing; discouraging; dissatisfying; inadequate; inapt; incapable; incompetent; ineffective; inferior; insufficient; lacking; unfit; unqualified; unsatisfactory; wanting.*

not a mean bone in (her) body A moribund metaphor (see page 21). *affable; agreeable; amiable; amicable; compassionate; friendly; gentle; good-hearted; good-natured; humane; kind; kind-hearted; personable; pleasant; tender; tolerant.*

not a snowball's chance in hell A moribund metaphor (see page 21). 1. *doubtful; dubious; farfetched; implausible; improbable; remote; unlikely; unrealistic.* 2. *hopeless; impossible; impracticable; impractical; infeasible; unrealizable; unworkable.*

not by a long shot A moribund metaphor (see page 21). *at no time; by no means; in no way; never; no; not; not at all; not ever; not in any way; not in the least.*

notch in (his) belt A moribund metaphor (see page 21). *achievement; attainment; success.*

not for all the tea in China A moribund metaphor (see page 21). *at no time; by no means; in no way; never; no; not; not at all; not ever; not in any way; not in the least.*

not for anything in the world A moribund metaphor (see page 21). *at no time; by no means; in no way; never; no; not; not at all; not ever; not in any way; not in the least.*

not for love or money A moribund metaphor (see page 21). *at no time; by no means; in no way; never; no; not; not at all; not ever; not in any way; not in the least.*

not for the world A moribund metaphor (see page 21). *at no time; by no means; in no way; never; no; not; not at all; not ever; not in any way; not in the least.*

nothing could be further from the truth A torpid term (see page 24). 1. *by no means; in no way; never; no; not; not at all; not ever; nothing of the sort; not in any way; not in the least.* 2. *be amiss; be astray; be deceived; be deluded; be erring; be erroneous; be fallacious; be false; be faulty; be inaccurate; be incorrect; be in error; be misguided; be misinformed; be mislead; be mistaken; be not correct; be not right; be untrue; be wrong.*

You would think that anyone who uses this phrase — anyone, that is, whose words or actions were being questioned or whose honor was being impugned — would choose to speak more eloquently. You would think that unfair or inaccurate accusations would elicit profound and persuasive expressions of denial. When they do not, as they certainly do not when a person resorts to *nothing could be further from the truth,* we have to wonder who is telling the truth and who is not. Formulaic responses like this may make us doubt the sincerity of those who use them

■ The premise put forth by the administration that employment must be sacrificed to protect the environment *could not be further from the truth.* REPLACE WITH *is erroneous.* ■ I know there will be Republicans who will try to say that because I'm not with you today in Chicago that I'm trying to distance myself from you, but *nothing could be further from the truth.* REPLACE WITH *they are mistaken.* ■ W. R. Grace makes use of my "model citizen" sound bite as though it were some sort of blanket absolution. *Nothing could be further from the truth.* REPLACE WITH *It is not.*

> They had been credited with attempting to stir up rebellion among the animals on neighbouring farms. Nothing could be further from the truth! — George Orwell, *Animal Farm*

nothing lasts forever A popular prescription (see page 23).

nothing to sneeze at A moribund metaphor (see page 21). *consequential; considerable; meaningful; momentous; significant; substantial; weighty.* ■ Two hundred thousand jobs is *nothing to sneeze at.* REPLACE WITH *considerable.*

nothing to write home about A moribund metaphor (see page 21). 1. *aver-*

age; common; commonplace; customary; everyday; fair; mediocre; middling; normal; ordinary; passable; quotidian; regular; standard; tolerable; typical; uneventful; unexceptional; unexciting; unremarkable; usual; workaday. 2. *anodyne; banal; barren; bland; boring; deadly; dreary; dry; dull; everyday; flat; humdrum; inanimate; insipid; jejune; lifeless; lusterless; mediocre; monotonous; prosaic; routine; spiritless; stale; tedious; tiresome; unexciting; uninteresting; vapid; wearisome.*

nothing ventured, nothing gained A popular prescription (see page 23).

not in (this) lifetime A moribund metaphor (see page 21). *at no time; by no means; in no way; never; no; not; not at all; not ever; not in any way; not in the least.*

not in (out of) the picture A moribund metaphor (see page 21). Some metaphors — so bloodless have they become — accommodate many different meanings. *Not in (out of) the picture* is one of them, for this pale expression could easily mean *dead* or *departed,* conceivably mean *forgotten* or *forgettable,* or imaginably mean *unmentionable* or *nameless.* SEE ALSO *in the picture.*

not on your life A moribund metaphor (see page 21). *at no time; by no means; in no way; never; no; not; not at all; not ever; not in any way; not in the least.*

not what (it) used to be A torpid term (see page 24). *deficient; disappointing; discouraging; dissatisfying; inadequate; inapt; incapable; incompetent; ineffective; inferior; insufficient; lacking; unfit; unqualified; unsatisfactory; wanting.*

not with a bang but with a whimper An infantile phrase (see page 20).

not worth a continental A moribund metaphor (see page 21). *barren; bootless; effete; feckless; feeble; fruitless; futile; impotent; inadequate; inconsequential; inconsiderable; ineffective; ineffectual; infertile; insignificant; inutile; meaningless; meritless; nugatory; null; of no value; pointless; powerless; profitless; sterile; trifling; trivial; unavailing; unimportant; unproductive; unprofitable; unserviceable; unworthy; useless; vain; valueless; weak; worthless.*

not worth a (tinker's) damn A moribund metaphor (see page 21). *barren; bootless; effete; feckless; feeble; fruitless; futile; impotent; inadequate; inconsequential; inconsiderable; ineffective; ineffectual; infertile; insignificant; inutile; meaningless; meritless; nugatory; null; of no value; pointless; powerless; profitless; sterile; trifling; trivial; unavailing; unimportant; unproductive; unprofitable; unserviceable; unworthy; useless; vain; valueless; weak; worthless.*

not worth a plugged nickel A moribund metaphor (see page 21). *barren; bootless; effete; feckless; feeble; fruitless; futile; impotent; inadequate; inconsequential; inconsiderable; ineffective; ineffectual; infertile; insignificant; inutile; meaningless; meritless; nugatory; null; of no value; pointless; powerless; profitless; sterile; trifling; trivial; unavailing; unimportant; unproductive; unprofitable; unserviceable; unworthy; useless; vain; valueless; weak; worthless.*

not worth a straw A moribund metaphor (see page 21). *barren; bootless; effete; feckless; feeble; fruitless; futile;*

impotent; inadequate; inconsequential; inconsiderable; ineffective; ineffectual; infertile; insignificant; inutile; meaningless; meritless; nugatory; null; of no value; pointless; powerless; profitless; sterile; trifling; trivial; unavailing; unimportant; unproductive; unprofitable; unserviceable; unworthy; useless; vain; valueless; weak; worthless.

not worth the paper it's written (printed) on A moribund metaphor (see page 21). *barren; bootless; effete; feckless; feeble; fruitless; futile; impotent; inadequate; inconsequential; inconsiderable; ineffective; ineffectual; infertile; insignificant; inutile; meaningless; meritless; nugatory; null; of no value; pointless; powerless; profitless; sterile; trifling; trivial; unavailing; unimportant; unproductive; unprofitable; unserviceable; unworthy; useless; vain; valueless; weak; worthless.* ■ I say to you that the governor's budget is *not worth the paper it's written on.* REPLACE WITH *useless.* ■ He went on to say that he did not believe in the United States Constitution, and that it was *not worth the paper it's printed on.* REPLACE WITH *nugatory.*

no use crying over spilt milk A popular prescription (see page 23).

no way An infantile phrase (see page 20). *at no time; by no means; in no way; never; no; not; not at all; not ever; not in any way; not in the least.*

no way José An infantile phrase (see page 20). *at no time; by no means; in no way; never; no; not; not at all; not ever; not in any way; not in the least.*

now it's my time (turn) A plebeian sentiment (see page 23). ■ I've done my family duty and brought up my children, and *now it's my turn.*

now you see it, now you don't An infantile phrase (see page 20).

null and void An inescapable pair (see page 20). *abolished; annulled; canceled; countermanded; invalid; null; nullified; recalled; repealed; rescinded; revoked; void; withdrawn; worthless.* ■ We aren't sure what the terms of the deal are, or what may be expected of them, or what may make them *null and void.* REPLACE WITH *invalid.*

(her) number is up A moribund metaphor (see page 21).

Ach, just my luck! Then the old fellow's number is up. — Isaac Babel, *Red Cavalry*

number-one A moribund metaphor (see page 21). *chief; foremost; leading; main; primary; prime; principal.*

number one (two) A wretched redundancy (see page 25). *first (second).* ■ *Number one,* I don't feel that qualifies her as black. *Number two,* a person's color shouldn't be worn on their sleeve. REPLACE WITH *First; Second.*

nuts and bolts A moribund metaphor (see page 21). *basics; essentials; facts; foundation; fundamentals; principles.* ■ In this text, we explore the *nuts and bolts* of radio production. REPLACE WITH *essentials.*

nuttier than a fruitcake A moribund metaphor (see page 21). *batty; cracked; crazy; daft; demented; deranged; fey; foolish; goofy; insane; lunatic; mad; maniacal;* *neurotic; nuts; nutty; psychotic; raving; silly; squirrelly; touched; unbalanced; unhinged; unsound; wacky; zany.*

object of one's affection An infantile phrase (see page 20). *admirer; beau; beloved; boyfriend (girlfriend); companion; darling; dear; flame; infatuate; inamorato (inamorata); lover; paramour; steady; suiter; swain; sweetheart; wooer.* SEE ALSO *significant other.*

obscene An overworked word (see page 22). *abhorrent; abominable; accursed; appalling; atrocious; awful; beastly; blasphemous; detestable; disagreeable; disgusting; dreadful; execrable; frightening; frightful; ghastly; grisly; gruesome; hateful; horrendous; horrible; horrid; horrifying; indecent; indelicate; inhuman; insulting; loathesome; monstrous; obnoxious; odious; offensive; repellent; repugnant; repulsive; revolting; tasteless; terrible; terrifying; unspeakable; unutterable; vulgar.* ■ Certain levels of expenditure are *obscene* and do a great injustice to our concept of social justice. REPLACE WITH *offensive.* ■ It's an *obscene* scenario that's being played out. REPLACE WITH *unspeakable.*

obviate the need for A wretched redundancy (see page 25). *obviate.* ■ If indicated, create a limited-access, safe unit to *obviate the need for* activity restriction. DELETE *the need for.*

247

(an) ocean of A moribund metaphor (see page 21). SEE ALSO *a barrage of.*

oceans of ink A moribund metaphor (see page 21).

> Those journalists who professed science, at war with those who professed wit, spilled oceans of ink in this memorable campaign ....
> — Jules Verne, *Twenty Thousand Leagues Under the Seas*

of biblical (epic) proportions A moribund metaphor (see page 21). *colossal; elephantine; enormous; epical; gargantuan; giant; gigantic; great; grand; huge; immense; impressive; legendary; mammoth; massive; monstrous; prodigious; stupendous; titanic; tremendous; vast.* ■ It has been called *a comeback of epic proportions.* REPLACE WITH *an epical comeback.* ■ He created a landmark television character whose suffering was *of biblical proportions.* REPLACE WITH *prodigious.*

> As if she'd made a cosmic announcement, her last word was followed by a trumpet blast of Biblical proportions that shook the windows. — Jill Churchill, *The Merchant of Menace*

(woman) of easy virtue A moribund metaphor (see page 21). *dissolute; immoral; licentious; loose; promiscuous; wanton.*

off and running A moribund metaphor (see page 21).

off base A moribund metaphor (see page 21). *amiss; astray; deceived; deluded; erring; erroneous; fallacious; false; faulty;* *inaccurate; incorrect; in error; misguided; misinformed; mislead; mistaken; not correct; not right; wrong.* ■ Given all the uncertainty surrounding the nation's economic future, no one is prepared to say the administration is *off base.* REPLACE WITH *incorrect.*

off (her) rocker A moribund metaphor (see page 21). *batty; cracked; crazy; daft; demented; deranged; fey; foolish; goofy; insane; lunatic; mad; maniacal; neurotic; nuts; nutty; psychotic; raving; silly; squirrelly; touched; unbalanced; unhinged; unsound; wacky; zany.*

off the beaten path (track) A moribund metaphor (see page 21). 1. *aberrant; abnormal; anomalistic; anomalous; atypical; bizarre; curious; deviant; different; distinct; distinctive; eccentric; exceptional; extraordinary; fantastic; foreign; grotesque; idiosyncratic; independent; individual; individualistic; irregular; novel; odd; offbeat; original; peculiar; queer; strange; uncommon; unconventional; unexampled; unique; unnatural; unorthodox; unusual; weird.* 2. *inaccessible; isolated; remote; secluded; unreachable.* ■ A lot of smaller towns of 800 to 3000 people are *off the beaten path.* REPLACE WITH *remote.*

off the cuff A moribund metaphor (see page 21). *extemporaneous; extempore; impromptu; improvised; spontaneous; unprepared; unprompted; unrehearsed.*

(go) off the deep end A moribund metaphor (see page 21). *batty; cracked; crazy; daft; demented; deranged; fey; foolish; goofy; insane; lunatic; mad; maniacal; neurotic; nuts; nutty; psychotic; raving; silly; squirrelly; touched; unbalanced; unhinged; unsound; wacky; zany.*

(let) off the hook A moribund metaphor (see page 21). *absolve; acquit; clear; condone; exculpate; excuse; exonerate; forgive; overlook; pardon; remit; vindicate.* ■ Confronting sexual issues is so taboo in most African culture that rapists are frequently *let off the hook* because few families will endure the public shame of acknowledging the abuse. REPLACE WITH *acquitted.* ■ But as news events in the scandal coverage ebb, the media have had to find new ways to *let Clinton off the hook.* REPLACE WITH *absolve Clinton.* ■ Now she's calling for Nicaragua and Honduras to be *let off the hook* for at least two years. REPLACE WITH *excused.*

off the record A moribund metaphor (see page 21). *classified; confidential; personal; private; privy; restricted; secret.*

off the top of (my) head A moribund metaphor (see page 21). *extemporaneous; extempore; impromptu; improvised; spontaneous; unprepared; unprompted; unrehearsed.*

off the wall A moribund metaphor (see page 21). *aberrant; abnormal; anomalistic; anomalous; atypical; bizarre; curious; deviant; different; distinct; distinctive; eccentric; exceptional; extraordinary; fantastic; foreign; grotesque; idiosyncratic; independent; individual; individualistic; irregular; novel; odd; offbeat; original; peculiar; puzzling; quaint; queer; rare; remarkable; separate; singular; strange; uncommon; unconventional; unexampled; unique; unorthodox; unparalleled; unprecedented; unusual; weird.*

off to the races A moribund metaphor (see page 21).

(goes) off track A moribund metaphor (see page 21). *amiss; astray; deceived; deluded; erring; erroneous; fallacious; false; faulty; inaccurate; incorrect; in error; misguided; misinformed; mislead; mistaken; not correct; not right; wrong.*

> An intelligent and beautiful girl from a loving family grows up in Orangetown, Ontario, her mother's a writer, her father's a doctor, and then she goes off the track. — Carol Shields, *Unless*

off (her) trolley A moribund metaphor (see page 21). *batty; cracked; crazy; daft; demented; deranged; fey; foolish; goofy; insane; lunatic; mad; maniacal; neurotic; nuts; nutty; psychotic; raving; silly; squirrelly; touched; unbalanced; unhinged; unsound; wacky; zany.*

oftentimes A wretched redundancy (see page 25). *frequently; often; repeatedly.* ■ *Oftentimes*, this results in overloading the office staff with the added responsibility of planning the company's meetings and events. REPLACE WITH *Often.*

(time is) of the essence A torpid term (see page 24). *critical; crucial; essential; important; key; significant; vital.*

> Time was of the essence — not only because of what those rival companies were up to, but also (and the Rani lowered her voice mysteriously) for Other Reasons. — Aldous Huxley, *Island*

of the first water A moribund metaphor (see page 21). *best; brightest; choice; choicest; elite; excellent; finest; first-class; first-rate; foremost; greatest; highest; highest quality; matchless; non-*

pareil; optimal; optimum; outstanding; paramount; peerless; preeminent; premium; prominent; select; superior; superlative; top; unequaled; unexcelled; unmatched; unrivaled; unsurpassed.

off (his) trolley A moribund metaphor (see page 21). *batty; cracked; crazy; daft; demented; deranged; fey; foolish; goofy; insane; lunatic; mad; maniacal; neurotic; nuts; nutty; psychotic; raving; silly; squirrelly; touched; unbalanced; unhinged; unsound; wacky; zany.*

ofttimes A withered word (see page 24). *frequently; often; repeatedly.*

of two minds A moribund metaphor (see page 21). *ambivalent; confused; divided; indecisive; in doubt; irresolute; neutral; torn; uncertain; uncommitted; undecided; unsure.*

O.K.? An infantile phrase (see page 20). ■ I don't have a lot of respect for people who judge others by their skin tone, *O.K.?* DELETE *O.K.?* ■ I have a master's degree, *O.K.?* but if I dress bad or speak bad, I'm treated bad, *O.K.?* DELETE *O.K.?* ■ Once that sperm hits that egg, *O.K.?* you have no rights after that, *O.K.?* DELETE *O.K.?* ■ What I did was wrong, *O.K.?* I shouldn't have done it, *O.K.?* I did my time for it, *O.K.?* DELETE *O.K.?*

old adage A wretched redundancy (see page 25). *adage.* ■ The *old adage* "The first half of our lives is ruined by our parents and the last half by our children" need not be and should not be. DELETE *old.*

old and decrepit An inescapable pair (see page 20).

(as) old as Adam An insipid simile. *aged; aging; ancient; antediluvian; antique; archaic; elderly; hoary; hoary-headed; old; patriarchal; prehistoric; seasoned; superannuated; venerable.*

(as) old as the hills An insipid simile. *aged; aging; ancient; antediluvian; antique; archaic; elderly; hoary; hoary-headed; old; patriarchal; prehistoric; seasoned; superannuated; venerable.*

(as) old as time An insipid simile. *aged; aging; ancient; antediluvian; antique; archaic; elderly; hoary; hoary-headed; old; patriarchal; prehistoric; seasoned; superannuated; venerable.*

> The family! Here was the old blackmail tactic, old as Time. — Joyce Carol Oates, *The Tattooed Girl*

old-boy network A moribund metaphor (see page 21).

old cliché A wretched redundancy (see page 25). *cliché.* ■ Working for these guys I feel like the *old cliché* "a cog in the wheel." DELETE *old.*

old enough to know better An infantile phrase (see page 20).

old enough to know better but young enough not to care An infantile phrase (see page 20).

(an) old hand A moribund metaphor (see page 21). *able; adept; apt; capable; competent; deft; dexterous; experienced; expert; practiced; proficient; seasoned; skilled; skillful; veteran.*

oldest story in the book A moribund metaphor (see page 21).

old habits never die A popular prescription (see page 23).

> Old habits never die. And when you've once been in the business of granting wishes, the impulse never quite leaves you. — Joanne Harris, *Chocolat*.

old hat A moribund metaphor (see page 21). 1. *antediluvian; antiquated; archaic; dead; obsolescent; obsolete; old; old-fashioned; outdated; outmoded; out of date; out of fashion; passé; superannuated.* 2. *anodyne; banal; barren; bland; boring; deadly; dreary; dry; dull; everyday; flat; humdrum; inanimate; insipid; jejune; lifeless; lusterless; mediocre; monotonous; prosaic; routine; spiritless; stale; tedious; tiresome; unexciting; uninteresting; vapid; wearisome.*

old maxim A wretched redundancy (see page 25). *maxim.* ■ A number of studies indicate that, in deciding what punishment is appropriate for different crimes, individuals typically rely on an *old maxim*: Let the punishment fit the crime. DELETE *old*.

old saw A wretched redundancy (see page 25). *saw.* ■ The claim is similar to the *old saw* from the tobacco industry, now proven false, that there is no direct link between cancer and smoking. DELETE *old*.

old saying A wretched redundancy (see page 25). *saying.* ■ The *old saying* "A picture is worth a thousand words" is usually true. DELETE *old*.

old wives' tale A moribund metaphor (see page 21).

on a ... basis A wretched redundancy (see page 25). ■ Meat production is the major use of goats *on a worldwide basis*. REPLACE WITH *worldwide*. ■ I am tortured *on a daily basis*. REPLACE WITH *daily*. ■ I see him for my treatment *on a regular basis*. REPLACE WITH *regularly*. ■ You meet the students *on a weekly basis*. REPLACE WITH *weekly*. ■ We should look at these issues *on a case by case basis*. REPLACE WITH *case by case*.

on account of the fact that A wretched redundancy (see page 25). *because; considering; for; given; in that; since.* ■ The former Beatle refused the award *on account of the fact that* he believes he is too young to receive it and does not want to be perceived as a washed-up has been. REPLACE WITH *because*. SEE ALSO *because of the fact that; considering the fact that; by virtue of the fact that; given the fact that; in view of the fact that; on account of the fact that.*

on a collision course A moribund metaphor (see page 21).

on a different wavelength A moribund metaphor (see page 21). *conflict; differ; disagree; disharmonize; feel differently; think unalike.*

on a dime A moribund metaphor (see page 21). *cheaply; economically; inexpensively.* ■ When it comes to interior design or decorating *on a dime*, you've got hundreds of tips and tricks to share with readers. REPLACE WITH *economically*.

(working) on all cylinders A moribund metaphor (see page 21). 1. *able; adept; apt; capable; competent; conversant; deft; dexterous; experienced; expert; familiar; practiced; proficient; seasoned; skilled; skillful; veteran.* 2. *adroit; astute; bright; brilliant; clever; discerning; effective; effectual; efficient; enlightened; insightful; intelligent; judicious; keen; knowledgeable; learned; logical; luminous; perceptive; perspicacious; quick; rational; reasonable; sagacious; sage; sapient; sensible; sharp; shrewd; smart; sound; understanding; wise.* ■ This rapid growth cycle is a challenge opportunity and needs good *people working on all cylinders* to take advantage of it. REPLACE WITH *capable people.*

on all fours (with) A moribund metaphor (see page 21). *analogous (to); equal (to); equivalent (to); identical (to).* ■ There's no circumstance in history that fits identically *on all fours* with subsequent circumstances. DELETE *on all fours.*

on an even keel A moribund metaphor (see page 21). *balanced; even; firm; fixed; stable; steadfast; steady; unfaltering; unwavering.*

on a ... note A wretched redundancy (see page 25). ■ *On a personal note,* I would not be all that appalled if my children were to perform well only 99 percent of the time. REPLACE WITH *Personally.*

on a roll A moribund metaphor (see page 21). *doing well; flourishing; prospering; succeeding; thriving.*

on a scale of 1 to 10 An infantile phrase (see page 20). The popularity of this phrase is further evidence of the delight some people have with numbers and counting and the distaste they have for words and concepts.

Of course, their fondness for numbers may not go much beyond the count of 10 — so too, perhaps, the number of words in their vocabulary.

■ *On a scale of 1 to 10,* how much does uncertainty surrounding laws and regulations in [COUNTRY] increase the risk of equities in that country? ■ *On a scale of 1 to 10,* just how good a student are you? ■ *On a scale of 1 to 10* (1 being the lowest, 10 being the highest) please rank the usefulness and intuitiveness of the website's navigational elements. ■ How would you rank your programming skills (in your best language) *on a scale of 1 to 10,* with 1 being lowest and 10 being highest? SEE ALSO *(for) a laugh; avid reader.*

on a shoestring A moribund metaphor (see page 21). *cheaply; economically; inexpensively.*

> He had been everywhere and he knew everything about traveling on a shoestring. — Laura Kalpakian, *Steps and Exes: A Novel of Family*

on automatic pilot A moribund metaphor (see page 21). *automatic; habitual; mechanical; routine.*

(come) on board A moribund metaphor (see page 21). ■ Some doctors are starting to *come on board,* but many haven't got a clue what's going on. REPLACE WITH *take alternative medicine seriously.*

on both sides (either side) of the equation A moribund metaphor (see page 21). ■ I believe there is little trust *on either side of the equation.* ■ Merrills tempers the super-cycle view to some extent however, by suggesting simply that there are risks *on either side of the equation.* ■ There is already a writer and producer attached to our first project, working *on both sides of the equation —* game and movie. ■ I have likewise seen the disconnect between people of color and law enforcement — the misconceptions *on both sides of the equation.*

on both sides of the fence A moribund metaphor (see page 21). *ambivalent; divided; indecisive; in doubt; irresolute; neutral; torn; uncertain; uncommitted; undecided; unsure.*

once bitten (burned), twice shy A popular prescription (see page 23).

once (and) for all A torpid term (see page 24). *conclusively; decisively; finally.* ■ Our broken judicial confirmation process must *be fixed once and for all.* REPLACE WITH *finally be fixed.*

once in a blue moon A moribund metaphor (see page 21). *hardly; infrequently; not often; occasionally; rarely; scarcely; seldom; sporadically; uncommonly.*

once in a lifetime (opportunity) A moribund metaphor (see page 21). *different; exceptional; extraordinary; incomparable; inimitable; matchless; nonpareil; notable; noteworthy; novel; odd; original; peculiar; peerless; rare; remarkable; singular; special; strange; uncommon; unequaled; unexampled; unique; unmatched; unparalleled; unrivaled;*
unusual; without equal. ■ This is a *once in a lifetime* opportunity. REPLACE WITH *singular.*

once upon a time An infantile phrase (see page 20).

> Once upon a time, in the rural South, there were farmhouses and farm wives who set tables where almost any passing stranger, a traveling preacher, a knife-grinder, an itinerant worker, was welcome to sit down to a hearty midday meal.
> — Truman Capote, *Music for Chameleons*

on cloud nine A moribund metaphor (see page 21). *blissful; blithe; buoyant; cheerful; delighted; ecstatic; elated; enraptured; euphoric; exalted; excited; exhilarated; exultant; gay; glad; gleeful; good-humored; happy; intoxicated; jolly; jovial; joyful; joyous; jubilant; merry; mirthful; overjoyed; pleased; rapturous; thrilled.*

on (our) doorstep A moribund metaphor (see page 21). *approaching; at hand; close; coming; expected; forthcoming; imminent; impending; looming; near; nearby.*

(the) one and only A wretched redundancy (see page 25). *one; only; sole.* ■ In the early days of any business, the *one and only* thing you understand is that the customer is king. REPLACE WITH *one* or *only.*

one and the same A wretched redundancy (see page 25). *identical; one; the same.* ■ Are you saying that submission and competition are *one and the same*? REPLACE WITH *the same.* ■ Some people believe that marketing and advertising are *one and the same*. REPLACE WITH *identical*.

on easy street A moribund metaphor (see page 21). *affluent; moneyed; opulent; prosperous; rich; wealthy; well-off; well-to-do.*

one big, happy family A suspect superlative (see page 24).

one foot in and one foot out A moribund metaphor (see page 21). *ambivalent; divided; indecisive; irresolute; torn; uncertain; uncommitted; undecided; unsure.*

(put) one foot in front of the other A moribund metaphor (see page 21).

one foot in the grave A moribund metaphor (see page 21). *decaying; declining; deteriorating; disintegrating; dying; ebbing; expiring; fading; failing; moribund; near death; sinking; very ill; waning.*

> She only used to marvel how so old and flabby a man, with one foot in the grave, came to be possessed of so fertile an imagination. — Esther Singer Kreitman, *Deborah*

one for the books A moribund metaphor (see page 21). *different; exceptional; extraordinary; incomparable; inimitable; matchless; nonpareil; notable; noteworthy; novel; odd; original; peculiar; peerless; remarkable; singular; special; strange; uncommon; unequaled; unexampled; unique; unmatched; unparalleled; unrivaled; unusual; without equal.*

one good turn deserves another A popular prescription (see page 23).

one hundred (100) percent An infantile phrase (see page 20). *absolutely; altogether; categorically; completely; entirely; fully; perfectly; positively; quite; roundly; thoroughly; totally; unconditionally; unreservedly; utterly; wholly.* ■ I agree with you *one hundred percent*. REPLACE WITH *unreservedly*.

one in a million A moribund metaphor (see page 21). *different; exceptional; extraordinary; incomparable; inimitable; matchless; nonpareil; notable; noteworthy; novel; odd; original; peculiar; peerless; remarkable; singular; special; strange; uncommon; unequaled; unexampled; unique; unmatched; unparalleled; unrivaled; unusual; without equal.* ■ One teacher commented that Philip is *one in a million*. REPLACE WITH *peerless*.

one man's meat is another man's poison A popular prescription (see page 23).

one man's trash is another man's treasure A popular prescription (see page 23).

one of a kind A torpid term (see page 24). *different; exceptional; extraordinary; incomparable; inimitable; matchless; nonpareil; notable; noteworthy; novel; odd; original; peculiar; peerless; remarkable; singular; special; strange; uncommon; unequaled; unexampled; unique; unmatched; unparalleled; unrivaled; unusual; without equal.*

one size fits all An infantile phrase (see page 20). *procrustean.* ■ We do not advocate a *one-size-fits-all* approach in making decisions about how students should be educated. REPLACE WITH *procrustean*.

one step at a time A popular prescription (see page 23).

(well) one thing led to another A grammatical gimmick (see page 19).

one-two punch A moribund metaphor (see page 21).

one-way street A moribund metaphor (see page 21).

one-way ticket to A moribund metaphor (see page 21).

on firm (solid) ground A moribund metaphor (see page 21). *firm; solid; sound; stable; sturdy.*

ongoing An overworked word (see page 22). *Ongoing* has superseded practically all of its synonyms. We have *ongoing basis; ongoing care; ongoing commitment; ongoing destruction; ongoing discussions; ongoing education; ongoing effort; ongoing investigation; ongoing plan; ongoing process; ongoing program; ongoing relationship; ongoing service; ongoing support;* and so many more.

Consider these synonyms: *ceaseless; constant; continual; continuing; continuous; endless; enduring; incessant; lifelong; long-lived; nonstop; progressing; unbroken; unceasing; unremitting.* ∎ With this new rehabilitation center, patients will no longer have to travel outside the community to receive the *ongoing* care they need. DELETE *ongoing*. ∎ Establishing paternity also may force more women into *ongoing* relationships with fathers who are abusive or violent. REPLACE WITH *lifelong*.

(up) on (her) high horse A moribund metaphor (see page 21). *arrogant; cavalier; condescending; contemptuous; despotic; dictatorial; disdainful; dogmatic; domineering; haughty; imperious; insolent; lofty; overbearing; overweening; patronizing; pompous; pretentious; scornful; self-important; supercilious; superior; vainglorious.*

on (its) last legs A moribund metaphor (see page 21). 1. *decaying; declining; deteriorating; disappearing; disintegrating; dying; ebbing; expiring; fading; failing; moribund; near death; sinking; vanishing; waning.* 2. *beat; bushed; debilitated; depleted; drained; drowsy; enervated; exhausted; fatigued; groggy; sapped; sleepy; sluggish; slumberous; somnolent; soporific; spent; tired; weary; worn out.* ∎ The battle for a smoke-free environment is hardly *on its last legs.* REPLACE WITH *moribund.*

(high) on (my) list of priorities A torpid term (see page 24).

> You were living with Amanda in New York and marriage wasn't high on your list of priorities, although on Amanda's it was. — Jay McInerney, *Bright Lights, Big City*

(the) only good (cat) is a dead (cat) A quack equation (see page 23).

only the strong survive A popular prescription (see page 23).

on (his) part A wretched redundancy (see page 25). *among; by; for; from; of; -s.* ∎ I think this is really irresponsible *on your part.* REPLACE WITH *of you.* ∎ I guess this is selfish *on my part.* REPLACE

WITH *of me*. ■ It's an incredible sacrifice *on her part and her family's part*. REPLACE WITH *from her and her family*. ■ This single one-page assignment made the point that Wilder's attitudes toward Native Americans and toward African Americans are problematic, and made it better than any amount of lecturing *on my part* could have done. REPLACE WITH *I*. SEE ALSO *on the part of*.

> All but Lucia, that is to say, whose throne had, quite unintentionally on Olga's part, been pulled smartly from under her, and her scepter flew in one direction, and her crown in another. — E. F. Benson, *Lucia in London*

on pins and needles A moribund metaphor (see page 21). *agitated; anxious; apprehensive; disquieted; distressed; disturbed; edgy; fretful; ill at ease; impatient; in suspense; nervous; on edge; restive; restless; troubled; uneasy; unquiet; unsettled; worried*. ■ Democrats — already *on pins and needles* over the release of Clinton's grand jury testimony — were scrambling yesterday with how to cope over the second tape. REPLACE WITH *uneasy*.

on (her) plate A moribund metaphor (see page 21). *awaiting (her); before (her); pending*.

on safe ground A moribund metaphor (see page 21). *guarded; protected; safe; secure; sheltered; shielded*.

on shaky ground A moribund metaphor (see page 21). *indefensible; shaky; unsound; unsustainable*.

on speaking terms A wretched redundancy (see page 25). *speaking*.

> For reasons they could no longer define clearly, Colin and Mary were not on speaking terms. — Ian McEwan, *The Comfort of Strangers*

(right) on target A moribund metaphor (see page 21). *accurate; correct; exact; irrefutable; precise; right; true*. ■ The Jan. 19 editorial identifying the inconsistent, but vociferous, antitax group as "the haters" is *right on target*. REPLACE WITH *irrefutable*.

on tenterhooks A moribund metaphor (see page 21). *agitated; anxious; apprehensive; disquieted; distressed; disturbed; edgy; fretful; ill at ease; impatient; in suspense; nervous; on edge; restive; restless; troubled; uneasy; unquiet; unsettled; worried*.

> Mick sat on tenterhooks, leaning forward in his chair, glaring at her almost hysterically: and whether he was more anxious out of vanity for her to say Yes! or whether he was more panic-stricken for fear she *should* say Yes! — who can tell? — D. H. Lawrence, *Lady Chatterley's Lover*

on the back burner A moribund metaphor (see page 21). *in abeyance; on hold; pending; suspended*.

on the ball A moribund metaphor (see page 21). 1. *alert; attentive; awake; aware; eagle-eyed; heedful; observant; vigilant; wakeful; watchful*. 2. *able; adroit; apt; astute; bright; brilliant; capable; clever; competent; discerning; effective;*

effectual; efficient; enlightened; insightful; intelligent; judicious; keen; knowledgeable; learned; logical; luminous; perceptive; perspicacious; quick; rational; reasonable; sagacious; sage; sapient; sensible; sharp; shrewd; smart; sound; understanding; wise.

on the basis of A wretched redundancy (see page 25). *after; based on; because of; by; due to; for; from; in; on; owing to; through; via; with.* ■ NABCO chooses material for this site *on the basis of* its timely and useful content. REPLACE WITH *based on.* ■ Exemption from IRB review and approval is determined *on the basis of* the risks associated with the study. REPLACE WITH *by.* ■ There shall be no discrimination against any individual *on the basis of* ethnic group, race, religion, gender, sexual orientation, age, or record of public offense. REPLACE WITH *because of.*

on the blink A moribund metaphor (see page 21). *broken; defective; in disrepair; not working; not functioning; out of order.*

on the brink of A moribund metaphor (see page 21). *about to; (very) close (to); (very) near (to).*

(right) on the button A moribund metaphor (see page 21). *accurate; correct; exact; irrefutable; precise; right; true.*

on the chopping block A moribund metaphor (see page 21). *at risk; endangered; imperiled; in danger; in jeopardy; in peril; in trouble; jeopardized.*

(ride) on the coattails of A moribund metaphor (see page 21).

on the cuff A moribund metaphor (see page 21). *on credit.*

on the cutting (leading) edge A moribund metaphor (see page 21). *first; forefront; foremost; leading; vanguard.*

on the day A torpid term (see page 24). *today;* delete. ■ He scored 16 points *on the day.* REPLACE WITH *today.* ■ The euro was flat *on the day* at 133.85 yen after it rose nearly 0.6 percent on Wednesday. REPLACE WITH *today.* ■ Even late in the fourth set, I was up a break to take it into a fifth set, and I just didn't quite play the big points as well as he did *on the day.* DELETE *on the day.*

Sports writers, known for mismanaging words, and financial analysts, known for mismanaging money, are especially fond of the expression *on the day.*

on the dot A moribund metaphor (see page 21). *on time; precisely; promptly; punctually.*

> They must be clean and neat about their persons and clothes and show up promptly — on the dot — and in good condition for the work every day. — Theodore Dreiser, *An American Tragedy*

on the drawing board A moribund metaphor (see page 21). ■ The university now has seven new schools *on the drawing board.*

on the edge of (their) seats A moribund metaphor (see page 21). *absorb; arrest; bewitch; captivate; charm; curious; divert; enchant; engage; engross; entertain; enthrall; entice; excite; fascinate; intrigue; rivet; spellbind; stimulate; tantalize.* ■

People are *on the edge of their seats* about this report. REPLACE WITH *fascinated*.

on the fast track A moribund metaphor (see page 21).

(sit) on the fence A moribund metaphor (see page 21). *ambivalent; divided; impartial; indecisive; irresolute; neutral; noncommittal; torn; uncertain; uncommitted; undecided; unsettled; unsure.*

on the firing line A moribund metaphor (see page 21).

on the fly A moribund metaphor (see page 21). *ad-lib; extemporize; improvise.*

on the fritz A moribund metaphor (see page 21). *broken; defective; in disrepair; not working; not functioning; out of order.*

on the front burner A moribund metaphor (see page 21). ■ While lawmakers continue their work, the governor is visiting schools across the state to keep the issue *on the front burner.*

on the front lines A moribund metaphor (see page 21).

on the go A moribund metaphor (see page 21). *absorbed; active; busy; employed; engaged; engrossed; going; immersed; involved; moving; occupied; preoccupied; wrapped up in.*

(hot) on the heels of A moribund metaphor (see page 21). *after; behind; ensuing; following; succeeding.* SEE ALSO *in the wake of.*

on the horizon A moribund metaphor (see page 21). *approaching; at hand;* *close; coming; expected; forthcoming; imminent; impending; near; nearby.*

(caught) on the horns of a dilemma A moribund metaphor (see page 21). *at risk; endangered; hard-pressed; imperiled; in a bind; in a dilemma; in a fix; in a jam; in a predicament; in a quandary; in danger; in difficulty; in jeopardy; in peril; in trouble; jeopardized.*

(take it) on the lam A moribund metaphor (see page 21). *abscond; clear out; decamp; depart; desert; disappear; escape; exit; flee; fly; go; go away; leave; move on; part; pull out; quit; retire; retreat; run away; take flight; take off; vacate; vanish; withdraw.*

on the level A torpid term (see page 24). *aboveboard; creditable; equitable; fair; genuine; honest; honorable; just; lawful; legitimate; open; proper; reputable; respectable; right; sincere; square; straightforward; truthful; upright; veracious; veridical.*

on the loose A torpid term (see page 24). *at large; at liberty; free; loose; unattached; unbound; unconfined; unrestrained; unrestricted.*

on the mark A moribund metaphor (see page 21). *accurate; correct; exact; precise; right; true.*

on the mend A torpid term (see page 24). *ameliorating; amending; coming round; convalescent; convalescing; gaining strength; getting better; healing; improving; looking up; meliorating; mending; rallying; recovering; recuperating; refreshing; renewing; reviving; strengthening.*

(right) on the money A moribund metaphor (see page 21). *accurate; correct; exact; fact; irrefutable; precise; right; true.* ■ I think it was *right on the money.* REPLACE WITH *irrefutable.*

on the nose A moribund metaphor (see page 21). *accurate; correct; exact; irrefutable; precise; right; true.*

> As usual, he gives me two hours with him, what will be two hours on the nose. — Binnie Kirshenbaum, *A Disturbance in One Place*

(on the) other side of the coin A moribund metaphor (see page 21). 1. *antithesis; contrary; converse; opposite; reverse.* 2. *but; in contrast; conversely; however; inversely; whereas; yet.* ■ *On the other side of the coin,* if you're astute you can occasionally buy them at big discounts. REPLACE WITH *But.*

on the part of A wretched redundancy (see page 25). *among; by; for; from; of; -s.* On the part of is a preposition phrase that apparently appeals to bombastic men and women who may not fully consider what they say, for they certainly do not consider how they say it. People use *on the part of* when they're too lazy to think of the proper, or even a better, word. This is a thoughtless person's phrase. ■ As a result, and following vigorous lobbying *on the part of* CFS victims, the disease is now called chronic fatigue immunodeficiency syndrome. REPLACE WITH *by.* ■ Open-ended questions require much more effort *on the part of* the person answering them. REPLACE WITH *from.* ■ There is some cultural resistance *on the part of* some U.S. racial and ethnic groups to govern-

ment-sponsored contraceptive programs. REPLACE WITH *from.* ■ *Misconduct on the part of the police* sometimes also violates the criminal law. REPLACE WITH *Police misconduct.* ■ It has also sometimes been attributed to an attitude *on the part of* health counselors that the poor are charity cases who should be satisfied with whatever they get since they are probably not paying for their own care. REPLACE WITH *among.* ■ If we are to get over the current crisis, *sacrifices on the part of everyone will have to be made.* REPLACE WITH *everyone will have to make sacrifices.* ■ Exhaustive questions reduce the *frustration on the part of the respondents.* REPLACE WITH *respondents' frustrations.* SEE ALSO *on (his) part.*

on the Q.T. A moribund metaphor (see page 21). *clandestinely; confidentially; covertly; furtively; mysteriously; in private; in secret; privately; quietly; secludedly; secretly; slyly; stealthily; surreptitiously; undercover.*

on the razor's edge A moribund metaphor (see page 21). *at risk; endangered; hard-pressed; imperiled; in danger; in difficulty; in jeopardy; in peril; in trouble; jeopardized.*

(start) on the right foot A moribund metaphor (see page 21). *auspiciously; favorably; positively; propitiously; well.*

on the right track A moribund metaphor (see page 21). *on target; on track.*

on the road A moribund metaphor (see page 21). *traveling.*

on the road to recovery A moribund metaphor (see page 21). *ameliorating; amending; coming round; convalescent; convalescing; feeling better; gaining strength; getting better; healing; improving; looking up; meliorating; mending; rallying; recovering; recuperating; refreshing; renewing; reviving; strengthening.* ■ His wife has been ill, but she's *on the road to recovery.* REPLACE WITH *improving.*

on the rocks A moribund metaphor (see page 21). *at risk; collapsing; endangered; failing; imperiled; in danger; in difficulty; in jeopardy; in peril; in trouble; jeopardized.* ■ Our marriage is *on the rocks.* REPLACE WITH *imperiled.*

on the ropes A moribund metaphor (see page 21). 1. *at risk; endangered; hard-pressed; imperiled; in danger; in difficulty; in jeopardy; in peril; in trouble; jeopardized.* 2. *defenseless; helpless; impotent; powerless.*

on the same page A moribund metaphor (see page 21). *agree; concur; feel similarly; harmonize; (be) in accord; (be) in agreement; (be) in harmony; like-minded; match; mesh; think alike. On the same page* is spoken or written by pawns and puppets who cannot think for themselves, who rely on others for how they should speak and what they should think; who prize the ease of agreement more than they do the entanglement of dissent; who turn few pages and read fewer books.
■ I believe we're all *on the same page.* REPLACE WITH *thinking alike.* ■ It gives us direction — everybody is *on the same page,* everybody knows where we want to get and how we want to get there. REPLACE WITH *in harmony.* ■ He usual-

ly gets his way, but we're usually *on the same page.* REPLACE WITH *in agreement.*

> He figured since Franklin hadn't responded to the idea with a gasp or an indignant speech they were on the same page. — Bill Fitzhugh, *Fender Benders*

on the same wavelength A moribund metaphor (see page 21). *agree; concur; feel similarly; harmonize; (be) in accord; (be) in agreement; (be) in harmony; like-minded; match; mesh; think alike.*

> He was the typical teacher on the same wavelength as his kids, since he himself didn't look a day over thirty, and the best part of it was that he wasn't some half-ass .... — Zoe Valdes, *Dear First Love*

on the ... side A wretched redundancy (see page 25). ■ Tuesday will be *on the chilly side.* REPLACE WITH *chilly.* ■ She is *on the thin side.* REPLACE WITH *thin.* ■ That means the 550,000 estimate is probably *on the low side.* REPLACE WITH *low.*

on the sly A torpid term (see page 24). *clandestinely; confidentially; covertly; furtively; mysteriously; in private; in secret; privately; quietly; secludedly; secretly; slyly; stealthily; surreptitiously; undercover.*

on the spot A torpid term (see page 24). 1. *at once; directly; forthwith; immediately; instantly; momentarily; promptly; right away; straightaway; summarily; without delay.* 2. *at risk; endangered; hard-pressed; imperiled; in danger; in difficulty; in jeopardy; in peril; in trouble; jeopardized.*

on the spur of the moment A wretched redundancy (see page 25). *impetuously; impulsively; spontaneously; suddenly; unexpectedly; without warning.*

on the table A moribund metaphor (see page 21). *before us; being considered; being discussed; considerable; discussable; under discussion.* Whoever speaks this expression speaks words scarcely worth hearing. Whoever writes this expression writes words scarcely worth reading. There are words that stir, words that persuade, words that compel; the expression *on the table* is not and is never among them.

■ A healthy dialog on value systems when there is no pressing issue *on the table* may help clear the air. REPLACE WITH *before us.* ■ There is nothing that is not *on the table.* REPLACE WITH *being considered.* ■ The White House could withdraw his nomination but say that option isn't *on the table.* REPLACE WITH *being discussed.*

(out) on the town A moribund metaphor (see page 21). *be merry; carouse; carry on; celebrate; debauch; disport; frolic; party; play; revel; riot; roister; rollick; romp; skylark.*

on the up-and-up A torpid term (see page 24). *aboveboard; creditable; equitable; fair; honest; honorable; just; lawful; legitimate; open; proper; reputable; respectable; right; sincere; square; straightforward; upright; veracious; veridical.*

on the warpath A moribund metaphor (see page 21). 1. *angry; bad-tempered; bilious; cantankerous; choleric; churlish; crabby; cranky; cross; curmudgeonly; disagreeable; dyspeptic; grouchy; gruff; grumpy; ill-humored; ill-tempered; irasci-*ble; *irritable; mad; peevish; petulant; quarrelsome; riled; roiled; short-tempered; splenetic; surly; testy; vexed.* 2. *aggressive; antagonistic; arguing; argumentative; battling; bellicose; belligerent; bickering; brawling; clashing; combative; contentious; fighting; militant; pugnacious; quarrelsome; querulous; squabbling; truculent; warlike; wrangling.*

on the wings of the wind A moribund metaphor (see page 21). *abruptly; apace; at once; briskly; directly; expeditiously; fast; forthwith; hastily; hurriedly; immediately; instantaneously; instantly; posthaste; promptly; quickly; rapidly; rashly; right away; speedily; straightaway; swiftly; wingedly.*

(start) on the wrong foot A moribund metaphor (see page 21). *adversely; inauspiciously; negatively; unfavorably; unpropitiously.*

on the wrong track A moribund metaphor (see page 21). *amiss; astray; deceived; deluded; erring; erroneous; fallacious; false; faulty; inaccurate; incorrect; in error; misguided; misinformed; mislead; mistaken; not correct; not right; wrong.*

(skate) on thin ice A moribund metaphor (see page 21). *chance; dare; endanger; gamble; hazard; imperil; jeopardize; make bold; peril; risk; venture.*

(keep) on (his) toes A moribund metaphor (see page 21). *(be) alert; (be) attentive; (be) awake; (be) aware; (be) heedful; (be) vigilant; (be) wakeful.*

(sitting) on top of the world A moribund metaphor (see page 21). 1. *advantageous; auspicious; blessed; charmed;*

enchanted; favored; felicitous; flourishing; fortuitous; fortunate; golden; in luck; lucky; propitious; prosperous; successful; thriving. 2. *blissful; blithe; buoyant; cheerful; delighted; ecstatic; elated; enraptured; euphoric; exalted; excited; exhilarated; exultant; gay; glad; gleeful; good-humored; happy; intoxicated; jolly; jovial; joyful; joyous; jubilant; merry; mirthful; overjoyed; pleased; rapturous; thrilled.*

onward and upward An inescapable pair (see page 20).

open and aboveboard A moribund metaphor (see page 21). *aboveboard; creditable; equitable; fair; honest; honorable; just; lawful; legitimate; open; proper; reputable; respectable; right; square; straightforward; upright; veracious; veridical.*

(an) open-and-shut case A moribund metaphor (see page 21). *apparent; clear; evident; open; plain; straightforward; unambiguous; uncomplex; uncomplicated.*

open (up) a Pandora's box A moribund metaphor (see page 21).

(an) open book A moribund metaphor (see page 21). 1. *apparent; clear; clear-cut; crystalline; evident; explicit; limpid; lucid; manifest; obvious; open; patent; pellucid; plain; translucent; transparent; unambiguous; uncomplex; uncomplicated; understandable; unequivocal; unmistakable.* 2. *aboveboard; artless; blunt; candid; direct; forthright; frank; genuine; guileless; honest; ingenuous; naive; sincere; straightforward; truthful; veracious; veridical.*

(the) opening (latest) salvo A moribund metaphor (see page 21).

(a) (an) (wide) open question A wretched redundancy (see page 25). *a question; debatable; disputable; moot; open; questionable; uncertain; unclear; undecided; undetermined; unknown; unsettled; unsure.* ■ Whether it's still possible for us to complete the project by next season is *an open question* at this point. REPLACE WITH *questionable.*

open the door for (on; to) A moribund metaphor (see page 21). *bring about; cause; create; effect; generate; give rise to; inaugurate; initiate; introduce; lead to; occasion; produce; provoke; result in; usher in.* ■ This breakthrough could *open the door to* a wide range of new varieties of important crops. REPLACE WITH *result in.* ■ Human embryo cells have been isolated and grown in the test tube for the first time, a development that could *open the door to* new drug therapies. REPLACE WITH *lead to.*

open the floodgates A moribund metaphor (see page 21).

operative A torpid term (see page 24). ■ The *operative* philosophy is spelled out early on: Winning is the most important thing in life.

opportunity knocks only once A popular prescription (see page 23).

(as) opposed to what? An infantile phrase (see page 20). SEE ALSO *(as) compared to what?; everything's (it's all) relative.*

opposites attract A popular prescription (see page 23).

or anything A grammatical gimmick (see page 19). ■ I didn't go beat her up, *or anything.* DELETE *or anything.* ■ Not to be rude *or anything*, but I don't think we should talk to each other. DELETE *or anything.* SEE ALSO *or anything like that.*

or anything like that A grammatical gimmick (see page 19). ■ He wasn't my first boyfriend *or anything like that.* DELETE *or anything like that.* ■ He didn't go out and say, "Who goes there?" *or anything like that.* DELETE *or anything like that.* ■ I really apologize if I was inappropriate or upset you *or anything like that.* DELETE *or anything like that.* SEE ALSO *or anything.*

(an) orgy of A moribund metaphor (see page 21). SEE ALSO *a barrage of.*

or (a; the) lack thereof A torpid term (see page 24). ■ He was ousted because the majority of voters believe he didn't do a good job as mayor — not because of his skin color, but because of his merit *or lack thereof.*

or something A grammatical gimmick (see page 19). As there are phrases that help us begin sentences, like *I'll tell you (something)*, so there are phrases that help us end them. *Or something, or something like that, or something or other* extricate us from having to conclude our thoughts clearly. Said as a person's thoughts end, but before his words do, *or something*, like its many relations, is a thoughtless phrase that reminds us only of our trembling humanity.
  ■ This is like something I'd wear in third grade, *or something.* DELETE *or something.* ■ It makes you mad when they make them sound like they're vicious people — that if you walk the street, they're going to grab you *or something.* DELETE *or something.* SEE ALSO *or something like that; or something or other.*

or something like that A grammatical gimmick (see page 19). ■ Why couldn't they have shot him in his arm or leg *or something like that?* DELETE *or something like that.* SEE ALSO *or something; or something or other.*

or something or other A grammatical gimmick (see page 19). ■ We might go to the movies *or something or other.* DELETE *or something or other.* SEE ALSO *or something; or something like that.*

or what A grammatical gimmick (see page 19). ■ Did you see an opportunity for escape, or plan it for a long time, *or what?* DELETE *or what.* ■ Was he being vulgar *or what?* DELETE *or what.* ■ Did you make enough money so you can retire *or what?* REPLACE WITH *or not.*

or whatever A grammatical gimmick (see page 19). ■ They say he corrupted my mind *or whatever.* DELETE *or whatever.* ■ Is it a good thing, is it a bad thing, is it useless, *or whatever?* DELETE *or whatever.* ■ She just wants the extra attention, *or whatever.* DELETE *or whatever.* ■ You can call this arrogance or way too much self-assurance *or whatever.* DELETE *or whatever.* ■ The percent remembered is the same whether the audience is a business audience, a college audience, a PTA audience, *or whatever.* DELETE *or whatever.*

or words to that effect A grammatical gimmick (see page 19).

(an) ounce of prevention A moribund metaphor (see page 21).

(an) ounce of prevention is worth a pound of cure A popular prescription (see page 23).

out and out A torpid term (see page 24). *absolute; compleat; complete; consummate; deadly; outright; perfect; thorough; thoroughgoing; total; unmitigated; unqualified; utter.*

out at the elbows A moribund metaphor (see page 21). 1. *disheveled; dowdy; frowzy; messy; ragged; run-down; seedy; shabby; slipshod; sloppy; slovenly; tattered; threadbare; unkempt; untidy; worn.* 2. *bankrupt; broke; destitute; distressed; impecunious; impoverished; indigent; insolvent; needy; penniless; poor; poverty-stricken; underprivileged.*

out for blood A moribund metaphor (see page 21). *revengeful; ruthless; vengeful; vindictive.*

out in left field A moribund metaphor (see page 21). 1. *amiss; astray; confused; deceived; deluded; erring; erroneous; fallacious; false; faulty; inaccurate; incorrect; in error; misguided; misinformed; mislead; mistaken; not correct; not right; uninformed; wrong.* 2. *ignorant; incognizant; insensible; nescient; unacquainted; unadvised; unapprised; unaware; unenlightened; unfamiliar; unintelligent; unknowing; unschooled; untaught; unversed.* ■ On this issue, feminists are truly *out in left field.* REPLACE WITH *misguided.*

(they're) out in the cold A moribund metaphor (see page 21). *abandoned; alone; assailable; attackable; defenseless; deserted; exposed; forsaken; obnoxious; penetrable; pregnable; stranded; undefended; unguarded; unprotected; unshielded; vulnerable.*

out in the sun too much A moribund metaphor (see page 21). *bewildered; con-*founded; confused; dazed; mixed up; muddled; perplexed.*

out like a light An insipid simile. 1. *asleep; dozing; napping; sleeping.* 2. *anesthetized; benumbed; comatose; insensate; insensible; insentient; oblivious; senseless; soporiferous; soporific; stuporous; unconscious.*

out of a clear blue sky A moribund metaphor (see page 21). *by surprise; suddenly; unexpectedly; without warning.*

out of circulation A moribund metaphor (see page 21). 1. *broken; defective; in disrepair; not working; not functioning; out of order.* 2. *afflicted; ailing; diseased; ill; indisposed; infirm; not (feeling) well; sick; sickly; suffering; unhealthy; unsound; unwell; valetudinarian.*

out of commission A moribund metaphor (see page 21). 1. *broken; defective; in disrepair; not working; not functioning; out of order.* 2. *afflicted; ailing; diseased; ill; indisposed; infirm; not (feeling) well; sick; sickly; suffering; unhealthy; unsound; unwell; valetudinarian.*

out of gas A moribund metaphor (see page 21). *beat; bushed; debilitated; depleted; drained; drowsy; enervated; exhausted; fatigued; groggy; sapped; sleepy; sluggish; slumberous; somnolent; soporific; spent; tired; weary; worn out.*

out of harm's way A moribund metaphor (see page 21). *guarded; protected; safe; secure; sheltered; shielded; undamaged; unharmed; unhurt; unscathed.*

out of it A moribund metaphor (see page 21). *ignorant; incognizant; insensi-*

ble; nescient; unacquainted; unadvised; unapprised; unaware; unenlightened; unfamiliar; uninformed; unintelligent; unknowing; unschooled; untaught; unversed.

out of kilter A moribund metaphor (see page 21). 1. *askew; awry; cockeyed; misaligned; skewed.* 2. *shaky; unbalanced; unsettled; unsound; unstable; wobbly.* 3. *broken; defective; in disrepair; not working; not functioning; out of order.*

In a further aside, I should just like to add here that I have observed in my sixty-four years that passion both erodes and enhances character in equal measure, and not slowly but instantly, and in such a manner that what is left is not in balance but is thrown desperately out of kilter in both directions. — Anita Shreve, *All He Ever Wanted*

out of line A moribund metaphor (see page 21).
1. *improper; inappropriate; inapt; indecorous; unbefitting; uncalled for; unfit; unfitting; unsuitable; unsuited.* 2. *boisterous; contrary; contumacious; disobedient; disorderly; fractious; insubordinate; misbehaving; obstreperous; rebellious; recalcitrant; refractory; rowdy; uncontrolled; undisciplined; unruly.*

out of reach A moribund metaphor (see page 21). 1. *inaccessible; remote; unapproachable; unreachable.* 2. *impossible; impracticable; improbable; unfeasible; unlikely; unworkable.*

out of sorts A moribund metaphor (see page 21). *angry; annoyed; cheerless; cross; dejected; depressed; despondent; discour-*

aged; dispirited; displeased; downcast; enraged; furious; gloomy; glum; grouchy; irate; irritated; mad; morose; peevish; riled; roiled; sad; testy; troubled; uneasy; unhappy; upset; vexed; worried.

out of sync A moribund metaphor (see page 21). 1. *askew; awry; cockeyed; misaligned; skewed.* 2. *shaky; unbalanced; unsettled; unsound; unstable; wobbly.* 3. *broken; defective; in disrepair; not working; not functioning; out of order.*

out of the blue A moribund metaphor (see page 21). *by surprise; suddenly; unexpectedly; without warning.*

out of the frying pan and into the fire A moribund metaphor (see page 21). *aggravate; complicate; exacerbate; heighten; increase; intensify; irritate; make worse; worsen.*

out of the game A moribund metaphor (see page 21).

out of the realm of possibility A wretched redundancy (see page 25). *implausible; imponderable; impossible; impracticable; inconceivable; infeasible; not likely; unbelievable; unconjecturable; unimaginable; unsupposable; unthinkable; unworkable.* ■ It's not *out of the realm of possibility* that he wants to embarrass the president. REPLACE WITH *unthinkable.*

out of the running A moribund metaphor (see page 21). *noncontender; not competing; not contending.*

out of the woods A moribund metaphor (see page 21). *guarded; protected; safe; secure; sheltered; shielded; undamaged; unharmed; unhurt; unscathed.*

out of thin air A moribund metaphor (see page 21).

out of this world A moribund metaphor (see page 21). *consummate; distinguished; eminent; excellent; exceptional; exemplary; exquisite; extraordinary; fabulous; fantastic; flawless; grand; great; ideal; illustrious; magnificent; marvelous; matchless; nonpareil; perfect; preeminent; remarkable; splendid; superb; superior; superlative; supreme; terrific; transcendent; tremendous; wonderful; wondrous.*

out of whack A moribund metaphor (see page 21). 1. *askew; awry; cockeyed; misaligned; skewed.* 2. *shaky; unbalanced; unsettled; unsound; unstable; wobbly.* 3. *broken; defective; in disrepair; not working; not functioning; out of order.*

(create) out of (the) whole cloth A moribund metaphor (see page 21). *fabricated; fake; false; falsified; fictional; fictitious; forged; invented; made-up; untrue.*

> She considered that she had created this man out of whole cloth, had thought him up, and she was sure that she could do a better job if she had to do it again. — John Steinbeck, *The Moon Is Down*

(go) out on a limb A moribund metaphor (see page 21). 1. *at risk; endangered; hard-pressed; imperiled; in a bind; in a dilemma; in a fix; in a jam; in a predicament; in a quandary; in danger; in difficulty; in jeopardy; in peril; in trouble; jeopardized.* 2. *abandoned; alone; assailable; attackable; defenseless; deserted; exposed; forsaken; obnoxious; penetrable; pregnable; stranded; undefended;*

unguarded; unprotected; unshielded; vulnerable. 3. *be adventuresome; be adventurous; be bold; be daring.*

output A torpid term (see page 24). SEE ALSO *(the) bottom line; feedback; input; interface; parameters.*

out the window A moribund metaphor (see page 21). 1. *abandoned; discarded; dismissed; jettisoned; rejected; repudiated; thrown out; tossed out.* 2. *dead; disappeared; dissolved; dispersed; evaporated; finished; forfeited; gone; inapplicable; inappropriate; inoperative; insignificant; irrelevant; lost; no longer applicable (apply); over; passed; scattered; unimportant; vanished.* ■ It's just that old rules are *out the window*, like most of last year's assumptions about Europe. REPLACE WITH *inapplicable.* ■ It's 1999 in America, a land where common sense went *out the window* long ago. REPLACE WITH *was jettisoned.*

out to lunch A moribund metaphor (see page 21). 1. *absent-minded; absorbed; abstracted; bemused; daydreaming; distrait; dreamy; faraway; lost; preoccupied.* 2. *forgetful; heedless; inattentive; lethean; neglectful; oblivious; unmindful.* 3. *ignorant; incognizant; insensible; nescient; unacquainted; unadvised; unapprised; unaware; unenlightened; unfamiliar; unintelligent; unknowing; unschooled; untaught; unversed.* 4. *amiss; astray; confused; deceived; deluded; erring; erroneous; fallacious; false; faulty; inaccurate; incorrect; in error; misguided; misinformed; mislead; mistaken; not correct; not right; uninformed; wrong.*

(put) out to pasture A moribund metaphor (see page 21). *discharge; dismiss; fire; lay off; let go; release; retire;*

sack; set aside; shelve. ■ Motors Inc. said Joe will be *put out to pasture* when it introduces next year's lineup of vehicles. REPLACE WITH *retired.*

over a barrel A moribund metaphor (see page 21). *defenseless; helpless; impotent; powerless.*

over and done with A wretched redundancy (see page 25). *completed; concluded; done; ended; finished; over; passed; through.* ■ But in reality, it is the same old story, one we'd like to think of as *over and done with.* REPLACE WITH *concluded.*

over (my) dead body A moribund metaphor (see page 21). *at no time; by no means; in no way; never; no; not; not at all; not ever; not in any way; not in the least*

overplay (his) hand A moribund metaphor (see page 21).

(go) over the edge A moribund metaphor (see page 21). *batty; cracked; crazy; daft; demented; deranged; fey; foolish; goofy; insane; lunatic; mad; maniacal; neurotic; nuts; nutty; psychotic; raving; silly; squirrelly; touched; unbalanced; unhinged; unsound; wacky; zany.*

over the hill A moribund metaphor (see page 21). *aged; aging; ancient; antediluvian; antique; archaic; elderly; hoary; hoary-headed; old; patriarchal; prehistoric; seasoned; superannuated; venerable.*

over the moon A moribund metaphor (see page 21). *blissful; blithe; buoyant; cheerful; delighted; ecstatic; elated; enraptured; euphoric; exalted; excited; exhilarated; exultant; gay; glad; gleeful; good-*

humored; happy; intoxicated; jolly; jovial; joyful; joyous; jubilant; merry; mirthful; overjoyed; pleased; rapturous; thrilled.

Over breakfast, expecting her to be over the moon, Paul had told her that she could give her notice in at the nursery, he'd fix her up a half share in a smart little business with the girlfriend of a friend of his. — Elizabeth Young, *Asking for Trouble*

over the transom A moribund metaphor (see page 21).

overworked and understaffed An inescapable pair (see page 20).

owing to the fact that A wretched redundancy (see page 25). *because; considering; for; in that; since.* ■ *Owing to the fact that* many companies are members of more than one EDI system, it is helpful if they all change in recognizable ways. REPLACE WITH *Since.* SEE ALSO *attributable to the fact that; due to the fact that.*

In the past she and I had seldom spoken to each other, owing to the fact that her 'one remaining joy' — her charming little Karl — had never succeeded in kindling into flame those sparks of maternity which are supposed to grow in great numbers upon the altar of every respectable female heart .... — Katherine Mansfield, *In a German Pension*

P

pack a punch (wallop) A moribund metaphor (see page 21). *cogent; convincing; dynamic; effective; effectual; emotional; energetic; ferocious; fierce; forceful; formidable; gripping; hard-hitting; herculean; impassioned; inspiring; intense; lively; mighty; moving; passionate; persuasive; potent; powerful; strong; vehement; vigorous; vital.* ■ No doubt hurricane Bonnie is still *packing a punch*. REPLACE WITH *mighty*.

packed in (trapped) like sardines (in a can) An insipid simile. *abounding; brimful; brimming; bursting; chock-full; congested; crammed; crowded; dense; filled; full; gorged; jammed; jam-packed; overcrowded; overfilled; overflowing; packed; replete; saturated; stuffed.*

> She gave me a rather disparaging look and took out a tin of Golden Virginia, which she opened to reveal a layer of tiny neat joints packed in like sardines. — Kate Atkinson, *Emotionally Weird*

pack to the gills A moribund metaphor (see page 21). *abounding; brimful; brimming; bursting; chock-full; congested; crammed; crowded; dense; filled; full; gorged; jammed; jam-packed; overcrowded; overfilled; overflowing; packed; replete; saturated; stuffed; swarming; teeming.* ■ Maybe we'll visit the Museum of Science, which will surely be *packed to the gills* and most unpleasant. REPLACE WITH *overcrowded*.

pack to the rafters A moribund metaphor (see page 21). *abounding; brimful; brimming; bursting; chock-full; congested; crammed; crowded; dense; filled; full; gorged; jammed; jam-packed; overcrowded; overfilled; overflowing; packed; replete; saturated; stuffed; swarming; teeming.*

pack up and leave A moribund metaphor (see page 21). *abscond; clear out; decamp; depart; desert; disappear; escape; exit; flee; fly; go; go away; leave; move on; part; pull out; quit; retire; retreat; run away; take flight; take off; vacate; vanish; withdraw.*

paddle (my) own canoe A moribund metaphor (see page 21). *be autonomous; be free; be independent; be self-reliant; be self-sufficient.* ■ I like to *paddle my own canoe* in life, but when you have holes in your canoe, it's hard to know what to do. REPLACE WITH *be self-reliant*.

pain and suffering An inescapable pair (see page 20). *agony; anguish; distress; grief; misery; pain; suffering; torment; worry.*

painfully shy An inescapable pair (see page 20). *afraid; apprehensive; bashful; coy; demure; diffident; distant; fearful; humble; introverted; meek; modest; pavid; quiet; reserved; reticent; retiring; sheepish; shrinking; shy; timid; timorous; tremulous; unassuming; unobtrusive; unsociable; unsocial; withdrawn.*

(a) pain in the ass (butt; rear) A moribund metaphor (see page 21). *affliction; annoyance; bane; bother; burden; curse; difficulty; inconvenience; irritant; irritation; load; nuisance; ordeal; pain; pest; plague; problem; torment; tribulation; trouble; vexation; weight; worry.*

(a) pain in the neck A moribund metaphor (see page 21). *affliction; annoyance; bane; bother; burden; curse; difficulty; inconvenience; irritant; irritation; load; nuisance; ordeal; pain; pest; plague; problem; torment; tribulation; trouble; vexation; weight; worry.*

> The do-gooder, the bleeding heart, the concerned citizen, the militant reformer: what a pain in the neck they are: always making us feel guilty about something. — Edward Abbey, *The Fool's Progress: An Honest Novel*

paint a (rosy) picture of A moribund metaphor (see page 21). *delineate; demonstrate; depict; describe; document; draw; evince; illustrate; indicate; paint; picture; portray; present; report; represent; reveal; show.* ■ The document will *paint a picture of* the nation's worsening financial system and warn that many large banks are near insolvency. REPLACE WITH *describe.* ■ Together, they *paint a picture of* hard times ahead. REPLACE WITH *portray.*

paint (himself) into a corner A moribund metaphor (see page 21). *at bay; catch; corner; enmesh; ensnare; entangle; entrap; net; snare; trap.*

paint the town red A moribund metaphor (see page 21). *be merry; carouse; carry on; celebrate; debauch; disport; frolic; party; play; revel; riot; roister; rollick; romp; skylark.*

paint with a broad brush A moribund metaphor (see page 21). *generalize; universalize.*

pair of (two) twins A wretched redundancy (see page 25). *twins.* ■ There were *two twins* at the mall who came up to him and asked him out. DELETE *two.*

(as) pale as death An insipid simile. *anemic; ashen; blanched; bloodless; cadaverous; colorless; deathlike; doughy; haggard; lusterless; pale; pallid; pasty; peaked; sallow; sickly; wan; whitish.*

> Her skin had turned as pale as death, after she'd been stuck in that blasted compartment of hers with a shade that only went up halfway, while the train rattled and shook, rattled and shook, day after day after day across the country. — John Sedgwick, *The Education of Mrs. Bemis*

(as) pale as a ghost An insipid simile. *anemic; ashen; blanched; bloodless; cadaverous; colorless; deathlike; doughy; haggard; lusterless; pale; pallid; pasty; peaked; sallow; sickly; wan; whitish.*

parameter An overworked word (see page 22). 1. *boundary; guideline; guidepost; limit; limitation; perimeter.* 2. *characteristic; factor.* ■ At this time, potential funding *parameters* may change in a variety of ways. REPLACE WITH *characteristics.* ■ We would like to send you our most recent catalog to see if any of our books fit within your reviewing *parameters.* REPLACE WITH *guidelines.* SEE ALSO *(the) bottom line; feedback; input; interface; output.*

pardon my French An infantile phrase (see page 20).

par excellence A foreign phrase (see page 19). *incomparable; preeminent.*

269

par for the course A moribund metaphor (see page 21). The people who say *par for the course* are *average; common; commonplace; customary; everyday; mediocre; middling; normal; ordinary; quotidian; regular; routine; standard; typical; uneventful; unexceptional; unremarkable; usual* users of the English language.

Though sports and even the word *sports* may make us imagine action and excitement, sports metaphors are among the most prosaic expressions available to us. Those who use them are precisely as dull and uninspired as are their words. ■ That is *par for the course* for foreign businesses here, which have descended upon the Soviet Union much as they descended upon China. REPLACE WITH *normal.* ■ It's *par for the course* for this administration to blame all of its troubles on someone else. REPLACE WITH *customary.*

> I'd heard of cleaning ladies with filthy houses, and of divorced marriage counselors, so maybe this was par for the course. — Susan Coll, *Rockville Pike*

part and parcel An inescapable pair (see page 20). *component; element; factor; part; portion.*

parting is such sweet sorrow A popular prescription (see page 23).

parting of the ways A moribund metaphor (see page 21). *altercation; argument; conflict; disagreement; discord; disputation; dispute; feud; fight; misunderstanding; quarrel; rift; row; spat; squabble.*

partner in crime A moribund metaphor (see page 21). *abettor; accessory; accomplice; affiliate; ally; assistant; associate; co-conspirator; cohort; collaborator; colleague; compatriot; compeer; comrade; confederate; consort; co-worker; crony; partner; peer.*

part of the landscape A moribund metaphor (see page 21). *average; common; conventional; customary; everyday; expected; familiar; habitual; natural; normal; ordinary; regular; routine; standard; usual; traditional; typical.* ■ In the Bay Area, bad traffic's *part of the landscape.* REPLACE WITH *expected.* ■ When does an exotic species become *part of the landscape*? REPLACE WITH *familiar.*

pass the buck A moribund metaphor (see page 21). *ascribe; assign; attribute; impute.*

pass the time of day A moribund metaphor (see page 21). *babble; blab; cackle; chaffer; chat; chitchat; chatter; confabulate; converse; gossip; jabber; palaver; prate; prattle; rattle; talk.*

pass with flying colors A moribund metaphor (see page 21). *ace; do well; excel; shine.*

past experience A wretched redundancy (see page 25). *experience.* ■ I know from *past experience* that a lot of you are not going to like what I have to say. DELETE *past.*

past history A wretched redundancy (see page 25). *history.* ■ We did not anticipate that the town would attempt to live off of its *past history.* DELETE *past.*

past (his) prime A torpid term (see page 24). *aged; aging; ancient; antediluvian; antique; archaic; elderly; hoary; hoary-headed; old; patriarchal; prehistoric; seasoned; superannuated; venerable.*

past the point of no return A moribund metaphor (see page 21).

> Until that last time, when I knew I had to go, when I knew that if I told my son I'd broken my nose, blacked my eyes, split my lip, by walking into the dining-room door in the dark, that I would have gone past some point of no return. — Anna Quindlen, *Black and Blue*

(as) patient as Job An insipid simile. *accepting; accommodating; acquiescent; complacent; complaisant; compliant; cowed; deferential; docile; dutiful; easy; forbearing; gentle; humble; long-suffering; meek; mild; obedient; passive; patient; prostrate; quiet; reserved; resigned; stoical; submissive; subservient; timid; tolerant; tractable; unassuming; uncomplaining; yielding.*

pat on the back A moribund metaphor (see page 21). *acclaim; accolade; acknowledgment; applause; appreciation; approval; compliment; congratulation; felicitation; homage; honor; plaudits; praise; recognition; tribute.* ■ The selections are a nice *pat on the back* for our talented staff around the world. REPLACE WITH *compliment.* ■ To me, it's *a pat on the back* for hard work well done. REPLACE WITH *an acknowledgment.*

pat (myself) on the back A moribund metaphor (see page 21). *acclaim; applaud; celebrate; cheer; commend; compliment; congratulate; extol; flatter; hail; honor; laud; plume; praise; puff; salute; self-congratulate.* ■ After *patting himself on the back*, he incidentally points out that many other people may have had something to do with it. REPLACE WITH *congratulating himself.*

pave the way (for) A moribund metaphor (see page 21). 1. *arrange; groom; make ready; plan; prepare; prime; ready.* 2. *bring about; cause; create; effect; generate; give rise to; inaugurate; initiate; introduce; lead to; occasion; produce; provoke; result in; usher in.* ■ Chartering all schools *paves the way* for a new way to organize public education. REPLACE WITH *prepares.*

pay (their) debt to society A moribund metaphor (see page 21).

pay (my) dues A moribund metaphor (see page 21).

pay the fiddler (piper) A moribund metaphor (see page 21). *pay; suffer.*

pay the price A moribund metaphor (see page 21). *pay; suffer.*

pay the ultimate price Like other euphemisms, other ludicrous expressions for death and dying, *pay the ultimate price* — for *be executed; be killed; be murdered; die* — diminishes death, often an avenging, merciless death. There is no reverence for the dead, or for death, in this dimwitted expression.

pay through the nose A moribund metaphor (see page 21). *costly; dear; excessive; exorbitant; expensive; high-priced.*

peace and harmony A wretched redundancy (see page 25). *harmony; peace.* ■ I want there to be *peace and harmony* between us. REPLACE WITH *harmony* or *peace.*

> When Ada reached the story's conclusion, and the old lovers after long years together in peace and harmony had turned to oak and linden, it was full dark. — Charles Frazier, *Cold Mountain*

peace and quiet An inescapable pair (see page 20). *calm; calmness; composure; equanimity; peace; peacefulness; poise; quiet; quietude; repose; rest; serenity; silence; stillness; tranquility.*

peaches and cream (complexion) A moribund metaphor (see page 21).

pea in (my) shoe A moribund metaphor (see page 21). *affliction; annoyance; bane; bother; burden; curse; difficulty; inconvenience; irritant; irritation; load; nuisance; ordeal; pain; pest; plague; problem; torment; tribulation; trouble; vexation; weight; worry.*

peaks and valleys A moribund metaphor (see page 21). *alterations; changes; erraticism; fluctuations; fortuitousness; inconstancies; shifts; uncertainties; vacillations; variations; vicissitudes.*

peanut gallery An infantile phrase (see page 20). *audience; spectators; viewers.*

pearls of wisdom A moribund metaphor (see page 21). *acumen; astuteness; erudition; insight; intelligence; perspicacity; sagacity; wisdom.* ■ In addition to the $50,000 fee, his *pearls of wisdom* will cost three first-class airplane tickets. REPLACE WITH *insights.*

pearly whites A moribund metaphor (see page 21). *teeth.*

> Then I saw him out of the corner of my eye, a little flash of pearly whites, a curl of chestnut hair, jawbones that could cut glass, and an entourage bigger than the crowd at my last birthday party. — Eric Garcia, *Cassandra French's Finishing School for Boys*

pencil pusher A moribund metaphor (see page 21). 1. *assistant; clerk; office worker; recorder; scribe; secretary; typist.* 2. *drudge; menial; scullion; toiler.*

(the) pen is mightier than the sword A moribund metaphor (see page 21).

penny pinching A moribund metaphor (see page 21). *cheap; economical; frugal; miserly; niggardly; parsimonious; stingy; thrifty.*

(a) penny saved is a penny earned A popular prescription (see page 23).

people are who (what) they are A quack equation (see page 23).

people who live in glass houses shouldn't throw stones A popular prescription (see page 23).

(as) per (your request) A torpid term (see page 24). *according to; as.* Quintessentially dimwitted, *(as) per (your request)* is used by brainless people who cannot manage to sustain an original thought. These are the people who rely on ready-made phrases and formulas; the people who unquestioningly do as they're told; the people who join mass movements because they themselves cannot bear the burden of making decisions; the people who hate on instruction and fear forever.

■ *As per your request*, you have been unsubscribed. REPLACE WITH *As you requested*. ■ Enclosed are chapters 1 through 6, *as per your request*. REPLACE WITH *as you requested*. ■ *As per usual*, he refuses to choose between his chief of staff and his chief of budget. REPLACE WITH *As usual*. ■ *Per our discussion*, please substitute the version developed in the earlier tool for all but the last two sentences of this. REPLACE WITH *As we discussed*. ■ OPEC crude production in the first half of 1989 was supposed to be 18.5 million b/d, *as per* the November 1988 agreement. REPLACE WITH *as stated in*. ■ *As per* the Semiconductor Industry Association, U.S. manufacturers accounted for nearly $137 billion in revenues during the year 1997. REPLACE WITH *According to*.

perception is reality A quack equation (see page 23). Perception is too often purblind for there to be much reality to this quack equation. Still, it is a formula, uttered by mountebanks and managers alike, that has done much to disturb the life and livelihood of people.

perchance A withered word (see page 24). 1. *conceivably; feasibly; maybe; perhaps; possibly*. 2. *accidentally; by chance*.

perennially popular An inescapable pair (see page 20).

(I'm a) perfectionist A suspect superlative (see page 24). Anyone who declares he is a perfectionist is most often someone who can barely manage his life, someone who trips over trying. SEE ALSO *I'm not perfect (you know); nobody's perfect*.

period An infantile phrase (see page 20). ■ The lesson of the women's movement is clearly that no one makes it on their own. *Period*. DELETE *period*. ■ I know some professional, single women who would not date married men. *Period*. DELETE *period*. SEE ALSO *no ifs, ands, or buts*.

period of time A wretched redundancy (see page 25). *period; time; while*. ■ I've been wanting to watch this movie for a long *period of time*. REPLACE WITH *time*. ■ Over a considerable *period of time*, this therapy gradually provides immunization. REPLACE WITH *period*.

> He enjoyed these exercises in increasing intimacy and was warmed by the knowledge that he would be able to remain for a period of time in the vicinity of the natural references that would move him. — Jane Urquhart, *A Map of Glass*

perish the thought An infantile phrase (see page 20).

> Perish the thought — such dark thoughts were too cynical and bleak to entertain. — Robert Traver, *Anatomy of a Murder*

personal friend A suspect superlative (see page 24). A *personal friend* is but a friend, and a friend, more often than not, but an acquaintance.

persona non grata A foreign phrase (see page 19). *undesirable*.

(as) phony (queer) as a three-dollar bill An insipid simile. *artificial; bogus; counterfeit; ersatz; fake; false; feigned; fic-*

titious; forged; fraudulent; imitation; mock; phony; pseudo; sham; simulated; spurious; synthetic.

phony baloney An infantile phrase (see page 20). *artificial; bogus; counterfeit; ersatz; fake; false; feigned; fictitious; forged; fraudulent; imitation; mock; phony; pseudo; sham; simulated; spurious; synthetic.*

physician, heal thyself A popular prescription (see page 23).

pick and choose An inescapable pair (see page 20). *choose; cull; decide; determine; elect; pick; select.* ■ For years, we could *pick and choose* where our students worked. REPLACE WITH *select.*

pick of the litter A moribund metaphor (see page 21). *best; choice; elite; excellent; finest; first-class; first-rate; foremost; greatest; highest; matchless; nonpareil; optimal; optimum; outstanding; paramount; peerless; preeminent; premium; prominent; select; superior; superlative; top; unequaled; unexcelled; unmatched; unrivaled; unsurpassed.*

pick up speed A moribund metaphor (see page 21). *accelerate; advance; bestir; bustle; hasten; hurry; precipitate; quicken; rush; speed up.*

pick up steam A moribund metaphor (see page 21). 1. *accelerate; advance; bestir; bustle; hasten; hurry; precipitate; quicken; rush; speed up.* 2. *advance; awaken; better; expand; flourish; gain; gain strength; grow; heal; improve; increase; pick up; progress; prosper; rally; recover; recuperate; refresh; renew; revive; rouse; strengthen; thrive.*

pick up (take) the ball (and run with it) A moribund metaphor (see page 21). *activate; bring about; cause; create; effect; enter on; generate; give rise to; inaugurate; initiate; instigate; introduce; lead to; occasion; produce; provoke; usher in.*

pick up the pace A moribund metaphor (see page 21). *accelerate; advance; bestir; bustle; charge; dash; go faster; hasten; hurry; quicken; run; rush; speed up; sprint.*

> Today, I'm running behind Greta, who picks up the pace just as we hit the twisted growth at the base of the mountain. — Jodi Picoult, *Vanishing Acts*

pick up the pieces A moribund metaphor (see page 21).

pick up the tab A moribund metaphor (see page 21). *pay (for).*

(a) picture is worth a thousand words A popular prescription (see page 23).

> If one picture's worth a thousand words, that's the first two thousand right there, two thousand minus the hi howareya nicetameetcha. — Francine Prose, *A Changed Man*

picture of health A moribund metaphor (see page 21). *fit; good; hale; hardy; healthful; healthy; hearty; robust; sound; strong; well.*

picture perfect A moribund metaphor (see page 21). *absolute; beautiful; consummate; excellent; exemplary; exquisite; faultless; flawless; ideal; impeccable; lovely; magnificent; matchless; nonpareil;*

model; peerless; perfect; pretty; pure; sublime; superb; supreme; transcendent; ultimate; unblemished; unequaled; unexcelled; unrivaled; unsurpassed; untarnished.

pièce de résistance A foreign phrase (see page 19).

(a) piece of cake A moribund metaphor (see page 21). apparent; basic; clear; clear-cut; conspicuous; distinct; easily done; easy; effortless; elementary; evident; explicit; facile; limpid; lucid; manifest; obvious; patent; pellucid; plain; simple; simplicity itself; straightforward; translucent; transparent; unambiguous; uncomplex; uncomplicated; understandable; unequivocal; unmistakable. Evoking only the silliest of images, a piece of cake ought to tell us that those who use this expression have nothing serious to say, and perhaps little thoughtful to think. ■ Choosing the menu for the wedding reception isn't always a piece of cake. REPLACE WITH easy. ■ Setting up a Palm device to use GoType! is a piece of cake. REPLACE WITH simplicity itself. ■ At my high school, preparing for college is not a piece of cake. REPLACE WITH effortless.

> Her job at UGP is a piece of cake, a lot of financial paper shuffling and occasional simultaneous interpreting of meetings between the polite and cold Swiss men in dark suits who run the front office and the hostile and sneering Arabs — known, I regret to say, as "towel heads" — who secretly control everything. — Katharine Weber, *Objects in Mirror Are Closer Than They Appear*

(a) piece of the action An infantile phrase (see page 20). ■ Similar to the U.S. model, it will give companies the capital and technology they need while giving employees a *piece of the action* and establishing a constituency for capitalism.

(a) piece (slice) of the pie A moribund metaphor (see page 21).

(a) piece of the puzzle A moribund metaphor (see page 21). clue; hint; inkling; pointer; sign.

(a) piece of work A moribund metaphor (see page 21). aberrant; abnormal; anomalistic; anomalous; atypical; bizarre; curious; deviant; different; distinct; distinctive; eccentric; exceptional; extraordinary; fantastic; foreign; grotesque; idiosyncratic; independent; individual; individualistic; irregular; novel; odd; offbeat; original; peculiar; puzzling; quaint; queer; rare; remarkable; separate; singular; strange; uncommon; unconventional; unexampled; unique; unnatural; unorthodox; unparalleled; unprecedented; unusual; weird.

pie in the sky A moribund metaphor (see page 21). artificial; capricious; chimeric; chimerical; delusive; dreamy; fanciful; fantastical; fictitious; frivolous; hallucinatory; illusory; imaginary; maggoty; phantasmal; phantasmic; unreal; whimsical. ■ The only alternatives to testing she proposes are scarcely more than *pie in the sky*. REPLACE WITH illusory. ■ Other predictions were laughably *pie-in-the-sky*. REPLACE WITH chimerical.

pillar of society (the church; the community) A suspect superlative (see page 24). It is the pillars of society —

whether powerful, knowledgeable, or moneyed — who are often the most wobbly among us.

Few who have power do not misapply it, few who have knowledge do not misuse it, and few who have money do not misspend it.

For these reasons and others, before long and before others, pillars totter and then topple.

■ But beware — you'll be going up against the well-informed dealer who might be viewed as *a pillar of the community.*

pillar (tower) of strength A moribund metaphor (see page 21). *constant; dependable; determined; faithful; fast; firm; fixed; inexorable; inflexible; loyal; obdurate; reliable; resolute; resolved; rigid; solid; stable; staunch; steadfast; steady; stern; strong; supportive; tenacious; true; trustworthy; trusty; unflinching; unwavering; unyielding.*

pin (his) ears back A moribund metaphor (see page 21). 1. *beat; better; cap; defeat; exceed; excel; outclass; outdo; outflank; outmaneuver; outperform; outplay; outrank; outsmart; outthink; outwit; overcome; overpower; prevail over; surpass; top; triumph over; trounce; whip; win out.* 2. *admonish; animadvert; berate; castigate; censure; chasten; chastise; chide; condemn; criticize; denounce; denunciate; discipline; impugn; objurgate; punish; rebuke; remonstrate; reprehend; reprimand; reproach; reprobate; reprove; revile; scold; upbraid; vituperate.*

pin the blame on A moribund metaphor (see page 21). *accuse; blame; censure; charge; condemn; criticize; implicate; incriminate; inculpate; rebuke; reprimand; reproach; reprove; scold.*

(the) pits A moribund metaphor (see page 21). 1. *abhorrent; abominable; appalling; atrocious; awful; beastly; detestable; disagreeable; disgusting; dreadful; frightening; frightful; ghastly; grisly; gruesome; horrendous; horrible; horrid; horrifying; inhuman; loathsome; objectionable; obnoxious; odious; offensive; repellent; repugnant; repulsive; revolting; terrible; terrifying; unspeakable; unutterable.* 2. *calamitous; deplorable; depressing; distressing; disturbing; grievous; lamentable; unfortunate; upsetting; sad; tragic; woeful.*

(a) place for everything and everything in its place A popular prescription (see page 23).

place the blame on (her) shoulders A moribund metaphor (see page 21). *accuse; blame; censure; charge; condemn; criticize; implicate; incriminate; inculpate; rebuke; reprimand; reproach; reprove; scold.*

plain and simple An inescapable pair (see page 20). *apparent; basic; clear; clear-cut; conspicuous; distinct; easily done; easy; effortless; elementary; evident; explicit; facile; limpid; lucid; manifest; obvious; patent; pellucid; plain; simple; simplicity itself; straightforward; translucent; transparent; unambiguous; uncomplex; uncomplicated; understandable; unequivocal; unmistakable.*

(as) plain as a pikestaff An insipid simile. *apparent; basic; clear; clear-cut; conspicuous; distinct; easily done; easy; effortless; elementary; evident; explicit; facile; limpid; lucid; manifest; obvious; patent; pellucid; plain; simple; simplicity itself; straightforward; translucent; transparent; unambiguous; uncomplex; uncomplicated;*

understandable; unequivocal; unmistakable.

(as) **plain as day** An insipid simile. *apparent; basic; clear; clear-cut; conspicuous; distinct; easily done; easy; effortless; elementary; evident; explicit; facile; limpid; lucid; manifest; obvious; patent; pellucid; plain; simple; simplicity itself; straightforward; translucent; transparent; unambiguous; uncomplex; uncomplicated; understandable; unequivocal; unmistakable.*

To a person that knew B. from hill's foot, it was just as plain as day that if that card laid on there in the office, Mr. Brightman would miss that important meeting in St. Louis in the morning. — Kate Chopin, *A Vocation and a Voice*

(as) **plain as the nose on (your) face** An insipid simile. *apparent; basic; clear; clear-cut; conspicuous; distinct; easily done; easy; effortless; elementary; evident; explicit; facile; limpid; lucid; manifest; obvious; patent; pellucid; plain; simple; simplicity itself; straightforward; translucent; transparent; unambiguous; uncomplex; uncomplicated; understandable; unequivocal; unmistakable.*

plain (smooth) sailing A moribund metaphor (see page 21). *apparent; basic; clear; clear-cut; conspicuous; distinct; easily done; easy; effortless; elementary; evident; explicit; facile; limpid; lucid; manifest; obvious; patent; pellucid; plain; simple; simplicity itself; smooth; straightforward; translucent; transparent; unambiguous; uncomplex; uncomplicated; understandable; unequivocal; unmistakable.*

plain vanilla A moribund metaphor (see page 21). *basic; common; conservative; conventional; customary; general; normal; ordinary; quotidian; regular; routine; standard; traditional; typical; uncreative; undaring; unimaginative; usual.* ■ He was uninterested in staying now that the bank has been limited to *plain vanilla* banking. REPLACE WITH *basic.*

plan ahead A wretched redundancy (see page 25). *plan.* ■ It's important that you *plan ahead* for your retirement. DELETE *ahead.*

plan for the worst, but hope for the best A popular prescription (see page 23).

plan of action A torpid term (see page 24). *action; course; direction; intention; method; move; plan; policy; procedure; route; scheme; strategy.*

plans and specifications A wretched redundancy (see page 25). *plans; specifications.* ■ Allowed expenditures include architectural and engineering services and related costs for *plans and specifications* for the renovation. USE *plans* or *specifications.*

play ball A moribund metaphor (see page 21). *agree; assent; collaborate; comply; concur; conspire; cooperate; join in; participate; work together.*

play both ends against the middle A moribund metaphor (see page 21).

play (your) cards right A moribund metaphor (see page 21).

play cat and mouse A moribund metaphor (see page 21). *fool; tease.*

play catch up A moribund metaphor (see page 21).

play (his cards) close to the chest (vest) A moribund metaphor (see page 21). *be clandestine; be confidential; be covert; be furtive; be mysterious; be private; be secretive; be secret; be sly; be stealthy; be surreptitious.*

play cupid A moribund metaphor (see page 21).

play fast and loose (with) A moribund metaphor (see page 21). *be careless; be dishonest; be disloyal; be false; be undependable; be unpredictable; be unreliable; be untrue; be untrustworthy.*

play games (with) A moribund metaphor (see page 21). *confuse; deceive; trick.*

play hardball A moribund metaphor (see page 21). *be demanding; be hardhitting; be harsh; be rough; be severe; be stern; be strict; be tough.*

play hard to get A moribund metaphor (see page 21). *be coy; be fickle.*

play (raise) havoc with A moribund metaphor (see page 21). *disturb; mess up; devastate; rack; ravage; ruin; shatter; smash; undo; upset; wrack; wreck.*

play hell (the devil) with A moribund metaphor (see page 21). *disturb; mess up; devastate; rack; ravage; ruin; shatter; smash; undo; upset; wrack; wreck.*

play hide and seek A moribund metaphor (see page 21).

(like) playing Russian roulette An insipid simile. ■ Licensees who sell on Sundays in violation of state law are *playing Russian roulette* with their licenses.

(will it) play in Peoria A moribund metaphor (see page 21).

play it by ear A moribund metaphor (see page 21). *ad-lib; extemporize; improvise.*

play musical chairs A moribund metaphor (see page 21).

play out A torpid term (see page 24). 1. *carry out; execute; perform; play.* 2. *develop; evolve; unfold.* ■ We will report to you how all this *plays out.* REPLACE WITH *unfolds.*

play possum A moribund metaphor (see page 21).

On other occasions, I had learned at great cost that it is always wiser, with grownups and with a crowd, to play possum, as if beneath the snout of a fierce animal. — Albert Memmi, *The Pillar of Salt*

play second fiddle A moribund metaphor (see page 21). *be ancillary; be inferior; be lesser; be lower; be middling; be minor; be second; be secondary; be second-rate; be subordinate; be subservient; be substandard.*

play the field A moribund metaphor (see page 21). *date.*

play the fool A moribund metaphor (see page 21). *be silly; clown; fool around; mess around.*

play the game A moribund metaphor (see page 21). *abide by; accommodate; accord; acquiesce; act fairly; adapt; adhere to; agree; behave; comply; concur; conform; correspond; follow; harmonize; heed; mind; obey; observe; submit; yield.*

play the waiting game A moribund metaphor (see page 21). *be patient; wait.*

play to the crowd A moribund metaphor (see page 21). *perform; play up; posture; show off.*

play (your) trump card A moribund metaphor (see page 21).

play with fire A moribund metaphor (see page 21). *chance; dare; endanger; gamble; hazard; imperil; jeopardize; make bold; peril; risk; venture.*

pleasant surprise An inescapable pair (see page 20).

(as) pleased as Punch An insipid simile. *blissful; buoyant; cheerful; delighted; elated; excited; gay; glad; gladdened; gleeful; good-humored; gratified; happy; jolly; jovial; joyful; joyous; jubilant; merry; mirthful; pleased; tickled.*

pleasingly plump An inescapable pair (see page 20). *ample; big; bulky; chubby; chunky; colossal; corpulent; dumpy; enormous; fat; flabby; fleshy; gigantic; heavy; hefty; huge; immense; large; mammoth; massive; obese; plump; portly; pudgy; rotund; round; squat; stocky; stout.*

plow new ground A moribund metaphor (see page 21). 1. *arrange; groom; make ready; plan; prepare; prime; ready.* 2. *bring about; cause; create; effect; generate; give rise to; inaugurate; initiate; introduce; lead to; occasion; produce; provoke; result in; usher in.*

(5:00) p.m. ... (in the) afternoon (evening) A wretched redundancy (see page 25). *(5:00) p.m.; (in the) afternoon (evening).* ■ The city school legislature was called to order at *2 p.m.* on a Monday *afternoon.* DELETE *afternoon.*

(he's) (a) poet but (he) doesn't know it An infantile phrase (see page 20).

poetry in motion A moribund metaphor (see page 21). *agile; graceful; limber; lissome; lithe; lithesome; nimble; supple.*

(a) point in time A wretched redundancy (see page 25). *a time.* ■ There comes *a point in time* when we all pass into adulthood. REPLACE WITH *a time.*

(the) point of no return A moribund metaphor (see page 21).

point the finger (of blame) at A moribund metaphor (see page 21). *accuse; blame; censure; charge; condemn; criticize; implicate; incriminate; inculpate; rebuke; reprimand; reproach; reprove; scold.* ■ When the problem is that severe, regulators have to *point the finger at* someone. REPLACE WITH *blame.*

poke (her) nose into A moribund metaphor (see page 21). *encroach; entrench; infringe; interfere; intrude; invade; meddle; pry; tamper; trespass.*

politics as usual A torpid term (see page 24). This is but a euphemism, a politic phrase, for words like *cheating; deceit; deceitfulness; deception; dishonesty; duplicity; falsehood; fraudulence; lying; mendacity; perfidy; self-interest; selfishness; tergiversation; treachery* or *backbiting; bad-mouthing; calumny; cruelty; defamation; denigration; infighting; insult; malevolence; malice; meanness; nastiness; slander; slur; spite; spitefulness; viciousness; vilification; vindictiveness.* ■ In the course of this election, there has been too much *politics as usual*. REPLACE WITH *dishonesty*. ■ Democrats have been somewhat more restrained than Republicans in returning to *politics as usual*, apparently because they don't want to be seen as undermining Bush during wartime. REPLACE WITH *backbiting*.

pomp and circumstance An inescapable pair (see page 20). *array; ceremony; circumstance; dazzle; display; fanfare; grandeur; magnificence; ostentation; pageantry; panoply; parade; pomp; resplendence; ritual; show; spectacle; splendor.*

(as) poor as a churchmouse An insipid simile. *bankrupt; broke; destitute; distressed; impecunious; impoverished; indigent; insolvent; needy; penniless; poor; poverty- stricken; underprivileged.*

(as) poor as sin An insipid simile. *bankrupt; broke; destitute; distressed; impecunious; impoverished; indigent; insolvent; needy; penniless; poor; poverty-stricken; underprivileged.*

> They would be poor as sin on his military pay, and then Teddy would just get himself killed and leave her stranded in California with nothing — or worse, with a baby. — Maile Meloy, *Liars and Saints*

poor cousin to A moribund metaphor (see page 21). ■ Independent TV stations were once viewed as *poor cousins to* network-owned stations and affiliates.

pose no immediate (imminent) danger (threat) A torpid term (see page 24). ■ And though the radioactive fuel may *pose no immediate threat*, the canisters continue to deteriorate.

positive (*n*) A torpid term (see page 24). *advantage; asset; benefit; gain; good; strength.* SEE ALSO *negative*.

positive effect (impact) A torpid term (see page 24). ■ The breakup doesn't undo any of the *positive effects*, and it doesn't mean I revert to the way I was 10 years ago. REPLACE WITH *goodness*. ■ A small but growing number of school programs on problem solving show *positive effects* in preventing depression. REPLACE WITH *success*. ■ It's a defeat for minority children who can't afford to attend private schools through grade 6, thus missing out on the *positive effect* of a private school education. REPLACE WITH *benefit*. SEE ALSO *negative effect (impact)*.

positive feelings A torpid term (see page 24). As the following variety of synonyms shows, *positive feelings* is a pulpous expression that arouses only our inattention: *affection; approval; blissfulness; courage; delectation; delight; ecsta-*

sy; enjoyment; fondness; friendliness; friendship; generosity; goodwill; happiness; hope; joy; kindness; lightheartedness; like; liking; love; loyalty; merriment; passion; peace; pleasure; rapture; relish; respect; warmth. ■ I feel she may have *positive feelings* for me, and I'd like to know for sure. REPLACE WITH *affection.* ■ The goal is to capture the *positive feelings* about making special purchases. REPLACE WITH *delectation.* ■ The better in touch you are with your *positive feelings* for each other, the less likely you are to act contemptuous of your spouse when you have a difference of opinion. REPLACE WITH *fondness and admiration.* SEE ALSO *in a good mood; negative feelings.*

(like) (the) pot calling the kettle black An insipid simile.

pot of gold A moribund metaphor (see page 21). *affluence; fortune; money; opulence; prosperity; riches; treasure; wealth.*

(exact) (a) pound of flesh A moribund metaphor (see page 21).

pound the pavement A moribund metaphor (see page 21). *hunt; look for; quest; ransack; rummage; scour; search; seek.*

pouring (down) rain A wretched redundancy (see page 25). *pouring; raining; storming.*

pour oil on troubled waters A moribund metaphor (see page 21). *allay; alleviate; appease; assuage; calm; compose; ease; mitigate; mollify; pacify; palliate; quiet; relieve; soothe; still; tranquilize.*

pour (rub) salt on (our) wounds A moribund metaphor (see page 21). *aggravate; complicate; exacerbate; heighten; increase; intensify; irritate; make worse; worsen.*

(the) power of the purse A moribund metaphor (see page 21).

practice makes perfect A popular prescription (see page 23).

practice what (you) preach A popular prescription (see page 23).

praise (them) to the skies A moribund metaphor (see page 21). *acclaim; applaud; celebrate; commend; compliment; congratulate; eulogize; extol; flatter; hail; laud; panegyrize; praise; puff; salute.*

precarious position An inescapable pair (see page 20).

pretty An overworked word (see page 22). *adequately; amply; enough; fairly; moderately; quite; rather; reasonably; somewhat; sufficiently; tolerably.* ■ She's a *pretty* bright woman. REPLACE WITH *reasonably.* ■ We're suffering some *pretty* devastating effects right now. DELETE *pretty.*

Pretty, in these senses, proclaims its users have a vocabulary of little more than disyllabic words. For a person who says *pretty* also says *little* and *logy, really* and *leery, input* and *impact.* And with so few words, only so much can be known, only so much can be conveyed.

(as) pretty as a picture An insipid simile. *appealing; attractive; beautiful; becoming; captivating; comely; cute; dazzling; exquisite; fair; fetching; good-looking; gorgeous; handsome; lovely; nice-look-*

ing; pleasing; pretty; pulchritudinous; radiant; ravishing; seemly; stunning.

(a) pretty picture A moribund metaphor (see page 21).

prevailing winds of A moribund metaphor (see page 21).

previous to A torpid term (see page 24). *before.* ■ *Previous to* meeting her, I showed no interest in women. REPLACE WITH *Before.* SEE ALSO *in advance of; previous to; subsequent to.*

prick (puncture) (his) balloon A moribund metaphor (see page 21). *abase; chasten; debase; decrease; deflate; degrade; demean; depreciate; depress; diminish; disgrace; dishonor; embarrass; humble; humiliate; lower; mortify; puncture; shame.*

prick up (her) ears A moribund metaphor (see page 21). *attend to; hark; hear; hearken; heed; listen; pay attention; pay heed.*

> I pricked up my ears, for it was positively the first time I had ever heard a foreign tongue. — Willa Cather, *My Antonia*

pride and joy An inescapable pair (see page 20).

prim and proper An inescapable pair (see page 20).

primrose path A moribund metaphor (see page 21).

(a) prince among men A suspect superlative (see page 24).

prince charming An infantile phrase (see page 20).

princely price An inescapable pair (see page 20). *costly; dear; excessive; exorbitant; expensive; high-priced.*

prioritize A torpid term (see page 24). *arrange; classify; list; order; place; put; rank; rate.* ■ He *prioritizes* this relationship above all his "after high school plans," such as going to college. REPLACE WITH *ranks.*

prior to A torpid term (see page 24). *before.* ■ Select only the cells to be printed *prior to* selecting the Print command. REPLACE WITH *before.* ■ Certain verbs in English require the use of a pronoun *prior to* and after an infinitive phrase. REPLACE WITH *before.* SEE ALSO *in advance of; previous to; subsequent to.*

prize(d) possession An inescapable pair (see page 20). ■ In an era of spiraling costs, a good indirect cost rate is a *prized possession.*

proactive A torpid term (see page 24). 1. *anticipatory; involved; participatory.* 2. *aggressive; assertive; enterprising.* ■ To educate parents to take this more *proactive* role in the education of their children, the board has authorized the creation of a parent-controlled Family Education Resources Center. REPLACE WITH *participatory.* ■ It is vital to obtain sell-through information from retailers so that you can take *proactive* steps to get a new order. REPLACE WITH *aggressive.* ■ A school needs a PR person to develop a *proactive* approach that anticipates problems before they develop. REPLACE WITH *enterprising.* ■ Smaller, specialty firms, such as Bath & Body

Works, or apparel stores, such as Bloomingdale's, Nordstrom, and Canada's famed Harry Rosen, teach their employees to *proactively* ask customers if they need assistance. DELETE *proactively.*

proceeded to A torpid term (see page 24). ■ The team *proceeded to develop* the recently generated ideas into a concrete curriculum. REPLACE WITH *developed.* ■ He then *proceeded to declare* his undying love for me. REPLACE WITH *declared.*

proceed forward A torpid term (see page 24). *advance; continue; develop; go on; grow; happen; improve; increase; make headway; make progress; move on; occur; proceed; progress; take place.* ■ Reducing operating losses in this business will give us increased flexibility to *proceed forward* with other endeavors. REPLACE WITH *proceed.* SEE ALSO *a step forward; a step (forward) in the right direction; go forward; move forward; move (forward) in the right direction.*

(the) promised land A moribund metaphor (see page 21). *Eden; El Dorado; Elysian Fields; Elysium; heaven; kingdom come; nirvana; paradise; utopia; Valhalla.*

(a) promise is a promise A quack equation (see page 23).

(the) proof of the pudding (is in the eating) A popular prescription (see page 23).

(as) proud as a peacock An insipid simile. *arrogant; cavalier; conceited; disdainful; egocentric; egotistic; egotistical; haughty; lofty; pompous; pretentious; prideful; proud; narcissistic; self-centered;* *self-important; self-satisfied; supercilious; superior; vain.*

proud parent An inescapable pair (see page 20).

pull a fast one A moribund metaphor (see page 21). *bamboozle; befool; beguile; bilk; bluff; cheat; con; deceive; defraud; delude; dupe; feint; fool; gyp; hoodwink; lead astray; misdirect; misguide; misinform; mislead; spoof; swindle; trick; victimize.*

pull a rabbit out of the hat A moribund metaphor (see page 21). *be creative; be ingenious; be inventive; be resourceful.*

pull (yank) (her) chain A moribund metaphor (see page 21). *bamboozle; befool; beguile; bilk; bluff; cheat; con; deceive; defraud; delude; dupe; feint; fool; gyp; hoodwink; jest; joke; kid; lead astray; misdirect; misguide; misinform; mislead; rib; spoof; swindle; tease; trick; trifle with.*

pull (my) leg A moribund metaphor (see page 21). *bamboozle; befool; beguile; bilk; bluff; cheat; con; deceive; defraud; delude; dupe; feint; fool; gyp; hoodwink; jest; joke; kid; lead astray; misdirect; misguide; misinform; mislead; rib; spoof; swindle; tease; trick; trifle with.*

(like) pulling teeth An insipid simile. *arduous; backbreaking; burdensome; difficult; exhausting; fatiguing; hard; herculean; laborious; not easy; onerous; severe; strenuous; toilful; toilsome; tough; troublesome; trying; wearisome.* ■ Getting these people to level with reporters is often *like pulling teeth.* REPLACE WITH *arduous.*

pull no punches A moribund metaphor (see page 21). *be blunt; be candid; be direct; be forthright; be frank; be open; be outspoken; be straightforward.*

pull (it) off A moribund metaphor (see page 21). *accomplish; bring about; do; carry out; perform; succeed.*

pull out all the stops A moribund metaphor (see page 21). *aim; attempt; endeavor; essay; exert; exhaust; labor; moil; strain; strive; struggle; toil; try hard; undertake; work at.*

pull strings A moribund metaphor (see page 21).

pull the plug (on) A moribund metaphor (see page 21). *abandon; abort; annul; arrest; ban; cancel; cease; check; conclude; derail; desert; desist; discontinue; end; forsake; halt; invalidate; leave; quit; repeal; rescind; revoke; stop; suspend; terminate; withdraw.* ■ Organizers say they'll *pull the plug* on the parade if a gay and lesbian group is allowed to participate. REPLACE WITH *cancel.* ■ Cellucci *pulled the plug on* the PAC last summer after learning it was being organized by inmates at some of the states' toughest prisons. REPLACE WITH *banned.*

> He thought about it, wondering if he really could pull the plug. — Christopher Bram, *Lives of the Circus Animals*

pull the rug out from under A moribund metaphor (see page 21). *capsize; founder; invert; overset; overthrow; overturn; reverse; sink; tip; topple; tumble; upend; upset.*

> For once the big dick of the law and government would not pull the rug out from under me. — Tim Miller, *Shirts & Skin*

pull the wool over (his) eyes A moribund metaphor (see page 21). *bamboozle; befool; beguile; bilk; bluff; cheat; con; deceive; defraud; delude; dupe; fake; feign; feint; fool; gyp; hoodwink; lead astray; lie; misdirect; misguide; misinform; mislead; misrepresent; pretend; spoof; swindle; trick; victimize.* ■ You also have a built-in B.S. detector, and you can tell if someone is attempting to *pull the wool over your eyes.* REPLACE WITH *mislead you.*

pull (yourself) up by (your) own bootstraps A moribund metaphor (see page 21).

pull up stakes A moribund metaphor (see page 21). *abscond; clear out; decamp; depart; desert; disappear; escape; exit; flee; fly; go; go away; leave; move on; part; pull out; quit; retire; retreat; run away; take flight; take off; vacate; vanish; withdraw.*

(can't) punch (his) way out of a paper bag A moribund metaphor (see page 21). *ham-fisted; inadequate; incapable; incompetent; ineffective; ineffectual; inefficacious; inept; lacking; not able; unable; unfit; unqualified; unskilled; useless; wanting.*

pure and simple An inescapable pair (see page 20). *basic; elementary; fundamental; pure; simple; straightforward; uncomplicated.*

(as) pure as the driven snow An insipid simile. 1. *decent; ethical; exemplary; good; honest; honorable; just; moral;*

pure; righteous; straight; upright; virtuous; wholesome. 2. celibate; chaste; immaculate; maidenly; modest; snowy; spotless; stainless; unblemished; unsoiled; untarnished; virgin; virginal; virtuous.

pursuant to A torpid term (see page 24). according to; by; following; under.

pursue (strive for) excellence A suspect superlative (see page 24). ■ *Striving for excellence* is not just a goal but a way of life. ■ The recipients had to prepare brief statements on what inspires them to *strive for excellence*. SEE ALSO *excellence*.

push and shove An inescapable pair (see page 20). bulldoze; drive; propel; push; shove; thrust.

(when) push comes to shove A moribund metaphor (see page 21).

push the envelope A moribund metaphor (see page 21). 1. be adventuresome; be adventurous; be bold; be daring. 2. beat; exceed; outdo; outstrip; surpass; top.

Like thousands of English idioms, *push the envelope* helps ensure that any article, any book in which it appears is mediocre and unmemorable.

Literature does not allow worn metaphors like this; bestsellers demand them.

> I push the envelope and put my right hand gently, softly, on his upper arm, inches away from his chin. — Alix Strauss, *The Joy of Funerals*

push the panic button A moribund metaphor (see page 21). be alarmed; be anxious; be excited; be frightened; be jumpy; be nervous; be panicky; be panic-stricken; be scared; be unnerved.

push the right buttons A moribund metaphor (see page 21).

pushed (me) to the wall A moribund metaphor (see page 21). 1. coerced; compelled; constrained; dictated; enforced; enjoined; forced; made; ordered; pressed; pressured; required. 2. at bay; caught; cornered; enmeshed; ensnared; entangled; entrapped; netted; snared; trapped.

put a bug in (his) ear A moribund metaphor (see page 21). allude to; clue; connote; cue; hint; imply; indicate; insinuate; intimate; prompt; suggest; tip off.

put a damper on A moribund metaphor (see page 21). check; dampen; deaden; depress; discourage; hinder; impede; inhibit; obstruct; repress; restrain.

put a gun to (my) head A moribund metaphor (see page 21). coerce; command; compel; constrain; demand; dictate; enforce; enjoin; force; insist; make; order; pressure; require. ■ Nobody *put a gun to your head*. REPLACE WITH *forced you*.

put a halt (an end; a stop) to A wretched redundancy (see page 25). cease; close; complete; conclude; derail; discontinue; end; finish; halt; settle; stop. ■ It's time we *put a stop to* all the violence. REPLACE WITH *stop*. SEE ALSO *call a halt (an end; a stop) to*.

put a lid on (it) A moribund metaphor (see page 21). 1. abandon; abort; annul; arrest; ban; cancel; cease; check; conclude; desert; desist; discontinue; end; forsake;

285

halt; leave; quit; stop; suspend; terminate.
2. *censor; hush up; muffle; quash; smother; squash; squelch; stifle.* 3. *be closed-mouthed; be quiet; be reticent; be silent; be speechless; be still; be taciturn; be uncommunicative; hush (up); keep quiet; shut up.* ■ *Put a lid on it.* REPLACE WITH *Be quiet.*

(don't) put all (your) eggs in one basket A moribund metaphor (see page 21).

put a sock in (it) A moribund metaphor (see page 21). *be closed-mouthed; be quiet; be reticent; be silent; be speechless; be still; be taciturn; be uncommunicative; hush (up); keep quiet; shut up.*

> I listened patiently to all this minutiae, never once wishing he'd put a sock in it. — Jane Heller, *Female Intelligence*

put a spin on A moribund metaphor (see page 21).

put (it) behind (us) A moribund metaphor (see page 21). ■ She is eager to testify before the grand jury and to *put this part of the investigation behind her.* SEE ALSO *get (go) on with (my) life.*

put (his) best foot forward A moribund metaphor (see page 21).

put (your) finger on A moribund metaphor (see page 21). *detect; discern; discover; distinguish; find; identify; know; locate; make out; note; notice; perceive; pick out; pinpoint; place; point out; recall; recognize; recollect; remember; see; specify; spot; think of.*

put (her) foot down A moribund metaphor (see page 21). 1. *hold fast; stand firm.* 2. *assert; command; decree; dictate; insist; order; require.* 3. *deny; disallow; forbid; prohibit; refuse; reject.* ■ I *put my foot down.* REPLACE WITH *refused.*

put (his) foot in (his) mouth A moribund metaphor (see page 21).

put forward A torpid term (see page 24). *advance; broach; introduce; offer; present; propose; propound; submit; suggest; tender.* ■ There is speculation that he opposed Moynihan's plan so he could *put forward* his own. REPLACE WITH *propose.* SEE ALSO *come forward (with).*

put (his) head in the lion's mouth A moribund metaphor (see page 21). *chance; dare; endanger; gamble; hazard; imperil; jeopardize; make bold; peril; risk; venture.*

put (our) heads together A moribund metaphor (see page 21). *collaborate; conspire; cooperate; work together.*

put (your) house (back) in order A moribund metaphor (see page 21). *correct; rectify; redress; remedy; restore; right.* ■ Ravaged by losses after it lost direction in a period of rapid growth, Phoenix is attempting to *put its house back in order.* REPLACE WITH *right itself.*

put in a plug for A moribund metaphor (see page 21). *acclaim; applaud; celebrate; commend; compliment; congratulate; eulogize; extol; flatter; hail; laud; panegyrize; praise; puff; salute.*

put (him) in bad light A moribund metaphor (see page 21).

put in cold storage A moribund metaphor (see page 21). *defer; delay; forget; hold off; hold up; ignore; pigeonhole; postpone; procrastinate; put aside; put off; set aside; shelve; suspend; table; waive.*

put in motion A moribund metaphor (see page 21). *begin; commence; embark; inaugurate; initiate; launch; originate; start; undertake.*

put (her) in (her) place A moribund metaphor (see page 21). *abase; chasten; debase; decrease; deflate; degrade; demean; depreciate; depress; diminish; disgrace; dishonor; embarrass; humble; humiliate; lower; mortify; puncture; shame.*

> Whenever he first spoke, whatever he said, one of us would have to put him in his place. — Karen Joy Fowler, *The Jane Austen Book Club*

put (yourself) in (her) place A moribund metaphor (see page 21). *be sorry for; commiserate; empathize; feel for; feel sorry for; identify with; pity; sympathize; understand.*

put (myself) in (his) shoes A moribund metaphor (see page 21). *be sorry for; commiserate; empathize; feel for; feel sorry for; identify with; pity; sympathize; understand.*

put (your) life on the line A moribund metaphor (see page 21). *chance; dare; endanger; gamble; hazard; imperil; jeopardize; make bold; peril; risk; venture.*

put money on A moribund metaphor (see page 21). *bet; gamble; wager.*

put (his) neck on the line A moribund metaphor (see page 21). *chance; dare;* *endanger; gamble; hazard; imperil; jeopardize; make bold; peril; risk; venture.*

put new life into A moribund metaphor (see page 21). *animate; energize; enliven; inspire; inspirit; invigorate; refresh; reinvigorate; rejuvenate; revitalize; revive; rouse; stimulate; stir; vitalize.*

put on airs A moribund metaphor (see page 21). *be affected; be arrogant; be conceited; be condescending; be contumelious; be disdainful; be egotistic; be egotistical; be haughty; be high-handed; be magisterial; be overbearing; be pompous; be pretentious; be proud; be prideful; be self-important; be snobbish; be supercilious; be superior.*

put on an act A moribund metaphor (see page 21). *affect; fake; feign; make believe; pretend; simulate.*

put (her) on a pedestal A moribund metaphor (see page 21). *adore; cherish; esteem; eulogize; exalt; extol; glorify; honor; idealize; idolize; laud; love; panegyrize; prize; revere; treasure; venerate; worship.*

put one over on (her) A moribund metaphor (see page 21). *bamboozle; befool; beguile; bilk; bluff; cheat; con; deceive; defraud; delude; dupe; feint; fool; gyp; hoodwink; lead astray; misdirect; misguide; mislead; spoof; swindle; trick; victimize.*

put on hold A torpid term (see page 24). *defer; delay; forget; hold off; hold up; ignore; pigeonhole; postpone; procrastinate; put aside; put off; set aside; shelve; suspend; table; waive.* ■ The agreement had been scheduled to go into effect on Tuesday, after being *put on hold* for 30 days. REPLACE WITH *delayed.*

put on ice A moribund metaphor (see page 21). *defer; delay; forget; hold off; hold up; ignore; pigeonhole; postpone; procrastinate; put aside; put off; set aside; shelve; suspend; table; waive.*

put on the back burner A moribund metaphor (see page 21). *defer; delay; forget; hold off; hold up; ignore; pigeonhole; postpone; procrastinate; put aside; put off; set aside; shelve; suspend; table; waive.* ■ She understands the necessity of *putting* her own emotional needs *on the back burner* when these would otherwise interfere with her goal. REPLACE WITH *waiving.*

put on the front burner A moribund metaphor (see page 21). *advance.* ■ They are all familiar with the lonesome efforts of Rev. Ladi Thompson's Macedonian Initiative which has strove for years to *put* the plight of northern Christians *on the front burner.*

put (us) on the map A moribund metaphor (see page 21). ■ At the time analysts thought Ames was just the tonic Zayre needed, and the deal *put* the 30-year-old Ames *on the map.*

put (it) on the table A moribund metaphor (see page 21). *be aboveboard; be candid; be forthright; be frank; be honest; be open; be straightforward; be truthful.*

put (it) out of (its) misery A moribund metaphor (see page 21). 1. *destroy; kill; murder; slay.* 2. *cease; close; end; finish; halt; shut off; stop; terminate; turn off.*

> She applied the parking brake, gently put the engine out of its misery, then held on for dear life as it convulsed, sputtered, and died with a sigh. — Rob Kean, *The Pledge*

put out to pasture A moribund metaphor (see page 21). 1. *cast off; discard; dismiss; drop; dump; eliminate; exclude; expel; jettison; lay aside; reject; retire; set aside; shed.* 2. *ax; discharge; dismiss; fire; let go; retire.* ■ Playing a hot-blooded parent helps you feel like you haven't yet been *put out to pasture.* REPLACE WITH *dismissed.*

put (his) pants on one leg at a time A moribund metaphor (see page 21). *average; common; commonplace; conservative; conventional; customary; everyday; mediocre; middling; normal; ordinary; quotidian; regular; routine; standard; traditional; typical; uneventful; unexceptional; unremarkable; usual.*

put pen to paper A moribund metaphor (see page 21). *author; compose; indite; inscribe; jot down; pen; scrabble; scratch; scrawl; scribble; scribe; write.*

put (your) shoulder to the wheel A moribund metaphor (see page 21). *drudge; grind; grub; labor; moil; slave; strain; strive; struggle; sweat; toil; travail; work hard.*

put (your) stamp of approval on A moribund metaphor (see page 21). *approve of; authorize; certify; endorse; sanction.* ■ To portray our community as *putting a stamp of approval on* the execution is inaccurate. REPLACE WITH *approving of.*

put that in your pipe and smoke it A moribund metaphor (see page 21).

put the brakes on A moribund metaphor (see page 21). *abandon; abort; arrest; block; bridle; cancel; cease; check; conclude; control; curb; derail; desert; desist; discontinue; disturb; end; forsake; halt; interrupt; leave; obstruct; quit; repress; restrain; stop; suppress; suspend; terminate.* ■ The parent's problems with its retail divisions effectively *put the brakes on* the project and helped stall other downtown projects as well. REPLACE WITH *stopped.* ■ It *put the brakes on* the decline of political talk radio. REPLACE WITH *checked.*

put the cart before the horse A moribund metaphor (see page 21). *backward; counterclockwise; inside-out; inverted; reversed; upside-down.*

put the best face on A moribund metaphor (see page 21). ■ In the aftermath, AT&T management tried to *put the best face on* an embarrassing and costly mix-up.

put the fear of God into (them) A torpid term (see page 24). *alarm; appall; benumb; daunt; frighten; horrify; intimidate; panic; paralyze; petrify; scare; shock; startle; terrify; terrorize.*

put the finger on A moribund metaphor (see page 21). *betray; deliver up; inform on; turn in.*

put the finishing touches on A moribund metaphor (see page 21). *complete; conclude; consummate; finish.*

put the genie back in the bottle A moribund metaphor (see page 21).

put the kibosh on A moribund metaphor (see page 21). *abort; annul; arrest; balk; block; bridle; cancel; check; derail; detain; end; foil; frustrate; halt; harness; neutralize; nullify; restrain; retard; stall; stay; stop; terminate; thwart.*

put the screws to A moribund metaphor (see page 21). *bulldoze; bully; coerce; compel; constrain; demand; drive; enforce; enjoin; goad; force; impel; incite; intimidate; make; necessitate; obligate; oblige; order; press; pressure; prod; require; threaten; tyrannize; urge.*

put the skids on A moribund metaphor (see page 21). *abandon; abort; arrest; cancel; cease; check; conclude; derail; desert; desist; discontinue; end; forsake; halt; leave; quit; stop; suspend; terminate.*

put through (her) paces A moribund metaphor (see page 21). *catechize; cross-examine; examine; grill; inquire; interrogate; pump; question; quiz; test.*

put through the wringer A moribund metaphor (see page 21). *catechize; cross-examine; examine; grill; inquire; interrogate; pump; question; quiz; test.*

put together the pieces of the puzzle A moribund metaphor (see page 21). *clear up; decipher; disentangle; explain; explicate; figure out; resolve; solve; unravel; untangle; work out.*

put (them) to the test A torpid term (see page 24). *catechize; cross-examine; examine; grill; inquire; interrogate; pump; question; quiz; test.*

put two and two together A moribund metaphor (see page 21). *comprehend; conclude; decipher; deduce; discern; draw;*

fathom; figure out; gather; grasp; infer; interpret; perceive; realize; reason; see; understand.

(like) putty in (my) hands An insipid simile. *accommodating; acquiescent; adaptable; agreeable; amenable; complacent; complaisant; compliant; deferential; docile; ductile; elastic; flexible; malleable; manageable; moldable; obedient; obliging; persuasible; pliant; responsive; submissive; tractable; trained; yielding.*

put up or shut up An infantile phrase (see page 20).

Q

queer fish A moribund metaphor (see page 21). *aberrant; abnormal; anomalistic; anomalous; atypical; bizarre; curious; deviant; different; distinct; distinctive; eccentric; exceptional; extraordinary; fantastic; foreign; grotesque; idiosyncratic; independent; individual; individualistic; irregular; novel; odd; offbeat; original; peculiar; puzzling; quaint; queer; rare; remarkable; separate; singular; strange; uncommon; unconventional; unexampled; unique; unnatural; unorthodox; unparalleled; unprecedented; unusual; weird.*

(as) quick and dirty An inescapable pair (see page 20). *crude; haphazard; improvised; makeshift; provisional; slapdash; temporary; tentative.*

(the) quick and the dead A moribund metaphor (see page 21).

(as) quick as a bunny An insipid simile. *brisk; expeditious; fast; fleet; hasty; hurried; immediate; instant; instantaneous; prompt; quick; rapid; speedy; spry; sudden; swift; winged.*

(as) quick as a flash An insipid simile. *brisk; expeditious; fast; fleet; hasty; hurried; immediate; instant; instantaneous; prompt; quick; rapid; speedy; spry; sudden; swift; winged.*

(as) quick as a wink An insipid simile. *brisk; expeditious; fast; fleet; hasty; hurried; immediate; instant; instantaneous; prompt; quick; rapid; speedy; spry; sudden; swift; winged.*

I showed her everything, and she got a job quick as a wink in my same factory, in a section where they made flexible mounts for the fifty-calibers. — Nancy E. Turner, *The Water and the Blood*

(as) quick as lightning An insipid simile. *brisk; expeditious; fast; fleet; hasty; hurried; immediate; instant; instantaneous; prompt; quick; rapid; speedy; spry; sudden; swift; winged.*

quick on (his) feet A moribund metaphor (see page 21). 1. *brisk; expeditious; fast; fleet; hasty; hurried; immediate; instant; instantaneous; prompt; quick; rapid; speedy; spry; sudden; swift; winged.* 2. *able; adroit; alert; apt; astute; bright; brilliant; capable; clever; competent; discerning; enlightened; insightful; intelligent; judicious; keen; knowledgeable; learned; logical; luminous; perceptive; perspicacious; quick; rational; reason-*

able; sagacious; sage; sapient; sensible; sharp; shrewd; smart; sound; understanding; wise; witty.

quick on the draw A moribund metaphor (see page 21). *fast; fast-acting; quick; rapid; speedy; swift.*

quid pro quo A foreign phrase (see page 19).

(as) quiet as a mouse An insipid simile. *dumb; hushed; motionless; mum; mute; noiseless; quiet; reticent; silent; speechless; stationary; still; stock-still; subdued; taciturn; unmoving; voiceless; wordless.*

quiet desperation An inescapable pair (see page 20).

> There was a look of quiet desperation on her face, just weeks into this new life, one she hadn't wanted. — Kathleen Cambor, *In Sunlight, in a Beautiful Garden*

quit the scene A torpid term (see page 24). *abscond; clear out; decamp; depart; desert; disappear; escape; exit; flee; fly; go; go away; leave; move on; part; pull out; quit; retire; retreat; run away; take flight; take off; vacate; vanish; withdraw.*

quit while (you're) ahead A popular prescription (see page 23).

quote, unquote An infantile phrase (see page 20). *as it were; so-called; so to speak; such as it is.* ■ It's too soon in the *quote, unquote* relationship for that. REPLACE WITH *so-called.* ■ I was referred to them by a friend of mine, *quote, unquote.* REPLACE WITH *as it were.*

R

(a) race to the finish (line) A moribund metaphor (see page 21).

(gone to) rack (wrack) and ruin An inescapable pair (see page 20). *broken down; crumbly; decayed; deteriorated; dilapidated; run-down; shabby.*

rack (wrack) (my) brains A moribund metaphor (see page 21). *endeavor; exert; labor; moil; slave; strain; strive; struggle; toil; try; work.*

radiantly happy An inescapable pair (see page 20). *blissful; blithe; buoyant; cheerful; delighted; ecstatic; elated; enraptured; euphoric; exalted; excited; exhilarated; exultant; gay; glad; gleeful; good-humored; happy; intoxicated; jolly; jovial; joyful; joyous; jubilant; merry; mirthful; overjoyed; pleased; rapturous; thrilled.*

> And both were radiantly happy because of old times' sake. — Theodore Dreiser, *An American Tragedy*

raid the cookie jar A moribund metaphor (see page 21). *filch; pilfer; pinch; purloin; rob; steal; take; thieve.*

raining cats and dogs A moribund metaphor (see page 21). *pouring; raining; storming.*

raining pitchforks A moribund metaphor (see page 21). *pouring; raining; storming.*

rain on (your) parade A moribund metaphor (see page 21). *blight; cripple; damage; disable; disrupt; disturb; harm; hurt; impair; incapacitate; lame; mar; mess up; rack; ruin; sabotage; spoil; subvert; undermine; vitiate; wrack; wreck.*

(come) rain or shine A moribund metaphor (see page 21). *no matter what; regardless.*

raise a (red) flag A moribund metaphor (see page 21). *alert; apprise; caution; forewarn; inform; notify; signal; warn.*

raise a stink A moribund metaphor (see page 21).

> What did trouble him was that he might not lie enough or in the right way to suit Washington, and that some eager beaver, or numbskull, or stooge might raise a stink that would cost Benny his job. — Patricia Highsmith, *Tales of Natural and Unnatural Catastrophes*

raise Cain A moribund metaphor (see page 21). 1. *bellow; bluster; clamor; complain; explode; fulminate; fume; holler; howl; object; protest; rage; rant; rave; roar; scream; shout; storm; thunder; vociferate; yell.* 2. *be merry; carouse; carry on; celebrate; debauch; disport; frolic; party; play; revel; riot; roister; rollick; romp; skylark.*

raise (some) eyebrows (of) A moribund metaphor (see page 21). *amaze; astonish; astound; awe; dumbfound; flabbergast; jar; jolt; shock; start; startle; stun; stupefy; surprise.* ■ An executive at one financial institution that participated in the bailout said Goldman Sachs's dual role *raised the eyebrows of* some participants. REPLACE WITH *surprised.*

raise hell A moribund metaphor (see page 21). 1. *bellow; bluster; clamor; complain; explode; fulminate; fume; holler; howl; object; protest; rage; rant; rave; roar; scream; shout; storm; thunder; vociferate; yell.* 2. *be merry; carouse; carry on; celebrate; debauch; disport; frolic; party; play; revel; riot; roister; rollick; romp; skylark.*

raise the dead A moribund metaphor (see page 21). *be merry; carouse; carry on; celebrate; debauch; disport; frolic; party; play; revel; riot; roister; rollick; romp; skylark.*

raise the flag A moribund metaphor (see page 21). *be delighted; be elated; be glad; be overjoyed; be pleased; celebrate; cheer; exult; glory; jubilate; rejoice; triumph.*

raise the hackles A moribund metaphor (see page 21). *acerbate; anger; annoy; bother; bristle; chafe; enrage; incense; inflame; infuriate; insult; irk; irritate; madden; miff; nettle; offend; provoke; rile; roil; vex.*

raise the roof A moribund metaphor (see page 21). 1. *bellow; bluster; clamor; complain; explode; fulminate; fume; holler; howl; object; protest; rage; rant; rave; roar; scream; shout; storm; thunder; vociferate; yell.* 2. *be merry; carouse; carry on; celebrate; debauch; disport; frolic; party; play; revel; riot; roister; rollick; romp; skylark.*

raison d'être A foreign phrase (see page 19).

rake over the coals A torpid term (see page 24). *admonish; animadvert; berate; castigate; censure; chasten; chastise; chide; condemn; criticize; denounce; denunciate;*

discipline; impugn; objurgate; punish; rebuke; remonstrate; reprehend; reprimand; reproach; reprobate; reprove; revile; scold; upbraid; vituperate.

rally 'round the flag A moribund metaphor (see page 21).

rank and file A moribund metaphor (see page 21). all; citizenry; commonage; commonalty; common people; crowd; everybody; everyone; followers; herd; hoi polloi; laborers; masses; mob; multitude; plebeians; populace; proletariat; public; rabble; workers.

rant and rave An inescapable pair (see page 20). bellow; bluster; clamor; explode; fulminate; fume; holler; howl; rage; rant; rave; roar; scream; shout; storm; thunder; vent; vociferate; yell.

rap (his) knuckles A moribund metaphor (see page 21). admonish; animadvert; berate; castigate; censure; chasten; chastise; chide; condemn; criticize; denounce; denunciate; discipline; impugn; objurgate; punish; rebuke; remonstrate; reprehend; reprimand; reproach; reprobate; reprove; revile; scold; upbraid; vituperate.

rara avis A foreign phrase (see page 19). aberrant; abnormal; anomalistic; anomalous; atypical; bizarre; curious; deviant; different; distinct; distinctive; eccentric; exceptional; extraordinary; fantastic; foreign; grotesque; idiosyncratic; independent; individual; individualistic; irregular; novel; odd; offbeat; original; peculiar; puzzling; quaint; queer; rare; remarkable; separate; singular; strange; uncommon; unconventional; unexampled; unique; unnatural; unorthodox; unparalleled; unprecedented; unusual; weird.

rarely (seldom) ever A wretched redundancy (see page 25). rarely (seldom). ■ We are brothers, but we rarely ever speak. DELETE ever.

rat race A moribund metaphor (see page 21).

(like) rats abandoning a ship An insipid simile.

rattle (their) cage A moribund metaphor (see page 21). 1. agitate; disquiet; disturb; excite; stir up; trouble; upset; work up. 2. goad; incite; inflame; needle; provoke; rouse; spur. 3. acerbate; anger; annoy; bother; bristle; chafe; enrage; incense; inflame; infuriate; insult; irk; irritate; madden; miff; nettle; offend; provoke; rile; roil; vex.

> Never, never had she met anyone who could rattle her cage with such quick thoroughness. — Susan Anderson, Obsessed

rave reviews A suspect superlative (see page 24). ■ The new LapLink for Windows is already getting rave reviews from both industry experts and users like you. ■ But it turned out Maximumrocknroll gave it a rave review. ■ In 1995, CeCe got rave reviews for her solo debut.

raving lunatic An inescapable pair (see page 20).

(a) ray of light (sunshine) A moribund metaphor (see page 21). anticipation; expectancy; expectation; hope; hopefulness; optimism; possibility; promise; prospect; sanguinity. ■ I don't see any ray of sunshine when we have all these interplaying forces in conflict. REPLACE WITH hope.

reach epidemic proportions A torpid term (see page 24). This phrase and journalistic junk of its kind — for example, *(breathe; heave) a collective sigh of relief* (SEE); *an uphill battle (fight)* (SEE); *deal a (crushing; devastating; major; serious) blow to* (SEE); *first (number-one; top) priority* (SEE); *grind to a halt* (SEE); *in the wake of; send a message (signal)* (SEE); *shocked (surprised) and saddened (dismayed)* (SEE); *weather the storm (of)* (SEE) — ensure the writers of them will never be seriously read, and the readers of them never thoroughly engaged.

■ The availability of guns on the street has *reached epidemic proportions.* ■ Dog bites among children are reportedly *reaching epidemic proportions.*

reach for the sky A moribund metaphor (see page 21). *exceed; excel; outclass; outdo; outrival; outshine; outstrip; shine; stand; surpass.*

reach out and touch (someone) An infantile phrase (see page 20).

> She sat in silence for a long moment, afraid he would reach out and touch her. — Tim Farrington, *The Monk Downstairs*

reach the end of (our) rope (tether) A moribund metaphor (see page 21). *exhausted; frazzled; harassed; stressed; stressed out; tense; weary; worn out.*

read between the lines A moribund metaphor (see page 21). *assume; conclude; conjecture; deduce; gather; guess; hypothesize; imagine; infer; presume; speculate; suppose; surmise; theorize; venture.*

read it and weep An infantile phrase (see page 20).

read (her) like a (an open) book An insipid simile. *empathize; identify with; know; sympathize; understand.*

read my lips An infantile phrase (see page 20).

read (him) the riot act A moribund metaphor (see page 21). *admonish; animadvert; berate; castigate; censure; chasten; chastise; chide; condemn; criticize; denounce; denunciate; discipline; excoriate; fulminate against; imprecate; impugn; inveigh against; objurgate; punish; rebuke; remonstrate; reprehend; reprimand; reproach; reprobate; reprove; revile; scold; swear at; upbraid; vituperate.*

ready, willing, and able An infantile phrase (see page 20). ■ She described her client as being *ready, willing, and able* to testify. REPLACE WITH *willing.* ■ We have a lot of social problems that need to be addressed, and I'm *ready, willing, and able* to do that. REPLACE WITH *ready.*

re- again A wretched redundancy (see page 25). *re-.* ■ I divorced him, and then I *remarried again.* DELETE *again.* ■ We missed the first ten minutes of his talk, so he *repeated* it *again* for us. DELETE *again.*

real An overworked word (see page 22). For example: *real contribution; real difference; real obvious; real possibility; real progress; real tragedy.*

reality check An infantile phrase (see page 20).

real, live An infantile phrase (see page 20).

really An overworked word (see page 22). If such an intensive is needed at all, alternatives to the word *really* include *consumedly; enormously; especially; exceedingly; exceptionally; extraordinarily; extremely; genuinely; particularly; remarkably; specially; truly; uncommonly; very*.

Often, however, such highlighting seems only to moderate the value of our statements. ■ At the *London Review* we take serious pride in our role as one of the *really* significant participants in the international exchange of ideas and information. DELETE *really*. ■ He did a *really* good job of convincing us to buy. DELETE *really*. ■ This speechlessness is *really* affecting his moods, his behavior, and his mental state. DELETE *really*. SEE ALSO *very*.

really? An infantile phrase (see page 20). SEE ALSO *you're kidding; you've got to be kidding*.

really (and) truly An infantile phrase (see page 20). ■ I *really and truly* love being in love. DELETE *really and truly*. ■ Do you *really truly* believe that your mom thinks you're a whore? DELETE *really*. ■ They *really and truly* thought I would never make it. DELETE *really and*. ■ She was, *really and truly*, only following orders. DELETE *really and truly*. ■ *Star* magazine is reporting that not only is Demi Moore *really and truly* pregnant with Ashton Kutcher's child, she's having a boy! DELETE *really and truly*.

> There I was with my parents and my sister and a serving plate layered with skewers of shish kabob, and I thought I was going to be ill. Really and truly ill. — Chris Bohjalian, *Before You Know Kindness*

(the) real McCoy A moribund metaphor (see page 21). *actual; authentic; genuine; legitimate; pure; real; sterling; true; unadulterated; unalloyed; veritable*. ■ When you are talking about classical scholarship, he is *the real McCoy*.

rear (its) (ugly) head A moribund metaphor (see page 21). *appear; emerge; materialize; surface*. ■ That hypocritical axiom, "Do as I say, not as I do" seems to have *reared its ugly head* on the editorial pages of the *Globe* once again. ■ None of us knows for sure whether there is another problem in this volatile environment which could *rear its ugly head* soon.

reasonable facsimile An inescapable pair (see page 20).

(the) reason (why) is because A wretched redundancy (see page 25). *because; reason is (that)*. ■ One of *the reasons why* people keep this to themselves *is because of* the stigma. REPLACE WITH *the reasons ... is*.

(the) reason why A wretched redundancy (see page 25). *reason*. ■ There is a *reason why* she is the way she is. DELETE *why*. ■ The researchers are not certain as to the *reason why*. DELETE *why*.

receive back A wretched redundancy (see page 25). *receive*. ■ DPL now communicates with Excel, sending the input values and *receiving back* the output value Profit. DELETE *back*.

reckless abandon An inescapable pair (see page 20).

record-breaking A wretched redundancy (see page 25). *record.* ■ We'll take a look at some *record-breaking* snowfalls. REPLACE WITH *record.* SEE ALSO *all-time record; record-high.*

record-high A wretched redundancy (see page 25). *record.* ■ In Concord, it was a *record-high* 12 degrees. REPLACE WITH *record.* SEE ALSO *all-time record; record-breaking.*

(as) red as a beet An insipid simile. 1. *beet-red; blood-red; burgundian; burgundy; cardinal; carmine; cerise; cherry; crimson; fire-engine-red; maroon; purple; purplish; red; reddish; rose; rose-colored; rosy; rubefacient; rubescent; rubicund; rubied; rubiginous; ruby; ruddy; rufescent; rufous; russet; sanguine; sanguineous; scarlet; vermilion; wine; wine-colored.* 2. *abashed; ashamed; blushing; chagrined; confused; discomfited; discomposed; disconcerted; embarrassed; flushed; flustered; mortified; nonplused; perplexed; red-faced; shamed; shamefaced; sheepish.*

(as) red as a cherry An insipid simile. 1. *beet-red; blood-red; burgundian; burgundy; cardinal; carmine; cerise; cherry; crimson; fire-engine-red; maroon; purple; purplish; red; reddish; rose; rose-colored; rosy; rubefacient; rubescent; rubicund; rubied; rubiginous; ruby; ruddy; rufescent; rufous; russet; sanguine; sanguineous; scarlet; vermilion; wine; wine-colored.* 2. *abashed; ashamed; blushing; chagrined; confused; discomfited; discom-*

posed; disconcerted; embarrassed; flushed; flustered; mortified; nonplused; perplexed; red-faced; shamed; shamefaced; sheepish.

(as) red as a rose An insipid simile. 1. *beet-red; blood-red; burgundian; burgundy; cardinal; carmine; cerise; cherry; crimson; fire-engine-red; maroon; purple; purplish; red; reddish; rose; rose-colored; rosy; rubefacient; rubescent; rubicund; rubied; rubiginous; ruby; ruddy; rufescent; rufous; russet; sanguine; sanguineous; scarlet; vermilion; wine; wine-colored.* 2. *abashed; ashamed; blushing; chagrined; confused; discomfited; discomposed; disconcerted; embarrassed; flushed; flustered; mortified; nonplused; perplexed; red-faced; shamed; shamefaced; sheepish.*

(as) red as a ruby An insipid simile. 1. *beet-red; blood-red; burgundian; burgundy; cardinal; carmine; cerise; cherry; crimson; fire-engine-red; maroon; purple; purplish; red; reddish; rose; rose-colored; rosy; rubefacient; rubescent; rubicund; rubied; rubiginous; ruby; ruddy; rufescent; rufous; russet; sanguine; sanguineous; scarlet; vermilion; wine; wine-colored.* 2. *abashed; ashamed; blushing; chagrined; confused; discomfited; discomposed; disconcerted; embarrassed; flushed; flustered; mortified; nonplused; perplexed; red-faced; shamed; shamefaced; sheepish.*

red herring A moribund metaphor (see page 21). *decoy; distraction; diversion; lure; ploy; trick.*

red in the face A moribund metaphor (see page 21). *abashed; ashamed; blushing; chagrined; confused; discomfited; discomposed; disconcerted; embarrassed; flushed; flustered; mortified; nonplused; perplexed; red-faced; shamed; shamefaced; sheepish.*

> They laughed together under-standingly; then, bending for-ward, he kissed her hastily on the cheek and went out, leaving her red in the face as if she were a young lass. — Catherine Cookson, *The Glass Virgin*

red-letter day A moribund metaphor (see page 21).

red light A moribund metaphor (see page 21). *ban; disallowance; enjoinment; exclusion; interdiction; prohibition; proscription; veto.* SEE ALSO *green light.*

red tape A moribund metaphor (see page 21). *bureaucracy; formalities; paperwork; procedures; regulations; rules.*

refer back A wretched redundancy (see page 25). *refer.* ■ *Refer back* to Chapter 4. DELETE *back.*

reflect back A wretched redundancy (see page 25). *reflect.* ■ Part of the energy is *reflected back* into medium 1 as a reflected ray, and the remainder passes into medium 2 as a refracted ray. DELETE *back.*

regardless of the fact that A wretched redundancy (see page 25). *although; but; even if; even though; still; though; yet.* ■ *Regardless of the fact that* these products are low in sucrose, they still contain energy from other nutrients. REPLACE WITH *Though.* SEE ALSO *despite the fact that; in spite of the fact that.*

(as) regular as clockwork An insipid simile. *cyclic; established; fixed; habitual; periodic; recurrent; recurring; regular; repetitive; rhythmic; rhythmical.*

> And week after week, regular as clockwork, LaShawndra comes over and raids Mother's kitchen like it's the Piggly Wiggly. — Tina McElroy Ansa, *You Know Better*

reinvent the wheel A moribund metaphor (see page 21).

relate back A wretched redundancy (see page 25). *relate.* ■ Like the Chicago School, anomie theory *relates back* to the European sociology of the 1800s. DELETE *back.*

relic of the past A wretched redundancy (see page 25). *relic.* ■ The very idea of a single, domestic market has become a *relic of the past.* REPLACE WITH *relic.*

(it) remains to be seen A torpid term (see page 24). *I don't know; (it's) not (yet) known; (that's) uncertain; (that's) unclear; (it's) unknown.* This phrase is often euphemistic for *(I) don't know* and similar admissions. ■ So much *remains to be seen.* REPLACE WITH *is unknown.* ■ It *remains to be seen* whether dietary soybeans can protect women against breast cancer. REPLACE WITH *We do not know.* ■ How the French public, fond of both cigarettes and alcohol, will respond *remains to be seen.* REPLACE WITH *is not yet known.* SEE ALSO *your guess is as good as mine; (just have to) wait and see.*

remedy the situation A torpid term (see page 24). Like all torpid terms, *remedy the situation* neither moves nor motivates us; its use practically ensures that nothing will be righted, nothing remedied.

An ill we might be moved to correct, a problem we might be inspired to solve, but a situation we might never be roused to remedy.

■ If the decisions actually turn out to hamper civil rights enforcement, obviously I would want to take steps to *remedy the situation*. ■ To *remedy the situation* — and make the process fairer, the SEC should require that voting be strictly confidential. ■ One issue has been bothering management for quite a while, but they feel somewhat helpless to *remedy the situation*. ■ The report again called on the government to *remedy this intolerable situation*. SEE ALSO *(a) situation*.

reminisce about the past A wretched redundancy (see page 25). *reminisce.* ■ She's now 89 years old and she spends most of her time *reminiscing about the past*. DELETE *about the past*.

remove the cotton from (my) ears A moribund metaphor (see page 21).

repay back A wretched redundancy (see page 25). *repay.* ■ She is *repaying* her debt *back* to society. DELETE *back*.

replace back A wretched redundancy (see page 25). *replace.* ■ When a change needs to be made, a developer reserves that file from the library, makes the change, and then *replaces* it *back*. DELETE *back*.

reports of (my) death are greatly exaggerated An infantile phrase (see page 20).

represent(s) A torpid term (see page 24). Increasingly, *represents* is being used for a sad, simple *is* (and *represent* for *are*). ■ The budgeted capacity level *represents* the level of expected business activity under normal operating conditions. REPLACE WITH *is*. ■ Newstar and BASYS currently *represent* the major newsroom computer systems in the broadcasting field. REPLACE WITH *are*. ■ Radiosurgery *represents* a major step forward in our ability to treat tumors that previously have been untreatable. REPLACE WITH *is*. ■ I think Ginger, Patty, and I *represent* three very hardworking, committed faculty members. REPLACE WITH *are*.

respond back A wretched redundancy (see page 25). *respond.* ■ The OPP will review each request and *respond back* within ten business days. DELETE *back*.

rest and relaxation An inescapable pair (see page 20). *calm; calmness; leisure; peace; peacefulness; quiet; quietude; relaxation; repose; rest; serenity; stillness; tranquility.*

(and) (the) rest is history An infantile phrase (see page 20).

rest on (her) laurels A moribund metaphor (see page 21).

restore back A wretched redundancy (see page 25). *restore.* ■ The new Undo feature allows you to *restore* the disk *back* to its original state. DELETE *back*.

return back A wretched redundancy (see page 25). *return.* ■ When SEU is exited, the user will be *returned back* to the Programmer Menu. DELETE *back*.

revenge is sweet A quack equation (see page 23).

revert back A wretched redundancy (see page 25). *revert.* ■ Scientists speculate that the rapid spread of the disease may be due to farmland *reverting back* to woodland. DELETE *back*. ■ Not knowing what to do, I would *revert right back* to my old eating habits. DELETE *right back*.

revolving door policy A moribund metaphor (see page 21).

(the) rich and famous A suspect superlative (see page 24). *The rich and famous infatuate only foolish people, who are as boring to themselves as they are barren of themselves.* ■ It has become a summer hideaway for *the rich and famous.* SEE ALSO *celebrity; fame and fortune.*

(as) rich as Croesus An insipid simile. *affluent; moneyed; opulent; prosperous; rich; wealthy; well-off; well-to-do.*

richly deserves An inescapable pair (see page 20). ■ Instead of vilifying him, we should be giving him the encouragement and support he *richly deserves.*

rich man, poor man, beggarman, thief A moribund metaphor (see page 21). ■ It doesn't matter whether you are *rich man, poor man, beggar, or thief,* if you are black, there's an artificial ceiling on your ambition.

ride herd on A moribund metaphor (see page 21). *control; direct; guard; manage; mind; watch over.*

ride off into the sunset A moribund metaphor (see page 21). *abscond; clear out; decamp; depart; desert; disappear; escape; exit; flee; fly; go; go away; leave; move on; part; pull out; quit; retire; retreat; run away; take flight; take off; vacate; vanish; withdraw.*

ride on (her) coattails A moribund metaphor (see page 21).

ride out the storm A moribund metaphor (see page 21).

ride roughshod over A moribund metaphor (see page 21). *boss; browbeat; brutalize; bully; dictate; domineer; enslave; master; oppress; overpower; overrule; reign over; repress; rule; subjugate; suppress; tyrannize.*

(as) right as rain An insipid simile. 1. *accurate; correct; exact; irrefutable; precise; right; true.* 2. *fit; good; hale; hardy; healthful; healthy; hearty; robust; sound; strong; well.*

(a case of) (the) right hand not knowing what the left hand is doing A moribund metaphor (see page 21).

(what's) right is right A quack equation (see page 23).

right off the bat A moribund metaphor (see page 21). *abruptly; apace; at once; briskly; directly; expeditiously; fast; forthwith; hastily; hurriedly; immediately; instantaneously; instantly; posthaste; promptly; quickly; rapidly; rashly; right away; speedily; straightaway; swiftly; wingedly.*

(on the) right track A moribund metaphor (see page 21).

ring a bell A moribund metaphor (see page 21). *be familiar; remind; sound familiar.*

ring down the curtain (on) A moribund metaphor (see page 21). *cease; close; complete; conclude; discontinue; end; finish; halt; settle; stop.*

ringing endorsement An inescapable pair (see page 20).

ringing off the hook A moribund metaphor (see page 21). *ceaselessly; constantly; continually; continuously; nonstop; perpetually; steadily.* ■ The phones are *ringing off the hook.* REPLACE WITH *constantly ringing.*

rip (tear) to shreds A moribund metaphor (see page 21). *demolish; destroy; devastate; obliterate; rack; ravage; ruin; shatter; smash; undo; wrack; wreck.*

rise from the ashes A moribund metaphor (see page 21). *rise anew.*

rise to the bait A moribund metaphor (see page 21). *get angry; react; rejoin; respond; retort.*

> My job was to look respectfully attentive without rising to his bait.
> — Gail Godwin, *Queen of the Underworld*

(a) rising tide of A moribund metaphor (see page 21). ■ The report found in the nation's public schools *a rising tide of* mediocrity. SEE ALSO *a barrage of.*

road less traveled A moribund metaphor (see page 21).

(the) road to hell is paved with good intentions A popular prescription (see page 23).

road to ruin A moribund metaphor (see page 21). ■ To permit lying is a step down the *road to ruin.*

roar (in) like a lion An insipid simile. *growl; roar.*

rob Peter to pay Paul A moribund metaphor (see page 21).

(the) rock of Gibraltar A moribund metaphor (see page 21). 1. *beefy; brawny; burly; energetic; firm; fit; hale; hardy; healthful; healthy; hearty; husky; manly; mighty; muscular; powerful; puissant; robust; rugged; sinewy; solid; sound; stalwart; stout; strapping; strong; sturdy; tough; vigorous; virile; well-built.* 2. *constant; dependable; determined; faithful; fast; firm; fixed; inexorable; inflexible; loyal; obdurate; resolute; resolved; rigid; solid; stable; staunch; steadfast; steady; stern; strong; tenacious; unflinching; unwavering; unyielding.*

rock the boat A moribund metaphor (see page 21). *agitate; confuse; disorder; disorganize; disquiet; disrupt; disturb; fluster; jar; jolt; jumble; mess up; mix up; muddle; perturb; rattle; ruffle; shake up; stir up; trouble; unnerve; unsettle; upset.*

(a) rogue's gallery of A moribund metaphor (see page 21).

(positive) role model A torpid term (see page 24). *archetype; example; exemplar; good example; good man (woman); guide; hero; ideal; inspiration; model; paragon; prototype.*

(like) (a) (an emotional) roller-coaster (ride) A moribund metaphor (see page 21). Without relentless amusement, endless diversions, people might manage to speak tolerably well. As it is, the need to be entertained so overcomes us that we can speak in little but laughable images. The expression *(like) a (an emotional) roller-coaster (ride),* one such image, results from and gives rise to only carnival-like conversation, sideshow prose. ■ But the next season, it's the same thing, a game filled with ups and downs; it really is *like a roller coaster ride.* ■ The stock market is *like a roller coaster ride.* ■ If you find that the everyday activities of your daily life are being interrupted by intense emotions or *a roller coaster* of emotions, call EAP Preferred to schedule a session. ■ When I started TTC again, I knew that this pregnancy would be a bit of *an emotional roller coaster,* but I had no idea just how terrified I would be.

> And so before it's too late I want to get it down for good: this roller-coaster ride of a single gene through time. — Jeffrey Eugenides, *Middlesex*

rolling in money A moribund metaphor (see page 21). *affluent; moneyed; opulent; prosperous; rich; wealthy; well-off; well-to-do.*

rolling over (smiling; turning over) in (his) grave A moribund metaphor (see page 21).

(a) rolling stone gathers no moss A popular prescription (see page 23).

roll in the aisles A moribund metaphor (see page 21). *cachinnate; cackle; chortle; chuckle; convulse; guffaw; hoot; howl; laugh; roar; shriek; whoop.*

roll out the red carpet A moribund metaphor (see page 21). *esteem; honor; respect; venerate; welcome.*

roll up (her) sleeves A moribund metaphor (see page 21). *drudge; grind; grub; labor; moil; slave; strain; strive; struggle; sweat; toil; travail; work hard.*

roll with the punches A moribund metaphor (see page 21). *abide by; accede to; accept; accommodate; acquiesce; adapt to; adhere to; adjust to; agree to; assent; be agreeable; be complacent; bend; be resigned; bow; comply with; concede to; concur; conform; consent to; fit; follow; reconcile; submit; succumb; yield.*

romantic interlude A suspect superlative (see page 24). *intercourse; love-making; sex.*

Rome wasn't built in a day A popular prescription (see page 23).

(the) roof fell in A moribund metaphor (see page 21). *break down; break up; collapse; crash; crumple; disintegrate; end; fail; fall apart; fold; stop.*

(a) roof over (their) heads A moribund metaphor (see page 21). *asylum; cover; harbor; harborage; haven; housing; lodging; protection; refuge; retreat; safety; sanctuary; shelter.*

root cause A wretched redundancy (see page 25). *cause; origin; reason; root; source.* ■ It does not truly solve the problem of rising health care costs since it does not address the *root cause* of the problem. REPLACE WITH *root.*

rootin', tootin', shootin' An infantile phrase (see page 20).

(money is) (the) root of all evil A popular prescription (see page 23).

(a) rose by any other name (would smell as sweet) A popular prescription (see page 23).

(a) rose is a rose (is a rose) A quack equation (see page 23).

rotten apple A moribund metaphor (see page 21). *bastard; blackguard; cad; charlatan; cheat; cheater; fake; fraud; impostor; knave; mountebank; phony; pretender; quack; rascal; rogue; scoundrel; swindler; undesirable; villain.*

rotten to the core A moribund metaphor (see page 21). *bad; base; contemptible; corrupt; crooked; deceitful; despicable; dishonest; evil; immoral; iniquitous; malevolent; mean; miserable; nefarious; pernicious; praetorian; rotten; sinister; underhanded; unethical; untrustworthy; venal; vicious; vile; wicked.*

rough and ready An inescapable pair (see page 20).

rough and tumble A moribund metaphor (see page 21). *boisterous; disorderly; raucous; riotous; rough; tempestuous; tumultuous; turbulent; uproarious; violent; wild.*

rough around the edges A moribund metaphor (see page 21). 1. *bad-mannered; boorish; coarse; crude; ill-mannered; loutish; oafish; rough; rude; uncouth; uncultured; unrefined; unsophisticated; vulgar.* 2. *imperfect; incomplete; unfinished.*

(a) round peg in a square hole A moribund metaphor (see page 21). *curiosity; deviant; eccentric; iconoclast; individual; individualist; maverick; misfit; nonconformist; oddball; oddity; renegade; undesirable.*

rousing success An inescapable pair (see page 20).

rub elbows (shoulders) with A moribund metaphor (see page 21). *associate; be involved with; consort; fraternize; frequent; hobnob; keep company; mingle; mix; see; socialize.*

rub (me) the wrong way A moribund metaphor (see page 21). 1. *acerbate; anger; annoy; chafe; gall; grate; irk; irritate; miff; nettle; provoke; rankle; rile; roil; upset; vex.* 2. *affront; agitate; bother; disrupt; disturb; fluster; insult; jar; offend; perturb; rattle; ruffle; shake up; stir up; trouble; unnerve; unsettle; upset.* ■ I wouldn't want to do anything that would *rub her the wrong way*. REPLACE WITH *annoy her.*

ruffle (her) feathers A moribund metaphor (see page 21). *affront; agitate; bother; disrupt; disturb; fluster; insult; jar; offend; perturb; rattle; ruffle; shake up; stir up; trouble; unnerve; unsettle; upset.*

(a) rule is a rule A quack equation (see page 23).

rules and regulations An inescapable pair (see page 20). *regulations; rules.* ■ You may have a player that's disappointed, but we're adhering to our *rules and regulations*. REPLACE WITH *regulations* or *rules.*

rules are made to be broken A popular prescription (see page 23).

(the) rule rather than the exception A torpid term (see page 24). *basic; common; commonplace; conventional; customary; general; normal; ordinary; quotidian; regular; routine; standard; typical; uneventful; unexceptional; unremarkable; usual.* ■ New advertising campaigns costing $5 million or even $10 million are becoming *the rule rather than the exception.* REPLACE WITH *common.*

(the) rules of the game A moribund metaphor (see page 21).

(the) rules of the road A moribund metaphor (see page 21).

rule the roost A moribund metaphor (see page 21). *administer; be in charge; be in command; be in control; boss; command; control; dictate; direct; dominate; govern; lead; manage; manipulate; master; order; overpower; oversee; predominate; preponderate; prevail; reign over; rule; superintend.* ■ High school football no longer *rules the roost.* REPLACE WITH *predominates.*

Each of the stories Ma told us about Papa reinforced the message that he was the boss, that he ruled the roost, that what he said went. — Wally Lamb, *I Know This Much Is True*

rule with an iron fist (hand) A moribund metaphor (see page 21). *authoritarian; authoritative; autocratic; cruel; despotic; dictatorial; dogmatic; domineering; hard; harsh; imperious; iron-handed; lordly; oppressive; overbearing; peremptory; repressive; rigorous; severe; stern; strict; tough; tyrannical.*

run a tight ship A moribund metaphor (see page 21). *controlled; ordered; organized; structured.*

run circles (rings) around A moribund metaphor (see page 21). *beat; better; cap; defeat; exceed; excel; outclass; outdo; outflank; outmaneuver; outperform; outplay;* *outrank; outsmart; outstrip; outthink; outwit; overcome; overpower; prevail over; surpass; top; triumph over; trounce; whip; win out.*

(a) run for (his) money A moribund metaphor (see page 21).

run (it) into the ground A moribund metaphor (see page 21).

running on empty A moribund metaphor (see page 21). *be exhausted; be fatigued; be spent; be tired; be weary; be worn out.*

running on fumes A moribund metaphor (see page 21).

run off at the mouth A moribund metaphor (see page 21). *babbling; blathering; chatty; facile; fluent; garrulous; glib; jabbering; logorrheic; long-winded; loquacious; prolix; talkative; verbose; voluble; windy.*

run of the mill A moribund metaphor (see page 21). *average; common; commonplace; customary; everyday; fair; mediocre; middling; normal; ordinary; passable; plain; quotidian; regular; routine; simple; standard; tolerable; typical; uneventful; unexceptional; unremarkable; usual; workaday.*

run out of steam A moribund metaphor (see page 21). *be exhausted; be fatigued; conclude; decline; deteriorate; die; droop; dwindle; end; expire; fade; fail; finish; flag; languish; perish; quit; regress; stop; tire; weaken; wear out.* ■ Market rallies within ongoing bear markets tend to *run out of steam* as soon as the market climbs back up to the vicinity of its 200-day moving average. REPLACE WITH *languish.*

(money) runs through (his) fingers A moribund metaphor (see page 21).

run the gauntlet A moribund metaphor (see page 21). *bear; endure; experience; face; suffer; undergo.*

run the show A moribund metaphor (see page 21). *administer; boss; command; control; dictate; direct; dominate; govern; in charge; in command; in control; manage; manipulate; master; order; overpower; oversee; predominate; prevail; reign over; rule; superintend.*

> He had called me sir more than enough times for me to have no hallucinations about who was running the show, and so I did leave, and, as I say, that was the end of it. — Philip Roth, *The Human Stain*

run with the pack A moribund metaphor (see page 21). *abide by; accommodate; accord; acquiesce; adapt; adhere to; agree; behave; comply; concur; conform; correspond; follow; harmonize; heed; mind; obey; observe; submit; yield.*

run with the hare and hunt with the hounds A moribund metaphor (see page 21).

S

sacred cow A moribund metaphor (see page 21).

sacrificial lamb A moribund metaphor (see page 21). *sacrifice; victim.*

safe and sound An inescapable pair (see page 20). *all right; unharmed; uninjured; safe.*

> They were going to pray that he come home safe and sound, with a minimum of mosquito bites. — William Kowalski, *The Adventures of Flash Jackson*

safe haven A wretched redundancy (see page 25). *asylum; haven; refuge; sanctuary; shelter.* ■ Massachusetts, which likes to think of itself as a liberal mecca, is no *safe haven*. REPLACE WITH *haven*.

safety net A moribund metaphor (see page 21).

said A withered word (see page 24). *that; the; these; this; those; delete.* ■ Therefore, the relative pronouns used to introduce clauses will retain *said* function. REPLACE WITH *this*.

sail (too) close to the wind A moribund metaphor (see page 21). *chance; dare; endanger; gamble; hazard; imperil; jeopardize; make bold; peril; risk; venture.*

sail under false colors A moribund metaphor (see page 21). *bamboozle;*

befool; beguile; belie; bilk; bluff; cheat; color; con; deceive; defraud; delude; disguise; dissemble; dissimulate; dupe; fake; falsify; feign; feint; fool; gyp; hoodwink; lead astray; masquerade; misdirect; misguide; misinform; mislead; misrepresent; pretend; simulate; spoof; swindle; trick.

(the) salt of the earth A moribund metaphor (see page 21).

(the) same A torpid term (see page 24). *it; one; them.* ■ Gemini critique partners are eager to assist, but steel yourself against their tendency to fire-off suggestions without consideration of your emotional reaction to *the same.* REPLACE WITH *them.* ■ Provide access aisle for first accessible parking space which lacks *same.* REPLACE WITH *it.*

(the) same but different An infantile phrase (see page 20). SEE ALSO *same difference.*

sans A withered word (see page 24). *bereft; lacking; without.* ■ He has a reckless streak, as revealed in his tendency to go swimming *sans* suit. REPLACE WITH *without a.* ■ Using this button will allow you to see what the dialog box will look like to the user, *sans* any personal or company information that you'll eventually add to it. REPLACE WITH *without.*

save A withered word (see page 24). *but; except.* ■ The room was quiet during his performance, *save* when he would take a deep breath and let out some of it. REPLACE WITH *except.* ■ In 1990, the Emirate of Kuwait — tiny in all respects *save* its role in oil affairs — was invaded by fellow OPEC and Arab League member Iraq. REPLACE WITH *but.*

saved by the bell An infantile phrase (see page 20).

save (it) for a rainy day A moribund metaphor (see page 21).

save (his) neck (skin) A moribund metaphor (see page 21).

save your breath A moribund metaphor (see page 21). *be quiet; be silent; be still; hush; keep quiet; keep still.*

(as) scarce (scarcer) as hen's teeth An insipid simile. *exiguous; inadequate; meager; rare; scant; scanty; scarce; sparse; uncommon; unusual.*

scare the (living) daylights out of (me) A moribund metaphor (see page 21). *alarm; appall; benumb; daunt; frighten; horrify; intimidate; panic; paralyze; petrify; scare; shock; startle; terrify; terrorize.*

scare the pants off (me) A moribund metaphor (see page 21). *alarm; appall; benumb; daunt; frighten; horrify; intimidate; panic; paralyze; petrify; scare; shock; startle; terrify; terrorize.*

scare to death A moribund metaphor (see page 21). *alarm; appall; benumb; daunt; frighten; horrify; intimidate; panic; paralyze; petrify; scare; shock; startle; terrify; terrorize.* SEE ALSO *to death.*

school of hard knocks A moribund metaphor (see page 21).

(just) scratch the surface A moribund metaphor (see page 21).

scream and yell An inescapable pair (see page 20). *bay; bawl; bellow; blare;*

caterwaul; clamor; cry; holler; hoot; howl; roar; screak; scream; screech; shout; shriek; shrill; squawk; squeal; vociferate; wail; whoop; yell; yelp; yowl. ■ If parents are *screaming and yelling* at each other, that causes fear in children. REPLACE WITH *yelling.* ■ It's very flattering that women *scream and yell* when you walk on stage. REPLACE WITH *scream.* SEE ALSO *yell and scream.*

scream (yell) at the top of (my) lungs A moribund metaphor (see page 21). *bay; bawl; bellow; blare; caterwaul; clamor; cry; holler; hoot; howl; roar; screak; scream; screech; shout; shriek; shrill; squawk; squeal; vociferate; wail; whoop; yell; yelp; yowl.*

scream (yell) bloody murder A moribund metaphor (see page 21). 1. *bay; bawl; bellow; blare; caterwaul; clamor; cry; holler; hoot; howl; roar; screech; shout; shriek; shrill; squawk; squeal; vociferate; wail; whoop; yell; yelp; yowl.* 2. *clamor; complain; explode; fulminate; fume; fuss; gripe; grumble; holler; howl; object; protest; rage; rant; rave; remonstrate; roar; scream; shout; storm; thunder; vociferate; yell.* ■ The Jones lawyers would have *screamed bloody murder*, and rightly so. REPLACE WITH *protested.*

screech to a halt A moribund metaphor (see page 21). *cease; close; complete; conclude; derail; discontinue; end; finish; halt; settle; stop.* ■ Work in 535 congressional offices *screeched to a halt.* REPLACE WITH *ceased.*

(a) sea of A moribund metaphor (see page 21). ■ He was surrounded by *a sea of* concerned women. DELETE *a sea of.* SEE ALSO *a barrage of.*

(the) second American Revolution A moribund metaphor (see page 21).

second banana A moribund metaphor (see page 21). *aide; assistant; associate; inferior; junior; minion; secondary; subordinate; underling.* ■ Murphy's greatest political need is to convince the public that she is a leader, and not just the governor's long-suffering *second banana.*

second of all A wretched redundancy (see page 25). *second.* ■ *Second of all*, you're going to get hurt if you continue this behavior. REPLACE WITH *Second.* SEE ALSO *first of all.*

second to none A torpid term (see page 24). *best; different; exceptional; extraordinary; finest; first; greatest; highest; incomparable; inimitable; matchless; nonpareil; notable; noteworthy; novel; odd; optimal; optimum; original; outstanding; peculiar; peerless; remarkable; singular; special; strange; superlative; uncommon; unequaled; unexampled; unique; unmatched; unparalleled; unrivaled; unusual; without equal.*

(plant) (the) seeds of A moribund metaphor (see page 21).

see eye to eye A moribund metaphor (see page 21). *agree; concur; think alike.* ■ We *see eye to eye* on most all matters. REPLACE WITH *agree.*

seeing is believing A quack equation (see page 23).

seek and you shall find A popular prescription (see page 23).

see red A moribund metaphor (see page 21). *acerbate; anger; annoy; bother; bris-*

tle; chafe; enrage; incense; inflame; infuriate; irk; irritate; madden; miff; provoke; rile; roil; vex.

see the glass half empty A moribund metaphor (see page 21). *cynical; dark; despairing; doubtful; gloomy; hopeless; morbid; pessimistic; sullen.*

see the light A moribund metaphor (see page 21). *appreciate; apprehend; comprehend; discern; fathom; grasp; know; make sense of; perceive; realize; recognize; see; understand.*

see the light of day A moribund metaphor (see page 21). 1. *be actualized; be carried out; be implemented; be initiated; be instituted; be realized; be undertaken.* 2. *be accomplished; be achieved; be completed; be consummated; be executed; be finished; be fulfilled.* ■ The proposal will never *see the light of day.* REPLACE WITH *be realized.*

seething mass of humanity A moribund metaphor (see page 21).

self-fulfilling prophecy A torpid term (see page 24). ■ If retailers think negatively and pessimistically in terms of Christmas, it's going to be a *self-fulfilling prophecy.*

sell (him) a bill of goods A moribund metaphor (see page 21). *cheat; deceive; defraud; dupe; fool; lie to; swindle; trick; victimize.* ■ We realize that we've been *sold a bill of goods.* REPLACE WITH *swindled.*

sell (him) down the river A moribund metaphor (see page 21). *betray; deliver up; inform on; turn in.*

send a (loud) message (signal) A torpid term (see page 24). This phrase is a favorite among journalists and politicians — scrawlers and stammerers — who are accustomed to expressing themselves with dead and indifferent words. And from such words, only the faintest of feelings and the shallowest of thoughts can be summoned.

■ The patent system that protects new drugs from competition *sends a message* to pharmaceutical companies: if you invest enough money and come up with a hit, you can make a killing. REPLACE WITH *says.* ■ We want to *send a message* that this kind of behavior will not be tolerated. REPLACE WITH *make clear.* ■ The police department *sent out a message* that we would not allow such looting to occur again. REPLACE WITH *made it known.* ■ By agreeing to act now, we are *sending a signal* that we do not want this plan to fail. REPLACE WITH *announcing.* ■ I think the MFA, by hosting this exhibit, is *sending the wrong message to* the public. REPLACE WITH *misguiding.* ■ A triple-spaced term paper *sends the loud message* that the writer probably has very little to say. REPLACE WITH *proclaims.* SEE ALSO *reach epidemic proportions.*

send chills (shivers) down (my) spine A moribund metaphor (see page 21). 1. *agitate; disquiet; disrupt; disturb; fluster; jar; jolt; perturb; rattle; ruffle; shake up; stir up; trouble; unnerve; unsettle; upset.* 2. *alarm; appall; benumb; daunt; frighten; horrify; intimidate; panic; paralyze; petrify; scare; shock; startle; terrify; terrorize.*

send (them) packing A moribund metaphor (see page 21). *discard; dismiss; discharge.*

send shock waves (through) A moribund metaphor (see page 21). *agitate; arouse; astound; bother; confuse; discomfit; disconcert; disquiet; disrupt; disturb; excite; jolt; shock; startle; stimulate; stir; stun; unsettle; upset.* ■ When Swiss pharmaceutical giant Roche Holding Ltd. announced that it would buy 60 percent of Genentech Inc., it *sent shock waves through* the biotechnology community. REPLACE WITH *shocked.*

send up a trial balloon A moribund metaphor (see page 21). *assess; check; explore; inspect; investigate; look into; probe; test; try.*

separate and distinct A wretched redundancy (see page 25). *distinct; separate.* ■ Nor are the stages *separate and distinct*; they may occur at the same time. REPLACE WITH *distinct.*

separate and independent A wretched redundancy (see page 25). *independent; separate.* ■ Since the audio and video in an Interactive Multipoint videoconference travel over *separate and independent* paths, the audio must be delayed to synchronize it with the video. REPLACE WITH *separate.*

separate out A wretched redundancy (see page 25). *separate.* ■ I don't think you can *separate out* those two things. DELETE *out.* ■ Our objective was to *separate out* the NLR from the continuum emission by subtracting the different filter images. DELETE *out.* ■ One of the things that became very clear to us early on was that you simply can't *separate out* issues like curriculum and teachers' professional development and learning and instruction. DELETE *out.*

separate the men from the boys A moribund metaphor (see page 21). *choose; cull; differentiate; discriminate; distinguish; divide; filter; isolate; pick; screen; segregate; select; separate; sieve; sift; sort; strain; weed out; winnow.*

separate the sheep from the goats A moribund metaphor (see page 21). *choose; cull; differentiate; discriminate; distinguish; divide; filter; isolate; pick; screen; segregate; select; separate; sieve; sift; sort; strain; weed out; winnow.*

separate the wheat from the chaff A moribund metaphor (see page 21). *choose; cull; differentiate; discriminate; distinguish; divide; filter; isolate; pick; screen; segregate; select; separate; sieve; sift; sort; strain; weed out; winnow.*

serious reservations An inescapable pair (see page 20).

set in concrete A moribund metaphor (see page 21). *eternal; everlasting; firm; immutable; invariable; irreversible; irrevocable; permanent; rigid; stable; unalterable; unchangeable; unchanging.*

set (her) teeth on edge A moribund metaphor (see page 21). 1. *acerbate; anger; annoy; bristle; chafe; enrage; incense; inflame; infuriate; irk; irritate; madden; miff; nettle; offend; provoke; rile; roil; vex.* 2. *agitate; bother; disconcert; disturb; fluster; perturb; unnerve; upset.*

The music runs clear up my spine and sets my teeth on edge. — Michael Lee West, *Crazy Ladies*

set the record straight A torpid term (see page 24). ■ There are a lot of things I can do in my book in terms of *setting* *the record straight.* ■ EPA believes it's time to *set the record straight* about an indisputable fact: secondhand smoke is a real and preventable health risk.

set the stage (for) A moribund metaphor (see page 21). *arrange; groom; make ready; plan; prepare; prime; ready.*

set the wheels in motion A moribund metaphor (see page 21). *begin; commence; embark; inaugurate; initiate; launch; originate; start; undertake.*

set the world on fire A moribund metaphor (see page 21). *amaze; animate; awe; captivate; dazzle; electrify; excite; exhilarate; fascinate; impress; intoxicate; thrill; overwhelm.*

settle the score A moribund metaphor (see page 21).

seventh heaven A moribund metaphor (see page 21). *bliss; delight; ecstasy; joy; rapture.*

(he's a) shadow of (his) former self A moribund metaphor (see page 21). *apparition; specter; wraith.*

shake to its foundations A moribund metaphor (see page 21). *agitate; disquiet; disrupt; disturb; fluster; jar; jerk; jolt; perturb; quake; quiver; rattle; ruffle; shake up; shudder; stir up; unnerve; unsettle; tremble; upset.*

shaking in (his) boots A moribund metaphor (see page 21). 1. *afraid; alarmed; apprehensive; cowardly; craven; diffident; faint-hearted; fearful; frightened; pavid; pusillanimous; recreant; scared; terror-striken; timid; timorous; tremulous.* 2. *jittery; jumpy; nervous; quivering; shaking; shivering; shivery; shuddering; skittish; trembling.*

shaking like a leaf An insipid simile. 1. *jittery; jumpy; nervous; quivering; shaking; shivering; shivery; shuddering; skittish; trembling.* 2. *afraid; alarmed; apprehensive; cowardly; craven; diffident; faint-hearted; fearful; frightened; pavid; pusillanimous; recreant; scared; terror-striken; timid; timorous; tremulous.*

shank's mare A moribund metaphor (see page 21). *by foot.*

share and share alike A popular prescription (see page 23).

(as) sharp as a razor An insipid simile. *able; adroit; apt; astute; bright; brilliant; capable; clever; competent; discerning; enlightened; insightful; intelligent; judicious; keen; knowledgeable; learned; logical; luminous; perceptive; perspicacious; quick; rational; reasonable; sagacious; sage; sapient; sensible; sharp; shrewd; smart; sound; understanding; wise.*

(as) sharp as a tack An insipid simile. 1. *dapper; neat; smart; trim; well dressed; well groomed.* 2. *able; adroit; apt; astute; bright; brilliant; capable; clever; competent; discerning; enlightened; insightful; intelligent; judicious; keen; knowledgeable; learned; logical; luminous; perceptive; perspicacious; quick; rational; reasonable; sagacious; sage; sapient; sensible; sharp; shrewd; smart; sound; understanding; wise.*

shed (throw) light on A moribund metaphor (see page 21). *clarify; clear up; describe; disentangle; elucidate; enlighten; explain; explicate; illume; illuminate; interpret; make clear; make plain; reveal; simplify.*

> But he had little faith that Dohmler would throw much light on the matter; he himself was the incalculable element involved. — F. Scott Fitzgerald, *Tender is the Night*

shift (swing) into high gear A moribund metaphor (see page 21). ■ The lawyer is *shifting into high gear*, summoning all his persuasive powers for a rhetorical flourish that will dazzle the jury and save his client a multimillion-dollar court award.

ship of fools A moribund metaphor (see page 21).

(like) (two) ships passing in the night An insipid simile.

> She became a ship passing in the night — an emblem of the loneliness of human life, an occasion for queer confidences and sudden appeals for sympathy. — Virginia Woolf, *The Voyage Out*

(my) ship to come in A moribund metaphor (see page 21).

(cost) (the) shirt off (my) back A moribund metaphor (see page 21).

shocked (surprised) and saddened (dismayed) A torpid term (see page 24). These are formulas that people — especially spokespeople and journalists it seems — use to express indignation. And, as formulas, the *shock and sadness,* the *shock and dismay,* the *shock and outrage* is scarcely heartfelt.

■ Gilda Radner's death from cancer *shocked and saddened* Hollywood. ■ I was *shocked and saddened* by the news of his death. ■ Shoppers and shop owners were also *shocked and saddened* by Mr. Stuart's suicide. ■ Relatives were *shocked and dismayed* by what they saw today. ■ When Kissinger was selected instead of the banking mogul, Rockefeller's staff were *shocked and dismayed.* ■ Sullivan says she is *surprised and saddened* by the recent turn of events. ■ We are *saddened and outraged* by the tragic death of a young man just starting to fulfill his life promise. ■ We are terribly *shocked and dismayed;* Ed was an active and important member of our community who will be missed by his colleagues. ■ Needless to say, my dear husband was, and is, *shocked and saddened.* ■ I am *shocked and saddened* by these allegations. ■ I want to begin by saying that Hillary and I are profoundly *shocked and saddened* by the tragedy today in Littleton. ■ The man who was at the heart of the Cape Verdean neighborhood leaves behind a wife, five children, and a *shocked and saddened* community.

A newspaper editor who has just learned of the mutilation of one of his female reporters in a strife-torn country remarks he is *saddened and distressed* by her death. This is the same soulless formula; anyone who has not surrendered to this dimwitticism would surely have said it differently. SEE ALSO *reach epidemic proportions.*

> Shocked and surprised as I was I agreed without hesitation, prompted both by curiosity as to his own feelings and a desire to discuss the transaction which concerned the child. — Lawrence Durrell, *Justine*

(the) shoe is on the other foot A moribund metaphor (see page 21).

shoot down A moribund metaphor (see page 21). *belie; confute; contradict; controvert; counter; debunk; deny; disprove; discredit; dispute; expose; invalidate; negate; rebut; refute; repudiate.*

shoot from the hip A moribund metaphor (see page 21). 1. *be aboveboard; be artless; be blunt; be candid; be direct; be forthright; be frank; be genuine; be guileless; be honest; be ingenuous; be naive; be outspoken; be sincere; be straightforward.* 2. *hasty; headlong; heedless; hot-headed; impetuous; impulsive; incautious; precipitate; rash; reckless; thoughtless; unthinking.* ■ Congress is feeling very ambivalent, there are very complicated questions of government here, and these *shoot-from-the-hip* folks already have their opinion locked in cement. REPLACE WITH *incautious.*

shoot full of holes A moribund metaphor (see page 21). *belie; confute; contradict; controvert; counter; debunk; deny; disprove; discredit; dispute; expose; invalidate; negate; rebut; refute; repudiate.*

(like) shooting fish in a barrel An insipid simile. *easily done; easy; effortless; elementary; facile; simple; simplicity itself; straightforward; uncomplex; uncomplicated.*

shoot the breeze (bull) A moribund metaphor (see page 21). *babble; blab; cackle; chaffer; chat; chitchat; chatter; confabulate; converse; gossip; jabber; palaver; prate; prattle; rattle; talk.* ■ He would come down every couple of weeks just to *shoot the breeze.* REPLACE WITH *chat.*

shoot the messenger A moribund metaphor (see page 21).

shoot the works A moribund metaphor (see page 21).

shop till you drop A moribund metaphor (see page 21).

short and sweet An inescapable pair (see page 20). *brief; compact; concise; condensed; curt; laconic; pithy; short; succinct; terse.*

short and to the point A torpid phrase. *brief; compact; concise; condensed; curt; laconic; pithy; short; succinct; terse.*

short end of the stick A moribund metaphor (see page 21).

(a) shot across the bow A moribund metaphor (see page 21). *admonition; caution; warning.*

shot heard around the world A moribund metaphor (see page 21).

shot (himself) in the foot A moribund metaphor (see page 21).

(a) shot in the arm A moribund metaphor (see page 21). *boost; encouragement; fillip; goad; impetus; impulse; incentive; incitation; incitement; inducement; jolt; motivation; motive; prod;*

provocation; push; shove; spur; stimulus; thrust; urge. ■ Their success will give *a shot in the arm* to the rest of the economy. REPLACE WITH *a thrust.*

(a) shot in the dark A moribund metaphor (see page 21). *appraisal; assessment; assumption; conjecture; estimate; estimation; guess; hypothesis; impression; opinion; presumption; speculation; supposition; surmise.*

shot to hell A moribund metaphor (see page 21). 1. *demolished; destroyed; devastated; obliterated; racked; ruined; shattered; smashed; wracked; wrecked.* 2. *damaged; decayed; decrepit; deteriorated; dilapidated; ragged; shabby; shopworn; tattered; worn.*

(stand) shoulder to shoulder A moribund metaphor (see page 21). *collaborate; comply; concur; conspire; cooperate; work together.*

shout (it) from the housetops (rooftops) A moribund metaphor (see page 21). *advertise; announce; broadcast; cry out; declaim; disseminate; exclaim; proclaim; promulgate; publicize; publish; shout; trumpet; yell.*

shove down (their) throats A moribund metaphor (see page 21). *bulldoze; bully; coerce; compel; constrain; demand; drive; enforce; enjoin; goad; force; impel; incite; intimidate; make; necessitate; obligate; oblige; order; press; pressure; prod; require; threaten; tyrannize; urge.*

show me a ... and I'll show you a ... An infantile phrase (see page 20). ■ *Show me a* person who's lived a normal, conventional life, *and I'll show you a* dullard.

(the) show must go on A popular prescription (see page 23).

(not a) shred of (evidence) A moribund metaphor (see page 21). ■ There was not a *shred of evidence* to support his contentions.

shrinking violet A moribund metaphor (see page 21). *diffident; quiet; reserved; retiring; self-effacing; shy; timid.*

shut (his) eyes to A moribund metaphor (see page 21). *brush aside; avoid; discount; disregard; dodge; duck; ignore; neglect; omit; pass over; recoil from; shrink from; shun; shy away from; turn away from; withdraw from.*

sick and tired (of) An inescapable pair (see page 20). 1. *annoyed; bored; discouraged; disgusted; exasperated; exhausted; fatigued; fed up; impatient; irked; irritated; sick; sickened; tired; wearied; weary.* 2. *cloyed; glutted; gorged; jaded; sated; satiated; surfeited.* ■ I'm *sick and tired* of seeing the welfare bashing in the newspaper. REPLACE WITH *weary.* ■ No matter how desperate and *sick and tired* and lonely I felt, I was also vibrant and alive. REPLACE WITH *discouraged.*

(as) sick as a dog An insipid simile. 1. *afflicted; ailing; diseased; ill; indisposed; infirm; not (feeling) well; sick; sickly; suffering; unhealthy; unsound; unwell; valetudinarian.* 2. *nauseated; nauseous; queasy; sick; squeamish; vomiting.*

sick to death A moribund metaphor (see page 21). *annoyed; bored; discouraged; disgusted; exasperated; exhausted; fatigued; fed up; impatient; irked; irritated; sick; sickened; tired; wearied; weary.* SEE ALSO *to death.*

(breathe; exhale; heave) a (collective) sigh of relief A torpid term (see page 24). *be allayed; be alleviated; be assuaged; be calmed; be comforted; be mollified; be palliated; be relieved; be soothed; calm down; quiet down; relax; rest; unwind.* People who *breathe a collective sigh of relief* also *welcome a breath of fresh air* (SEE). They expire fetid words and inspire foolish thoughts.

■ Investors *breathed a sigh of relief* there was nothing more in the report than they expected. REPLACE WITH *were relieved.* ■ Emergency workers were *breathing a collective sigh of relief.* REPLACE WITH *relieved.* ■ Every morning when I come in and see them, I *breathe a sigh of relief.* REPLACE WITH *relax.* ■ After holding its breath for days, the city finally *exhaled a sigh of relief.* REPLACE WITH *relaxed.* ■ You are probably *breathing a sigh of relief knowing* that you won't have to mangle code any longer to render a display of a list within a list. REPLACE WITH *relieved to know.* SEE ALSO *reach epidemic proportions.*

(a) sight for sore eyes A moribund metaphor (see page 21).

signed, sealed, and delivered A moribund metaphor (see page 21). *completed; concluded; consummated; ended; executed; finished; fulfilled; made final; terminated.*

significant An overworked word (see page 22). For example: *significant development; significant effect; significant impact; significant progress.* SEE ALSO *meaningful.*

significant other A torpid term (see page 24). The use of this dispassionate expression will likely result in a blood-less relationship with whomever it is used to describe. Any one of the following words is a far better choice: *admirer; beau; beloved; boyfriend (girlfriend); companion; confidant; darling; dear; dearest; familiar; family member; flame; friend; husband (wife); inamorata (inamorato); infatuate; intimate; love; lover; paramour; partner; spouse; steady; suitor; swain; sweetheart.*

The term *significant other* (SO) gives rise to sentiments like this:

Lover: I love you SO.

Loved: I love you so, SO.

■ Whether it be with instructors, *significant others,* children, or bosses, you practice the art of gentle persuasion continually. REPLACE WITH *spouses.* ■ My *significant other* is always calling me a spoil sport because I won't compromise on things. REPLACE WITH *lover.* ■ Men trying to use it to cheat on their *significant others* should know that a pager number will work on a woman for only a short time. REPLACE WITH *girlfriends or wives.* ■ I am being stalked by a former *significant other.* REPLACE WITH *boyfriend.* SEE ALSO *object of one's affection.*

(a) significant part (portion; proportion) A wretched redundancy (see page 25). *a good (great) deal; a good (great) many; almost all; many; most; much; nearly all.* ■ Many programmers spend *a significant portion* of their working day maintaining software. REPLACE WITH *a good deal.* SEE ALSO *a substantial part (portion; proportion).*

silence is golden A quack equation (see page 23).

(as) silent as the dead An insipid simile. *dumb; hushed; mum; mute; noiseless; quiet; reticent; silent; speechless; still; stock-still; taciturn; voiceless; wordless.*

(the) silent majority A moribund metaphor (see page 21). *all; citizenry; commonage; commonalty; common people; crowd; everybody; everyone; followers; herd; hoi polloi; masses; mob; multitude; plebeians; populace; proletariat; public; rabble.*

(as) silly as a goose An insipid simile. *absurd; asinine; childish; comical; farcical; fatuous; flighty; foolhardy; foolish; frivolous; giddy; idiotic; immature; inane; laughable; ludicrous; nonsensical; ridiculous; senseless; silly.*

silver lining A moribund metaphor (see page 21).

simultaneously at the same time A wretched redundancy (see page 25). *at the same time; simultaneously.* ■ This machine does four welds *simultaneously at the same time.* REPLACE WITH *at the same time* or *simultaneously.* SEE ALSO *while at the same time; while simultaneously.*

(a) sine qua non A foreign phrase (see page 19). *critical essential; indispensable; necessary; requisite; vital.* ■ A comprehensive neurologic assessment is *a sine qua non* in assessing cases of cerebral palsy. REPLACE WITH *indispensable.*

sing a different tune A moribund metaphor (see page 21).

singe (your) wings A moribund metaphor (see page 21). *be harmed; be injured; be wounded.*

sing for (her) supper A moribund metaphor (see page 21).

sing from the same hymn sheet A moribund metaphor (see page 21).

single best (biggest; greatest; highest; largest; most) A wretched redundancy (see page 25). *best (most).* This expression is a good example of how people pay scant attention to what they say or write. Idiom or no, superlatives like *best* and *most* need not be qualified by the word *single.* People attend more to what others say — copying, as they do, one another's words — than to what they themselves say.
■ The *single most* important problem is discrimination among one another. DELETE *single.* ■ Good records are the *single best* way to avoid having deductions disallowed in the event you are audited. DELETE *single.* ■ The *single biggest* issue is the cost of upgrading a substandard system. DELETE *single.* ■ The school committee and the superintendent place student safety as their *single highest* priority. DELETE *single.*

sing like a bird An insipid simile. *dulcet; harmonious; melodic; melodious; pleasant-sounding; sonorous; sweet.*

sing (his) praises A torpid term (see page 24). *acclaim; applaud; celebrate; commend; compliment; congratulate; eulogize; extol; flatter; hail; laud; panegyrize; praise; puff; salute.*

(enough to) sink a ship A moribund metaphor (see page 21). *a big (brobdingnagian; colossal; enormous; gargantuan; giant; gigantic; grand; great; huge; immense; large; massive; monstrous; prodigious; tremendous; vast) amount; a great deal; a lot.*

sink or swim A moribund metaphor (see page 21).

sink (my) teeth into A moribund metaphor (see page 21). 1. *absorb; engage; engross; immerse; involve; plunge; submerge.* 2. *brood over; cogitate on; consider; contemplate; deliberate on; dwell on; excogitate on; meditate on; mull over; ponder; reflect on; study; think about.* ■ If you can *sink your teeth into* a good role, and the end result is anything like what you hope it's going to be, it's really satisfying. REPLACE WITH *plunge into.* ■ Rarely does a recording of such grace and elegance also offer so much to *sink your teeth into.* REPLACE WITH *contemplate.*

> She can' t get into it. It' s not at all like sinking your teeth into a foreign language. — Nancy Zafris, *The Metal Shredders*

sit on (her) duff A moribund metaphor (see page 21). *be idle; be inactive; be lazy; be unemployed; be unoccupied; dally; dawdle; loaf; loiter; loll; lounge; relax; repose; rest.*

sit on (their) hands A moribund metaphor (see page 21). *be idle; be inactive; be lazy; be unemployed; be unoccupied; dally; dawdle; loaf; loiter; loll; lounge; relax; repose; rest.*

sit on the fence A moribund metaphor (see page 21). *ambivalent; divided; indecisive; in doubt; irresolute; neutral; torn; uncertain; uncommitted; undecided; unsure.* ■ If you're *sitting on the fence* or your answer is yes, you're in luck. REPLACE WITH *undecided.*

sit tight A moribund metaphor (see page 21). *be patient; hold on; wait.*

(a) sitting duck A moribund metaphor (see page 21).

sitting on a gold mine A moribund metaphor (see page 21).

(a) situation An overworked word (see page 22). For example: *crisis situation; difficult situation; life-threatening situation; push-pull situation; no-lose situation; no-win situation; open-ended situation; problematic situation; sad situation; tragic situation; win-win situation.* ■ It's really *a* pathetic *situation.* DELETE *a situation.* ■ If there is an emergency *situation,* then that person can exit as well. DELETE *situation.* ■ It's nice to be *in a situation where you are* recognized for the work you're doing. DELETE *in a situation where you are.* ■ The *air conditioning situation* is currently under repair. DELETE *situation* or REPLACE WITH *air conditioner.* ■ The network approach *is a win-win situation for* all involved. REPLACE WITH *benefits.* SEE ALSO *remedy the situation.*

(sit) with (his) head in (his) hands A moribund metaphor (see page 21). *brood; despair; despond; mope.*

(it's) six of one, half dozen of the other A moribund metaphor (see page 21). *either; either way; it doesn't matter; no matter.*

(the) $64,000 question An infantile phrase (see page 20). ■ That's *the $64,000 question* for a number of people.

skate on thin ice A moribund metaphor (see page 21). *chance; dare; endanger; gamble; hazard; imperil; jeopardize; make bold; peril; risk; venture.*

skeletons in the closet (cupboard) A moribund metaphor (see page 21). *secret; surprise.*

(all) skin and bones A moribund metaphor (see page 21). *asthenic; attenuated; bony; cachectic; emaciated; gaunt; lank; lanky; lean; narrow; rail-thin; scraggy; scrawny; skeletal; skinny; slender; slight; slim; spare; spindly; svelte; sylphid; thin; trim; wispy.*

(as) skinny as a stick An insipid simile. *asthenic; attenuated; bony; cachectic; emaciated; gaunt; lank; lanky; lean; narrow; rail-thin; scraggy; scrawny; skeletal; skinny; slender; slight; slim; spare; spindly; svelte; sylphid; thin; trim; wispy.*

(the) sky's the limit A moribund metaphor (see page 21).

(a) slap in the face A moribund metaphor (see page 21). *abuse; affront; contempt; contumely; derision; disappointment; disdain; dishonor; impertinence; indignity; insult; offense; outrage; rebuff; rebuke; rejection; scorn; slap; slight; slur; sneer; snub.* ■ Megan's mother called the judge's decision *a slap in the face.* REPLACE WITH *an insult.* ■ The document is *a slap in the face* to the democratic principles that Americans expect their leaders to uphold. REPLACE WITH *an affront.*

> The fact that my father would spend even a nickel more than necessary was a slap in the face for all of the effort my mother put in trying to support us. — Brett Ellen Block, *The Grave of God's Daughter*

slap on the wrist A moribund metaphor (see page 21). *admonish; animadvert; berate; castigate; censure; chastise; chide; condemn; criticize; denounce; discipline; objurgate; punish; rebuke; remonstrate; reprehend; reprimand; reproach; reprobate; reprove; revile; scold; upbraid; vituperate.* ■ When the story proved false, Oliver and Smith were fired, but Arnett was *slapped on the wrist* and retained by CNN. REPLACE WITH *chided.*

sleep like a log An insipid simile. *doze; nap; rest; sleep; slumber.*

sleep like a top An insipid simile. *doze; nap; rest; sleep; slumber.*

sleep the sleep of the just A moribund metaphor (see page 21). *doze; nap; rest; sleep; slumber.*

slice of life A moribund metaphor (see page 21).

slim and trim An inescapable pair (see page 20). *asthenic attenuated; bony; cachectic; emaciated; gaunt; lank; lanky; lean; narrow; rail-thin; scraggy; scrawny; skeletal; skinny; slender; slight; slim; spare; spindly; svelte; sylphid; thin; trim; wispy.*

slings and arrows A moribund metaphor (see page 21). 1. *assault; attack; blow.* 2. *adversity; bad luck; calamity; catastrophe; hardship; ill for-*

tune; misadventure; mischance; misfortune; mishap; reversal; setback.

(the) slings and arrows of outrageous fortune A moribund metaphor (see page 21).

slip of the lip (tongue) A moribund metaphor (see page 21). *blunder; error; gaffe; mistake; slip.*

> It sometimes happens that when you make a slip of the tongue you don't want to correct it. You try to pretend that what you said was what you meant. — V. S. Naipaul, *Half a Life*

slipped (my) mind A moribund metaphor (see page 21). *be forgetful; be heedless; be inattentive; be lethean; be neglectful; be negligent; be oblivious; be remiss; be thoughtless; be unmindful; be unthinking.*

> An appointment was made with a counselor but the day came and went and they both pretended it had slipped their minds. — Kevin Guilfoile, *Cast of Shadows*

(as) slippery as an eel An insipid simile. 1. *elusive; ephemeral; evanescent; evasive; fleeting; fugitive; passing; short-lived; slippery; volatile.* 2. *crafty; cunning; deceitful; dishonest; foxy; shifty; slick; tricky; wily.*

slippery character (customer) A moribund metaphor (see page 21). *bastard; blackguard; cad; charlatan; cheat; cheater; fake; fraud; impostor; knave; mountebank; phony; pretender; quack; rascal; rogue; scoundrel; swindler; undesirable; villain.*

slippery slope A moribund metaphor (see page 21). *declivity.*

slip through (our) fingers A moribund metaphor (see page 21). *abscond; clear out; decamp; depart; desert; disappear; escape; exit; flee; fly; go; go away; leave; move on; part; pull out; quit; retire; retreat; run away; take flight; take off; vacate; vanish; withdraw.*

slip through the cracks A moribund metaphor (see page 21). *discount; disregard; elide; ignore; leave out; miss; neglect; omit; overlook; slight.*

slow and steady wins the race A popular prescription (see page 23).

(as) slow as molasses (in January) An insipid simile. *crawling; dallying; dawdling; deliberate; dilatory; faltering; hesitant; laggardly; lagging; leisurely; methodical; plodding; procrastinating; slothful; slow; slow-paced; sluggardly; sluggish; snaillike; systematic; tardy; tortoiselike; unhurried.*

(a) slow boat to China (nowhere) A moribund metaphor (see page 21).

slow(ly) but sure(ly) An inescapable pair (see page 20).

slower than molasses (in January) A moribund metaphor (see page 21). *crawling; dallying; dawdling; deliberate; dilatory; faltering; hesitant; laggardly; lagging; leisurely; methodical; plodding; procrastinating; slothful; slow; slow-paced; sluggardly; sluggish; snaillike; systematic; tardy; tortoiselike; unhurried.*

smack dab in the middle of An infantile phrase (see page 20). ■ It puts readers *smack dab in the middle of* the action.

(a) small army of A moribund metaphor (see page 21). ■ *A small army of* labor leaders came to Washington for a final assault against the agreement. SEE ALSO *a barrage of.*

small potatoes A moribund metaphor (see page 21). *immaterial; inappreciable; inconsequential; inconsiderable; insignificant; meaningless; minor; negligible; niggling; nugatory; petty; trifling; trivial; unimportant; unsubstantial.* ■ And 10,000 cases is *no small potatoes.* REPLACE WITH *not insignificant.*

(as) smart as a whip An insipid simile. *able; adroit; alert; apt; astute; bright; brilliant; capable; clever; competent; discerning; enlightened; intelligent; judicious; keen; knowledgeable; learned; logical; luminous; perceptive; perspicacious; quick; quick-witted; rational; reasonable; sagacious; sage; sapient; sensible; sharp; shrewd; smart; sound; understanding; wise.*

smart cookie A moribund metaphor (see page 21). *able; adroit; apt; astute; bright; brilliant; capable; clever; competent; discerning; enlightened; intelligent; judicious; keen; knowledgeable; learned; logical; luminous; perceptive; perspicacious; quick; rational; reasonable; sagacious; sage; sapient; sensible; sharp; shrewd; smart; sound; understanding; wise.*

smell a rat A moribund metaphor (see page 21).

smell fishy A moribund metaphor (see page 21). *doubtful; dubious; questionable; shady; shaky; suspect; suspicious.*

smoke and mirrors A moribund metaphor (see page 21). *artfulness; artifice; chicanery; cover-up; cozenage; craftiness; cunning; deceit; deceiving; deception; dissembling; dissimulation; duplicity; feigning; fraud; guile; pretense; shamming; trickery; wile.*

smokes like a chimney An insipid simile.

smoking gun A moribund metaphor (see page 21). *evidence; proof.*

(as) smooth as glass An insipid simile. 1. *burnished; even; glassy; glossy; greasy; lustrous; oily; polished; satiny; silky; sleek; slick; slippery; smooth; velvety.* 2. *apparent; basic; clear; clear-cut; conspicuous; distinct; easily done; easy; effortless; elementary; evident; explicit; facile; limpid; lucid; manifest; obvious; patent; pellucid; plain; simple; simplicity itself; smooth; straightforward; translucent; transparent; unambiguous; uncomplex; uncomplicated; understandable; unequivocal; unmistakable.*

(as) smooth as silk An insipid simile. 1. *burnished; even; glassy; glossy; greasy; lustrous; oily; polished; satiny; silky; sleek; slick; slippery; smooth; velvety.* 2. *apparent; basic; clear; clear-cut; conspicuous; distinct; easily done; easy; effortless; elementary; evident; explicit; facile; limpid; lucid; manifest; obvious; patent; pellucid; plain; simple; simplicity itself; smooth; straightforward; translucent; transparent; unambiguous; uncomplex; uncomplicated; understandable; unequivocal; unmistakable.*

smooth (her) feathers A moribund metaphor (see page 21). *allay; appease; assuage; calm; comfort; compose; concili-*

ate; console; moderate; modulate; mollify; pacify; placate; propitiate; quiet; soften; soothe; still; temper; tranquilize.

snake in the grass A moribund metaphor (see page 21). *animal; barbarian; beast; brute; degenerate; fiend; knave; lout; monster; rake; rascal; reptile; rogue; ruffian; savage; scamp; scoundrel; villain.*

snatch victory from the jaws of defeat A moribund metaphor (see page 21).

snow job A moribund metaphor (see page 21). *deception; dishonesty.*

(as) snug as a bug in a rug An insipid simile. *comfortable; cosy; habitable; homey; inhabitable; livable; safe; snug.*

(like a) soap opera An insipid simile. *exaggerated; excessive; histrionic; hyperbolic; maudlin; mawkish; melodramatic; overblown; overdone; overemotional; sensational; sentimental; soppy.*

(as) sober as a judge An insipid simile. 1. *dignified; earnest; formal; grave; pensive; reserved; sedate; self-controlled; self-restrained; serious; severe; sober; solemn; somber; staid; stern; strict; subdued; thoughtful.* 2. *abstemious; sober; teetotal; temperate.*

social butterfly A moribund metaphor (see page 21). *fin-lover; gadabout; pleasure-seeker.*

(as) soft as velvet An insipid simile. *delicate; downy; feathery; fine; fluffy; satiny; silken; silky; smooth; soft; velvety.*

soft landing A moribund metaphor (see page 21). ■ The airline industry's problem is trying to determine whether this

is a *soft landing* for the economy or a recession.

soft touch A moribund metaphor (see page 21).

(as) solid as a rock An insipid simile. 1. *adamantine; firm; granitelike; hard; petrified; rock-hard; rocklike; rocky; solid; steellike; steely; stonelike; stony.* 2. *athletic; beefy; brawny; burly; firm; fit; hale; hardy; hearty; husky; manly; mesomorphic; mighty; muscular; powerful; puissant; robust; rugged; sinewy; solid; stalwart; stout; strapping; strong; sturdy; tough; vigorous; virile; well-built.* 3. *constant; dependable; determined; faithful; fast; firm; fixed; inexorable; inflexible; loyal; obdurate; resolute; resolved; rigid; solid; stable; staunch; steadfast; steady; stern; strong; tenacious; unflinching; unwavering; unyielding.*

some of my best friends are A plebeian sentiment (see page 23).

(thirty)-something An infantile phrase (see page 20). ■ But they're not the typical self-absorbed, *30-something* crowd. ■ If you give a speech on social security, your purpose will vary for audiences made up of *twenty-something, forty-something,* or *seventy-something* individuals.

(there's) something in the wind A moribund metaphor (see page 21).

(there's) something rotten in the state of Denmark A moribund metaphor (see page 21).

(like) something out of a (Norman Rockwell painting) An insipid simile. ■ Li River cruises can take your clients past dreamlike rock formations; they *look like something out of a Salvador Dali painting.*

(it's) something to do A plebeian sentiment (see page 23). SEE ALSO *(it) gives (me) something to do; (it) keeps (me) busy; (it) keeps (me) out of trouble.*

(it's) something to look forward to A plebeian sentiment (see page 23). Those who use this phrase acknowledge the future appeals to them more than does the present, as they do the apparent pallor of their lives.

(it's) something to think about A plebeian sentiment (see page 23). SEE ALSO *food for thought.*

(a) sometime thing A torpid term (see page 24). *erratic; fitful; haphazard; inconsistent; intermittent; irregular; occasional; random; sometime; spasmodic; sporadic; unpredictable.*

song and dance A moribund metaphor (see page 21). 1. *pattern; routine.* 2. *deception; dissimulation; duplicity; equivocation; evasion; excuse; fabrication; falsehood; fib; invention; lie; mumbo-jumbo; nonsense; prevarication.*

son of a gun A moribund metaphor (see page 21). *brute; degenerate; fiend; knave; lout; rake; rascal; rogue; ruffian; scamp; scoundrel; villain.*

sooner rather than later A torpid term (see page 24). 1. *before long; presently; shortly; soon.* 2. *abruptly; apace; at once; briskly; directly; expeditiously; fast; forthwith; hastily; hurriedly; immediately; instantaneously; instantly; posthaste; promptly; quickly; rapidly; rashly; right away; speedily; straightaway; swiftly; wingedly.* ■ These people will die unless help arrives *sooner rather than later.* REPLACE WITH *soon.* ■ That, more than BSE or foot and mouth disease, is why McDonald's is pushing so hard to get an animal ID system in place *sooner rather than later.* REPLACE WITH *swiftly.*

(the) sooner the better A quack equation (see page 23).

sorely missed An inescapable pair (see page 20). Let us not die only to have it said we will be *sorely missed.* We should prefer silence to such insipidity. More disturbing still is that we should be spoken of so blandly, so, indeed, badly. This is hardly the wording of a tribute, hardly an encomium. ■ He is going to be *sorely missed* by his teammates. ■ He will be *sorely missed* by those of us who were privileged to call him our friend. ■ He will be *sorely missed* by his family, friends and neighbors.

sound and fury An infantile phrase (see page 20).

> It seemed a poor catch, for all their sound and fury, and Mr. Murphy would be glad to let them have it.
> — Kevin Baker, *Dreamland*

(as) sound as a bell An insipid simile. 1. *cogent; convincing; intelligent; judicious; just; logical; prudent; rational; reasonable; sensible; sound; telling; valid; well-founded; well-grounded; wise.* 2. *athletic; beefy; brawny; energetic; fit; good; hale; hardy; healthful; healthy; hearty; lanky; lean; manly; mesomorphic; muscular; powerful; robust; shapely; sinewy; slender; solid; sound; stalwart; strong; sturdy; thin; trim; vigorous; virile; well; well-built.*

(as) sound as a dollar An insipid simile. 1. *cogent; convincing; intelligent; judicious; just; logical; prudent; rational; reasonable; sensible; sound; telling; valid; well-founded; well-grounded; wise.* 2. *athletic; beefy; brawny; energetic; fit; good; hale; hardy; healthful; healthy; hearty; lanky; lean; manly; mesomorphic; muscular; powerful; robust; shapely; sinewy; slender; solid; sound; stalwart; strong; sturdy; thin; trim; vigorous; virile; well; well-built.*

(she) sounds like a broken record An insipid simile.

(as) sour as vinegar An insipid simile.

sour grapes A moribund metaphor (see page 21). *bile; bitterness; resentment; umbrage.*

sour note A moribund metaphor (see page 21).

so what else is new? An infantile phrase (see page 20).

sow the seeds of A moribund metaphor (see page 21). *circulate; disseminate; distribute; propagate; sow; spread.*

sow (his) wild oats A moribund metaphor (see page 21). *be dissolute; be licentious; be wild; have sex.*

spare the rod and spoil the child A popular prescription (see page 23).

(a) spate of A moribund metaphor (see page 21). ■ The legislation was proposed in response to *a spate of* violent incidents. SEE ALSO *a barrage of.*

speaks volumes A moribund metaphor (see page 21).

(she's) special A suspect superlative (see page 24).

(that) special someone A suspect superlative (see page 24). *admirer; amorist; beau; boyfriend; flame; gallant; girlfriend; inamorata; inamorato; lover; paramour; steady; suitor; swain; sweetheart; wooer.* ■ I still haven't met *that special someone*, but I am confident it will happen soon. REPLACE WITH *a girlfriend.*

(the) specter of A moribund metaphor (see page 21). ■ The Troika's standard response to all who raised *the specter of* diminished social services has been insult, invective, and ire.

spick and span An inescapable pair (see page 20). *antiseptic; clean; cleansed; disinfected; germ-free; hygienic; immaculate; neat; orderly; sanitary; sanitized; scoured; scrubbed; spotless; spruce; stainless; sterile; tidy; unblemished; unsoiled; unspotted; unsullied; untarnished; washed.*

> He was secretly orderly and in person spick and span — his friends declared that they had never seen his hair rumpled. — F. Scott Fitzgerald, *The Beautiful and Damned*

spilled milk A moribund metaphor (see page 21).

spill (his) guts A moribund metaphor (see page 21). *broadcast; confess; disclose; divulge; expose; make known; proclaim; publicize; reveal; talk; tell; uncover; unveil.*

> Nor do I covet the mute commiseration of friends who *don't know what to say* and so leave me to spill my guts by way of making conversation. — Lionel Shriver, *We Need to Talk About Kevin*

spill the beans A moribund metaphor (see page 21). *confess; disclose; divulge; leak; make known; reveal; tell.*

spinning (my) wheels A moribund metaphor (see page 21). *mired; stalled; stuck.*

spit and image (spitting image) An inescapable pair (see page 20). *clone; copy; counterpart; doppelgänger; double; duplicate; exact likeness; match; twin.*

spit and polish A moribund metaphor (see page 21).

spoil rotten A moribund metaphor (see page 21). *coddle; gratify; humor; indulge; mollycoddle; overindulge; overprotect; pamper; spoil.*

spread (himself) too thin A moribund metaphor (see page 21).

sprout up like mushrooms An insipid simile. *breed; multiply; proliferate; propagate; reproduce; spread.*

(on the) spur of the moment A moribund metaphor (see page 21). *abrupt; extemporaneous; extempore; immediate; impromptu; improvised; impulsive;* *instant; quick; rash; spontaneous; sudden; unexpected; unprepared; unprompted; unrehearsed.*

square peg in a round hole A moribund metaphor (see page 21). *aberrant; abnormal; anomalistic; anomalous; atypical; bizarre; curious; deviant; different; distinct; distinctive; eccentric; exceptional; extraordinary; fantastic; foreign; grotesque; idiosyncratic; independent; individual; individualistic; irregular; novel; odd; offbeat; original; peculiar; puzzling; quaint; queer; rare; remarkable; separate; singular; uncommon; unconventional; unexampled; unique; unnatural; unorthodox; unparalleled; unprecedented; unusual; weird.*

squeaky clean A moribund metaphor (see page 21). *high-minded; moralistic; principled; strait-laced; upright; upstanding.*

(the) squeaky wheel gets the grease A popular prescription (see page 23).

stab (her) in the back A moribund metaphor (see page 21). 1. *assail; attack; badmouth; complain; criticize; denounce; knock; put down.* 2. *abuse; harm; hurt; injure; maltreat; mistreat; wound.* ■ If I stop trusting people because they may *stab me in the back*, I could miss out on some valuable and enriching friendships. REPLACE WITH *mistreat me.*

stack the cards (deck) A moribund metaphor (see page 21). ■ While such efforts must invariably fail, the climate of distrust and fear *stacks the deck* against individuals who must move into a hostile environment.

(the) staff of life A moribund metaphor (see page 21). *bread.*

(the) stage has been set A moribund metaphor (see page 21). ■ *The stage has been set* for a contract that will have to contain genuine reforms.

(old) stamping (stomping) ground A moribund metaphor (see page 21). *hangout; haunt; rendezvous.*

stamp of approval A moribund metaphor (see page 21). *approval; authorization; certification; endorsement; sanction.*

stand (their) ground A moribund metaphor (see page 21). 1. *hold fast; persevere; persist; stand firm; stick with.* 2. *be adamant; be balky; be bullheaded; be cantankerous; be contrary; be contumacious; be dogged; be headstrong; be inflexible; be intractable; be mulish; be obdurate; be obstinate; be ornery; be perverse; be refractory; be resolute; be rigid; be stubborn; be unyielding; be willful.*

stand on (his) own two feet A moribund metaphor (see page 21). *assured; confident; independent; self-assured; self-confident; self-contained; self-governing; self-reliant; self-ruling; self-sufficient; self-supporting; sure.*

stand on the sidelines A moribund metaphor (see page 21). ■ Surgeons who have been *standing on the sidelines* are beginning to take up the procedure themselves.

stand out from (in) the crowd (pack) A moribund metaphor (see page 21). *aberrant; abnormal; anomalistic; anomalous; atypical; bizarre; curious; deviant; different; distinct; distinctive; eccentric; exceptional; extraordinary; fantastic; foreign; grotesque; idiosyncratic; independent; individual; individualistic; irregular; novel; odd; offbeat; original; peculiar; puzzling; quaint; queer; rare; remarkable; separate; singular; strange; uncommon; unconventional; unexampled; unique; unnatural; unorthodox; unparalleled; unprecedented; unusual; weird.*

stand (stick) out like a sore thumb An insipid simile. *apparent; arresting; blatant; conspicuous; evident; flagrant; glaring; gross; manifest; noticeable; observable; obtrusive; obvious; outstanding; patent; prominent; salient.*

(his) star is on the rise A moribund metaphor (see page 21).

(has) stars in her eyes A moribund metaphor (see page 21). *dreamy; happy; idealistic; optimistic; starry-eyed.*

start the ball rolling A moribund metaphor (see page 21). *begin; commence; enter on; initiate.*

start with a clean slate A moribund metaphor (see page 21). *begin anew; start afresh; start over.*

state of siege A moribund metaphor (see page 21).

staying power A moribund metaphor (see page 21). *determination; durability; endurance; firmness; fortitude; permanence; permanency; perseverance; resolution; resolve; spunk; stability; stamina; steadfastness; tenacity.*

stay on target A moribund metaphor (see page 21).

stay the course A moribund metaphor (see page 21). *advance; continue; go on; grow; make progress; move on; occur; press on; proceed; progress.*

■ Maeng says she knows that West Point, the oldest military academy in the country, will be challenging; however, she plans to *stay the course.* ■ The congressman wants to *stay the course* until the farm bill comes up for its scheduled review in a few years. ■ If parents *stay the course* and recognize God's confidence and trust in their parenting skills, then life will be fine throughout the world.

> There was nothing to do but patch himself up as well as he could, stay the course, not be depressed. — Jonathan Franzen, *The Corrections*

(as) steady as a rock An insipid simile. *constant; dependable; determined; faithful; fast; firm; fixed; inexorable; inflexible; loyal; obdurate; reliable; resolute; resolved; rigid; solid; stable; staunch; steadfast; steady; stern; strong; supportive; tenacious; true; trustworthy; trusty; unflinching; unwavering; unyielding.*

steal the show A moribund metaphor (see page 21).

steal (her) thunder A moribund metaphor (see page 21).

steer clear (of) A moribund metaphor (see page 21). *avoid; bypass; circumvent; dodge; elude; evade; shun; sidestep; skirt.* ■ It was a signal to the new mayor to *steer cleer of* divisiveness and cliquishness. REPLACE WITH *shun.*

steer wrong A moribund metaphor (see page 21). *beguile; betray; deceive; lead astray; misdirect; misguide; mislead.* ■ I trust that you won't *steer* them *wrong.* REPLACE WITH *mislead.*

stem the flow A moribund metaphor (see page 21). *abort; arrest; block; check; curb; decelerate; delay; end; halt; hamper; hinder; impede; obstruct; plug; quash; quell; retard; slow; squash; stay; stem; stop; suspend; terminate.*

stem the tide A moribund metaphor (see page 21). *abort; arrest; block; check; curb; decelerate; delay; end; halt; hamper; hinder; impede; obstruct; plug; quash; quell; retard; slow; squash; stay; stem; stop; suspend; terminate.* ■ But twenty years of effort have failed to *stem the tide of* environmental degradation. REPLACE WITH *retard.*

> It was the inability to speak openly about them, and thus to devise ways and means to stem the tide until they could re-form their ranks. — Lawrence Durrell, *Constance*

(a) step backward A torpid term (see page 24). *backset; reversal; setback.*

(a) step forward A torpid term (see page 24). *advancement; betterment; development; furtherance; growth; headway; improvement; progress.* ■ This is *a step forward* for us all. REPLACE WITH *betterment.* For some writers, *a step forward* isn't positive enough: ■ Although the IFS interface is *a positive step forward* for DOS, it remains in a sort of twilight zone. REPLACE WITH *an advancement.* SEE ALSO *a step (forward) in the right direction; go forward; move forward;*

move (forward) in the right direction; proceed forward.

(a) step (forward) in the right direction A torpid term (see page 24). *advancement; betterment; development; furtherance; growth; headway; improvement; progress.* Like many dimwitticisms, *a step forward in the right direction* is an ungainly creation. The English language is wonderfully expressive and infinitely flexible, but this phrase is stiff, wooden, awkward. ■ Incentives to attract and retain nurses would be *a step in the right direction.* REPLACE WITH *an improvement.* ■ Mr Singh described the arrests of Mr Saeed and other militants as *a step forward in the right direction* but said more action was necessary. REPLACE WITH *progress.* SEE ALSO *a step forward; go forward; move forward; move (forward) in the right direction; proceed forward.*

step on (his) toes A moribund metaphor (see page 21). *abuse; affront; anger; annoy; bother; displease; harm; hurt; insult; irk; irritate; offend; outrage; provoke; rile; roil; slap; slight; smart; trouble; upset; vex; wound.* ■ During his five months as acting mayor, he *stepped on many people's toes.* REPLACE WITH *offended many people.*

step up to the plate A moribund metaphor (see page 21). 1. *aim for; attempt; endeavor; engage; participate; pursue; seek; strive for; try.* 2. *advance; appear; approach; come forth; come forward; emerge; rise; show; surface; transpire.* 3. *act; perform; speak; talk.* 4. *be accountable; be answerable; be responsible.* ■ Rumors of an imminent buyout circulated, but no one *stepped up to the plate.* REPLACE WITH *came forward.* ■

Industry is *stepping up to the plate on* this. REPLACE WITH *pursuing.* ■ Because his public presence has been tainted greatly, she's going to have to *step up to the plate* and do more. REPLACE WITH *come forward.*

stewed to the gills A moribund metaphor (see page 21). *besotted; crapulous; drunk; inebriated; intoxicated; sodden; stupefied; tipsy.*

stew in (her) own juice A moribund metaphor (see page 21). *brood; fret; mope; stew; worry.*

stick in (my) craw (throat) A moribund metaphor (see page 21). *acerbate; anger; annoy; bother; bristle; chafe; enrage; envenom; exacerbate; gall; incense; inflame; infuriate; insult; irk; irritate; madden; miff; nettle; offend; provoke; rankle; rile; roil; vex.*

stick (your) neck out A moribund metaphor (see page 21). *chance; dare; endanger; gamble; hazard; imperil; jeopardize; make bold; peril; risk; venture.* ■ They do not *stick their necks out* to initiate change — they are followers. REPLACE WITH *venture.*

sticks and stones will break my bones, but words will never hurt me An infantile phrase (see page 20).

stick to (your) guns A moribund metaphor (see page 21). 1. *hold fast; persevere; persist; stand firm; stick with.* 2. *be adamant; be balky; be bullheaded; be cantankerous; be contrary; be contumacious; be dogged; be headstrong; be inflexible; be intractable; be mulish; be obdurate; be obstinate; be ornery; be perverse; be refractory; be resolute; be rigid; be stubborn; be unyielding; be willful.*

stick to (your) ribs A moribund metaphor (see page 21). *fill; sate; satiate; satisfy.*

stick to the knitting A moribund metaphor (see page 21).

sticky wicket A moribund metaphor (see page 21). *affliction; annoyance; bane; bother; burden; curse; difficulty; inconvenience; irritant; irritation; load; nuisance; ordeal; pain; pest; problem; tribulation; trouble; vexation; weight; worry.*

(as) stiff as a board An insipid simile. 1. *firm; inelastic; inflexible; rigid; stiff; unbending; unmalleable; unpliable; unyielding.* 2. *awkward; ceremonious; constrained; formal; precise; priggish; prim; proper; prudish; punctilious; puritanical; reserved; starched; stiff; stilted; strait-laced; stuffy; unrelaxed; uptight.*

still and all A wretched redundancy (see page 25). *even so; still; yet.* ■ *Still and all,* I love her. REPLACE WITH *Even so* or *Still.*

(as) still as a mouse An insipid simile. *dead; dormant; dull; immobile; immovable; inactive; inanimate; indolent; inert; inoperative; languid; latent; lethargic; lifeless; listless; motionless; noiseless; phlegmatic; quiescent; quiet; silent; sluggish; soundless; stagnant; static; stationary; still; stock-still; torpid; unresponsive.*

To placate him, I sit as still as a harvest mouse (*Micromys minutus*), and after about fifteen minutes of silent work he relents. — Sally Beauman, *The Sisters Mortland*

(as) still as death An insipid simile. *dead; dormant; dull; immobile; immovable; inactive; inanimate; indolent; inert; inoperative; languid; latent; lethargic; lifeless; listless; motionless; noiseless; phlegmatic; quiescent; quiet; silent; sluggish; soundless; stagnant; static; stationary; still; stock-still; torpid; unresponsive.*

still kicking A moribund metaphor (see page 21). *alive; animate; breathing; live; living.*

still waters run deep A popular prescription (see page 23).

stink like hell An insipid simile. *reek; smell; stink.*

stir up a hornet's nest A moribund metaphor (see page 21). SEE ALSO *hornet's nest.*

stitch in time A moribund metaphor (see page 21).

(a) stitch in time saves nine A popular prescription (see page 23).

(a) stone's throw (away) A moribund metaphor (see page 21). *accessible; at hand; close; close by; handy; near; nearby; neighboring; not far from; vicinal.*

stop and smell the flowers (roses) A moribund metaphor (see page 21). *be idle; be inactive; be lazy; be unemployed; be unoccupied; dally; dawdle; loaf; loiter; loll; lounge; relax; repose; rest.*

stop (him) (dead) in (his) tracks A moribund metaphor (see page 21). *arrest; check; freeze; halt; hold; immobilize; restrain; stop.*

> But there was one photo that stopped me in my tracks, that had me standing unsmiling before it for a long time. — Elizabeth Berg, *The Art of Mending*

stop the world I want to get off An infantile phrase (see page 20).

storm brewing A moribund metaphor (see page 21).

(a) storm of A moribund metaphor (see page 21). SEE ALSO *a barrage of.*

(the) story of (my) life A plebeian sentiment (see page 23). ■ I've always felt like an outcast; it's *the story of my life.*

straddle the fence A moribund metaphor (see page 21). *ambivalent; divided; indecisive; in doubt; irresolute; neutral; torn; uncertain; uncommitted; undecided; unsure.*

(the) straight and narrow (path) A moribund metaphor (see page 21). *decent; ethical; exemplary; good; honest; honorable; just; moral; pure; righteous; straight; upright; virtuous; wholesome.*

(as) straight as an arrow An insipid simile. 1. *direct; lineal; linear; straight.* 2. *decent; ethical; exemplary; good; honest; honorable; just; moral; pure; righteous; straight; upright; virtuous; wholesome.*

straight from the horse's mouth A moribund metaphor (see page 21).

straight from the shoulder A moribund metaphor (see page 21). *bluntly; candidly; directly; forthrightly; frankly; man to man; openly; outspokenly; plainly; straightforwardly; unambiguously; unequivocally.*

straight shooter A moribund metaphor (see page 21). *decent; ethical; forthright; honest; just; moral; righteous; straight; trustworthy; upright; virtuous.*

strange An overworked word (see page 22). *aberrant; abnormal; anomalistic; anomalous; atypical; bizarre; curious; deviant; different; distinct; distinctive; eccentric; exceptional; extraordinary; fantastic; foreign; grotesque; idiosyncratic; independent; individual; individualistic; irregular; novel; odd; offbeat; original; peculiar; puzzling; quaint; queer; rare; remarkable; separate; singular; uncommon; unconventional; unexampled; unique; unnatural; unorthodox; unparalleled; unprecedented; unusual; weird.* SEE ALSO *weird.*

strange bedfellows A moribund metaphor (see page 21).

(the) straw that broke the camel's back A moribund metaphor (see page 21).

stretch the point (truth) A moribund metaphor (see page 21). *elaborate; embellish; embroider; enhance; enlarge; exaggerate; hyperbolize; inflate; magnify; overdo; overstress; overstate; strain; stretch.*

strike (touch) a chord A moribund metaphor (see page 21). *be familiar; remind; sound familiar.* ■ These words *struck a familiar chord* with many of the 6,000 conference participants.

strike gold A moribund metaphor (see page 21).

strike while the iron is hot A moribund metaphor (see page 21). *capitalize on; exploit.*

strings attached A moribund metaphor (see page 21). *conditions; limitations; preconditions; prerequisites; provisions; qualifications; requirements; stipulations; terms.*

stroll down memory lane A moribund metaphor (see page 21). *be nostalgic; recall; recollect; remember; reminisce; think back.*

(as) strong as a horse An insipid simile. *athletic; beefy; brawny; burly; energetic; fit; hale; hardy; healthful; healthy; hearty; husky; manly; mesomorphic; mighty; muscular; powerful; puissant; robust; rugged; sinewy; solid; sound; stalwart; stout; strapping; strong; sturdy; vigorous; virile; well-built.*

(a) stroll (walk) in the park A moribund metaphor (see page 21). 1. *casual; easily done; easy; effortless; elementary; facile; simple; simplicity itself; straightforward; uncomplex; uncomplicated.* 2. *agreeable; beguiling; charming; delightful; enchanting; engaging; enjoyable; fun; glorious; gratifying; inviting; joyful; joyous; pleasant; pleasing; pleasurable.* ■ Building high-rise buildings, dams, and bridges isn't exactly *a walk in the park.* REPLACE WITH *simple.* ■ Compared to NetWare 3.x, installing Windows NT Server is *a stroll in the park.* REPLACE WITH *effortless.*

(as) strong as a lion An insipid simile. *athletic; beefy; brawny; burly; energetic; fit; hale; hardy; healthful; healthy; hearty; husky; manly; mesomorphic; mighty; muscular; powerful; puissant; robust; rugged; sinewy; solid; sound; stalwart; stout; strapping; strong; sturdy; vigorous; virile; well-built.*

(as) strong as an ox An insipid simile. *athletic; beefy; brawny; burly; energetic; fit; hale; hardy; healthful; healthy; hearty; husky; manly; mesomorphic; mighty; muscular; powerful; puissant; robust; rugged; sinewy; solid; sound; stalwart; stout; strapping; strong; sturdy; vigorous; virile; well-built.*

(as) stubborn as a mule An insipid simile. *adamant; balky; bullheaded; cantankerous; contrary; contumacious; dogged; headstrong; inflexible; intractable; mulish; obdurate; obstinate; ornery; perverse; refractory; resolute; rigid; stubborn; unyielding; willful.*

stuff and nonsense An inescapable pair (see page 20). *absurdity; fatuousness; folly; foolishness; ludicrousness; nonsense; preposterousness; ridiculousness; rubbish; silliness.*

(the) stuff dreams (legends) are made of A moribund metaphor (see page 21).

(the) stuff of (legends) A moribund metaphor (see page 21). ■ His mumbo-jumbo about the war on terror was *the stuff of* prime time television. ■ The abuse of this child truly is *the stuff of* nightmares. ■ Lance Armstrong's record seventh win of the Tour de France is *the stuff of* true legends. ■ Being in the Hambletonian is *the stuff of* dreams — and obituaries.

> That was the stuff of others' lives.
> — Annie Proulx, *The Shipping News*

stuff to the gills A moribund metaphor (see page 21). *abounding; brimful; brimming; bursting; chock-full; congested; crammed; crowded; dense; filled; full;*

gorged; jammed; jam-packed; overcrowded; overfilled; overflowing; packed; replete; saturated; stuffed; swarming; teeming.

(major) stumbling block A moribund metaphor (see page 21). *barrier; hindrance; hurdle; impediment; obstacle; obstruction.* ■ Modernization of the Chinese HRM system is fraught with significant *stumbling blocks.* REPLACE WITH *obstacles.*

stupid An overworked word (see page 22). This epithet, along with others as common, is much overused. Let's do our best to convince *stupid* people that they are by calling them, instead, *addlebrained; addleheaded; addlepated; Boeotian; bovine; cretinous; decerebrate; doltish; dull-witted; dunderheaded; fatuous; fat-witted; harebrained; hebetudinous; imbecilic; incogitant; insensate; ludicrous; moronic; muddled; nescient; obtuse; oxlike; pedestrian; phlegmatic; sluggish; torpid; vacuous; witless.*

(as) sturdy as an oak An insipid simile. *athletic; beefy; brawny; burly; energetic; fit; hale; hardy; healthful; healthy; hearty; husky; manly; mesomorphic; mighty; muscular; powerful; puissant; robust; rugged; sinewy; solid; sound; stalwart; stout; strapping; strong; sturdy; vigorous; virile; well-built.*

subsequent to A torpid term (see page 24). *after; following.* ■ *Subsequent to* the initiation of the Ethics Committee investigation, the senator took back some tapes in my possession which I had not yet transcribed. REPLACE WITH *Following.* SEE ALSO *in advance of; previous to; subsequent to.*

(a) substantial part (portion; proportion) A wretched redundancy (see page 25). *a good (great) deal; a good (great) many; almost all; many; most; much; nearly all.* ■ It is unconscionable that *a substantial proportion* of our population does not have adequate access to health care. REPLACE WITH *much.* ■ I assume that Boston will be eligible for *a substantial portion* of the distressed communities fund. REPLACE WITH *a good deal.* SEE ALSO *a significant part (portion; proportion).*

such is life A plebeian sentiment (see page 23). SEE ALSO *that's how (the way) it goes; that's how (the way) the ball bounces; that's how (the way) the cookie crumbles; that's life; that's life in the big city; that's show biz; what are you going to do; what can you do.*

suck the life out of A moribund metaphor (see page 21). *bleed dry; deplete; drain; exhaust; sap; suck dry.*

suddenly and without warning A wretched redundancy (see page 25). *impetuously; impulsively; spontaneously; suddenly; unexpectedly; without warning.*

sufficient enough A wretched redundancy (see page 25). *enough; sufficient.* ■ Just tell them your new number, and that should be *sufficient enough.* REPLACE WITH *sufficient* or *enough.* SEE ALSO *adequate enough.*

(a) sufficient number (of) A wretched redundancy (see page 25). *enough.* ■ Effective groups contain *a sufficient number of* members to ensure good interaction. REPLACE WITH *enough.* SEE ALSO *a ... number (of).*

sugar and spice A moribund metaphor (see page 21).

sum and substance An inescapable pair (see page 20). *basis; center; core; crux; essence; gist; heart; kernel; pith; substance; sum.*

(the) summer (winter) of (our) discontent A moribund metaphor (see page 21).

(the) sun, the moon, and the stars A moribund metaphor (see page 21).

(as) sure as death An insipid simile. *assured; certain; destined; established; fated; fixed; foreordained; ineluctable; inescapable; inevitable; inexorable; irresistible; irreversible; irrevocable; ordained; prearranged; predestined; predetermined; sure; unalterable; unavoidable; unchangeable; unpreventable; unstoppable.*

(as) sure as death and taxes An insipid simile. *assured; certain; destined; established; fated; fixed; foreordained; ineluctable; inescapable; inevitable; inexorable; irresistible; irreversible; irrevocable; ordained; prearranged; predestined; predetermined; sure; unalterable; unavoidable; unchangeable; unpreventable; unstoppable.*

survival of the fittest A popular prescription (see page 23).

swallow (her) pride A moribund metaphor (see page 21). *abase; chasten; debase; degrade; demean; disgrace; dishonor; embarrass; humble; humiliate; lower; mortify; shame.*

swan song A moribund metaphor (see page 21). *farewell; good-bye.*

swear by all that's holy A moribund metaphor (see page 21). *affirm; asseverate; assert; attest; aver; avow; declare; pledge; promise; swear; testify; vow; warrant.*

swear like a sailor (trooper) An insipid simile. *abusive; blackguardly; coarse; crude; fescennine; foul-mouthed; indecent; lewd; obscene; profane; ribald; scurrilous; thersitical; vulgar.*

swear on a stack of bibles A moribund metaphor (see page 21). *affirm; asseverate; assert; attest; aver; avow; declare; pledge; promise; swear; testify; vow; warrant.*

sweat bullets A moribund metaphor (see page 21). 1. *excrete; exude; ooze; perspire; sweat; swelter; wilt.* 2. *be afraid; be agitated; be anxious; be apprehensive; be distraught; be distressed; be fearful; be fretful; be impatient; be nervous; be panicky; be tense; be uneasy; be worried.* 3. *drudge; grind; grub; labor; moil; slave; strain; strive; struggle; sweat; toil; travail; work hard.*

sweep off (her) feet A moribund metaphor (see page 21). *amaze; astonish; astound; awe; dazzle; dumbfound; flabbergast; overpower; overwhelm; shock; startle; stun; stupefy; surprise.*

sweep (it) under the (carpet) rug A moribund metaphor (see page 21). 1. *brush aside; avoid; discount; disregard; dodge; duck; ignore; neglect; omit; pass over; recoil from; shrink from; shun; shy away from; turn away from; withdraw from.* 2. *camouflage; cloak; conceal; cover; disguise; enshroud; harbor; hide; keep secret; mask; screen; shroud; suppress; veil; withhold.* ■ The strategy was to *sweep it under the rug.* REPLACE WITH *ignore it.*

sweep (it) under the table A moribund metaphor (see page 21). 1. *brush aside; avoid; discount; disregard; dodge; duck; ignore; neglect; omit; pass over; recoil from; shrink from; shun; shy away from; turn away from; withdraw from.* 2. *camouflage; cloak; conceal; cover; disguise; enshroud; harbor; hide; keep secret; mask; screen; shroud; suppress; veil; withhold.* ■ We see the word *anti-Semitism* every day in our secular newspapers, but the word *anti-Catholic* is *swept under the table.* REPLACE WITH *brushed aside.*

(as) sweet as honey An insipid simile. 1. *honeyed; luscious; saccharine; sugary; sweet; sweetened; syrupy.* 2. *agreeable; ambrosial; beguiling; celestial; charming; delectable; delicious; delightful; divine; enchanting; engaging; enjoyable; fun; heavenly; glorious; gratifying; inviting; joyful; joyous; luscious; pleasant; pleasing; pleasurable.*

(as) sweet as pie An insipid simile. 1. *honeyed; luscious; saccharine; sugary; sweet; sweetened; syrupy.* 2. *agreeable; ambrosial; beguiling; celestial; charming; delectable; delicious; delightful; divine; enchanting; engaging; enjoyable; fun; heavenly; glorious; gratifying; inviting; joyful; joyous; luscious; pleasant; pleasing; pleasurable.*

sweeten the pot A moribund metaphor (see page 21). *add to; augment; enhance; improve; increase; supplement.*

sweeter than honey A moribund metaphor (see page 21). 1. *honeyed; luscious; saccharine; sugary; sweet; sweetened; syrupy.* 2. *agreeable; ambrosial; beguiling; celestial; charming; delectable; delicious; delightful; divine; enchanting; engaging; enjoyable; fun; heavenly; glorious; gratify-*

ing; inviting; joyful; joyous; luscious; pleasant; pleasing; pleasurable.

sweet smell of success A moribund metaphor (see page 21).

(as) swift as an arrow An insipid simile. *brisk; expeditious; fast; fleet; hasty; hurried; immediate; instant; instantaneous; prompt; quick; rapid; speedy; spry; sudden; swift; winged.*

swim against the current (tide) A moribund metaphor (see page 21). 1. *drudge; grind; grub; labor; moil; slave; strain; strive; struggle; sweat; toil; travail; work hard.* 2. *battle; fight; tussle; wrestle.*

swim like a fish An insipid simile.

swim upstream A moribund metaphor (see page 21).

swim with the tide A moribund metaphor (see page 21).

T

tabula rasa A foreign phrase (see page 19).

(a case of) (the) tail wagging the dog A moribund metaphor (see page 21). *backward; in reverse.*

take a back seat A moribund metaphor (see page 21). *be ancillary; be inferior; be lesser; be lower; be minor; be second; be*

secondary; be subordinate; be subservient.
■ Just a few years after this work, machine learning *took a back seat* to expert knowledge systems. REPLACE WITH *became subordinate.* ■ As in most races for most offices, issues have *taken a back seat* to personality, image, footwork, money, and most important, field organization. REPLACE WITH *became ancillary.* ■ Power based on expertise frequently *takes a back seat* to power based on position. REPLACE WITH *is second.*

take a bath A moribund metaphor (see page 21). *lose money.*

take a beating A moribund metaphor (see page 21). 1. *be beaten; be conquered; be crushed; be defeated; be outdone; be overcome; be overpowered; be overwhelmed; be quelled; be routed; be trounced; be vanquished.* 2. *be assailed; be assaulted; be attacked; be battered; be beaten; be cudgeled; be flagellated; be flogged; be hit; be lambasted; be lashed; be licked; be mangled; be pounded; be pummeled; be struck; be thrashed; be trounced.*

take a breather An infantile phrase (see page 20). *be idle; be inactive; be lazy; be unemployed; be unoccupied; dally; dawdle; loaf; loiter; loll; lounge; relax; repose; rest.*

She stops to take a breather, picks up the ringing phone. — Kate Moses, *Wintering*

take a dim view of A moribund metaphor (see page 21). *deprecate; disapprove; dislike; frown on; object; protest.*

take a fancy (shine) to A moribund metaphor (see page 21). *delight in; enjoy; fancy; like; relish.*

take a front seat A moribund metaphor (see page 21). *prevail; rise above; surmount; triumph.*

Yesterday she way ready to pick up the phone, call Jeff, and tell him off for all he was worth. This morning, family took a front seat. — Margaret Johnson-Hodge, *Warm Hands*

take a gander (at) An infantile phrase (see page 20). *gaze; glance; glimpse; look; observe; stare; watch.*

take a haircut A moribund metaphor (see page 21). *lose money.* ■ He suggested what has been plain for some time — that holders of $1.7 billion in junk bonds would probably *take a haircut.* REPLACE WITH *lose money.*

take a hit A moribund metaphor (see page 21). *be assailed; be assaulted; be attacked; be battered; be beaten; be cudgeled; be flagellated; be flogged; be hit; be lambasted; be lashed; be licked; be mangled; be pounded; be pummeled; be struck; be thrashed; be trounced.*

take a leaf (page) out of (their) book A moribund metaphor (see page 21). *copy; duplicate; emulate; follow; imitate; mimic.*

take a load off (your) mind A moribund metaphor (see page 21). *acknowledge; admit; affirm; allow; avow; concede; confess; disclose; divulge; expose; grant; own; reveal; tell; uncover; unveil.*

take a long, hard look (at) A torpid term (see page 24). *analyze; assay; check out; delve into; examine; investigate; probe; scrutinize; study.* ■ We need leaders with the will and the determination to *take a long, hard look at* the structure of our government. REPLACE WITH *examine.*

take a nose dive A moribund metaphor (see page 21). *collapse; crash; dive; drop; fall; nose-dive; plummet; plunge.*

take a powder A moribund metaphor (see page 21). *abscond; clear out; decamp; depart; desert; disappear; escape; exit; flee; fly; go; go away; leave; move on; part; pull out; quit; retire; retreat; run away; take flight; take off; vacate; vanish; withdraw.*

take a turn for the better A moribund metaphor (see page 21). *ameliorate; amend; come round; convalesce; gain strength; get better; heal; improve; look up; meliorate; mend; rally; recover; recuperate; refresh; regain strength; renew; revive; strengthen.*

take a turn for the worse A moribund metaphor (see page 21). *decay; decline; degenerate; deteriorate; disintegrate; ebb; erode; fade; fall off; languish; lessen; wane; weaken; wither; worsen.*

take (my) ball (toys) and go home An infantile phrase (see page 20).

take (your) breath away A moribund metaphor (see page 21). *amaze; astonish; astound; awe; dazzle; dumbfound; flabbergast; overpower; overwhelm; shock; startle; stun; stupefy; surprise.*

take by storm A moribund metaphor (see page 21). *amaze; animate; awe; captivate; dazzle; electrify; excite; exhilarate; fascinate; impress; intoxicate; thrill; overwhelm.* ■ In the two years since it was introduced as the newest drug for depression, Prozac has *taken* the mental health community *by storm.* REPLACE WITH *captivated.*

take each day as it comes A popular prescription (see page 23).

take exception to A wretched redundancy (see page 25). *challenge; demur; disagree with; disapprove of; dispute; find fault with; object to; oppose; protest; question; resent.* ■ I *take exception to* your analysis of his difficulties. REPLACE WITH *disagree with.* SEE ALSO *take issue with.*

take (him) for a ride A moribund metaphor (see page 21). *bamboozle; befool; beguile; bilk; bluff; cheat; con; deceive; defraud; delude; dupe; feint; fool; gyp; hoodwink; lead astray; misdirect; misguide; misinform; mislead; spoof; swindle; trick; victimize.*

take (my) hat off to A moribund metaphor (see page 21). *acclaim; applaud; commend; compliment; congratulate; extol; hail; laud; praise.*

take (a lot of) heat A moribund metaphor (see page 21).

take into account A wretched redundancy (see page 25). *allow for; consider; contemplate; examine; inspect; investigate; look at; ponder; provide for; regard; scrutinize; study; think over; weigh.* ■ The character of the army is also an important factor to be *taken into account.* REPLACE WITH *considered.* SEE ALSO *take into consideration.*

take into consideration A wretched redundancy (see page 25). *allow for; consider; contemplate; examine; inspect;*

investigate; look at; ponder; provide for; regard; scrutinize; study; think over; weigh. ■ All this will be *taken into consideration,* and financial analysis will be done. REPLACE WITH *examined.* SEE ALSO *take into account.*

take issue with A wretched redundancy (see page 25). *challenge; demur; disagree with; disapprove of; dispute; find fault with; object to; oppose; protest; question; resent.* ■ Some *take issue with* the state requiring people to use seat belts. REPLACE WITH *object to.* SEE ALSO *take exception to.*

take it as it comes A popular prescription (see page 23).

(I) take it (that) back An infantile phrase (see page 20). 1. *be incorrect; be in error; be misguided; be misinformed; be mislead; be mistaken; be not right; be wrong.* 2. *disavow; recant; renounce; repudiate; retract; withdraw.* ■ Joanie is in third place; no, *I take it back* — it's another runner. REPLACE WITH *I'm wrong.* ■ I always wanted to be with someone more respectable; not respectable, *I take that back,* professional. REPLACE WITH *I retract that.*

take it one day (step) at a time A popular prescription (see page 23).

take it on the chin A moribund metaphor (see page 21). 1. *be beaten; be conquered; be crushed; be defeated; be flattened; be outdone; be overcome; be overpowered; be trampled; be trounced; be vanquished.* 2. *abide; accept; bear; brook; endure; stand; stomach; suffer; take; tolerate; withstand.*

take (her) life in (her) hands A moribund metaphor (see page 21). *chance; dare; endanger; gamble; hazard; imperil; jeopardize; make bold; peril; risk; venture.*

take (his) lumps A moribund metaphor (see page 21). ■ We fought our way back to profitability after *taking our lumps.*

take (their) medicine A moribund metaphor (see page 21).

taken aback A moribund metaphor (see page 21). *amazed; astonished; astounded; flabbergasted; shocked; staggered; stunned; surprised.*

take off the table A moribund metaphor (see page 21). *dismiss; not consider; reject; set aside; shelve.* ■ I don't think we should ever *take* a nuclear response *off the table.*

take the bait A moribund metaphor (see page 21).

> I almost take the bait and then decide, no, if I start talking about the boss, taking him apart, it will never quit. — Louise Erdrich, *Tales of Burning Love*

take the bit between (in) (her) teeth A moribund metaphor (see page 21). *defy; disobey; rebel; resist; revolt; take charge; take control.*

take the bitter with the sweet A popular prescription (see page 23).

take the bull by the horns A moribund metaphor (see page 21). *meet head-on.*

take the cake A moribund metaphor (see page 21). 1. *be best; be finest; be first; be first-rate; be outstanding; win.* 2. *be absurd; be disgraceful; be inane; be lowest; be outrageous; be poorest; be preposterous; be ridiculous; be worst.* ■ I am accustomed to being shocked by John Ellis, but "Beyond manifest destiny" *takes the cake.* REPLACE WITH *is outrageous.*

take the high road A moribund metaphor (see page 21). 1. *be beneficent; be benevolent; be broad-minded; be charitable; be civil; be courteous; be gracious; be high-minded; be kind; be liberal; be magnanimous; be noble.* 2. *be decent; be ethical; be exemplary; be good; be honest; be honorable; be just; be moral; be pure; be respectful; be righteous; be straight; be upright; be virtuous; be wholesome.*

take the money and run A moribund metaphor (see page 21). *abscond; clear out; decamp; depart; desert; disappear; escape; exit; flee; fly; go; go away; leave; make off; move on; part; pull out; quit; retire; retreat; run away; steal away; take flight; take off; vacate; vanish; withdraw.*

take the plunge A moribund metaphor (see page 21). *dive in; do it; jump in.*

take the wind out of (his) sails A moribund metaphor (see page 21). 1. *abase; chasten; debase; decrease; deflate; degrade; demean; depreciate; depress; diminish; disgrace; dishonor; embarrass; humble; humiliate; lower; mortify; puncture; shame.* 2. *arrest; balk; block; bridle; check; curb; derail; detain; end; foil; frustrate; halt; harness; hold up; impede; inhibit; obstruct; restrain; retard; slow; stall; stay; stop; suppress; terminate; thwart.*

(to) take this opportunity (to) An ineffectual phrase (see page 19). On the podium and before others, people speak what they're expected to say. Alone and on their deathbeds, they moan that no one knew who they were. *(To) take this opportunity (to)* is one of the phrases that people learn to mimic before they know to moan.

■ I would like *to take this opportunity* to apologize to my family and friends. DELETE *to take this opportunity.* ■ I'd like *to take this opportunity* to renew our commitment to you — to provide you with superior service. DELETE *to take this opportunity.* ■ Let me *take this opportunity to* thank our most inspirational guest. DELETE *take this opportunity to.* ■ As we wind down the current year, I would like to *take this opportunity to* thank you for your hard work on the Tech Communications Workshop this past academic year. DELETE *take this opportunity to.*

take to (his) heels A moribund metaphor (see page 21). *abscond; clear out; decamp; depart; desert; disappear; escape; exit; flee; fly; go; go away; leave; move on; part; pull out; quit; retire; retreat; run away; take flight; take off; vacate; vanish; withdraw.*

take (him) to task A torpid term (see page 24). *admonish; animadvert; berate; blame; castigate; censure; chasten; chastise; chide; condemn; criticize; denounce; denunciate; discipline; impugn; objurgate; punish; rebuke; remonstrate; reprehend; reprimand; reproach; reprobate; reprove; revile; scold; upbraid; vituperate.* ■ In polite, carefully chosen words, the auditors *take* management *to task* for a multitude of sins. REPLACE WITH *censure.*

take (her) to the cleaners A moribund metaphor (see page 21).

take (them) to the woodshed A moribund metaphor (see page 21). *admonish; animadvert; berate; castigate; censure; chasten; chastise; chide; condemn; criticize; denounce; denunciate; discipline; excoriate; fulminate against; imprecate; impugn; inveigh against; objurgate; punish; rebuke; remonstrate; reprehend; reprimand; reproach; reprobate; reprove; revile; scold; swear at; upbraid; vituperate.*

take with a grain (pinch) of salt A moribund metaphor (see page 21). *be suspicious; be wary; disbelieve; distrust; doubt; have doubts; have misgivings; have reservations; mistrust; question; suspect; wonder.* ■ But this pane's data should be *taken with a grain of salt.* REPLACE WITH *doubted.*

> But Tim Paddy hinted that this story should be taken with a pinch of salt. — William Trevor, *Fools of Fortune*

(like) taking candy from a baby An insipid simile. *apparent; basic; clear; clear-cut; conspicuous; distinct; easily done; easy; effortless; elementary; evident; explicit; facile; limpid; lucid; manifest; obvious; patent; pellucid; plain; simple; simplicity itself; straightforward; translucent; transparent; unambiguous; uncomplex; uncomplicated; understandable; unequivocal; unmistakable.*

> It was a situation tailor-made for Eden, who would've considered it just slightly more challenging than taking candy from a baby and then pushing the buggy off a cliff. — Antoinette Stockenberg, *Safe Harbor*

(like) taking lambs to the slaughter An insipid simile.

a tale never loses in the telling A popular prescription (see page 23).

(tell) tales out of school A moribund metaphor (see page 21). ■ A lot of people thought they were *telling tales out of school.*

> I oughtn't to tell tales out of school but it's a long time ago now and I'm glad Sarah has found happiness, but in those days it was well-known in Pankot that Susan was always pinching her elder sister's young men .... — Paul Scott, *Staying On*

talk a blue streak A moribund metaphor (see page 21). *babbling; blathering; chatty; facile; fluent; garrulous; glib; jabbering; logorrheic; long-winded; loquacious; prolix; talkative; verbose; voluble; windy.*

talk (my) ear (head) off A moribund metaphor (see page 21). *babbling; blathering; chatty; facile; fluent; garrulous; glib; jabbering; logorrheic; long-winded; loquacious; prolix; talkative; verbose; voluble; windy.*

talk is cheap A quack equation (see page 23).

talk (speak) out of both sides of (his) mouth A moribund metaphor (see page 21). *be ambivalent; be indecisive; be irresolute; be uncertain; be unsure; be wishy-washy; dodge; doubletalk; equivocate; evade; fence; hedge; palter; prevaricate; quibble; shuffle; sidestep; tergiversate; waffle.*

(he) talks a good game A moribund metaphor (see page 21).

talk through (his) hat A moribund metaphor (see page 21). *babble; blather; jabber; prate; prattle.*

talk turkey A moribund metaphor (see page 21).

tan (warm) (her) hide A moribund metaphor (see page 21). *spank.*

tar and feather A moribund metaphor (see page 21). *admonish; animadvert; berate; castigate; censure; chasten; chastise; chide; condemn; criticize; denounce; denunciate; discipline; impugn; objurgate; punish; rebuke; remonstrate; reprehend; reprimand; reproach; reprobate; reprove; revile; scold; upbraid; vituperate.*

tar (him) with the same brush A moribund metaphor (see page 21).

teach (me) the ropes A moribund metaphor (see page 21). *coach; educate; initiate; instruct; teach; train; tutor.*

team player A suspect superlative (see page 24). This term is much favored by those in the business world for an employee who thinks just as others do and behaves just as he is expected to. A *team player* is a person who has not the spirit to think for or be himself.

Of course, nothing new, nothing innovative is likely to be realized by insisting, as the business world does, on objectivity and consensus.

A team player is often no more than a *bootlicker;* no more than a *fawner,* a *flatterer,* a *follower;* no more than a *lackey,* a *minion,* a *stooge;* no more than a *sycophant,* a *toady,* a *yes-man.* ■ Mulvey,

whose termination is perhaps the most striking — he was one of the bank's stellar performers — was not regarded as a *team player.*

tear (out) (my) hair A moribund metaphor (see page 21). 1. *acerbated; angry; annoyed; bothered; cross; displeased; enraged; furious; grouchy; incensed; inflamed; infuriated; irate; irked; irritated; mad; miffed; peeved; provoked; riled; roiled; testy; upset; vexed.* 2. *agitated; anxious; apprehensive; distraught; distressed; fearful; frustrated; nervous; panicky; stressed; stressful; tense; tormented; troubled; uneasy; worried.*

teeter on the brink (of) A moribund metaphor (see page 21).

tell it like it is An infantile phrase (see page 20). *be blunt; be candid; be forthright; be frank; be honest; be open; be truthful.* ■ He's not whining; he's just *telling it like it is.* REPLACE WITH *being honest.* ■ These videos may be informative and *tell it like it is* but are far too explicit and do not belong in a coed classroom. REPLACE WITH *truthful.*

tell it to the Marines A moribund metaphor (see page 21).

tell (her) off A torpid term (see page 24). *admonish; animadvert; berate; castigate; censure; chasten; chastise; chide; condemn; criticize; denounce; denunciate; discipline; impugn; objurgate; punish; rebuke; remonstrate; reprehend; reprimand; reproach; reprobate; reprove; revile; scold; upbraid; vituperate.*

tell (them) where to get off A torpid term (see page 24). *admonish; animadvert; berate; castigate; censure; chasten;*

chastise; chide; condemn; criticize; denounce; denunciate; discipline; impugn; objurgate; punish; rebuke; remonstrate; reprehend; reprimand; reproach; reprobate; reprove; revile; scold; upbraid; vituperate.

tempest in a teapot A moribund metaphor (see page 21).

terra firma A foreign phrase (see page 19).

terrific An overworked word (see page 22). *Terrific* means *causing terror* or *terrifying*, but of late, it means only *very bad* or, annoyingly, *very good*. ■ I have a *terrific* stomachache. REPLACE WITH *very bad*. ■ We had a *terrific* time at the party. REPLACE WITH *very good*. SEE ALSO *awesome; awful*.

(the) temper of our time A moribund metaphor (see page 21).

test the waters A moribund metaphor (see page 21).

thank goodness it's Friday An infantile phrase (see page 20).

thanks but no thanks An infantile phrase (see page 20). *thanks; thanks all the same; thanks anyway; thanks just the same.*

thank you A plebeian sentiment (see page 23). Even *thank you* — once a sure sign of civility — becomes part of the plebeian patois when it is spoken mechanically.

Only a spectacularly thoughtless person would thank others for having been abused or berated by them, for having been refused or rejected by them. SEE ALSO *excuse me?; I'm sorry*.

thank(ing) you in advance A plebeian sentiment (see page 23). These phrases are more than plebeian, they are impudent. Only the lowbred or harebrained would presume to thank another for something while requesting it of him. ■ We *thank you in advance* for your understanding in this situation. ■ *Thank you in advance* for taking the time to help us. ■ *Thanks in advance* for your cooperation. ■ I have contacted the folks at ArtistDirect as well, and wanted to *thank you in advance* for your compliance in this matter.

And now variations of this phrase are being used in other, even more facile and sillier, constructions: ■ If I offend any man, woman, beast, or anything in between, *I apologize in advance*. ■ He *apologizes in advance* to those with a more normal sense of humor.

that makes two of us An infantile phrase (see page 20). *as I do; I do too; neither do I; no more do I; nor do I; so do I.*

that's for me to know and you to find out An infantile phrase (see page 20). SEE ALSO *it's a long story*.

that's how (the way) it goes A plebeian sentiment (see page 23). *That's how (the way) it goes* and other expressions of resignation are often spoken by some people and rarely, if at all, spoken by others.

It is dimwitted people who are too often resigned when they should be complaining, too often resigned when they should be demanding, too often resigned when they should be raging. SEE ALSO *such is life; that's how (the way) the ball bounces; that's how (the way) the cookie crumbles; that's life; that's life in the big city; that's show biz; what are you going to do; what can you do.*

> The window was open so the skinny bird flew in. Flappity-flap with its frazzled black wings. That's how it goes. — Bernard Malamud, *Idiots First*

that's how (the way) the ball bounces A plebeian sentiment (see page 23). SEE ALSO *such is life; that's how (the way) it goes; that's how (the way) the cookie crumbles; that's life; that's life in the big city; that's show biz; what are you going to do; what can you do.*

that's how (the way) the cookie crumbles A plebeian sentiment (see page 23). SEE ALSO *such is life; that's how (the way) it goes; that's how (the way) the ball bounces; that's life; that's life in the big city; that's show biz; what are you going to do; what can you do.*

that's interesting A plebeian sentiment (see page 23). *That's interesting,* like *that's nice* (SEE), is most often a witless response to what a person has said. As such, it is no more than an acknowledgment of having been bored, an admission of not having listened, or a confession of having nothing clever to say. SEE ALSO *every effort is being made; interesting.*

that's life A plebeian sentiment (see page 23). SEE ALSO *such is life; that's how (the way) it goes; that's how (the way) the ball bounces; that's how (the way) the cookie crumbles; that's life in the big city; that's show biz; what are you going to do; what can you do.*

that's life in the big city A plebeian sentiment (see page 23). SEE ALSO *such is*

life; that's how (the way) it goes; that's how (the way) the ball bounces; that's how (the way) the cookie crumbles; that's life; that's show biz; what are you going to do; what can you do.

that's nice A plebeian sentiment (see page 23). This phrase is used to dismiss what a person has said. *That's nice* is a perfunctory response that, though it suggests interest in a person, actually reveals indifference to the person. SEE ALSO *every effort is being made; that's interesting.*

that's show biz A plebeian sentiment (see page 23). SEE ALSO *such is life; that's how (the way) it goes; that's how (the way) the ball bounces; that's how (the way) the cookie crumbles; that's life; that's life in the big city; what are you going to do; what can you do.*

that's the thing An ineffectual phrase (see page 19). SEE ALSO *here's the thing; the thing about (of) it is; the thing is.*

that's what it's all about A popular prescription (see page 23). ■ It's the little things, not the big things — like playing with my son — *that's what it's all about.*

that's where (you) enter the picture A moribund metaphor (see page 21).

that would be An infantile phrase (see page 20). ■ So, how much carbon does a typical car add to the atmosphere each year, anyway? *That would be* about 30 pounds. DELETE *That would be.* ■ Who is the tour guide? *That would be* me. DELETE *That would be.* ■ In a state that still flies the Confederate battle flag on its statehouse grounds, could a

Democratic governor grant clemency to a white man convicted of killing a black man? *That would be* a big no. DELETE *That would be.* ■ Do you recognize the handwriting and initials? *That would be* my handwriting. *That would be* my initials. USE *That is; These are.* ■ What is the first storm of the season? *That would be* Arthur. DELETE *That would be* ■ Who sat back here? Oh *that would be* Charles Thomas. DELETE *that would be.*

thence A withered word (see page 24). 1. *from that place; from there.* 2. *from that time.* 3. *hence; therefore; thus.* ■ Saudi Arabia pumps some crude through the IPSA pipeline to the Red Sea and *thence* through the Suez canal. REPLACE WITH *from there.*

there are no words to describe (express) A plebeian sentiment (see page 23). There are many more words than people seem to think, and far more is expressible with them than people seem to imagine.

Those who depend on dimwitticisms to convey thought and feeling are more apt to believe *there are no words to describe* ..., for these people are, necessarily, most frustrated by the limits of language.

Dimwitticisms do permit us to describe our most universal feelings, our most banal thoughts, but they prevent us from describing more individual feelings, more brilliant thoughts. These are reserved for a language largely unknown to everyday speakers and writers. SEE ALSO *words cannot describe (express).*

there are other fish in the sea A moribund metaphor (see page 21).

there are two sides to every (question) story A popular prescription (see page 23).

thereby hangs a tale A torpid term (see page 24).

there's a first time for everything A popular prescription (see page 23).

there's a time and a place for everything A popular prescription (see page 23).

there's more than one way to skin a cat A popular prescription (see page 23).

there's no accounting for taste A popular prescription (see page 23).

there's no fool like an old fool A popular prescription (see page 23).

there's no (such thing as a) free lunch A popular prescription (see page 23).

there's no going back A popular prescription (see page 23).

there's no harm in trying A popular prescription (see page 23).

there's no place like home A popular prescription (see page 23).

there's no rest for the weary A popular prescription (see page 23).

there's nothing new under the sun A popular prescription (see page 23).

there's no time like the present A popular prescription (see page 23). ■ They say *there's no time like the present* and that's never been truer.

there's nowhere to go but up A popular prescription (see page 23).

there's safety (strength) in numbers A popular prescription (see page 23).

thick and fast An inescapable pair (see page 20).

> Lenina was left to face the horrors of Malpais unaided. They came crowding in on her thick and fast.
> — Aldous Huxley, *Brave New World*

(as) thick as molasses An insipid simile. *concentrated; congealed; gelatinous; gluey; glutinous; gooey; gummy; inspissated; jellied; jellified; jellylike; mucilaginous; sticky; thick; viscid; viscous.*

(as) thick as thieves An insipid simile. *amiable; amicable; attached; brotherly; chummy; close; confidential; devoted; familiar; friendly; inseparable; intimate; loving; thick.*

(as) thin as a reed An insipid simile. *asthenic; attenuated; bony; cachectic; emaciated; gaunt; lank; lanky; lean; narrow; rail-thin; scraggy; scrawny; skeletal; skinny; slender; slight; slim; spare; spindly; svelte; sylphid; thin; trim; wispy.*

(as) thin as a rail An insipid simile. *asthenic attenuated; bony; cachectic; emaciated; gaunt; lank; lanky; lean; narrow; rail-thin; scraggy; scrawny; skeletal; skinny; slender; slight; slim; spare; spindly; svelte; sylphid; thin; trim; wispy.*

(the) thin end of the wedge A moribund metaphor (see page 21).

(a) thing An overworked word (see page 22). ■ The mind is *an* amazing *thing*. DELETE *an thing*. ■ It's *a* very important *thing*. DELETE *a thing*. ■ We have won the battle, but the war is *an* ongoing *thing*. DELETE *an thing*. ■ I think that change is *a* good *thing*. DELETE *a thing*. ■ You do this by comparing something your listeners know a lot about with something they know little or nothing about in order to make the unfamiliar *thing* clear. DELETE *thing*.

(the) thing about (of) it is An ineffectual phrase (see page 19). ■ *The thing about it is* it's humiliating and destructive to the psyche to be hit. DELETE *The thing about it is*. ■ *The thing about it is* what they say or do has no influence on what I do. DELETE *The thing about it is*. ■ *The thing about it is* I could never tell her anything. DELETE *The thing about it is*. SEE ALSO *here's the thing; that's the thing; the thing is.*

(the) thing is An ineffectual phrase (see page 19). ■ *The thing is* we know sexual orientation is discovered prior to adolescence. DELETE *The thing is*. ■ *The thing is* I work two jobs, and when I get home I want to relax. DELETE *The thing is*. ■ But *the thing is*, there's always someone who knows where they are. DELETE *the thing is*. SEE ALSO *here's the thing; that's the thing; the thing about (of) it is.*

(a) thing of beauty is a joy forever A popular prescription (see page 23).

(a) thing of the past A torpid term (see page 24). 1. *ceased; completed; concluded; dead; deceased; defunct; departed; done; ended; exanimate; expired; extinct; extinguished; finished; gone; inanimate; lifeless; no more; over; perished; stopped; termi-*

nated. 2. *antediluvian; antiquated; archaic; dead; obsolescent; obsolete; old; old-fashioned; outdated; outmoded; out of date; out of fashion; passé; superannuated.*
■ All agree that the days of students being able to work their way through college are *a thing of the past.* REPLACE WITH *over.* ■ The 8-hour day has become *a thing of the past.* REPLACE WITH *obsolete.* ■ Is the civil rights movement still alive in the United States or *a thing of the past?* REPLACE WITH *dead.*

> He was often on our campus, invited to address Municipal Government seminars on corruption. He told students that corruption was a thing of the past. — Saul Bellow, *More Die of Heartbreak*

think outside the box A torpid term (see page 24). *be creative; be innovative; be inventive; be original.*

Think outside the box is an uninspired way of saying *be creative.* Using it is the antithesis of what is means to be clever. Only the dull and hopeless use *think outside the box.*

thinly veiled An inescapable pair (see page 20).

> There is a thinly veiled tremble in her voice that tells him she is anything but okay. — John Searles, *Strange But True*

this and that A grammatical gimmick (see page 19).

this can't be happening (to me) A plebeian sentiment (see page 23).

this is the first day of the rest of your life A popular prescription (see page 23).

this is to inform you that An ineffectual phrase (see page 19). ■ *This is to inform you that* your credit application has been approved and your account is now open. DELETE *This is to inform you that.* SEE ALSO *(please) be advised that; (please) be informed that.*

thorn in (my) flesh (side) (of) A moribund metaphor (see page 21). *affliction; annoyance; bane; blight; bother; burden; curse; difficulty; inconvenience; irritant; irritation; load; nuisance; ordeal; pain; pest; plague; problem; torment; tribulation; trouble; vexation; weight; worry.* ■ Inventory collateral valuations have been *a thorn in the side of* the agricultural industry for years. REPLACE WITH *bane to.*

> Professor Emerson Sillerton was a thorn in the side of Newport society .... — Edith Wharton, *The Age of Innocence*

those who can, do; those who can't, teach A popular prescription (see page 23).

(the) three musketeers An infantile phrase (see page 20).

three sheets to the wind A moribund metaphor (see page 21). *besotted; crapulous; drunk; inebriated; intoxicated; sodden; stupefied; tipsy.*

> At Holtzman's place, in the two webbed lawn chairs they had set up on the sparse grass of the front lawn because the low steps where they had sat for so many nights when they were young were now too hard on their aging backs and sent pins and needles into their legs, Billy leaned forward, three sheets to the wind, and told Dennis that bitterness, then, was all that was left to it. — Alice McDermott, *Charming Billy*

three strikes and you're out An infantile phrase (see page 20).

thrilled to death A moribund metaphor (see page 21). *blissful; blithe; buoyant; cheerful; delighted; ecstatic; elated; enraptured; euphoric; exalted; excited; exhilarated; exultant; gay; glad; gleeful; good-humored; happy; intoxicated; jolly; jovial; joyful; joyous; jubilant; merry; mirthful; overjoyed; pleased; rapturous; thrilled*. SEE ALSO *to death*.

> Eveline was thrilled to death, but they got Eric Egstrom to come along too, on account of Frenchmen having such a bad reputation. — John Dos Passos, *The 42nd Parallel*

thrills and chills An inescapable pair (see page 20).

through thick and thin A moribund metaphor (see page 21).

throw (a dog) a bone A moribund metaphor (see page 21).

throw (her) a curve A moribund metaphor (see page 21). *bamboozle; befool; beguile; bilk; bluff; cheat; con; deceive; defraud; delude; dupe; feint; fool; gyp; hoodwink; lead astray; misdirect; misguide; misinform; mislead; spoof; swindle; trick; victimize*.

throw a monkey wrench into the works A moribund metaphor (see page 21). 1. *agitate; confuse; disorder; disorganize; disquiet; disrupt; disturb; fluster; jar; jinx; jolt; jumble; mix up; muddle; perturb; rattle; ruffle; shake up; stir up; trouble; unnerve; unsettle; upset.* 2. *blight; cripple; damage; disable; harm; hurt; impair; incapacitate; lame; mar; mess up; rack; ruin; sabotage; spoil; subvert; undermine; vitiate; wrack; wreck*.

throw a wet blanket on A moribund metaphor (see page 21). *bridle; check; constrain; contain; curb; curtail; dampen; discourage; foil; harness; hinder; impede; inhibit; obstruct; quell; repress; restrain; restrict; retard; stifle; subdue; suppress; thwart; weaken*. SEE ALSO *throw cold water on*.

throw caution to the wind A moribund metaphor (see page 21). 1. *be adventuresome; be adventurous; be audacious; be bold; be brave; be courageous; be daring; be dauntless; be fearless; be intrepid; be mettlesome; be plucky; be stalwart; be unafraid; be valiant; be valorous; be venturesome.* 2. *be careless; be foolhardy; be hasty; be heedless; be impetuous; be incautious; be precipitate; be rash; be reckless; be thoughtless*.

throw cold water on A moribund metaphor (see page 21). *bridle; check; constrain; contain; curb; curtail; dampen; discourage; foil; harness; hinder; impede; inhibit; obstruct; quell; repress; restrain; restrict; retard; stifle; subdue; suppress;*

thwart; weaken. SEE ALSO *throw a wet blanket on.*

throw down the gauntlet (glove) A moribund metaphor (see page 21). *affront; brave; call; challenge; confront; dare; defy; encounter; face; meet.*

throw dust in (your) eyes A moribund metaphor (see page 21). *bamboozle; befool; beguile; bilk; bluff; cheat; con; deceive; defraud; delude; dupe; feint; fool; gyp; hoodwink; lead astray; misdirect; misguide; misinform; mislead; spoof; swindle; trick; victimize.*

throw enough dirt, and some will stick A moribund metaphor (see page 21).

throw for a loop A moribund metaphor (see page 21). *amaze; astonish; astound; awe; dazzle; dumbfound; flabbergast; overpower; overwhelm; shock; startle; stun; stupefy; surprise.*

throw (toss) (his) hat in the ring A moribund metaphor (see page 21). 1. *join; run.* 2. *commence; begin; enter into; start; undertake.*

throw (toss) in the sponge (towel) A moribund metaphor (see page 21). *abdicate; accede; acquiesce; bow; capitulate; cede; concede; give in; give up; quit; relinquish; retreat; submit; succumb; surrender; yield.* ■ The bloated bureaucracy remains unscathed, spending continues uncontrolled, and the House leadership has *thrown in the towel* to the governor. REPLACE WITH *acquiesced.* ■ If I get any more overwhelmed, I'm going to *throw in the towel.* REPLACE WITH *quit.*

throw (them) off the scent A moribund metaphor (see page 21). *bamboozle; befool; beguile; bilk; bluff; cheat; con; hoodwink; lead astray;; deceive; defraud; delude; dupe; feint; fool; gyp; misdirect; misguide; misinform; mislead; spoof; swindle; trick.*

throw out the baby with the bath water A moribund metaphor (see page 21).

throw (toss) out the window A moribund metaphor (see page 21). *abandon; chuck; discard; dismiss; dump; jettison; reject; repudiate; throw out; toss out.* ■ Everything I tried to teach them about getting along and togetherness has been *thrown out the window.* REPLACE WITH *jettisoned.*

throw the book at A moribund metaphor (see page 21). *admonish; animadvert; berate; castigate; censure; chasten; chastise; chide; condemn; criticize; denounce; denunciate; discipline; excoriate; fulminate against; imprecate; impugn; inveigh against; objurgate; penalize; punish; rebuke; remonstrate; reprehend; reprimand; reproach; reprobate; reprove; revile; scold; swear at; upbraid; vituperate.*

throw (them) to the dogs (wolves) A moribund metaphor (see page 21). 1. *forfeit; sacrifice; surrender.* 2. *endanger; imperil; jeopardize.*

I remember his ex-partner at the hospital saying he'll be thrown to the hounds, and I can only hope he's wrong, that the guards will look out for one of their own, though I feel like I'm lying to myself thinking this. — Andre Dubus III, *House of Sand and Fog*

throw (his) weight around A moribund metaphor (see page 21). *awe; browbeat; bully; frighten; intimidate; menace; push around; scare; threaten; torment.*

thumb (his) nose (at) A moribund metaphor (see page 21). *contemn; deride; despise; detest; disdain; jeer at; laugh at; mock; ridicule; scoff at; scorn; shun; slight; sneer; snub; spurn.* ■ We burden our own banks with record keeping and reporting while offshore bankers *thumb their noses* at us. REPLACE WITH *mock.*

> He's breaking the rules, under their noses, thumbing his nose at them, getting away with it. — Margaret Atwood, *The Handmaid's Tale*

(turn) thumbs down A moribund metaphor (see page 21). *decline; deny; disallow; disapprove; forbid; nix; prohibit; proscribe; refuse; reject; rule out; say no; turn down; veto.*

thunderous applause An inescapable pair (see page 20).

tickled pink A moribund metaphor (see page 21). *blissful; buoyant; cheerful; delighted; elated; excited; gay; glad; gladdened; gleeful; good-humored; gratified; happy; jolly; jovial; joyful; joyous; jubilant; merry; mirthful; pleased; tickled.*

tickled to death A moribund metaphor (see page 21). *blissful; buoyant; cheerful; delighted; elated; excited; gay; glad; gladdened; gleeful; good-humored; gratified; happy; jolly; jovial; joyful; joyous; jubilant; merry; mirthful; pleased; tickled.* SEE ALSO *to death.*

(a) tidal wave of A moribund metaphor (see page 21). ■ There's just *a tidal wave of* vital information that gets delivered by telephone. SEE ALSO *a barrage of.*

(the) tide of A moribund metaphor (see page 21). SEE ALSO *a barrage of.*

tied to (her) apron strings A moribund metaphor (see page 21). *clinging; dependent; subject; subordinate; subservient.*

tie the knot A moribund metaphor (see page 21). *marry; wed.*

tie up loose ends A moribund metaphor (see page 21).

(as) tight as a drum An insipid simile. *firm; snug; strained; stretched; taut; tense; tight.*

tighten (our) belts A moribund metaphor (see page 21). *reduce costs; save money.* ■ We are constantly looking for ways to *tighten our belts.* REPLACE WITH *save money.*

tighten the screws A moribund metaphor (see page 21). *coerce; command; compel; constrain; demand; dictate; enforce; enjoin; force; insist; make; order; press; pressure; push.*

tight rein on A moribund metaphor (see page 21).

(talk) till (I'm) blue in the face A moribund metaphor (see page 21). *always; ceaselessly; constantly; continually; continuously; endlessly; eternally; everlastingly; evermore; forever; forevermore; immortally; indefinitely; interminably; permanently; perpetually; persistently; unceasingly; unremittingly.*

till (until) (her) dying days A moribund metaphor (see page 21). *always; ceaselessly; constantly; continually; continuously; endlessly; eternally; everlastingly; evermore; forever; forevermore; immortally; indefinitely; interminably; permanently; perpetually; persistently; unceasingly; unremittingly.*

till (until) hell freezes over A moribund metaphor (see page 21). *always; ceaselessly; constantly; continually; continuously; endlessly; eternally; everlastingly; evermore; forever; forevermore; immortally; indefinitely; interminably; permanently; perpetually; persistently; unceasingly; unremittingly.*

till (until) it's coming out (of) (my) ears A moribund metaphor (see page 21). *excessively; exorbitantly; extravagantly; immoderately; in excess; inordinately; profligately; unrestrainedly.*

till kingdom come A moribund metaphor (see page 21). *always; ceaselessly; constantly; continually; continuously; endlessly; eternally; everlastingly; evermore; forever; forevermore; immortally; indefinitely; interminably; permanently; perpetually; persistently; unceasingly; unremittingly.*

> I let out a great bellow such as cattle do and would have gone on bellowing till Kingdom Come had not some sinner taken my ear and turned me to look under Johnson's devilish table. — Jeanette Winterson, *Sexing the Cherry*

till (until) the cows come home A moribund metaphor (see page 21). *always; ceaselessly; constantly; continually; continuously; endlessly; eternally; everlast-*

ingly; evermore; forever; forevermore; immortally; indefinitely; interminably; permanently; perpetually; persistently; unceasingly; unremittingly. ■ You can press Escape *until the cows come home*, and it will do nothing. REPLACE WITH *unceasingly.*

tilt at windmills A moribund metaphor (see page 21).

time and effort An inescapable pair (see page 20). ■ He still puts a lot of *time and effort* into his commercials.

time and energy An inescapable pair (see page 20). ■ Boiling water also is cheaper than buying bottled water, but it takes more *time and energy.*

time and tide wait for no man A popular prescription (see page 23).

time flies when you're having fun A popular prescription (see page 23).

(the) time has come A torpid term (see page 24). ■ *The time has come* to recognize that personal diaries must be accorded greater protection than business records.

time heals all wounds A popular prescription (see page 23).

time is a great healer A popular prescription (see page 23).

time is money A quack equation (see page 23).

time period A wretched redundancy (see page 25). *period; time.* ■ Would you go along with this for a *time period?* REPLACE WITH *period* or *time.*

time was when A torpid term (see page 24). *before; earlier; formerly; long ago; once; previously.*

(the) time will come A torpid term (see page 24).

time will tell A moribund metaphor (see page 21). ■ We have made many changes in attitude and practice, and only *time will tell* whether these are for the ultimate good or merely more mischief.

tip (my) hat to A moribund metaphor (see page 21). 1. *acknowledge; flag; greet; hail; recognize; salute; wave to; welcome.* 2. *acclaim; applaud; cheer; commend; compliment; congratulate; hail; praise; salute; support; toast.* ■ I *tip my hat to* Mayor Menino for having the vision to see that Boston does not require a professional football team to remain a world-class city. REPLACE WITH *salute.* ■ I'd also like to *tip my hat to* Jeff Staples for his fast editing and feedback. REPLACE WITH *acknowledge.*

(a) tip of the hat A moribund metaphor (see page 21).

tip of the iceberg A moribund metaphor (see page 21). *beginning; commencement; foundation; inauguration; inception; least of it; onset; start.* The monstrous and omnipresent *tip of the iceberg*, like so many other dimwitted usages, alerts us to an inarticulate speaker, a tentative writer. ■ We have just seen the *tip of the iceberg* of corporations that have loaded up with too much debt and gone broke because of the merger and takeover wars. REPLACE WITH *beginning.* ■ I feel these issues and programs are just the *tip of the iceberg*. REPLACE

WITH *start.*

And here are a couple of examples no less than wonderful: ■ It's difficult to tell whether my study is the iceberg and the tip is yet to be found, or whether my study was the *tip of the iceberg*. ■ These attacks are only the *tip of the iceberg*; they are the part of the iceberg that is visible above the water, in clear view — but as everyone knows, the largest part of the iceberg, and possibly the most dangerous, lies beneath the surface of the water and is difficult to detect.

tip the scales A moribund metaphor (see page 21).

(as) tired as a dog An insipid simile. *beat; bushed; debilitated; depleted; drained; drowsy; enervated; exhausted; fatigued; groggy; sapped; sleepy; sluggish; slumberous; somnolent; soporific; spent; tired; weary; worn out.*

to all intents and purposes A wretched redundancy (see page 25). *effectively; essentially; in effect; in essence; practically; virtually.* ■ *To all intents and purposes*, you were dating two women at a time. REPLACE WITH *In effect.* SEE ALSO *for all intents and purposes; for all practical purposes; to all intents and purposes; to all practical purposes.*

to all practical purposes A wretched redundancy (see page 25). *effectively; essentially; in effect; in essence; practically; virtually.* ■ The ruling Unionist party is, *to all practical purposes*, a Protestant party. REPLACE WITH *in essence.* SEE ALSO *for all intents and purposes; for all practical purposes; to all intents and purposes.*

(the) toast of the town A moribund metaphor (see page 21).

to a T A moribund metaphor (see page 21). *accurately; correctly; exactly; faultlessly; flawlessly; ideally; just right; perfectly; precisely; rightly; strictly; to perfection; unerringly; very well.*

> Like all Whiting males, C.B. was a short man who disliked drawing attention to the fact, so the low-slung Spanish architecture suited him to a T. — Richard Russo, *Empire Falls*

to beat the band A moribund metaphor (see page 21). *actively; aggressively; dynamically; emphatically; energetically; fast; ferociously; fervently; fiercely; forcefully; frantically; frenziedly; furiously; hard; intensely; intently; mightily; passionately; powerfully; robustly; savagely; spiritedly; strenuously; strongly; vehemently; viciously; vigorously; violently; wildly; with vigor.* ■ When you wake up, it should be snowing *to beat the band*. REPLACE WITH *mightily*.

to burn A moribund metaphor (see page 21). 1. *enormous; great; huge; immense; large; massive; monstrous; prodigious; tremendous; vast.* 2. *excessive; exorbitant; extreme; immoderate; inordinate; undue.* ■ And Mrs. Dole has *Southern charm to burn*. REPLACE WITH *immense Southern charm*.

today is the first day of the rest of (your) life A popular prescription (see page 23).

to death A moribund metaphor (see page 21). *consumedly; enormously; exceedingly; excessively; exorbitantly; extraordinarily; extremely; greatly; hugely; immensely; immoderately; inordinately; intemperately; intensely; mightily; prodigiously; unreasonably; unrestrainedly; very much.* ■ I love him *to death*. REPLACE WITH *prodigiously*.

And as if *to death* were not persuasive enough: ■ The DoD and VA appeared content to study Gulf War illnesses *literally to death*. REPLACE WITH *unrestrainedly*.

to each (his) own A popular prescription (see page 23).

to err is human A popular prescription (see page 23).

to err is human, to forgive divine A popular prescription (see page 23).

toe the line (mark) A moribund metaphor (see page 21). *abide by; accede; accommodate; accord; acquiesce; adapt; adhere to; agree; behave; comply; concur; conform; correspond; follow; harmonize; heed; mind; obey; observe; submit; yield.*

(leveraged) to (their) eyebrows A moribund metaphor (see page 21).

(smell) to high heaven A moribund metaphor (see page 21). *decidedly; mightily; greatly; forcefully; hugely; powerfully; strongly; terribly; tremendously.*

to make a long story short A torpid term (see page 24). *briefly; concisely; in brief; in short; in sum; succinctly; tersely.*

(with) tongue in cheek A moribund metaphor (see page 21). *facetiously; humorously; in fun; in jest; in play; jocosely; jokingly; kiddingly; playfully; teasingly.*

(set) tongues wagging A moribund metaphor (see page 21). *babble; blab; cackle; chaffer; chat; chitchat; chatter; confabulate; converse; gossip; jabber; palaver; prate; prattle; rattle; talk.*

too big for (his) breeches A moribund metaphor (see page 21). *arrogant; cavalier; condescending; contemptuous; despotic; dictatorial; disdainful; dogmatic; domineering; haughty; imperious; insolent; lofty; overbearing; overweening; patronizing; pompous; pretentious; scornful; self-important; supercilious; superior; vainglorious.*

(she's) too good for (him) A suspect superlative (see page 24).

too hot to handle A moribund metaphor (see page 21).

(you) took the words (right) out of (my) mouth A moribund metaphor (see page 21).

too many chiefs (and not enough Indians) A moribund metaphor (see page 21).

too many cooks spoil the broth (brew) A popular prescription (see page 23).

too smart for (his) own good A plebeian sentiment (see page 23).

(fight) tooth and nail A moribund metaphor (see page 21). *actively; aggressively; dynamically; emphatically; energetically; ferociously; fervently; fiercely; forcefully; frantically; frenziedly; furiously; hard; intensely; intently; mightily; passionately; powerfully; robustly; savagely; spiritedly; strenuously; strongly; vehement-*

ly; viciously; vigorously; violently; wildly; with vigor. ■ Bank of Boston, the state's largest bank, lobbied *tooth and nail* against the interstate law. REPLACE WITH *intensely.*

toot (your) own horn A moribund metaphor (see page 21). *acclaim; applaud; bluster; boast; brag; celebrate; cheer; commend; compliment; congratulate; crow; extol; flatter; gloat; hail; honor; laud; praise; puff; salute; self-congratulate; strut; swagger.* ■ Engineers are the world's worst at *tooting their own horn.* REPLACE WITH *applauding themselves.* ■ Even so, the group president of Lucent Technologies' Global Service Provider business division isn't the type to *toot her own horn.* REPLACE WITH *boast.*

top brass A moribund metaphor (see page 21). *administrator; boss; brass; chief; commander; director; executive; foreman; head; headman; leader; manager; master; (high) muckamuck; officer; official; overseer; president; principal; superintendent; supervisor.*

(a) torrent of A moribund metaphor (see page 21). SEE ALSO *a barrage of.*

> They crossed the street and O'Keefe bought an Irish Times and moved jauntily over the bridge, both filled with a torrent of words bled from O'Keefe's excitement and memories of Dublin. — J. P. Donleavy, *The Ginger Man*

toss and turn An inescapable pair (see page 20).

> Heaven knew how he missed her and how many nights he remained awake tossing and turning while thinking about her. — Ha Jin, *Waiting*

to tell you the truth An ineffectual phrase (see page 19).

(march) to the beat of a different drummer A moribund metaphor (see page 21). *aberrant; abnormal; anomalistic; anomalous; atypical; bizarre; curious; deviant; different; distinct; distinctive; eccentric; exceptional; extraordinary; fantastic; foreign; grotesque; idiosyncratic; independent; individual; individualistic; irregular; novel; odd; offbeat; original; peculiar; puzzling; quaint; queer; rare; remarkable; separate; singular; strange; uncommon; unconventional; unexampled; unique; unnatural; unorthodox; unparalleled; unprecedented; unusual; weird.*

to the bone A moribund metaphor (see page 21). *altogether; completely; entirely; fully; perfectly; quite; roundly; thoroughly; totally; unreservedly; utterly; wholly.*

to the ends (far reaches) of the earth A moribund metaphor (see page 21). 1. *always; ceaselessly; constantly; continually; continuously; endlessly; eternally; everlastingly; evermore; forever; forevermore; frequently; interminably; nonstop; permanently; perpetually; persistently; recurrently; regularly; repeatedly; unceasingly; unremittingly.* 2. *all during; all over; all through; everyplace; everywhere; throughout.*

(up) to the hilt A moribund metaphor (see page 21). *altogether; completely; entirely; fully; perfectly; quite; roundly; thoroughly; totally; unreservedly; utterly; wholly.*

to the letter A moribund metaphor (see page 21). *accurately; correctly; exactly; faultlessly; flawlessly; ideally; just right; perfectly; precisely; rightly; strictly; to perfection; unerringly.*

(dressed) (up) to the nines A moribund metaphor (see page 21). *elaborately; elegantly; extravagantly; fashionably; flamboyantly; flashily; gaudily; lavishly; ostentatiously; profusely; richly; showily; smartly; stylishly.* ■ The house was decorated *to the nines.* REPLACE WITH *lavishly.*

> Happily enough, it did not rain next day, and after morning school everybody dressed up to the nines. — Evelyn Waugh, *Decline and Fall*

to the point of (that; where) A wretched redundancy (see page 25). *so; so far (that); so much (that); so that; to; to when; to where.* ■ It's gotten *to the point that* I even flirt with operators. REPLACE WITH *so that.* ■ But it has now evolved *to the point where* they do it all the time. REPLACE WITH *to where.*

to the teeth A moribund metaphor (see page 21). *altogether; completely; entirely; fully; perfectly; quite; roundly; thoroughly; totally; unreservedly; utterly; wholly.*

to the tune of A wretched redundancy (see page 25). ■ It cost him *to the tune of* $4,500 to buy his new computer system. DELETE *to the tune of.*

to the victor belong the spoils A popular prescription (see page 23).

to thine own self be true A popular prescription (see page 23).

touch and go A moribund metaphor (see page 21). *dangerous; precarious; risky; uncertain.*

touch base with A moribund metaphor (see page 21).

(as) tough as leather An insipid simile. 1. *athletic; beefy; brawny; burly; energetic; firm; fit; hale; hardy; hearty; healthful; healthy; husky; leathery; manly; mesomorphic; mighty; muscular; powerful; puissant; robust; rugged; sinewy; solid; sound; stalwart; stout; strapping; strong; sturdy; tough; vigorous; virile; well-built.* 2. *constant; dependable; determined; faithful; fast; firm; fixed; inexorable; inflexible; loyal; obdurate; resolute; resolved; rigid; solid; stable; staunch; steadfast; steady; stern; strong; tenacious; unflinching; unwavering; unyielding.*

(as) tough as nails An insipid simile. 1. *athletic; beefy; brawny; burly; energetic; firm; fit; hale; hardy; healthful; healthy; hearty; leathery; manly; mesomorphic; mighty; muscular; powerful; puissant; robust; rugged; sinewy; solid; sound; stalwart; stout; strapping; strong; sturdy; tough; vigorous; virile; well-built.* 2. *constant; dependable; determined; faithful; fast; firm; fixed; inexorable; inflexible; loyal; obdurate; resolute; resolved; rigid; solid; stable; staunch; steadfast; steady; stern; strong; tenacious; unflinching; unwavering; unyielding.*

tough sledding A moribund metaphor (see page 21). *arduous; backbreaking;* *burdensome; difficult; exhausting; fatiguing; hard; herculean; laborious; not easy; onerous; severe; strenuous; toilful; toilsome; tough; troublesome; trying; wearisome.*

(it's) tough to teach an old dog new tricks A moribund metaphor (see page 21).

towering inferno An infantile phrase (see page 20). *blaze; conflagration; fire; holocaust; inferno.*

(proven) track record A moribund metaphor (see page 21).

tread water A moribund metaphor (see page 21). ■ He is now *treading water*, deciding what to do next.

treat (us) like royalty An insipid simile.

très A foreign phrase (see page 19). *very.* ■ She is *très* happy now that she is working. REPLACE WITH *very.* ■ Two New Yorkers we recently sent out on a discount shopping spree were *très* impressed with the hippness quotient. REPLACE WITH *very.*

trials and tribulations An inescapable pair (see page 20). *adversity; affliction; calamity; catastrophe; difficulty; distress; hardship; misadventure; misfortune; ordeal; trial; tribulation; trouble; woe.* ■ It also presents a first-hand account of the *trials and tribulations* of living in a lesbian family. REPLACE WITH *ordeal.*

tried and true An inescapable pair (see page 20). 1. *constant; dependable; faithful; firm; loyal; reliable; solid; staunch; steadfast; strong; true; trustworthy; trusty.*

2. *authentic; authenticated; established; reliable; substantiated; sound; verified; well-founded; well-grounded.*

trim (her) sails A moribund metaphor (see page 21).

trip the light fantastic A moribund metaphor (see page 21). *dance.*

triumphant return An inescapable pair (see page 20).

trouble in paradise A moribund metaphor (see page 21).

(a) trouble shared is a trouble halved A popular prescription (see page 23).

true blue A moribund metaphor (see page 21). *constant; dependable; faithful; firm; loyal; reliable; solid; staunch; steadfast; strong; true; trustworthy; trusty.*

true facts A wretched redundancy (see page 25). *facts; truth.* ■ Sometimes I wish the papers would print the *true facts*. REPLACE WITH *facts* or *truth*.

true love A suspect superlative (see page 24).

(the course of) true love never runs smooth A popular prescription (see page 23).

truthfully honest A wretched redundancy (see page 25). *honest; truthful.* ■ To be *truthfully honest*, I do want to be her friend. REPLACE WITH *truthful*.

truth is stranger than fiction A popular prescription (see page 23).

truth, justice, and the American way An infantile phrase (see page 20).

(the) truth of the matter is An ineffectual phrase (see page 19). ■ *The truth of the matter is* half of the people who get married end up divorced. DELETE *The truth of the matter is*. ■ *The truth of the matter is*, I don't understand it, but I'm against it. DELETE *The truth of the matter is*. SEE ALSO *(the) fact of the matter is*.

(the) truth will set you free A popular prescription (see page 23).

(a) tug of war A moribund metaphor (see page 21). ■ There's *a tug of war* between people who like the economy and people who are afraid.

(a) turn on A moribund metaphor (see page 21). *animating; arousing; bracing; enlivening; exciting; exhilarating; inspiring; inspiriting; invigorating; provoking; refreshing; rousing; stimulating; vivifying.*

try it, you'll like it An infantile phrase (see page 20).

try, try again A popular prescription (see page 23).

turn a blind eye to (toward) A moribund metaphor (see page 21). *brush aside; avoid; discount; disregard; dodge; duck; ignore; look away from; neglect; omit; overlook; pass over; shrink from; shun; shy away from; turn away from; withdraw from.* ■ And Chile, at least, is learning the risks of *turning a blind eye* to the past. REPLACE WITH *ignoring*. ■ Yet some of Bolt's advertisers, while lured by the site's demographics, may be *turning a blind eye* to content they normally find questionable in other media.

REPLACE WITH *overlooking*. ■ The donors have *turned a blind eye* toward allegations of corruption. REPLACE WITH *disregarded*.

> The scholarly badger, who hated contradiction and despised the Socratic method, would cast a blind eye to the twitching braid until her pupil's gasps became too insistent to ignore. — George Hagen, *The Laments*

turnabout is fair play A popular prescription (see page 23).

turn a (the) corner A moribund metaphor (see page 21). 1. *advance; awaken; better; expand; flourish; gain; gain strength; grow; heal; improve; increase; pick up; progress; prosper; rally; recover; recuperate; refresh; renew; revive; rouse; strengthen; thrive.* 2. *adjust; alter; change; modify; transform.* ■ Our No. 1 goal is to reestablish reliability and customer satisfaction, and we think we have started *to turn the corner*. REPLACE WITH *improve*.

> Two weeks was only one day more than thirteen days, but I felt we'd turned a corner that shouldn't have been turned, and I couldn't get myself out of bed. — Ann Packer, *The Dive From Clausen's Pier*

turn a deaf ear to A moribund metaphor (see page 21). *brush aside; avoid; discount; disregard; dodge; duck; ignore; neglect; omit; pass over; recoil from; shrink from; shun; shy away from; turn away from; withdraw from.* ■ Wilson should *turn a deaf ear to* HMO lobbyists and sign it. REPLACE WITH *dis-regard*. ■ Congress has *turned a deaf ear to* the public and taken the next step to unplug PBS and NPR. REPLACE WITH *ignored*.

turn a negative into a positive A torpid term (see page 24). ■ The revolution in traditional family ties has *turned a negative into a positive* for most singles today. SEE ALSO *negative; positive*.

turn (their) back on A moribund metaphor (see page 21). *abandon; abdicate; avoid; brush aside; deny; desert; disavow; discount; disinherit; disown; disregard; dodge; drop; duck; forgo; forsake; give up; ignore; leave; neglect; omit; pass over; quit; recoil from; reject; relinquish; renounce; shrink from; shun; shy away from; snub; surrender; turn away from; withdraw from; yield.* ■ It will be unfortunate, indeed, if the countries of Western Europe *turn their backs on* their Eastern neighbors. REPLACE WITH *disregard*.

turn back the clock (of time) A moribund metaphor (see page 21).

turn (your) dreams into reality A popular prescription (see page 23).

turn inside out A moribund metaphor (see page 21). *agitate; confuse; disorder; disorganize; disquiet; disrupt; disturb; fluster; jar; jolt; jumble; mess up; mix up; muddle; perturb; rattle; ruffle; shake up; stir up; trouble; unnerve; unsettle; upset.*

turn into (to) stone A moribund metaphor (see page 21). *calcify; fossilize; harden; petrify; solidify.*

turn like the weather An insipid simile. *capricious; changeable; erratic; fickle;*

fitful; flighty; fluctuating; haphazard; inconsistent; inconstant; intermittent; irregular; mercurial; occasional; random; sometime; spasmodic; sporadic; unpredictable; unsettled; unstable; unsteady; vacillating; volatile; wavering; wayward.

(another) turn of the screw A moribund metaphor (see page 21).

turn over a new leaf A moribund metaphor (see page 21). *alter; begin again; change; convert; improve; metamorphose; modify; reform; remake; remodel; rethink; transform.*

turn sour A moribund metaphor (see page 21). ■ Banks caught in the euphoria of a construction boom have watched the economy *turn sour.*

turn (my) stomach A moribund metaphor (see page 21). *appall; disgust; horrify; nauseate; offend; outrage; repel; repulse; revolt; shock; sicken.*

turn tail A moribund metaphor (see page 21). *abscond; clear out; decamp; depart; desert; disappear; escape; exit; flee; fly; go; go away; leave; move on; part; pull out; quit; retire; retreat; run away; take flight; take off; vacate; vanish; withdraw*

turn the other cheek A moribund metaphor (see page 21).

turn the tables (on) A moribund metaphor (see page 21).

turn the tide A moribund metaphor (see page 21).

turn up (her) nose A moribund metaphor (see page 21). *contemn; deride; despise; detest; disdain; jeer at;*

laugh at; mock; ridicule; scoff at; scorn; shun; slight; sneer; snub; spurn.

turn up the heat A moribund metaphor (see page 21). *coerce; command; compel; constrain; demand; enforce; force; goad; impel; importune; incite; induce; insist; instigate; make; oblige; press; pressure; prod; push; spur; urge.*

(the) twelfth of never An infantile phrase (see page 20).

24/7 An infantile phrase (see page 20). *always; ceaselessly; constantly; continually; continuously; endlessly; eternally; everlastingly; evermore; forever; forevermore; frequently; interminably; nonstop; permanently; perpetually; persistently; recurrently; regularly; repeatedly; unceasingly; unremittingly.*

Nothing recommends this silly phrase — especially when so many other words, true words, mean as much. *24/7* is favored by people who find words unwieldy and thought distasteful.

(sit and) twiddle (our) thumbs A moribund metaphor (see page 21). *be idle; be inactive; be lazy; be unemployed; be unoccupied; dally; dawdle; loaf; loiter; loll; lounge; relax; repose; rest.*

twilight zone A moribund metaphor (see page 21).

twist (his) arm A moribund metaphor (see page 21). *bulldoze; bully; coerce; compel; constrain; demand; drive; enforce; enjoin; exhort; goad; force; impel; incite; insist; intimidate; make; necessitate; obligate; oblige; order; press; pressure; prod; require; threaten; tyrannize; urge.*

twist (wrap) (him) around (her) little finger A moribund metaphor (see page 21). *administer; boss; command; control; dictate; direct; dominate; domineer; govern; in charge; in control; in command; manage; manipulate; master; misuse; order; overpower; oversee; predominate; prevail; reign over; rule; superintend; tyrannize; use.*

twist of fate A moribund metaphor (see page 21).

twists and turns (of fate) A moribund metaphor (see page 21).

twist slowly in the wind A moribund metaphor (see page 21). *afflict; agonize; crucify; excruciate; harrow; martyr; persecute; rack; torment; torture.*

two heads are better than one A popular prescription (see page 23).

(like) two peas in a pod An insipid simile. *akin; alike; correspondent; corresponding; equal; equivalent; identical; indistinguishable; kindred; like; matching; one; same; selfsame; similar; twin.*

two's company, three's a crowd A popular prescription (see page 23).

two-way street A moribund metaphor (see page 21).

two wrongs don't make a right A popular prescription (see page 23).

U

(as) ugly as a toad An insipid simile. *deformed; disfigured; disgusting; displeasing; distorted; freakish; frightful; ghastly; gorgonian; grisly; grotesque; gruesome; hideous; homely; horrendous; horrible; horrid; monstrous; offensive; plain; repellent; repulsive; revolting; ugly; unsightly.*

(as) ugly as sin An insipid simile. *deformed; disfigured; disgusting; displeasing; distorted; freakish; frightful; ghastly; gorgonian; grisly; grotesque; gruesome; hideous; homely; horrendous; horrible; horrid; monstrous; offensive; plain; repellent; repulsive; revolting; ugly; unsightly.*

ugly duckling A moribund metaphor (see page 21). *deformed; disfigured; disgusting; displeasing; distorted; freakish; frightful; ghastly; gorgonian; grisly; grotesque; gruesome; hideous; homely; horrendous; horrible; horrid; monstrous; offensive; plain; repellent; repulsive; revolting; ugly; unsightly.*

unbeknownst A withered word (see page 24). *unbeknown; unknown.* ■ *Unbeknownst to his girlfriend, he made a videotape of them having sex.* REPLACE WITH *Unknown.*

unbelievable An overworked word (see page 22). 1. *beyond belief; beyond comprehension; doubtful; dubious; implausible; imponderable; improbable; incomprehensible; inconceivable; inexplicable; questionable; unfathomable; unimaginable; unthinkable.* 2. *astonishing;*

astounding; breathtaking; extraordinary; fabulous; fantastic; marvelous; miraculous; overwhelming; prodigious; sensational; spectacular; wonderful; wondrous.

uncharted waters A moribund metaphor (see page 21).

under a cloud A moribund metaphor (see page 21). *discredited; disfavored; disgraced; dishonored; distrusted; in disfavor; in disgrace; in disrepute; in ignominy; in shame; suspect; under suspicion.* ■ He became the only vice president to leave *under a cloud.* REPLACE WITH *in disgrace.* ■ He left the police department *under a cloud of suspicion.* REPLACE WITH *under suspicion.*

under (my) belt A moribund metaphor (see page 21). *background; education; experience; grooming; grounding; instruction; learning; knowledge; maturity; practice; preparation; qualifications; schooling; seasoning; skill; teaching; training.*

(come) under fire A moribund metaphor (see page 21). *be admonished; be assailed; be attacked; be castigated; be censured; be chastised; be chided; be condemned; be criticized; be denounced; be rebuked; be reprimanded; be reproached; be reproved; be scolded; be set on; be upbraided.*

(keep) under lock and key A moribund metaphor (see page 21). 1. *confined; imprisoned; in jail; locked up.* 2. *guarded; protected; safe; secure; sheltered; shielded.*

under (his) own steam A moribund metaphor (see page 21).

understaffed and overworked An inescapable pair (see page 20).

under the gun A moribund metaphor (see page 21). *be at risk; be at stake; be endangered; be imperiled; be in danger; be in jeopardy; be jeopardized; be menaced; be threatened.* ■ The American way of life, long taken for granted, was *under the gun.* REPLACE WITH *being threatened.*

under the same roof A moribund metaphor (see page 21). *be as one; be indissoluble; be indivisible; be inseparable; be together.* ■ The who's who of world power, gathered *under the same roof* in a public place, poses an unparalleled security headache for Italian authorities. REPLACE WITH *together.* ■ While he understands those living in the house could live anywhere in the community, he sees a danger in putting them all together *under the same roof.* DELETE *under the same roof.*

> I hold it singular, as I look back, that I should never have doubted for a moment that the sacred relics were there; never have failed to feel a certain joy at being under the same roof with them. — Henry James, *The Aspern Papers*

under the sun A moribund metaphor (see page 21). *in existence; known.*

under the table A moribund metaphor (see page 21). *clandestinely; confidentially; covertly; furtively; mysteriously; in private; in secret; privately; quietly; secludedly; secretly; slyly; stealthily; surreptitiously; undercover.*

under the weather A moribund metaphor (see page 21). 1. *afflicted; ail-*

ing; debilitated; diseased; enervated; feeble; frail; ill; indisposed; infirm; not (feeling) well; sick; sickly; suffering; unhealthy; unsound; unwell; valetudinarian. 2. *besotted; crapulous; drunk; inebriated; intoxicated; sodden; stupefied; tipsy.* ■ It doesn't matter if some days I'm feeling a little low or *under the weather.* REPLACE WITH *unwell.*

under the wire A moribund metaphor (see page 21).

under (his) thumb A moribund metaphor (see page 21). *dependent; subject; subordinate; subservient; under.*

under (his) wing A moribund metaphor (see page 21).

(keep) under wraps A moribund metaphor (see page 21). *camouflage; clandestine; cloak; conceal; cover; covert; disguise; enshroud; harbor; hide; out of sight; secret; mask; screen; shroud; suppress; surreptitious; veil; withhold.* ■ Radcliffe tried, and failed, to keep its list *under wraps.* REPLACE WITH *hidden.* ■ Negotiations have been kept largely *under wraps.* REPLACE WITH *secret.*

uneasy calm An inescapable pair (see page 20). ■ By midafternoon, an *uneasy calm* returned to much of the capital.

uneasy lies the head that wears a crown A popular prescription (see page 23).

united we stand (divided we fall) A popular prescription (see page 23).

unite in holy wedlock (marriage) A wretched redundancy (see page 25). *marry; wed.*

unless and (or) until A wretched redundancy (see page 25). *unless; until.* ■ I am opposed to the imposition of any new taxes *unless and until* major cuts in spending have been implemented. REPLACE WITH *unless* or *until.*

unmitigated gall An inescapable pair (see page 20).

untenable position An inescapable pair (see page 20).

until and (or) unless A wretched redundancy (see page 25). *unless; until.* ■ *Until and unless* these two conditions are met, the second rule does not fire. REPLACE WITH *Unless* or *Until.*

until such time as A wretched redundancy (see page 25). *until.* ■ Lessee shall not be liable for any rent *until such time as* Lessor can deliver possession. REPLACE WITH *until.* ■ The FBI would cooperate but play a subordinate role *until such time as* it became evident that the explosion was caused by a criminal act. REPLACE WITH *until.*

up a blind alley A moribund metaphor (see page 21). 1. *at risk; endangered; hard-pressed; imperiled; in a bind; in a dilemma; in a fix; in a jam; in a predicament; in a quandary; in danger; in difficulty; in jeopardy; in peril; in trouble; jeopardized.* 2. *caught; cornered; enmeshed; ensnared; entangled; entrapped; netted; snared; trapped.*

up a creek A moribund metaphor (see page 21). *at risk; endangered; hard-pressed; imperiled; in a bind; in a dilemma; in a fix; in a jam; in a predicament; in a quandary; in danger; in difficulty; in jeopardy; in peril; in trouble; jeopardized.*

up against the wall A moribund metaphor (see page 21). 1. *at risk; desperate; endangered; frantic; hard-pressed; imperiled; in a bind; in a dilemma; in a fix; in a jam; in a predicament; in a quandary; in danger; in difficulty; in jeopardy; in peril; in trouble; jeopardized.* 2. *caught; cornered; enmeshed; ensnared; entangled; entrapped; netted; snared; trapped.*

(right) up (her) alley A moribund metaphor (see page 21).

up and running A moribund metaphor (see page 21). 1. *at work; functioning; going; in action; in operation; operational; operating; performing; producing; running; working.* 2. *able-bodied; active; fit; healthy; robust; strong; vigorous; well.* ■ We intend to have a smoothly functioning, well-integrated unit *up and running* when we start in February. REPLACE WITH *in operation.* ■ This country needs massive amounts of aid to get these people *up and running.* REPLACE WITH *well.*

> Everyone, even Liam, offered their expertise to get her up and running. — Rebecca Bloom, *Tangled Up in Daydreams*

up a tree A moribund metaphor (see page 21). 1. *at risk; endangered; hard-pressed; imperiled; in a bind; in a fix; in a jam; in a predicament; in danger; in difficulty; in jeopardy; in peril; in trouble; jeopardized.* 2. *caught; cornered; enmeshed; ensnared; entangled; entrapped; netted; snared; trapped.*

up close and personal An infantile phrase (see page 20).

(an) uphill battle (fight) A moribund metaphor (see page 21). 1. *an endeavor; an undertaking; a struggle; a task; drudgery; hard work; labor; moil; toil; travail; work.* 2. *arduous; difficult; hard; laborious; strenuous.* ■ Even though it's been *an uphill battle*, I've learned a lot. REPLACE WITH *difficult.* SEE ALSO *reach epidemic proportions.* ■ Alleging sexual harassment against a supervisor is *an uphill battle.* REPLACE WITH *a struggle.*

up in arms A moribund metaphor (see page 21). 1. *agitated; alarmed; angry; annoyed; aroused; choleric; enraged; fierce; fuming; furious; incensed; indignant; inflamed; infuriated; irate; irked; irritable; mad; maddened; raging; resentful; splenetic; vexatious.* 2. *factious; insubordinate; insurgent; mutinous; rebellious; seditious.* ■ The nurses were *up in arms* because of their work conditions. REPLACE WITH *incensed.*

up in the air A moribund metaphor (see page 21). *confused; dubious; indecisive; in doubt; irresolute; open; questionable; tentative; uncertain; unconcluded; undecided; undetermined; unknown; unresolved; unsettled; unsure.* ■ The issue is still very much *up in the air* despite a series of rulings in the 1980s. REPLACE WITH *unsettled.*

> Or depending on his work schedule, which was now up in the air, he could urinate on them at whatever time he got up. — James Whorton, *Approximately Heaven*

ups and downs A moribund metaphor (see page 21). *alterations; changes; erraticism; fluctuations; fortuitousness; inconstancies; shifts; uncertainties; vacillations; variations; vicissitudes.* ■ A community that can meet many of its needs by using locally available natural, human, and financial resources will be less affected by the *ups and downs* of the national and global economies. REPLACE WITH *vicissitudes*.

upset the apple cart A moribund metaphor (see page 21). *confuse; damage; disorder; disrupt; disturb; jumble; mess up; mix up; muddle; ruin; scramble; spoil; upset.*

up the ante A moribund metaphor (see page 21).

up the creek (without a paddle) A moribund metaphor (see page 21). 1. *at risk; endangered; hard-pressed; imperiled; in a bind; in a dilemma; in a fix; in a jam; in a predicament; in a quandary; in danger; in difficulty; in jeopardy; in peril; in trouble; jeopardized.* 2. *caught; cornered; enmeshed; ensnared; entangled; entrapped; netted; snared; trapped.*

up till (until) A wretched redundancy (see page 25). *till (until).* ■ *Up until* the day he left, they hoped that he would play a major role in the new company as a key senior executive. REPLACE WITH *Until.*

I'd given him the pipe for Father's Day. Up until then he had never even smoked. — Sue Monk Kidd, *The Mermaid Chair*

up till (until) this point (time) A wretched redundancy (see page 25). *until now.* ■ *Up until this point* we have been working in the dark. REPLACE WITH *Until now.*

(step) up to bat A moribund metaphor (see page 21). 1. *aim for; attempt; endeavor; engage; participate; pursue; seek; strive for; try.* 2. *advance; appear; approach; come forth; come forward; emerge; rise; show; surface; transpire.* 3. *act; perform; speak; talk.* 4. *be accountable; be answerable; be responsible.* ■ In this regard, one campus organization has *stepped up to bat.* REPLACE WITH *emerged.* ■ First *up to bat* is Philip Cercone, director of McGill-Queen's University Press. REPLACE WITH *to speak.*

So now Lora comes up to bat and tells a story that is basically the same as mine but utterly different.... — David Margolis, *The Stepman*

up to (my) ears A moribund metaphor (see page 21). 1. *bury; deluge; flood; glut; immerse; infest; inundate; overburden; overload; overpower; overrun; overwhelm; sate; swamp.* 2. *altogether; completely; entirely; fully; perfectly; quite; roundly; thoroughly; totally; unreservedly; utterly; wholly.*

up to (my) eyeballs (eyebrows; eyes) A moribund metaphor (see page 21). 1. *bury; deluge; glut; immerse; infest; inundate; overburden; overload; overpower; overrun; overwhelm; sate; swamp.* 2. *altogether; completely; entirely; fully; perfectly; quite; roundly; thoroughly; totally; unreservedly; utterly; wholly.* ■ The campaigns' organizations are all *up to their eyeballs* with delegate-counting. REPLACE WITH *overrun.* ■ We are in this now, *up to our eyebrows* and for the long haul. REPLACE WITH *fully.*

up to par A moribund metaphor (see page 21). 1. *average; common; commonplace; customary; everyday; mediocre; middling; normal; ordinary; quotidian; regular; routine; standard; typical; uneventful; unexceptional; unremarkable; usual.* 2. *acceptable; adequate; fine; good; good enough; healthy; passable; satisfactory; sufficient; suitable; tolerable; well.*

up to scratch A moribund metaphor (see page 21). *acceptable; adequate; fine; good; good enough; healthy; passable; satisfactory; sufficient; suitable; tolerable; well.*

up to snuff A moribund metaphor (see page 21). *acceptable; adequate; fine; good; good enough; healthy; passable; satisfactory; sufficient; suitable; tolerable; well.*

up to speed A moribund metaphor (see page 21). *acceptable; adequate; fine; good; good enough; healthy; passable; satisfactory; sufficient; suitable; tolerable; well.*

use and abuse An inescapable pair (see page 20). ■ We all agree that we have been racially *used and abused*. ■ Lil Franklin said her son had been *used and abused* by two fundamentalist ministers.

utilize A torpid term (see page 24). *apply; employ; make use of; use.* ■ I utilize my bike for nearly everything. REPLACE WITH *use.* ■ These are all expository techniques that you will be *utilizing* once you have mastered the basics of writing. REPLACE WITH *using.* SEE ALSO *finalize.*

valuable asset An inescapable pair (see page 20). This phrase is, like many inescapable pairs, also redundant, for an *asset* is *valuable.*

variations on a theme A torpid term (see page 24).

> Once she allowed herself to think that, then there was no stopping a flood of other suspicions — primarily variations on the theme of the power and ubiquity of Ray's "friends." — Jane Smiley, *Duplicate Keys*

variety is the spice of life A popular prescription (see page 23).

various and sundry An inescapable pair (see page 20). *assorted; diverse; sundry; varied; various; varying.* ■ I tried *various and sundry* ways to get her to see me. REPLACE WITH *various.* SEE ALSO *all and sundry.*

vehemently oppose An inescapable pair (see page 20). ■ MCA *vehemently opposed* Sony's Betamax and the VCR invasion.

verboten A foreign phrase (see page 19). *banned; disallowed; enjoined; forbidden; prohibited; proscribed.* ■ But once everything was set up, my analog modem worked on a previously *verboten* digital phone. REPLACE WITH *disallowed.*

verily A withered word (see page 24). *actually; indeed; in fact; in faith; in reality; in truth; truly.*

very An overworked word (see page 22). The word *very* is often a needless intensive, but preceding words like *excellent, major,* and *delightful,* it is ludicrous. ■ I think that's a *very* excellent thought. DELETE *very.* ■ It's a *very* major plus for our state and our region. DELETE *very.* ■ You seem *very* delightful. DELETE *very.* ■ She's a biochemist and *very* brilliant. DELETE *very.* ■ If the test cells were to be shut down, it would be *very* detrimental to the operation. DELETE *very.* ■ Moreover, the wind at the peak can be *very* deadly. DELETE *very.* SEE ALSO *really.*

viable alternative An inescapable pair (see page 20).

vicious circle An inescapable pair (see page 20).

vicious rumor An inescapable pair (see page 20).

vim and vigor An inescapable pair (see page 20). *animation; ardor; dash; dynamism; élan; energy; fervor; force; intensity; liveliness; passion; potency; power; spirit; stamina; strength; verve; vigor; vitality; vivacity; zeal.*

virtue is its own reward A popular prescription (see page 23).

vis-à-vis A foreign phrase (see page 19).

viselike grip A moribund metaphor (see page 21).

visible (invisible) to the eye A wretched redundancy (see page 25). *visible (invisible).* SEE ALSO *audible (inaudible) to the ear.*

(a) vision of (loveliness) A moribund metaphor (see page 21).

> After talking for a couple of minutes, I asked Bruce who this vision of ebony beauty was. — E. Lynn Harris, *Invisible Life*

vive la différence A foreign phrase (see page 19).

voice (crying) in the wilderness A moribund metaphor (see page 21).

vote with (their) feet A moribund metaphor (see page 21). ■ People are *voting with their feet,* and politicians know this.

wages of sin A moribund metaphor (see page 21).

(just have to) wait and see (what happens) A torpid term (see page 24). *I don't know; (it's) not (yet) known; (that's) uncertain; (that's) unclear; (it's) unknown.* SEE ALSO *(it) remains to be seen; your guess is as good as mine.*

wait for the ax to fall A moribund metaphor (see page 21).

wait for the other shoe to drop A moribund metaphor (see page 21).

waiting for Godot An infantile phrase (see page 20).

waiting in the wings A moribund metaphor (see page 21).

wake the dead A moribund metaphor (see page 21). *blaring; boisterous; booming; deafening; earsplitting; fulminating; loud; noisy; obstreperous; piercing; plangent; resounding; roaring; shrill; stentorian; strident; thundering; thunderous; tumultuous; vociferous.*

wake up and smell the coffee A moribund metaphor (see page 21). *be alert; be attentive; be awake; be aware; be cognizant; be conscious; be mindful; be perceptive; be sentient; be wakeful.*

wake-up call A moribund metaphor (see page 21). *admonition; caution; warning.* ■ The priest sexual scandal is a *wake-up call* for the church.

walk a fine line A moribund metaphor (see page 21).

walk a tightrope A moribund metaphor (see page 21). *chance; dare; endanger; gamble; hazard; imperil; jeopardize; make bold; peril; risk; venture.*

walk away from A moribund metaphor (see page 21). *abandon; abdicate; avoid; brush aside; deny; desert; disavow; discount; disinherit; disown; disregard; dodge; drop; duck; forgo; forsake; give up; ignore; leave; neglect; omit; pass over; quit; recoil from; reject; relinquish; renounce; shrink from; shun; shy away from; snub; spurn; surrender; turn away from; with-*draw from; yield.* ■ The state cannot *walk away from* that obligation. REPLACE WITH *disregard.*

(the) walking dead A moribund metaphor (see page 21).

(a) walking, talking An infantile phrase (see page 20).

walk on air A moribund metaphor (see page 21). *blissful; blithe; buoyant; cheerful; delighted; ecstatic; elated; enraptured; euphoric; exalted; excited; exhilarated; exultant; gay; glad; gleeful; good-humored; happy; intoxicated; jolly; jovial; joyful; joyous; jubilant; merry; mirthful; overjoyed; pleased; rapturous; thrilled.*

walk on eggs (eggshells) A moribund metaphor (see page 21). ■ For years, Robinson *walked on eggshells* as the first black baseball player in the major leagues.

(all) walks of life A moribund metaphor (see page 21).

walk softly and carry a big stick A popular prescription (see page 23).

walk (me) through A moribund metaphor (see page 21). *clarify; clear up; describe; disentangle; elucidate; enlighten; explain; explicate; illume; illuminate; interpret; make clear; make plain; reveal; simplify.* ■ Can you *walk me through* the process of how you wrote it? USE *explain.* ■ Middle-school students will be told the details of the drill in advance, and their teachers will *walk them through* the steps on the day of the event. USE *describe.*

wall of silence A moribund metaphor (see page 21).

(the) walls have ears A moribund metaphor (see page 21).

want to bet? An infantile phrase (see page 20).

war clouds A moribund metaphor (see page 21).

war is hell A quack equation (see page 23).

(as) warm as toast An insipid simile. *heated; lukewarm; mild; temperate; tepid; toasty; warm; warmish.*

warm the cockles of (my) heart A moribund metaphor (see page 21).

warn in advance A wretched redundancy (see page 25). *warn.* ■ Management should be *warned in advance* that fines are no longer the way to satisfy the system for a careless disaster. DELETE *in advance.* SEE ALSO *advance warning; forewarn.*

war of words A moribund metaphor (see page 21). *altercation; argument; bickering; conflict; contention; controversy; disagreement; disputation; dispute; feud; polemics; quarrel; row; spat; squabble; strife; wrangle.* ■ Yesterday's *war of words* seemed like a replay of the bitter 1988 campaign. REPLACE WITH *squabble.*

wash (their) dirty linen in public A moribund metaphor (see page 21).

(all) washed up A moribund metaphor (see page 21). *beaten; condemned; con-* *quered; cowed; cursed; damned; defunct; doomed; fated; finished; gone; lost; ruined; vanquished.*

wash (her) hands of (it) A moribund metaphor (see page 21). *abandon; abdicate; avoid; brush aside; deny; desert; disavow; discount; disinherit; disown; disregard; dodge; drop; duck; forgo; forsake; give up; ignore; leave; neglect; omit; pass over; quit; recoil from; reject; relinquish; renounce; shrink from; shun; shy away from; snub; surrender; turn away from; withdraw from; yield.*

> The gambler apparently had washed his hands of me, but he didn't seem to hold any stubbornness against me. — Dashiell Hammett, *Red Harvest*

waste not, want not A popular prescription (see page 23).

(a) watched pot never boils A popular prescription (see page 23).

(like) watching grass grow An insipid simile. *banal; barren; bland; boring; deadly; dreary; dry; dull; everyday; flat; humdrum; inanimate; insipid; jejune; lifeless; lusterless; mediocre; monotonous; prosaic; routine; spiritless; stale; tedious; tiresome; unexciting; uninteresting; vapid; wearisome.*

watch (him) like a hawk An insipid simile. *be alert; be attentive; be awake; be aware; be eagle-eyed; be heedful; be informed; be keen; be observant; be vigilant; be wakeful; be watchful.*

water over the dam A moribund metaphor (see page 21). 1. *completed; concluded; done; ended; finished; over;*

passed; through. 2. *history; the past; yesterday.*

water (runs) under the bridge A moribund metaphor (see page 21). 1. *completed; concluded; done; ended; finished; over; passed; through.* 2. *history; the past; yesterday.*

A lot of water runs under the bridge, a lot of it dirty. — Thomas Savage, *The Sheep Queen*

(the) wave of the future A moribund metaphor (see page 21).

(like) waving a red flag (rag) in front of a bull An insipid simile.

wax and wane An inescapable pair (see page 20).

ways and means An inescapable pair (see page 20). *approaches; means; mechanisms; methods; techniques; ways.*

(the) way to a man's heart is through his stomach A popular prescription (see page 23).

(as) weak as a baby An insipid simile. *dainty; debilitated; delicate; enervated; feeble; fragile; frail; infirm; nonmuscular; puny; sickly; unhealthy; unwell; valetudinarian; weak; weakly.*

(as) weak as a kitten An insipid simile. *dainty; debilitated; delicate; enervated; feeble; fragile; frail; infirm; nonmuscular; puny; sickly; unhealthy; unwell; valetudinarian; weak; weakly.*

weak in the knees A moribund metaphor (see page 21). *dizzy; faint; giddy; lightheaded; weak.*

wears (her) heart on (her) sleeve A moribund metaphor (see page 21). *demonstrative; emotional; emotive; sensitive; sentimental.*

(the) weak link (in the chain) A moribund metaphor (see page 21).

wear the pants A moribund metaphor (see page 21). *administer; boss; command; control; dictate; direct; dominate; govern; in charge; in command; in control; manage; manipulate; master; order; overpower; oversee; predominate; prevail; reign over; rule; superintend.*

weather the storm (of) A moribund metaphor (see page 21). ■ A tremendous thank you goes out to each of you who has helped our family *weather this storm.* SEE ALSO *reach epidemic proportions.*

weighs a ton An insipid simile. *bulky; heavy; hefty; weighty.*

weight in proportion (proportionate) to height A torpid term (see page 24). Men should eschew women (and women, men) whom they've not yet met and who describe their physiques as *weight in proportion (proportionate) to height.*

Let us men prefer an *athletic; brawny; firm; fit; medium-build; mesomorphic; muscular; robust; sinewy; toned; well-built* woman or a *bony; ectomorphic; lanky; lean; petite; rail-thin; scraggy; scrawny; skeletal; skinny; slender; slight; slim; small; spare; spindly; svelte; sylphid; thin; tiny; trim; wispy* woman or a *big-boned, big-breasted, big-bellied,* or *big-bottomed; bulbous; bulky; busty; buxom; chubby; chunky; corpulent; curvaceous; curvy; dumpy; endomorphic; enormous;*

fat; flabby; fleshy; full-figured; globular; heavy; heavyset; hefty; huge; large; obese; plump; portly; pudgy; rotund; round; squat; steatopygic; stocky; stout; voluptuous; zaftig woman — if not for her *womanliness* then at least for her *words*.

weird An overworked word (see page 22). *aberrant; abnormal; anomalistic; anomalous; atypical; bizarre; curious; deviant; different; distinct; distinctive; eccentric; exceptional; extraordinary; fantastic; foreign; grotesque; idiosyncratic; independent; individual; individualistic; irregular; novel; odd; offbeat; original; peculiar; puzzling; quaint; queer; rare; remarkable; separate; singular; strange; uncommon; unconventional; unexampled; unique; unnatural; unorthodox; unparalleled; unprecedented; unusual.* SEE ALSO *strange.*

(all) well and good A wretched redundancy (see page 25). *adequate; all right; excellent; fine; good; O.K.; satisfactory; well.* ■ That's *all well and good* for the hobbyist running a bulletin board or the IT worker who does side programming jobs in his off-hours at home. REPLACE WITH *good.* ■ Well, this is *all well and good*, but who's going to pay for it — not my insurance company! REPLACE WITH *fine.* ■ This is *all well and good*, but what do experts say? REPLACE WITH *good.* ■ That's *all well and good*, but what about my son? REPLACE WITH *fine.* SEE ALSO *fine and dandy; still and all.*

well-nigh A withered word (see page 24). *almost; nearly.*

wet behind the ears A moribund metaphor (see page 21). *artless; awkward; callow; green; guileless; immature; inexperienced; inexpert; ingenuous; innocent; naive; raw; simple; undeveloped; unfledged; unskilled; unskillful; unsophisticated; untaught; untrained; unworldly.*

wet (my) whistle A moribund metaphor (see page 21). *drink; guzzle; imbibe; quaff.*

we've all got to go sometime A popular prescription (see page 23).

we've got to stop meeting like this An infantile phrase (see page 20).

what a difference a day makes A torpid term (see page 24).

what are you going to do A plebeian sentiment (see page 23). This is still another expression of resignation. Though phrased as a question, it is rarely spoken interrogatively, so resigned, so hopeless are those who use it. SEE ALSO *such is life; that's how (the way) it goes; that's how (the way) the ball bounces; that's how (the way) the cookie crumbles; that's life; that's life in the big city; that's show biz; what can you do.*

what can I say? An infantile phrase (see page 20).

what can I tell you? An infantile phrase (see page 20).

what can you do A plebeian sentiment (see page 23). SEE ALSO *such is life; that's how (the way) it goes; that's how (the way) the ball bounces; that's life; that's life in the big city; that's show biz; what are you going to do.*

what (he) doesn't know won't hurt (him) A popular prescription (see page 23).

whatever An infantile phrase (see page 20). As a one-word response to another's comment or question, *whatever* is as dismissive as it is ill-mannered. SEE ALSO *excuse me.*

whatever happens happens An infantile phrase (see page 20). SEE ALSO *it just happened; what(ever) must (will) be, must (will) be.*

what goes around, comes around A popular prescription (see page 23). This is the secular equivalent of "as you sow, so shall you reap." As such, it is nonetheless a moralistic prescription — intoned by those who think in circles — that too easily explains the way of the world.

what goes up must come down A popular prescription (see page 23).

what happened (is) An ineffectual phrase (see page 19). ■ *What happened was* I woke up one morning and just decided to leave. DELETE *What happened was.* ■ *What happened was* we applied for welfare. DELETE *What happened was.* ■ *What happened was* when I said that to him he got upset and left in a huff. DELETE *What happened was.* ■ *What has happened is,* my identity has gotten lost in this ordeal. DELETE *What has happened is.* SEE ALSO *what is.*

what ... is An ineffectual phrase (see page 19). ■ *What* you want *is* someone who will stand by his work once it is completed. DELETE *What is.* ■ *What* we are finding *is* that they want to measure up to our standards of integrity. DELETE *What is.* ■ *What* this course is about *is* empowerment. DELETE *What is.* ■ *What* we have *is* a program that asks

some important questions. DELETE *What is.* SEE ALSO *what happened (is).*

what is the world coming to? A plebeian sentiment (see page 23).

what's done is done A quack equation (see page 23). ■ *What's done is done,* but rethinking the choice now will help you make a better choice next time.

what's good for (the goose) is good for (the gander) A popular prescription (see page 23).

what will they think of next? A plebeian sentiment (see page 23).

what you don't know can't (won't) hurt you A popular prescription (see page 23).

what you see is not always what you get A quack equation (see page 23).

what you see is what you get A quack equation (see page 23).

wheel and deal An inescapable pair (see page 20). *bargain; contrive; deal; do business; negotiate; plan; plot; scheme.*

when and if A wretched redundancy (see page 25). *if; when.* ■ People are asking *when and if* there will be a democratic government. REPLACE WITH *if* or *when.* SEE ALSO *if and when; if, as, and when; when and whether; when, as, and if; whether and when.*

when and whether A wretched redundancy (see page 25). *when; whether.* ■ She will decide *when and whether* and under what circumstances she'll become a mother. REPLACE WITH *when* or *whether.* SEE ALSO *if and when; if, as, and when; when and if; when, as, and if; whether and when.*

when, as, and if A wretched redundancy (see page 25). *if; when.* SEE ALSO *if and when; if, as, and when; when and if; when and whether; whether and when.*

whence A withered word (see page 24). 1. *from where.* 2. *from what source.* 3. *from which.*

when (you) come right down to it A wretched redundancy (see page 25). *all in all; all told; altogether; eventually; finally; in all; in the end; on the whole; overall; ultimately.*

when hell freezes over A moribund metaphor (see page 21). *never; no; not at all; not ever; not in any way; not in the least.*

when in Rome (do as the Romans do) A popular prescription (see page 23). *abide by; accede; accommodate; accord; acquiesce; adapt; adhere to; agree; behave; comply; concur; conform; correspond; follow; harmonize; heed; mind; obey; observe; submit; yield.*

when it comes to A wretched redundancy (see page 25). *about; as for; as to; concerning; for; in; of; on; over; regarding; respecting; to; toward; when; with.* ■ I feel I'm more experienced *when it comes to* looking for a job. REPLACE WITH *in.* ■ I'm an expert *when it comes to* marriage. REPLACE WITH *about.* ■ *When it comes to* middle-age dating, there are four stages. REPLACE WITH *As for.* ■ She is not reasonable *when it comes to* me. REPLACE WITH *with.*

when it rains, it pours A moribund metaphor (see page 21).

when push comes to shove A moribund metaphor (see page 21). ■ *When push comes to shove*, liberalism collapses, society polarizes itself, and the gloves are removed.

when the cat's away, the mice will play A moribund metaphor (see page 21).

when the going gets tough, the tough get going A popular prescription (see page 23).

where angels fear to tread A moribund metaphor (see page 21).

whereat A withered word (see page 24). *at which point.*

wherefore A withered word (see page 24). 1. *why.* 2. *for which.* 3. *therefore.*

wherein A withered word (see page 24). *how; in what way.*

where ... is concerned A wretched redundancy (see page 25). *about; as for; as to; concerning; for; in; of; on; over; regarding; respecting; to; toward; with.* ■ Our gangs are just getting off the ground *where* violence *is concerned.* REPLACE WITH *concerning.* ■ Obviously, time doesn't heal all wounds, especially *where* the Red Sox *are concerned.* REPLACE WITH *regarding.* SEE ALSO *as far as ... (goes; is concerned).*

whereon A withered word (see page 24). *on what; on which.*

where's the beef? An infantile phrase (see page 20).

where there's a will, there's a way A popular prescription (see page 23).

where there's smoke there's fire A popular prescription (see page 23).

where the rubber hits the road A moribund metaphor (see page 21). ■ That, for Christians, is *where the rubber hits the road* — where we intersect with people who are poor or marginalized.

wherethrough A withered word (see page 24). *through which.*

whereto A withered word (see page 24). *to what; to which.*

whereunto A withered word (see page 24). *to what; to which.*

wherewith A withered word (see page 24). *with what; with which.*

whet (my) appetite A moribund metaphor (see page 21).

whether and when A wretched redundancy (see page 25). *when; whether.* ■ Lee will be the one to determine *whether and when* he isn't up to the job. REPLACE WITH *when* or *whether*. SEE ALSO *if and when; if, as, and when; when and if; when and whether; when, as, and if.*

which way the wind blows A moribund metaphor (see page 21).

while at the same time A wretched redundancy (see page 25). *at the same time; while.* ■ It provides us with an opportunity to honor his memory *while at the same time* assisting future students. REPLACE WITH *at the same time* or *while*. SEE ALSO *simultaneously at the same time; while simultaneously.*

> Once in the elevator, it was important to stand in silence beside the bags, to erase oneself behind the dignity of the uniform, while at the same time not seeming cold or indifferent and indeed remaining alert to any sign of helplessness in the traveler. — Steven Millhauser, *Martin Dressler*

while simultaneously A wretched redundancy (see page 25). *simultaneously; while.* ■ So you can work on applications *while simultaneously* watching TV in a resizable window. DELETE *simultaneously*. SEE ALSO *simultaneously at the same time; while at the same time.*

whilst A withered word (see page 24). *while.* ■ *Whilst* it delivers the required protection, most users will probably feel strangely unsatisfied after some hard use. REPLACE WITH *While*. ■ Some imply a functional relationship between variables *whilst* others are of a more exploratory nature. REPLACE WITH *while.*

whip into a frenzy A moribund metaphor (see page 21). *acerbate; anger; annoy; bother; bristle; chafe; enrage; incense; inflame; infuriate; irk; irritate; madden; miff; provoke; rile; roil; vex.*

whip into shape A moribund metaphor (see page 21).

whistle in the dark A moribund metaphor (see page 21).

whistling Dixie A moribund metaphor (see page 21).

(as) white as a ghost An insipid simile. 1. *anemic; ashen; blanched; bloodless; cadaverous; colorless; deathlike; doughy; haggard; lusterless; pale; pallid; pasty; peaked; sallow; sickly; wan; whitish.* 2. *achromatic; alabaster-white; albescent; bleached; chalky; colorless; ivory; milk-white; milky; niveous; pearly; pearly-white; snow-white; snowy; uncolored; whitish.*

> He tells me that the Dictator was receiving all this in silence, but that he was as white as a ghost. — Thornton Wilder, *The Ides of March*

(as) white as a sheet An insipid simile. 1. *anemic; ashen; blanched; bloodless; cadaverous; colorless; deathlike; doughy; haggard; lusterless; pale; pallid; pasty; peaked; sallow; sickly; wan; whitish.* 2. *achromatic; alabaster-white; albescent; bleached; chalky; colorless; ivory; milk-white; milky; niveous; pearly; pearly-white; snow-white; snowy; uncolored; whitish.*

(as) white as snow An insipid simile. 1. *achromatic; alabaster-white; albescent; bleached; chalky; colorless; ivory; milk-white; milky; niveous; pearly; pearly-white; snow-white; snowy; uncolored; whitish.* 2. *anemic; ashen; blanched; bloodless; cadaverous; colorless; deathlike; doughy; haggard; lusterless; pale; pallid; pasty; peaked; sallow; sickly; wan; whitish.*

(like) white on rice An insipid simile. 1. *congenital; fundamental; genetic; hereditary; inborn; inbred; ingrained; inherent; inherited; innate; intrinsic; native; natural.* 2. *all over; everywhere; omnipresent; ubiquitous.*

whither A withered word (see page 24). 1. *where.* 2. *wherever.*

(the) whole ball of wax A moribund metaphor (see page 21). *aggregate; all; all things; entirety; everything; gross; lot; sum; total; totality; whole.*

(my) whole, entire (life) An infantile phrase (see page 20). ■ People like you laughed at me *my whole, entire life.* ■ With this on, you will attract more women than you have in *your whole, entire lives.*

(the) whole is greater than the sum of its parts A popular prescription (see page 23).

(the) whole nine yards A moribund metaphor (see page 21). *aggregate; all; all things; entirety; everything; gross; lot; sum; total; totality; whole.* ■ You've won the Sony TV, the VCR, the stereo system, the camcorder, *the whole nine yards.* REPLACE WITH *everything.*

(the) whole shebang A moribund metaphor (see page 21). *aggregate; all; all things; entirety; everything; gross; lot; sum; total; totality; whole.*

(the) whole shooting match A moribund metaphor (see page 21). *aggregate; all; all things; entirety; everything; gross; lot; sum; total; totality; whole.*

who let the cat out of the bag? A moribund metaphor (see page 21).

whoop it up A moribund metaphor (see page 21). 1. *be merry; carouse; carry on; celebrate; debauch; disport; frolic; party; play; revel; riot; roister; rollick; romp; skylark.* 2. *bay; bawl; bellow; blare;*

caterwaul; cheer; clamor; cry; holler; hoot; howl; roar; screak; scream; screech; shout; shriek; shrill; squawk; squeal; vociferate; wail; whoop; yell; yelp; yowl.

who's minding the store? A moribund metaphor (see page 21).

who would have (ever) thought A plebeian sentiment (see page 23).

why didn't (I) think of that? A plebeian sentiment (see page 23).

why me? A plebeian sentiment (see page 23).

(the) why and (the) wherefore A wretched redundancy (see page 25). *aim; cause; design; end; goal; intent; intention; motive; object; objective; purpose; reason.*

wide of the mark A moribund metaphor (see page 21). *erroneous; false; incorrect; inexact; mistaken; untrue; wrong.*

wild and crazy An inescapable pair (see page 20).

> However wild and crazy they may be, they stand by their friends. — Matthew Reilly, *Scarecrow*

wild and woolly An inescapable pair (see page 20).

wild blue yonder A moribund metaphor (see page 21). *air; atmosphere; biosphere; empyrean; ether; firmament; heaven; heavens; outer space; sky; space; stratosphere.*

wild goose chase A moribund metaphor (see page 21).

> Copulatory leads to copulation, the union of the sexes in the art of generation and I don't know what that means and I'm too weary going from one word to another in this heavy dictionary which leads me on a wild goose chase from this word to that word and all because the people who wrote the dictionary don't want the likes of me to know anything. — Frank McCourt, *Angela's Ashes*

wild horses couldn't (keep me away) A moribund metaphor (see page 21).

wild horses couldn't drag it from (me) A moribund metaphor (see page 21).

window dressing A moribund metaphor (see page 21).

window of opportunity A moribund metaphor (see page 21). *chance; occasion; opening; opportunity; possibility; prospect.* Only able writers know that *window of opportunity* is unable to influence or involve us. *Window of opportunity* is a language that lulls and then deadens.
   ■ I think we have a terrific *window of opportunity* to make progress this year. REPLACE WITH *chance.* ■ There may be *a window of opportunity* between 12 and 1 for us to talk. REPLACE WITH *time.* ■ One redesign of an ASIC can cause the system vendor to completely miss the *window of opportunity* for a particular product. REPLACE WITH *opportunity.* ■ On the conflict in Darfur, the High Commissioner said he saw a *window of opportunity* to reach a political settle-

ment for the strife-torn region. REPLACE WITH *chance.* SEE ALSO *a barrage of.*

window on the (world) A moribund metaphor (see page 21).

winds of change A moribund metaphor (see page 21).

wine and dine An inescapable pair (see page 20).

win hands down A moribund metaphor (see page 21). *beat; conquer; crush; defeat; outclass; outdo; overcome; overpower; overwhelm; prevail; quell; rout; succeed; triumph; trounce; vanquish; win.*

win, lose, or draw A moribund metaphor (see page 21). *regardless.*

win (his) spurs A moribund metaphor (see page 21).

wipe the slate clean A moribund metaphor (see page 21). *begin anew; start afresh; start over.*

-wise A grammatical gimmick (see page 19). We fasten the suffix *-wise* to words when we have not sufficiently thought about what we want to say or, even more so, how we want to say it. With -*wise,* though there may be some substance to our thought, there is scant style.

■ I've been very successful *businesswise.* REPLACE WITH *in business.* ■ *Burialwise,* I don't feel they're responsible enough to take care of *my wishes.* REPLACE WITH *my burial wishes.* ■ I do have a photo of a model *who resembles me bodywise.* REPLACE WITH *whose body resembles my own.* ■ And *academicwise,*

he's made the honor role every year. REPLACE WITH *academically.* ■ She is attractive and much smaller *sizewise* than me. DELETE *sizewise.* ■ I'll let you know *what I get from them informationwise.* REPLACE WITH *what information I get from them.* ■ By spending our development time, future ads will be very *reasonable pricewise.* REPLACE WITH *reasonably priced.*

> The cream of the East and Middle West, engineering-wise and managerwise, was met in the amphitheater of the Meadows. — Kurt Vonnegut, Jr., *Player Piano*

(as) wise as Solomon An insipid simile. *astute; bright; brilliant; clever; discerning; enlightened; insightful; intelligent; judicious; keen; knowledgeable; learned; logical; luminous; penetrating; perceptive; perspicacious; rational; reasonable; sagacious; sage; sapient; sensible; sharp; shrewd; smart; sound; understanding; wise.*

wit and wisdom An inescapable pair (see page 20).

with a big (capital) (A) An infantile phrase (see page 20). ■ It's crisp, *with a capital C.* DELETE *with a capital C.* ■ He loves conversation — *with a big C.* DELETE *with a big C.* ■ These establishments offer *dining with a capital D.* REPLACE WITH *elegant dining.*

> So he knew a little bit about Beauty too. Beauty with a capital B: not just a pretty face or a picturesque landscape, ... — Robert Hellenga, *Philosophy Made Simple*

(go over) with a fine-toothed comb A moribund metaphor (see page 21). *analyze; canvass; comb; examine; explore; filter; forage; hunt; inspect; investigate; look for; probe; quest; ransack; rummage; scour; scrutinize; search; seek; sieve; sift; winnow.*

with a heavy hand A moribund metaphor (see page 21). *coercively; draconianly; harshly; oppressively; severely.*

with all (my) heart A moribund metaphor (see page 21). *earnestly; fervently; genuinely; heartily; honestly; sincerely; unreservedly; wholeheartedly.*

with an open hand A moribund metaphor (see page 21). *altruistically; beneficently; bountifully; charitably; generously; liberally; munificently; unselfishly; unstintingly.*

with a vengeance A moribund metaphor (see page 21). *actively; aggressively; dynamically; emphatically; energetically; fast; furiously; fervently; fiercely; forcefully; frantically; frenziedly; furiously; hard; intensely; intently; mightily; passionately; powerfully; robustly; savagely; spiritedly; strenuously; strongly; vehemently; viciously; vigorously; violently; wildly; with vigor.*

with a wink and a nod A moribund metaphor (see page 21). *clandestinely; confidentially; covertly; furtively; mysteriously; in private; in secret; privately; quietly; secludedly; secretly; slyly; stealthily; surreptitiously; undercover.* ■ Boston's most infamous criminal partnership began *with a wink and a nod.* REPLACE WITH *furtively.*

with bated breath A moribund metaphor (see page 21). *agitatedly; anxiously; apprehensively; excitedly; fearfully; nervously; suspensefully; timidly; timorously; tremulously; worriedly.*

with bells on A moribund metaphor (see page 21). *animatedly; eagerly; ebulliently; effervescently; effusively; enthusiastically; excitedly; lively; spiritedly; sprightly; vivaciously.*

with (their) eyes wide open A moribund metaphor (see page 21). *by design; consciously; deliberately; intentionally; knowingly; on purpose; purposely; willfully; with intent.* ■ They did this *with their eyes wide open.* REPLACE WITH *deliberately.*

with flying colors A moribund metaphor (see page 21). *beautifully; brilliantly; dazzlingly; excellently; grandly; impressively; magnificently; marvelously; outstandingly; splendidly; sublimely; successfully; superbly; triumphally; triumphantly; victoriously; wonderfully.*

with (her) heart in (her) mouth A moribund metaphor (see page 21). *anxiously; apprehensively; fearfully; pavidly; timidly; timorously; tremblingly; tremulously.*

within a hair's breadth of A moribund metaphor (see page 21). *(very) close (to); (very) near (to).* ■ Some visionaries are *within a hair's breadth of* achieving unattended computer center operation. REPLACE WITH *close to.*

(beaten) within an inch of (his) life A moribund metaphor (see page 21). *brutally; cruelly; ferociously; fiercely; harshly; mercilessly; ruthlessly; severely; viciously; violently.*

> Alderman Schlumbohm, heckled to within an inch of his life, followed to the council door by three hundred of his fellow-citizens, was there left with the admonition that they would be waiting for him when he should make his exit.
> — Theodore Dreiser, *The Titan*

within a whisker of A moribund metaphor (see page 21). *(very) close (to); (very) near (to).*

(handle; treat) with kid gloves A moribund metaphor (see page 21). *carefully; cautiously; delicately; gently; gingerly; mildly; sensitively; tactfully; with care.*

with machinelike precision An insipid simile. *accurately; easily; exactly; excellently; faultlessly; flawlessly; flowingly; impeccably; indefectibly; methodically; perfectly; precisely; regularly; smoothly; systematically; well.*

with might and main A moribund metaphor (see page 21). *actively; aggressively; dynamically; emphatically; energetically; ferociously; fervently; fiercely; forcefully; frantically; frenziedly; furiously; hard; intensely; intently; mightily; passionately; powerfully; robustly; savagely; spiritedly; strenuously; strongly; vehemently; viciously; vigorously; violently; wildly; with vigor.*

with (her) nose in the air A moribund metaphor (see page 21). *arrogant; cavalier; condescending; contemptuous; despotic; dictatorial; disdainful; dogmatic; domineering; haughty; imperious; insolent; lofty; overbearing; overweening; patronizing; pompous; pretentious; scornful; self-important; supercilious; superior; vainglorious.*

(welcome) with open arms A moribund metaphor (see page 21). *affectionately; cheerfully; eagerly; enthusiastically; gladly; happily; joyously; readily; unreservedly; warmly.* ■ We have welcomed them *with open arms*. REPLACE WITH *cheerfully*. ■ I hope I am welcomed back *with open arms*. REPLACE WITH *unreservedly*.

(went off) without a hitch A moribund metaphor (see page 21). *accurately; easily; exactly; excellently; faultlessly; flawlessly; flowingly; impeccably; indefectibly; methodically; perfectly; precisely; regularly; smoothly; systematically; well.*

without cost or obligation A wretched redundancy (see page 25). *free.*

without further ado An infantile phrase (see page 20). *at once; directly; forthwith; immediately; instantly; promptly; right away; straightaway; summarily; unfalteringly; unhesitatingly; without delay.*

Of course, any speaker who drones *without further ado* at the end of his prefatory remarks probably ought never himself to be introduced.

without missing a beat A moribund metaphor (see page 21). *accurately; easily; exactly; excellently; faultlessly; flawlessly; flowingly; impeccably; indefectibly; methodically; perfectly; precisely; regularly; smoothly; systematically; well.*

without rhyme or reason A moribund metaphor (see page 21). *decerebrate; foolish; idiotic; illogical; incomprehensible; meaningless; nonsensical; senseless; stupid; unintelligent; unintelligible.*

with (my) tail between (my) legs A moribund metaphor (see page 21). *abjectly; ashamedly; humbly; ignobly; ignominiously; ingloriously; in humility; in shame; meekly; shamefully; submissively.* ■ But she was not happy at the school and left before graduation *with her tail between her legs.* REPLACE WITH *ingloriously.*

Anne came home with her tail between her legs and slumped into her father's smoking chair. — Elle Eggels, *The House of the Seven Sisters*

with the exception of A wretched redundancy (see page 25). *apart from; aside from; barring; besides; but for; except; except for; excepting; excluding; other than; outside of.* ■ We found that our first 50 patients were wide awake and alert the next day *with the exception of* one patient. REPLACE WITH *except for.*

woefully inadequate An inescapable pair (see page 20). Little is *inadequate* that isn't *woefully* so.

(the) wolf at the door A moribund metaphor (see page 21).

wolf in sheep's clothing A moribund metaphor (see page 21). *apostate; charlatan; deceiver; dissembler; fake; fraud; hypocrite; impostor; knave; mountebank; pharisee; phony; pretender; quack; rascal; recreant; renegade; scoundrel; swindler; tergiversator; traitor.*

(a) woman's place is in the home A popular prescription (see page 23).

(a) woman's work is never done A popular prescription (see page 23).

(the) wonderful world of A moribund metaphor (see page 21).

(he) won't bite A moribund metaphor (see page 21).

won't budge (an inch) A moribund metaphor (see page 21). *adamant; close-minded; contumacious; firm; immovable; immutable; inflexible; intransigent; invariable; obstinate; resolute; resolved; rigid; steadfast; stubborn; unalterable; unbending; unchangeable; unchanging; unwavering; unyielding.*

won the battle but lost the war A moribund metaphor (see page 21).

won't take no for an answer An infantile phrase (see page 20). *insist.*

(the) (F)-word An infantile phrase (see page 20). ■ Many men have trouble with *the C-word.* REPLACE WITH *commitment.* ■ During the holidays, many people write and ask about *the D-word,* depression. DELETE *the D-word.* ■ Nearly everyone involved with the contract was using *the H-word,* "historic," to describe it. DELETE *the H-word.* ■ Journalists agonized over asking about the *"A" word.* REPLACE WITH *affair.* ■ For most middle-aged women, *the M-word* is not a laughing matter. REPLACE WITH *menopause.* ■ The see-through Clinton has three schemes in his playbook to divert us all from *the "M" word.* REPLACE WITH *Monica.*

words cannot describe (express) A plebeian sentiment (see page 23). ■ *Words cannot express* the terrible emptiness we feel or how much we miss her. SEE ALSO *there are no words to describe (express).*

work (my) butt (tail) off A moribund metaphor (see page 21). *drudge; grind; grub; labor; moil; slave; strain; strive; struggle; sweat; toil; travail; work hard.*

work (his) fingers to the bone A moribund metaphor (see page 21). *drudge; grind; grub; labor; moil; slave; strain; strive; struggle; sweat; toil; travail; work hard.*

(a) work in progress A torpid term (see page 24). *A work in progress* is often periphrastic for something or someone undone, unfinished, incomplete. ■ Islamicizing liberal democracy is still *a work in progress.* ■ Georgia State is *a work in progress.* ■ She's *a work in progress* and a person to whom we can all relate.

working stiff A moribund metaphor (see page 21). *aide; apparatchik; assistant; cog; dependent; drudge; flunky; helper; hireling; inferior; junior; minion; secondary; servant; slave; subaltern; subordinate; underling; vassal.*

work like a dog An insipid simile. *drudge; grind; grub; labor; moil; slave; strain; strive; struggle; sweat; toil; travail; work hard.*

(the) world is (his) oyster A moribund metaphor (see page 21).

> Suburbs are the best of both worlds, all you need is a car and the world is your oyster, your Edsel, your Chrysler, your Ford. — Ann-Marie MacDonald, *The Way The Crow Flies*

(a) (whole new) world of A moribund metaphor (see page 21). ■ Mail merge can make your word processor more useful and can open up *a whole new world of power.* SEE ALSO *a barrage of.*

(and) (the) world will beat a path to (your) door A moribund metaphor (see page 21).

worlds apart A moribund metaphor (see page 21).

worn threadbare A moribund metaphor (see page 21). 1. *banal; bromidic; common; commonplace; hackneyed; overused; overworked; pedestrian; platitudinous; prosaic; stale; trite.* 2. *damaged; decayed; decrepit; deteriorated; dilapidated; ragged; shabby; shopworn; tattered; worn.*

worried to death A moribund metaphor (see page 21). *agitated; anxious; apprehensive; distraught; distressed; fearful; nervous; panicky; stressed; stressful; tense; tormented; troubled; uneasy; worried.* SEE ALSO *to death.*

(looks) (the) worse for wear A moribund metaphor (see page 21). 1. *broken-down; crumbly; damaged; decayed; decrepit; depleted; deteriorated; dilapidated; dingy; dirty; exhausted; filthy; flimsy; foul; frayed; grimy; grubby; grungy; ragged; ramshackle; rickety; seedy; shabby; shaky; soiled; sordid; sullied; squalid; tattered; tired; tottering; unclean; unsound; used up; washed-out; worn; worn-out.* 2. *aged; aging; elderly; hoary; old; seasoned.*

> The conferees had, by that time, acquainted themselves with the accommodation provided in one of the University's halls of residence, a building hastily erected in 1969, at the height of the boom in

higher education, and now, only ten years later, looking much the worse for wear. — David Lodge, *Small World: An Academic Romance*

(he) worships the ground (I) walk on A moribund metaphor (see page 21). *adore; cherish; esteem; eulogize; exalt; extol; glorify; honor; idealize; idolize; laud; love; panegyrize; prize; revere; treasure; venerate; worship.*

worst-case scenario An overworked word (see page 22). ■ The *worst-case scenario* would be for Question 3 to pass and for Question 5 to fail. ■ The indictment of a top executive on child-porn charges represents a *worst-case scenario* for any company and its IT managers. ■ He could ultimately be a progressive's *worst-case scenario.*

Sometimes the worst-case scenario comes true. But, of course, it wasn't the worst-case scenario at all: she could have died; she could have been paralyzed from the neck down rather than the waist; she could have been disfigured as well. — Daniel Stolar, *The Middle of the Night*

(every parent's) worst nightmare A moribund metaphor (see page 21). ■ It's *every mother's worst nightmare.* ■ This defendant is *every person's worst nightmare.* ■ Being a stepparent is *my worst nightmare.* ■ Perhaps the cliché is true about its being a woman's greatest fantasy and *a man's worst nightmare.* SEE ALSO *it was a nightmare.*

Mariah awakens to her worst nightmare: Ian Fletcher has disappeared with Faith. — Jodi Picoult, *Keeping Faith*

(the) worst of all (possible) worlds A moribund metaphor (see page 21).

worth (her) salt A moribund metaphor (see page 21). *advantageous; beneficial; cost-effective; effective; effectual; efficacious; gainful; lucrative; productive; profitable; serviceable; useful; valuable; worthwhile.*

worth (its) weight in gold A moribund metaphor (see page 21). 1. *costly; dear; expensive; inestimable; invaluable; precious; priceless; prized; valuable.* 2. *advantageous; beneficial; effective; effectual; efficacious; essential; helpful; indispensable; profitable; serviceable; useful; valuable; vital; worthwhile.*

would appear (hope; imagine; seem; submit; suggest; suspect; think) A wretched redundancy (see page 25). *appear (hope; imagine; seem; submit; suggest; suspect; think).* ■ I *would think* so. DELETE *would.* ■ I *would hope* a decision would be reached before the term of office expires. DELETE *would.* ■ It *would appear* that the state wants to jeopardize the project. REPLACE WITH *appears.*

Not only is the *would* in *would appear (hope; imagine; seem; submit; suggest; suspect; think)* superfluous, it calls into question the accuracy and knowledge of whoever uses the phrase. Only the intellectually timorous, the dimwitted, need to so qualify their words.

wouldn't be caught (seen) dead A torpid term (see page 24). 1. *abhor; abom-*

inate; detest; hate; loathe. 2. *averse; disinclined; loath; opposed; reluctant; unwilling.*

> Jason wouldn't take her on dates, wouldn't be caught dead holding hands with her in public or stepping onto a dance floor. — Tom Perrotta, *Little Children*

wouldn't hurt a flee (fly) A moribund metaphor (see page 21). 1. *affable; agreeable; amiable; amicable; compassionate; friendly; gentle; good-hearted; good-natured; humane; kind; kind-hearted; personable; pleasant; tender; tolerant.* 2. *dovish; irenic; nonviolent; pacific; pacifist; pacifistic; peaceable; peaceful; peace-loving; unbelligerent; uncontentious.*

(I) wouldn't touch it with a ten-foot pole A moribund metaphor (see page 21).

wrapped up in (herself) A moribund metaphor (see page 21). *egocentric; egoistic; egotistic; egotistical; narcissistic; self-absorbed; selfish; solipsistic.*

wreak havoc An inescapable pair (see page 20). *demolish; destroy; devastate; injure; obliterate; rack; ravage; ruin; shatter; smash; undo; wrack; wreck.* ■ A handful of companies is *wreaking havoc on* the rest of the industry. REPLACE WITH *ravaging.*

wreathed in smiles A moribund metaphor (see page 21). *beaming; glowing; smiling.*

(it's) written all over (you) A moribund metaphor (see page 21).

wrong end of the stick A moribund metaphor (see page 21).

(what's) wrong is wrong A quack equation (see page 23).

(the) wrong side of the tracks A moribund metaphor (see page 21).

(he) wrote the book (on) A moribund metaphor (see page 21).

X, Y, Z

x marks the spot A moribund metaphor (see page 21).

year in (and) year out A moribund metaphor (see page 21). *always; ceaselessly; constantly; continually; continuously; endlessly; eternally; everlastingly; evermore; forever; forevermore; immortally; indefinitely; interminably; permanently; perpetually; persistently; unceasingly; unremittingly.*

(62) years young An infantile phrase (see page 20). ■ I'm 43 *years young.* DELETE *years young.*

yell and scream An inescapable pair (see page 20). *bay; bawl; bellow; blare; caterwaul; clamor; cry; holler; hoot; howl; roar; screak; scream; screech; shout; shriek; shrill; squawk; squeal; vociferate; wail; whoop; yell; yelp; yowl.* ■ Two months later, he'd lost all his hair, and his wife started *yelling and screaming* about my not making him continue. REPLACE WITH *scream* or *yell*. SEE ALSO *yell and scream*.

yell (her) head off A moribund metaphor (see page 21). *bay; bawl; bellow; blare; caterwaul; clamor; cry; holler; hoot; howl; roar; screak; scream; screech; shout; shriek; shrill; squawk; squeal; vociferate; wail; whoop; yell; yelp; yowl.*

yes, Virginia, (there is) An infantile phrase (see page 20).

(the) yin and the yang A moribund metaphor (see page 21).

you are what you eat A popular prescription (see page 23).

you can catch more flies with honey than with vinegar A popular prescription (see page 23).

you can fool some of the people some of the time, but you can't fool all of the people all of the time A popular prescription (see page 23).

you can lead a horse to water, but you can't make (him) drink A popular prescription (see page 23).

you can make a difference A popular prescription (see page 23).

you can say that again An infantile phrase (see page 20).

you can't be all things to all people A popular prescription (see page 23).

you can't buy love A popular prescription (see page 23).

you can't change the world in a day A popular prescription (see page 23).

you can't fight city hall A popular prescription (see page 23).

you can't fit a square peg in a round hole A popular prescription (see page 23).

you can't get blood from (out of) a stone A popular prescription (see page 23).

you can't get there from here An infantile phrase (see page 20).

you can't go home again A popular prescription (see page 23).

you can't have everything A popular prescription (see page 23).

you can't have it both ways A popular prescription (see page 23).

you can't have something for nothing A popular prescription (see page 23).

you can't have your cake and eat it too A popular prescription (see page 23).

you can't judge a book by its cover A popular prescription (see page 23).

you can't live on love alone A popular prescription (see page 23).

you can't live with (them) and you can't live without (them) A popular prescription (see page 23).

you can't lose what you never had A popular prescription (see page 23).

you can't make a silk purse out of a sow's ear A popular prescription (see page 23).

you can't please everyone A popular prescription (see page 23).

you can't put new wine in old bottles A popular prescription (see page 23).

you can't serve God and mammon A popular prescription (see page 23).

you can't take it with you A popular prescription (see page 23).

you can't teach an old dog new tricks A popular prescription (see page 23).

you can't win them all A popular prescription (see page 23).

(so quiet) you could hear a pin drop A moribund metaphor (see page 21). 1. *dumb; hushed; motionless; mum; mute; noiseless; quiet; reticent; silent; soundless; speechless; stationary; still; stock-still; subdued; taciturn; unmoving; voiceless; wordless.* 2. *becalmed; calm; halcyon; irenic; pacific; peaceable; peaceful; placid; quiescent; reposeful; serene; tranquil.*

you don't miss what you never had A popular prescription (see page 23).

you do the best you can A suspect superlative (see page 24). Dwelling on our failures is no better than dismissing them, but *you do the best you can,* still another expression of resignation, may too easily excuse us for our missteps and mistakes, our failures and inadequacies. Here, *the best* is surely suspect.

you (have to) do what you have to (do) A popular prescription (see page 23).

you get what you pay for A popular prescription (see page 23).

you had to be there A grammatical gimmick (see page 19). This is merely an admission of having badly told a tale.

you have everything to gain and nothing to lose A popular prescription (see page 23).

you have nothing to lose A popular prescription (see page 23).

you have to give to get A popular prescription (see page 23).

you have (got) to start somewhere A popular prescription (see page 23).

you have to understand (that) An ineffectual phrase (see page 19). ■ First of all, *you have to understand that* many black men are in prison. DELETE *you have to understand that.* SEE ALSO *it is important to understand (that).*

(do) you know? An ineffectual phrase (see page 19). ■ I felt like I was enlightened, *you know?* DELETE *you know?* ■ You never know what's going to happen, *you know?* DELETE *you know?* ■ The translation sounded too straightforward, *you know?* DELETE *you know?* ■ To an extent, I think everybody is racist. *You know?* DELETE *You know?* SEE ALSO *(you) hear what I'm saying? (you) know what I mean? (you) know what I'm saying? (you) know what I'm telling you?*

you learn something new every day A plebeian sentiment (see page 23). It's the event of having learned something — something taught, not thought — that gives rise to the remark.

you made your bed, now lay in it A popular prescription (see page 23).

you name it A grammatical gimmick (see page 19). *and others; and so forth; and so on; and the like; etc.* ■ Today, in our state, those who do the public's work — teachers, cops, public-health nurses, social workers, highway builders, prison guards, *you name it* — are held up to ridicule.

you never know A plebeian sentiment (see page 23).

you never know till you try A popular prescription (see page 23).

young and foolish An inescapable pair (see page 20).

you owe it to yourself A popular prescription (see page 23). ■ Believe me, *you owe it to yourself* to take advantage of this exciting opportunity.

you're (only) as old as you feel A popular prescription (see page 23).

you're either part of the solution or part of the problem A popular prescription (see page 23).

you're either with (me) or against (me) A popular prescription (see page 23).

you're kidding An infantile phrase (see page 20). This expression is among the most banal we utter. We say it uncontrollably — less in stupefaction than in stupidity — and without a moment's reflection.

The more commonplace the words you use, the more commonplace the person you are. SEE ALSO *really? you've got to be kidding.*

you're not alone A plebeian sentiment (see page 23). ■ Feeling depressed, lonely, restless, bored, upset? *You're not alone.*

you're not the only one An infantile phrase (see page 20). *as I do; I do too; neither do I; no more do I; nor do I; so do I.*

you're only young once A popular prescription (see page 23).

your guess is as good as mine An infantile phrase (see page 20). *I don't know; (it's) not (yet) known; (that's) uncertain; (that's) unclear; (it's) unknown.* SEE ALSO *(it) remains to be seen; (just have to) wait and see.*

yours truly An infantile phrase (see page 20). *I; me.* ■ And you can bet that *yours truly* will do something crazy. REPLACE WITH *I*.

you scratch my back, I'll scratch yours A popular prescription (see page 23). ■ It's an approach that resonates equally with businessmen steeped in the win-win jargon of negotiations and politicians deep in the pragmatic *you-scratch-my-back-I'll-scratch-yours* conversations that make Washington run.

you think too much A plebeian sentiment (see page 23). *You think too much* is, of course, commentary that only those who rarely think could ever offer. These are the people who cower from consciousness. SEE ALSO *I (just) don't think about it.*

you've come a long way (baby) An infantile phrase (see page 20).

you've got to be kidding An infantile phrase (see page 20). SEE ALSO *really? you're kidding.*

you win a few (some), you lose a few (some) A popular prescription (see page 23).

zigs and zags An inescapable pair (see page 20).

(a) zillion(s) (of) An infantile phrase (see page 20). Doubly infantile are the phrases *ba-zillion* and *ga-zillion.* ■ I'll bet their mothers spent *a zillion* hours trying to get their sons to clean up after themselves. REPLACE WITH *countless.* ■ I made *a zillion* mistakes. REPLACE WITH *innumerable.* ■ There may be grating aspects to 20- and 30-somethings earning *kazillion*-dollar bonuses, but at least wealth gives them the self-confidence to ask for a date. REPLACE WITH *million.*

The Vocabula Review

If you've enjoyed The Dimwit's Dictionary, you may want to subscribe to The Vocabula Review (www.vocabula.com). Twelve monthly issues of The Vocabula Review cost only $15.00.

Mail this page with your check or money order — made payable to The Vocabula Review — to:

The Vocabula Review
5A Holbrook Court
Rockport, MA 01996
United States

Name: _____

Email address: _____
(please print clearly)

Once we've received your payment, we will email you a password so that you can read The Vocabula Review's pages.

The Vocabula Review
www.vocabula.com

Acknowledgments

Having the private use of a dive boat was indispensable for our work in Bimini. Close friends John and Laura Smith of Jacksonville, Florida provided the *Pocahontas* in 1995, Scuba Bimini allowed us to use the *Blenny* in 1996 and 1997, and our South Bimini neighbors, Dr. W. J. "Pete" Morse and Helen Swallow, made the *Big Hellie* available to us in 1998. Their generosity provided the freedom to study the fishes at our own pace. I am especially grateful to Bill and Phoebe Foster of York Harbor, Maine, two of the loveliest people I know, for the use of their delightful island home Wen-Mar on South Bimini. I'm indebted to James Bohnsack, Anne-Marie Eklund, Michael Domeier and Chris Koenig for sharing details of their past and present research projects. I must mention my close working relationship with the dedicated staff of the Reef Environmental Education Foundation (REEF): Laddie Akins, Deena Wells-Feeley, John Pitcairn, Dr. Cristina Pattengill-Semmens and Denise Mizell who provided valuable fish survey data and personal observations. On his visits to Bimini, good friend Richie Collins kept our boat engines running, and, as always, provided stimulating companionship. A special thanks to the Rosenstiel Marine Library and their pleasant, professional staff. Chris Mills drew and Jose Levy provided the isopod drawings on page 112 and Wesley Strong provided the hammerhead drawing on page 303. Lee Petersen at Marine Camera Distributors and Toshikazu Kozawa assisted with underwater camera housings. I am especially grateful to the hands-on people who helped put the book together: Paul Humann, Eric Riesch, Fred McConnaughey, Nancy DeLoach, Dr. Emily Schmitt-Lavin, Ken Marks, Michael O'Connell and Sean Keeler. My gem of a wife Anna - so smart, lovely and full of energy — was with me on every dive and library junket. The insight of Paul Humann my trusted friend, mentor and tireless partner touches every page.

And last, I wish to express my sincere gratitude to the marine biologists and ecologists whose years of research are the heart of this book.

PHOTOGRAPHY:

The photographs in this book show species in their natural habits. Many outstanding underwater photographers contributed their work. I appreciate their skills and assistance in making this collection of photographs as comprehensive as possible.

Charles Arneson - 128, 177, 241, 343. **Andrew Bruckner** - 294, 295. **Nick Caloyianis** - 305, 306&307. **David Cubbin** - 309 b. **Jim Church** - 97. **Ned DeLoach** - Front cover, 8, 9 t&b, 10 t&b, 14, 15, 16, 17 t&b, 22, 23, 26, 28 t&b, 29 l&r, 32, 33, 38 tl&tr&ml&mr&bl, 39 tl&tr&mr, 40 t&b, 41, 44 t&b, 45 tl&bl&br, 46 b, 52, 53, 54, 55, 58 b, 56 b, 57 t&b, 58 b, 60 tl&tr, 61 tl&tr, 63 t, 64, 65 t&b, 66, 67 t&b, 69, 70 tr, 72 t&ml&mr&b, 73, 74,75 tl&tr, 76 t&m, 79, 81, 82 tl&tr, 89 ms&mr&bl&br, 90 tl,91 t&m,92 t&m, 93 t&b, 94 tl&tr&ml&mr&bl&br, 95 l&r, 98, 101 b, 102 tr&mr&br, 103 tl&tr&bl&br, 104 t, 105, 106 t&b, 107, 108, 110, 111 t, 114, 119 t, 122, 123 ms&mr, 124, 127, 138, 140, 144, 147, 148, 149 l&r, 152, 153, 156 t&lb&rb, 157, 158 tl&tr&b, 159, 160 tl&tr, 161, 162, 163, 164, 165 t&b, 166, 167 t&b, 168, 169, 170 t&b, 171, 172, 173, 174 tl&tr, 178, 179 t&b, 183 t&b, 184, 185, 186, 187 t&b, 189 t&m&bl&br, 190, 191 br, 192, 194 r, 195, 196, 199 l, 200 t&b, 201 t&b, 202, 203, 204, 205, 206, 207 t&b, 208, 209, 210 t&m&b, 211 t&b, 214, 215 t&m&b, 216 t&m&b, 217, 222, 226, 229 ml, 231, 245 t, 247, 250 t&b, 251 tl&m&b, 253, 254 t&b, 255, 258, 259, 260 bl, 262, 264, 265, 266, 268, 270, 271, 272, 273, 274, 275, 276 tl&tr, 277 t&b, 278 tl&tr, 279 t&b, 283, 284, 286, 291, 292 b, 297, 298, 299, 311 t&b, 312, 313 t&m&b, 314 l&r, 315 t&br, 319, 317 t&b, 319 t&ml&mr&br, 320 t&b, 321 t&b, 327, 328, 331 t&br, 334, 340 t&b, 342, Back cover tl&-bl&-tr&-br. **Michael Domeier** - 245 b. **Rick Frehsee** - 232. **Debbie Fugitt** - 77. **Mike Haber** - 45 tr. **Pam Hardie** - 4. **Paul Humann** - 1, 7, 11,12 t&b, 13 t&b, 19, 36 l&r, 37 l&r, 38 br, 39ml&bl&br, 47, 48, 58 t, 61 ml&mr&bl&br, 63 m&b, 70 tl&bl&br, 77 t, 78, 80, 83, 84, 86, 87 t&b, 88 t&b, 89 tl&tr, 90 tr&bl&br, 92 b, 96, 99, 100 l&r, 101 t, 102 tl&ml&bl, 104 b, 109 t&m&b, 111 b, 115, 116 t&b, 117 l&r, 118 b, 119 b, 121 t&br, 123 tl&tr,bl&br, 125, 139 tl&tr&mr&mr&bl, 143, 146, 150, 154 t&b, 155, 160 b, 176, 181 ml&mr&bl&br, 191 t&bl, 194 l, 199 r, 212, 218, 223 b, 225 t&b, 228, 229 tl&tr&mr&bl&br, 230, 234, 239, 252, 257 tl&tr&bl&br, 260 tl&tr&br, 261 bl&br, 267, 284, 287, 300, 301, 304 b, 310, 315 br, 322, 323 t&m&b, 326, 330 bl, 332 tl&tr&m&b, 335 t&b, 336, 337, 338 t&bl&br, 339 t&bl&br, 340. **Mike Kelly** - 118 t. **Ken Marks** - 56 t, 142. **Woody Mayhew** - 76 b, 219, 220,221, 223 t, 224. **Doug Perrine** - 20, 21, 30,46T, 59t, 121 bl, 180, 236, 237 t&b, 240, 242, 247 t&b, 280, 281, 292t, 308. **Scott Michael** - 18, 68, 227, 267. **Mike Seale** - 139 br. **Wayne Shoemake** - 31. **Walt Sterns** - 50, 51, 62, 71, 75 b. **Wesley Strong** - 302, 304 t. **Carlos Villoch** - 309 t. **Dick Zingula** - 35 t&b.

Author's Note

Anna & Ned DeLoach

Reef Fish Behavior is intended as an overview of what is presently known about the nature of reef fishes inhabiting the waters of Florida, the Caribbean and Bahamas. It is also meant to serve as a companion reference to Paul Humann's *Reef Fish Identification* – a comprehensive guide to the fishes in the same region. Both volumes are the result of an expanding and productive partnership between the scientific and the recreational diving communities.

The information included in the text came from two primary sources – four summers of underwater observation and photography in Bimini, Bahamas and many hours of research in the library at the Rosenstiel School of Marine and Atmospheric Science, University of Miami. Extended stays in Bonaire, Belize, the Florida Keys and shorter visits to Roatan, the Cayman Islands, Puerto Rico, Walker Cay Bahamas, New Providence Island Bahamas, St. Lucia, St. Vincent and the Grenadines, and Barbados rounded out five years of research and regional travel. Video images, recorded by my wife Anna, were used extensively to analyze behavior described in the text. Anecdotal observations gleaned from conversations with fish aficionados in the scientific, marine management, conservation, aquarium and diving fields add insight and spice to an otherwise data-dominated narrative. Entries beginning with "we" were personal observations made by Anna, my partner Paul Humann or me. In the text, I chose to do the following: capitalize common fish and invertebrate names to set them apart from descriptive adjectives; enter a species' scientific name only the first time it appears in a section; and, in all but two instances (the common names of the Fairy Basslet and the Yellowtail Parrotfish), we followed the recommendations of *Common and Scientific Names of Fishes* published by the American Fisheries Society.

Anna and I thoroughly enjoyed every facet of gathering material for this book but our four extended stays in South Bimini were magical times, when, as John Steinbeck wrote "the world spun in well-greased grooves." While in Bimini we had the luck of living at Wen-Mar – a rustic, thick-walled white concrete cottage built in the 1940s at the very edge of the sea. Our times there revolved around a small, brightly-lit sitting room that faced west toward the Gulf Stream. On clear nights we could see the glow of Miami from the room's glass doors and, while enjoying coffee in the cool of morning, we watched Brown Pelicans dive and Eagle Rays jump in our front yard. Afterwards, I would settle into an ocean-facing futon surrounded by stacks of copied research papers and dog-eared references and read about fishes or hammer away at my laptop until noon.

We dived seven days a week, except during prolonged westerly blows. Our borrowed boat (the *Pocahontas*, the *Blenny* or the *Big Hellie* – depending on the year) invariably pulled away from the dock at one with Capt. Anna at the helm. Thirty-minutes later, we were happily underwater. From among the dozens of excellent dive sites that edge the islands, we consistently returned to the same six. The locations, ranging in depth from 14 to 55 feet, allowed us to observe several different fish communities on a semi-regular basis over extended periods of time. When we were studying new behavior or trying to capture a difficult image, we often returned to the same location daily for weeks. During these periods, when we were "on to something," we worked the hardest, stayed underwater the longest and were the happiest.

Although we observed interesting fish behavior throughout the day, we found fish watching best at sunset when the large predators prowl and many fishes court and spawn. Our most productive dusk dives had a marked tendency to occur on the evenings of the seventh through the ninth day after the full moons of early spring to early summer.

Anna carried a Sony 3-chip video camera, and I lugged along a Nikon F 3 with a 60 mm macro lens and a Nikonos III with a 20 mm lens both connected to a single Ikelite Substrobe 200. We typically made three dives each afternoon, the last beginning 45 minutes before sunset and ending with just enough light left on the horizon to help Anna navigate home. Even before showering, we had the day's videotape turning in the VCR and reviewed our afternoon's exploits while sipping rum and taking notes.

When we began our research we had little idea how much, or what, is known about reef fishes. At the Rosenstiel Marine Library, we dived into the journal-packed stacks with the same enthusiasm that kept us underwater for hours on end. We quickly discovered that, unlike terrestrial animals that have been observed and documented for centuries, the study of coral reef animals is in its infancy. With little choice before the birth of Scuba, just a half-century ago, marine biologists based much of their early research on preserved specimens fished from the reef. Their inability to observe the fishes and invertebrates in their natural habitat left large gaps in our understanding of the behavior and ecology of reef animals. Today's diving naturalists, whether scientifically trained or inquisitive amateurs, are pioneers chronicling the last great undocumented natural history on earth. It is an exciting time to be a diver.

Following Page: *A school of Horse-eye Jack circling –*
a common behavior that has yet to be explained.

Contents

Reproduction

*The rapid upward spawning rise of Redband Parrotfish
ends with an explosive release of gametes.*

When searching for sex on the reef, there is no better time to be underwater than dusk. Unfortunately, divers traditionally are hanging up their wet suits or preparing for dinner when the mating rituals of reef fishes go into high gear. During the last hour of daylight, straddling sunset, numerous species release hundreds of free-floating gametes into the water column, where the eggs and sperm mix and disperse in the currents. This reproductive strategy, known as **pelagic** or **broadcast spawning**, ordinarily involves male-female pairs; but a few species spawn in groups that can number in the thousands. The pelagic spawners' upward **spawning rises** are typically split-second rocket-blasts culminating in an explosive release of **gametes** (eggs and sperm) that are abandoned by the parents. The visible portion of the milky gamete clouds left behind is sperm; the thousands of transparent eggs are virtually invisible. A second spawning strategy, **benthic egg laying**, generally begins at sunrise with lively courtship preceding the females' laying eggs in nests prepared, tended and guarded by males. Divers rarely see **internal fertilization** and **live bearing**, a much less common reproductive method typical of sharks and rays.

Sperm is little more than DNA with a tail; but eggs packed with fat to nourish the yolk-sac larvae require a large amount of energy to produce. This energy imbalance makes it possible for males to spawn far more frequently than females. With an almost unlimited supply of sperm and without the burden of parental care, **polygamy** (multiple mates) is the practice of choice for the majority of pelagic spawning males. The males' penchant for promiscuity and the dangers involved in traveling in search of mates combine to make **harems** the preferred social system of small, site-attached pelagic spawners. Dominant territorial males vigorously defend boundaries encompassing several females with whom they attempt to mate exclusively. Of course, harems have their costs – it takes plenty of energy to isolate mates from rivals, and food and shelter, nearly always in short supply, must be shared.

Group-spawning Bluehead Wrasse.

Although spawning rises are brief, the extended courtships leading to the wild finales are often entertaining, passion-packed melodramas. Courtship behavior varies but always revolves around a basic theme: A revved boy fish relentlessly chases, cajoles, corners, nudges and shows-off to a seemingly indifferent girl fish. To an untrained eye courtship often appears as nothing more than fish milling near the bottom. But after observing one or two fish trysts, the signs become unmistakable. Clues can be subtle or conspicuous, including color and pattern changes, body twitches, fin displays, swollen abdomens, females hovering in mid-water, and males rapidly swimming in and out of an area and aggressively chasing away competitors. While the males arrive at spawning sites prepared to shed sperm, females require additional time for their eggs to hydrate sufficiently before release. Prolonged courtship offers suitors the opportunity to assess their partners' readiness to spawn and possibly hastens egg preparation. When ready, the females become more receptive to the males' advances and normally initiate spawning rises by slowly by hovering a few feet above the bottom.

Sergeant Major laying and fertilizing eggs on a rock bottom.

Reproduction

Pelagic-spawning Redband Parrotfish.

Not all pelagic spawners wait until twilight to mate. Several common species, notably parrotfishes and wrasses, spawn during the day. The timing of a species' daily spawning period, which typically lasts from one to two hours, varies between regions in the Caribbean, but occurs locally at the same time each day. If there is such a thing as a typical courtship and pelagic spawning scenario, the Redband Parrotfish, *Sparisoma aurofrenatum*, provides a good example. From two to seven females gather late each afternoon at a traditional spawning site within the feeding territory of an excited male. While the swollen females graze, the male blazes about with his fins folded and his tail arched upward. The feisty suitor briefly approaches his mates with his fins spread and his body jerking and assesses the females' readiness to spawn before speeding out of the area. With each subsequent approach courtship intensifies until willing females rise eight to ten feet above the bottom and pause. The male circles slowly, occasionally voiding plumes of waste as he analyzes the situation. When a hovering female begins a steep rise, the male dashes to her side and together the pair skyrocket toward the surface and simultaneously release gametes, separate, then dive for the bottom. Males often

A male Redband Parrotfish (right) courts a female.

spawn with two or three partners in succession before swimming away, only to return minutes later to repeat the process. Spawning can continue in this manner for nearly an hour.

Species vary in their reactions to the close approach of divers during reproduction. After courtship begins, nothing seems to bother wrasses, flounders and small sea basses, but parrotfishes refuse to spawn with observers nearby. At dusk, the beam from a diver's handlight easily distracts courting fishes. When we approached a pair of Scrawled Filefish, *Aluterus scriptus*, during their slow, spiraling spawning ascent, the fish broke apart. One partner fled immediately, leaving the other alone in mid-water. Confused, it settled to the seafloor and released a stream of gametes next to a sea fan.

A number of species, including most members of the wrasse, parrotfish and sea bass families, are **sequential hermaphrodites**, born with the ability to change sex. This strategy allows a species to maintain a desired sex ratio under varying social and environmental conditions. Sex changes, once completed, are irreversible. In the Caribbean, nearly all sex-changing species are **protogynous hermaphrodites**, switching from females to males after reaching a certain size or age or when social situations, such as the loss of the harem's dominate male, warrant. Snook, *Centropomus undecimalis*, are one of the few species in the Caribbean documented to be **protandrous hermaphrodites**, changing from males to females. The factors triggering sex reversal have yet to be determined for most species.

Graysby, *Epinephelus cruentatus*, common, moderate-sized, protogynous sea basses, have a straightforward pattern of sex reversal. All individuals are born female. After reaching a length of eight inches during their fourth or fifth year, females change into males and establish harems. However, things are much more complicated for wrasses and parrotfishes. Nearly all the species in the two families have two visually distinct types of reproductive adults. The most numerous are the young, sexually mature individuals in the **initial phase** who, depending on their species, can be either males or females but are generally females. The sexes resemble each other in size, color, markings and general behavior. Initial phase males are either **primary males** (born males) or **secondary males** (sex-changed females). **Terminal males**, the largest, most colorful and least numerous individuals in a population, are typically secondary males; but in a few species, primary males also transform into the terminal phase.

The Graysby, a common, protogynous sea bass, has a straightforward pattern of sex change.

Reproduction

Although the social systems of parrotfishes and wrasses appear chaotic, their strict, size-oriented pecking orders promote stability. The majority of terminal males join harems as young females and, with growth, rise through the hierarchy until positioned next in line to change sex and take control. The ability to transform quickly into males is essential for establishing dominance in a harem and for discouraging neighboring terminal males from taking advantage of a sudden power vacuum.

Bluehead Wrasse, *Thalassoma bifasciatum*, one of the Caribbean's most abundant and thoroughly studied reef fishes, do not form harems. Instead, the terminal males take temporary control of traditional spawning sites, usually along the periphery of forereefs, where they spawn for a one- to two-hour period each afternoon. When ready to mate, females migrate from their feeding grounds to favored spawning sites, each controlled by one of the larger terminal males in the population. During a research project that removed all the terminal Bluehead Wrasse from an isolated reef, the larger females immediately displayed aggression among themselves. Within minutes, a few initiated male courtship behavior. Later the same day, the ranking females attempted to spawn as males and exhibited a slight darkening of their heads, a unique terminal phase coloration. After three days the same fish displayed obvious **transitional color patterns**, intermediate to the two phases. Recently sex-changed

Young initial phase Bluehead Wrasse.

A female shows an early transitional color pattern as she begins to change into a male.

Bluehead males grow 50 percent faster than females, but it takes a minimum of four months before they are large enough to experience significant reproductive success.

It would be death defying for non-ranking sequential hermaphrodites to buck the system and change sex before social order dictates. Offenders would be driven from their feeding grounds and would be unable to establish territories of their own or to join other harems. However, there always seems to be a twist on the reef. Within the small harems of the Rock Beauty, *Holacanthus tricolor*, one of two sex-changing angelfishes in the Caribbean, the ranking females regularly switch sex without the loss of the harems' dominant males or the opportunity to control nearby territories. These **bachelor males**, as they are called, possibly escape the wrath of the much larger dominant males by keeping low profiles. Even though they are unable to reproduce for a short period, their premature transformations have benefits. Bachelor males are in a better position to change quickly into a dominant role if the opportunity arises, and, like transitional Bluehead Wrasse, their rate of growth is accelerated – no small matter in a world where size means everything.

On reef systems with small communities of Bluehead Wrasse, Yellowtail Parrotfish, *Sparisoma rubripinne*, and Striped Parrotfish, *Scarus croicensis*, terminal males of each species control spawning activities exclusively. As populations grow, the number of initial phase males increases substantially

A late-stage transitional pattern. By this time the individual is probably functioning as a male.

Terminal phase Bluehead Wrasse.

Reproduction

putting competitive pressure on the dominance of terminal males. On these reefs, both harems and roving bands of initial phase males and females exist together. To boost their reproductive success, the young males participate in alternate spawning strategies. They not only interfere with the pair spawning activities of terminal males but also spawn in groups. Several aggregations, some with as many as 50 young males, gather just upcurrent from traditional spawning sites and waylay egg-swollen females on their way to mate with terminal males. Other initial phase males use stealth to get in on the action. Because they resemble females, small males, known as **streakers**, are able to hang around a harem undetected while waiting for an opportunity to streak in and join the spawning rise of a terminal male. **Sneakers**, on the other hand, secretly court and spawn with females inside the territories of terminal males. When recognized, the impostors are immediately chased, but often cover their escapes by disappearing into a passing initial phase herd. Controlling spawning territories is no easy task; on average, site-holders chase interfering males three times each minute during the two-hour reproductive periods. Occasionally terminal males can no longer fend off the competitors, who overrun spawning sites and mate with the waiting females. As populations grow, competition can become so heated that terminal males are forced to abandon their prime sites and reestablish territories on the periphery of initial phase group-spawning activities.

Females do have some say in these male-dominated domains. In an attempt to acquire a worthy set of genes for their eggs, many choose to mate only with the largest and most conspicuous males. To help the females make their decisions, terminal males often display bright colors. Most polygamous species are either permanently or temporarily **dichromatic** (the sexes exhibit different color patterns). Fishes with terminal and initial phases, such as many parrotfishes and wrasses, are generally considered to be permanently dichromatic. Most temporarily dichromatic species change colors and patterns only during reproductive periods. These temporary **spawning patterns** are common among damselfishes and many large sea basses. Ordinarily monogamous species, without the need to attract multiple mates, are **monochromatic** (the sexes exhibit the same permanent color

The Sailfin Blenny uses his enlarged dorsal fin to attract mates and to intimidate rivals.

A male Elliptic Flounder (foreground) extends his elongate pectoral fin during courtship.

pattern). Some species are **dimorphic**, with males obviously larger or developing physical features absent in females. Three-inch male Sailfin Blenny, *Emblemaria pandionis*, rise above the sea floor flaunting dorsal fins larger than their bodies in spirited shows to attract prospective mates. Lancer Dragonet, *Paradiplogrammus bairdi*, and several flounders display enlarged fins as markers of hereditary fitness.

Although it seems obvious that bright colors play an important role in sexual selection, there is little evidence supporting the idea. To date, only the vigor of a male's courtship displays has been directly correlated to reproductive success. Female Bluehead Wrasse have been found to select male partners because of their control of preferred spawning locations rather than for their flamboyance. When dominant males were removed from a reef or switched to nearby locations, their former female partners remained faithful to their previous spawning sites even when they were appropriated by less colorful males. Bright male colors and distinctive features, however, appear to play a role in intrasexual competition. Several members of the wrasse family display brilliant colors when engaged in territorial disputes. Sailfin Blenny, Lancer Dragonet and flounders erect their oversized fins when confronting rivals.

Some polygamists willingly mate with any obliging female that happens along, while others show a preference for the largest females, apparently because of their greater egg production. Studies have shown that male Bluehead Wrasse and Bucktooth Parrotfish, *Sparisoma radians*, allocate more sperm during spawning rises with larger females. And in proportion to body weight, initial phase males have larger testes than terminal phase males, a significant advantage when sneaking and streaking or competing in group spawns. However, terminal phase Bluehead males are estimated to be from 20 to 50 times more reproductively successful than the smaller males.

Reproduction

A large dominant male Spanish Hogfish (foreground) approaches members of his harem who hover above the reef ready to spawn.

Because of constant competitive pressure, terminal males of most species can defend successfully no more than seven females at any one time. Late one afternoon we observed the break-up of an unusually large harem of 13 Spanish Hogfish, *Bodianus rufus*, by a small, probably recently sex-changed male who took advantage of the unmanageable situation. Unlike other Caribbean wrasses, Spanish Hogfish are monochromatic, wearing the same purple-and-gold coats throughout life. The harem's dominant male was identified easily by his large size, but the sex of the smaller harem members was impossible to determine. Two similar-sized harem members squaring off with their jaws flared, provided our first clue that something unusual was taking place.

Courtship began when the females gathered loosely at the side of a reef. Moments later the terminal male made a close pass, prompting three females to rise above the reef and curve their bodies into an S-shape, signaling their readiness to mate. The unenthusiastic male casually pair spawned with each before wandering away. When he returned several minutes later, five additional females were waiting to mate, but the aloof male obliged only two before once again leaving. As soon as the terminal male was out of sight, the smaller male made his play. Flaring his fins and jerking his body, he repeatedly nudged the waiting females. When the terminal male returned and attempted to spawn, the young male streaked in and joined the rising pair. The large male instantly turned on the upstart and chased him down to the reef, where he disappeared among a cluster of similar-sized females. By the time this problem seemed in hand, a second large terminal male appeared on the scene. The harem-master

A male Spanish Hogfish positions next to a small female during a spawning rise.

instantly gave chase. In his absence the young male quickly spawned with two females, and, with the dominant male still occupied, he and three females fled as a group toward deeper water.

Several small sea basses have both functioning ovaries and testes, which allows them to spawn as males, females or both. These **simultaneous hermaphrodites** pull off this odd life style by **egg trading**. Unlike most pelagic-spawning females that typically discharge their entire load in one spawn, egg

Similar-sized Spanish Hogfish attempt to establish rank in their harem.

Reproduction

The passionate spawning clasp of egg-trading hamlets.

traders parcel out their energy-expensive cargo a portion at a time. This behavior ensures that their partners will reciprocate by releasing eggs which they, in turn, fertilize. Palm-sized egg-trading hamlets, *Hypoplectrus* spp., offer one of the most entertaining peep shows on the reef. An hour before sunset, the solitary sea basses leave their small feeding territories for a nightly rendezvous with customary mates. The courting couples display fins, alter colors, twitch and chase about the sea floor. The partners taking the female role always act as the aggressors. Just as the sun sets, the pairs rise above coral mounds and intertwine like clasping hands for a count of three before releasing gametes and popping apart. Each pair spawns from two to 12 times before separating for the night.

Of course, not all reef fishes are hermaphroditic or polygamist. Most species are **gonochorist**, remaining the same sex for life. And although **monogamy** (mating with a single partner) was once believed to be rare on the reef, new evidence indicates otherwise. It is difficult to substantiate the fidelity of mated pairs over time, but stable relationships lasting several breeding cycles have been documented for some species of butterflyfishes; Gray Angelfish, *Pomacanthus arcuatus*; French Angelfish, *P. paru*; egg-trading hamlets; Harlequin Bass, *Serranus tigrinus*; pipefishes and the egg-laying Cocoa Damselfish, *Stegastes variabilis*. Mouth-brooding male jawfishes and cardinalfishes, with limited capacities to incubate young, have marked tendencies toward monogamy. Because mated pairs of butterflyfishes and angelfishes feed together throughout much of the day, they are the most conspicuous twosomes sighted by divers. Gray and French Angelfish even seem affectionate, rising to circle returning mates. Having only a single reproductive partner limits a male's ability to distribute his genes, but ready access to a mate does offer advantages. However, complete monogamy appears to be rare. Scattered reports have noted male butterflyfishes straying into adjacent territories to spawn and permanently paired angelfishes joining in group sex. Even egg-trading Harlequin Bass and hamlets occasionally spawn with other mates.

Taking promiscuity to extremes, several species of pelagic spawners migrate to traditional spawning sites along outer reef shelves. There they participate in mass spawning events that, for some species, can involve thousands of individuals. There are two types of spawning groups: **resident spawning aggregations** involving small grazers, plankton-pickers or mobile invertebrate feeders who travel a few hours or less to their local spawning areas, and **transient spawning aggregations** composed of the large predatory groupers and snappers that, in many cases, migrate for days and, possibly, more than 100 miles to traditional spawning grounds. Species known to form resident aggregations include the Bluehead Wrasse; Striped Parrotfish; Yellowtail Parrotfish; Ocean Surgeonfish, *Acanthurus bahianus*; Blue Tang, *A. coeruleus*; Spotted Goatfish, *Pseudupeneus maculatus*; and egg-laying Brown Chromis, *Chromis multilineata*. With additional fieldwork, other species will undoubtedly be added to this list.

A resident aggregation of Blue Tang estimated between 6,000 and 7,000 individuals was observed for a four-year period by researchers in Puerto Rico. The gathering of Blue Tang always occurred in late afternoon around the full and new moon at a site in 60 feet of water. The huge, dome-shaped cloud of fish would rise slowly, ten or more feet, then settle back to the bottom. Eventually subgroups of four to 15 males following single females broke from the main group in spawning rises that carried them near the surface. An aggregation estimated to include 20,000 Ocean Surgeonfish spawned nearby in a similar fashion every afternoon from December through March. All resident-spawning species achieve the majority of their reproductive success pair spawning

Resident spawning aggregations of Blue Tang assemble late each afternoon.

Reproduction

outside aggregations. The advantages, if any, of group spawning are not understood. Published hypotheses include increased fertilization rates, limiting predation of eggs and adults and enhanced genetic recombination.

Synchronized by the lunar cycle, large, generally solitary groupers and snappers migrate long distances once or twice each year to reproduce at traditional spawning grounds for multi-day periods. During the week before the full moons of two consecutive winter months (usually December and January), Nassau Grouper, *Epinephelus striatus*, become restless and move out of their home ranges. Groups of up to 500 fish have been sighted swimming along the shelf edge toward spawning grounds. For several days arriving fish gather in small groups across a large area of moderately deep bottom. Spawning takes place in late afternoon for three to four consecutive days. Shortly before sunset the fish, wearing dramatic spawning colors, form into a spiraling mass that rises high off the sea floor. Small subgroups form and dash upward at steep angles, leaving visible gamete clouds at the apex of their rises. Because species participating in these semiannual reproductive events are not believed to spawn outside aggregations, these great gatherings probably represent their total reproductive output for the year.

Mutton Snapper, *Lutjanus analis*; Dog Snapper, *L. jocu*, and Cubera Snapper, *L. cyanopterus*, normally form large, transient spawning aggregations during consecutive months in late spring and early summer. However, one team of researchers studying a gathering of Nassau Grouper in Belize in January unexpectedly discovered an aggregation of Dog Snapper estimated from 500 to 1,000 individuals milling about the bottom in 90 feet of water 600 feet from the grouper. The snapper did not exhibit spawning patterns, but a few were noticeably darker than normal. When approached by divers, the scattered group dropped over a ledge to 160 feet, then ascended, forming a comet-shaped cloud. At 30 feet the rising snapper compressed into a compact ball before disappearing back into the depths. A few grouper displaying their distinct black-and-white spawning colors were mixed in with the throng. Although the

Left and right: *A transient spawning aggregation of Dog Snapper, numbering between 500 and 1,000 individuals, gathers in 90 feet of water near an outer reef bank.*

Reproduction

rising fish appeared to make a spawning rush, gamete release for this and other snapper aggregations has never been substantiated, leading to speculation that gametes are released after dark.

The question of how fishes know when and where to gather has prompted considerable research and debate. One hypothesis suggests that sites and times are selected to maximize survival of eggs and larvae. Possible benefits to offspring could include rapid dispersal of eggs, protection from predators, placement of larvae in optimal conditions to find food in the open ocean and increased chances for offspring to return to their reefs of origin. A second hypothesis focuses on possible social and reproductive advantages for adults, such as using tidal and daylight cycles to coordinate spawning schedules. To date, little evidence supports any of these ideas. It seems likely that factors from both schools of thought drive site selection and timing of reproduction.

There appears to be a tendency among pelagic spawners to release gametes during conditions favorable for their survival. Many pelagic-spawning species migrate to the outer, downcurrent edges of reefs or island shelves, where they spawn at dusk hypothetically to protect their progeny from the many egg predators on the reef. Water column feeders, such as Brown Chromis and Creole Wrasse, *Clepticus parrae*, which pick plankton above the reef throughout much of the day, move closer to the bottom as light fades. Their departure creates a window of opportunity for clouds of fresh spawn to dissipate unmolested. A few pelagic spawners, notably parrotfishes and smaller wrasses, spawn during daylight hours when feeding in the water column is intense. However, even though their conspicuous courtship behavior signals impending spawns, few planktivores feed directly on their clouds of gametes. Only Yellowtail Snapper, *Ocyurus chrysurus*, and Sergeant Major, *Abudefduf saxatilis*, regularly lurk around spawning activities.

Spawning fishes leaving the secure cover of the bottom to place their gametes above the reef brazenly expose themselves to nearby piscivores. Under these circumstances, speed would seem essential. Studies have demonstrated a correlation between the body size of spawners and their rate of ascent. Larger species less vulnerable to predation, such as Stoplight Parrotfish, *Sparisoma*

Yellowtail Snapper and Sergeant Major occasionally feed on the gamete clouds of pelagic spawners.

viride, often climb over 15 feet. Whitespotted Filefish, *Cantherhines macrocerus*, immune to most predators because of size and deep bodies, ascend high off the sea floor in slow, graceful, head-to-tail spiraling spawning rises. At the opposite end of the size scale, three-inch Peppermint Bass, *Liopropoma rubre*, barely rise above their coral cover to release gametes. These tactics must work: few successful attacks on spawning fish have been documented.

The slow spiraling spawning rise of Whitespotted Filefish.

If spawning on outgoing tides offers survival benefits for offspring, the strategy is not adopted by many species. Small and medium-sized site-attached pelagic spawners seldom coordinate reproduction with the lunar cycle, which in turn controls the tides. Of 22 pelagic spawners from eight families documented, only five species, all large predators which migrate to distant spawning grounds, were found to have lunar spawning cycles. However, in regions with pronounced tidal flow, there are indications that a few daytime spawners alter their reproductive schedules to spawn with outgoing tides. In areas with minimal tides, the same species reproduce at established times each day.

Reproduction

Most reef fishes have long reproductive seasons with one or more annual peaks. These peaks tend to occur during the cool-water months of late winter and early spring. Whether spawning in pairs or groups, daily, seasonally or annually, pelagic spawners rendezvous faithfully at traditional sites during specific times. Generally pair-spawning individuals and resident-spawning groups migrate to customary sites typically near three- to five-foot structures such as tall coral heads, sponge clusters or gorgonians. Some of these sites have been documented to be in continuous use for at least three decades. It was originally proposed that raised features act as launching platforms, facilitating higher spawning ascents. However, when elevated structures are absent from an area, no decrease in spawning activities occurs. The spawning grounds of transient aggregations are generally associated with distinct promontories jutting seaward from the insular shelf. Several of these sites are known to have been active for more than 50 years and are often used by different species at different times. Dyes and surface floats used to track the dispersal of eggs from the resident spawning sites of Bluehead Wrasse and the transient spawning grounds of Nassau Grouper produced little evidence of eggs leaving inshore waters from either location. It was the researchers' conclusion that, at least in some instances, reef fishes do not spawn at superior dispersal sites or at the best times for their offspring to be swept to sea. Today, many researchers lean toward the idea that prominent topographical features act simply as landmarks to help widely dispersed individuals locate each other during spawning periods.

A long-range study of isolated Bluehead Wrasse populations demonstrated that tradition, rather than resource assessment, is the strongest influence in the spawning site selection process. For 12 years, encompassing four generations, the same sites were used continually for daily spawning even though the area had an abundance of alternate sites. When entire populations were removed from three separate reefs and replaced with like numbers and sex ratios of Blueheads, it was discovered that the previously used sites were no more likely to be selected than any other suitable sites in the area. However, when the manipulated populations were themselves replaced a month later, the new populations demonstrated a strong tendency to reuse the sites selected after the first manipulation. This led the researchers to suspect that, in the absence of tradition, resource assessment, possibly for optimal egg transport, plays a dominant role in mating site selection.

Like nearly all reef fishes, Bluehead Wrasse settle out of the plankton to reefs where they remain for their maximum three-year life span. The tiny juveniles, quite susceptible to predation, remain close to shelter greatly limiting their ability to migrate or to assess their surroundings. Therefore it would seem almost certain that individuals learn the routes to mating sites by following members of the existing population rather than by trial-and-error. After researchers replaced a population, it took three to four days before the new residents began to spawn. It can be hypothesized that if interruptions on a small scale cause such confusion, then they should create even greater disruption for large spawning aggregations. Many scientists fear that when transient aggregations are repeatedly overfished, too few experienced adults remain to teach succeeding generations how to locate spawning grounds. This could have a devastating effect on the large species of groupers and snappers that are believed to concentrate their entire reproductive efforts during the two mass-spawning events each year.

With so many species of pelagic spawners placing gametes in the water column, it seems inevitable that occasional hybrids would occur. And, in fact, cross-fertilization among fishes in the wild is fairly common. The mixed offspring are almost precisely intermediate in body structure and color patterns to parental species. The more closely related, the better the chance two species have of crossbreeding. It is extremely rare for members of different genera to mix, but four cases of such natural crosses between western Atlantic fishes have been documented. The most peculiar occurred in Bermuda between two members of the sea bass family. The two species, Creole-fish, *Paranthias furcifer*, and Coney, *Epinephelus fulvus*, are not only classified in separate genera but do not even share the same habitat. Creole-fish, reported to form loose spawning aggregations, are plankton-pickers who feed high in the water column. Coneys inhabit bottom territories where they pair spawn within harems. The three other recorded hybrids are crosses between Yellowtail Snapper and three species of snappers in the genus *Lutjanus* (Schoolmaster, *L. apodus*; Gray Snapper, *L. griseus*; and Lane Snapper, *L. synagris*). The Yellowtail Snapper-Lane Snapper hybrids were once classified as a valid species, the Cuban Snapper, *L. ambiguus*. In an experiment in the late 1980s a Lane Snapper and a Yellowtail Snapper were crossed in the laboratory. When examined 16 months later, the offspring had the same morphology and coloration as individuals previously described as Cuban Snapper. The research points to the apparent ease with which Yellowtail Snapper cross in the wild with *Lutjanus*, bringing into question the validity of *Ocyurus* as a legitimate genus.

It seems unlikely that the sperm and eggs of different species, released separately, would find each other in the currents. The hybrids were more likely engendered when Yellowtail Snapper joined the spawning activities of the three *Lutjanus*. Like the Nassau Grouper involved in the spawning ball of Dog Snapper in Belize, Yellowtail Snapper could accompany the spawning rises of *Lutjanus*. We have twice observed Yellowtails spawning in groups of ten or twelve individuals in late afternoon in summer. The fish circled a few feet off the bottom before suddenly charging straight up 15 to 20 feet, where they left visible gamete clouds. This behavior could be easily assimilated in the spawning activities of other snappers.

Because of the close physical and behavioral similarities between Striped Parrotfishes, *Scarus croicensis*, and Princess Parrotfish, *S. taeniopterus*, researchers have long expected to find a natural hybrid of the species. Interestingly, Princess Parrotfish are one of the few pelagic spawners who reproduce in the early morning; the look-alike Striped Parrotfish spawn in the more traditional late afternoon. This is probably the factor limiting cross-fertilization between the two.

Although most hybrids are born sterile or die before reaching sexual maturity, crosses between Queen Angelfish, *Holacanthus ciliaris*, and Blue Angelfish, *H. bermudensis*, occur regularly where the ranges of the two species overlap in Florida and the western Bahamas. Their hybrid offspring, once incorrectly classified as the Townsend Angelfish, *H. townsendi*, are fertile and frequently **backcross** (mating with either parent species), creating a variety of

intermediate color forms. In rare cases, crosses between species can lead to the formation of new species. The importance of this evolutionary process to reef fishes is still being investigated.

Benthic Egg Laying

Although pelagic spawning predominates on tropical reefs, benthic egg laying is widespread. As a general rule, egg-layers are small and numerous. Prevalent among their ranks are damselfishes, cardinalfishes, blennies and gobies. A few members of the triggerfish family are the only large egg-laying species on the reef. As benefits, egg-layers do not have to make dangerous openwater ascents to release their eggs, search for mates or make risky migrations to distant spawning sites. However, substantial energy costs are required of the parental males to prepare nests, fin-fan clutches, pluck out bacteria and dead eggs, and keep aggressive egg-bandits at bay. The males' care pays dividends. Unlike the eggs of their pelagic-spawning counterparts that hatch in little more than 24 hours as nothing more than tiny yolk sacs with tails, the larvae of egg-layers emerge after six or seven days with eye pigment, developed fins and the ability to fend for themselves. Hatching usually occurs during the first hour after sunset. Many egg-layers spawn with the lunar cycle. Of these, the majority follow biweekly timetables believed to correspond with the new and full moon. However, only limited correlation has been found between hatching times and optimal tidal flows that would quickly carry the hatchlings away from the reef.

The eggs of most species are spawned at daybreak inside holes, crevices, abandoned shells, under rocks and around gorgonian stems. Most damselfishes lay compact, single-layer patches of eggs, known as **clutches**. Each female repeatedly skims over the nest, extruding a single row of eggs at a time from an extended organ, known as a **papilla**. Females periodically move to the side, allowing males to fertilize in a similar manner. The process continues from minutes to an hour before a circular patch a few inches across and containing possibly as many as 5,000 eggs is abandoned by the female. Nests normally contain several clutches, often deposited by different females. Blue Chromis, *Chromis cyanea*, Brown Chromis, *C. multilineata*, and Sergeant Major, *Abudefduf saxatilis*, lay and fertilize eggs in open nests during daylight hours. Female Brown Chromis, less discriminating than other family members, scatter tiny eggs in crudely prepared nest sites, often located on small algal bushes or exposed rocks. As many as ten females may contribute to a single nest. The purple egg patches of Sergeant Major are laid in well prepared nests, usually located in open areas where they are actively guarded by males who turn a dark blue for the occasion.

Some triggerfishes (Queen Triggerfish, *Balistes vetula*, and Sargassum Triggerfish, *Xanthichthys ringens*) are pelagic spawners, but other family members lay eggs in shallow depressions blown in the sand. The egg-laying triggerfishes are not only the largest reef fishes to lay eggs but also the only

Left: *Purple Reeffish spawning in the algal turf of a reef crevice.*

Reproduction

Black Durgon use teamwork to defend their sand nest from numerous nimble egg-predators.

species known to provide maternal protection. Lacking the agility of smaller egg-laying fishes, large triggerfishes have a difficult time keeping pace with darting egg-raiders. One afternoon we watched three Black Durgon, *Melichthys niger*, probably members of the same harem, guarding an egg nest in a sand channel between coral ridges. The triggerfishes were kept alert

An Ocean Triggerfish blows a shallow egg-nest in the open sand.

A male cardinalfish uses his mouth to incubate his clutch.

Male jawfishes regularly aerate and mix their clutches.

by scrappy packs of wrasses and damselfishes circling just out of reach of their snapping beaks. When we approached, the triggerfishes moved several feet away and watched anxiously. In a sand basin no more than an inch deep and a foot across, we found a two-inch flattened circular mass of gelatinous eggs mixed with sand. Before the wrasses attacked we backed away allowing the guardians to regain control. Fortunately, the eggs of triggerfishes hatch quickly, possibly within one or two days after being laid. On two consecutive days, we observed 15 to 20 large, normally solitary Ocean Triggerfish, *Canthidermis sufflamen*, gathered in the water column above a bed of Manatee Grass, *Syringodium filiforme*, in 55 feet of water. While most of the large graceful fish cruised about, a few individuals blew shallow, two- to three-foot wide nests in the grass bed below. The fish were wary and often displayed darkened faces and backs. We did not observe spawning or find eggs in the nests.

Male jawfishes and several species of cardinalfishes take parental responsibilities to extremes by incubating eggs inside their mouths. During the eggs' five- to seven-day development, male jawfishes seldom feed and only momentarily leave their charges unattended within the security of their burrows. Male seahorses and pipefishes brood fertilized eggs within an abdominal body pouch until hatching.

Live-Bearing

The majority of bony fishes are **oviparous** – releasing gametes for external fertilization. Cartilaginous fishes are typically **viviparous** – bearing live offspring. Male sharks, rays and skates fertilize their mates internally **(copulation)**. They transfer sperm into the **cloaca** (a ventral opening used for reproduction and excretion) of their mates with **claspers**, organs modified from the inner edge of each pelvic fin. The presence of claspers can be used to

Reproduction

distinguish males. The ends of claspers, often equipped with hooks and spines, flare when inside a female to help secure a hold. Sperm passes through grooves in the claspers, fertilizing a few large eggs.

The developing embryos of viviparous species receive nourishment in various ways, but most absorb food directly from their mother's uterine wall, much like mammals. Members of the hammerhead and requiem shark families reproduce in this manner. In a version known as **cannibal viviparity**, Sand Tiger, *Eugomphodus taurus*, produce two pups – one developing in each of two separate uteri. The first young devours its sibling before consuming its mother's continued production of eggs. A hardy, three-foot pup is born after an eight or nine month gestation period. **Ovoviviparous** species, stingrays for example, carry their fertilized, yolk-rich eggs throughout gestation. After the embryos consume the yolk, they eat food secreted from the uterus. Skates are the only rays that do not bear live offspring. Females lay durable, leathery cases, commonly known as mermaid's purses, that attach to bottom structures by tendrils. Each packet contains a fertilized egg and several months' supply of yolk.

Little is known about the reproductive behavior of sharks. Bite marks on the pectoral and dorsal fins of females attest to the aggressive nature of the encounters. During breeding season, males swim behind potential mates with their snouts close to the females' cloacas to assess their reproductive status. When ready to copulate the males bite the females' sides and fins, a courtship

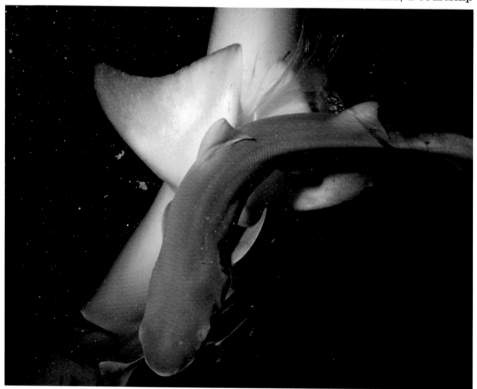

The live birth of a Lemon Shark.

*A female
Black Brotula
packed with
embryos.*

behavior believed to elicit a compliant response from their mates. With the females' pectoral fins firmly clenched in their mouths, the males turn on their sides and insert sperm through a clasper. Six to 22 months later, fully formed pups, able to fend for themselves and large enough to avoid most predation, are born in the shallows.

A few species of brotulas in family Bythitidae are the only Caribbean bony fishes known to be viviparous. The 70 or so species of these curious little fishes inhabit a variety of habitats worldwide, including freshwater caves, estuaries, reefs and the deep sea. Black Brotula, *Stygnobrotula latebricola*, secretive three-inch reef dwellers, are occasionally sighted in pairs at night, inside crevices and under overhangs of shallow reefs. Brotulas swim by undulating fins encircling the length of their bodies. The males' copulatory organs, located behind the anus and surrounded by two pairs of pseudoclaspers, are apparently derived from the anal fin. Embryos, closely packed like cordwood, develop inside the females' ovaries. It is not known whether the offspring disperse in the currents or remain near their birthplace.

Toadfishes, in family Batrachoididae, another oddity, are the only bony fishes known to care for free-swimming offspring. As many as 60 one-inch juveniles have been counted around the den of a single male. One male was observed tending three different broods during a five-month period. Because they lack a dispersal mechanism, toadfishes are restricted to the continental shelf of their birth and only rarely inhabit islands.

Life Cycles &
Reef Fish Communities

A settling triggerfish finds temporary refuge next to a suspended light.

The majority of reef fishes begin life in gamete clouds launched high above the reef. This hedge against the hungry mouths living below is the only assistance offspring receive before being carried off by currents on one of the most perilous odysseys in the animal kingdom. If one considers that to sustain population numbers each adult needs to reproduce itself only once or twice during a lifetime, and that a single female typically produces tens of thousands of eggs annually, it's easy to comprehend the odds against surviving a journey in the vast pelagic realm. Weeks later and possibly hundreds of miles from their origins, the survivors surf toward shore during the night on incoming tides and **settle** to the shallow sea floor. Over the next several hours to days, the well-traveled oceanic larvae metamorphose into site-attached juvenile reef fishes who, with growth and continued luck, will one day shed their own gametes above the reef. This endless cycle of prolific spawning and unpredictable recruitment is responsible for structuring fish communities on coral reefs around the world.

Amazingly, before 1980 reef ecologists were generally unaware of the great "pelagic orphanage" and its profound importance. Instead of gathering detailed natural history data, early researchers, often former bird ecologists, simply adopted the classic niche theory, the accepted model of terrestrial ecology. They believed that under water, as on land, most animals live in "closed" communities saturated with an endless supply of their own offspring. Constant competition for limited food and space, and the forces of predation ultimately shape the final assemblies. Pioneering reef ecologists were so enamored of their pet hypothesis that nearly everyone failed to note that marine fisheries researchers in Europe and the United States had, for eight decades, been working with a different set of population dynamics. Their "open" non-equilibrium model focused on a correlation between adult stock size and random waves of larval recruits arriving from the open ocean. As early as 1914, Norwegian fisheries biologist Johan Hjort indicated the potential importance of recruitment to adult populations of marine organisms. In 1950 and 1966, Gunnar Thorson stated that marine invertebrates have a planktonic phase and a "settled" juvenile phase. He also pointed out that such species are subject to large-scale fluctuations in abundance. However, these and other early insights played no role in molding the favored ecological theory of the day.

Thinking back, it is easy to understand how everyone was seduced by the niche theory. It seems to make such good sense when observing a reef fish community in action. To an unsophisticated eye, a never-ending turf war appears to be taking place. Every niche in a reef's craggy face houses an animal ready to protect itself, its territory and its food supply. It simply was assumed that the local offspring of spawning reef fishes quickly found protected corners in their home reefs or were eaten or driven away.

During the late 1970s and early 1980s, when evidence supporting an open system no longer could be ignored, marine ecologists scrambled to get on the bandwagon even though the new hypothesis was, and remains, difficult to demonstrate. Although field studies in the pelagic realm are logistical maelstroms that more often than not produce perplexing variations in nearly every set of data, ecologists have made great strides in improving larval collection methods and gaining a better understanding of physical oceanography over the last two decades. Scattered findings indicate that larvae are retained occasionally near their home reefs by tidal fronts, current gyres and enclosed bays, leading to the possibility that reef systems may vary in their degree of openness. But, for the most part, research supports the concept that the vast majority of fish larvae settles far from where they were spawned.

A juvenile jack.

Life Cycles

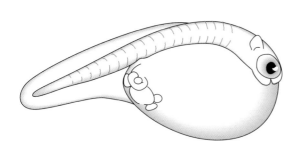

A typical yolk-sac fish larva.

The daily otolith aging technique introduced by Giorgio Panella in 1971 aided everyone's research efforts. This significant new tool makes it possible to learn the age of a fish from embryo to adult by counting concentric layers of protein-rich and protein-poor materials embedded in tiny calcium carbonate structures known as **otoliths**. The three tiny stones, used for balance and sound detection, are found within the semicircular canal at the base of the braincase of all bony fishes. After preparation for observation, the structures' matrix of protein appears similar to the growth rings of a tree. Although the legibility of time-markers varies among species, daily increments are sufficiently distinct to be deciphered on most larval and juvenile fishes. The technique provides a wealth of indispensable information, including the duration of a fish's planktonic larval stage and the ability to determine the day it was spawned.

Despite recent advances in knowledge, much of the early life history of reef fishes remains a mystery. It is known that within 24 hours the buoyant fertilized eggs develop into tiny fishes with long tails and distended bellies packed with a store of fat. The tiny **yolk-sac larvae**, alternating between long vigorous swims and rest, are high-energy eating machines that must locate a food source within two to three days or starve. Fortunately, the ocean transports random clouds of concentrated food, known as **patches**, near the surface. If these patches didn't exist, food particles would be so widely distributed that larvae of all types would perish.

In tropical water, patches begin on warm, calm days when an upwelling brings cool water barreling up from deep below. The sudden mixture of nutrient-rich water and sunlight creates a wild bloom of single-celled plants or simple chains of plant cells known as **phytoplankton**. Single-celled **diatoms**, encased in intricate silica shells, are the most prevalent pelagic algae. These simple plants, forming the base of the food web, are a favorite food of oceanic **copepods**, the most abundant group of animals on earth. When the tiny pelagic crustaceans begin to gorge, they multiply by the millions. Soon, mollusks, salps, larvaceans – a distant relative of tunicates – and other pelagic herbivores add their biomass to the ever-thickening biological soup. The banquet is joined by macro-carnivores whose numbers are dominated by flat, elongate arrow worms, with formidable mouths ringed with teeth and grasping hooks capable of ripping chunks from egg-yolk larvae. These microscopic oceanic animals are collectively known as **zooplankton** or **zooplankters**. They are joined by jellyfishes, and siphonophores trailing deadly mops of stinging tentacles. Schools of fast-swimming fishes including tunas regularly cut through the moveable feast. Even though this savage pelagic world should seem a nightmare to our cherubic fish larvae, their instincts indicate otherwise. For the next few weeks, this drifting patch of snapping-jaw hell will be home sweet home, stocked with a full cupboard of food only a tail-thrust away.

In the beginning, young fish larvae consume a variety of foods, including phytoplankton, larval copepods and mollusks and, in some cases, siblings. When potential prey is sighted the larval fishes curve into an S shape and scull forward with their pectoral fins until close enough to engulf the victim with quick open-mouthed lunges. As they mature, body mass increases by a third each day, and each species begins to select a more specialized diet.

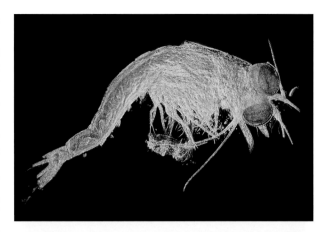

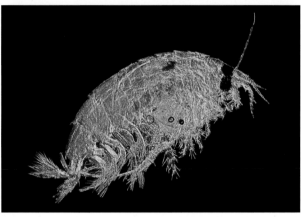

Microscopic pelagic crustaceans, members of the zooplankton community.

Fortunately, evolution hasn't forsaken the little fishes during these dangerous times. As the yolk sac disappears, larvae develop elaborate morphological adaptations that attain a state of complexity that delights the imagination. Spikes, spines and spinelets, streaming fins bristling with barbs, bulbous heads sporting enormous jaws and stalked eyes are a few adaptations designed to deter and deceive predators. Silver or transparent bodies aid in this death-defying game of openwater hide-and-seek.

The size of drifting patches, without defined borders or even distribution of food, varies horizontally from meters to miles depending on the stability of the surface waters. When storms brew, wind and waves break patches apart; during periods of calm, they retain their size or even enlarge as they occasionally coalesce. Nearly all larval fishes inhabit the upper 600 feet, with members of different families inhabiting specific depth ranges during the day. At night, these strata often lose definition as larvae move toward the surface to feed. The purpose of these daily migrations is uncertain. Possibly the cooler water below preserves energy by lowering metabolism or the fishes descend into the dark to escape visual predators during the day. Whatever the reason, it must be important. The 600-foot journey for a two-millimeter larva is equivalent to a 120-mile trip for humans.

Life Cycles

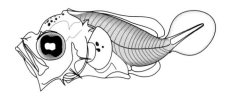

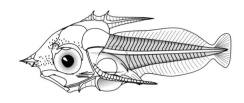

Larval Cherubfish, 2.8 mm.   *Larval squirrelfish, 3 mm.*

Adult Cherubfish.   *Adult Longjaw Squirrelfish.*

A typical larval voyage in the Caribbean lasts between 14 and 30 days but many continue for 60 days or more. Before settling to the sea floor, some larvae undergo a second dramatic morphological shift; others change little more than color. The Queen Triggerfish, *Balistes vetula*, one of the largest species retaining pelagic features at settlement, measures two inches after spending 75 days in the plankton. The smallest, a reef drum called the Cubbyu, *Equetus umbrosus*, is only four millimeters when it ends its pelagic existence after 14 days. A few species, including puffers, chubs, bigeyes, Gray Triggerfish, *Balistes capriscus*, and Sergeant Major, *Abudefduf saxatilis*, develop into juveniles prior to settlement. Most semi-pelagic species such as jacks never settle. Instead, juveniles mature into adults in the plankton, often in association with rafts of *Sargassum*, jellyfishes or openwater predators like barracudas and sharks.

Most larvae must locate a specific type of bottom habitat to survive. Some species settle on high-profile reefs; others search for sand flats, rubble fields, shallow patch reefs, grass beds, estuaries, mangroves or surf zones. A few can be quite choosy: larval Nassau Grouper, *Epinephelus striatus*, find sanctuary in algae-covered clumps of dead finger corals inside shallow mangrove lagoons. Settlement-stage fishes have well-developed senses, including sight, taste and smell, as well as significant behavioral and swimming abilities; yet it is unknown how these are used to locate suitable habitats. Certain species are now known to seek out or to avoid members of their own species during the settlement process by sensing dissolved chemical cues. The same ability also may be used to steer clear of predators. The new recruits make easy targets. To protect themselves while changing into

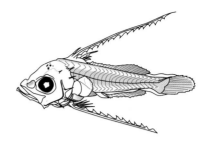

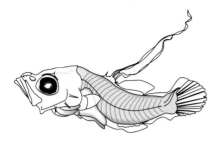

Larval Peppermint Bass, 3.6 mm.

Larval grouper, 4 mm.

Adult Peppermint Bass

Adult Scamp.

juveniles, wrasses and eels burrow into the sand. Others evade predators by schooling, hiding inside a reef or within rubble fields.

Although many species settle randomly throughout the year, recruitment reaches its peak in the summer when patches spread along narrow fronts paralleling the shore. During the dark nights around the new moon, when the threat of predation is least, concentrations of larval fishes known as pulses ride the flood tide toward the shallows. We have been underwater at night as **pulses** passed over the reef. One moment the water was clear, and in the next instant the beams from our handlights attracted a blizzard of darting small creatures as strange little fishes rained down. Surgeonfishes the size of quarters with polished

A recently settled Queen Triggerfish - one of the largest reef fish at settlement.

A recently settled drum - one of the smallest reef fish at settlement.

Life Cycles

Flying Gunard

Settling postlarvae.

Juveniles.

Adult.

Foureye Butterflyfish

Settling postlarvae.

Juvenile.

Adult.

Life Cycles

Blue Tang

Settling postlarvae.

Juvenile.

Adult.

Jackknife Fish

Settling postlarvae.

Juvenile.

Adult.

Life Cycles

Instead of settling, larval and juvenile jack associate with flotsam, such as Sargassum.

heads and bodies so clear you could count their ribs, bounced along the bottom; transparent eel-like fishes squirmed into the sand; and tiny, silver-burnished butterflyfishes paused as if collecting their bearings before disappearing into the reef. Back at the boat we found refugees from the plankton hovering next to the down lines. Moving closer, we recognized a miniature trunkfish no larger than a jellybean and the unmistakable shape of a filefish next to the underwater strobe. Ten to 15 minutes later the patch moved on, leaving behind a new generation of fishes.

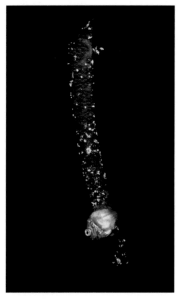

A postlarval fish hovers near a floating blade of grass.

If the proper bottom is not encountered, some species can prolong their presettlement mode for days or even months. Surgeonfishes have been reported to settle anywhere from 18 to 65 days after hatching, and a few reef fishes put themselves in a holding pattern for up to 100 days. But even with this capacity, it is possible that a large percentage of larvae are never carried near shore and drift aimlessly until death. It would seem that the amount of time a species is capable of spending in the open sea would have a direct relation to its distribution, but such relationships are not as clear-cut as they might appear and have been substantiated only for a few species of wrasses. Another way to think of a species' range of distribution is by **metapopulations**, a mosaic of widely spaced settlement sites separated by open sea and bottom unsuitable for recruitment. These systems of distinctly separate populations, linked in various degrees by larval dispersal, allow species to colonize reefs across vast regions.

After two decades of study, the only thing reef ecologists agree on is that "larval fishes arrive at different reefs at different rates and at different times." Recruitment varies not only among fishes, but also among family members and even within the same species. Although similarities in the timing and magnitude of annual settlement often occur across a region, recruitment prediction at any scale remains haphazard at best. Seasonal pulses bearing the greatest influx of larval recruits are loosely synchronized with the moon's phases and with spawning dates. However, these patterns appear to be disrupted by fluctuating meteorological and hydrological events and unknown biological processes in the plankton. And making interpretation of data even more difficult, every region has its own system of hydrology and topography influencing dispersal patterns of local offspring. Settlement peaks of Bluehead Wrasse, *Thalassoma bifasciatum*, were found to consist of individuals spawned over an extended period of weeks which, for unknown reasons, aggregated before being swept toward shore.

Occasionally, a species settles in mass-recruiting episodes. In Panama, Queen Triggerfish larvae traditionally arrive in low numbers. During a single week in 1985, however, the species settled at a rate 50 times higher than the total for any previous year. For less common long-lived species a dramatic influx such as this may increase the size of a local population for a decade, while poor recruitment often causes local extinction for extended periods. Further complicating matters, high rates for one species have no bearing on the success of other species. Even when consistent across a region, settlement is often erratic among neighboring sites. During a 24-hour period the recruitment of a common damselfish varied 12-fold between two patch reefs separated by only 50 feet. And two species of recently settled damselfishes were found to have a ten-fold variation among patch reefs just 400 yards apart. These local fluctuations may result from aggregating behavior, forced concentration by local hydrodynamics or the random size and movement of patches.

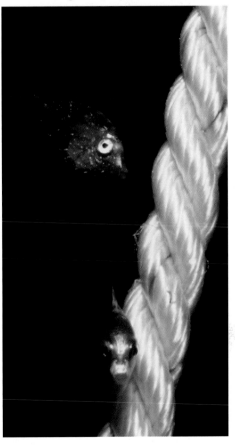

Settling filefish and trunkfish.

Life Cycles

Reef Fish Community Structures

Reef ecologists agree that the distribution and abundance of reef fish populations are controlled to some degree by larval supply, but to what degree remains in question. Those researchers favoring the recruitment limitation hypothesis believe that the numbers of arriving larvae will have a direct relationship to adult abundance. Their case is built on the concepts that settling larvae rarely exceed the carrying capacity of a reef and that a species seldom colonizes every area of suitable habitat. Others argue that competition for space, shelter, food and the rate of predation after settlement hold the keys to understanding population dynamics. Studies investigating the effect of predation after settlement tend to bolster this view, but such research is difficult to substantiate. General estimates place mortality between 25 and 50 percent for the first month. Research on Caribbean reefs, where piscivores often make up a large percentage of biomass, estimated that juvenile grunts experience 90 percent mortality during their first month. Bluehead Wrasse juveniles suffer 22 percent mortality for each of the first three days after appearing on the reef, and adults lose 13 percent of their population each month. Reefs where large predators had been eliminated by spearfishing were found to have a higher abundance of small species such as Bluehead Wrasse.

Few studies have analyzed the long-term effects of larval recruitment on the structure of reef fish communities, and to date, these studies have produced varying results. For example, in Barbados recruitment of Redlip Blenny, *Ophioblennius atlanticus*, does not appear to be limited by larval supply but rather by competition between settling larvae and residents for available space. However, recruitment rates and the post-recruitment survivorship of damselfishes in Australia and of both the Bluehead Wrasse and damselfishes in Panama show no correlation to the density of resident populations. It is possible that the behavior of different species predisposes them to space limitation or recruitment limitation. Although research forges ahead in the Pacific and Caribbean, such an intricate set of interacting processes is at work that it might well be some time before this perplexing riddle is solved.

Not all larval fishes settle in what will become their adult habitat. In the Caribbean, mangrove forest, seagrass meadows and inshore shallows function as nursery grounds for a number of species. With growth and changing dietary needs, the young fishes make what are known as **ontogenetic shifts** to intermediate habitats or to their final home ranges. For example, larval grunts settle in grass beds where they hide among the blades to avoid predators. After a few weeks they move to a reef and form mixed schools near sea urchins or protective pockets. Later they join schools of larger juveniles above coral structures. Finally, as adults, the grunts become permanent members of aggregations, resting by day and moving in shoals each evening to feed in distant seagrass beds.

Nearly all reef fishes are strongly site-attached throughout their benthic life cycle. The few exceptions are species making daily migrations to feeding grounds, sleeping shelters or spawning aggregations. Territorial species may remain in one area to protect food resources, or because of strong social and reproductive bonds with small groups known as harems but the fear of predation is what keeps most reef fishes at home. Few dare venture far from their familiar set of hiding-holes. For most fishes, even a short excursion across open bottom, much less to a neighboring reef, would be extremely dangerous.

Determining the maximum age and growth rates of wild fishes is difficult. Fisheries researchers making stock assessments of groupers and snappers generally employ one of three methods, each with interpretation problems. The most widely used technique, the length-frequency analysis, is possibly the least reliable. It measures the growth of fishes by extrapolating a large population sample with mathematical formulas. The tag-and-recapture method provides information on the rate of growth between two dates. Analysis of scales, spines, vertebrae and otoliths presents the troubling problem of distinguishing time-markers from incidental marks. Otoliths work extremely well as markers during the first five to six months of life for many reef fishes, but later their usefulness varies among species.

Growth and age studies show a marked difference among fish populations in the Caribbean, where water temperatures remain relatively constant, and in the southeastern United States, where temperatures drop each winter. The data indicate that species from cooler climes typically live longer and grow larger and more slowly. However, these results might be skewed by different sampling techniques. The Caribbean specimens usually were taken from shallow reefs by trawls and traps that capture fishes only to a certain size. Fishes sampled in the southeastern United States are primarily caught by hook and line at various depths including the deeper offshore banks where the larger and older specimens typically live. Gray Snapper, *Lutjanus griseus*, from Cuba were found to live seven to nine years and grow to 22 inches; in Florida the oldest individuals live 21 years and reach a length of 35 inches. Basically, the larger a species is, the longer it lives. Little gobies and blennies may live only a season; small wrasses, such as Blueheads, three years; angelfishes and other medium-sized fishes average ten years, while large groupers survive 15 to 20 years. Jewfish, *Epinephelus itajara*, the largest of all reef fishes, have been aged to 37 years.

Feeding

A seemingly uninterested Great Barracuda swims casually among potential prey.

After visiting a coral reef packed with schools of fish lazing in the shadows and notorious predators swimming past potential prey with no apparent interest, divers often leave the water with the impression that fishes seldom eat. Nothing could be further from the truth. Most reef fishes spend the majority of their time locating, stalking, capturing and digesting prey. In fact, the driving

Bluestriped Grunt resting in a defensive school during the day.

force behind every fish is to maximize its reproductive capacity by obtaining as much energy as possible from food. The inactive schools lingering close to protective structures are taking well-deserved rests after long nights scouring the grass flats for crustaceans, and the seemingly unenthusiastic predators are biding their time until twilight, when the odds of making successful strikes turn in their favor. As divers become more familiar with the feeding behaviors of fishes, they will begin to understand the subtle rhythms of life and death on the reef.

Feeding

Fishes are placed in broad categories according to what they eat: **herbivores** primarily feed on plants; **carnivores** prey on animals; **omnivores** consume both animals and plants, and **detritivores** ingest decaying organic matter that accumulates on the sea floor. Some carnivores are further categorized as **planktivores** that pick tiny transparent animals (zooplankton) from open water, and **piscivores** that primarily eat fishes. The shape, size and position of a species' mouth generally indicate its feeding category. The mouths of bottom-feeding carnivores are downturned, and typically surrounded by strong blubbery lips or decked with prominent incisors. Piscivores have large mouths either expandable, like groupers, or lined with sharp teeth, like barracudas,

Prominent incisors of a carnivore.

Tooth-lined mouth of a piscivore.

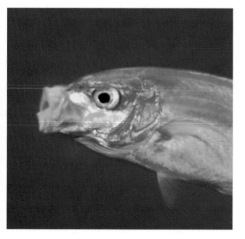

Protrusible mouth of a planktivore.

Beak of an algae-eating parrotfish.

sharks and needlefishes. The small terminal mouths of planktivores shoot forward to secure prey. The teeth of parrotfishes are fused into a beak to scrape algae from rocks, and angelfishes use overlapping rows of tightly packed needlelike teeth to cut through the tough tissue of sponges.

Feeding

An algae-eating Blue Tang switches from its typical diet to take advantage of a temporary bloom of Sea Thimbles.

The diets of reef fishes are normally quite varied and customarily change as they grow. Most species begin life as planktivores feeding on tiny animals in the open sea. After settling to shallow-water habitats, they transform into carnivorous juveniles foraging for small crustaceans before finally switching to their adult diets. Even after maturity, nearly all fishes readily abandon their daily diets to take advantage of temporarily abundant food supplies. For example, in the early summer small jellyfish known as Sea Thimble, *Linuche unguiculata*, bloom in such profusion that they form rafts which wash over reefs. The sudden influx of jelly-plankton provides easy pickings for numerous species, including Blue Tang, *Acanthurus coeruleus*, which normally eat algae. Only a species' mouth size and structure and digestive capabilities limit the foods eaten. A fish's flexible eating habits and tendency to consume the most accessible prey maximizes energy gains with minimum energy expenditure. This strategy, known as the **optimal foraging theory**, is the guiding principle of fish-feeding ecology.

A Red Hind rapidly expands its mouth creating suction to draw in prey.

The Great Barracuda uses a primitive mouth structure lined with sharp teeth to sever the bodies of fishes with a single strike.

Because all reef fishes are to some extent opportunistic feeders, the frequently used terms specialists, generalists and opportunists are somewhat misleading and should be used only to describe temporary feeding behaviors. **Specialist** refers to species that typically concentrate on a single food source. **Generalists** eat a variety of foods without a specific preference for one type. **Opportunists** willingly eat foods not included on their normal menus. The ability to convert from one food to another is made possible in great part by suction feeding, a universal characteristic of fishes. Even though mouth structures vary, food, whether algae, zooplankton or crustaceans, is ingested by suction when the jaws rapidly open and the gill covers flare. A few piscivores, such as the Great Barracuda, *Sphyraena barracuda*, are exceptions: using a primitive mouth structure lined with sharp teeth, the swift hunters sever fishes with a single strike, then circle back to pick up the pieces.

Even specialists may permanently alter their diets if their preferred food becomes scarce. Two species of western Caribbean toadfishes provide an illustration of a specialist's ability to adapt. Both reef-dwelling species dined almost exclusively on Long-spined Urchin, *Diadema antillarum*, before 1983, when an unidentified pathogen wiped out more than 95 per cent of the abundant echinoderms throughout the tropical western Atlantic. After the loss of their long-time food supply, both species quickly became generalists. One switched to a diet of fishes and hermit crabs, and the other began hunting mobile, bottom-dwelling invertebrates. Neither species suffered a population decline.

Some specialists have difficulty adjusting to a rapid decline in their customary food. Spotted Eagle Ray, *Aetobatis narinari*, forage over sand flats for hard-shelled clams, oysters and large gastropods which are crushed by specialized dental plates. The spectacular fish suffered a marked decline in the

Feeding

Cayman Islands after commercial interests overharvested their primary food, Queen Conch, *Strombus gigas*. But after the government mandated no-take reserves for Queen Conch, the tasty mollusks made a dramatic rebound. With their primary food supply reestablished, the islands' population of Spotted Eagle Rays also made a strong recovery.

Individual members of many fish species stake claims to and vigorously defend areas of the bottom, known as **territories**. This strategy conserves energy by transferring the cost of searching for food to the less demanding duties of defense. Territories also provide for the protection of mates, nests and reproductive sites and offer residents the advantage of knowing where every

A Spotted Eagle Ray hunts the sand for buried mollusks.

hiding hole is located. Once a territory is established, most individuals remain almost exclusively within its boundaries. A few, however, commute to and from alternate sleeping locations, and others migrate to distant spawning sites. **Home range**, a term frequently confused with territory, refers to the entire area an individual frequents but does not defend.

Typically fishes occupy territories in relation to their size with small fishes, blennies, gobies, jawfishes and juveniles, defending a few inches or feet of turf, while large species, such as angelfishes and Hogfish, *Lachnolaimus maximus*, partition tracts the size of football fields. The territories of some fishes lie side-by-side, covering a large area of the sea floor; those of other species are distributed randomly. Territorial boundaries are defined by the extent of the occupants' defensive efforts. The size of an individual's territory appears to be more closely related to intra-species competition than to protecting food supplies. When the defender of an adjoining territory disappears, nearby territory holders compete for the vacant turf. However, even after acquiring additional feeding resources, the victors' food consumption seldom increases.

Territories are frequently established and defended by a single inhabitant, as in the case of algae-eating damselfishes. These spunky herbivores single-handedly challenge intruders – including divers – who approach their personal algal gardens. Parrotfishes, wrasses and several smaller sea basses form harems with a single dominant male overseeing a large area encompassing the territories of several females. Each group member participates in defensive duties by challenging similar-sized or smaller members of their own species. Intruders, usually food competitors or members of the same species, are challenged by lateral fin displays, chases, sounds, parallel-swimming, and occasional nips. These showdowns, generally lasting less than a minute, seldom cause injuries.

Mated pairs of Gray Angelfish, *Pomacanthus arcuatus*; French Angelfish, *P. paru*, and Harlequin Bass, *Serranus tigrinus*, share territories and the responsibility of protecting their mutually held feeding grounds. In a more complex arrangement, the boundaries of Yellowtail Damselfish, *Microspathodon chrysurus*, incorporate the smaller territories of several Dusky Damselfish, *Stegastes fuscus*, and Redlip Blenny, *Ophioblennius atlanticus*. The three herbivores feed from the same field of filamentous algae without conflict, but the smaller Duskies are expected to expend the greatest amount of energy defending the communal algal crop.

Approximately one-half to two-thirds of the species in a reef fish community forage by day, and one-quarter to one-third feed during the night. The hunting activities of many piscivores peak during the low-light hours of dawn and dusk. For daytime feeders, vision and vigilance hold the keys to survival. Every reef fish is well aware of just how far it can wander away from a shelter hole and expect not to be eaten. This sphere of relative safety greatly limits the size of a species' feeding grounds.

By the time the sun rises the profiles of feeding planktivores fill the water column. But only the streamlined species designed for speed, such as Brown Chromis, *Chromis multilineata*, and Creole-fish, *Paranthias furcifer*, dare to venture high above the reef where the richest plankton streams flow; the smaller, deep-bodied plankton-pickers must be satisfied to dine in the less fertile water closer to hiding holes. Sand-dwelling planktivores such as Yellowhead Jawfish, *Opistognathus aurifrons*, and Hovering Goby, *Ioglossus helenae*, nab passing specks just above the safety of their sand burrows. Crustacean-eating carnivores, including wrasses, goatfishes and porgies, spend their daylight hours rooting in sand only a short sprint away from the safety of the reefs' fringes. Cleanerfishes, juvenile wrasses and gobies pick parasitic crustaceans from client fishes at cleaning stations. Because of their utilitarian behavior, the little carnivores are graced with a degree of immunity from predators. Large parrotfishes, emboldened by size, range widely scraping algae from coral rock, while smaller, more vulnerable family members feed in loose groups near cover. Deep bodies, tough skin and a formidable, stilettolike foredorsal spine provide triggerfishes and filefishes a substantial degree of protection while they nibble algae and search for bottom-dwelling invertebrates.

Feeding

Barracudas, groupers and other piscivores hang around the reef during the day, but their ability to make successful strikes is severely limited by the excellent vision of their prey. If reef fishes remain alert, do not stray too far from cover or allow themselves to become distracted or confused, the odds of escaping an attack are decidedly in their favor. However, when opportunities present themselves, large piscivores will not hesitate to attack in broad daylight.

A Great Barracuda with a freshly killed Stoplight Parrotfish.

During their safety stop, a group of divers were casually watching a five-foot Great Barracuda hovering just under the surface. The large predator suddenly angled downward aiming its elongate body at two initial phase Stoplight Parrotfish, *Sparisoma viride*, moving across a wide stretch of open sand 40 feet below. The barracuda bowed into an S-shape, and, as if shot from a cannon, streaked toward the bottom in a blur completely severing the body of one of the Stoplights in the attack. Quickly circling, the predator grabbed the head section off the sand, bit down on the fresh kill repeatedly, and casually swam away with its bleeding prey.

Piscivores often hunt as a team to gain an advantage. Mated pairs of Harlequin Bass hunt together within their small territories. One partner momentarily distracts a shrimp or other small crustacean while its companion sneaks in from the opposite direction. Coney, *Epinephelus fulvus*; Graysby, *E. cruentatus*; and other medium-size predators join forces with prowling morays or octopuses. As the limber crevice-creepers create panic inside the reef, the groupers take positions near openings in the hope of capturing fleeing fishes. An underwater photographer diving in the Los Rocas Islands, Venezuela spent 20 minutes observing a group of ten Comb Grouper, *Mycteroperca rubra*, working in concert to keep schooling silverside minnows corralled above a knoll where the grouper fed. From a position under the school the groupers raised their bodies upward at a 45-degree angle and shot up through the mass in open-mouth rushes. Each time the minnows dispersed the predators herded them back into a concentrated school above the killing-zone and continued to feed.

When daylight begins to fade and vision becomes less reliable, feeding fishes grow restless and even more cautious, and with good reason, for this is when the odds begin to swing in favor of the piscivores. The smaller, more vulnerable species are first to retire for the night, larger fishes follow, and the big parrotfishes bed down last. During the last 20 minutes before complete darkness the low-light conditions are so favorable for the big predators that the water above the reef is virtually devoid of fish life. This precarious interval, known as the **quiet period**, precedes the emergence of nocturnal foragers.

The night-feeders – cardinalfishes, bigeyes and squirrelfishes – are easily recognized by their large eyes facilitating better vision and reddish hues that make them more difficult to see in the dark. With fewer piscivores around, the nocturnal foragers have little need to aggregate or remain near shelters. Many

Comb Grouper work as a team to keep the silversides in a concentrated school.

Feeding

species range freely over open sand flats where their daytime counterparts wouldn't dare feed. Small cardinalfishes ascend by the thousands into the water column to feed on microscopic reef-dwelling animals that, like themselves, hide within the reef during the day. As the quiet period ends grunts, snappers, squirrelfishes and sweepers make nightly pilgrimages to distant feeding grounds. Grunts, wearing muted night colors, leave the reef in streaming schools and feed randomly as they travel over open terrain toward grass flats. Some of these migration routes take the fishes a mile or more from their home reefs. After arriving the fishes fan out and forage for crustaceans until just

Just after sunset grunts, such as these Tomtate, stream away from the reef and begin feeding as they migrate to customary nightly hunting grounds.

before dawn, when they gather once again for the return trip to their home reefs. Several species of squirrelfishes leave the reef just after the grunts, traveling individually to the same seagrass meadows. Glassy Sweeper, *Pempheris schomburgki*, journey to seaward reef banks to feed on zooplankton. Unless the sky is heavily overcast, these migrations, synchronized by light intensity, occur at a predictable time each evening.

Detritus is a potpourri of decomposing plant and animal matter mixed loosely with sand. Much of the content is made up of single-celled plants called diatoms and the organic waste of fishes. Pockets of the matter harbor a variety of living organisms, ranging from bacteria and fungi to tiny worms. Only a few reef associated fishes, primarily mullets and bottom-dwelling gobies, consume sufficient amounts to be considered detritivores, but many secondary consumers, especially bottom-grazing herbivores, ingest varying amounts of detritus when foraging.

Opportunistic carnivores are extremely fond of human food. Yellowtail Snapper, *Ocyurus chrysurus*; Sergeant Major, *Abudefduf saxatilis*, and Bermuda Chub, *Kyphosis sectatrix*, hang out in the shade of dive boats and piers waiting for handouts or garbage. To entertain customers, divemasters and tour guides often attract swarms of fishes by chumming. At sites such as shallow snorkeling reefs where fish feeding is routine, fishes mob divers whether they are carrying food or not. At times the fishes can be intimidating, nipping hair, scalp and hands. On the other hand, being close to so many wild creatures is exhilarating. Reef visitors generally enjoy the experience, and the fishes certainly aren't complaining. However, some ecologists argue that these free lunches might permanently alter the fishes' ability to search for more traditional foods. This seems unlikely. Remember, these are opportunistic feeders; if their free meals suddenly come to a halt, they are certainly not going to starve.

Our favorite fish-feeding story occurred in a palm-lined lagoon on the Caribbean coast of Yucatan, Mexico. As usual, a tour group loaded with stale bread for the fishes arrived from a cruise ship. One young tourist, tiring of his frequent swims to shore for handfuls of bread, stuffed half a loaf inside his trunks and headed back into the boil of feeding fishes. It wasn't pretty, but the vacationer did survive more or less intact.

Carnivores and Omnivores

The first step in understanding the nature of fishes is to know the foods they eat. And there is no better source for such information than *Food Habits of Reef Fishes of the West Indies* by John E. Randall. During the seven-year study (1958 to 1965), Randall and his colleagues analyzed and cataloged the stomach contents of 5,526 specimens representing 212 species of fishes. To insure a complete picture of a species' food habits, specimens were collected from a variety of reef-related habitats in Puerto Rico and the Virgin Islands. Thirty years later, the unprecedented work remains a standard of reef fish ecology.

The majority of reef fishes are generalized carnivores which, as a group, eat just about every animal on the reef, including such unsavory fare as sponges, firecorals and hydroids. The Sergeant Major, *Abudefduf saxatilis*, provides a good

example of just how diverse a carnivore's diet can be. The species' indiscriminate feeding habits allow the little damselfish to proliferate in a variety of habitats. They are equally at home picking zooplankton above the reef, nipping algae from rocks or plucking marine animals off the reef. Randall's analysis of 35 specimens taken at 13 stations showed that the Sergeant Major's diet consisted of 43 percent zoanthid polyps; 14 percent pelagic copepods; nine percent algae; seven percent tunicates; five percent Lettuce Sea Slug, *Tridachia crispata*; five percent fish eggs; four percent minnow-sized herring; three

Sergeant Major feed in a varity of habitats.

Feeding

percent shrimp larvae; three percent barnacle appendages, and about one percent each winged ants, feather duster plumes and jelly plankton.

Generalized carnivores can be categorized by the types of foods they typically eat. The more specialized feeders – planktivores and piscivores – are discussed later in this chapter, and cleanerfishes are discussed separately in the Symbiosis chapter. The remaining carnivores eat primarily from one of three invertebrate groups: mobile invertebrates, attached (sessile) invertebrates, or hard-shelled mollusks. The species eating mobile invertebrates typically have the most extensive diets, often including a substantial portion of fishes.

Shrimps, crabs and lobsters are the most frequently eaten reef animals. Fishes commonly consuming crustaceans include snappers in the genus *Lutjanus* (except the Cubera Snapper, *L. cyanopterus*, a piscivore); sea basses, *Epinephelus* spp.; hamlets, *Hypoplectrus* spp.; mojarras; goatfishes; Sand Tilefish, *Malacanthus plumieri*; Slippery Dick, *Halichoeres bivittatus*; the larger jawfishes, *Opistognathus* spp.; night-feeding squirrelfishes, grunts and the Spotted Drum, *Equetus punctatus*.

A Chain Moray hunts the sun-splashed shallows for crabs, its favorite food.

The Chain Moray, *Echidna catenata*, is the king of the crab-eaters. The golden-streaked eels match the dark, sun-splashed tidal rocks where crabs congregate. The eels, accustomed to hunting in a world of both water and air, think nothing of being temporarily stranded while waves go out. During low tide they often wedge into pockets of pools well away from the water's edge. Crabs are also the favorite food of snake eels and Flying Gurnard, *Dactylopterus volitans*, that use modified ventral fins to turn rocks when hunting. At night, foraging squirrelfishes, grunts and snappers plunder crab-rich grass beds. Shrimps top the food list of most scorpionfishes, jawfishes and smaller sea basses, including hamlets and Harlequin Bass, *Serranus tigrinus*. Mantis shrimps have been found in the stomachs of over 40 fishes but never in large numbers. Few fishes eat lobsters because of their size, but they are the main food of the largest fish on the reef, the Jewfish, *Epinephelus itajara*. Dog Snapper, *Lutjanus jocu*, and Nassau Grouper, *E. striatus*, occasionally eat smaller lobsters.

54

Sea urchins and brittle stars have good reason to hide deep within crevices: the brittle echinoderms are regularly wrestled from the rocks by wrasses and other carnivores armed with conspicuous incisors. However, few fishes go to the trouble of eating the urchins' tough-skinned relatives, sea stars and sea cucumbers. Only the entrails of a sea cucumber were found inside a Spotted Trunkfish, *Lactophrys bicaudalis*, leading to speculation that the echinoderm might have been harassed by the trunkfish until it expelled its intestines, a last-resort defensive tactic. In times of plenty, opportunistic carnivores can change their preferences quickly. Spearfishermen discovered dozens of inch-long juvenile sea cucumbers packed inside a Sheepshead, *Archosargus probatocephalus*, a member of the porgy family inhabiting inshore temperate zones.

The diet of Slippery Dick is representative of carnivores feeding on small, mobile prey. Randall found that the fast-moving, cigar-shaped wrasse consumed 22 percent crabs; 18 percent echinoderms; 12 percent gastropods, including more than 20 species; seven percent brittle stars; four percent bivalves; four percent shrimps; three percent chitons; three percent fish remains; three percent mantis shrimps, and one percent hermit crabs.

Omnivores primarily eat attached invertebrates and a substantial amount of plant material. Commonly sighted omnivores include Black Durgon, *Melichthys niger*; Scrawled Filefish, *Aluterus scriptus*; Orangespotted Filefish, *Cantherhines pullus*; Whitespotted Filefish, *C. macrocerus*; French Angelfish, *Pomacanthus paru*, and the Sharpnose Puffer, *Canthigaster rostrata*. Although animals in the phylum Cnidaria, which includes stony and soft corals and hydroids, are the most abundant attached invertebrates on the reef, they are not important sources of food in the Caribbean. Only random fragments of stony coral, thought to be accidentally ingested, have been found in a few fishes. However, Stoplight Parrotfish, *Sparisoma viride*, and Queen Parrotfish, *Scarus vetula*, have been documented to take just over nine percent of their grazing bites from living Boulder Star Coral, *Montastraea annularis*, and, to a lesser extent, two species of brain corals. The damage, which leaves open white lesions, often requires several weeks to heal, while the tissue removed by smaller bites can regenerate in less than five days. Although grazing seldom causes the death of an entire colony, it is responsible for the largest amount of

The sharp incisors of the Slippery Dick indicate its preference for mobile prey.

Feeding

Scrawled Filefish venture into the water column to dine on a Moon Jellyfish.

chronic tissue loss by Boulder Star Coral. Gorgonians avoid heavy predation by giving off pungent odors. Only Scrawled Filefish were found with significant amounts of gorgonian polyps (12 percent) in their stomachs. The same species also dines on the horny, nematocyst-filled skeletons of fire corals, *Millepora* spp. Hydroids and anemones are nibbled only sparingly; but the polyps of zoanthids are important in the diets of Sergeant Major; Foureye Butterflyfish, *Chaetodon capistratus*, and Banded Butterflyfish, *C. striatus*. Jellyfishes, siphonophores and comb jellies, collectively known as jelly plankton, are picked at from time to time by Scrawled Filefish; Creole Wrasse, *Clepticus parrae*; Boga, *Inermia vittata*; Ocean Surgeonfish, *Acanthurus bahianus*; Yellowtail Snapper, *Ocyurus chrysurus*, and other water-column feeders.

Only a few species, including the Queen Angelfish, eat tough, distasteful sponges.

Sponges, covered with tough fibrous exteriors and filled with tiny indigestible mineralized supports and repellent chemicals, are distasteful food. Only 11 fish species regularly eat the primitive multicellular animals. It is interesting to note that all of the sponge-eating species, including the Atlantic Spadefish, *Chaetodipterus faber*; four angelfishes; boxfishes and two filefishes, evolved in recent geological time, possibly as a response to increased competition for food on coral reefs. Numerous attached worms, feather dusters and Christmas Tree Worm, *Spirobranchus giganteus*, are popular food items for butterflyfishes, grunts and boxfishes. The protruding mouths of butterflyfishes are ideal for nipping off the featherlike crowns of

The blubbery lips of a Permit – a gastropod eater.

worms before they can withdraw into their protective tubes.

Atlantic Spadefish, offer an example of the diverse diets of bottom-picking carnivores. The seven specimens dissected by Randall contained 33 percent sponges; 19 percent zoanthid polyps; 14 percent Magnificent Feather Duster, *Sabellastarte magnifica*; 13 percent pelagic tunicates; six percent gorgonian polyps; five percent algae; three percent gastropod eggs and two percent sea grasses. Less than one percent each of crabs, lobsters, and shrimp larvae and a

Atlantic Spadefish consume a diverse diet of bottom-dwelling invertebrates.

Feeding

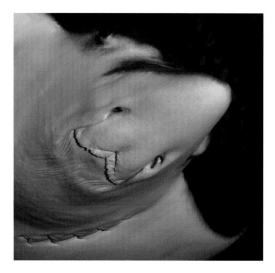

The shell-crushing mouth of a Spotted Eagle Ray.

half-inch fragment of live stony coral, *Oculina diffusa*, were also found in the specimens.

Fishes that feed on thick-shelled gastropods have powerful mouths with big lips or beaklike jaws for crushing. Notable shell-crackers include Spotted Eagle Ray, *Aetobatus narinari*; Black Grunt, *Anisotremus surinamensis*; Spanish Grunt, *Haemulon macrostomum*; Caesar Grunt, *H. carbonarium*; Jolthead Porgy, *Calamus bajonado,* and, to a lesser extent, other members of the porgy family. Other gastropod-eaters include Queen Triggerfish, *Balistes vetula*; the Trunkfish, *L. trigonus;* the Hogfish, *Lachnolaimus maximus,* and several members in the spiny puffer family. Permit, *Trachinotus falcatus*, also have blubbery lips and strong jaws indicative of their preference for gastropods. The stomachs of eight specimens contained 48 percent gastropods; 25 percent echinoderms; 17 percent bivalves; six percent hermit crabs and four percent true crabs.

Although most large carnivores feed alone, many smaller species regularly forage for brief periods in roving bands of mixed species. Yellowhead Wrasse, *Halichoeres garnoti*; Yellowtail Snapper, Bar Jack, *Caranx ruber,* and porgies often follow goatfishes as they probe the sand for hidden prey. A diver can quickly

Bottom-feeding carnivores improve their capture rate when feeding with goatfishes.

A Bar Jack turns black as it shadow-feeds with a Southern Stingray.

attract an enthusiastic group of bottom-feeders by fanning the sand. Solitary Bar Jack commonly hunt in association with Southern Stingray, *Dasyatis americana*, and Spanish Hogfish, *Bodianus rufus*, in a behavior known as **shadow-feeding**. Whether foraging in pairs or groups, the rate of strikes increases substantially for the participants. We watched one piggybacking Bar Jack shadow a Spanish Hogfish for over an hour. While near the bottom, the Bar Jack's normal openwater coat of silver turned deep bronze. Every minute or so the pair made simultaneous strikes, moving with such speed and intensity that sand flew.

A Bar Jack shadow-feeding with a Spanish Hogfish.

Feeding

Bluehead Wrasse devouring damselfish eggs.

Fishes enthusiastically pick gametes from a spawning star coral.

Every carnivore delights in a meal of fat-filled fish eggs. When a Sergeant Major's nest is full, as they often are, packs of young Bluehead Wrasse, *Thalassoma bifasciatum*, periodically test the male's guardianship abilities. If defenses are overwhelmed, the wrasse swarm the nest. Nearby carnivores immediately join the rout. Yellowtail Snapper, Black Durgon and Sergeant Major hang around courting pairs of pelagic spawners, waiting for a chance to dart through a freshly released gamete cloud. During the annual mass coral spawn of summer, many carnivores stay up past their bedtimes to grab packets of coral gametes released just after dusk. We have watched greedy little Foureye Butterflyfish pull gametes from the polyps of Giant Star Coral, *Montastrea cavernosa*, before they were even released.

Piscivores

Even though prey and predators share reefs, it is uncommon to see a fish eat another fish. Barracudas and groupers seldom waste energy making random strikes in broad daylight. Their prey are too accomplished at surviving in a world of big mouths and sharp teeth for the hunters' conspicuous attacks to be effective. The grunts hovering together next to the reef instinctively understand, like all schooling fishes, that there is security in numbers. Their close parallel formation and bold stripes make it difficult for predators to single out targets. Every eye tracks the movement of passing piscivores; before a split-second strike can meet its mark, the prey vanish inside the reef. Small solitary fishes, aware of their vulnerability, seldom wander far from a hiding hole.

Predation not only affects behavior but also influences the shape, color and markings of reef fishes. To discourage attacks, the bodies of reef fishes have evolved into tall, flat and difficult-to-bite shapes or become streamlined for speedy escapes. Some protect themselves by displaying menacing sets of spines, inflating their bodies with water, wearing confusing markings or custom-designing their wardrobes to match their backgrounds. Others learned to build burrows or to dive beneath the sand to colonize open bottom.

Right page: *Fishes have evolved numerous defensive strategies against piscivores.*

Flat bodies offer protection.

Blackbar Soldierfish schooling for safety.

A defensive foredorsal spine.

A burrfish inflates its body.

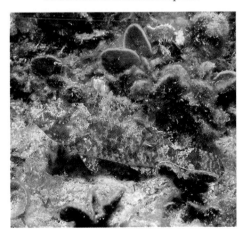

Redband Parrotfish rely on camouflage.

Razorfish escape into the sand.

Feeding

Fish-eating species are divided into two groups according to their hunting technique. **Roving predators** such as barracudas; sea basses in the genus *Mycteroperca;* sharks; mackerels; jacks; morays in the genus *Gymnothorax;* Tarpon, *Megalops atlanticus*; needlefishes; Trumpetfish, *Aulostomus maculatus*; Tobaccofish, *Serranus tobacarius*, and several snappers, stalk or chase prey. The **lie-in-wait predators** – frogfishes, lizardfishes and scorpionfishes – ambush prey from concealed positions.

Longlure Frogfish.

Under normal circumstances reef fishes are virtually impossible to capture. However, a predator's capture rate increases dramatically when it takes advantage of abnormal situations. Concentrating hunting efforts during the brief, low-light period of twilight has proven to be a productive strategy. During the remainder of the day, roving predators have two basic options for acquiring food: they can wait patiently for disturbances to occur naturally or they can create distracting situations.

Raiding parties of large Yellow Jack, *Caranx bartholomaei*, and Bar Jack, *C. ruber*, are masters of pandemonium. We have watched packs ranging from six to 20 big jacks terrorize reefs on numerous afternoons. Seconds before the hunters appear, schooling reef fishes tighten ranks and begin to swirl while solitary fishes inch toward shelters. At times the jacks make only a few cursory passes, but on other afternoons they come flying in toward the reef, cutting fast and with authority.

Sand Diver - a lizardfish.

Left page: *A Black Grouper makes repeated rushes into silversides.*

Spotted Scorpionfish.

Feeding

A hunting pack of Bar Jack attempting to disrupt the schooling behavior of grunts.

The packs circle schools of grunts, attempting to splinter the groups before slashing through the escaping fishes. In the confusion, the panicked prey dodge into overcrowded hiding holes, where the big predators come crashing in behind. In the swirls of sand and fleeing fishes, it is difficult to determine success; but an occasional jack rises off the reef compulsively working its jaws. The more aggressive the attack, the longer it lasts. Some forays are over after one or two quick strikes. Others continue for ten minutes or more as the hunters work up and down a reef line, continually disrupting schools before they are able to regroup.

On two occasions we have watched jacks flush Spotted Moray, *Gymnothorax moringa*, out of the reef. The frenzied fishes pounded the terrified eels as they dashed for cover. Even after the morays disappeared back into the reef, the jacks continued to lunge at the openings where the eels disappeared. One hunting party chased an eel out of five different shelters during a ten-minute period before losing interest. It appears that the jacks take pleasure from the chase rather than attempting to kill or eat the eels. If they had wanted, it seems the jacks could have torn the eels to shreds – but maybe not; a moray's skin is as tough as rawhide.

Two common reef predators, Graysby, *Epinephelus cruentatus*, and Coney, *E. fulvus*, have a much more favorable attitude toward morays. The two small sea basses increase their odds of capturing elusive prey by forming hunting confederations with the Spotted Moray and Goldentail Moray, *G. miliaris*, the

64

After splintering schools of grunts, the predators feed on prey that packs into overcrowded hiding holes.

only two morays that hunt during daylight hours. We have observed a similar set of predators hunting in the same manner with the Common Octopus, *Octopus vulgaris*. The hunting parties are occasionally joined by Trumpetfish; Mutton Snapper, *Lutjanus analis*; Yellowtail Snapper, *Ocyurus chrysurus*; young Black Grouper, *Mycteroperca bonaci*; Nassau Grouper, *Epinephelus striatus*, and Bar Jack. We have counted as many as seven predators accompanying a single eel. Hiding holes in the reef keep small fishes safe from all major predators except one, the eel. Morays, with long, slender, malleable bodies and one of the keenest senses of smell in the animal kingdom, are well suited for home invasions. When a feeding eel slips inside a coral head, resident fishes know exactly where the exits are located; but if escape is blocked by the hungry mouth of a waiting grouper, the fishes panic and bounce around inside the dark like pinballs – an abnormal situation and a predator's dream.

Sand swirls as a pack of Yellow Jack attempts to flush a moray from the reef.

Feeding

A Trumpetfish and a Coney, both piscivores, hunt with a Goldentail Moray— a behavior known as nuclear hunting.

We first became aware of the behavior late one afternoon, when our attention was drawn to three Graysby and a Coney resting on the bottom, staring intently at a small opening in a limestone ledge. Graysby are usually shy, but this bunch was so intent on their business they didn't even notice us. Moments later the head of a Spotted Moray appeared in the entrance. To our amazement one of the Graysby moved forward and rested its beefy little ten-inch body next to the eel's head. The odd couple remained cheek-to-cheek for nearly a minute before the moray calmly withdrew. The Graysby backed away and resettled to the bottom, intently staring at the vacated hole like a puppy longing for a lost squeaky toy. When the eel reappeared, a second Graysby stationed itself next to the eel's head and quivered slightly. The moray didn't appear to be concerned in the least by the close proximity of the fishes. Without warning the moray shot forward and raced across the open sand, with one grouper shadowing its head and the others trailing close behind. Ten feet away, the eel slithered inside an opening at the base of a brain coral. Two fishes poked their snouts into the same crevice while the others moved anxiously around the structure, peering first in one undercut and then another. Presently, the speckled head of the moray reappeared. One Graysby moved forward and nudged the moray with its snout, while the others hovered just off the bottom. The eel dodged back into the dark pocket but almost immediately reappeared and streaked off to another crevice, with

A Coney perches next to a Goldentail Moray waiting for it to make a run.

its entourage close behind. After several runs the moray finally settled under a ledge with only its head exposed. While the minutes passed and light faded, two groupers remained nearby and two lost interest and slipped away. Soon three Ocean Surgeonfish, *Acanthurus bahianus*, passed on their way to night shelter. Strangely, one of the algae-eaters swam down and lay briefly against the eel's head much like the groupers.

This feeding behavior, known as **nuclear hunting**, has been reported from the Gulf of California, the Red Sea and the Caribbean. Each study described small reef predators following day-feeding morays. The Caribbean report also mentioned Ocean Surgeonfish and a Princess Parrotfish, *Scarus taeniopterus*, both herbivores, involved in "rubbing and posing" similar to what we had seen,

A Coney shadows a Goldentail Moray as it dashes to a new hunting location.

Feeding

Six species nuclear hunt with a prowling Sharptail Eel.

but the papers didn't venture an explanation of the peculiar behavior. After watching the hunting groups on several occasions, we finally began to see a pattern emerge. The eel nearly always waits for a grouper to position itself next to its body before making a break across the bottom. In every instance, the fish in contact at the beginning of a run shadows the moray's head. It appears that the two animals cooperate to insure that they arrive at the next coral head simultaneously so the grouper can cover an escape route while the eel invades the dark interior.

Although the groupers made frequent strikes into the dark holes occupied by foraging eels, it was a long time before we finally confirmed a capture. Three Coney and a Trumpetfish were following a very active Goldentail Moray. On a short run across the sand, a Coney crowded the eel's head as usual, while the other fishes trailed close behind. As soon as the moray disappeared inside a coral head, one of the larger Coney started jumping eagerly from one opening to another. Suddenly the Coney made a strike that sent sand flying. The piscivore appeared from the cloud with a tail protruding from its mouth. When the hunter tried to reposition its catch, the prey, a three-inch Orangespotted Filefish, *Cantherhines pullus*, popped free and rocketed away. The grouper pounced, recapturing its victim. But nothing comes easy in the sea. The little filefish locked its piercing foredorsal lancet firmly into the roof of the predator's mouth. The Coney, unable to swallow, swam sluggishly over to a sea fan, settled hard on the bottom, and with its mouth awkwardly bulging and eyes glazed over, rolled to one side and slowly changed into its blotched night-colors. When we left the area 10 minutes later, the Coney had still not swallowed the filefish.

Of course morays also hunt alone, and sometimes they hunt each other. We had the opportunity to view an extraordinary piece of video showing a Spotted Moray hunting a shallow reef crest of Finger Coral, *Porites porites*, in St. Lucia. It was apparent that the eel was following the scent of prey by the way it tracked across the coral, periodically thrusting its head into openings. Suddenly the hunter plunged into a fissure, struggled, and pulled out a Chain Moray, *Echidna catenata*, half its length, tightly gripped in its jaws. The desperate moray reached around and bit its captor across the eyes. Intertwined, the two maddened eels spun violently. The larger moray thrust its tail into the reef to gain traction, then raked its head through coral branches to break the blinding grip. After pulling free, it swallowed its prey in less than ten seconds.

Day in and day out, Trumpetfish are the most entertaining piscivores on the reef. Stealth is their game, and persistence is their strength. Their long, thin bodies scarcely throw shadows as the solitary hunters cautiously weave their way through a maze of bottom structures in search of prey. Disguising their positions by aligning with branching gorgonians and sponges and shadow-feeding with foraging fishes are favorite tricks. The elongate hunters occur in three basic color patterns: brown to reddish brown, tan to gray with blue to purple snouts, and yellow. Each type is inclined to shadow-feed with fishes of similar colors. Brownish individuals associate with groupers and parrotfishes, and yellow types prefer Spanish Hogfish, *Bodianus rufus*. Individuals with blue snouts join swarming feeding aggregations of Blue Tang, *Acanthurus coeruleus*, to take advantage of the general confusion caused when the herbivores mob damselfish gardens. Trumpetfish are seldom welcomed as hitchhikers. On occasions, parrotfishes and groupers attempt to lose the predators by swimming erratically and brushing against bottom structures.

Trumpetfish hunt throughout the day, only occasionally taking time out to visit cleaning stations. While on the move, they generally swim horizontally just above the bottom but quickly assume a vertical pose to conceal their presence or position for a strike. They often remain poised straight up with their mouths just inches from the bottom for minutes at a time while waiting for a holed-up fish to reappear. Downward strikes generated from bowed bodies are short and lighting-quick. Their mouths flare like trumpets to engulf fishes, which generally measure less than two inches, although a five-inch squirrelfish was once found inside a two-foot specimen. Bicolor Damselfish, *Stegastes partitus*, larval fishes, blennies, cardinalfishes and juvenile grunts are their most frequent victims. The elongate hunters also pursue groups of foraging fishes while parallel to the bottom and occasionally lie on their sides or turn upside down to gain an advantage. A feeding study recorded eight successful Trumpetfish strikes in 45 attempts during 19 hours of observed stalking.

A Trumpetfish - the reef's most prevalent piscivore.

Feeding

The same study analyzed the response of Threespot Damselfish, *Stegastes planifrons*, to models of Trumpetfish manipulated by observers. The research found the Threespots (prey) most vigilant when the models (predators) were large, close or held vertically. When the Threespots sight horizontally swimming predators moving in their direction, they stop feeding, rise slightly off the bottom and swim toward the threat. This behavior is possibly meant to better assess the danger or to let the predators know they have been seen. The damselfish then drop to the bottom and retreat. If the predators continue or assume vertical positions, the prey disappear inside hiding holes. After the predators pass, the damselfish often chase after the adversaries and nip at their tails. Large damselfishes frequently charge and occasionally nip Trumpetfish simply swimming near their territories. These attacks are quite effective, causing the Trumpetfish to jump and quickly leave the area. However, once poised in a vertical strike position, the hunters seem impervious to damselfish assaults.

Shadowing a Princess Parrotfish.

Shadowing a Spanish Hogfish.

Shadowing a Nassau Grouper.

Oops! A bit of confusion.

Feeding

The expanded mouth of a Trumpetfish illustrates the source of the predator's common name.

Four Trumpetfish stalk the same prey.

Postured for a strike.

Lying flat on the sand– an unusual stalking position.

Coney regularly stalk small fishes during daylight hours. Once in pursuit, the groupers' intensity and persistence are reminiscent of terriers after rats. The hunters often lie motionless on their sides for minutes at a time, with their snouts thrust under rocks to keep an eye on their intended victims. During one encounter, a determined Coney worked a targeted goby for ten minutes before moving eight feet away and settling to the sea floor as if no longer interested. Moments later, when the goby made a dash for a nearby rock, the Coney sprang into action, nabbing the fleeing prey well before it reached safety. One afternoon we watched a lengthy standoff between a Bicolor Damselfish and a Coney. There was no obvious reason why the predator singled out its prey; the damselfish didn't appear injured, and there were numerous larger and smaller Bicolors around the same isolated coral mound. The Coney stared intently at a hole where the prey hid for long stretches, then moved several feet away. Each time the one-inch fish attempted to rise into the water column the Coney instantly charged, driving the damselfish back into the hole. One hour and nine unsuccessful attacks later, the stalemate continued.

A piscivore's fortunes are not always what they appear. When a fish makes a strike, food competitors rush to the scene. To avoid injury and sharing their prey, most piscivores stalk fishes small enough to fit inside their mouths.

A Red Hind dashes across the sand with a freshly caught Bigeye.

However, if an opportunity arises to capture prey too large to swallow easily few predators can resist. While descending to a 30-foot patch reef we noticed a 20-inch Red Hind, *Epinephelus guttatus*, rapidly cutting across a sand channel with the back half of a bright red Bigeye, *Priacanthus arenatus*, projecting awkwardly from its mouth. Even before we could settle to the sea floor, the successful hunter was joined by a smaller Red Hind that made a grab for the prey. With a toss of its head that sent sand swirling, the hunter defended its catch and accelerated toward the cover of a ledge.

At that instant, the first of several Queen Triggerfish, *Balistes vetula*, appeared. It struck with the speed and intent of a dive-bomber, burying its beak deep into the Bigeye's flesh. The unexpected jolt broke the grouper's hold.

Feeding

The smaller Red Hind pounced but was knocked clear by the enraged hunter. To secure a better grip, the larger Red Hind unhinged its jaws and flared its gills, drawing in the Bigeye with such powerful suction that the outgoing blast sent sand flying. Just as the prey was secured, the water darkened with the swooping silhouettes of a large strike force of triggerfish intent on a free lunch. Their usual pastel shading of purple, blue, turquoise and yellow darkened to a menacing black. In this belligerent state, the triggerfish relentlessly attacked the Bigeye's exposed tail until the hapless prey, again wrenched from the grouper's mouth, lay on the sand, pale and eyeless, in two tattered pieces.

The Red Hind, now joined by three Coney and a Graysby, formed a circle around the kill just out of reach of the flying circus of snapping triggerfish beaks. While the groupers waited for an opportunity to make a move, a school of

We counted 38 fishes attemping to hijack the Red Hind's freshly caught prey.

algae-eating Blue Tang, for some unexplained reason, added their numbers to the ever-growing feeding frenzy that swirled in a chaotic cloud ten feet off the bottom. Kneeling just outside the vortex of flying fishes and sand, we quickly counted 38 Queen Triggerfish, Tang, Yellowtail Snapper, grouper and Black Durgon, *Melichthys niger*. Suddenly, the big Red Hind dashed forward, grabbed the head segment and took off in the direction of a ledge with a streaming column of irate fishes in chase.

The Red Hind disappeared under a limestone overhang. Just as it appeared that the big fellow was finally going to reap a portion of his just reward, several pursuing triggerfish, without so much as breaking stride, turned on their sides and dived under the ledge. A sandstorm rose from the narrow opening as three lobsters wisely fled. It took 20 minutes before the sand settled, the last of the fishes dispersed, and the lobsters marched back across the flat to their lair.

Even though piscivores must know better, they occasionally succumb to temptation and grab small fishes protected by piercing dorsal spines. We have seen both a frogfish and a scorpionfish engulf heavily spined butterflyfishes and immediately blow them back out. An Indigo Hamlet, *Hypoplectrus indigo*, made

An Indigo Hamlet having trouble swallowing a Slender Filefish.

A Yellowhead Wrasse exploits the hamlet's dilemma.

the mistake of plucking a dainty little Slender Filefish, *Monacanthus tuckeri*, from where it hid among the branches of a gorgonian. The half-swallowed prey locked its elongate foredorsal spine inside the predator's widely stretched mouth. A Yellowhead Wrasse, *Halichoeres garnoti*, swooped down and, in a single bite,

clipped off the filefish's exposed tail then returned and chased the hapless hamlet in circles attempting to steal more of its meal. A Nassau Grouper dashed six feet off the bottom to take a Black Durgon in midwater. The triggerfish extended its single foredorsal spine on impact momentarily preventing it from being taken into the grouper's mouth. The grouper repositioning and shoved the prey against the bottom for five minutes before it was finally swallowed.

Few piscivores, other than sharks, morays, Tarpon and Greater Soapfish, *Rypticus saponaceus* are believed to feed regularly after dark. However, under favorable circumstances such as bright moonlit nights, or when an unusual

A Black Durgon's erect foredorsal spine makes it difficult for the Nassau Grouper to swallow.

Feeding

Spoon-nose Eel waiting for prey.

Lunging from the sand.

abundance of nocturnal prey is present, the opportunistic predators freely extend their daytime feeding hours. Fishermen report taking Nassau Grouper on live bait well after dark, even though the species is commonly thought of as a daytime feeder. Night-stalking piscivores are quite resourceful. One evening a Greater Soapfish grabbed five cardinalfishes in succession before we realized that the predator was using our light beams to locate the prey. We also have heard accounts of a Great Barracuda, *Sphyraena barracuda*; Mutton Snapper, *Lutjanus analis*, and Tarpon using divers' lights to find food. It is interesting to note that some researchers believe that potential nighttime prey can anticipate the oncoming rushes of piscivores from flashes of bioluminescence activated by an attack.

Hiding behind large mouths and camouflage coats, lie-in-wait predators patiently wait for small fishes to mistakenly swim too close. Prey is captured with an explosive lunge and suction created by a rapidly opening mouth. Frogfishes, not satisfied with waiting for prey

Spoon-nose Eel with captured prey.

to happen by, entice small fishes with a dangling lure attached to the end of a modified foredorsal spine. Peacock Flounder, *Bothus lunatus*, not only ambush prey from camouflaged positions, but also actively stalk small fishes, often striking like cobras. Lizardfishes are possibly the most aggressive bottom predators. They prowl the sea floor, stopping to rest on coral, sponges or sand for minutes at a time before moving to a new location a short distance away. Instead of changing colors to match their background, the slender piscivores often bury in the sand with only their

Peacock Flounder with mouth extended.

eyes and large mouths exposed. Their high-speed attacks make short work of juvenile grunts and other small fishes passing overhead. Although the feeding strategies of Caribbean lizardfishes have not been studied in detail, the Engelman's Lizardfish, *Synodus engelmani*, a family member from the Indo-Pacific, was found to average one strike every 35 minutes with an 11 percent success rate.

Night-feeding fishes generally rest in schools for protection during the day. By far, the largest and most spectacular of these gatherings are the teeming schools of herrings and anchovies, collectively known as silversides, that swirl

Sand Diver with Blackbar Soldierfish.

Feeding

Tarpon slashing through a polarized school of silversides.

together in the entrances of coral caves and open wrecks in polarized schools. These minnow-sized silvery fishes have good reason to congregate; they are the most frequently eaten fishes on the reef. By joining together, their odds of survival improve dramatically. The continually moving and flashing schools make difficult targets for hunters. An attack from any direction is signaled through a school at twice the speed of the oncoming rush, setting into motion one of several synchronized evasion tactics. Using vision, otoliths and lateral lines to maintain position, the fishes can open a hole around an advancing predator, contract into balls or explode into a thousand shimmers. Attacks become more profitable at dusk, when the schools begin to disperse and the silversides no longer glint and gleam at every turn.

Planktivores

One or two species from nearly every major fish family have evolved the physical features necessary to feed on zooplankton swept to the reef from open sea. Zooplankters are primarily swimming crustaceans so small they cannot be detected easily by the unaided eye. Most are clear, shrimplike copepods less than two millimeters in size, that hop erratically as they swim. There are two basic types of planktivores: particulate feeders, usually reef associated species that use binocular vision to focus on oncoming specks which are ingested one at time, and filter feeders that swim with opened mouths, engulfing large volumes of water containing prey.

Particulate feeders, also known as plankton-pickers, have small, upturned, protrusible, fine-toothed mouths that shoot forward to reach and draw in prey with suction. Long, closely spaced gill rakers keep the minute particles, which are typically swallowed whole, from passing through the gill openings. A growing number of researchers believes that mucus coating the gill rakers plays an important role in entrapping particles. Even with these specialized modifications, plankton-pickers are able to capture only the larger zooplankters with conspicuous pigmented eyes or body parts. Surprisingly, daytime planktivores seldom feast on the swarms of tiny Mysid Shrimp, *Mysidium* spp., associated with reef structures. It seems that planktivores are unable to focus on an individual within the swarms.

Reef-related planktivores feeding high in the water column developed sleek bodies and deeply forked tails necessary to evade the strikes of openwater predators such as jacks and mackerels. Their trim forms also allow them to maintain stationary positions in brisk currents. The most noticeable planktivores, Brown Chromis, *Chromis multilineata*; Creole Wrasse, *Clepticus parrae*, and, in the southern Caribbean, Creole-fish, *Paranthias furcifer*, gather in large aggregations in the current-swept waters over outer reefs, where the greatest number of transient zooplankters occur.

When threatened, the clouds of feeding fishes close ranks and ease away. If attacked, they disappear into the reef below. Water-column foragers such as Striped Grunt, *Haemulon striatum*, and Boga, *Inermia vittata*, which feed in polarized schools, flee en masse rather than seeking protection in the reef. A few plankton feeders, including Black Durgon, *Melichthys niger*, and Sergeant Major, *Abudefduf saxatilis*, have taken an alternate route to survival by relying on deep flat bodies and sharp spines to discourage predation. On overcast days and during the low light of late afternoon, all planktivores feed lower in the water column than normal.

Brown Chromis feeds on plankton with its protrusible mouth.

Those smaller planktivores with deeper bodies, indicative of less speed, such as Bicolor Damselfish, *Stegastes partitus*; Fairy Basslet, *Gramma loreto*; Masked Goby, *Coryphopterus personatus*, and Purple Reeffish, *Chromis scotti*, feed alone or in small groups within restricted areas close to the reef. Planktivores inhabiting open sand, including Yellowhead Jawfish, *Opistognathus aurifrons*; Hovering Goby, *Ioglossus helenae*, and Brown Garden Eel, *Heteroconger halis*, rise only immediately above their burrows to feed on passing zooplankters.

As darkness falls and the daytime crew heads for night shelter, an entirely new set of planktivores enters the water column to dine. The most common species include cardinalfishes; bigeyes; Blackbar Soldierfish, *Myripristis jacobus*; Glassy Sweeper, *Pempheris schomburgki*, and silversides. These large-eyed night feeders, unable to see the small transient zooplankters in low light, consume the larger resident copepods and mysids that ascend from the reef after dark. With their food source distributed randomly and predators limited, there is little need to aggregate. Most feed alone or in small groups near their daytime hiding places, except for Glassy Sweeper which make migrations from inshore ledges and caves to outer reefs each night.

The filter-feeding planktivores vary in size from small, minnowlike herrings to Whale Shark, *Rhincodon typus*, the largest fish in the sea reported to reach a length of 55 feet. While maintaining a stationary position, herrings employ pump filtration, using rapid bouts of suction to draw in water and prey. Manta, *Manta birostris*, the largest ray, feed by ram filtration. The great fish swim

Above: *Terminal phase male Creole Wrasse feeding on plankton.*
Left : *Creole Wrasse feeding in the rich plankton stream above the outer reef.*

Feeding

Manta filter feeding.   *Whale Shark filter feeding.*

through clouds of microscopic plankton with their oval-shaped mouths opened wide. Gill rakers sieve out food particles as the water exits through flared gill covers. Extensions of the pectoral fins, known as cephalic lobes, funnel food toward their mouths. The lobes fold out of the way when not in use. While feeding in concentrated clouds of plankton, the fish often perform graceful loops. Whale Shark use both filtration methods to sustain their massive size. They typically swim near the surface, engulfing plankton and small fishes as they go, but, when feeding in thick patches of plankton, they hover and pump food into their mouths.

Herbivores

Herbivores transfer energy from plants to animals higher in the food chain. This pattern holds true for coral reefs, where roughly 25 percent of the fishes eat plants. Large populations of plant-eating marine fishes are essentially restricted to tropical reef and seagrass environments. Why herbivores have not become better represented in subtropical or temperate waters is not clearly understood. In the Caribbean, parrotfishes and surgeonfishes, the two major families of plant consumers, feed from an abundant supply of fast-growing filamentous algae. Using powerful beaklike mouths, parrotfishes scrape the short (1 - 2 mm) algal turf from dead coral and rock with flurries of bites. During the process, significant amounts of calcium carbonate are ingested. In contrast, surgeonfishes browse selectively, taking quick, deliberate bites. Because algae provide few nutrients, herbivores must harvest and process large quantities of plant material to meet their growth and energy demands.

The rapid growth of turf algae makes shallow forereefs extremely productive habitats. Marine herbivores are estimated to consume between 50 and 100 percent of the primary production – the highest grazing rate on earth. Without herbivores to harvest the rapidly growing algae, coral reefs could not exist in their present form. If left ungrazed, the competitively superior algae would quickly smother existing corals and blanket reef rock, leaving nowhere for coral larvae to settle and establish new colonies. When plastic-mesh cages were placed over porous clay tiles during herbivore exclusion studies in the Florida Keys, tiny filaments of red algae, typically found in mats of algal turf, changed structure, growing into fleshy upright plants. After the cages were removed months later, parrotfishes and surgeonfishes picked the lush growth clean in less than two hours.

Parrotfishes and surgeonfishes are not the only plant-eaters on the reef. Algae dominate the diets of Goldspot Goby, *Gnatholepis thompsoni*; Bridled Goby, *Coryphopterus glaucofraenum*; Redlip Blenny, *Ophioblennius atlanticus*; Cherubfish, *Centropyge argi*, and several species of bottom-dwelling damselfishes. Numerous invertebrates also eat algae. Microherbivores, limpets, amphipods and small gastropods keep tiny foraging areas clear of growth. Clinging crabs, *Mithrax* spp., also depend on plants for food. But by far the most important algae-eating invertebrate in the tropical western Atlantic is the Long-spined Urchin, *Diadema antillarum*. A single urchin, using its complicated five-part mouth structure known as an Aristotle's Lantern, keeps a square yard of rock or reef clear of algae. The abundant, shallow-water night-feeders consumed so much algae that they were a major food competitor of herbivorous fishes before 1983-84, when a Caribbean-wide epidemic almost eliminated the species. Following the die-off, parrotfish and surgeonfish populations monitored in St. Croix increased two- to four-fold in response to the additional food supply. However, in Jamaica, where parrotfishes and surgeonfishes had been severely overfished for decades, the loss of *Diadema* had a devastating effect on the island's northern reefs. Without the urchins' help, the depleted fish stocks were unable to keep the burgeoning algal crop in check. Corals, which had already experienced severe damage from Hurricane Allen in 1980, were overwhelmed. Living coral coverage plummeted in three short years from 45 to 55 percent to

Terminal phase Stoplight Parrotfish scraping filamentous algae from reef rock.

Feeding

five to 15 percent. Although they may be dense in a few isolated locations, urchins are unfortunately making a slow recovery in Jamaica, as well as across most of the Caribbean Basin. Because of the scarcity of *Diadema,* coupled with continued overfishing and nutrient-rich runoff from coastal development and agriculture, algae continue to dominate the reefs in many areas.

Instead of foraging freely over the bottom, several species of damselfishes spend considerable energy tending and defending private algal patches. The little farmers weed out unwanted plants, leaving a luxuriant turf that grows one- and one-half to three- and one-half times taller than the unprotected algae on surrounding rocks. Although individual plots measure only a few feet across, up to 70 percent of a reef's surface can be covered with contiguous territories, greatly increasing the habitat's primary production. The thick mats harbor thriving colonies of tiny invertebrates and support secondary gardens of appetizing diatoms and other epiphytes. It is not known if, or to what extent, the damselfishes' diet depends on the hidden fauna for protein, but encroaching carnivores and herbivores are chased with equal vigor.

Grazing is so intense in shallow water that 30-foot plant-free sand zones, known as halos, are created around inshore patch reefs. Their margins represent the limit to which herbivores dare to venture from the reef's protection. As algal biomass decreases with depth, the number of foraging

Blue Tang feeding in an aggregation.

herbivores also declines. However, there is a tendency toward a surplus of ungrazed plants on the deeper reefs. This disparity might be brought about by a greater threat of predation in the lower light. The density and diversity of herbivore populations remains stable throughout the year, even though grazing increases significantly during the warm-water periods of summer and early fall. In the Florida Keys, where there is a marked difference in seasonal water temperatures, grazing rates are six times greater during summer than winter.

Feeding

Digesting plant material is not easy. Chemicals break down the rather selective diets of damselfishes and surgeonfishes as the food passes quickly through their thin-walled, elastic stomachs and winding guts. In contrast, the digestive process of parrotfishes has been characterized as a concrete mixer, grinding plants and calcareous sediment with flattened pharyngeal teeth, known as the pharyngeal mill. The chalky mixture moves rapidly through a stomachless gut before discharging in long, white plumes of sand. In fact, it has been estimated that a large parrotfish may produce a ton of sand annually! How the large herbivores obtain sufficient protein for growth from their diets is still under study. Adults could possibly acquire the necessary nutrients from organic waste, microorganisms or small invertebrates that accumulate in algal turf. Whatever the source, it is effective; parrotfishes grow quickly, reaching maturity in three to five years and live for perhaps eight to 12 years.

It has long been assumed that parrotfishes are strict herbivores. However, a recent study reported that three members of the genus *Sparisoma*, Redtail Parrotfish, *S. chrysopterum*; Redband Parrotfish, *S. aurofrenatum*, and Stoplight Parrotfish, *S. viride*, consume several species of crevice-dwelling sponges. Each time researchers removed the sponges from the crevices, the parrotfishes eagerly devoured the colonies. They even chased one another from the sponges, although they never defend their customary food. It was obvious from the parrotfishes' enthusiastic response that the cryptic sponges would be exterminated if they didn't inhabit inaccessible crevices.

Reef algae are divided into four groups based primarily on their morphological structure. **Crustose** coralline are unpalatable, highly calcified encrustations that form important protective coverings and function as an adhesive for the reef's structure. **Calcareous** species are green, leafy upright plants that avoid predation by calcification and chemical deterrents. **Turf** or **filamentous** species form the primary food source of herbivores although some species are chemically defended. **Frondose** or fleshy algae, typically vulnerable to grazing, grow primarily on reef flats and in back-reef areas.

Calcareous leaf algae in the genus *Halimeda* provide an interesting example of how one group of marine plants has evolved defenses to survive on the reef. These rich green clumps and vines not only reduce their nutritional value by calcification, but also produce chemical compounds repugnant to many herbivores. The plants use their deterrents judiciously. On reefs with an abundance of herbivores, the chemicals produced by *Halimeda* are much more potent than those manufactured by the same species in areas with few grazers. The plants have also adapted to grow their tender, uncalcified leaf tips at night, when herbivorous fishes sleep. The new growth, produced without sunlight for photosynthesis, is packed with high concentrations of toxins until the tips develop calcification. When researchers coated blades of Turtle Grass, *Thalassia testudinum*, with *Halimeda* toxin, Bucktooth Parrotfish, *Sparisoma radians*, avoided the treated blades but readily ate unmanipulated control grasses. Chemical deterrents are far from foolproof, however. The toxic compounds that repel one species have limited, or no, effect on others.

Colors & Camouflage

The bright "poster colors" of a Queen Angelfish.

Reef fishes are known for their exquisite colors and markings. Adding even more variety to the reef's catalog of wonders, many species display different colors and patterns during various life phases and also have the ability to change their regular patterns within seconds and to lighten or darken at will. Generally the brightest, most conspicuous patterns are used to communicate reproductive readiness or aggression, whereas dull, broken markings provide a protective cloak of camouflage. When stimulated by nerves or, in some cases hormones, pigments in irregularly shaped cells known as **chromatophores** either concentrate in the core, causing the fish to pale, or expand through radiating branches, intensifying colors. Chromatophores containing different pigments overlaying each other in the skin produce colors in the longer wavelengths – red, yellow, orange, black and brown. Those species displaying the most brilliant or complex patterns have higher densities of chromatophores. Many fishes display permanent structural colors of shorter wave lengths – greens, blues, pinks, silvers and iridescence – by reflecting light from crystals inside cells called **iridophores**. Silvery fishes have several layers of iridophores that mirror nearly all the light striking their bodies.

Several of the large groupers in the genus *Mycteroperca*, including Black Grouper, *M. bonaci*; Yellowmouth Grouper, *M. interstitialis*; Tiger Grouper, *M. tigris*, and the Yellowfin Grouper, *M. venenosa*, can pale, darken, display various patterns or flush red, depending on their moods or activities. Some of

A Yellowfin Grouper displays its typical color pattern.

Yellowfin Grouper often change their color scheme radically, such as developing reddish blotches when near the bottom.

the most skilled color-changers are lie-in-wait predators such as flounders, frogfishes and scorpionfishes. These masters of disguise, whose livelihood depends on camouflage, are replete with chromatophores. Within seconds of settling in new locations flounders can vanish like mirages by using visual cues to expand or contract their chromatophores to match the colors and patterns of the seafloor where they rest. Although frogfishes sometimes take hours to alter their colors to correspond with new surroundings, any experienced fish watcher can attest to their genius at hiding in the open. The Sargassum Frogfish, *Histrio histrio*, and Sargassum Pipefish, *Syngnathus pelagicus*, inhabitants of the floating weed for which they are named, display color patterns to match their drifting homes. The remarkable little frogfishes even acquire the shape of the surrounding stems and leaves. The fleshy tabs and cirri on the head and chin of the bottom-dwelling Spotted Scorpionfish, *Scorpaena plumieri*, develop to resemble the algae where these predators often wait in ambush. The disguise is so realistic that many casual observers believe algae actually grow on the sedentary fish.

Colors & Camouflage

The cryptic pattern of a Sargassum Pipefish blends well with its floating home.

A Sargassum Frogfish.

Some small fishes use color-changing camouflage to hide from big mouths. Instead of diving for cover when threatened, initial phase Redband Parrotfish, *Sparisoma aurofrenatum*, drop to the bottom and blend with the background. Slender Filefish, *Monacanthus tuckeri*, keep low profiles by hanging out within the branches of gorgonians, grass blades or algal bushes, and alter both colors and patterns to disappear among the branches. Some bottom-oriented species like Slippery Dick, *Halichoeres bivittatus*, and Rock Hind, *Epinephelus adscensionis*, lighten or darken as they move from light sandy areas to darker sections of the reef.

Right: *Many small reef fishes use color-changing camouflage to hide from big mouths.*

Female Sailfin Blenny.

Juvenile Trumpetfish.

Slender Filefish.

Slender Filefish.

Juvenile Green Razorfish.

Initial phase Bucktooth Parrotfish.

Colors & Camouflage

A Hogfish with its normal color pattern.   *A Hogfish with bottom feeding colors.*

Males of many species crank up their chromatophores during courtship. Unfortunately, their eye-catching patterns also attract predators. To strike a balance between reproductive success and untimely death, males of many small, vulnerable fishes flaunt their brightest hues only during brief courtship bouts. This behavior is most notable among seagrass residents, who must be extremely cautious when away from readily accessible hiding holes. Male Bluelip Parrotfish, *Cryptotomus roseus*, flash their neon-bright panels of gold, pink, blue and green only when swooping down to court females grazing in the grass. As they move away they quickly revert to their drab, camouflaged initial phase pattern. Even the bright permanent coats of Clown Wrasse, *H. maculipinna*, and Yellowhead Wrasse, *H. garnoti*, acquire an extra luster during spawning activities.

While it seems logical to assume that the varied markings and colors of reef fishes benefit survival, advantages are not always readily apparent. For instance, there is little agreement on why so many fishes display such vibrant colors and patterns. Famed Austrian naturalist Konrad Lorenz coined the term "poster

A Bluelip Parrotfish displaying   *A Bluelip Parrotfish turns on*
its normal pattern.   *its bright courtship colors.*

The nocturnally active Bigeye normally displays a solid red coat.

A group of Bigeye temporarily blanches while hovering just above the bottom during the day.

colors" to describe brightly colored fishes, a phrase in common usage today. In his 1960s best-selling book, *On Aggression*, Lorenz hypothesized that the flamboyant colors act as no-trespassing signs announcing territorial sovereignty. Further research has proven his idea too simple to explain fully the purpose of conspicuous colors, but no one has yet offered a more convincing argument. It has been suggested that the bright colors worn by spiny, deep-bodied species such as butterflyfishes and angelfishes deter predation by advertising the fishes as bony, low-quality, difficult-to-swallow meals. Others have proposed that the graphic colors might serve to help gregarious species remain in contact with one another.

Several recurring colors and patterns are more easily explained. Nocturnal species are customarily red, an obscure color in the low light of night or depth. However, for an unknown reason, reddish representatives of the bigeye, squirrelfish and cardinalfish families regularly pale to a pinkish white. Many fishes, especially openwater species, use countershading to conceal their movements. When observed from above, their dark backs blend with the dimness below, while their light bellies viewed from below tend to be lost in the surface light. The bold horizontal stripes of schooling species help individuals to orient visually with their neighbors and at the same time make it difficult for predators to single out individuals from a shifting panorama of lines. When Hogfish, *Lachnolaimus maximus*, porgies, snappers and many other bottom-foragers settle to the sea floor to feed, they often acquire vague bars that instantly vanish as they rise back into the water column. The bars help mask the bottom-feeders' profiles when they are viewed against a backdrop of vertical structures such as gorgonian branches.

Colors & Camouflage

Juvenile Banded Butterflyfish display eyespots and eyebars.

Predators routinely key on the eyes of intended prey to evaluate their size and likely direction of escape. Dark **eyebars** worn by many species help conceal the eye's location. False **eyespots** in the form of dark spots with a contrasting outer ring, typically located near the tail, may misdirect attacks away from the head or cause the predator to misjudge the direction of the prey's escape. Butterflyfishes

A Red Hind in its sleeping colors.

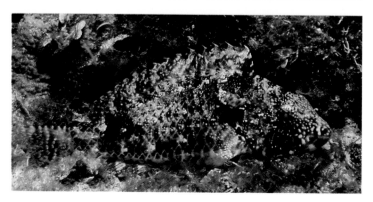

Initial phase Redband Parrotfish change their colors and pattern dramatically when sleeping at night.

are well known for their eye camouflage. All five Caribbean species have eyebars. The Foureye Butterflyfish, *Chaetodon capistratus*, and a few butterflyfish juveniles display eyespots. Residents of shallow habitats typically display more eye camouflage than deep-water species. While living among mangrove roots, young Gray Snapper, *Lutjanus griseus*, and Schoolmaster, *L. apodus*, wear distinct eyebars that are lost when they move to deeper water.

During the night most daytime species sleep inside the protection of the reef or bury in the sand, but a few bed down in the open and display bizarre night colors. The complexions of slumbering parrotfishes and groupers change so radically that it is difficult to identify the sleeping individuals. Their blotched patterns, so striking when illuminated by light beams, possibly function as disruptive coloration in the low light of night. Several members of the butterflyfish family, which typically sleep just inside ledges at the edge of the reef, develop vague bars and eyespots during the night. Creole Wrasse, *Clepticus parrae*, intensify their already gaudy purple, yellow and red colors while sleeping deep within the protection of tube sponges.

As they mature, most parrotfishes and wrasses change color patterns three or four times to indicate a new sexual or social status. However, most reef-associated species wear the same general wardrobes throughout their benthic lifecycles and a few species make only a single transition from juveniles into adults. Plankton-feeders, nocturnal species and small bottom-foragers rarely have separate juvenile patterns, whereas larger bottom-foragers, especially territorial species, typically have distinct juvenile and adult colorations. It has

A terminal phase Redband Parrotfish bedding down on the open sand changes into its nighttime wardrobe.

An Ocean Surgeonfish in night colors.

Colors & Camouflage

Solid adult pattern.

Bicolor adult pattern.

Golden adult pattern.

Transitional phase - juvenile to adult.

Juvenile golden pattern.

Juvenile mottled pattern.

Resting and night pattern.   *Male courtship pattern.*

been hypothesized that by wearing different color patterns the youngsters conceal species membership which, in turn, protects them from the attacks of adults. Because of their susceptibility to predation, juveniles are often more cryptically patterned than their elders. Young Green Razorfish, *Xyrichtys splendens*, and Great Barracuda, *Sphyraena barracuda*, are well patterned for hiding in the vegetation where they customarily live. However, the juveniles of a few species are far more colorful than the adults. This is especially true of territorial damselfishes. Many of these conspicuous juveniles, who live isolated from other members of their species, are extremely territorial. It is possible that, like Lorenz's "poster color" hypothesis, eye-catching colors serve to space individuals from one another.

The Coney, *Epinephelus fulvus*, a common medium-sized sea bass, runs the gamut of color patterns. Juveniles display a cryptic mottled reddish brown-and-white pattern or, in direct contrast, a bright golden color scheme. Adults are most commonly reddish brown with a scattering of blue or pale dots, although a few individuals are golden. This striking **xanthic coloration**, believed to result from a single recessive gene, occurs sporadically in a few other species, including Trumpetfish, *Aulostomus maculatus*, and the Smooth Trunkfish, *Lactophrys triqueter*. It is not known if golden Coney juveniles mature only into golden adults, but it appears doubtful because there is a much higher ratio of golden juveniles than of golden adults in a given population. Individuals in the reddish brown pattern frequently change into a bicolor phase. When making the transition, which in some instances occurs quite rapidly, the fish pass through an intermediate pattern. While sleeping at night, individuals develop an irregular barred and blotched pattern. Finally, courting males pale and become blotched, with a tan streak extending from behind their pectoral fins to their tails.

Left & above: *Various color patterns displayed by Coney.*

Symbiosis

Tiger Grouper attend a cleaning station.

Symbiosis, or "living together," refers to a close interrelationship between two species. There are three primary types of symbiosis: **mutualism** – two species forming an alliance for the well-being of both; **commensalism** – one species benefits while the other is unharmed by the association, and **parasitism** – one species benefits at the expense of a host species. In **mimicry**, a special category of symbiosis, a species imitates the colors, patterns and, in some cases, the behavior of another species to gain benefit. The advantages of cleaning symbiosis, a common relationship between parasite-picking fishes and shrimps and numerous reef fishes, are still under investigation.

Cleaning Symbiosis

Many species, particularly groupers, are plagued by an assortment of external parasites, so small they can hardly be seen. The creepy little bloodsuckers, mainly isopods and copepods, armed with razor-edged mandibles, burrow into the tissue around the eyes and nostrils, under scales and even invade the tender, blood-rich lining of gills and mouths. To keep their infestations under control, **client fishes** spend significant amounts of time at sites known as **cleaning stations**, where they often assume stationary trancelike poses while parasite-eating fishes and shrimps dine on their pests. In the process, the **cleaners** also remove dead or injured skin and mucous and now and again take a bite of healthy tissue.

Cleaning behavior is not exclusive to the marine world; some terrestrial animals also form similar associations. Galapagos finches pick parasites from marine iguanas; Oxpeckers feast off the backs of hoofed mammals on the African savanna, and Black-tailed Deer, responding to the calls of Scrub Jays, hold still and extend their ears while the birds remove ticks. However, most cleaning occurs underwater where animals have inherent difficulty removing their parasites. At first glance, the alliance appears to be a model of mutualism: the cleaners tap a renewable food source, and the clients obtain a dependable means of pest control. But as researchers regularly discover, the behavior of animals is not always what it seems.

Cleaning symbiosis between fishes was originally described during the early part of the century but was not linked to the removal of parasites until the mid-50s. The behavior gained widespread attention after the publication of a detailed account by Conrad Limbaugh in a 1961 issue of *Scientific American*. The author described a modest field experiment conducted in the Bahamas where he removed all the cleaning organisms from two small, isolated reefs. His reported results were dramatic. Limbaugh wrote, "Within a few days the number of fish was drastically reduced; within two weeks all except the territorial fishes had disappeared. The experiment also demonstrated the importance of cleaning symbiosis in maintaining the health of the marine populations. Many of the fish remaining developed fuzzy white blotches, swelling, ulcerated sores and frayed fins." Limbaugh concluded, "From the standpoint of the philosophy of biology, the extent of cleaning behavior in the ocean emphasizes the role of co-operation in nature as opposed to the tooth-and-claw struggle for existence." Almost overnight, the glowing portrayal of the cooperative behavior captured the hearts and minds of both the public and the scientific community. But at the same time, Limbaugh's article unwittingly planted some broad, untested generalizations about the remarkable behavior that remain with us today.

A Bar Jack extends its mouth while being cleaned by a juvenile French ˄

Symbiosis

A decade later, marine biologists thousands of miles away in Hawaii began conducting their own cleaner-removal experiments on Pacific reefs. Their controlled studies revealed the relationship to be more complex than first believed. Far from duplicating Limbaugh's celebrated results, the new findings showed insignificant changes in the abundance of fishes and no increase in their rates of parasites or disease. Suddenly, everyone's favorite example of cooperation in the animal kingdom was open to reevaluation. And sure enough, the scattering of research papers published on the subject in the 70s and 80s laid siege to the conventional wisdom. One line of reasoning proposed that cleaners have only limited effect on parasite control and actually act as parasites themselves, removing bits of flesh and mucous. In his 1987 paper *Cleaning Symbiosis*, George Losey, a biologist at the University of Hawaii, presented an idea of interest, supported by intriguing evidence. Losey wrote, "Cleaners are nothing but very clever behavioral parasites ... [that] perhaps have taken advantage of the rewarding aspects of tactile stimulation, found in nearly all vertebrates. They may have parasitised this reward system to train hosts to visit them for rewarding stimulation and, at the same time, provide a dining table for the cleaners." During aquarium experiments, fishes, whether infested or not, reacted to objects rubbed against their sides in the same manner they responded to cleaners. Fishes have been observed repeatedly posing for cleaners even when free of ectoparasites.

A puzzling behavior, termed **pseudo-cleaning**, also supports this concept. Four species of Caribbean parrotfishes – Stoplight Parrotfish, *Sparisoma viride*; Redband Parrotfish, *S. aurofrenatum*; Redtail Parrotfish, *S. chrysopterum*, and Blue Parrotfish, *Scarus coeruleus* – often assume classic, head-up cleaning poses within the upright branches of two species of sea plume, *Pseudopterogorgia americana*, and *P. rigida*. The fishes remain in zombielike states for seconds or

An initial phase Redband Parrotfish assumes a classic head-up cleaning pose within the branches of a gorgonian – a puzzling behavior known as pseudo-cleaning.

even minutes at a time, often repeating the behavior in the same gorgonian bushes throughout the day. Close inspections did not find cleaners in the vicinity. Could the caress of waving branches prompt the peculiar behavior? In the long run, it might turn out that tactile stimulation and parasite control are not mutually exclusive. The pleasure of touch could well be the primary incentive for clients to attend cleaning stations, which by having parasites removed, possibly improves their health and ultimately, reproductive success.

A Tiger Grouper flushes red and opens its mouth while attending a cleaning station.

Additional research is necessary before even fundamental questions concerning cleaning symbiosis can be answered. It appears likely that rates of parasitism and the benefits of cleaning vary considerably between regions, with studies from one area having little or no relationship to those made elsewhere. For instance, more external parasites were found on reef fishes in Puerto Rico than in Hawaii. Additional cleaner-removal studies would be useful, but the manipulation of infestation in the field would possibly be of even greater value. A change in the rate of parasitism should have a direct impact on the time clients spend at cleaning stations. Presently, a few commercial salmon farms use wrasses as an alternative to chemicals for the control of sea lice. Findings from this enterprise should provide interesting details about the extraordinary behavior.

Symbiosis

Cleaning symbiosis is a widespread marine behavior in tropical and temperate seas as well as in freshwater habitats. In the Pacific, the Cleaner Wrasse, *Labroides dimidiatus*, is the most prevalent cleaner and the subject of several research papers. Four primary cleaning organisms occur in the tropical western Atlantic: gobies in the genus *Gobiosoma*; juvenile Spanish Hogfish, *Bodianus rufus*; initial phase Bluehead Wrasse, *Thalassoma bifasciatum*, and Pederson Cleaner Shrimp, *Periclimenes pedersoni*. Several other fishes and shrimps also participate in regular cleaning activities, but are considered secondary cleaners because of their limited numbers. In addition, the juveniles of numerous fishes, all bottom-picking carnivores, act as incidental cleaners, taking occasional nips at stationary fish resting nearby.

The slender, one-inch gobies cluster on the tops or sides of large brain, star and plate corals. They generally service fish resting on the bottom. Although six genus members have been reported to act as cleaners, the Sharknose Goby, *G. evelynae*; the Neon Goby, *G. oceanops*; and the Cleaner Goby, *G. genie*, are most active.

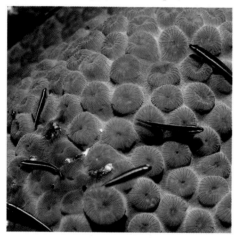

Cleaning gobies.   Juvenile Spanish Hogfish.

Juvenile Spanish Hogfish, ordinarily measuring only an inch or two, prefer to clean hovering fishes. Up to seven of the purple-and-gold wrasse form cleaning stations in the general vicinity of tall coral structures. The agile cleaners pick here and there along the sides and fins and, now and then, explore under gill covers or dart inside opened mouths. Some of their nips, usually directed at the tail, are evidently painful, causing the client to flinch and abruptly swim away or, in rarer cases, turn and chase the offending cleaners. It is not known whether these bites are necessary to dislodge well attached isopods or are intended to remove pieces of flesh. But it is interesting to note that they nearly always occur well away from a client's mouth.

Bluehead Wrasse, one of the most common parasite-pickers on Caribbean reefs, account for only ten percent of cleaning activities. The bulk of their diet is obtained by plucking plankton from currents or foraging for crustaceans on the sea floor. Many cleaning stations established by other species have a group of the young wrasse buzzing about, but they also form independent cleaning

Initial phase Bluehead Wrasse account for ten percent of the cleaning activity on Caribbean reefs.

clusters above gorgonian bushes and coral formations. The bright yellow juveniles work quickly, momentarily swarming clients suspended in open water before moving on to their next customer. Unlike the other primary cleaning species, which have immunity from predation, blueheads are regularly eaten. This is probably a strong factor in the species' reluctance to clean piscivores. Although it is generally believed that mature wrasse do not function as cleaners because of their well-developed teeth, we have observed solitary terminal males cleaning in association with adults in the initial phase, and in small groups with other terminal phase Blueheads.

Pederson Cleaner Shrimp live within the protective tentacles of the Corkscrew Anemone, *Bartholomea annulata*, and the Giant Anemone, *Condylactis gigantea*. As many as 13 of the wispy little transparent shrimp with lavender markings colonize a single anemone. To solicit prospective clients, the cleaners prance about on the ends of tentacles, waving long, conspicuous antennae twice the length of their bodies. Clients must take a position within a few inches of an anemone before the shrimp venture out to pick parasites.

A Pederson Cleaner Shrimp (with an abdomen full of eggs) is the most common cleaning shrimp in the Caribbean.

Symbiosis

Juvenile French Angelfish.

Juvenile Spotfin Hogfish.

Juvenile Porkfish.

Juvenile Spotted Drum.

Fairy Basslet.

Juvenile Rock Beauty.

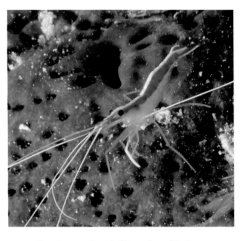

Scarlet-striped Cleaning Shrimp.

Banded Coral Shrimp.

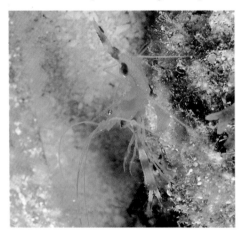

Golden Coral Shrimp.

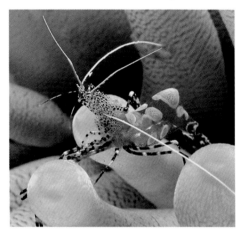

Spotted Cleaner Shrimp.

Several additional species of Caribbean fishes and shrimps act as secondary cleaners. Juvenile Gray Angelfish, *Pomacanthus arcuatus*, and French Angelfish, *P. paru*, obtain 20 percent of their diet from ectoparasite-plucking. We have on rare occasions observed cleaning behavior by juvenile Rock Beauty, *Holacanthus tricolor*; Spotted Drum, *Equetus punctatus*, and Spotfin Hogfish, *Bodianus pulchellus*. Once, in the Gulf of Mexico, we watched Spotted Soapfish, *Rypticus subbifrenatus*, picking parasites from Jewfish, *Epinephelus itajara*. Published accounts describe cleaning by juvenile Porkfish, *Anisotremus virginicus*; Fairy Basslet, *Gramma loreto*, and Black Brotula, *Stygnobrotula latebricola*. Caribbean cleaning shrimps include Scarlet-striped Cleaning Shrimp, *Lysmata grabhami*; Banded Coral Shrimp, *Stenopus hispidus*, a circumtropical species; Golden Coral Shrimp, *S. scutellatus*, and Spotted Cleaner Shrimp, *Periclimenes yucatanicus*.

Left: *A gallery of fishes reported to be secondary cleaners.*
Above: *Shrimps known to act as cleaners.*

Symbiosis

Although it has not been reported, we suspect that Red Snapping Shrimp, *Alpheus armatus*, are cleaning organisms. Usually one, but in some cases a pair, of the stocky, one- to two-inch crustaceans with large, single snapping claws, share Corkscrew Anemone with Pederson Cleaner Shrimp. Whenever we rest a hand within a half-inch of an anemone, the shrimp will pick at our fingertips for several minutes. Even after repeated attempts with numerous individuals, we were never able to coax them away from the anemone's protective tentacles. Unfortunately, the fishes that we believe are being cleaned by the shrimp lie flat over the opening of the anemone, blocking our view of the activity.

Red Snapping Shrimp share a home with Pederson Cleaner Shrimp within the stinging tentacles of Corkscrew Anemone. Although not documented to be a cleaner species, Red Snapping Shrimp readily pick at extended fingers.

Remoras in the family Echeneidae, well known for hitching long-term rides on large fishes such as sharks, are recognized as part-time cleaners of their hosts. We watched a seven- to eight-inch juvenile Sharksucker, *Echeneis* sp. nimbly slipping inside the gill cavity of a resting Nurse Shark, *Ginglymostoma cirratum*. Each time water pumped through the gill slits, the spry little Sharksucker darted in, grabbed a bite and backed out in less than two-seconds. After a series of successful forays, luck ran out when the cover slammed shut just as the cleaner's head emerged. The instant the flap reopened the Sharksucker made a beeline for the back of the shark, where it huddled next to the rear dorsal fin for the remainder of our observation.

Sharksucker, recognized as part-time cleaners, hitch long-term rides with a variety of fishes.

Right: *A Yellow Goatfish, with barbels extended, hovers head-down while being cleaned by a juvenile Spanish Hogfish.*

Symbiosis

Tomtate gather around a juvenile Spanish Hogfish in the hopes of having their mouths cleaned.

Perhaps half of the fish species on a Caribbean reef spend part of their day at cleaning stations. The cleaners' best customers are typically groupers; parrotfishes; surgeonfishes; Brown Chromis, *Chromis multilineata*, and Creole Wrasse, *Clepticus parrae*. Members of different families have customary posing styles. Some rest on the bottom, while others maintain stationary positions in mid-water with their heads angled upward. Goatfishes hang with their heads and barbels pointed straight down; surgeonfishes and grunts hover horizontally.

Bluestriped Grunt open their mouths to be cleaned by an adult Porkfish even though only juveniles of the species act as cleaners.

Two common planktivores, the Brown Chromis and the Creole Wrasse, often converge on cleaning stations in groups. On outer reef banks, where the plankton-pickers feed in large aggregations, up to a dozen Creole Wrasse stream into stations and pose head-down in tight clusters, while Blueheads hastily shuttle from one to the other.

We have watched aggressive hunting packs of large Yellow Jack, *Caranx bartholomaei*, wildly working their way down a reef, slamming under ledge after ledge in pursuit of hiding fishes, when suddenly one of the big predators stopped cold in the midst of the frenzy and assumed a head-up cleaning pose while a two-inch Spanish Hogfish calmly picked at its side. Tightly packed schools of resting grunts are regularly serviced by patrolling squadrons of young Spanish Hogfish. Frequently the grunts gang around the two-toned cleaners simultaneously opening their mouths as wide as choirboys in the hopes of having parasites plucked from their throats. In what must be an innate reaction to the typically bright colors of cleaners, we have seen Bluestriped Grunt, *Haemulon sciurus*, open their mouths to adult Porkfish over twice their size, even though only juvenile Porkfish act as cleaners.

Small cleaners enter the mouths of larger client fishes without fear.

Bottom oriented species such as groupers, Hogfish, *Lachnolaimus maximus*, flounders, morays and lizardfishes, are most commonly cleaned by gobies and shrimps. These cleaning stations tend to be regulated by dominance hierarchies dictated by size. Large groupers regularly chase smaller groupers away from cleaning stations, even if they are not interested in being cleaned at the moment. Clients settle to the sea floor within inches of a station and list in the direction of the cleaners. Groupers often open their jaws and gills so wide that daylight can be

Symbiosis

Gobies scamper over the head of a reverse-phase Spotted Moray.

seen when looking into their mouths. A few species change colors. Tiger Grouper, *Mycteroperca tigris*, occasionally turn deep red; Yellowmouth Grouper, *M. interstitialis*, become so dark their spotted pattern is obscured; and Hogfish display rust-colored body bars. The purpose of the color shifts is not understood. Perhaps the color changes make parasites easier for the cleaners to see or they may function as a signal to the cleaners indicating a desire to be cleaned.

Once settled, the predators appear oblivious to their surroundings but are actually quite alert. When divers approach the fish become uneasy, shifting slightly and often moving away. To get a closer view, pause at least ten feet away for a few minutes before making a slow approach. Occasionally, large groupers remain in place for more than an hour, but most clients leave within minutes. When ending cleaning sessions, groupers and other fishes twitch insuring the gobies and shrimps a safe passage back to their home bases before the clients move away.

Patient divers can usually entice Pederson Cleaning Shrimp and gobies to briefly clean their outstretched hands. Your best bet is to look for shrimps advertising for business by waving their antennae. Slowly extend the back of

Gobies stream from a coral head to clean a Yellowmouth Grouper.

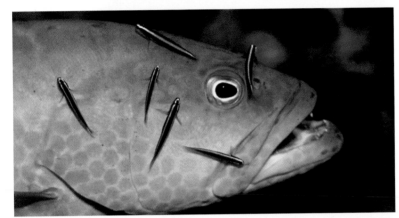

When client fishes are ready to leave a cleaning station, they give a brief twitch as a signal to the cleaners.

A Yellowmouth Grouper at a cleaning station. Client fishes appear to relax and enjoy being cleaned.

Symbiosis

your open hand with the palm angled slightly away. The shrimp usually make tentative contact with their antennae before hopping aboard, picking around the nails or at rough or broken skin. The gobies are quite cautious and only smaller individuals fall for the ruse, but at times we have had several of the tiny fish scampering over our hands.

Another possible benefit from cleaning organisms is wound-healing. A researcher made extensive observations of the healing process of three severely wounded Blue Tang, *Acanthurus coeruleus*, and a small Yellow Jack. During the first five days after injury, the Blue Tang spent an average of 25 minutes each hour at cleaning stations with gobies, juvenile Spanish Hogfish and Blueheads. Two weeks later, after the wounds completely crusted over, the time was reduced to less than two minutes an hour. The cleaners picked at loose muscle threads, the edges and, to a lesser extent, the surfaces of the fresh wounds. Their bites often caused the injured fishes to jump and, at times, move from the station. In four weeks the

Cleaner shrimps attend to an injured Viper Moray.

black scabs covering the injuries disappeared, leaving only slight indentations. The small Yellow Jack, a non-reef resident, arrived at the patch reef missing one-third of the muscle tissue from its left side. It spent an average of just over 18 minutes an hour in a cleaning station of gobies and juvenile Spanish Hogfish. After 16 days, just four days after the massive wound sealed over, the jack left the area. A juvenile Gray Angelfish picked at an open wound on the leg of an observer for as long as 20 minutes on three successive days. At times the nips were painful. Over a three-day period, we observed Pederson Cleaner Shrimp and Banded Coral Shrimp picking at wounds on the head of a Viper Moray, *Gymnothorax nigricans*, who repeatedly jerked, causing his cleaners to retreat temporarily.

There has been little research on how ectoparasites affect reef fishes. One study conducted in the Exuma Cays Land and Sea Park in the Bahamas removed external parasites from 63 groupers representing four species (44 were

A Brown Chromis hovers within reach of Golden Coral Shrimp.

Nassau Grouper, *Epinephelus striatus*). The fishes were captured in mesh traps, dipped in an anesthetic, immersed in a freshwater bath for five minutes to remove the parasites, injected with an antibiotic, tagged and released where captured. Four species of crustaceans, three from Order Isopoda and one species from Subclass Copepoda, and a single worm from Phylum Platyhelminthes, were recovered and examined. As many as 60 ectoparasites were removed from a single specimen, although a few fishes appeared to be free of infestation.

Typically, isopods are flat on top and bottom, with no definition between body sections. Four hundred fifty parasitic forms infest fishes and invertebrates. The three isopods attached to the infested groupers were free-living species that spend only a portion of their life cycle as parasites. Two species attach to hosts as egg-laying females, temporarily feeding on blood before returning to the bottom. Isopod *Excorallana* sp., live in intertidal areas of rubble, sea grasses sponges and corals; *Alcirona krebsii* inhabit sponges and dead corals. The third isopod, planktonic larvae of *Gnathia* sp., attach to the inside of the mouths and gills of fishes and feed on blood while maturing. After metamorphosis, the adults drop off and burrow into sponges, sediment or algae, where they reproduce.

A Pederson Cleaner Shrimp leaves the protection of an anemone to clean a Blue Chromis.

Symbiosis

Ectoparasites
of
Reef Fishes

Isopod,
Excorallana *sp., 6 mm.*

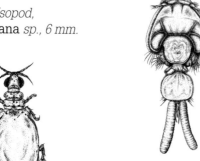

Isopod,
Alcirona krebssi, *6 mm.*

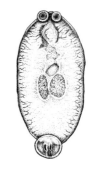

Copepod,
Lepeophtheirus *sp.,*
4 mm.

Isopod,
Gnathia *sp., 3 mm.*

Platyhelminth,
Neobenedenia *sp., 2 mm.*

*Once
settled, a
client fish,
such as this
Nassau
Grouper,
may remain
at a cleaning
station for
an hour.*

Although not reported as cleaners, a terminal phase Bluehead Wrasse cleans the mouth of a Stoplight Parrotfish.

Copepods display diverse body shapes but are generally cylindrical with a division between the head and thorax. More than 1,800 species are known to infest marine and freshwater fishes. Nearly 100 species have been described in the genus *Lepeophtheirus*, to which the specimens collected in the Bahamas belong. If there is a typical shape for copepods, these species certainly don't fit the mold. Flattened bodies offer ease of movement; great head-shields ringed with suckerlike organs provide attachment; and sharp mandibles penetrate into the flesh below. Two sausage-shaped egg sacs trail from the abdomen. These four-millimeter brutes were the most prevalent parasites found during the study.

The single specimen from Phylum Platyhelminthes was identified to genus *Neobenedenia*. The free-swimming ciliated larvae of the tiny two-millimeter worms attach permanently to the body or gills, where they feed on mucous and blood. A genus member, *N. melleni*, causes considerable problems for the tropical aquarium fish and cultured fish trades.

A Coney scraps against the bottom – a behavior known as flashing, believed to ease the aggravation of parasites.

113

Symbiosis

It is believed, but as yet unconfirmed, that hosts employ different cleaning organisms to relieve infestations of specific parasites. Some fishes attempt to eliminate or relieve the irritation of pests themselves. Flashing occurs when a fish swimming along the bottom suddenly turns on its side, arches laterally and scrapes against the sea floor. The spectacular water-clearing leaps of Manta, *Manta birostris*, and Spotted Eagle Ray, *Aetobatus narinari*, culminating in great belly flops are possibly intended to relieve parasitation.

Mutualism

A straightforward mutualistic relationship exists between Orangespotted Goby, *Nes longus*, and a snapping shrimp from genus *Alpheus*. The nearly blind shrimps typically excavate burrows in shallow mud or sandy bottoms near mangroves or along the sloping edges of canals. The sediment-filtering crustaceans have little to worry about while underground, but once above the surface they become easy pickings for hungry carnivores hunting the sand. Gobies also find life difficult on the open sand. They have no problem seeing potential predators, but finding a suitable place to hide is another matter. To adapt, the blurry-eyed shrimps and the homeless gobies join forces for their mutual benefit.

From dawn to dusk, the tiny, nearsighted shrimps maintain winding burrow tunnels connecting two or three enlarged chambers by hauling dirt up from below. The gobies perch on furrows leading from burrow openings, except now and again, when they dart a few inches away to grab a mouthful of sand that is filtered for food and discarded through the gill openings. When above ground, the shrimps always keep at least one antenna in contact with the gobies, usually near the tail. Signals range from a slight tail twitch, indicating caution, to a thrash for alarm. Once a warning is given, the time it takes for everyone to disappear can be measured in tenths of a second. But even in panic there are proprieties – the shrimp always enters the burrow first. The subterranean passages where they hide are typically one inch in diameter, two to four feet long and run a few inches under the surface. The instability of the upper sections creates constant maintenance, and new openings must be dug frequently.

An Orangespotted Goby lives in a mutualistic relationship with a near-blind snapping shrimp. The goby keeps guard for the shrimp who, in turn, keeps a burrow in good repair for both animals.

Because of their vigilant nature, the duos are difficult, but not impossible, to approach closely. Once a goby is sighted, remain still for a minute or two before moving slowly in its direction. The reward of watching the shrimps bulldozing their entranceways is worth a wait. The shrimps battle the shifting sands like single-minded power robots – heaving and hoisting, jamming and cramming, poking and plowing. Using their single enlarged snapping claws, they lift shell fragments twice their weight.

A mated pair of Cymothoid isopods clings to the head of a Coney.

Commensalism

Large, segmented isopods from the family Cymothoidae attach to the heads or internal gill structures of several common reef fish species. Unlike their flesh-burrowing brethren, Cymothoids attach to the skin with seven pairs of hooklike legs and benignly scavenge specks of floating food. Far from killing the hosts, their long-term associations cause only minor skin discoloration, scale erosion or, at worst, slight bone deformities. These monster isopods, sometimes growing to three inches, begin life as tiny, one-eighth-inch, free-swimming males. Once associated with a fish, they lose their ability to swim and remain where they settle for life.

Typically only a single female or a mated pair colonize a host. To increase their odds of finding mates, male Cymothoids have the ability to transform into females. When a male settles on a host with a female already in place, it mates

Symbiosis

Cymothoid isopods are quite particular about which species they infest and the exact location on the fish where they attach.

with the larger female. Later, after the female dies, the male changes sex and awaits the arrival of a young male. If a mate is not present at settlement, a male accelerates growth and prematurely changes into a female. The largest and darkest individuals are invariably brooding females, sometimes incubating more than 100 juveniles inside their bulky ventral pouches. When fully

Cymothoid isopods only attach under the eyes of Foureye Butterflyfish.

developed, the offspring emerge one at a time. While collecting Cymothoids, researchers discovered that each time they speared a fish carrying a pregnant female, the isopod instantly discharged her entire brood. This behavior, termed a burst release, is evidently intended to save the offspring during attacks on hosts. The vulnerable youngsters are fair game while searching for a compatible host, and even after settling they continue to suffer predation from cleaner fishes and shrimps until they begin to grow. Like all crustaceans, isopods must molt to grow; however, if their entire exoskeleton were shed at one time they would lose their life-sustaining grip. The parasites resolve their dilemma by first molting the front half of their bodies, and later, after their legs harden, slough off the remaining shell.

Although Cymothoid isopods inhabit tropical seas around the world, divers most frequently observe the large external species while exploring the coral reefs of the tropical western Atlantic. To date, 12 species from two genera have been classified from the Caribbean. The nine members of genus *Anilocra* are broadly distributed, but the different species tend to inhabit specific regions. While diving in the southern Caribbean, you might find them attached to Creole-fish, *Paranthias furcifer*; in the Bahamas they are most frequently sighted on Coney, *Epinephelus fulvus*, and Blackbar Soldierfish, *Myripristis jacobus*. The three species in genus *Renocila* are restricted to isolated sites off Puerto Rico and the Dominican Republic.

The large isopods are quite choosy about their hosts. Of the nine *Anilocra*, eight infest a specific fish species or the members of a single genus. One associates with three genera in the grunt and sea bass families. The isopods' scientific names are derived from the host. For example, *A. abudefdufi* associate with Sergeant Major, *Abudefduf saxatilis*; *A. myripristis* with Blackbar Soldierfish and *A. chromis* with Brown and Blue Chromis, *Chromis multilineatus* and *C. cyanea*. Other infested fishes include four species of butterflyfishes; four species of sea basses; nine species of grunts; Squirrelfish, *Holocentrus adscensionis*; Doctorfish, *Acanthurus chirurgus*; Ocean Surgeonfish, *A. bahianus*; Bicolor Damselfish, *Stegastes partitus*, and the Rock Beauty, *Holacanthus tricolor*. In addition, *Renocila* infest two cardinalfishes and the Harlequin Bass, *Serranus tigrinus*. *Anilocra* also are quite particular about where they attach. *A. abudefdufi* always settles beneath the eyes of Sergeant Major; *A. acanthuri* fastens under the pectoral fins of surgeonfishes; and *A. myripristis* make their homes between the eyes of Blackbar Soldierfish. Of the thousands of *Anilocra* observed by researchers, only four females were located in abnormal positions.

An isopod fastens to the lower lip of a Sunshinefish.

A damselfish carries an isopod behind its gill cover.

Symbiosis

A Greenbanded Goby finds a safe haven within the protective spines of an urchin.

The isopod *A. chromis*, which is known to infest both Blue Chromis and Brown Chromis, for a yet unexplained reason, attaches only to Blue Chromis in a range extending from south Florida through the Bahamas to the Dominican Republic. In the U.S. Virgin Islands and Puerto Rico the same species avoids the Blue Chromis and attaches exclusively to the Brown Chromis, even though both fishes are well represented in each of the two regions. To test regional compatibility, researchers performed an experimental transfer of parasites between the two species of *Chromis*. Isopods were removed from Brown Chromis captured in the U.S. Virgin Islands and reattached to previously uninfested Brown Chromis and to Blue Chromis, a non-compatible host in the area. Then both sets were released back to their home reefs. The Blue Chromis reacted violently to the isopods, and most of the 22 experimental fish had ditched their pests by the end of the first day. All were lost after day two. However, the Brown Chromis seemed undisturbed by the freshly attached females, and all but three still carried the isopods at the end of the seven-day experiment. The study indicates that host species appear to be predisposed to accept the presence of the hulking pest. This might explain why fishes don't go berserk attempting to dislodge the brawny freeloaders.

Other commensal relationships occur on the reef and in the open ocean. The Greenbanded Goby, *Gobiosoma multifasciatum*, shelters within the protective spines of sea urchins, and the Diamond Blenny, *Malacoctenus boehlkei*, often

Diamond Blennies often seek sanctuary within the tentacles of Giant Anemone. Apparently the blennies are unaffected by the anemones' stinging cells.

takes refuge among the tentacles of the Giant Anemone, *Condylactis gigantea*, apparently unaffected by the stinging cells. In open water, small fishes often travel in the company of large fishes and invertebrates. Juvenile jacks regularly convoy near the heads of Great Barracuda, *Sphyraena barracuda*, and sharks. They also cluster within the draping tentacles of jellyfishes. Schools of Man-of-War Fish, *Nomeus gronovii*, live beneath the purplish, gas-filled floats of the Portuguese Man-of-War, *Physalia physalis*, scavenging bits of food captured by their hosts' toxic tentacles. If food is scarce the fish are occasionally devoured by the deadly siphonophores. Boldly banded Pilot Fish, *Naucrates ductor*, accompany sharks, rays and whales.

For protection in the open sea, juvenile jack cluster within the draping tentacles of jellyfishes.

The Conchfish, *Astrapogon stellatus*, a member of the cardinalfish family, inhabits the mantle cavities of living Queen Conch, *Strombus gigas*, during the day. It is not known if the mollusk benefits from the association. The one- to two-inch fish only venture out after dark to feed on planktonic crustaceans just above the bottom or in the water column, often up to 25 feet away from the protection of their hosts. Before sunrise they return, normally entering their hosts through the anterior siphon canal, whether the mantle cavity is open or closed. Most populations occur on the leeward side of islands. Only a single Conchfish inhabits most hosts, but as many as 16 have been found crowded inside a single conch. The small fish have also

A cardinalfish, known as the Conchfish, inhabits the mantle cavities of living Queen Conch.

Symbiosis

been discovered inside penshells and helmet shells, but tests show they prefer living in the Queen Conch. Eggs have been found year-round inside the mouths of brooding males.

The letter-opener-shaped Pearlfish, *Carapus bermudensis*, and the sluggish, bottom-dwelling Five-toothed Sea Cucumber, *Actinopyga agassizi*, form one of the most peculiar commensal relationships in the Caribbean. The elongate, two- to five-inch fish wriggles, head or tail first, through the anus of the sea cucumber and spend its days inside the alimentary canal of its host. At night, it exits the same opening to feed on an assortment of shrimps and other small crustaceans. While inside their hosts, Pearlfish cannibalize recently settled larvae or juveniles of their own species seeking sanctuary inside the same sea cucumber. Probably for this reason, only solitary individuals inhabit most hosts, although researchers have found as many as ten Pearlfish infesting a single sea cucumber. Other than occasionally raising the rear portions of their bodies as the fish make their entries, the sea cucumbers seem unaffected by the association. *C. bermudensis*, the only shallow-water member of the pearlfish family, Carapidae, in the Caribbean, has also been found in limited numbers inside Donkey Dung Sea Cucumbers, *Holothuria mexicana*, and Three-rowed Sea Cucumbers, *Isostichopus badionotus*, in depths below 100 feet. Pearlfish produce jellylike rafts of elliptical eggs that hatch in open water. The elongate pelagic larvae with streaming tail fins settle to the sea floor approximately three months later. Those finding vacant sea cucumbers shrink to one-third of their presettlement length before changing into their definitive shape.

Mimicry

Mimicry is employed in two primary ways: **aggressive mimicry**, where the mimic imitates the appearance and behavior of a harmless species to gain closer access to unsuspecting prey, and **Batesian mimicry**, where a harmless species imitates a predator for protection. Several criteria must be fulfilled to distinguish between true mimicry and the chance resemblance of two species. The mimic and model must share the same habitat and range; the mimic must be less abundant than the model; it must alter its behavior to enhance the resemblance; and it must gain an advantage from the resemblance.

The Wrasse Blenny, *Hemiemblemaria simulus*, is an excellent imitator of the initial phase Bluehead Wrasse, *Thalassoma bifasciatum*. Not only do Wrasse Blenny bear a close visual resemblance to Blueheads, but they are also the only blenny in the Caribbean that, like wrasses, swim with their pectoral fins. These solitary little impersonators hang out in abandoned wormholes in coral heads with only their heads protruding. When herds of Blueheads swim close by, the blennies join the feeding packs. It is still uncertain whether this mimicry is aggressive, Batesian or both. Wrasse Blenny mimic Blueheads possibly because they are part-time cleaners, which may grant a degree of immunity from predation. On the other hand, their mimicry may be aggressive, enabling them to approach unsuspecting prey more easily. The Wrasse Blenny's disguise is so effective that only sharp-eyed fish watchers can pick them out of Bluehead herds. Subtle clues – a red rather than yellow iris, a larger mouth and a scaled body – help distinguish the impostors.

Initial phase Bluehead Wrasse are believed to be models for mimicry because of their role as cleaners.

Wrasse Blenny.

Juvenile Tiger Grouper.

A second mimic of initial phase Bluehead Wrasse, juvenile Tiger Grouper, *Mycteroperca tigris*, closely resemble their models' yellow bodies and broad, dusky midbody stripes. When mixing with foraging Blueheads or when small fishes approach, juvenile Tiger Grouper begin swimming with their pectoral fins and collapse their medial fins for a more wrasselike appearance. The disguise works. A researcher watched a juvenile Tiger Grouper slip into a group of one-inch juvenile Redband Parrotfish, *Sparisoma aurofrenatum*, without causing a flight reaction and capture one of the fish. The young groupers change into adult colors between four and five inches, at about the same size that initial phase Blueheads make their transition to the terminal phase.

One study proposes that Yellowtail Snapper, *Ocyurus chrysurus*, are aggressive mimics of the Yellow Goatfish, *Mulloides martinicus*. These two species are the only reef fishes in the region with bold, bright yellow lateral stripes joining forked yellow tail fins. Although Yellowtail Snapper grow larger than goatfishes, nearly 90 percent are approximately the same size as the goatfish with which they associate. Goatfish scour open sand plains for buried invertebrates in groups of up to 20 individuals. By mixing in with the similar-appearing goatfish, snapper were found to be nearly twice as successful in capturing small fishes such as juvenile Slippery Dick, *Halichoeres bivittatus*, that do not flee from passing goatfish groups or other carnivores attracted to the groups' sand clouds.

Senses & Sound Communication

Schooling fish use vision and lateral lines to maintain their position within a group.

In the clear water world of coral reef fishes, life and death revolve around good vision. Correspondingly, most species have excellent eyesight. Their eyes are much like those of humans, with external corneas and lenses that focus light on retinas packed with photoreceptor cells. However, there are a number of important differences. Because water rapidly absorbs sunlight, fishes in general, and nocturnal-feeders in particular, have large eyes with extremely clear spherical lenses to gather the scarce light. Like our eyes, the retinas of fishes contain rod-shaped and cone-shaped photoreceptors. Species with more rods can see better in low-light situations, whereas fishes with more cones can see details better in bright daylight. Cones provide color vision in humans, but their presence does not mean that fishes distinguish colors as we do. There is a tendency for the cones of reef fishes to be blue-and-green-sensitive, a good combination to contrast targets against the blue backlighting of tropical reefs but not for discriminating among a wide spectrum of colors.

Fish eyes bulge from the head, providing an arching panoramic field of vision that extends almost completely behind the fish. Round lenses positioned in the center of oval-shaped eyeballs allow nearsightedness directly ahead and farsightedness to the side. Fishes such as plankton-pickers, with eyes set close together, have overlapping binocular vision with good depth perception to focus on incoming specks. Those species with eyes farther apart have a wider range

Jewfish eye.

Nassau Grouper eye.

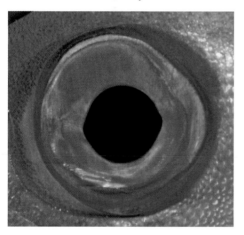

Bigeye eye.

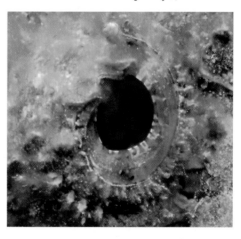

Scorpionfish eye.

Stalked flounder eyes.

Atlantic Flashlightfish eye.

Senses & Sound Communication

The lateral lines of Common Snook are quite obvious.

of vision. As fishes grow, vision improves. Bluehead Wrasse, *Thalassoma bifasciatum*, a plankton-feeding species with high cone density for better resolution, were found to detect particles at greater distances as they matured.

Several nocturnal species, including reef sharks, have a reflecting layer behind the retina known as the **tapetum lucidum**. The tapetum reflects light back through the photoreceptors greatly enhancing low-light vision. During the day the light-sensitive reflective layer is covered to prevent overload and requires about an hour after sunset to regain its full potential. It is this layer that creates the dazzling eyeshine in members of the bigeye and sweeper families when their eyes are illuminated by light beams at night.

The Atlantic Flashlightfish, *Kryptophanaron alfredi*, the only Caribbean representative of family Anomalopidae. The three- to four-inch, primarily deep-dwelling nocturnal fish have a crescent-shaped light organ under each eye. On dark nights individuals occasionally ascend from the depths and temporarily inhabit caves and overhangs along steep slopes and walls as shallow as 40 feet. The organs' blue-green glow, which is believed to either attract or illuminate prey, is generated by a colony of bacteria. The fish turn the light on and off by rotating the organ and simultaneously covering it with a skin fold.

Although eyesight is used primarily to capture prey, smell, taste and electroreception also are used in varying degrees by different species to locate food. Most reef fishes have two paired sets of nasal openings **(nares)** on each side of their heads. Damselfishes, with two single nares, and members of the puffer family, with no nasal openings, are exceptions. Depending on the species, ciliated cells, a pumping action or the force of water pressure when swimming carries water into one of the paired openings. Incoming odors pass along a canal and over a series of epithelial lobes lined with olfactory receptor cells **(olfactory bulbs)** before exiting the second nare. All animals, including reef fishes, exude amino acids known as pheromones from their skin and excretions. Fishes use their keen sense of smell to trace these chemical markers when locating prey and mates or avoiding predators. During courtship, males of most species repeatedly approach and often nudge the vents of egg-laden females to assess their readiness to spawn. It has been shown in laboratory experiments that male Bicolor Damselfish, *Stegastes partitus*, do not respond to nearby spawn-ready females if the pairs are kept chemically isolated by glass partitions.

Morays and sharks, both night-feeders with highly developed senses of smell, have much longer olfactory bulbs than day-feeding fishes. Morays, with virtually no eyesight, have large, obvious incurrent nares on their snouts, often in the form of tubes, and excurrent openings under their eyes. Nurse sharks and hammerhead sharks, with widely separated nares, home in on a distant food source by angling toward the side receiving the strongest olfactory clues. Sharks have been found to respond to fish extracts diluted to as much as one part per ten billion parts of water. Taste buds located in the mouth and on the lips also detect chemical stimuli. The elongate **barbels** of goatfishes are loaded with taste cells, providing a means of "distant taste" when the carnivores scour the sand's surface for hidden invertebrates.

Sharks and rays use electroreception to detect prey at close range. Numerous pores located on the snout, head and lower jaw open into canals filled with electrically conductive gel that lead to clusters of hair-lined chambers known as **ampullae of Lorenzini**. When a hunting shark or ray passes its head within a foot of prey, even if buried, it is able to sense bioelectric energy generated primarily by muscle tissue. The system also is believed to function in some way as an electromagnetic compass to aid navigation.

Because fishes do not have external ear openings, it is often assumed that they are unable to hear. In fact, bony fishes have an elaborate inner ear system consisting of a series of interconnected semicircular fluid-filled canals. These structures, located next to the brain, typically detect sounds of lower frequency than can be perceived by humans. The same system also controls equilibrium. Each of two lower "hearing chambers" widens to house a crystalline calcium carbonate **otolith**, or ear stone, nestled in a bed of hairlike sensory cells. The density of water carries sound in the form of vibrations nearly five times faster and farther than air. These sound waves, when produced at close range, cause

Goatfishes use paired chin barbels to scour the sand for hidden invertebrates.

Senses & Sound Communication

the fish to shift ever so slightly. The ear stones, three times denser than the fish, do not move as readily, causing them to contact surrounding hairs which, in turn, transmit signals to the auditory center of the brain. In many fishes, gas-filled swim bladders behind the inner ear amplify many distant or weak sounds sufficiently to move the otoliths. Three upper canals, each angling in a different direction from a common base and housing a third ear stone, are used to maintain balance and to monitor acceleration. They function like the auditory chamber: movement from side-to-side, up and down or forward shifts fluids creating pressure on sensory hair receptors.

Fishes also have the ability to detect water displacement by a system of hairlike sensory receptors similar to those used in the internal ear. Each tightly packed bundle of protruding hairs, known as a **neuromast**, is encased in a jellylike sheath. A few "free" neuromasts are scattered about the head and body, but most lie within two canals called **lateral lines**. A single canal runs just beneath the skin along each side of the body from the head to the base of the tail. A series of pores, opening to the surface, appears as distinct lines on the sides of many species. A single neuromast extends into the liquid-filled channel between each set of adjoining pores. External water movement creates pressure at the pore opening causing the canal fluid to bend the receptors in a way that allows a fish to sense nearby disturbances and objects and to identify their general locations. Because the sensory cells are housed internally, the system functions when a fish is on the move. Although schooling fishes primarily use vision to maintain their precise positioning, the lateral line is also believed to assist in the process, but exactly how or to what extent has yet to be determined.

When swimming, each species of fish generates a unique sound. It has been proposed that the internal ear system, the lateral line or a combination of the two senses detects approaching predators. Researchers have observed Slippery Dick, *Halichoeres bivittatus*, diving into the sand at the same instant that hydrophones intercepted the sound of an advancing school of Blue Runner, *Caranx crysos*. We have often observed a similar defensive response from schooling grunts. Seconds before hunting packs of jacks come into view, the fish draw closer together and begin to swirl.

Sound Communication

A few fishes use a limited number of sounds to communicate with members of their own and other species. Hard body parts rubbing together (**stridulation**) produces most sounds. The swim bladder, located next to, or connected by taut muscles to the sound-producing structure, serves as an amplifier. Vibrating muscles surrounding the swim bladder also generate sound in a few species. The deep rumblings of grunts, drums and croakers are so distinctive they became the origin of the fishes' common family names. Grunts produce sounds by grinding their flat pharyngeal teeth together. Drums and croakers communicate during the spawning season by vibrating muscles. Because the majority of fish sounds are transmitted at low frequencies, they are seldom heard by divers, but there are a few noteworthy exceptions. Large Nassau Grouper, *Epinephelus striatus*; Black Grouper, *Mycteroperca bonaci*, and

Territorial conflicts between Longspine Squirrelfish, including grunts, shaking and fin displays, end with the fish pressing their rear bodies and tails together.

Jewfish, *E. itajara*, produce loud "booms" when startled or cornered. A first-time encounter with a thundering grouper can be quite startling. The loud sounds possibly could be intended to frighten predators, but this idea has never been substantiated. Jewfish also produce similar sounds during courtship, and researchers have heard juveniles in mangrove shallows boom before taking bait, conceivably to stun small prey. No one will forget a night dive during the spawning season of toadfishes. The amorous males send forth a cacophony of whistling calls, measured to be 30 to 40 decibels louder than any other known sound produced by fishes.

By using hydrophones accommodating lower frequencies, researchers have substantiated that Longjaw Squirrelfish, *Holocentrus marianus*; Longspine Squirrelfish, *H. rufus*, and possibly other members of the family are major sound-producers. The calls, resonating from air bladders, reach a peak during dawn and dusk. Night-foraging squirrelfishes, intensely territorial by day, routinely challenge fishes approaching their hiding holes. Neighboring squirrelfishes are met with a grunt or two, fin displays, head-shaking and nipping lunges. An end to the bickering is generally signaled when the antagonists assume parallel positions and briefly press their rear bodies together. Single calls are directed at small or neighboring fishes, whereas bursts of staccato grunts greet larger intruders.

Without question the most sophisticated vocalists on Caribbean reefs are damselfishes, particularly the highly social Bicolor Damselfish, *Stegastes partitus*. The one- to two-inch plankton-pickers use a combination of displays, color changes, chemical clues and a repertoire of calls to communicate with other members of their size-related hierarchies. Territorial males constantly challenge similar-sized rivals for social position. Hovering head down an inch or so off the bottom, the contestants face one another and emit a series of combative pops. During courtship, inspired males wearing black masks perform a series of eye-catching dips, each accompanied by a chirp. Females respond to these acoustical courtship overtures from as far as 20 feet away. Interested females are not only able to distinguish the locations of the callers but also to differentiate between suitors and to assess their relative sizes.

Marine Wildlife Management

Nassau Grouper trapped during their spawning aggregation.

Commercial and recreational fishermen have long enjoyed a tradition of virtually unrestricted access to the sea that many of them believe to be their inherent right. Their vocal opposition to management policies, including the establishment of no-take reserves, has closely paralleled the rapid decline of inshore fisheries stocks during the last decades of the 20th Century.

Recent evidence that many grouper and snapper spawning aggregations have been exploited to the point of collapse and that reef fish communities are open systems, often relying on larval recruits from distant reefs has only added fuel to the arguments on both sides of the long-simmering management debate. Opponents contend that it would be foolish to limit access to reef tracts or restrict fishing at spawning aggregations if the offspring simply float off to someone else's reefs. Fisheries officers, marine biologists and conservation groups counter in a united voice that no-take reserves are the only realistic solution for managing multispecies fisheries. As usual, the fishing lobby continues to couch its arguments by claiming that the scientific community does not have conclusive evidence supporting the benefits of marine reserves.

Current ecological data may not be conclusive, but is compelling. In the few areas where no-take reserves have been established and monitored, local fisheries stocks have increased, in some instances dramatically. No-take reserves also provide much needed sanctuary for larger, genetically superior members of a species' breeding population. These "ol' mamas and papas" have been documented to be hundreds of times more prolific than smaller individuals just reaching sexual maturity. For instance, a single 25-pound snapper can produce nine million eggs per spawn; it would take 212 smaller snappers to generate an equivalent number. Yet these same great fishes, the primary target of harvesters, go unprotected.

It has become obvious that traditional management strategies are insufficient to cope with the accelerating declines in fisheries stocks. Imposed size-limits, based on the minimum reproductive length of a species, have proven ineffective partly because of the high mortality rate for released fishes. Evaluation of minimum size regulations implemented in Florida during the early 1980s found no obvious increase in the size of Nassau Grouper, *Epinephelus striatus*, and Black Grouper, *Mycteroperca bonaci*. Catch quotas, which are difficult to determine and monitor, also have proven problematic.

Groupers and snappers have suffered more than any other reef fishes. In the 1960s, when divers first began extensive exploration of Caribbean reefs, numerous large groupers were regularly sighted on every dive. Things were quick to change. Within only a few years, spearfishing, fish traps, powered fishing boats and an ever-growing demand for market fish began to take a heavy toll on every grouper species in the region. The big predators, with few natural enemies, had little or no innate fear of men carrying spears. Instead of hiding, the curious fishes often swam off the reef to get a closer look at the approaching oddities. Those surviving the initial slaughter quickly learned to flee from their new enemies or relocated to deeper reefs. At the same time, a proliferation in the use of wire-mesh fish traps by small-scale island fisheries removed substantial numbers of juvenile groupers from inshore areas. However, the deadliest blow dealt the beleaguered groupers has been the overharvesting of their annual spawning aggregations. With thousands of large reproductive groupers simultaneously gathering from miles around into restricted areas at predictable times, it was like catching fish in a barrel. The annual economic boom for local fisheries spelled disaster for the groupers.

Although a small number of inshore spawning aggregations had been harvested since the early years of the twentieth century, a sufficient number of remote locations remained unmolested, helping to sustain breeding stock. But by the 1960s, even the distant breeding grounds began to suffer from advanced technology and growing fishing fleets. In just a few years, many heavily fished aggregations, which may have existed for centuries, no longer reformed.

All grouper species have shown marked decreases in the average size of individuals and population numbers. Aggregate spawning groupers, including Red Hind, *Epinephelus guttatus;* Jewfish, *E. itajara;* Gag, *Mycteroperca microlepis,* and Scamp, *M. phenax,* have suffered heavily; but none has declined as precipitously as Nassau Grouper. Its populations have been so devastated in the past four decades that the species is considered commercially extinct in the continental United States, U. S. Virgin Islands, Puerto Rico and Bermuda. Since the 1970s numerous spawning aggregations, some estimated between 30,000 and 100,000 fish before heavy fishing pressures began, have ceased to reform in the Cayman Islands, Dominican Republic, Jamaica, Mexico and the Bahamas. In Bermuda, Nassau Grouper landings declined by 95 percent between 1975 and 1981. Comparable declines have been reported throughout much of the Caribbean Basin and the Bahamas.

Marine Wildlife Management

Marine ecologists under joint sponsorship of The Florida Department of Environmental Protection and National Marine Fisheries Service recently conducted extensive research on Gag, Scamp and Red Grouper, *E. morio,* populations to better understand how the species' reproductive behavior affects their susceptibility to overexploitation. Each of these three commercially important grouper species in the Gulf of Mexico and the southeastern United States has been confirmed to be protogynous hermaphrodites (changing from females to males), with a naturally female-heavy sex ratio. However, while Gag and Scamp migrate in large numbers to annual spawning grounds, Red Grouper remain in their home ranges and spawn at a variety of depths in small, widely scattered groups unsusceptible to concentrated fishing. Gag, reproductively active between February and April, gather over the sea floor in depths ranging from 150 to 375 feet and form into numerous subgroups numbering between ten and 100 individuals. During the remainder of the year, females inhabit shallow inshore areas apart from the deeper-dwelling males. Scamp often share the same offshore reefs with Gag during breeding periods, but the two groups do not intermix. The reproductive behavior of both species is quite similar except for the longer spawning season of Scamp, from February until June.

Comparison of recent commercial landing data with catches made 15 to 30 years earlier reveals that Gag and Scamp, both aggregate spawners, have suffered a marked decline in numbers and mean size. But a substantial change in the sex ratios of both species is even more disturbing. Prior to 1980 the Gag population off South Carolina contained 17 percent males, but by the mid 1990s the number of males had dropped to less than four percent. The patterns for Scamp are similar but less dramatic. At the same time Red Grouper, just as heavily fished, show negligible decreases in size and almost no difference in sex ratio. Although the exact mechanisms creating the imbalance are not known, it appears that unregulated fishing of spawning aggregations is a key factor in the declining populations of both Gag and Scamp.

Theoretically, protogyny should compensate for the loss of males by increasing the transition of females into males. But evidently this isn't happening with Gag and other aggregate-spawning groupers. One possible explanation is that fishing pressures select for males, removing them faster than they can be replaced. Both males and transitional males are known to take a hook more aggressively than females. It is generally believed that social mechanisms, rather than size or age, influence the timing of sexual transition. If this is the case, the rapid removal of so many individuals from spawning aggregations could disrupt the cues necessary to initiate sexual transition. And because males and females coexist only during reproduction, the cues are most likely passed during the brief period when the sexes are together in aggregations.

Today, with the sex ratio of Gag populations so out of balance, more and more females, even though well fed, are unable to reach their reproductive potential. Increasing numbers of females remain inshore during spawning periods. Others migrating to breeding grounds fail to have their eggs fertilized because of a shortage of males or they spawn incompletely or not at all. Atresia, the reabsorption of unspawned eggs, common in underfed populations, has recently been detected in healthy Gag and Scamp, possibly another negative effect of fewer males.

Marine Wildlife Management

At the turn of the 21st Century, Bermuda, the Bahamas and the Dominican Republic are the only governments to ban harvesting of grouper aggregations. Other countries have tiptoed around the problem by implementing half-measures – compromises following opposition from commercial fishing interests. The Cayman Islands have closed aggregation fishing to all but local fishermen using hook and line. Mexico has prohibited the use of spearguns along the Yucatan coastline since 1990; in Belize, gear restrictions apply at spawning aggregations, and Cuba has placed a harvesting quota on Nassau Grouper since 1985.

In the 1980s the United States, armed with strong evidence of an impending population collapse, took a timid step by instituting a minimum size limit of 12 inches for Nassau Grouper, with plans to increase the limit by one inch each year until reaching a length of 24 inches in the mid 1990s. The increments were designed to ease economic hardships on commercial fishermen. It was not until 1990, however, when there were essentially no more Nassau Grouper of any size to protect, that a moratorium prohibiting their harvest was finally imposed. If a far-reaching management strategy is not implemented throughout the Bahamas and Caribbean Basin, Nassau Grouper may soon become the first major reef fish to go the way of the Passenger Pigeon. And if harvesting continues at its present rate, several other grouper species could quickly follow their path to extinction.

Three large shallow-water species of snapper, Mutton Snapper, *Lutjanus analis;* Dog Snapper, *L. jocu,* and Cubera Snapper, *L. cyanopterus,* also gather in exploitable spawning aggregations. We once counted more than 60 fishing boats anchored over a Mutton Snapper aggregation just west of Bimini, Bahamas. Fishermen worked the site from morning until two hours after sunset, with a reported peak in harvesting activities just before dark. How long this and dozens of other heavily fished aggregations will continue to reform each summer is hard to predict. In 1991, researchers visiting a Mutton Snapper aggregation in the Dry Tortugas Islands, Florida, which had been heavily fished by commercial vessels for several years, found only a scattering of fish. Although the specimens collected were heavy with sperm or hydrated eggs, no spawning formations were observed. The site, known as Riley's Hump, is now closed to harvesting during the spawning season. Only time will tell if overharvested snapper aggregations will reestablish, once protected.

Groupers and snappers are only two market fishes in decline. According to the World Wide Fund for Nature, fisheries are in trouble around the world. The Fund estimates that 60 percent of the 200 most valuable species, including many reef fishes, are presently overfished or fished to the limit. As the largest and most commercially valuable piscivores are overexploited, fisheries harvest lower on the food chain, further degrading ecosystems. It is increasingly obvious that the current level of global fishing pressure is unsustainable, leaving fisheries management with few options but to impose harvesting bans for extended periods. Even though every recent fisheries study calls for the immediate establishment of additional no-take areas, less than one percent of the world's fishing grounds are protected at present.

Coral reefs provide the only source of protein for many economically deprived coastal societies in the tropics. For them sustaining marine resources is a matter of life or death. A ten-year fish population study from 1983 to 1993 at two islands in the Philippines provides valuable insight into the effects of subsistence fishing on local reefs. The researchers estimated that 15 percent of the fish biomass is removed annually at one island and 25 percent at the other. Even with such heavy harvesting, species diversity was little affected. Only a marked decline in top predators was evident, although this did not cause a proliferation of prey species. Even though the communities' biomass was lowered, primarily because of targeting of large individuals, no loss in relative abundance was noted. The researchers concluded that the local reef fish population's long-term resilience was due to four factors: an open system with a healthy upstream recruitment supply; the absence of keystone species; the use of non-destructive harvesting methods, and the relatively non-selective catches of the fishermen.

Those species whose loss causes a profound change in the community structure are known as keystone species. An example is the relationship between herbivorous fishes and sea urchins. A major Caribbean-wide die-off of Long-spined Urchins, *Diadema antillarum*, in 1983 left an abundance of ungrazed algae which caused an increase in parrotfish and surgeonfish populations in most locations. In Jamaica, however, where overfishing had previously eliminated the two primary families of herbivorous fishes, unchecked algal blooms in the absence of urchins smothered many coral reefs. In Kenya, overfishing of triggerfishes, a natural predator of urchins, allowed the urchin population to increase rapidly, putting severe competitive pressure on herbivorous fishes. Interestingly, preliminary investigations indicate that major predators are not keystone species. It is believed that because the big piscivores are opportunistic feeders, regularly taking a wide variety of fishes, their selective removal from a reef community seldom increases the abundance of prey species.

In 1983, after a nine-year closure, one of two reserves in the Philippines study area was reopened to fishing. More than 100 fishermen began harvesting the reef with hook and line, spears, bamboo fish traps, gill nets and extremely destructive explosives and drive-nets. A gallon canister of explosives dropped with a delay fuse obliterates standing corals for 15 feet in every direction and kills every fish and invertebrate across a much broader area. Drive-netting involves a chain of humans, each equipped with a weighted scare-line which is dropped repeatedly as the workers herd fishes toward a bag net. By the time the reserve was closed again a year-and-a half-later, 40 percent of the area's coral garden lay in rubble, and parrotfishes and small plankton-eating wrasses had replaced the majority of local predators, damselfishes, butterflyfishes and fusiliers. Six years after re-closing, the reserve once again supported an abundant fish population, but the destruction of coral did not allow the reef to regain its previous community structure.

The Philippines study indicates that subsistence fisheries are sustainable without altering the reef fish community if a wide range of species is harvested in proportion to their abundance and if non-destructive fishing methods are used. The authors caution that their ten-year study was brief in relation to the maximum life expectancy of many reef fishes and that substantial shifts in populations can occur if harvesting becomes excessive.

In a fishing-impact study closer to home, Florida and federal fisheries researchers built a series of 22 experimental artificial reef sites in the Gulf of Mexico. Each reef consisted of 24 or 96 prefabricated 36-inch concrete cubes with open horizontal cores arranged in hexagonal formations. The structures were deployed between 1990 and 1993 in 40 feet of water 16 miles west from the mouth of Florida's Suwannee River. An extensive survey of the flat sand bottom prior to the project found few Gag grouper, the study species, in the area. After five years it was estimated that more than 400 Gag resided on each of the larger artificial reefs. In 1996 nine sites were opened experimentally to public fishing. As predicted, the Gag were hit hard. In less than eight months 40 percent of the resident populations, accounting for 77 percent of the biomass, were gone, leaving virtually no legal-sized Gag at several reefs.

The project provided scientific information to help resolve the "attraction-production issue" surrounding the use of artificial reefs. For over two decades, an assortment of structures has been placed on the sea floor in the belief that additional habitat would increase fish populations. Today, most marine ecologists have come to the conclusion that populations are limited more by fluctuating larval recruitment than by habitat restriction. A Japanese study published in 1989 concluded that artificial reefs increased populations only for octopuses. It demonstrated that recruitment fluctuated with the number of arriving larvae and that the adult fishes living on the study's reefs were attracted from surrounding waters. This supports the thinking of several researchers, who have long contended that artificial reefs act as nothing more than fish attractors for anglers. This certainly appears to have been the case in the Gulf of Mexico Gag study.

Today, fisheries managers are far more sophisticated in their use of artificial habitats. If utilized properly, artificial reefs work well for testing ecological theories and models, enhancing low-relief hard-bottom areas, increasing the density of juveniles and, when designed for specific fishes, reducing predation and increasing foraging efficiency of targeted species. Harmful practices such as deploying unstable materials and sinking large vessels with explosives are out of favor. Instead, managers are using structures that more closely imitate natural reefs and have fewer tendencies to break apart or move during storms. Lessons learned from the Gag project include the importance of designing small, complex structures scaled to the target species, spacing structures far apart and, above all, not advertising their location to the public.

It seems only right that a percentage of coral reefs around the world should be set aside as wilderness areas, much like national parks on land. The reefs' diverse collections of exotic animals are irresistible attractions for thousands of sightseers year after year. Yet only a handful of governments have seen fit to manage their reefs for the benefit of visitors. The few Caribbean governments with the vision to manage their marine ecosystems are reaping benefits today. In the 1980s, the reefs of the Cayman Islands were protected by a series of replenishment zones and marine parks which are teeming with sea life today. Paul Humann, who captained the Caribbean's first live-aboard dive vessel, the *Cayman Diver*, and pioneered many of the area's popular dive sites during the 1970s, revisited the islands nearly 30 years later. While diving along the wall, he sighted far more Spotted Eagle Rays, *Aetobatus narinari*, than he had ever seen. It was only later, when he saw several of the great fish feeding in the shallow-water replenishment zone, that he made the connection. One of the Spotted Eagle Ray's primary foods is Queen Conch, *Strombus gigas*, a species making a strong comeback in the islands since being protected from harvesting. Humann felt that the adoption of a

Marine Wildlife Management

marine management program had resulted in more fishes inhabiting the reefs now than during the early days of recreational diving on the island.

Even small marine reserves have proven successful for fishermen and tourists. A reef-lined cove set aside as a no-take reserve on the eastern Caribbean island of St. Lucia has, in only a few years, become a hit with visitors and has increased the catch rate of local fishermen in the waters outside the reserve's boundaries.

Reserve opponents often point to the perceived difficulties of policing no-take zones. Fortunately, enforcement has not yet presented a significant problem. Without official monitoring of any form, there has been 68 per cent compliance by harvesters just after the establishment of reserves, and compliance increases with time. In New Zealand commercial fishermen became the unauthorized enforcers of boundaries – their attitude is that if the area is off limits to their then it is certainly not going to be fished by their competitors. In attempts to limit public support, fishing lobbies often call for the exclusion of divers and snorkelers from no-take reserves, citing the damage inflicted on living corals by underwater sightseers. Unfortunately, there is considerable misinformation about divers' negative impact on corals. While careless or uncaring visitors do on rare occasion break branching corals and sponges or mar the surface of boulder-type corals, the damage is mostly aesthetic and rarely jeopardizes the health of the affected colony. Branching corals propagate asexually from breakage, and the living veneer of coral tissue, relatively impervious to incidental diver contact, typically heals in a matter of days. This is not to say that contact with coral is acceptable or should be ignored. We certainly would not think of walking across a flower bed in a public park. Environmental etiquette and buoyancy control skills should be encouraged and practiced. But restricting divers from protected marine reserves makes as much sense as limiting hunting in Yellowstone Park but not allowing anyone in to appreciate the natural resources. If it were not for the economic impact and the environmental concerns of underwater sightseers, there would be few, if any, protected reefs in the Caribbean. Those fortunate enough to visit a coral garden become the reefs' most ardent advocates. If there were twice as many divers and snorkelers coral reefs would be twice as safe, not the other way around.

Misapprehension also exists concerning the use of mooring buoys to prevent anchor damage at heavily dived reef sites. Concentrated underwater activities do create a disproportionate amount of wear and tear around moorings, but the damage is minimal when measured against the destruction caused by dropping and retrieving anchors. The use of moorings correlates well with the practice of cutting public trails in land parks. In both cases, the harm to a limited area is easily outweighed by the long-term benefit to the surrounding habitat.

Although reef fishes seldom migrate far from where they settle, the offspring of most species are carried by currents to populate distant reefs. Likewise, most reefs are dependent upon larval recruits spawned miles upcurrent. This interconnective process of give-and-take maintains population size and biodiversity on coral reefs across widespread regions. The concept makes it easy to understand how the continued overharvesting of local breeding stocks adversely affects the fisheries of downcurrent neighbors. The most practical solution for everyone would be a system of strategically placed no-take reserves. Each should protect at least ten percent of the coral reefs of every nation in an interconnected larval transport chain – an idea that best fits what we know about the reproduction and recruitment of marine populations.

By taking human consumption out of the equation, reefs will manage themselves. No-take reserves have already proven to increase the density of breeding populations, protect the larger, more prolific individuals and elevate fertilization rates. However, doing the right thing is not always easy. A map (following page) of the region's prevailing surface currents – the probable routes of larval transport – paints a clear picture of the geo-political implications of managing a vast interdependent resource. To sell such a politically sensitive idea, politicians will need a simple, easy-to-understand master plan, the cooperation of partner nations and the example of a working model with a proven track record.

The first geographic guideline for establishing a Caribbean-wide network of reserves was proposed by Callum Roberts in *Science*. To work effectively the reserves must be close enough to receive an adequate larvae supply from upcurrent sources and, at the same time, deliver larvae effectively to downcurrent reserves and intervening reefs. Roberts calculated that the average minimum and maximum inter-reserve distances should be 90 and 125 miles respectively. These distances were computed by multiplying the local rate of current flow by 30- and 60-day envelopes – the average periods larvae remain as plankton before settlement. Using a series of maps, Roberts indicates the probable larval dispersal routes for 18 locations. At the low end of the scale are isolated reef systems, such as Barbados in the far eastern Caribbean and the Flower Gardens in the Gulf of Mexico, which are totally dependent on self-recruitment. Andros Island in the Bahamas and the middle Florida Keys, both bathed by currents from numerous upstream reefs, represent the opposite end of the spectrum. Roberts' approach makes the assumption that larvae are basically passive planktonic travelers, a matter still under study, and he also disregards the possible relevance of nearshore countercurrents and seasonal gyres on the distribution process. However, the plan represents a much-needed beginning for managing a long-neglected resource.

The majority of the 18 larval transport chains detailed by Roberts spans the waters of multiple nations. Reserve networks represented by the 30-day envelope involve from one to six national management partners, with an average of just over two. Expanding to the 60-day envelope, the average escalates to 3.5 nations per network. For example, using the 30-day model, partners of the U.S. Virgin Islands include Puerto Rico and the British Virgin Islands; the 60-day envelope reaches west, encompassing St. Martin, Anguilla and the Netherlands Antilles. Convincing so many partner nations to cooperate in such a political complex might appear impractical were it not for one common bond – declining reef fish populations.

Possibly the best promotion for a system of reserves would be an example of an established network already at work. Unfortunately, it would require traveling all the way to New Zealand, which has 12 no-take reserves scattered around the country, and to South Africa, with eight, to find even a semblance of a "system." And even though these nations are trendsetters, their protected areas were established for a variety of reasons and without a clear policy for

Marine Wildlife Management

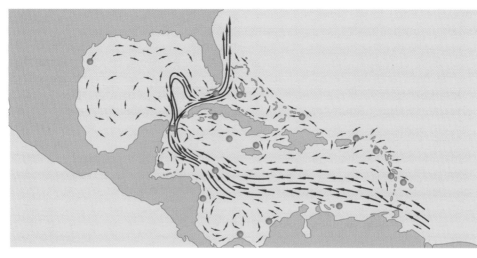

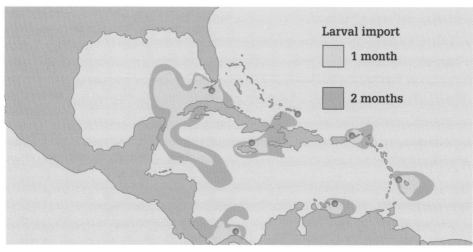

Larval import

1 month

2 months

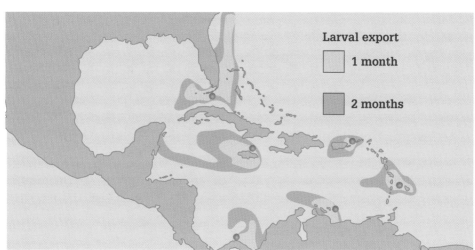

Larval export

1 month

2 months

creating additional reserves. Things in the Western Hemisphere are much worse. In fact, the few no-take areas are widely separated independent reserves located in Belize, Bonaire, the Exuma Islands in the Bahamas, Honduras, Saba and one embarrassingly small, site in the Florida Keys Marine Sanctuary.

The United States lost a banner opportunity to set the standard for marine conservation when Congress created the 3,674-square-mile Florida Keys National Marine Sanctuary in 1990. The concerted efforts of marine scientists, conservation groups and Florida and federal agencies to implement a system of no-take reserves within the Sanctuary turned out to be no match for the fishing lobby. The original management plan, allocating ten percent of the Sanctuary for three no-take reserves was, after an initial campaign, whittled down to six percent. Still dissatisfied, the fishermen rallied the support of local residents and turned their self-serving crusade nasty and personal. Sanctuary managers and fisheries personnel were embarrassed, ridiculed and hanged in effigy. During six years of contention the number and size of the reserves steadily dwindled until the final draft contained only the single 9-square-nautical mile Western Sambos Ecological Reserve, an area encompassing less than one-half of one percent of the Sanctuary.

Commercial fishermen tend to be an independent lot with little patience for rules, regulations and paperwork. As fishing methods mechanize, competition multiplies, regulations encroach and fish stocks plummet, they become more defensive. Commercial and recreational fishermen, more than any other groups, have witnessed the sharp decline of fish stocks in recent decades. In their heart of hearts, both groups must realize that no-take reserves are not only inevitable but also an urgent necessity to protect their long-term interests. If breeding stocks continue to be exploited at the present rate, even more fisheries will collapse. If this occurs it could be a long time, if ever, before the species make a comeback to sustainable numbers. However, with wise fisheries management, it is possible that limited-yield fishing could continue indefinitely.

But what about marine fishes that do not have commercial value? What about the damselfishes, the trunkfishes, the gobies, the blennies and the hundreds of other irreplaceable fishes? It is hard to believe that their fates, as well as those of all other creatures on the reef, are not intrinsically linked to gamefishes and market fishes. A system of protected and properly administered no-take marine reserves, extending from inshore habitats to offshore depths not only would be a boon for the "ol' mamas and papas" and spawning aggregations, but also would provide reef fishes with the diverse habitats required for survival of their larval recruits.

The number of fish larvae carried off to distant reef systems, often outside a nation's boundaries, and the number caught in gyres and spun back to their reefs of origin, remains unknown. But if we wait for all the answers before taking action, it will be too late to save much of our remaining marine wildlife. Systems of no-take reserves are the last best hope for reef fishes around the world.

(A) Major surface current patterns in the wider Caribbean region. The thickness of arrows are approximately proportional to a current's strength. Few of the weak nearshore countercurrents, common to most coastlines, are shown. (B) One- and two-month envelopes of potential larval transport indicating the probable upstream larval sources for six of the 18 locations studied. (C) From the same six locations, one- and two-month envelopes of potential larval transport showing downstream areas where larvae could settle.

Angelfishes
Family Pomacanthidae

Rock Beauty.

Large, graceful and bedecked with fins, angelfishes – the quintessential tropical reef residents – constantly attract the diver's eye. Even though western Atlantic waters host only seven of the world's 74 Angelfishes, the seven are spectacular species from three genera. One of the most exquisite, the Queen Angelfish, *Holacanthus ciliaris*, is regularly sighted on coral reefs across the region, while the large and lovable Gray Angelfish, *Pomacanthus arcuatus*; the spirited Rock Beauty, *H. tricolor*; and the delightful little Cherubfish, *Centropyge argi*, add a touch of class to any reef scene. Interestingly, each of these Atlantic species, with the exception of the Rock Beauty, has a closely related and similar-appearing counterpart. Queen Angelfish are so closely allied with Blue Angelfish, *H. bermudensis*, that the two species often interbreed, producing fertile hybrids. French Angelfish, *P. paru*, and Grays are not only similar in size and appearance, but also share habitats and many of the same foods. Cherubfish are comparable to the Flameback Angelfish, *C. aurantonotus*, in size, behavior, diet and basic color scheme.

Until the mid-70s, angelfishes were considered to be a subfamily of butterflyfishes, Chaetodontidae. The two groups certainly have many things in common: both are round, laterally compressed, have continuous dorsal fins, swim alike and even behave in much the same way. A well-developed preopercular spine on the gill covers of angelfishes differentiates family members from butterflyfishes. Fish watchers can make a quicker identification

Queen Angelfish.

Blue Angelfish.

Gray Angelfish.

French Angelfish.

Cherubfish.

Flameback Angelfish.

Angelfishes

by noting the extended rear dorsal and anal fins common to most angelfishes but absent on butterflyfishes.

At first glance, slow-moving angelfishes would seem to be easy targets for predators, but the family's typically large size and thin round bodies present awkward mouthfuls for those interested in a quick meal. On the other hand, the darting, reclusive nature of the small juvenile Rock Beauty and Cherubfish attests to their vulnerability. French and Gray Angelfish juveniles have taken an alternate route to self-preservation by becoming cleaners who move freely in open water picking annoying ectoparasites from reef fishes. Their conspicuous black and golden markings – strikingly different from the patterns they will wear as adults – advertise their role as cleaners, a strategy that greatly increases their chances of escaping predation.

Only 11 Caribbean fishes are known to feed regularly on sponges; five are angelfishes.

Sponge-eating species, including angelfishes, evolved during recent geological time, possibly as a response to increased competition for food on coral reefs. Sponges by their nature are a distasteful food. The primitive organisms are laced with tiny internal supports of indigestible and irritating calcareous and siliceous spicules. Repellent chemicals and tough, fibrous exteriors add to their repugnance. Nonetheless, the tissue from a wide variety of sponges makes up 95 percent of the food consumed by species in the genus *Holacanthus* (Rock Beauty, Queen and Blue Angelfish) and 70 percent in *Pomacanthus* (Gray and French Angelfish). Two of the most frequently eaten sponges contain the least amount of spicules, but many of the angelfishes' choices are packed with the mineralized structures. Several species toxic to humans are also regularly eaten. Angelfishes seldom devour an entire sponge. Instead, they follow timeworn paths leading from colony to colony, taking a few bites from each as they go. The sponge-eaters have developed strong, protracting jaws lined with overlapping rows of tightly packed teeth to shear through the sponges' tough fiber. A thick coating of mucus secreted around lumps of food helps to protect their stomachs during digestion. Algae is the primary food of juveniles and adult Cherubfish and Flameback Angelfish. Juveniles acting as cleaners obtain only 25 percent of their food by volume from picking parasites off fishes; the remaining 75 percent is filamentous algae.

The five larger species establish territories to defend mates rather than to protect food supplies. Trespassing juveniles and adults of the same species are quickly chased, while other fishes, even with similar diets, are generally ignored. Even though they brim with sponges and other foods, uninhabited areas just outside established territories often go ungrazed. The two little *Centropyge* species constantly guard their turf from other small algae-eating species but, because their small territories are widely spaced, they seldom have reason to defend their harems from neighboring males.

Not much is known about the reproductive behavior of Atlantic angelfishes, and the little information available is often based on contradictory observations. Family members share a few similarities: all spawn at sunset during a limited period; spawning always occurs between a single male and female; pelagic eggs are shed in the water column after a spawning rise; spawning periods are not based on the lunar calendar and possibly take place during all seasons. Gray and French Angelfish are believed to be monogamous, perhaps forming lifelong bonds, but there have been a few reports of promiscuous spawning events for both species. It is possible that each species follows two reproductive agendas, or perhaps populations in one region spawn differently from those in another. This may be the case with Cherubfish, who maintain multifemale harems dominated by a single male in the southern and eastern Caribbean, while in Florida and the Bahamas many individuals appear to live as monogamous pairs.

The three species of *Holacanthus* and two species of *Centropyge* are protogynous hermaphrodites that typically live in harems. There, the largest female changes sex after the disappearance of a dominant male. Large sex-changed males mate exclusively with from one to four females living within defended territories. To keep tabs on their mates, males visit each in turn throughout the day and briefly forage at their sides before continuing on their rounds. Boundaries are regularly patrolled to maintain territorial sovereignty.

Species that form harems participate in similar courtship and spawning behavior. Every evening, dominant males spawn with females living in their harems. Courtship begins with males repeatedly presenting themselves laterally while displaying erect fins. Subsequent visits intensify and lengthen. Before actually mating, females make several false spawning rises, but each time the males attempt to position next to their sides, the females dart back to the bottom. When finally ready to shed their eggs, females ascend higher than

Angelfishes

before. The males approach from below and place their snouts on or near the females' genital openings and gently nudge them up into the water column. A sudden push on the females' abdomens forces the eggs to discharge. In the same instant, the males roll on their sides, placing their genital openings close to the females and shed sperm. The pairs quickly separate and dive for the bottom, where the females briefly nip or chase the males. The transparent clouds of gametes mix and disperse with the currents. Fertilized eggs hatch into slender larvae within 15 to 20 hours. Three to four weeks later, they settle in shallow water habitats and quickly transform into juveniles.

The sex of Gray and French Angelfish remains unchanged throughout life (gonochorism). Similar-sized pairs form extended, possibly lifelong, monogamous relationships. The lovely courtship of Gray Angelfish seems affectionate – during their slow spawning rises, the females gently flutter their tails against the faces of their mates.

Gray Angelfish
Pomacanthus arcuatus
&
French Angelfish
Pomacanthus paru

There is not a more amiable character on the reef than the stately Gray Angelfish. The slow-swimming, dinner-plate-sized fish seem to enjoy the companionship of divers, often following them closely for minutes at a time, snapping at bubbles or peering at their image in a face plate or camera port as if admiring their regal reflections. The frugally colored grayish fish, accentuated

A juvenile Gray Angelfish cleans needlefish.

A mated pair of French Angelfish.

by white lips, are reported to reach a length of two feet, but few grow to over 16 inches. Mated pairs live within large territories averaging more than 2,400 square yards that often slope seaward from ten to 80 feet. Territories are protected from members of their own species, who are challenged and chased. The species is known to congregate occasionally in groups of up to 20 individuals that move about together in loose formations within a customary area. The function of these gatherings remains unexplained.

Gray Angelfish seldom take shelter as they roam their territories in the company of their similar-sized mates, who typically remain by their sides for nearly half the day. When reunited after extended separations the pairs circle enthusiastically, as if pleased to be back together. They often swim well off the bottom, dropping down occasionally to forage at the leisurely rate of three or four bites per minute. Four terraced rows of slender, pointed, tightly packed teeth, shear chunks of fibrous tissue from a variety of sponges – their favorite food. Gorgonian polyps also make up a significant portion of their diet, and other invertebrates, including zoanthids, bryozoans and hydroids, are occasionally eaten. Although algae forms less than ten percent of their stomach content, the food source requires over a third of their foraging time to harvest.

Reproductive seasons and behavior have not been well documented. The similarity of size between mated pairs and the exclusion of juveniles from territories lead to the conclusion that the species is usually monogamous and does not change sex. On two consecutive September evenings, we observed a pair of Gray Angelfish participating in a lengthy courtship and spawning ritual above a low-profile reef bank in 30 feet of water. The pair arrived on site about 30 minutes before sunset and immediately began slowly circling and cavorting together near the bottom. Every few minutes, the presumed female would

Angelfishes

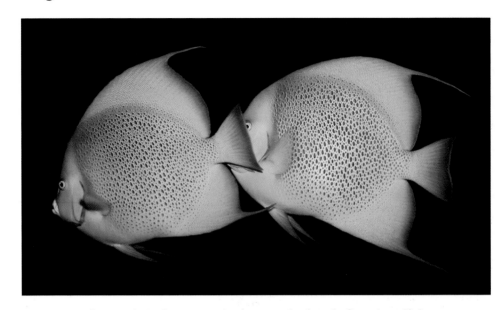

During their slow spawning ascent, the female Gray Angelfish flutters her tail constantly against her mate's face.

gradually ascend three to five feet, closely followed by the male, who attempted to place his snout close to the female's rapidly fluttering tail fin. After rising together for only a few feet, the female prematurely broke for the bottom, followed by the male, and they again began to circle and chase. This routine continued uninterrupted for over 20 minutes, with subsequent false spawning rises taking the pair further above the flat sea floor. Finally, just after sunset and with little light remaining, the pair continued their rise 15 feet into the water column. During their slow ascent, the female's constantly fluttering tail gently caressed the male's face. At the apex the couple abruptly rolled to their sides in an apparent spawn, although a gamete cloud was not visible. Soon after making a quick dash to the sea floor, the fish left the area together.

A promiscuous spawning behavior in waters off the San Blas Islands, Panama has also been documented. A late afternoon gathering of eight to 14 Gray Angelfish was monitored for a two-week period. Beginning an hour before sunset several individuals, believed to be males because of their slightly larger size, peacefully circled over a group of unsettled females who milled about the bottom, chasing each other and making grunting sounds. The males developed a dark vertical bar behind their gill covers. Eventually one or two females, displaying darkened bellies and pale backs, moved off, followed by a single male. These subgroups were at times aggressively pursued and disrupted by other females. When a pair finally was able to isolate itself, they hovered calmly, with the male positioned slightly above the female for as long as ten minutes. Eventually, the male began a slow circling ascent followed by the female. Charging males often broke up the spawning rises. If uninterrupted, the pairs would rise ten feet before separating and returning to the substrate. No gamete clouds were observed.

French Angelfish, occasionally confused with the similar-appearing and closely related Gray Angelfish, can be readily differentiated by their bright, golden-rimmed scales. The juveniles are much more difficult to distinguish and can be identified to species only by a subtle differences in markings on their snouts and tails. Young Grays have a clear, flat tail margin, while those of the French are rounded and lined in gold. The two angelfishes are also closely allied in their social, feeding and reproductive behavior. Mated pairs of French Angelfish also live in large territories spanning a broad range of depths, where they feed on many of the same sponge species eaten by Grays. French Angelfish, however rely less on gorgonian polyps and algae in their diet.

Juveniles of both species act as cleaners until about three inches in length. The smallest of the tiny black and gold-barred youngsters move about with an extravagant fluttering of oversized fins. Filamentous algae are their primary food, with parasitic copepods picked from client fishes making up only 25 percent of their diet. The little fishes also eat a few free-living copepods. As adults they switch roles, spending nearly ten percent of their time attending cleaning stations.

Although French Angelfish do not change sex and are believed to be monogamous, the details of their reproductive behavior have not been established. Two observations of apparent spawning have been published. The first, occurring late one afternoon off Grand Bahama Island, Bahamas, involved five to eight similar-sized pairs and three or four smaller individuals. Each pair aggressively chased other pairs or individuals that came within 20 feet of where they swam side-by-side just off the bottom. This hostile behavior, often with the aggressors rolling laterally during an attack, kept the pairs evenly spaced across the sea floor. One closely observed couple displayed no obvious courtship behavior or distinctive color pattern, but ten minutes after sunset they rose together at a low angle that carried them 20 to 30 feet forward and seven to ten feet above the bottom. Throughout the rise their abdominal regions were angled slightly toward one another. After separating at the end of their rise, no cloud of spawn was visible. The other pairs behaved in a similar fashion, without interference. What appeared to be spawning behavior between a single pair of French Angelfish also was observed in Puerto Rico. The two fish rose in the water column for several feet, with one fish positioned just below the other. At the top of their rise, the pair parted and returned to the bottom; again, no gamete cloud was observed.

Two conflicting reports examine the relationship between Gray and French Angelfish. One documents pairs of both species peacefully sharing overlapping home ranges in Florida and the Bahamas. However, aggressive behavior by Grays toward a French Angelfish was observed in Panama. In this instance, from one to three Grays were seen chasing a solitary French Angelfish whenever it approached within 100 feet. No sightings of mixed groups or pairs have been documented, indicating that the two species are incompatible. And, unlike Queen Angelfish and Blue Angelfish who regularly crossbreed, no wild hybrids of French and Grays have been documented. Hybrids of the two species have been artificially produced in aquariums, however, demonstrating the possibility of such an occurrence.

Angelfishes

Queen Angelfish
Holacanthus ciliaris
&
Blue Angelfish
Holacanthus bermudensis

Queen Angelfish, considered by many to be the most beautiful reef fish in the Caribbean, wear a striking array of blues, greens, yellows and oranges accentuated by streaming dorsal and anal fins. Unfortunately, the species frequently seeks shelter during the day and is somewhat skittish when closely approached. Lengths of 18 inches have been reported, but individuals over 14 inches are considered rare. Although primarily a shallow water fish, Queens have been recorded below 200 feet. Their sexual development has not been studied extensively, but both Queen and Blue Angelfish are assumed to be protogynous hermaphrodites. Females forage in separate areas of the males' large home ranges. During the day the dominant males regularly visit the solitary females in turn, approaching rapidly and circling before settling down and feeding by their sides for five to ten minutes. Ninety-seven percent of their diet comes from 33 genera of sponges. The remaining tidbits include algae, tunicates, hydroids and bryozoans. Solitary juveniles primarily eat algae until they reach sexual maturity and join harems.

The species' reproductive behavior has not been well documented. The few reported spawnings involve a single male courting members of his harem just before sunset within territorial boundaries. The observed male rolled laterally and repeatedly flicked his pectoral fins, then held them extended as he circled above two females. Much like Rock Beauties, *Holacanthus tricolor*, and Cherubfish, *Centropyge argi*, a female, when ready to release eggs, moves into the water column where she is joined by a male, who nudges her from below with his snout.

The Blue Angelfish, similar-appearing and closely related to the Queen Angelfish, is primarily a continental species inhabiting the tropical and temperate waters of Florida and up the eastern seaboard to the Carolinas. The

The Townsend Angelfish, a regularly occuring hybrid of the Queen Angelfish and the Blue Angelfish.

species also occurs in Bermuda and along the western fringes of the Bahama Bank. In south Florida, where the range of Blues overlaps that of Queens, the two species occasionally interbreed, producing a hybrid that was once described as a separate species, the Townsend Angelfish, *H. townsendi*. The hybrids are fertile and often cross-spawn with Queens and Blues and other hybrids, producing an infinite variety of color variations.

Courtship between a Queen Angelfish (right) and a Blue Angelfish.

In Bimini, Bahamas, seven days after the full moon of May and one hour before sunset, we followed a Blue Angelfish obviously distended with hydrated eggs. After foraging for 20 minutes, the fish moved across the bottom toward deeper water, where a pair of Queen Angelfish joined her. The Blue rose six feet off the bottom and jerked her body several times. One of the Queens left its partner and swam off with the swollen Blue female. Each time the pair paused the Blue lifted off the bottom, tilted her head up, extended her fins and shuddered but appeared to be ignored by the feeding Queen. After following a circuitous route for ten minutes, the pair briefly joined a single Blue before moving off together once again. Five minutes after sunset, the female Blue rose ten feet off the sea floor, where she was approached from below by the Queen, who nudged her abdomen with his snout before the fishes parted, swimming hurriedly away in different directions. There was no visible sign of a gamete cloud.

Rock Beauty
Holacanthus tricolor

Rock Beauties, with their distinctive yellow and black markings, add a bold splash of color to nearly every high-profile reef of moderate depth in the Caribbean. Known to be protogynous hermaphrodites, Rock Beauties live in harems dominated by a single large male, who mates exclusively with from two to four smaller females. Juveniles less than two inches in length are brilliant yellow with a single black spot ringed in blue on their sides. The solitary youngsters are extremely shy, spending much of their day in hiding. As they mature, the black enlarges until it covers much of their bodies. At approximately three and a half inches females become sexually mature and join harems. The transformation to male occurs at about five inches. Older males, reported to reach a foot in length, develop streamers from their dorsal, anal and tail fins. Other than size, the only difference between the sexes is a small red dot on the tails of most males.

The territories of males, averaging just over 1,000 square yards, encompass the smaller territories of females. The large territories are randomly distributed

147

Angelfishes

A male Rock Beauty nuzzles a female's vent during their slow spawning rise.

across the sea floor, often leaving substantial, uninhabited gaps. Such large, untapped areas filled with plentiful food and shelter indicate that these resources are not a factor in limiting population size. However, males are quick to protect their turf from encroaching males who often display darkened faces.

Interestingly, when two females differ in size by more than 15 percent, they often share all or part of their territorial area without conflict. Their peaceful coexistence appears to be related to the social order of haremic life, where only the largest female can transform into a male. The larger fish seem willing to accept the smaller females, who may one day become part of their harems. On the other hand, similar-sized females, who might at a later date challenge the right to dominate the harem, do not tolerate one another and never share any portion of their territories.

Unlike most protogynous species, whose sex reversal is prompted by the disappearance of a dominant male, the largest females in harems of Rock Beauties regularly change sex before there is an opportunity to dominate females. In other species, bachelor males would be promptly driven from the territory and, as competitive outcasts, would be unable to join another harem. However, the fish hide within their territories, well out of view of the dominant males while undergoing their premature sex change. It is believed that, even though unable to reproduce, the new males, unhampered by the daily burden of egg production, undergo a rapid growth spurt. This puts them in an advantageous position to take control of harems when opportunities arise.

While moving about their territories, individuals feed periodically as they follow specific paths. For an unknown reason, Rock Beauties spend as much as half their time hiding in one of a dozen or more shelter sites. Two females sharing an overlapping home range typically use the same hiding places. Rock Beauties primarily feed on sponges and algae. They forage at a slow rate, taking fewer than three bites each minute. Even though nearly half of their feeding time is spent scraping algae, stomach analyses reveal that more than 95 percent of the diet is sponge and only four percent is plant material. The large amount of time and effort required to harvest such a small amount of algae indicates that plants, even in small quantities, must play a significant role in their nutritional needs. The remaining one percent of their food is made up of invertebrates and eggs.

Males regularly visit their females during the day and casually forage at their sides without making courtship overtures. About thirty minutes before sunset during most evenings of the year, females move to an established spawning site

Males regularly develop black faces during courtship.

A male assesses a female's readiness to spawn.

inside the males' home ranges. These sites are typically associated with prominent structures such as coral mounds or gorgonian bushes. While the females meander near the bottom, the males, displaying darkened faces, court with increased enthusiasm as daylight fades. Each female is approached with an exaggerated swimming motion, then circled rapidly and repeatedly presented with a lateral fin display. Before spawning, a female often rises several feet off the bottom as if ready to mate; but when approached from below by a courting male, she bolts back to the bottom, followed closely by the eager male, who again begins to circle and display. After one or two false rises a female finally holds still while the male positions himself underneath and pushes his snout firmly against the female's genital region. The pair slowly rises a few feet before suddenly dashing upward, quivering and shedding a visible cloud of gametes. The pair immediately separates and dives to the bottom, where the female chases the male briefly. Males typically spawn with several or all their mates each evening. Spawning activities are completed by ten minutes after sunset, when females return to their territories and bed down for the night inside coral cover.

Angelfishes

Cherubfish
Centropyge argi

Cherubfish, delightful miniature angelfish seldom exceeding two and one-half inches, are distributed throughout much of the tropical western Atlantic. In the southern Caribbean where most common, the species is found in shallow depths from 15 to 50 feet, but in the Bahamas and southern Florida, they typically live below 80 feet. In the southeastern Caribbean, from Curacao to Barbados, their range overlaps with a similar-appearing genus member, *Centropyge aurantonotus*, the Flameback Angelfish, that replaces the Cherubfish south to Brazil. In the northern region, Cherubfish typically live in pairs or small groups composed of a large male and female and several smaller, possibly immature,

Cherubfish.

individuals. These groups often make their homes in the rubble piles of Sand Tilefish, *Malacanthus plumieri*, on the sand plains extending seaward from coral-fringed drop-offs. In the U.S. Virgin Islands, harems reside within five-by 12-foot territories established along coral-shrouded banks. Each social unit includes a single dominant male and from one to four smaller females. The lovely little blue angelfish with golden trim flit and dart about the bottom, often dodging inside one of their many shelter holes for minutes at a time. They are typically shy and difficult to approach. The species' color pattern varies slightly among individuals but not between the sexes. Juveniles are identical to adults except for a dark spot just above the pectoral fin base. Within harems single dominant males are only slightly larger than the females, but may be smaller than the females in an adjacent harem, leading to speculation that sex change is socially induced in this species.

Females, who show little hostility toward other members of their sex, set up housekeeping near the centers of their small territories. Throughout the day males busily follow established routes, leading from one female to another. During rounds, they occasionally wander out to territorial boundaries to reassert authority. Possibly because harems are seldom established close to one another, males have little reason to display aggression toward neighbors. Most hostility is directed toward small damselfishes who share the Cherubfishes' algal diet. Nearly half of the little herbivores' stomach content is made up of fine sand particles picked up while grazing during the day in territorial pastures.

Male Cherubfish begin life as females. As with most protogynists living in harems, when a dominant male is lost, the largest female changes sex and takes his place. Spawning occurs each evening throughout the year. As darkness settles, males decrease foraging and pick up their pace of female visitations, following the same paths every two to six minutes. Females wait in or near favorite shelter holes along the males' routes. On initial approaches males do not linger, but if females are hidden, they take the time to search them out. Females are seldom coy, often swimming enthusiastically toward oncoming males, who proudly present them with lateral displays of erect fins and audible chirps, believed to be answered by the females. After brief interludes lasting but seconds, males proceed to their next mates. During subsequent visits, courtship efforts become more intense and prolonged. With fins spread and bodies curved laterally, frenzied males swim in tight circles around females. They frequently stop abruptly in mid-circle with their heads angled upward and flutter their outstretched pectoral and ventral fins. At this stage of courtship, anxious females occasionally pursue the males to their next mates. On rare occasions, two, or even three, females converge at a single site. This so exhilarates the males that they attempt to spawn prematurely but are aggressively interrupted by competing females.

Spawning generally takes place within ten minutes of sunset. After several courtship encounters and false spawning rises, females, finally ready to release eggs, spread their fins, become blanched and, with paired fins fluttering, rise several inches. Males ascend from below at a 45-degree angle and place their snouts near the genital openings of the horizontal females who extend their pectoral fins downward. The nuzzling males slowly push the females' quivering bodies upward four to 12 inches with rapidly beating pectoral and ventral fins. A mass of eggs occasionally can be seen bulging from the females' genital openings. At the top of the rise, males push their snouts into the females, forcing the release of their cargo. Faster than the eye can follow, males flip laterally, position their ventral regions next to the females' and bathe the eggs in sperm. With males leading, the pairs dive back to the bottom. Spent females immediately take cover, while males move on to their next partners. An entire spawning episode, beginning with the females' rise and ending with their rush back to the bottom, takes between four and six seconds; the explosive discharge of gametes requires less than a quarter-second. After completing their reproductive duties, males calmly patrol their territories for a few minutes before retiring for the night.

Females discharge just over 100 eggs with each spawn. The thrust of the tail fins from the pairs' dive for the bottom swirls the gamete mass, aiding fertilization and dispersal. The tiny eggs, only 0.6 millimeter in diameter, are among the smallest planktonic eggs yet recorded for marine fishes. Yolk sac larvae hatch in 30 to 32 hours. Little is known about settlement or the juvenile stage of Cherubfish. From aquarium observations it is believed that adults can live at least eight years.

Basslets
Family Grammatidae

Like most basslets, Fairy Basslet swim upside-down under the ledges they inhabit.

The Fairy Basslet, *Gramma loreto*, also commonly known as Royal Gramma, is one of the most exquisite fishes inhabiting Caribbean coral reefs. The common two- to three-inch violet-and-yellow fish reach their population zenith at depths of 40 to 50 feet, but occasionally inhabit clearwater reefs as shallow as ten feet, and have been reported at depths of 200 feet. The small planktivores, living in colonies of a dozen or more individuals, hover near high vertical corals, under overhangs or just inside coral caves and fissures. Like many cave-dwelling fishes, Fairy Basslet orient their bellies to the ceiling when beneath ledges. The species ranges from Bermuda south through the Bahamas, to Venezuela and west to Central America but, for some reason, is absent in Florida waters.

Colony members seldom venture far from small defended territories that encompass their personal hiding-holes. Small species, including Masked Goby, *Coryphopterus personatus*, and Threespot Damselfish, *Stegastes planifrons*, believed to be potential competitors for their sleeping holes, are frequently chased. Colonies typically consist of one or two large breeding males that mate with three to nine females. Young males, conserving their energies for rapid growth, do not spawn. Large males assert their dominance over colony members by chasing smaller individuals and occasionally engaging in mouth-to-mouth power struggles with similar-sized males. Although its social system is similar to that of many sex-changing protogynous species, the Fairy Basslet has been determined to be gonochoristic, with individuals remaining the same sex throughout life.

The species is reproductively active from January or February until June and possibly for a brief period in mid-October. To prepare their nests for eggs, reproductive males pluck tangles of algae, which are blown in and out of the mouth, possibly to remove microinvertebrates, then added to cushionlike mats built in the deepest section of small holes or narrow crevices used for nesting. Harvested algae is also used to conceal the entranceways to nesting holes. Mouthfuls of silt are periodically removed from the nests and spit into open water.

On consecutive days beginning just before dawn and continuing for an hour, three to seven females lay eggs in a male's algal nest. The negatively buoyant one-millimeter eggs, clinging together by tendrils and intertwined with algae, form flat one- to four-square-inch multi-layered masses. Guarding males hover in front of their nests or rest inside the entranceway with only their heads protruding. If

Members of a Fairy Basslet colony feeding on plankton.

approached, they generally retreat inside and gaze out the opening. On rare occasions approaching fishes are nipped. Based on the behavior of other egg-laying species, in-nest care would include fanning and the removal of infertile, infected or dead eggs. Field-collected eggs raised in well-aerated tanks suffered a high mortality rate, suggesting the importance of parental care. Three- to four-millimeter larvae with silvery eyes and well-developed jaws hatch in ten or 11 days. It is assumed the larvae are pelagic; however, the species has never been captured in plankton tows.

The Grammatidae family includes nine species in two genera. The three *Gramma*: the Fairy Basslet, the Blackcap Basslet, *G. melacara*, and the Yellowcheek Basslet, *G. linki*, are partitioned by depth, often with as little as a ten-foot overlap between species. Depending on location, the Blackcap Basslet typically displaces the Fairy Basslet at 40 to 100 feet. It, in turn, is supplanted by the Yellowcheek Basslet below 250 feet. In Puerto Rico and Haiti, where the Blackcap Basslet is absent, Yellowcheek Basslet have been collected as shallow as 80 feet.

Members of genus *Lipogramma* also are partitioned by depth. The Threeline Basslet, *L. trilineatum*, inhabiting the shallowest depths, has been collected

Basslets

Large male Fairy Basslet occasionally compete for colony dominance.

between 25 and 200 feet but typically lives in the 60- to 70-foot range. The shy one- to two-inch fish customarily swim upside-down near the ceilings of caves. A Threeline Basslet living in an aquarium hid and slept inside a double-ended shelter tunnel built of algae. Similar structures have not been found in the field. Below 200 feet, the species is replaced by the beautiful, but elusive Heliotrope Basslet, *L. klayi.* Several additional family members, discovered well below safe diving limits, have been classified recently.

Blennies
Family Blenniidae – Combtooth Blennies, Clinidae – Clinid Blennies, Tripterygiidae – Triplefins, Chaenopsidae – Tube Blennies

Saddled Blenny, family Clinidae.

A golden phase Seaweed Blenny, family Blenniidae.

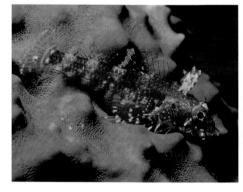

Triplefin, Tripterygiidae *sp.*

Blennies are small, elongate bottom-dwelling fishes that live in a variety of habitats ranging from tide pools to deep reefs. Because of their appealing little faces and animated behavior, blennies are favorites with fish watchers. The diverse group of fishes has undergone two major family revisions and still has taxonomists scratching their heads. Today, blennies are generally separated into four families by anatomical features. Blenniidae, or combtooth blennies, have a single row of close-set teeth lining their jaws, scaleless bodies, blunt heads capped with large goggle eyes and prominent lips. Most family members consume a combination of algae and tiny benthic invertebrates. Members of the more specious Clinidae family have scale-covered bodies. Although their tiny scales are difficult to see, the little crustacean-eaters can be distinguished by pointed snouts, small mouths and, in many species, tall foredorsal fins. Triplefins, in the genus *Enneanectes*, true to their common name, have three-part dorsal fins. The five Caribbean species are striking fishes less than an inch in length. Each species displays a slightly different version of five dark body bars. Their small size and similar appearance make the relatively common fishes difficult to find and identify. The exotic Chaenopsidae family, including some of the most entertaining fishes on the reef, are notable for spectacular dorsal fins and their fierce mouth-to-mouth combat.

Most blennies have fleshy, often multi-branching appendages called cirri above their eyes and on their snouts that help disguise their head profiles. Blennies are easily confused with similar-sized bottom-dwelling gobies in the family Gobiidae. Gobies can be distinguished by their stiff bodies, two-part dorsal fins and lack of cirri, which differ from the blennies' flexible bodies and single, continuous dorsal fins.

Comprehensive field surveys in Belize and Honduras identified 60 different blennies. Each species lived almost exclusively within one of 11 distinct habitats — drop-offs, spur and groove reefs, shallow forereefs, patch reefs, rubble/algae, tidepools, mangroves, shallow seagrass, deep seagrass, mainland rocks and offshore rocks. The largest number of species (20) were associated with live coral in shallow surge-swept forereefs. Limited food resources, reproductive behavior and vulnerability to predators possibly contribute to the need for such strict habitat partitioning among the species.

Chaenopsidae – Tube Blennies

The Chaenopsid blennies reside exclusively in the Western Hemisphere, with 33 species in eight genera living in the western Atlantic. The family consists of many delightful characters, including nine tiny, hole-dwelling planktivores in genus *Acanthemblemaria*; the free-ranging, fish-eating Arrow Blenny, *Lucayablennius zingaro*; the stealthy Wrasse Blenny, *Hemiemblemaria simulus*, that mimics the behavior and coloration of the juvenile Bluehead Wrasse, *Thalassoma bifasciatum*; the high-flying Sailfin Blenny, *Emblemaria pandionis*, and four species of eccentric pikeblennies. A fascinating fish family indeed!

Secretary Blenny.

Blennies

Spinyhead Blenny.

Roughhead Blenny.

Tube-dwelling blennies fight among themselves to acquire better hole locations.

Acanthemblemaria make their homes inside abandoned wormholes in dead corals, reef pavement and sponges. The Spinyhead Blenny, *A. spinosa;* the Roughhead Blenny, *A. aspera;* and the Secretary Blenny, *A. maria,* are the most common and widely distributed genus members. Each species prefers to live close together to insure an adequate supply of mates. Some white limestone rocks are so peppered with protruding blenny heads that the sites are fondly known as blenny condos. Every few minutes the tiny fishes pop partially out of their holes to grab passing specks of plankton or dart across the rock to nab benthic microcrustaceans.

Individuals occasionally attempt to displace neighbors occupying larger, more favorable holes higher on the coral rock where planktonic food is more plentiful and the threat of predation less. With dorsal fins flying, challengers grab the heads of hole-owners in their jaws and spin wildly. These ferocious takeover attempts,

A golden phase Roughhead Blenny darts out of its shelter tube to nab a speck of floating zooplankton.

often lasting several minutes, are seldom successful but appear to be fundamental to the social structure of densely clustered communities. Females, which are smaller and less numerous but otherwise similar in appearance to males, lay eggs inside the males' shelter tubes. After hatching in a few days, the yolk-sac larvae rise to become plankton for an unknown period. Recently settled juveniles take cover in small crevices until they can find a vacant hole associated with a colony.

To study the nature of *Acanthemblemaria* communities, researchers removed residents, transplanted individuals and drilled additional holes in existing colonies. They discovered that the larger individuals tended to occupy the more spacious worm tubes on top of the colony permanently, while underlings competed for positions in lower sections. When superior holes became available, residents participated in their own version of musical holes by each resituating in a slightly larger home. Vacated holes near the lower boundaries of the communities were quickly filled by immigrants leading to the conclusion that a surplus of "floaters" lived nearby in less desirable locations.

Within two weeks after 11 of the 22 resident Spinyheads were removed from one coral head, three residents moved to larger holes and six blennies had immigrated to the site. The new blennies averaged three-quarters of an inch in length, compared to the one-inch average size of removed residents. When all 15 blennies were removed from a second coral head, only five new fish moved into the vacated colony during the same time period, indicating the species' preference for saturated colonies.

Possession of a shelter hole appears to be necessary for survival. When researchers added 30 new Spinyheads to three colonies lacking vacant holes, only three were able to acquire residences. Within an hour, Redspotted Hawkfish, *Amblycirrhitus pinos*, and lizardfishes consumed ten of the homeless arrivals. To test the Spinyheads' homing instincts, 11 individuals were moved 16 feet from their homes. Seven reoccupied their prior holes within two days. However, when a number of individuals were moved 65 feet from their homes, none made it back to their previous holes.

Blennies

Papillose Blenny.

Papillose Blenny display.

Most chaenopsid blennies live in specific habitats, typically within a restricted depth range. In the U.S. Virgin Islands, Spinyheads inhabit depths between 12 and 65 feet, whereas Secretary Blennies live in six to 18 feet of water. Occasionally Roughhead Blennies co-occur with Spinyheads at the same depths and, at times, even share the same coral rocks. In these joint habitations, Spinyheads occupy the upper sections with Roughheads relegated to lower positions. After researchers removed the Spinyheads from shared rocks, the Roughheads moved into the preferred upper holes. In Belize, similar microhabitat partitioning occurs between Spinyheads and Greenfield Blennies, *Acanthemblemaria greenfieldi*, with the larger Greenfields occupying the horizontal surfaces and Spinyheads living below.

Papillose Blenny, *A. chaplini*, a less common member of the genus, normally inhabit holes in reef pavement. We found a group of more than a dozen individuals living among Sailfin Blennies in 15 feet of water off Bimini, Bahamas. We had been observing the Sailfins regularly for over a month before discovering the Papillose. The wispy one- to two-inch brownish blennies blended so well with their surroundings that they were difficult to see with only their heads sticking out from the bottom. They first caught our attention while scampering about among the algal bushes. We were never certain whether the cryptic fishes had been at the site all along, or if they had recently arrived. In any case, when we finally noticed them, we saw them regularly. We were never sure of the prowling blennies' sex, but when their forays took them near the occupied holes of other Papillose, it meant certain war. The residents rose out of the rock bottom, arching and

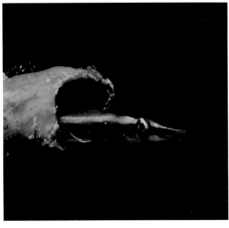

An Arrow Blenny resting in a sponge.

swaying menacingly and flaring their gill covers until their heads appeared to be three times larger than normal size. Attacks were instantaneous and ferocious. Clamped together mouth-to-mouth, the rivals spun and thrashed until it seemed their delicate bodies would break. In seconds all was over as the challengers scampered off, leaving the homesteaders panting with fury. In the five battles witnessed, we never saw a resident displaced. We also never observed reproductive behavior, although one afternoon we discovered an individual with a bright orange head that we interpreted as a dichromatic display of a breeding male.

The Arrow Blenny breaks from its family's hole-dwelling tradition, spending most of the day hovering inside shallow undercuts at the base of reefs in depths from 40 to 100 feet. Either as solitary individuals or in small unorganized groups, the splendid one- to two-inch fish generally live in association with their favorite food, Masked Gobies, *Coryphopterus personatus*. With tails cocked for thrust, the blennies move slowly in a start-and-stop fashion, propelled by fluttering pectoral fins. When within four to five inches of prey their tails spring straight, shooting them toward their victims. The slender blennies have been seen consuming gobies half their length. One goby was struck with such force that the paralyzed prey drifted toward the bottom, where it was seized mid-body, repositioned and swallowed headfirst. More in tune with other genus members, Arrow

An Arrow Blenny hovers with its tail cocked for a rapid attack.

Blennies occasionally rest in holes or small sponge openings with only their heads exposed. The Wrasse Blenny, another free-swimming Chaenopsid, is discussed in the mimicry section of the Symbiosis chapter.

Blennies

A male Yellowface Pikeblenny leans from his shelter tube toward an approaching rival.

Yellowface Pikeblenny
Chaenopsis limbaughi

We made our first discovery of a pikeblenny while lying on the sand searching the bottom for signs of life. Our gaze caught a flick of unfamiliar movement off in the distance near a stand of Manatee Grass, *Syringodium filiforme*. After inching forward slowly for several feet, we spied the well-camouflaged Daffy Duck profile of a Yellowface Pikeblenny staring back from the opening of its buried shelter tube. Every now and then, the two- to three-inch blenny disappeared inside, only to reappear after a second or two, preceded by its distinctive yellow bill. It is easy to understand why the rather common little fish are so difficult to locate. When sitting inside their tubes with only their heads above the sand, their slender upright bodies resemble the stems of dead algal bushes and grass stubble scattered about their sandy habitat.

Soon the blenny lost interest in us and swam free from its tube to peck in the sand for buried invertebrates and to snap at minute specks of zooplankton floating overhead. After a minute, the little predator scampered back to its hole, turned, located the entrance with its finely finned puff of a tail and slipped inside backwards, leaving only its head exposed. Almost as an afterthought, we placed a hand mirror inches from the hole. Our comical cartoon fish instantly underwent a radical attitude adjustment, ascending from the sand like a cobra from a basket. Menacingly, it spread an imposing dorsal fin, flared gill covers and weaved from side to side. Fast as a flash, the blenny shot its three-inch body forward and confronted its image in fierce mouth-to-mouth combat. As soon as the mirror was removed the blenny calmed, returned to the shelter tube and slipped out of sight.

Unfortunately, we made our find in June on the last day of an extended stay in Bimini, Bahamas. Adding to our dilemma, the blenny was in 55 feet of water, greatly limiting observation time. When we returned to Bimini the following spring, pikeblennies topped our underwater agenda, but after two one-hour searches, none were to be found. Our consolation prize came in Belize that September, when we located a colony of Bluethroat Pikeblenny, *Chaenopsis ocellata*, in the shallow grass that rings the country's famous Blue Hole.

Back in Bimini the next May, we hit the jackpot, finding 13 Yellowface Pikeblennies spaced randomly about the sand and along the edge of the grass

bed exactly where we had located the lone individual the previous year. Each of the five males and eight slightly smaller and less ornate females rested with their heads and bodies extending at various heights from abandoned parchmentlike soda-straw-sized worm tubes. As we visited the site throughout the summer, we discovered that the colony was far more extensive and individuals more mobile than we had expected.

Out of their holes the fish appear delicate, vulnerable and easy targets for fish-eating predators that prowl the sand. Fortunately, the keen-eyed blennies are well aware of their situation. When Yellowtail Snapper, *Ocyurus chrysurus*, or Bar Jack, *Caranx ruber*, patrol nearby, the pikeblennies remain in their holes. However, when the coast is clear they are regularly out and about, often making long forays that take them ten to 20 feet from their homes. During outings they swim snakelike in quick spurts just above the bottom, expertly blending with the background. If danger appears, they always seem to know where to find a nearby unoccupied shelter tube.

Bluethroat Pikeblennies inhabit shallow sea grass beds.

Blennies

A high-flying male Yellowface Pikeblenny attempts to attract a mate.

Occasionally the slender carnivores perch on algal tops to survey their surroundings. On one extended excursion a female stalked and captured a tiny razorfish feeding at the edge of the grass. The species consumes primarily planktonic copepods, but unidentified fish remains, shrimp larvae, shrimps and a single polychaete worm also were found during a scientific study that examined their stomach content.

We quickly discovered that the most rewarding blenny watching takes place from mid-to-late afternoon. During these hours, the females swim free in search of food and a bit of social life. And when the gals are out, the guys go nuts. The

A female Yellowface Pikeblenny stalks and captures a razorfish.

first indication that the sand-colored females are on the move is signaled by ever-watchful males, who make it their business to know such things. As soon as a female leaves her tube, males flush black, intensify the color of their yellow beaks, pop their impressive dorsal fins taut and bob up and down while remaining in contact with their tubes. If a wandering female comes anywhere near, suitors soar from their holes in graceful, high-flying eight- to ten-inch arches. The most enthusiastic remain aloft for seconds at a time. Unhappily, their acrobatics are seldom rewarded. We never saw a spawn but, according to

aquarium observations, an obliging female simply follows a male into his tube and quickly deposits a few eggs for the male to fertilize and tend. Pikeblenny eggs hatch within days. Weeks later the larvae settle back to the sand and metamorphose into transparent half-inch juveniles.

As summer advanced and more pikeblennies appeared, confrontations between residents begin to erupt in the once peaceful colony. For a brief period, the blennies were in such a high state of agitation that even our outstretched fingers elicited attacks. Unfurled dorsals flew like battle flags during conflicts. Gray fins proclaimed aggression, black defense. It was not clear whether individuals were competing for dwindling food resources, favored mates or choice shelter tubes, but for almost a week in August, afternoons were packed with aggressive encounters.

A male Yellowface Pikeblenny exhibits for a nearby female.

165

Blennies

The first altercation we witnessed took us completely by surprise. While we were watching a large male trying to attract the attention of running females, a second, equally large male came sailing over the sand in a direct line for the happily dancing blenny. The defender instantly arched from his hole to counter the onrush. For several seconds the mini-titans clashed in a madcap mouth-to-mouth wrestling match before the attacker retreated to a shelter tube not two feet away from a smaller male who also was busily attempting to lure a female his way. Like lighting the troublemaker charged, bowling the youngster backwards, and flinging him from his hole. Somehow during the ensuing melee the smaller blenny regained his tube and hunkered down while the attacker, poised and ready for round two, glared from inches away. In a brazen show of misplaced ego, the small blenny popped from his hole, spread a defiant black dorsal and danced in his rival's face. The assailant pounced, sending the upstart scrambling deep inside his tube.

Nearly a minute passed before the rounded tip of his yellow beak reappeared in the opening. Without waiting to see more, the larger blenny dived into the tube, forcing his way inside with a wildly lashing tail. Unable to turn within the narrow chamber, the intruder looped his body, inserting his tail into the hole for leverage, which allowed his head to slip back into the open. Three times the hole-owner reappeared; three times the large blenny drove him back before finally retreating to a nearby shelter tube to catch his breath. Moments later, the embattled youngster poked his head into the open and peered about tentatively. Noting the withdrawal, he expanded his blackened dorsal into its full glory and began to display with even more moxie than before. Enraged, the attacker rose from his tube. Even this slight bluff was sufficient to send the defender back underground. But with no assault forthcoming, he quickly reappeared and continued his taunts. This was more than the larger blenny could endure. In an attack faster than our eyes could follow, he arrived at the hole in a cloud of sand just as the panicked upstart disappeared. With time

Female Yellowface Pikeblennies on the run.

Male Yellowface Pikeblennies fight for control of a shelter tube located near females.

running out on our computers, we reluctantly lifted off the bottom and drifted in the direction of the mooring line while keeping our eyes glued to the ongoing fray. The following afternoon we found the little blenny perched high in his hole, intently scouting the terrain for running females as if nothing had happened. His brawny rival was nowhere to be found.

After nearly four months of weekly observations, we left Bimini at the end of August. When we returned two weeks later the water temperature was at its annual peak, and patches of nasty red algae pocked the pikeblennies' white sand home. We found the number of resident blennies at less than half of previous numbers. The females were especially hard hit. Although the remaining males occasionally displayed, it was obvious that the colony's vim and vigor were gone.

During the two seasons that we randomly surveyed the pikeblenny colony population numbers increased from zero to well over 20 and declined again. During the same time frame we noticed a similar trend in a colony of closely related Sailfin Blennies, *Emblemaria pandionis* (discussed in the next section). Our initial spring Sailfin survey revealed a thriving group of 28 inhabiting a 50- by 75-foot rock bottom in 15 feet of water. Like the pikeblennies, as summer progressed their population grew, and as

Rivals lock jaws and spin violently.

Blennies

numbers swelled, male fighting and displaying increased correspondingly. Another similarity was a noticeable, almost overnight increase in female Sailfins followed by increasing female hostility.

The only published study describing the ecology or behavior of pikeblennies involved a 13-month program of monitoring a population of Orangethroat Pikeblennies, *Chaenopsis alepidota*, in the Sea of Cortez. The findings indicate that Orangethroats are also quite mobile and that low-density, noncombative populations, rather than high-density, territorially aggressive colonies, are the norm. There is no mention made of sudden increases of females and, contrary to our observations, the Orangethroat Blennies spent more time foraging in the morning than in the afternoon. The study's data suggest that the species is annual, with the prosperity of colonies determined by habitat conditions and reproductive success.

Male Sailfin sitting in his shelter tube.

Sailfin Blenny
Emblemaria pandionis

Our attention was so intently focused on the tiny, dark head protruding from an algae-tufted sea floor that we hardly noticed the Spotted Eagle Ray, *Aetobatus narinari*, patrolling the reef line. We were patiently waiting for an equally impressive marine wildlife show from a fidgety two-inch male Sailfin Blenny balancing on elongate ventral fins at the edge of its hole, less than three feet from our face masks. Our awkward presence and thunder of bubbles had no effect on the typically wary fish; at that moment, in the late afternoon, he had nothing but sex on his mind.

Without warning, the diminutive suitor shot skyward with a great flurry of fins. The undistinguished crustacean-eating bottom-dweller instantly transformed into a majestic high-flying Don Juan, vying for the affections of a female Sailfin perched impassively a few feet away. The little guy needed all the charm he could muster because he was not alone. Before he could settle back into his hole, a neighboring male made his play soaring straight up well over a foot. Further away, across the gradually sloping limestone plain, others began popping up, seemingly out of nowhere.

Our first encounter with the small, cryptically colored blennies provided us with a search image that made it easy to find Sailfins in many shallow rocky habitats we later surveyed in Florida and the Caribbean. Most individuals live

Right: *At the approach of a female, a male Sailfin Blenny sails from his shelter tube.*

Blennies

A male dives for his hole after a jump.

inside irregular-shaped holes formed by worms, bivalves, snapping shrimps or erosion in the bottom or on the sides of low-lying limestone rock. Research provides little information about *Emblemaria pandionis* other than its range, which extends across the tropical waters of the western Atlantic and into the Gulf of Mexico.

Even though we spent hours observing the Sailfins we never tired of their antics. In fact, the more we watched the more fascinated and perplexed we became by their behavior. Our initial survey, in Bimini, Bahamas, located 28 resident blennies inside a 50- by 75-foot plot that stretched across a flat, 15-foot, algae-tufted terrain. The majority appeared to be males. We noted that, although sporadic jumping began at dawn and continued throughout the day, most displays occurred between 4:30 PM and dusk. If females were holed-up nearby or on the move, males launched a series of jumps that carried them from three to 24 inches above the sea floor before they suddenly collapsed their fins and dive-bombed back into their holes.

It soon became apparent that even though most individuals remained in a favorite hole, some movement was going on. An explanation for a few of the

Females clash in a territorial dispute.

A runner attempts to evict a combative hole-owner.

changes in address became apparent late one afternoon when we saw a Sailfin making a mad dash across the seafloor. The little fellow looked vulnerable and out of place in the open. His color changed from black to light brown to better match the bottom, and the magnificent dorsal lay awkwardly collapsed across his back. A round, rapidly fluttering tail fin propelled the slender body just above the bottom. This was our first observation of what we came to call runners. After several minutes of crazy zigzags the runner arrived at a hole occupied by a slightly smaller male, and a miniature version of a marine *Jurassic Park* commenced.

With dorsal fins flared and mouths agape, both the intruder and defender paled to gray with primordial rage. No quarter was given. Sand and algae flew as the combatants locked jaws and slung each other about. After a brief pause, not even long enough for sand to settle, another attack commenced. But this time the defender made a quick move to the side, skillfully parried the interloper and backed into his hole. Undeterred, the aggressor followed, plunging in after the threatened hole-owner driving him down and out of sight. Only the tip of the invader's wildly thrashing tail was visible. With a puff of sand, they reappeared. Another charge, then suddenly both disappeared inside the hole. Within seconds they popped into view once again, but it was obvious that the tide of battle had turned.

The smaller blenny made one last half-hearted lunge before retreating to the top of a nearby algae clump. There he perched, panting for several minutes before slowly moving off. The victor backed into the hole, turned jet black and raised his dorsal in triumph. The dispossessed male tested several depressions before settling into a hole only a few feet away. Soon home improvements began. As he was busily spitting mouthfuls of sand into his new front yard, his dark color gradually returned. Of the several clashes we witnessed between runners and residents, this was the only successful eviction observed.

Blennies

The Sailfins did not seem to spend a lot of time feeding. Occasionally an individual dashed across the bottom and appeared to grab something from a nearby algal bush. One male shot straight up over four feet and nabbed a speck from open water. When we arrived at its hole, the blenny was clutching a transparent shrimp crosswise in its mouth. Although at first we had a bit of difficulty distinguishing the females from the males, we soon learned to make the distinction. Male Sailfins perched in their holes – as they generally are – are nearly always black with, in many cases, a row of white squares along their sides. The males' dorsal fins are also larger, taller, more rounded and sometimes have an orange spot on the leading edge. Females are mottled brown and have a generally smaller dorsal fin with a series of thin, broken diagonal lines. Any confusion came from young males an inch or less in length, male runners and frightened males that acquired mottled brown complexions similar to females.

A female Sailfin Blenny reacts aggressively to her reflection in a mirror.

The true Sailfin gender test came when we placed a small mirror in front of a blenny hole. Surprisingly, males that fought so valiantly among themselves showed little or no interest in their own reflections; however, females went ballistic. Their color immediately changed to gray, gill covers flared and, with fins flicking aggressively, they lunged from their holes and darted wildly back and forth along the glass with their open mouths pressed against the image. Seconds later, the bewildered females briefly backed into their holes for respite. Then out they came again with equal vigor. Occasionally females ran off the length of the mirror and stopped dead at the sudden disappearance of their imaginary rivals. When they moved back toward their holes and saw their image, the battle was on once again.

Females occasionally left the protection of their shelter tubes to make rounds. As they prowled the bottom, nearby males danced like demons, but to no avail. The females had eyes only for trouble, and it came each time another female was discovered. After furious but brief clashes, the troublemakers scurried on to receive similar receptions at a succession of occupied holes before their paths finally led them home.

Even though we made several dawn dives when mating has been reported to occur, we never, at any

A shrimp captured from open water.

hour, observed anything even remotely resembling foreplay. To the contrary, the brief encounters we chanced to witness between males and females were more along the lines of professional wrestling than romance. Finally, after weeks of anticipation, when we had begun to doubt there would ever be a new generation of Sailfins, it happened.

During the last light of dusk, we spotted a rather small male sitting high in his hole, frantically fluttering his great fin. Sure enough, a female perched nearby. After several minutes, the female approached the dancing male. We expected a typical scuffle, but to our delight the male moved aside, allowing the female to slide out of sight inside his shelter tube. The male immediately followed. After several seconds his dark head reappeared. He sat briefly in the opening, as if in a daze, before moving clear of the entrance. The female immediately jumped out, and without even a backward glance, scampered off into the approaching night.

Unfortunately, by the end of our two summers of observation dives in our Sailfin sanctuary, we had more questions than answers about the feisty little blennies' nature. For instance, why on earth is it that males ignore their reflections but won't tolerate the approach of another male? And exactly what were the prowling females up to? But our biggest puzzler concerned display-jumping.

What little we gleaned from the few mentions of *Emblemaria pandionis* in scientific literature indicates that their jumping behavior is used only to lure prospective females for mating. But we both felt, after our brief time among the Sailfins, that the display was also a kind of macho thing. It seems to us that those putting on the biggest show are most frequently the targets of attack. But for whatever reason, the spectacular jumps, that can last for seconds and occasionally carry the blennies more than three feet above their holes, are one of the most entertaining marine life behaviors observed by divers.

Blennies

Redlip Blenny – dark phase.　　　　*Redlip Blenny – pale phase.*

Family Blennidae

Redlip Blenny
Ophioblennius atlanticus

Redlip Blennies, common residents of shallow fringing rock reefs and coral crests, spend their days grazing on filamentous algae and detritus within their small territories. The delightful two- to four-inch, chocolate-brown fish with blunt heads and large red lips occasionally come in pale morphs with shell-white bodies and reddish brown heads. Two decades of research in Barbados have extensively documented the social structure and behavior of the island's Redlip population.

Males and females, represented in equal numbers in a given area, are indistinguishable except during reproductive periods. Both sexes vigorously patrol and defend territories averaging from approximately five square feet in February and March, when population densities are low, to half that size following heavy recruitment in May. Individuals seldom venture far from their personal patches of reef rock for fear of predation or the good possibility of losing a portion of their territory while away. Even females leaving for periods as short as an hour to lay eggs often return to find a section of their turf appropriated. Flurries of nips usually oust intruders.

Males prepare nesting sites within their territories by removing sand, bits of rock and debris from protective crevices. Occasionally nests are situated inside living coral or under flat rocks. Reproduction peaks a few days before and after the full moons of spring, but spawning possibly occurs year-round. The three-hour courtship and spawning periods begin just after sunrise when females leave their territories to lay eggs in the nests of preferred males. These dangerous treks can take ripe females up to 16 feet from the safety of their territories — a substantial distance in blenny terms. While females are on the move, eager males show interest by hovering briefly in front of their nests with their dorsal and anal fins spread. After giving a quick quiver, they dodge back to cover. Females arriving at the males' boundaries elevate their bodies at a 45-degree angle to display their ripe, swollen bellies. As many as three females may display before a single male at the same time. During these prenuptial interludes the red lips and faces of both sexes brighten considerably.

When males find females to their liking, they approach with fins erect and peck the tops of their selected mates' heads. Then, as if to show the females exactly where to go, they dart in and out of their nests. The females disappear inside and begin moving back and forth across the walls, laying adhesive eggs as they go. From time to time the males fertilize the eggs in a similar manner. During the 15- to 20-minute egg-laying episodes the males periodically dash outside, turn and peck the females' heads if they are exposed, and return. At other times they lift their forebodies off the bottom at a 60-degree angle, flex fins and curve into an exaggerated S-posture. If females approach while spawning is underway, the males chase the late-comers away. After finishing, the females may attempt to spawn with other males but usually swim back to their territories, provoking a series of chases by territory-holders as they pass.

During each multi-day reproductive period males receive from zero to 21 clutches, often from several females. On some mornings, as many as three females lay eggs in the same nest. Brooding males repeatedly fin-fan and pick at the single layer of eggs covering their nest walls, but guarding their charges from roving packs of egg-predators, especially young Bluehead Wrasse, *Thalassoma bifasciatum*, is their primary concern.

Both female and male Redlip Blennies prefer large spawning partners. Females were found to approach the nests of larger males more frequently, spawn with them more often and, while there, deposit more eggs. By chasing away smaller females and accepting only the larger more prolific egg-layers, males were calculated to increase their reproductive success. Females are believed to select larger suitors because they spend more time guarding their nests, therefore losing fewer clutches than smaller males. Larger males also tend their nests for more days during each reproductive period. Larger males, at or near their maximum growth potential, are probably better able to sacrifice feeding time than their smaller, rapidly growing rivals.

The spherical eggs, less than one millimeter in diameter, hatch during the night of the fifth day after fertilization, one of the shortest incubation periods known for blennies. The yolk-sac larvae rise to the surface, where they catch a seaward ride on an outgoing tide. Approximately 45 days later the transparent torpedo-shaped fish bearing large recurved teeth settle into crevices in adult habitats. In Barbados, ninety percent of recruits arrive in May. Researchers there have been unable to find Redlip recruits other than in areas colonized by adults. While metamorphosing into juveniles, the settled larvae feed on fat stored in enlarged livers. Juveniles attempt to establish territories near where they settle. As the juveniles emerge after metamorphosis, competition for territories increases, with most attacks directed at the recent arrivals. With shelter sites at a premium, young fish unable to retain their niches become easy victims of predators. Still, their mortality rate of 33 percent during the first month after settlement is extremely low, compared with recruits of other species. Redlips become sexually active about two months after settling, at a length of two inches. Those that are able to establish territories have a life expectancy of about one year.

Butterflyfishes
Family Chaetodontidae

Spotfin Butterflyfish regularly feed together in, what are believed to be, mated pairs.

Butterflyfishes generally flit about the bottom in pairs, using keen eyesight and protruding terminal mouths lined with fine teeth to pluck dinner from the substrate. The sexually indistinguishable mated pairs, which live together inside large home ranges, are believed to be companions for extended periods, possibly for a lifetime. Territorial defense is seldom evident except late in the day, close to the courtship period, when the customarily mild-mannered fishes occasionally chase neighbors.

The Caribbean is home to only seven butterflyfishes. The majority of the worldwide tropical family of 120 species resides in the Pacific and Indian Oceans. Although the Caribbean butterflyfishes, all in the genus *Chaetodon*, eat anthozoids, primarily from hard and soft corals, and zoanthids, each species tends to have its own favorite foods. The Foureye Butterflyfish, *Chaetodon capistratus*, ranges widely over the reef platform, compulsively nipping at nearly every bottom structure it passes. The common species is particularly fond of gorgonian polyps. Banded Butterflyfish, *C. striatus*, spend their day harvesting exposed polychaete appendages on shallow reef crests and patch reefs. Reef Butterflyfish, *C. sedentarius*, and Spotfin Butterflyfish, *C. ocellatus*, live slightly deeper, generally near high-profile reefs, where they dine on tubeworms, hydroids and small crustaceans, including shrimps. The protracted snouts of Longsnout Butterflyfish, *C. aculeatus*, are used to nip the exposed radioles of Christmas Tree Worms, *Spirobranchus giganteus*, usually on deeper drop-offs and complex coral structures from 40 to 200 feet. In the southern Caribbean, Longsnouts often live as shallow as 20 feet. The rarely sighted Bank Butterflyfish, *C. aya*, seldom found in less than 100 feet of water, ranges from eastern Florida to North Carolina and the Gulf of Mexico. The Threeband Butterflyfish, *C. guyanensis*, inhabits Caribbean reefs below 200 feet.

Butterflyfishes also consume bits of tunicates and eggs. During annual coral spawns Foureye Butterflyfish and Banded Butterflyfish flock around erupting coral heads, gobbling down fat-filled gamete bundles. We have observed Foureyes greedily pulling gametes from Giant Star Coral, *Montastraea cavernosa*, even before they were released.

Butterflyfishes depend on their laterally compressed bodies and prominent arsenal of dorsal spines to deter predators. Dark eye-concealing bands and false eyespots, prominent on juveniles and the Foureye, help to misdirect attacks. Although they are slow swimmers who seldom seek shelter, their defenses must work well – few butterflyfishes have been found in the stomachs of piscivores. As night falls, most adults bed down deep within protective structures. Only the Foureye, a restless sleeper who develops a vague pattern of bars at night, is regularly sighted after dark.

Little is known about the spawning behavior or reproductive seasons of the Caribbean butterflyfishes. The majority of reported spawnings occurred at sunset during the cool-water months from February until May, but a few ripe females and sporadic courtship behavior have been noted in the fall. (Noting the swollen bellies of egg-laden females is the only way to visually distinguish between the sexes.) Only isolated pair spawning events between what appear to be monogamous couples have been documented to date. During reproductive peaks Longsnouts are believed to spawn every other day at alternating sites within their home ranges. Ten minutes before sunset, a pair, or occasionally a male with two mates, rendezvous near a prominent feature rising from the sea floor. Courtship is brief and unspectacular. While slowly rising, the male laterally circles the female with his snout caressing her tail fin. Just before gamete release, the female pauses in a head-up stance while the male positions his snout next to her vent from below. After simultaneous release, the male moves forward, leaving the female and a gamete cloud behind. When two females are involved, the male spawns with his second partner less than a minute after spawning with the first.

Courting Longsnout Butterflyfish.

Butterflyfishes

The purpose of Foureye Butterflyfish aggregations is not understood.

On three consecutive evenings, a researcher observed a savage wound-inflicting rivalry between Longsnouts when a solitary male challenged a pair attempting to court. The paired-male, at times assisted by his swollen partner, repeatedly attempted to drive the stranger away before the males finally squared-off inches apart. With their sharp foredorsal spikes directed at one another, the fish attacked repeatedly driving needle-sharp spines into his opponent's fins and body until both fish, showing obvious injuries, retreated. The next evening the trio arrived at the same site, but the female, minus her bulging abdomen apparently was not worth fighting over. On the third evening, with the female once again ripe, it was war. After another bloodletting the challenger suddenly departed, allowing the pair to spawn unmolested.

Pairs of Foureye Butterflyfish have been observed spawning on alternate evenings in much the same manner as Longsnouts. However, their spawning rise carries them somewhat higher above their spawning landmark and, instead of explosively releasing clouds of gametes, the eggs discharge in a thick stream. In regions with concentrated populations Foureye Butterflyfish may also participate in group spawns. On numerous occasions, we have observed up to a dozen individuals moving about the reef together in Bimini, Bahamas. Similar gatherings also have been reported in Puerto Rico, Jamaica and the Cayman Islands. The lively groups swim rapidly about in loose formations, nipping, pecking and chasing among themselves. From time to time pairs and foursomes break away, only to rejoin the constantly moving assemblies later. This gregarious behavior seems to be most prevalent in late afternoon shortly before the traditional pair-spawning period, but we have also seen group behavior in the morning.

The less frequent reproductive activities of Banded Butterflyfish were observed by researchers once in February and again in March in Puerto Rico.

Two solitary pairs, each with a visibly swollen female, swam steadily about the bottom of a large area, gradually moving closer to one another as darkness settled. The males occasionally brushed their mates' tail fins with their snouts. Neither pair associated with a raised bottom structure, and both made several false starts before finally ascending more than 20 feet above the bottom to spawn. The Spotfin Butterflyfish and Reef Butterflyfish have not been observed spawning. A partially distended Spotfin female was captured at dusk in May in the Bahamas. Her eggs were found to be only partially hydrated, leading to speculation that the species might spawn in the early morning.

Foureye Butterflyfish dine on the gamete bundles of spawning coral.

Depending on the size of the female, several hundred to a few thousand eggs are released with each spawn. The buoyant, spherical eggs, less than one millimeter across, hatch into tiny larvae with large yolk sacs between 24 and 48 hours later. Three days after hatching pigmented eyes are evident, and the yolk is gone. As the larvae mature they develop deep, laterally compressed bodies and a series of clear armorlike plates covering their heads and forebodies. This feature, unique among fishes, is so unusual that the silvery little quarter-inch creatures have been given their own name, tholichthys. The amount of time the different species remain pelagic has not been determined.

The button-sized larvae settle to the sea floor at night and make a rapid transformation into juveniles. Most juvenile butterflyfishes are creamy white with yellow fin highlights, distinctive ocellated eyespots and barred patterns. The skittish youngsters generally inhabit shallow habitats, taking up residence in sand pockets, around isolated coral and sponge formations, in grass beds and among mangrove roots. They lead solitary lives until they reach sexual maturity in approximately one year at a length of about four inches.

A juvenile Spotfin Butterflyfish finds protection under urchin spines.

Damselfishes
Family Pomacentridae

The threat of nips from a Threespot Damselfish turns away a Queen Angelfish.

Any diver who has explored a Caribbean reef is well aware of the disagreeable disposition of damselfishes. Several species of the palm-sized fishes are driven by a compulsion to attack everything that comes near their personal pieces of the reef, including divers. Fortunately, their tiny mouths lined with fine teeth are designed for nipping algae, and even their worst bites fail to leave a mark. Of the 14 species from the tropical western Atlantic, only four are primarily responsible for giving the family its infamous reputation, though every damselfish is territorially assertive to some degree, especially males guarding egg nests. Three characteristics define family membership: a single nostril hole on each side of the snout rather than the usual two, scales that extend onto the fins, and an interrupted lateral line. Over 315 damselfishes have been classified worldwide. While the majority inhabit the tropical reefs of the Indo-Pacific, a few species have invaded temperate waters. Males and females of every species are difficult, if not impossible, to distinguish visually except during breeding periods when one or both sexes, but usually males, exhibit distinct spawning patterns and behavior.

Though there probably has been more behavioral research on Pomacentrids than any other group of reef fishes, their taxonomy is still in question. Even the name of the most populous Atlantic genus, originally known as *Eupomacentrus* and switched along the way to *Pomacentrus*, is now being challenged by *Stegastes*. And there remains a shortage of information about the common Longfin Damselfish, *Stegastes diencaeus*, long confused with the similar-appearing Dusky

Damselfish, *S. fuscus*. In fact, into the early 1980s, the juvenile Longfin was still classified incorrectly as a separate species, *Eupomacentrus mellis*, and commonly known as the Honey Gregory.

Caribbean damselfishes are divided into four genera: *Stegastes*, the largest group, represented by six species; *Abudefduf*, with two species, the Sergeant Major, *A. saxatilis*, and Night Sergeant, *A. taurus*; *Microspathodon*, which includes only the Yellowtail Damselfish, *M. chrysurus*; and the semi-pelagic, plankton-picking *Chromis*, with five species, including the slender Brown Chromis, *C. multilineata*, and Blue Chromis, *C. cyanea*. Four species, the Dusky Damselfish; the Longfin Damselfish; the Threespot Damselfish, *S. planifrons*; and the Yellowtail Damselfish farm and defend permanent territories of filamentous algae that surround their centrally-located hiding holes. These are the notorious nippers, and there is good reason for their aggressive nature: the reef is rife with algae-eating parrotfishes and surgeonfishes that covet the damselfishes' well-kept lawns. Even wrasses and other bottom-pickers will, if given the chance, gladly savage a damselfish garden for the wealth of tiny

Threespot Damselfish - genus Stegastes.

Sergeant Major - genus Abudefduf.

Yellowtail Damselfish - Microspathodon.

Brown Chromis - genus Chromis.

Damselfishes

invertebrates living within the tangled algal strands. The bulk of the damselfishes' diet does not come from eating the lawns, but from the garden of tiny epiphytic blue-green algae and associated detritus that clings to the filaments. Incidental animal matter, taken while grazing, is believed to supply the remainder of their nutritional needs. The hyper little fishes often go to such lengths protecting their turf that a four-inch defender will chase a three-foot parrotfish six feet into the water column. However, Blue Tang, *Acanthurus coeruleus*, one of the reef's most abundant algae-grazers, have learned to penetrate their defenses by feeding in large, swarming groups, often including a variety of other bottom-feeding species. Algae-farming damselfishes hover in horror as the battalion of clicking jaws makes it way down the reef line. When under siege, the overmatched tenant dashes about frantically, biting first one invader and then another until it gives up, moves to the side and watches its prized crop being ravaged. In less than a minute all is over as the mob moves on to its next victim.

Never-ending border wars played out daily between homesteading damselfishes and free-ranging herbivores create a mosaic of heavily matted oases surrounded by rock scraped bare of filamentous algae. Defended territories are stable through time, with one generation after another tending the same sites. The damselfishes' thick algal mats prevent the growth of coralline algae and corals – organisms indispensable for bonding the reef's framework. Over the years, the reef rock underneath loosens and crumbles from the constant forces of erosion. At the same time, the lush growth is responsible for much of the reef's productivity through nitrogen fixation, a process necessary to form proteins in marine animals and plants, including zooxanthellae, the symbiotic algae essential for coral growth.

The ubiquitous Sergeant Majors and the rarely observed Night Sergeant also consume plant material, but they, like most family members, do not make their living by defending feeding territories. Night Sergeants live in rocky inshore surge zones with plenty of rapidly growing algae and few competitors, so there is no need to expend energy protecting crops. Sergeant Majors have a diverse diet with only ten percent from plants and the remainder coming from benthic invertebrates, small fishes, eggs, and zooplankton picked from the currents. Plankton is also the primary food of Bicolor Damselfish, *S. partitus*, the lone plankton-eating *Stegastes*, and of all five species in the genus *Chromis*.

Damselfishes inhabit nearly every type of reef structure, from the shallows to depths well beyond safe diving limits. Although most species are found in a single habitat, others readily adapt to a variety of surroundings, and a few coexist with one or two other damselfish species. For example, Threespots prefer to establish their territories within the three-dimensional maze of Staghorn Coral, *Acropora cervicornis*, branches but regularly reside in Lettuce Coral, *Agaricia agaricites*, and large boulder corals. Cocoa Damselfish, *S. variabilis*, who live in extended home ranges that are too large to defend aggressively, favor massive boulder corals in deep water but also thrive in shallow groves of Staghorn Coral. Large female Yellowtail Damselfish are typically associated with Elkhorn Coral, *Acropora palmata*, on reef crests, while the males occupy deeper rubble zones.

An interesting example of cohabitation involves Yellowtails, who reach their greatest abundance when sharing feeding resources with smaller Duskys or

A Threespot Damselfish tends its private algal garden.

The damselfishes' luxuriant turf of filamentous algae supports a secondary garden of appetizing diatoms and other epiphytes.

Damselfishes

Threespots. Large Yellowtails, which grow to over eight inches, superimpose their broad feeding areas over the territories of several Duskys. Both species protect the same resources from the same herbivores, but the smaller, submissive tenants are expected to perform the lion's share of the defensive duties. A similar, size-related dominance occurs with smaller Threespots; however, large adults are able to expel the less-aggressive Yellowtails from their turf.

Unlike their reef-oriented relatives, the Brown and the Blue Chromis have adapted to a semi-pelagic way of life to gain access to the rich plankton streams that flow above the reef. Both species feed much of the day in small to large groups, maintaining ties with the reef only to elude predators, sleep, spawn and patronize cleaning stations. Interestingly, these two species and Sergeant Majors, the region's only schooling damselfish, are the only family members to visit cleaning stations. The less numerous Blue Chromis tend to collect in small groups in shallower water and remain closer to the reef, while Brown Chromis assemble in massive aggregations that often fill the water column high above outer reef banks.

Brown Chromis often pick zooplankton from open water in thick aggregations.

Occasionally the species integrate and at times are joined by Creole Wrasse, *Clepticus parrae*, the region's other abundant plankton-picker. The three remaining members of the genus generally inhabit deeper water. The two- to three-inch adult Purple Reeffish, *Chromis scotti*, and Sunshinefish, *C. insolata*, and their brightly colored juveniles typically congregate in small groups in shallow pockets on walls and reef slopes. Yellowtail Reeffish, *C. enchrysurus*, also live deep but prefer flat, heavily contoured bottoms and artificial reef sites. All three rely on plankton diets but never feed far from the reef's protection.

Half of the damselfish species, the six *Stegastes* and the lone *Microspathodon*, patrol and defend permanent territories throughout the year. However, the breeding males of the remaining seven species, the five *Chromis* and two *Abudefduf*, temporarily defend spawning sites during reproductive periods. Though the size of permanent territories varies considerably among species, each is the exclusive dominion of a single adult and functions to protect food resources, shelter holes and, in the case of males, nest sites and eggs. But not every adult in a population maintains its own personal area. These so-called wanderers, including both females and non-reproductive males, suffer a higher predation rate. Their presence, however, provides a pool of individuals ready to repopulate vacated territories, helping to maintain a constant population density.

Permanent territories have three basic components: a core, peripheral areas and pathways. The core is usually a small, intensely defended feeding area around the most frequently used shelter hole. The same hole also serves as a nighttime retreat and nest site. Encompassing the core is a much larger irregularly shaped peripheral sector,

Juvenile Sunshinefish.

defined by the limits of a territory-holder's defensive efforts. Territories adjacent to those of members of the same species are patrolled to maintain sovereignty. Paths, closely following protective ledges and outcroppings, are habitually used as routes of travel through the periphery.

Not all fishes are equal in the eyes of territorial damselfishes; during non-breeding periods the most forceful attacks are directed at their own species and algae-eating surgeonfishes and parrotfishes. When males guard eggs the intensity of attacks elevates dramatically, and known egg-bandits are encountered further from the core than at other times. While brooding, even normally mellow Sergeant Major males will sail up to ten feet above their nests to confront passing divers.

All damselfishes are benthic egg-brooders that follow a standard reproductive regime. It begins with males selecting and preparing nest sites, followed by courtship, egg-laying, and males tending and protecting the nests until hatching. Spawning occurs throughout the year, but the pace picks up in the spring, reaches its pinnacle during summer months and tapers off as fall progresses. Monthly peaks, lasting several days, are linked to lunar or semilunar cycles. Nearly all courtship and spawning by species holding permanent territories takes place during the first hour of daylight, while those maintaining temporary nesting sites become reproductively active in the afternoon.

Intra-species communications are important to the social organization of damselfishes. Each species employs color changes and body language to signal aggression, submission, territorial dominance and sexual readiness; and all, except members of the genus *Chromis,* communicate with sound. The majority of messages come into play during reproduction. While courting, for instance, male Bicolors develop a striking black mask/black tail pattern and perform a series of swooping dips, producing a chirping sound with each motion.

Before courtship begins, nests are prepared to receive eggs. Most territorial damselfishes select a hard surface inside their shelter holes. Algae, invertebrates and debris are removed by mouth. Long-spined Urchins, *Diadema antillarum,* are chased away by biting off the tips of their spines. *Chromis* never clear surfaces but repeatedly fan open areas on the reef, in algae bushes and even on the sand in

Damselfishes

preparation for spawning. When all is ready, males assume their courtship colors and set about wooing mates during the early hours of the morning. Spawning patterns vary among species, but typically the upper region of the back from behind the head to the tail lightens noticeably. If males are lucky, females approach their nests; but in most instances, the suitors must travel outside their territories and employ a mixed bag of tactics to coax potential partners back to their nest sites. The standard device is the signal jump, a common courtship behavior employed by members of several fish families: the males, in full spawning colors, dash almost straight up, turn and quickly swim back to the starting point. These eye-catching moves are usually performed in a series over the nest site but also, on occasion, outside their territories. In an attempt to encourage females to follow them to their nests, courting males circle females, perform figure 8s, lead, shove, bump, nudge and, from time to time, nip flanks to get them moving in the proper direction. Each solicitation is executed with an exaggerated swimming style, characterized by increased body flexion. Once at the nests, quite a few females leave without spawning, forcing the undaunted males to repeat their high-spirited nuptial routine.

Compact clusters of eggs, called clutches, are laid in a single layer by females repeatedly dragging their extended cone-shaped urogenital papillae over the nests. This maneuver, also used by males to fertilize eggs, is known as skimming. When not in use the white, fleshy papilla, which can be seen during spawning, retracts into a recessed abdominal groove between the anus and the first spine of the anal fin. Occasionally pairs spawn in the same nest at the same time, side-by-side, but in most circumstances, the males fertilize the eggs while their mates are away from the nests. When, as often happens, more than one female spawns in a nest during the same day the fresh eggs are added to the same clutch. Eggs laid the following day are nearly always placed contiguous to those of the previous day. However, if clutches have been in the nest for more than one day, new eggs customarily are deposited on the opposite side of the nests. Males can fertilize every morning throughout a reproduction cycle, but females must take a few days off before spawning again.

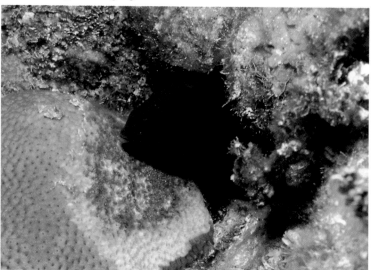

A male Longfin Damselfish guards his nest of eggs from predators.

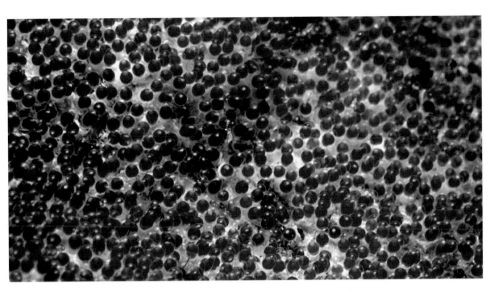

Close-up of a Sergeant Major's egg nest.

Once eggs are in the nests, the responsibility for their well-being is left entirely to the males. Eggs are attentively picked at to remove debris, bacteria and infertile capsules. Occasionally males place their mouths around small groups of eggs and gently agitate them. Clutches are regularly fanned to move water over their surfaces. Some damselfishes turn laterally to the eggs and scull with a single pectoral fin, while others face the eggs and direct water forward by alternating pectoral fins. A few males sweep across the eggs with their anal and tail fins. The *Chromis*, whose eggs are often scattered in algae bushes, wedge themselves between the blades and sway back and forth. For an unknown reason, swarming clouds of tiny, transparent Mysid Shrimp, *Mysidium spp.*, commonly hover in the entranceways of nests containing eggs.

A male Sergeant Major keeping his nest tidy.

187

Damselfishes

The number of clutches received by males varies considerably. Why one male is more successful than another is not completely understood. Unlike other fish species which provide parental care, female damselfishes do not favor mates because of their larger physical size, quality of nest preparation or the number of eggs already in place. In fact, the only attribute correlated directly with mating success for any species of damselfish is an increased rate and number of dips performed by courting Bicolors.

Researchers recently documented a surprising new dynamic at work in the little Bicolors' mate selection process that probably applies to other family members as well. Often, egg-laden females pass several courting males en route to a preferred partner. It has also been noted that once reproductive cycles begin, female Bicolors, as well as females of other damselfish species, routinely inspect nest sites during nonreproductive hours of the day. Further observations established that approximately 20 percent of unhatched eggs, in most cases entire clutches, disappear from the Bicolors' nests. A quarter of these losses could be attributed to cannibalism by guardians. Such behavior, typical of many damselfishes, only occurs after new eggs are laid in nests already containing two or more clutches. However, the majority of eggs disappear at night, when males no longer guard their nests.

The culprit was discovered to be the nocturnally active Blunt-spined Brittle Star, *Ophiocoma echinata*. These five-armed egg-pirates hide in confined passages and wiggle out to dine only after dark. It now appears that the females' daytime excursions are utilized to monitor a nest site's susceptibility to egg predation. Females generally show a marked fidelity to a single partner, spawning with him 70 percent of the time. However, those females who discover a clutch missing or detect the lingering scent of a brittle star almost always select a new site to deposit subsequent clutches.

An adhesive matrix of microscopic strands secures each elliptical egg in its nest. Throughout spawning, both parents periodically fan the clutch to force the eggs into an upright position, which allows them to move slightly on their individual holdfast. Egg sizes vary among species, with those of the Brown Chromis and Blue Chromis the smallest, measuring just under 0.6 mm in length, while Beaugregory, *S. leucostrictus* eggs, the largest, measure 1.28 mm long. Eggs generally begin to hatch at dusk three to seven days after fertilization. The tiny, transparent larvae immediately enter the pelagic stage of their life cycle. The time damselfishes spend as plankton is shorter and fluctuates less when compared to other families of reef fishes. The duration between hatching and settlement back to a shallow-water environment ranges from 17 to 34 days.

With the exception of the Sunshinefish, the juveniles of plankton-feeding damselfishes closely resemble and commonly live in association with adults. By contrast, the juveniles of the territorial bottom-feeders exhibit bright patterns distinctly different from their typically drab elders. This dichromatism between the age groups is believed to suppress the aggressive drive of adults. The colorful youngsters spend their early months in isolated, shallow-water areas well away from established feeding territories. Only with sexual maturity will they venture into adult habitats. It is believed that *Stegastes*, other than Bicolors, become sexually active by their second or third year and probably live for six to eight years.

Adult Brown Chromis.

Recently settled Brown Chromis juveniles. Like most planktivores, juvenile Brown Chromis bear a close resemblance to adults.

Adult Longfin Damselfish.   *Juvenile Longfin Damselfish.*

Damselfishes

Bicolor Damselfish
Stegastes partitus

Bicolor Damselfish are well represented in nearly every part of the tropical western Atlantic. Where prolific, the two- to three-inch black and white fish establish territories on virtually every available coral structure, sponge, conch shell and rocky outcrop from shallow back reefs to the edge of plunging depths. Bicolors form into distinct colonies comprising every size individual and both sexes. The species' ability to communicate with a broad repertoire of movements, color patterns and sounds makes it an interesting subject for behavioral biologists and fish watchers.

Throughout much of the day adult Bicolors feed in the water column, plucking tiny copepods, pelagic tunicates and larvae from the currents. The feeding height is limited by an individual's size, with even the largest males rising no further than five feet above the protection of their personal shelter holes. When predators or divers approach, the fish drop to the bottom and remain near cover until the threat passes.

Colonies are strict, size-related hierarchies governed by a dominant high-spirited male – always the largest fish who oversees the largest territory. His quasi-submissive subjects typically include two or three lesser males holding much smaller domains, a few females with limited, less-defined territories and a scattering of half-inch juveniles who spend their time cloistered near protective shelters. The social order is maintained by a seemingly endless succession of chases and challenges. Chases are nearly always directed at the next smaller individual, while challenges consist of rather weak-willed stands of defiance by subordinates after being driven back to their hiding holes. The more passive females have their own pecking order with fewer and less-intense chases aimed at other females and juveniles. It is

Bicolor Damselfish picking zooplankton from the currents.

A Bicolor Damselfish – typical color phase.

believed that the smallest female acts as a lightning rod for the frustrations of the entire colony. During reproductive periods, when the males' movements are restricted by egg-tending and competition for mates is running high, everyone vents anger at the lowly female, especially higher-ranking males. Only her ability to maneuver rapidly within restricted areas keeps her alive.

Even though Bicolors do not have to protect their planktonic food source, both males and females routinely defend their territories from prowling fishes. When eggs are in nests, attacks from guardian males increase in both number and intensity. The most frequent recipients of their wrath are the notorious egg-eating Bluehead Wrasse, *Thalassoma bifasciatum*, and Slippery Dick, *Halichoeres bivittatus*. Occasionally, a large Bicolor male from a neighboring area takes temporary refuge in another colony. Such a serious breach of sovereignty is handled exclusively by the colony's dominant male. In a grand show of bravado he immediately switches on a vertical white bar of aggression and confronts the rival with a ritualistic suite of intimidating behaviors, including close parallel swimming, frontal and lateral displays and tail-backs, where he turns and backs toward the intruder with spread fins and a wildly beating tail.

The Bicolors' impressive inventory of communication skills is divided into three basic categories: body movements and postures, color patterns and

Black mask pattern of courting males.

White body bar of aggression.

Damselfishes

sounds. At crucial points in every significant interaction at least one, but in most instances a medley, of communicative exchanges comes into play. Depending on circumstances, Bicolors produce either chirps, grunts or pops. For instance, the face-off described above between two dominant males would possibly include as many as six to ten pops. Unfortunately, nearly all of the sounds are undetectable by underwater observers.

Both male and female Bicolors reach sexual maturity within a year, and if they survive, breed from two to three additional years. The prolific species spawns in all but the coolest months, with lunar peaks occurring during seven-day periods following the full moons of May through October. Even though females spawn only in the early morning and on specific days, males exhibit courtship behavior in every season and throughout much of the day. Their persistent displays attest to the females' control over the mating schedule. During spawning periods courtship begins at sunrise, when males acquire distinctive "black mask" patterns that turn their faces and tails jet black and their midbodies a bright contrasting white. Decked out in their eye-catching, two-tone wardrobe, males swim up to 20 feet from their territories to lure females back to their nests. As they approach a prospective mate, males execute a series of tilts and dips, a behavior similar to the signal jumps of other species. When a male starts to dip, no matter what time of day, others in the vicinity quickly follow suit, and with good reason – those males performing the most frequent dips receive the most clutches. Dip sequences are typically repeated three to five times in a row, with each moving the males closer

*A male Bicolor Damselfish protects his egg nest, inside the conch shell,
from a hungry swarm of Bluehead Wrasse.*

to prospective mates. Chirps accompany each series. Experiments reveal that females are not only able to identify the sounds of individual males but can also distinguish the size of the singing males.

When females show interest by moving toward dipping males, the suitors fall in behind and encourage them to move forward with a nudge or two. They then zip around in front and eagerly lead intended mates in the right direction. Once at a nest, most females leave without spawning, forcing the males to repeat the entire tilting-dipping-nudging-and-leading cycle. It ordinarily takes repeated attempts before partners are persuaded to spawn, but in some cases females travel to nest sites and spawn without prompting.

Having decided to spawn, the females darken noticeably, and the males position themselves nose-down next to their nests and quiver. The pairs spread fins and circle side-by-side for five to 15 seconds while the males make occasional grunting noises. The males dart to their nests and briskly skim the surface. Like many damselfishes, the nests of Bicolors are hidden from view inside small holes, narrow crevices or conch shells. Once spawning begins, it generally takes the female from 20 to 40 minutes to lay between 500 and 5,000 eggs. The number of eggs corresponds to a female's size. Now and again females move briefly from the nests, allowing males to fertilize. While waiting, the males busy themselves by circling the sites, chasing away all comers and occasionally courting nearby females. Generally only one female spawns in a nest, but nearly a third of nests contain a single clutch with the eggs of two or even three females. During a weeklong reproductive cycle, females spawn once every two days and, in 70 percent of cases, at the same nest site.

Parental males do not spend as much time grooming and fanning eggs as other damselfishes, but they are accomplished nest-defenders. When first laid, the eggs appear white, changing to dull yellow by the end of day one, pink on day two, and finally purple on the third day. At dusk, three and one-half days after fertilization, the eggs begin to hatch, and the larvae enter the pelagic realm for 27 to 31 days before ready to settle to a shallow sea floor. Clusters of recently settled juveniles often inhabit the rubble mounds of Sand Tilefish, *Malacanthus plumieri*.

Threespot Damselfish
Stegastes planifrons

Threespot Damselfish lay claim to virtually every substantial thicket of Staghorn Coral, *Acropora cervicornis*, in the Caribbean. However, if a reef lacks their favorite habitat, these highly adaptable three- to five-inch fish willingly establish their permanent feeding territories on patch reefs, massive coral mounds, Elkhorn Coral, *A. palmata*, dock pilings and fields of large-sized rubble. Males dominate the Staghorn Coral groves, with the larger individuals controlling territories in the center while smaller males and a few females reside in the less desirable outer branches. Excluded females and subordinate males spill over into surrounding habitats.

Many Staghorn colonies are filled to capacity with contiguous Threespot territories, each with its own protected algae garden growing on dead interior branches. Although space is at a premium, conflicts between neighbors are limited.

Damselfishes

Adult Threespot Damselfish.

Spawning pattern.

Algae-eating intruders, however, are confronted throughout the day. Because of their more vulnerable situation, defenders on the outskirts challenge prowlers more frequently. Continued advances by a surgeonfish will provoke a squadron of high-strung Threespots to rise above their territories in a united front. Smaller residents from the periphery regularly scout the colony's interior for vacant or poorly defended territories, but the newcomers are not allowed to remain unless they are equal in size to neighboring territory holders. Through this slow process, long-lived individuals eventually gain access to the favored real estate in the colony's interior.

Like most damselfishes, spawning occurs in every season, with increased activity during warmer months. Peak periods begin four to seven days after the full moon. In Staghorn, nest sites are prepared by resident males on dead tips of cylindrical algae-covered branches. In other habitats nests are located on the ceilings of overhangs and rock caves. At the first light of dawn, either females or males initiate spawning. Females with territories in coral mounds often cross open terrain to mate in Staghorn colonies. Courting males acquire a dark diffuse blotch across their sides, their cheeks flush pale, and the spot at the base of each pectoral fin darkens. In large colonies, courtship is contagious; the first signal jump sets off a frenzy of jumping males across the maze of branches. Once aroused, males leave their territories with only one thought in mind. Females are approached and circled with an embellished swimming style, accompanied by clicking sounds. Males energetically lead, herd and nudge their choices toward their nests. Once near, they dart back and forth from nests to mates, perform signal jumps and mock spawning runs, indicating where eggs are to be placed. When females initiate spawning, their backs pale to brownish yellow and their bellies lighten as they approach the males. Once positioned next to their partners the females are led to the nest sites, where the pairs simultaneously make slow circular spawning passes. In this manner, between 2,000 and 10,000 eggs are laid in a single nest.

The males fan and tend the eggs every few minutes, but their best parental attribute is nest-guarding. Nothing that comes near the Threespots' egg-laden nests leaves unchallenged. Smaller fishes are immediately chased, while larger intruders are forewarned with lateral displays, exaggerated swimming, headstands and clicking sounds before a barrage of well-placed nips is delivered to the eyes and fins.

The fresh yellow eggs turn green as they mature. Hatched larvae remain in their planktonic stage for 17 to 25 days. The bright yellow juveniles stay close to cover, feeding on a diet evenly divided between algae and bottom-dwelling copepods. With growth, they become more dependent on plant material. Unlike most damselfish juveniles, they seldom inhabit shallow inshore areas, choosing instead small patch reefs and the shelter of fire coral ridges in deeper water.

Dusky Damselfish
Stegastes fuscus

Dark, olive-brown Dusky Damselfish inhabit a variety of bottom structures from shallow to moderate depths. The four- to six-inch fish prefer areas of large rubble, but regularly inhabit reef structures. Smaller individuals frequent shallow sandy slopes and bare rock in back-reef areas. Both males and females aggressively defend permanent feeding territories ranging from four to 20 square feet. The species reaches its highest population density inside Elkhorn Coral, *Acropora palmata*, gardens, where it shares feeding turf with large Yellowtail Damselfish, *Microspathodon chrysurus*, which dominate the smaller Duskys.

The species spawns year-round between the new and full moon, with synchronized peaks occurring sporadically every two to four days. Females spawn several times within each lunar cycle, at intervals of from one to nine days. It is not yet understood what prompts spawning peaks. At daybreak females travel to prepared nest sites in secluded areas of the males' territories. The backs of courting males pale as they perform a series of signal jumps that occasionally attract multiple mates. In rare cases as many as three females lay eggs together, but most prefer waiting their turn. Eggs are deposited in several installments, each lasting from one to 20 minutes. Between bouts, females often return to their territories for brief periods while the males fertilize. The final product is a compact, single-layer clutch. Males frequently defend and tend as

A Dusky Damselfish, in spawning colors, fertilizes his egg nest.

Damselfishes

many as four clutches in a nest, each laid on a separate day. Eggs begin hatching at dusk four days after fertilization, and the larvae settle back to the reef between 20 and 23 days later.

Beaugregory
Stegastes leucostictus

Beaugregories typically inhabit calm inshore bottoms of sand and rubble. They are quite common in boat channels, bays, jetties and around dock pilings where they often find shelter in empty conch shells and cans. Those inhabiting reefs generally take sanctuary in rubble-strewn back-reef surge zones or occasionally reef fronts, most frequently in depths of less than 20 feet. Juveniles often take refuge inside small, isolated structures on open sand, while adolescents live in areas of sand and rubble; adults prefer rubble bottom. Because of the large amount of eggs, worms, fishes, crabs and shrimps in their diet, and the limited volume of algae (just over 20 percent), the species is considered to be carnivorous, with no need to protect algae patches.

The bright, horizontal, two-tone blue and yellow color pattern of the juveniles remains through sexual maturity. Individuals take on olive-brown overtones only after moving into rubble with older adults. Half of the males maintain large, weakly defended permanent territories with several widely spaced shelter holes. The remaining adult males move freely from place to place. A shortage of good locations to build nests in rubble possibly accounts for the surplus of unstable males. Females are even more mobile and far less aggressive than territorial males.

Spawning occurs to some degree year-round, with peaks around the full moons of January through October. Breeding males prepare and defend nest sites in small rubble caves, conch shells, concrete blocks and cans. Hard interior surfaces are picked clean of algae and sponge. Thrashing tails remove sand from entranceways and often create trenches encircling nests. Occasionally unsolicited females come

A young adult Beaugregory makes its home inside an abandoned Queen Conch shell.

to spawn, but in most cases males leave their territories and travel up to 30 feet to woo females. Courting males lighten noticeably across their backs as they signal jump, circle perspective mates and herd them back to their territories. The closer they get to their nests the more hyperactive males become – darting, dipping and attempting to herd the females inside by swimming next to their sides. Spawning is brief, lasting only 10 to 20 seconds. Often nests receive multiple clutches over several days. Guarding males remain close to the nests' entrances, now and again darting inside to fan the eggs. Defense is spirited; wrasses and damselfishes are chased at distances of three to four feet from the nests. Male Saddled Blenny, *Malacoctenus triangulatus*, often take advantage of the Beaugregories' fish-chasing skills by locating their egg nests next to the clutches of brooding male's.

The eggs, the largest laid by the damselfishes in the region, are bright yellow when fresh, later changing to green. Depending on the number of clutches present, a single nest may accommodate between 4,000 and 25,000 eggs at one time. A clutch begins to hatch four and one-half to five days after fertilization. The planktonic phase of the life cycle lasts from 19 to 21 days.

Cocoa Damselfish
Stegastes variabilis

Cocoa Damselfish weakly defend rather large home ranges in a variety of habitats, from inshore patch reefs to deep coral-strewn sandy slopes, where they often wander about the bottom for hundreds of yards. The species' temperate disposition allows it to share habitat with Threespot Damselfish, *Stegastes planifrons*, and Bicolor Damselfish, *S. partitus*. Cocoas consume a mixture of soft bottom materials, including algae, crowns of feather duster worms, tunicates, anemones and isopods.

Breeding increases during summer months, with multiday peaks beginning two weeks after the full moon. During spawning periods, breeding males defend nests on the ceilings and vertical walls of small coral recesses. When females come near, courting males approach them with a head-up display. If the females continue to advance, males perform a quick series of dips before rushing back and executing an impressive set of high signal jumps directly over their nests. Next, males tightly circle the females before herding them to their nests with an exaggerated swimming motion. After pairs enter nests, the males skim briefly before the females begin to lay eggs. Brooding males frequently chase small egg-eating wrasses, but don't seem disturbed by fishes too large to enter the nests. Eggs are regularly inspected, fanned and mouthed. Usually, only a single clutch is present at any one time. The hatched larvae settle 22 to 25 days later.

Yellowtail Damselfish
Microspathodon chrysurus

An Elkhorn Coral, *Acropora palmata*, garden wouldn't be complete without a flourishing community of Yellowtail Damselfish. Fortunately for divers, these large damselfish, which often reach a length of seven inches, are among the family's least-aggressive members. Their lovely juveniles, still referred to in the

Damselfishes

aquarium trade as Jewelfish, display a scattering of iridescent blue dots over rich cobalt bodies. The tiniest have translucent tail fins that become yellow as they mature. Adults retain the basic juvenile patterns but in less vibrant tones. Males and females are visually indistinguishable except during courtship and spawning, when their colors change temporarily.

Large females reign over widespread territories of varying sizes on reef crests, while males typically occupy deeper zones of Elkhorn rubble. Deeper territories tend to be larger, but the circumference of a Yellowtail's territory does not appear to relate to the individual's size. Boundaries regularly encompass several territories of either Dusky Damselfish, *Stegastes fuscus*, or Threespot Damselfish, *S. planifrons*. The smaller species share the harvest of epiphytic diatoms that grow in profusion on the protected algal lawns. The large, dominant Yellowtails rely almost exclusively on their more aggressive cohabitants to keep algae-eating intruders away from their mutual feeding grounds.

In areas with dense population, where there never seems to be sufficient habitat to go around, larger Yellowtails have a distinct advantage in staking territorial claims. Smaller individuals of both sexes are forced to become wanderers. These nonterritorial individuals graze within the boundaries of established residents, who generally offer only token resistance as long as the visitors exhibit a submissive posture. The weak-willed defense of territory-holders is primarily directed toward neighboring Yellowtails and wanderers late in the day.

A peak four- to five-week spawning period occurs in February-March and again in July-August, with decreasing activity during the three following months. Males over four-and-one-half inches long with permanent territories begin readying nests at the onset of each breeding period. Sites are generally located in 20 to 35 feet of water, near the center of territories on the inclined surfaces of exposed Elkhorn rubble or around the base of gorgonian stems. Males use their teeth to rasp algae and invertebrates free from one or, in rare cases, as many as four nests. Just before sunrise, ripe females migrate up to 300 feet to spawn. When they arrive, their light gray heads darken to a deep blue and their yellow tails brighten – colors that remain throughout courtship and spawning. By contrast, courting males wear dull gray coats that lighten as they become increasingly motivated.

Excited males attempt to lead potential partners back to their nests by swimming in a series of increasingly shorter figure-eight patterns. The maneuvers may take them up to 30 feet from their territories. If their first attempts fail, they begin butting and herding the females in the proper direction. Once close, the enamored males perform several signal jumps near their nests. With pectoral fins fluttering, cooperative females rub their abdomens in a circular path over the cleared surfaces, laying eggs as they go. If an area is too small for all the eggs, females continue at a second, nearby nest. While spawning, which can take from three to 90 minutes, the males chase intruders and frequently circle their partners. Every few minutes females swim to the side allowing males to fertilize the deposited eggs. After each pause the males once again signal jump and, if necessary, drive the females back to their duties. When females are finished, the males chase them from the area. As females flee back toward shallow water, smaller courting males enthusiastically vie for their attention. During peak breeding season, females typically spawn once every three days; however, their fidelity to a particular partner has yet to be established.

The light golden color pattern of a courting male.

Yellowtail Damselfish juveniles were once incorrectly known as Jewelfish.

As many as four or, in rare cases, five separate clutches incubate at one time inside a male's nest or nests. During the day guardians continually fan, mouth and pick at the brood to remove algae, tiny invertebrates and infertile or hatched egg cases. With their nests full of eggs, the traditionally passive males become quite temperamental, often confronting egg-eating fish several feet from the nest. Grunts and occasional nips regularly accompany chases. The advances of neighboring Yellowtails pose little threat and are easily thwarted by brief displays of spread fins. Eggs failing to hatch with their clutch during the night are eaten by males the following day as they prepare their nests for additional spawns. Just over ten percent of eggs disappear in this manner.

Three days after fertilization the reddish brown eggs turn gray, and the encased embryos begin wiggling in a circular motion. The following evening the tiny larvae break through tears in their egg cases and begin the 21- to 27-day pelagic phase of their life cycle. They are believed to settle in shallow patch reefs, where the brightly colored juveniles take up temporary residence near the flat branches of Blade Fire Coral, *Millepora complanata*, which makes up the bulk of their early diet. Although we have never observed the behavior, it has been reported that Yellowtail juveniles occasionally act as cleaners.

Sergeant Major
Abudefduf saxatilis

A diverse diet allows Sergeant Major to thrive in a variety of inshore habitats, from coral gardens to jetties and mangroves. The opportunistic feeders are equally at home picking plankton from currents, nibbling tender algae, plucking invertebrates and eggs off rocks, nabbing floating insects or, on occasion, taking

Damselfishes

An aggregation of Sergeant Majors swims rapidly across open terrain.

tiny fishes. When hand-fed from a boat or dock the scrappy fish boil the surface like piranhas, and, during the annual coral spawn, they are first on the scene to gobble up the windfall. In fact, any shallow bottom with shelter and a source of food seems to suit their fancy.

Sexually mature adults tend to cluster in loose groups within home ranges covering a few hundred square feet of sea floor. The boldly barred black and yellow males and females are visually indistinguishable except during courtship and spawning, which occur sporadically throughout the year with a slight peak in early summer. During multiday spawning bouts, triggered by unknown clues, groups move to nearby nesting areas. Mature males prepare nests on barren walls and beneath overhangs or, as a last resort, on the hard sea floor. Premium locations provide better protection from silting and predation. As soon as sites are selected, the once mild-mannered males turn steel-blue and aggressively territorial – a color and attitude that stays with them throughout much of their six- to eight-day nest preparation, courtship, spawning and egg-brooding cycle. Each male first sets about the long, meticulous task of clearing a two- to three-foot circular surface for a

A male and female Sergeant Major place gametes on a rock shelf.

nest. Living materials, such as hydroids, tubeworms, mollusks and algae, are removed by mouth. Large objects are dragged or head-butted to the side. Repeated fin-fanning sweeps away sand and debris. When nests are as slick as dinner plates, males begin advertising for egg-laden females.

Courtship occurs at random throughout the day when blue males suddenly begin to dart erratically back and forth across their nesting territories. As courtship becomes intense, white patches appear on the suitors' heads and cheeks. During spawning additional white blotches

Male courtship colors.

often appear on the males' bodies, and similar markings occasionally show on females. To attract distant mates, males perform repeated loops that carry them two to four feet off the bottom. Persistence pays – frequently dozens of jumps are required to entice egg-laden females.

Usually single, but in some cases, multiple partners show up to spawn, but only one remains. Mating pairs skim in circular patterns over the nests, with the males positioned next to and slightly behind their partners' outside flanks. When males leave to chase an approaching predator, females frequently flee. Males pursue them up to 15 feet and once again perform a series of loops to rekindle interest. Occasionally, well-placed nips help prompt a quick return. It is common for females to be lured back repeatedly before spawning. Males generally remain near the nests, keeping watchful eyes on their partners, during the hour-long spawnings. Now and again they dart in to shed streams of milt. When females slow, an encouraging peck on the fins usually quickens their pace. If neighbors approach, outraged males place themselves between mates and rivals with their bodies angled down and heads touching the bottom.

A Sergeant Major builds a nest in the sand.

Damselfishes

A single female can lay up to 20,000 eggs, and as many as four different females may contribute to a single nest. Each fresh clutch is placed adjacent to the most recent batch. The elliptical pink-to-red globules are extruded in single, continuous side-by-side rows from an extended papilla that brushes along the bottom. Throughout spawning both parents periodically fan the eggs to position them upright so each can sway on its individual holdfast. When finished, the females leave their broods to the exclusive care of the males.

Protecting a nest is a high-energy endeavor. Males not only fan and regularly remove damaged and infertile eggs, but must also remain on constant alert for bandits. Bottom scavengers like nothing better than a dinner of rich, plump fish eggs. The most frequent thieves are Slippery Dick, *Halichoeres bivittatus*; Bluehead Wrasse, *Thalassoma bifasciatum*; Bluestriped Grunt, *Haemulon sciurus*; Redlip Blenny, *Ophioblennius atlanticus*, and other Sergeant Major. Even crabs and sea urchins are not to be trusted.

On several occasions we have watched swarming aggregations of young wrasses overwhelm the males' defenses and storm nests. Once underway, nearby fish joined in the routs. In each case it took the frenzied guardian minutes to restore order. It has been reported that males, unable to chase off attackers, occasionally join the feast. A marine biologist reported watching a Schoolmaster, *Lutjanus apodus*, lurk near a besieged nest picking off small wrasses on their way to the free-for-all.

Males tend their nests for six to eight days, depending on the number of clutches involved. As the yolk is absorbed and eye pigments enlarge, the reddish eggs turn green and begin to hatch. Once underway, it takes about 12 hours before all of a clutch's tiny larvae wiggle free. As soon as males abandon their nests, the eggs' tattered remains are quickly picked clean by nearby fishes. Within days the sites are once again cloaked in a cover of algae and silt.

Three days after hatching, the large-headed, big-jawed, tenth-of-an-inch larvae actively swim and eagerly consume tiny copepods. Between 17 to 20 days after hatching, the planktonic larvae have grown to nearly a half inch and are ready to seek shelter in floating rafts of *Sargassum*, tide pools and mangrove banks. The tiny juveniles, miniature versions of their elders, group together for protection as they grow. In a matter of months they will be ready to join adult populations in shallow coastal waters.

Young Sergeant Major cluster around fire coral in the shallows.

Night Sergeant
Abudefduf taurus

If you want to see the largest of all Caribbean damselfishes, you will have to leave the reef and move inshore to rocky surf-swept shallows or steep shore embankments where Night Sergeants live. These rather reclusive, six- to ten-inch fish subsist almost exclusively on a diet of rapidly growing filamentous algae nipped from rocks. The fish regularly associate with up to eight individuals. When divers arrive, the cagey fish dart under ledges or swim out of the area but usually return after a few minutes. They resemble their genus-mate, the Sergeant Major, *A. saxatilis*, except for their larger size and less colorful countershadings of browns and brownish greens.

Night Sergeant.

From April through September, males prepare nests on the hidden undersides of rocks or inside small holes the day before spawning. They darken for courtship and mating and occasionally while guarding clutches. Females turn dark only while on the nest. When females approach, males perform several signal jumps. With great ceremony, interested females spread their fins, beat their tails briskly, and approach the males laterally with their bodies angled downward. While the females spawn, the males stand guard, chasing away other damselfishes and blennies. When the females leave periodically, the males fertilize until their mates return to lay additional eggs. Spawning, beginning at first light, often continues for two hours. Occasionally, two females skim the same nest together. The two-and-a-half-to three-inch clutches, each containing from 2,000 to 10,000 eggs, are guarded continually by the males until hatching six or seven days later. After 20 to 23 days in open sea, the larvae settle and promptly metamorphose into tiny, miniature versions of adults.

Genus *Chromis*

The five species of damselfishes in the genus *Chromis* that make their home in the region's waters can be separated easily into two distinct groups.

The first is made up of a pair of the Caribbean's most abundant reef fish, the Brown Chromis, *Chromis multilineata*, and Blue Chromis, *C. cyanea*. Both four-inch fish have developed slender profiles and elongated scissorlike tails enabling them to feed on zooplankton high above the reef, where speed equals survival. The Yellowtail Reeffish, *C. enchrysurus*; Purple Reeffish, *C. scotti*; and

Damselfishes

Sunshinefish, *C. insolata*, still retain the classic, laterally-compressed damselfish shape. All three favor deepwater habitats. The Purple Reeffish and Sunshinefish congregate in small mixed groups including juveniles on reef slopes below 80 feet, where they feed on zooplankton passing close to the reef. Yellowtail Reeffish are more commonly found on deeper patch reefs and around artificial wreck sites.

Where brisk currents run, Brown Chromis gather for hours high in the water column to pick plankton. Small groups work the shallow reefs while vast aggregations, numbering in the hundreds, throng to the rich currents above deep reef slopes. Microscopic pelagic animals, mainly copepods, comprise the bulk of their diet. Synchronized beats of translucent pectoral fins shuttle them about as, now and again, their entire mouth structure shoots forward to nab floating specks of food. When openwater piscivores such as jacks or mackerels approach, the widespread clouds of fish close and slowly ease away; if the predators advance to within 20 feet, the school dives as one for the reef. As evening approaches, the fish feed closer to the reef. Most find shelter for the night, while others bed down on the open sand and acquire blotched night colors.

The Brown Chromis has two reproductive strategies: pair spawning in temporarily defended territories and mass spawning aggregations. Reproduction occurs in all seasons with distinct peaks for ten-day periods following each full moon. Solitary males begin three-day spawning bouts by staking claims to sections of the reef and preparing crude nest sites on exposed ledges, crevice walls, gorgonian stems, sponges or *Sargassum* blades. The males repeatedly fan their future nests with rapidly-beating pectoral fins. When ready to spawn, they perform a few brief three-foot vertical signal jumps to attract mates. Often as many as ten fish of both sexes gather at the same site. At first every fish is chased, but soon the females reveal their gender by turning their tails toward the males and exposing their ventral regions.

A small spawning aggregation of Brown Chromis.

Pair spawning Brown Chromis.

Partners are led to the nest by a series of quick dashes. When near, the females are herded, butted and nipped into place. Sometimes clusters of females hover above the nests, but only one at a time enters to lay eggs. The males frequently join their mates, but wait until the females finish before actually fertilizing. One busy male was reported to have spawned 30 times with different partners within 45 minutes.

Males guard, fan and mouth the eggs for three days before they hatch. Rival males approaching the nest are challenged with lateral and head-on displays of spread fins and flared gill covers. Every now and then males face off only inches apart and joust back and forth, occasionally touching mouths. Wrasses, small grunts and other damselfishes are attacked as far as four or five feet from the nests. If a threatening aggregation of wrasses approaches, males assume defiant head-down positions at the entrances to their nests.

Group spawnings, sometimes involving a thousand individuals, occur once each lunar cycle in areas with large populations. One or two days preceding spawning, small groups of large adults settle to the reef to fan the bottom, dispersing in less than an hour. By the morning of day three, the bottom is covered with vigorously fanning adults. After an hour, a few random signal jumps herald the beginning of a five- to six-hour orgy of wildly skimming fish. It is believed that females spawn in several nests. The hatched larvae drift off with the currents for 24 to 30 days before they are ready to settle to the reef. Recently settled juveniles, who look almost identical to adults, often cluster just inside the lips of rock ledges.

Damselfishes

Unlike their more numerous counterparts, Blue Chromis typically inhabit slightly shallower depths and prefer to feed alone or in small groups no more than six to eight feet above the reef. More than half of their diet consists of planktonic algae; the balance comes from pelagic animal matter, primarily copepods, eggs, tunicates and larval fishes. The juveniles' diet contains only 20 percent planktonic algae, which increases to nearly 80 percent for young adults, and then decreases to under 65 percent with maturity. Adults maintain permanent territories around a single small hiding hole, where they flee from danger and sleep each night. The availability of hiding places tends to have a direct bearing on the species' distribution. Blue Chromis are usually well represented in reef areas with substantial structure and occasionally inhabit tangles of Staghorn Coral, *Acropora cervicornis*. Their prudent habit of feeding close to the reef and seeking safe sleeping quarters serves the species well. Stomach content

A male confrontation during spawning.

analysis of Graysbys, *Epinephelus cruentatus*, a common, small grouper, revealed 50 Brown Chromis for every Blue Chromis.

Reproduction occurs year-round with two-week peaks straddling the full moons of March through July. Males seem unconcerned about where nests are located and often select a different spot within their territories for each spawning period, showing no preference for protected areas. Individuals living in low-density populations often spawn on open sand in the vicinity of their hiding holes, while those in heavily populated areas prefer algae-covered coral. Spawning females turn blue-black; courting males darken their backs and sides, which contrasts sharply with their bright white bellies. Only pair spawning has been observed in this species. Often males have to travel 50 or 60 feet to find females to court. Males perform a series of signal jumps and dips before leading interested females to nest sites. Several females customarily lay eggs in a single nest. Like those of the Brown Chromis, the eggs are tiny, clear, scattered and impossible to see. Nests are guarded by males for three days before hatching. The pelagic larva stage lasts for 27 to 34 days. Clusters of juveniles often hover near the protection of the reef.

The spawning behavior of the three deepwater *Chromis* are quite similar. Each species pair spawns on leaf algae or the bare walls of rock depressions. Nest sites are probably prepared within the males' preexisting feeding territories,

Courtship pattern of the male Blue Chromis.

generally spaced at least 15 feet apart. Group spawning has never been reported for the three species. Nest preparation consists of little more than the males fanning sand off small algae bushes. During courtship and spawning males develop pale blotches across their backs that, in the case of Purple Reeffish, often cover the soft portion of their rear dorsal fins and tails. The blotches become more intense with increased reproductive activity. Males leave their nest sites to solicit females by actively dipping, chasing and herding. Once back with mates, males perform one- to two-foot signal jumps above their sites. Several females are usually attracted during a single spawning period, but only one at a time enters a nest. The males customarily enter and circle the nest first, followed by the females, who deposit eggs for several minutes, often with males positioned by their sides. Spawning involves quite a bit of shaking and quivering causing considerable disturbance in the algae. When the females leave, the males continue to fertilize and fan the eggs. It is believed that all the eggs in a nest are laid in a single day. Guarding males usually hover a few feet from their nests, as if disguising the eggs' exact location. Chasing is vigorous; wrasses and large parrotfishes are challenged four to five feet from the nest sites. A guarding Sunshinefish was seen nipping a piece from the trailing anal fin streamer of a Blue Angelfish, *Holacanthus bermudensis*, as it fled. When other fish are not in the vicinity, eggs are inspected, fanned and mouthed.

The female turns black when laying eggs, while a male waits to fertilize his nest.

Dragonets
Family Callionymidae

Male dragonets signal sovereignty by displaying their tall dorsal fins.

Lancer Dragonet
Paradiplogrammus bairdi

Territorial disputes and courtship behavior of the small, three-quarter- to two-inch Lancer Dragonet take place on shallow sand flats and algae-tufted terrain. These tiny algae-eating bottom-dwellers are so cleverly concealed by their brown camouflage that only short, intermittent sprints across the sand give them away. Bubble-eyes set high on a wide flattened head and a pointed snout lined with thin yellow lips give the odd little fish an engaging appeal. Males can be distinguished easily from females by their larger size and a tall, golden foredorsal fin that snaps erect from time to time. Similarly patterned females display a somewhat smaller foredorsal fin edged in black.

Lancer Dragonets can be quite common in the sand around shallow patch reefs but are seldom seen without a search. From a prone or kneeling position, look carefully across the sand plain. When dragonets are in the area, you will soon catch a glimpse of their darting movements as the little fish scoot across the sand, stopping periodically to peck at pieces of algae. Once sighted, they can be trailed closely without disturbing their routine. If you are following a male, he might just lead you to a good fight.

When another male is sighted, the traveling male usually pauses just long enough to flash his tall dorsal fin in a defiant message of sovereignty before continuing on his way. Occasionally, however, these encounters lead to dramatic confrontations that can last from 15 to 30 minutes. One afternoon, a male we had been following suddenly charged a nearby male of comparable size. The attacker stopped short when his opponent stubbornly held ground. Once side-by-side, both curved and stiffened their bodies, flared fan-shaped tails, puckered their tiny mouths into tight little "O's" and, with much ceremony, began to circle one another slowly. After three tight turns, without so much as bumping a fin, the antagonist darted to a nearby algae clump and nonchalantly began nibbling greenery. His opponent, apparently buoyed by success, flicked his fin and followed. Once close, he stopped and began to graze a short distance away.

After a few minutes the fish spread their fins, puckered and began to circle once again. Immediately after circling, the rivals faced off, locked jaws and glared eye-to-eye. Neither appeared to twitch a muscle. Seconds later, the challenger, almost imperceptibly, began to lose purchase. With a final flurry, he was flipped onto his back. The two little dragonets, still joined mouth-to-mouth, floated calmly away in a mild current. The instant they settled to the sand, the humbled aggressor fled.

In the Bahamas from May until September, we were able to find courting dragonets nearly every afternoon during the hour before sunset. In the fall, when the water temperature dropped, we never encountered the behavior. When a male dragonet happens upon a female during the day, he pauses just long enough to display his golden fin a time or two before moving on. As the day's

The rivals circle one another slowly.

Dragonets

After locking jaws, males remain unmoving for seconds.

Still locked mouth-to-mouth, the combatants float off the bottom.

One dragonet gains control and flips his opponent over.

light begins to fade, interest in the opposite sex escalates. During this period, prowling accelerates. Generally a male's advances are rebuffed by two or three different females before he finally invests time in a prolonged courtship effort.

From the instant a male's golden dorsal signals interest, a female plays her role as coquette with nothing short of brilliance. Her admirer prances and dances and sashays to her side. Showing no concern, she

Female dragonets can be distinguished from males by their smaller, darker dorsal fins.

nonchalantly continues to nibble. Undaunted, he spreads his fins, arches his back and goes rigid with passion. The female occasionally offers a modest fin-flick before scampering off across the sand. The eager male races behind, attempting to block her path. Once stopped, she passively begins to nibble once again while he enthusiastically continues to strut his stuff. This cat-and-mouse routine often continues for 15 to 20 minutes before the female finally indicates willingness by holding her black fin erect. He instantly positions himself parallel and pushes against her side. Still coy, she turns away again and again, making him repeatedly spin to reposition. Finally, at or just after the sun sets, she allows him to remain pressed to her body. With ventral fins wildly churning, the two fish slowly lift free of the bottom and, as if in a dream, sway together above the sea floor. In a dramatic finale the lovers explode apart, leaving behind gossamer strands of spawn.

In a few cases we have seen the same pair spawn two or three times in succession. More often, however, the male, after a single spawn, dashes off in pursuit of a second mate for the evening. When darkness falls, the little fish quickly vibrate belly-first into the sand, often leaving only their large eyes exposed.

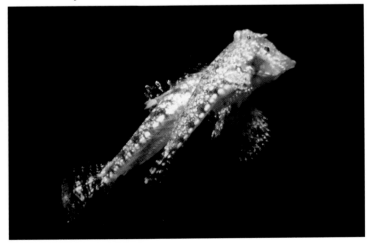

The smaller female finally allows the male to remain by her side and together the pair lift off the bottom in a slow spawning rise.

Flounders
Family Bothidae

Territorial flounder spend much of their day chasing neighbors.

Living on the open sand is risky business. To avoid being eaten, sand-dwelling fishes have adapted a variety of strategies. Jawfishes build deep burrows lined with rocks where they retreat at the first sign of danger. Sand Tilefish, *Malacanthus plumieri*, cover their shallow sand hideaways with mounds of stones and shells to keep out invaders. Garden eels and snake eels use their sharp tails to corkscrew backwards into the sand, and hatchet-headed razorfishes power-dive beneath the surface. But flounders, one of the oddest of the oceans' many oddities, are, far and away, the most masterful of all the sand-flat survivalists.

Flounders belong in the Order Pleuronectiformes, the flatfishes, which also includes halibuts, soles, whiffs, sanddabs, plaice, turbot and tonguefishes. Species have been placed in one of three families principally by the location of their eyes. Bothidae, or lefteye flounders, are mainly shallow-water tropical species with both eyes on their left sides; righteye flounders, Pleuronectidae, primarily live in temperate or deep waters, and Soleidae, the sole and tonguefishes, have eyes on their left sides but slightly out of alignment. A few species from both families have "reversed" individuals whose eyes are located on the contrasting side.

To ready themselves for a hazardous life on open bottom, flatfishes pull off one of the animal kingdom's most astonishing feats of developmental biology. While adrift in offshore currents, larval flounders have typical bilateral fish-shaped bodies, properly aligned fins and pigmented eyes, one on each side of the head. Weeks later, sometime before settling to a shallow sea floor, muscles, skin, blood vessels and bones inexorably shift into the flattened shape of dime-sized benthic juveniles. During the magical metamorphosis, one eye migrates across the head until next to the other, backs darken, bellies lighten, swimbladders disappear, the dorsal and anal fins line the flatfishes' oval bodies, and a lone pectoral fin, often quite long on the males, extends from the center of their backs.

The flatfishes' thin horizontal profile not only hides them from predators and prey but also allows them to bury quickly in the sand, leaving only their stalked, independently functioning, 180-degree-rotating, pariscopic eyes exposed. But without question, the tropical flounders' best defensive strategy is rapid adaptive camouflage. When moving from one bottom location to another, they can change body patterns within seconds to match their new surroundings. Once settled, visual cues from their immediate environment are transmitted via nerves to thousands of irregular-shaped cells in the skin known as chromatophores. Chromatophores pale when pigments converge in their cores, and darken as the pigments expand throughout radiating cell branches. Red, yellow, orange, black and brown can be produced by activating overlapping chromatophores containing different pigments. Fishes capable of displaying the most complex patterns such as the Peacock Flounder, *Bothus lunatus*, a common shallow-water Caribbean flatfish, have higher concentrations of chromatophores.

Although it has long been known that flatfishes change patterns to match backgrounds, little research supports the concept. The few studies of their camouflaging abilities have used species from temperate rather than tropical waters for their experiments. An early reference, published in 1911, reported that the backs of flatfishes placed on checkered patterns for several days appeared to mimic the checks. Two subsequent researchers, also experimenting with temperate species, refuted the earlier findings, concluding, "flatfishes simply have a universal texture allowing them to blend into any environment."

In the early 90s, researchers from the University of California, San Diego, using the Peacock Flounder as their subject species, were the first to extensively investigate the camouflaging abilities of a tropical flatfish. They first tested the idea that the rapid color and pattern changes seen in the wild were simply illusions. Early photographic experiments put a quick end to this hypothesis. Five specimens rotated through a series of five bottom patterns – yellow sand, course gravel, one-centimeter and two-millimeter checkerboard squares and a solid gray sheet – closely matched the backgrounds in 91 percent of the trials. Even more impressive, most changes were complete in just two to eight seconds.

In the most dramatic experiment, flounders placed on the larger checkerboard squares quickly developed splotches closely mimicking the checks. However, the markings did not bear an exact spatial relationship with the pattern. In other words, the fishes' splotches were not aligned with the checks they rested on. Fish gently moved to a different position on the checkerboard retained their previous markings. When a piece of gray cardboard was slipped under the fish, the subjects' adapted wardrobes remained unchanged. It was also noted that each time a specimen was reintroduced to a particular design, it developed a corresponding pattern more rapidly than before.

Flounders

Colors worn by a swimming Peacock Flounder.

During another set of experiments, flounder placed on a white background with widely spaced black polka dots paled significantly, leaving only solitary, dark, centrally located eyespots and a dusky blotch encircling their eyes. White dots of the same size on a black background caused the fish to darken, leaving only a series of white blotches along the edges of their bodies. These sparse patterns required minutes rather than seconds to complete. The researchers also observed that the fishes' entire bodies instantly blanched when the fish were frightened.

Microscopic analysis revealed that six sets of independently controlled markings are responsible for the myriad designs. Individual markings include a series of H-shaped splotches edging the body; small dark rings; light-colored rings encircling dark dots; thin scrawled lines; a central eyespot, and a spectacle frame around the eyes. By mixing and matching and varying the contrast of different sets, the fish are able to blend expertly with any natural background.

When settled in their surroundings, the classic lie-in-wait predators are indistinguishable to prey. Peacock Flounder primarily eat fishes, usually small minnowlike species. On occasion they snap up a mantis shrimp or even octopuses. The stomach of one 12-inch individual contained two small four-inch jacks. The author of a feeding study found six herrings and two anchovies inside one specimen which was collected on the bottom 25 feet below a school of the small fishes swimming on the surface. He speculated that the flounder caught the minnows when they fed near the bottom, rather than making a feeding rush to the surface. However, we once observed a three-inch Eyed Flounder, *B. ocellatus*, powered by an undulating skirt of fins, swim eight feet off the bottom to nab an insect floating on the surface at night under a dock light.

Flounder watching is at its best at dusk. During the hour before sunset the Peacock Flounder, the Eyed Flounder and the Elliptic Flounder, *B. ocellatus*, a common sand-flat resident of the southern and eastern Caribbean, court and spawn in harems controlled by large territorial males. The three species, all pelagic spawners, shed their gametes above the bottom in male-female pairs. Dominant Peacock and Elliptic males are larger than females and also have much longer pectoral fins, prominently displayed during courtship and male-to-male rivalries. Both male and female Eyed Flounder have short pectoral fins, but the sexes of the small two-to three-inch species can be differentiated by the females' eyestalks that are set closer together than those of the males. Fortunately, during courtship flounders take little notice of inquisitive divers; flashlight beams, however instantly alter their behavior.

Each time a Peacock Flounder settles in a new location, it quickly changes colors and pattern.

Two researchers from Texas A&M University compiled extensive observational data on the social and reproductive behavior of Eyed Flounder during two winter seasons in Bonaire. By coincidence, their shallow-water study site inshore from the old town pier was the same location where we observed and photographed the species a few years later. The researchers found that Eyed Flounder harems consist of from one to six females occupying small sub-territories within the larger 50- to 350-square-yard territories of dominant males. Typically the territories of several males lie side-by-side, often covering large expanses of shallow sandy terrain.

Females are jealously guarded from neighboring males who are always looking for an opportunity to increase the size of their harems and territories, even at the expense of a tussle. Male-to-male confrontations occur just before

Flounders

A courting male raises his dorsal fin.

A male attempts to move under his mate.

Once positioned, the pair lift off the sand.

and during courtship. Trespassing males typically flee when chased, but on rare occasions they stand their ground facing each other across the sand with raised forebodies arching toward their opponents like striking snakes. Attacks are swift and vicious, with combatants locking jaws and slinging each other about. Mature rivals often battle for five minutes or more before matters are settled.

Male Eyed Flounder spawn once or, in a few cases, twice every evening with each female in their harems. Courtship begins about 40 minutes prior to sunset, with males following established routes as they make repeated visits to each of their mates in turn. Initial meetings are brief, with the males pausing just long enough to inspect swollen bellies and possibly sniff pheromones to evaluate the females' readiness to release eggs. From time to time the males perch atop sand mounds to scout for predators. On a few evenings, lingering piscivores such as jacks or lizardfishes prompt harem members to dive under the sand for extended periods, preempting the evening's spawning activities. As an evasive tactic, the escaping flounder may flip completely over once under the sand, ending up facing in the opposite direction with only their eyestalks exposed.

As courtship continues male Eyed Flounder become more impassioned, often touching their mates' sides with their snouts, laying forebodies across the females' backs and vigorously pursuing fleeing mates. Eventually the females comply, allowing the males to wiggle beneath their bodies. Once stacked like pancakes and with fins aflutter, the pairs rise slowly off the sand. At some point, between six to 30 inches above the bottom, the males suddenly contract, releasing clouds of sperm, and immediately dive for the sea floor. A second later the arching

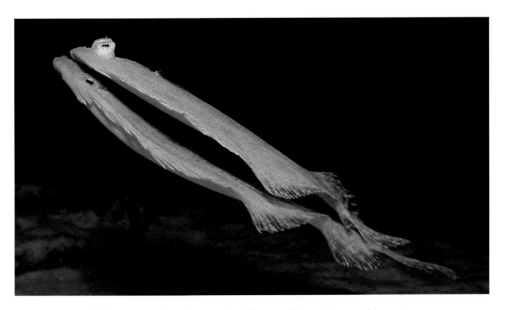

A slow spawning rise ends with a sudden release of gametes.

females discharge transparent eggs into the males' dissipating sperm and streak back to the bottom. As soon as the females are settled, the males inspect their partners' abdomens to be certain all of the eggs were released. If females are still swollen, a second spawning rise is initiated; if not the males zip off to spawn with other mates.

Males typically make repeated overtures before being allowed to slip beneath their partners' bellies, and even then, the females often break away prematurely during the spawning rise. Occasionally a lucky male simply sidles up and the female obliges by lifting her flat body in acceptance or even by hopping onto the suitor's back. After shedding eggs, females leave their daytime territories to sleep in deeper water. Males head off in the opposite direction, leisurely picking at bits on the bottom as they meander toward the shallows where they bed down in the same patches of sand each evening.

The larger Elliptic and Peacock Flounders (males reach nine and 12 inches in length respectively) court and spawn in a similar fashion. However, the males' tall pectoral fins add grand spectacle to the event. The males of both species appear to oversee harems of no more than two females. The instant male Peacock Flounder approach a prospective mate, their pectoral fins pop upright. There is little nuzzling, and the females' bellies are not obviously distended with eggs, like those of the Eyed Flounder. When the males near, the partners glide toward one another, stop, arch their forebodies off the sand and briefly touch snouts before the coquettish females turn and swim away, continually flicking their small pectoral fins as they go. The excited males, with fins still flying high, sprint to their sides. As the pairs swim side-by-side just off the bottom, the males suddenly collapse their pectoral fins and slip beneath the bellies of moving females. Their slow spawning rises, lasting over 12 seconds, carry the blissful pairs up six or seven feet before they simultaneously release gametes.

Frogfishes
Family Antennariidae

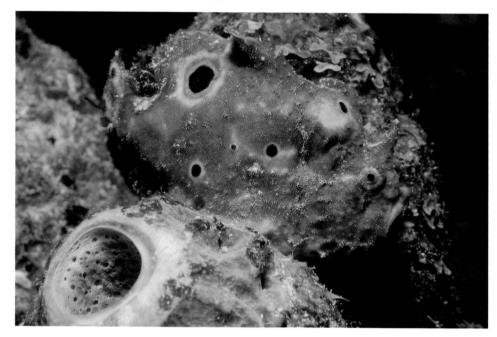

The occelated spots on Longlure Frogfish mimic the outcurrent siphons of the sponge colonies where they typically perch.

Although frogfishes are little more than fist-sized stomachs with large mouths, the oddball eating-machines are among the most sought after fishes on the reef. The trouble is finding them. The same lumpy texture and color-changing camouflage that conceal frogfishes from predators and prey also hide them from divers. Nestled within a stand of sponge, the Longlure Frogfish, *Antennarius multiocellatus* – the Caribbean's most common family member – mimics its perch down to its ocellated markings resembling the sponge colony's outcurrent siphons. If the same fish moves to an algae-covered ledge, it will, over a period of weeks, alter its color and pattern to mimic the turf-covered rocks just as cleverly.

The frogfishes' ability to change their appearance has led to the formal description of 165 species even though today taxonomists recognize only 43 species worldwide: six of which inhabit the waters of the tropical western Atlantic. Although found across the Caribbean, the largest frogfish populations occur in Bonaire, Barbados, St. Vincent, St. Lucia, Dominica and St. Croix. Interestingly, seahorses also reach their population peaks at many of these same islands. All frogfishes are globular, with rough skin formed by modified scales, tiny eyes and a small tubular gill opening behind each pectoral fin. The fin rays of

Right: Frogfishes periodically stretch their mouths open – a behavior common to most predatory fishes.

Frogfishes

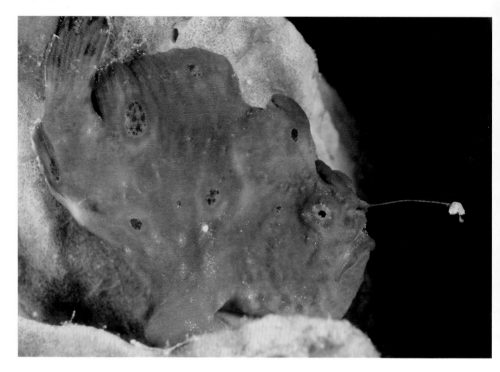

To attract fish prey, frogfishes dangle lures in front of their jaws.

the rounded dorsal, anal and tail fins are buried beneath thick flesh, and the two sets of paired fins (pectoral and pelvic) resemble stumpy legs complete with toes. Topping off the outlandish outfit, the first spine of the dorsal fin is modified into a thin, whiplike rod tipped with a lure. With the pole, known as an illicium, and the bait, called an esca, the lie-in-wait predators fish for dinner by dangling the baits enticingly in front of their jaws.

When potential meals are nearby, the rod swings forward from its resting place on the head and jiggles the bait. As curious prey enters its strike zone, the frogfish lowers slightly and, as if shot by a cannon, blows its mouth out to 12 times normal size. The victim, along with a considerable volume of water, is sucked through the mouth and into the stomach as the pectoral fins simultaneously clamp the tiny gill openings shut. Measured at six milliseconds, the strike is the fastest recorded for any vertebrate predator. Attacks are so swift that schooling fishes seldom react to the sudden loss of a neighbor.

If hunting is good, individuals remain for days or even weeks at the same ambush site. Ambushing from beds of filamentous algae offers the added benefit of attracting herbivores. As algae-eating fishes are consumed the surrounding growth flourishes, attracting even more prey. Frogfishes are not picky eaters. Although small fishes top their food list, they also consume crabs, mantis shrimps and other crustaceans. Not all victims are small. A Longlure Frogfish was reported to have consumed a squirrelfish a quarter longer than its own

Right: A Longlure Frogfish angles for dinner.

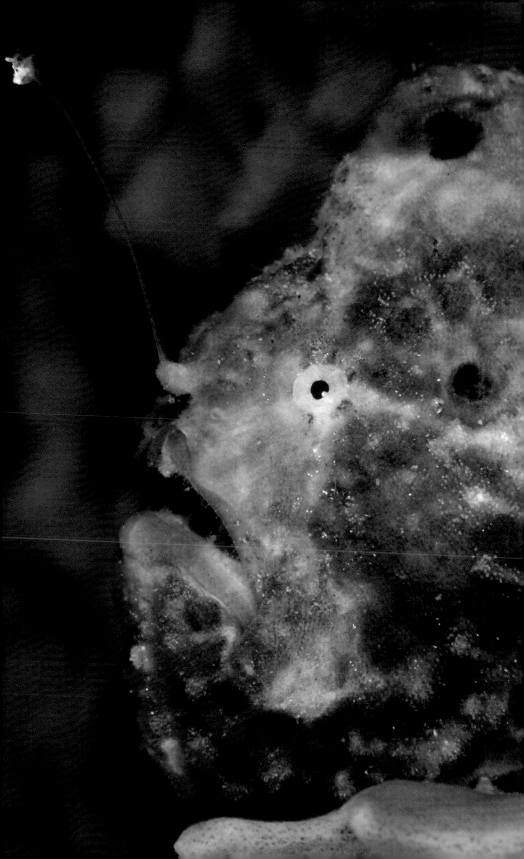

Frogfishes

A frogfish perches on rope sponge, high above the reef.

body. Captured prey too large to pass directly into the stomach is held by recurved conical teeth while being positioned for swallowing. Frogfishes are so voracious that they regularly grab fishes too difficult to handle. We watched an individual cough out a spine-laden butterflyfish just seconds after capture, and an aquarium specimen was found floating dead with an inflated porcupinefish inside its stomach. However, frogfishes appear to be immune to the poisonous spines of scorpionfishes, a regular item on their menu.

Fishing is used in about 80 percent of captures. In some cases, curiosity rather than hunger attracts victims to the dancing bait. At other times, small territorial neighbors associate the movement as a threat and attack. Some victims, believing that the frogfish is part of the substrate, unwittingly swim into its range. Surprisingly, frogfishes fish at night. In the dark, the lateral-line sensors of cardinalfishes and other nocturnal feeders pick up the vibrations of the wiggling bait. Chemical attractants may also help to attract prey. By the nature of their use, the thin pole and fleshy lure take a beating. When not in use, the rod is laid across the head and the lure is tucked close to the dorsal fin. After an illicium and its attached esca were experimentally removed, the appendage showed signs of regeneration in five days; in six months it had grown to its original size and shape.

Even though their success as hunters depends, in great part, on remaining motionless, frogfishes occasionally stalk prey. With dorsal fins raised and walking on their paired fins, the hunters approach rapidly at first, but slow, crouch and lower their dorsals as they near the target. In rare instances frogfishes pursue prey while

The adaptive color patterns of Longlure Frogfish vary widely.

Frogfishes

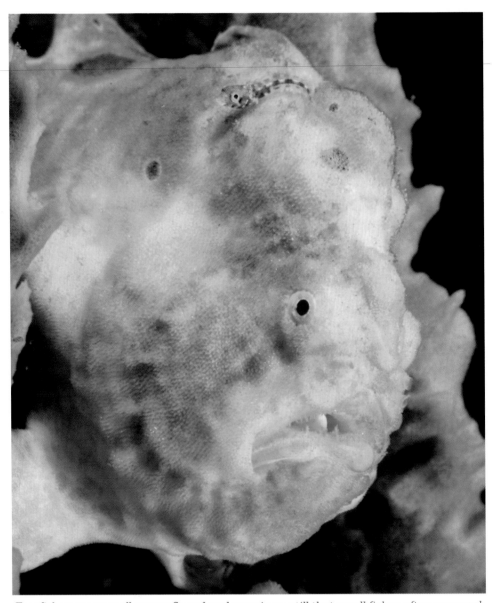

Frogfishes are so well camouflaged and remain so still that small fishes often approach their ambush sites unaware of the lurking predators.

fishing. As many aquarists can attest, frogfishes are gluttons, consuming large amounts of whatever food is provided and, if precautions are not taken, other fishes in the tank. One four-inch specimen readily gobbled down two to three goldfish each day for an extended period without showing ill effects. If given a chance, frogfishes will eat their own kind. Sargassum Frogfish, *Histrio histrio*, are regularly found with a dozen or more smaller individuals inside their stomachs. In an aquarium, one of two equal-sized specimens ate the other.

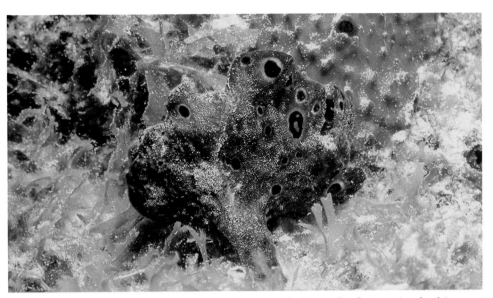

Ambush sites in filamentous algae provide the added benefit of attracting herbivores.

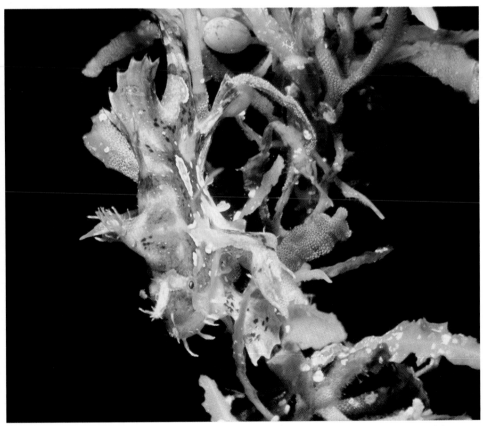

The bodies of Sargassum Frogfish match the color and shape of Sargassum foliage.

Frogfishes

Except during courtship and spawning, frogfishes tend to be solitary. If approached closely by another individual, the defender will take a position in front of its ambush site, raise on its pectorals, spread its medial fins, lighten, open its mouth, quiver and lean in the direction of the trespasser. In most confrontations the intruder will move away slowly, but occasionally will respond with a similar display. In rare instances, threatened frogfishes have been known to gulp water to increase their size.

Given their awkward, saclike shape, it is a wonder frogfishes can move about at all. In addition to hunting, they also move to find new ambush sites, search for mates and to flee when threatened. As one might imagine, their gaits are ungainly. The two leglike pectoral fins are used for force, and the much weaker paired pelvic fins, located close together under the throat, provide support. In "crutching" – the most frequently used walk – the pectoral fins push the body forward until the weight rests temporarily on the extended pelvic fins, allowing the pectoral fins to swing forward for the next stride. During a "modified walk" the pectoral fins alternate strides, much like terrestrial vertebrates, with the pelvic fins providing little more than support.

Frogfishes swim in three ways. The most frequently used style employs a rhythmic waving of the body and tail that moves the fish at a rate of a body length per second. Frogfishes can jet away at about the same speed by forcibly funneling large mouthfuls of water through their restricted gill openings. When panicked, frogfishes thrash their tails, force water out their gill openings and

A courting male, the smaller of the pair, remains close to his mate for several days as she distends with eggs.

A released egg raft retains the scroll-like shape of the female's ovaries.

stroke furiously with their pectoral fins. The all-out effort causes the fishes to dart erratically at a rate of five body lengths per second.

Spawning in the wild has not been documented, but numerous aquarium observations of the behavior have been published. Female frogfishes release large, gelatinous rafts of eggs wound in the scroll-like shape of their ovaries. Within 48 hours the tightly wound ribbons, which contain between 48,800 and 288,000 eggs, soften and unroll to measure approximately four inches wide and three to four feet in length. Days later, the eggs hatch into one-millimeter pelagic yolk-sac larvae.

Courtship consists of the male, usually the smaller of the pair, staying close to a ripe female for the few days it takes her to swell with eggs. Periodically displaying erect fins, the male nudges, nibbles, leans on and presses his pectoral fins against the ballooning female. As spawning nears, the male spends more time nudging her vent. When spawning is imminent the female lumbers across the substrate followed closely by the male who frequently noses around beneath her raised tail. Just before release, the female's abdomen contracts violently. Without warning she dashes upward followed closely by her mate. In a fraction of a second, the entire egg mass erupts from her body. The male streaks past ejecting sperm which is absorbed into the pores of the egg structure along with seawater. The exhausted female returns to the bottom where she staggers about before regaining her steadiness a short while later.

Groupers & Sea Basses
Family Serranidae

Black Grouper, members of genus Mycteroperca, *primarily eat fish.*

In the tropical western Atlantic, the sea bass family encompasses species ranging from giant groupers, genera *Epinephelus* and *Mycteroperca*, to small sea basses measuring less than two inches, genus *Serranus*. Also sharing the family name are such curiosities as the small, cryptic, torpedo-shaped cave basses, genus *Liopropoma*, night-prowling soapfishes, genus *Rypticus*, and the enigmatic hamlets, genus *Hypoplectrus* – a group of anatomically similar fishes, who, for yet inexplicable reasons, come in an array of color patterns. Although most sea basses are solitary carnivores feeding primarily on fishes and crustaceans, two species, the Creole-fish, *Paranthias furcifer*, and the tiny Chalk Bass, *Serranus tortugarum*, pick plankton from open water.

The word grouper, describing medium and large bottom-dwelling serranids, comes from the Portuguese "garrupa," a derivation of a name native Brazilian fishermen used for large species of sea basses. Most inhabit shallow tropical seas, but a few species survive in temperate waters and several, including Snowy Grouper, *Epinephelus niveatus*; Misty Grouper, *E. mystacinus*; and Warsaw Grouper, *E. nigritus*, generally live well below safe diving limits. The distribution of juveniles is much wider than adults. Small Gag, *Mycteroperca microlepis*, have been reported as far north as New England, but few, if any, survive the area's harsh winters.

Right: *Members of the sea bass family vary considerably in size and shape.*

Orangeback Bass – genus Serranus.

Shy Hamlet – genus Hypoplectrus.

Cave Bass – genus Liopropoma.

Greater Soapfish – genus Rypticus.

Creole-fish, a planktivore.

Chalk Bass, a planktivore.

Groupers & Sea Basses

The strapping, top-level predators are secretive but curious fishes that, in the days before spearfishermen, would swim confidently over to have a look at an approaching diver. A well-developed air bladder allows the bulky predators to calmly hover or maneuver easily through caves or overhangs within their home ranges, typically located around high-profile coral reefs and wrecks that attract food, provide shelter and have cleaning stations. Enjoying the services of cleaning shrimps and fishes is a favorite and often prolonged pastime. Mature groupers show a strong homing tendency; most tagged specimens released far from their ranges make their way back to the area where originally captured.

A Tiger Grouper with mouth open and fins flared – a customary cleaning pose.

Nearly all groupers can switch colors and body patterns quickly and can also lighten or darken radically. These often striking transitions are triggered by changes in habitat, water depth, light levels or the fishes' disposition. Changes in patterns frequently occur when groupers feed, attend cleaning stations, spawn, rest or signal members of their own species. Their many appearances can make identification tricky. For example, Yellowfin Grouper, *M. venenosa*, most frequently show a series of tan body blotches and spots superimposed over a light background, but they can swiftly brighten to red or turn so dark the blotches disappear completely. The brown undercoat of Rock Hind, *E. adscensionis*, pales when the bottom-hugging species slips off the reef and

230

A juvenile Snowy Grouper hovers near the protection of an abandoned conch shell. Only the juveniles of this deep-water species make their homes in shallow water. Adults inhabit depths below 800 feet.

moves over white sand. Red Grouper, *E. morio*, who normally wear tobacco-brown coats with a scattering of white dots, acquire irregular blotches of white across their heads and bodies when resting on sand. Coney, *E. fulvus*, exquisitely beautiful small grouper, change between a solid reddish brown and a distinct bicolor pattern. Their two-tone attire is generally displayed in the early morning, again late in the afternoon, or while stalking prey. Several groupers modify their appearance during reproduction. The courtship patterns of Nassau Grouper, *E. striatus*, are the most dramatic. The species exhibits at least four distinct patterns, but the most impressive is the flamboyant black and white coat worn late in the day when spawning is imminent.

Giant groupers begin life as pelagic eggs spawned annually. The eggs hatch into translucent larvae that quickly develop elongate spines and large mouths. After drifting with the currents for 25 to 45 days, the larvae, at approximately one-inch, settle to the bottom in species-specific, shallow-water habitats where they hide while completing their metamorphosis into juveniles. Nassau Grouper begin life on the sea floor hiding inside algae-covered coral clumps in mangrove lagoons; Red Grouper in grass beds; Jewfish, *E. itajara*, in mangrove forests; while Gag and Black Grouper, *M. bonaci*, swept inshore by tides, settle on oyster reefs in high-salinity estuaries.

Little is known about the juveniles' growth rates, feeding habits or habitat shifts as they mature. During early development, most species feed almost exclusively on crustaceans. One study of the early life stages of Nassau Grouper found that an increasing demand for food forces rapidly growing juveniles to leave their original settlement sites at approximately two inches. By six inches the youngsters take up a second temporary residence in protective breaks in the sea floor. They next relocate to shallow patch reefs or conch shells in grass flats and later move to more complex reef structures. Most large, sex-changed males resettle in deeper water, leaving a virtually all-female contingent in the shallower end of the species' depth range.

Although difficult to establish, the maximum age of several grouper species has been extensively examined because of their importance to commercial fisheries. Jewfish, the largest Atlantic sea bass, have been documented to live for

Groupers & Sea Basses

Mass spawning aggregations of Nassau Grouper numbered in the tens of thousands before overharvesting.

37 years; Nassau Grouper 28; Red Grouper over 25; Scamp, *M. phenax*, 21; Red Hind, *E. guttatus*, 17; Gag 16; Yellowfin Grouper 15; Black Grouper 14; and Graysby, *E. cruentatus*, and Coney nine years.

Groupers are ambush hunters who feed on fishes, crustaceans and cephalopods throughout much of the day, with a sharp increase in activity during the low-light periods of dawn and dusk. Small grunts and parrotfishes make up the bulk of their fish diet, while crabs top their list of crustaceans. Members of genus *Mycteroperca* primarily eat fishes, whereas the species in genus *Epinephelus* prefer crustaceans. A quick forward lunge, accompanied by rapidly expanding jaws and flaring gill covers, vacuums prey into the mouth, to be swallowed whole. The forceful suction of Jewfish and other big groupers is sufficient to suck lobsters from crevices. Coney and Graysby regularly hunt with eels and octopuses. This behavior, known as nuclear feeding, is discussed in the Feeding chapter.

The majority of Serranids are protogynous hermaphrodites. This sexual development strategy allows individuals to reproduce first as females and later, at a larger size, change into males when certain unidentified social or environmental factors are met. This form of sex-switching is considered by many to be a superior reproductive tactic, enabling populations to adapt more easily to short-term environmental fluctuations. Sea basses have adapted two basic versions of hermaphroditism. Most larger species are sequential hermaphrodites, with the majority of individuals in a given population making a complete and non-reversible sex change. Many of the smaller family members are simultaneous hermaphrodites, able to function actively in both the male and female role. Within each of these methods are numerous variations on the theme. Hamlets, *Hypoplectrus* spp., and Harlequin Bass, *S. tigrinus*, two simultaneous hermaphrodites, spawn as both males and females each night in a monogamous relationship known as egg trading. Lantern Bass, *S. baldwini*, reproduce in small harems, with one large dominant individual spawning as a male with several other hermaphrodites who function only as females.

Many larger groupers believed to be sequential hermaphrodites – Nassau Grouper; Tiger Grouper, *M. tigris*; Black Grouper; Yellowfin Grouper; Jewfish and the intermediate-sized Red Hind, Gag and Scamp – travel many miles during one or two months each year to mate in huge spawning aggregations at breeding grounds used for centuries by their ancestors. A Nassau Grouper was documented to journey over 60 miles in the Bahamas. Another Nassau Grouper in Belize relocated nearly 150 miles to join a breeding aggregation, and a Gag traveled more than 350 miles along the coast of the southeastern United States in a possible spawning migration.

The migrations to the immense aggregations, often involving hundreds or thousands of fish, are synchronized by the onset of the full moon, typically during the cooler winter months. The traditional rendezvous sites are generally located near promontories along outer reef shelves at depths over 100 feet. Many basic questions remain unanswered about these great "grouper runs" which were first reported in scientific literature in 1972. For instance, it is still unknown whether individuals migrate each time their species gathers to spawn, if additional spawning activities occur outside aggregations or even if adults reproduce each year.

For several days prior to the actual spawning, incoming fish collect at aggregation sites and mill about nervously near the bottom. Females, obviously swollen with eggs, huddle close to the protection of bottom structures. Shortly before the full moon, courtship behavior and color patterns intensify as afternoons progress. Spawning takes place at or just before sunset within subgroups whose sexual composition varies among species. Female Nassau Grouper and Red Hind form discrete groups serviced by a single male who possibly spawns with multiple groups. Scamp, medium-sized grouper, assemble in subgroups with up to 20 females attended by a lone male. The same species occasionally forms into clusters of more than 50 females and several males. Male Tiger Grouper and Yellowfin Grouper, who often aggregate at the same sites as Nassau Grouper but in different months, defend small territories where they are approached by females ready to spawn. As the late afternoon spawning time approaches, males more aggressively defend their areas of bottom from other males. Not all common, shallow-water groupers aggregate to reproduce: Red Grouper, Coney and Graysby pair spawn in small clusters on their home reef.

A Jewfish hovers near a cleaning station.

Jewfish
Epinephelus itajara

Without question, Jewfish are the largest reef fish in the region and one of the two largest species of groupers in the world. The massive monsters, growing to eight feet in length and weighing more than 700 lbs., were frequently sighted by divers until the late 1960s. Then the top-level predators began to fall victim to spearfishermen armed with explosive powerheads who could easily swim right up to the fearless fish. For nearly a decade, huge carcasses of the magnificent creatures, hoisted high on block and tackle, gathered sightseers and flies at marinas from Florida to Mexico. By the 1980s, the few Jewfish remaining on inshore reefs were so wary of divers that they fled whenever approached. During the same period, many of the species' annual breeding aggregations, unmolested for centuries, were overexploited to the point of collapse by line fishing. The harvesting was so excessive that an emergency ruling was enacted in 1990, making it unlawful to harvest or possess Jewfish along Florida's Gulf Coast, the historical population center of the species. During the same year the no-harvest moratorium was extended to all federal waters, and the U.S. Virgin Islands followed suit in 1993.

By 1995, the laws protecting the slow-growing, long-lived species began to show positive effects. Many inshore wreck sites in the western Gulf of Mexico were once again homes to a small but growing population of Jewfish. Along

Florida's southeast coast and in the upper Keys, areas where the species had not been reported by recreational divers for nearly 20 years, Jewfish sightings began to trickle in. Today, Florida's charter boat fleet is transporting a new generation of divers to locations where they can see the great fish. Fortunately, no one carries spearguns this time around.

Epinephelus itajara ranges across the Gulf of Mexico, Caribbean and Bahamas, up the Atlantic coast possibly as far as the Carolinas, south to Brazil and along much of Africa's western shore. In the eastern Pacific, it is found from the Gulf of California to Peru. The big fish can be identified quickly by size and a scattering of small dark spots over their bodies and fins. Adults are typically shallow-water dwellers, although individuals have been reported as deep as 280 feet. Before their populations dwindled, Jewfish, the only grouper able to survive extended periods in brackish water, regularly entered harbors, bays and estuaries. Fishermen have reported seeing the large fish feeding in tidal mangrove swamps so shallow that their tails thrashed the surface.

No one knows exactly how Jewfish stalk their prey. Although generally sedentary and sluggish, they are capable of moving short distances with amazing speed. Prey is drawn into their cavernous mouths by suction created when they suddenly expand their jaws and flare gill covers. The force of the water passing through the mouth is so powerful that thick clouds of sand and debris swirl behind the rush of a feeding fish. Spiny and slipper lobsters make up the bulk of their diet, but an examination of eight specimens revealed an array of food items, including Southern Stingray, *Dasyatis americana*, Honeycomb Cowfish, *Lactophrys polygonia*, spiny puffers, crabs, octopuses and a small sea turtle. One fish had five lobsters in its gut. Juveniles subsist mainly on shrimps, crabs and small fishes. Large Jewfish have been known to grab a spearfisherman's catch. In the early 1970s, a young underwater hunter related that he made the mistake of getting between a hungry Jewfish and food. While he trailed a mesh bag containing three lobsters around a wreck site off Tampa, Florida, a 200 to 300 lb. Jewfish came up from behind and in a rush engulfed both the bag and the diver's right leg. In his struggle to free himself, the hunter lost his crustacean dinner, a new flipper, and two-thirds of the skin from his knee to his toes.

The species is known for the loud "booming" sound produced by its swim bladder and surrounding muscles. The booms are believed to be territorial warnings. A resident Jewfish will often emit the thunderous sound if startled by an approaching diver. Researchers have also heard juveniles boom before taking bait, indicating a possible use to stun prey when feeding.

Research is only beginning to improve our understanding of the species' early life. Large expanses of mangrove forest have been found to be vital for both settling pelagic larvae and juveniles until they reach 30 lbs. The lack of such habitat in the Eastern Caribbean is believed to be the reason for the species' limited population there. Ten Thousand Islands in the southwestern corner of the Florida Everglades, adjacent to the species' historic population center, is home to the largest concentration of young Jewfish yet discovered. Juveniles, with large pronounced spots and four or five dark bars, seek protection under the deep shelves created by the area's numerous mangrove islands.

Groupers & Sea Basses

Known to live for 37 years, Jewfish grow slowly. Outside spawning periods, there is no visual difference between the sexes. There is some evidence of protogynous hermaphroditism in the species, with a few individuals possibly passing through an immature female stage before maturing as males, but there have yet to be any specimens found in a transitional phase. Both males and females are sexually mature by age seven, at a length of approximately four feet. Outside of reproductive periods, adult Jewfish are not particularly gregarious, usually establishing claim to a protected location within a wreck or cave and remaining in the vicinity for extended periods of time.

Spawning aggregations of Jewfish occur around the full moons of late summer.

Members of the species gather in spawning aggregations around the time of the full moons in August and September. On different occasions research divers have observed a series of behaviors believed to be part of courtship activities; however, an actual spawn has not been documented to date. The locations of only a small number of aggregations are presently known. Of those, most have significantly declined in numbers or failed to reform into reproductive groups for the past several years. Aggressive harvesting off the southwest coast of Florida has reduced counts of 25 to 150 fish in 1982, when first fished, to between zero and five in 1989.

The courtship behavior of Jewfish has been documented only a few years; spawning has yet to be observed.

The few recorded observations of courtship have been made during the last decade at wreck sites at approximately 100 feet in the Gulf of Mexico between 60 to 80 miles west of Naples, Florida. Today, most are small gatherings consisting of fewer than a dozen individuals, estimated to range from 130 to over 300 lbs. While assembled, the fish either remain close to the bottom near the wreck or hover ten to 20 feet up in the water column. An extended courtship period lasts from late morning to the middle of the afternoon. As males approach females their entire forebodies from pectoral fins forward turn pale, contrasting sharply with their dark bodies. Females exhibit no significant color change, remaining in a characteristic blotched pattern.

While gathered in spawning aggregations, Jewfish emit low-frequency booming sounds clearly audible more than 100 feet away.

Groupers & Sea Basses

Two apparent courtship behaviors are repeated from time to time throughout the period. The first, "vent nuzzling," occurs when a male moves slowly alongside a female from the rear and appears to inspect or nudge her vent area at the posterior of the abdomen. As the male approaches the female rolls her body, angling her vent region away from the suitor. The male, usually persistent, swims underneath and attempts the same strategy from the opposite side. At this point, the female generally eases away. In the second courtship behavior, "turn and rise," a male approaches directly toward the side of a female, who is either hovering off the bottom or slowly rising. Once near, he positions himself parallel, and the couple slowly rotates together as much as a half turn before the female swims off. The male then moves to another female and repeats the maneuver. Throughout the courtship period, especially when approaching females, males emit low-frequency booming sounds clearly audible more than 100 feet away. When courtship peaks, the booms can occur every 15 to 20 seconds.

Unfortunately, short bottom times at depths of 100 feet or more severely restrict researchers' ability to study the Jewfish's reproductive behavior, and lessens the chance of being on location when a spawn takes place. The lack of courtship activity both in the early morning and late afternoon points to the mid- to late-afternoon, when courtship is at its height, as the most likely time for spawning to occur. At times single males, accompanied by one to three females, have been sighted moving away from an aggregation. This suggests that Jewfish reproduce in harems away from the main courting group.

Nassau Grouper
Epinephelus striatus

Although Nassau Grouper are the most widely studied sea bass, many important gaps in our knowledge of the species' ecology and behavior remain. The distinctive fish, with five irregular, olive-brown body bars over a light background and a prominent saddle-spot on the upper tail base, have been documented to weigh more than 55 lbs. and reach a length of three feet. The solitary predators live within large home ranges in clear inshore waters with a high-profile bottom, but larger males often inhabit depths to 300 feet. The species is indigenous to the tropical western Atlantic and ranges from Bermuda through the Bahamas, down Florida's east coast, across the Caribbean and along the eastern coastline of Brazil. It is absent from much of the Gulf of Mexico. Historical records, established by examination of fossilized otoliths, indicate the fishes' presence in Florida waters as far back as 2000-1000 BC. Recently expanding research related to the behavior and ecology of Nassau Grouper has been driven by the species' unprecedented decline in population numbers and size during the last two decades.

The species has long been one of the most important market-fish harvested in the tropical western Atlantic. The first official survey of Puerto Rican fisheries, compiled in 1900, found the Nassau Grouper to be "a common and very important food fish, reaching a weight of 50 lbs. or more." As recently as the 1970s, it was the fourth most common shallow-water fish landed in Puerto Rico. A 1968 reef fish biodiversity and abundance study at Alligator Reef near

Marathon in the Florida Keys recorded multiple Nassau Grouper sightings on every survey dive. Today, however, the species' numbers have plummeted so drastically that it is considered commercially extinct in Puerto Rico and the U. S. Virgin Islands, and so threatened in Florida that a no-harvest moratorium was imposed in 1990. In 1994 volunteer research divers from the Reef Environmental Education Foundation logged only 19 sightings in 145 dives in Key Largo, where spearfishing has been banned since 1960, and five sightings from 158 dives in Key West. Only 18 sighting were made from 204 dives in the Dry Tortugas, a region considered to be one of the species' historic population centers.

A Nassau Grouper displays the species' typical color pattern.

There are no visual distinctions between the sexes except during courtship and spawning. Nassau Grouper were believed until recently to be protogynous hermaphrodites. However, because there is a significant size overlap between the sexes and at least some individuals are born as primary males, this view is now questioned. Recent studies have disclosed that juveniles go through a bisexual phase before reaching sexual maturity, then lose most of the gonadal tissue of one sex. Because individuals retain remnants of their bisexual phase, it is difficult to confirm a sexual transition later. If sex change occurs, it does not appear to be governed by a specific size requirement, as is the case with many hermaphroditic species, and possibly requires yet unidentified social conditions.

Although all large grouper populations have decreased during the last 20 years, none has declined more quickly or dramatically than the Nassau Grouper. The downfall of this relatively large apex predator appears to be directly related to its annual mass-spawning behavior, which makes it a sitting duck for

Groupers & Sea Basses

overexploitation. Nassau Grouper migrate long distances to traditional spawning grounds during one-week reproductive periods that fall around the full moons of two consecutive winter months. Groups of dozens, or hundreds, of the otherwise solitary grouper join together before the full moon and swim along outer reef banks to the distant sites. One tagged fish traveled 60 miles and another 140 miles from their home ranges to spawn. Groups form into massive aggregations that, until the recent heavy exploitation, often numbered up to 100,000 fish, ranging between 18 inches and three feet in length. The moon is believed to cue the phenomenal gatherings, but there are strong indications that a water temperature of about 77 degrees also plays a critical role. In Bermuda, at the northern extent of the species' range, aggregations occur later in the year, from May to July, when the water reaches the desired

As sunset approaches, aggregating Nassau Grouper rise 30 to 40 feet off the bottom and begin to display spawning patterns.

temperature. In the Bahamas, spawning takes place in December and January; but in the warmer waters of the Cayman Islands, it is not until January and February, after temperatures drop sufficiently, that the grouper gather. The fish assemble in great milling masses near the bottom, at depths ranging from 60 to 150 feet. Spawning sites tend to be on or near prominent drop-offs offshore from the ends of islands, or near underwater promontories jutting toward open ocean from substantial reef lines.

240

Minutes before spawning, most Nassau Grouper exhibit a striking bicolor pattern. The display, worn by males and females, vanishes in seconds if the fish are disturbed.

Courtship and spawning begin at sunset two days before the full moon, while migrating groups are still arriving, and continue for several days. Aggregations are composed of three to five females for every male. Breeding fish exhibit one of four distinct color and marking patterns that can be integrated or quickly changed from one to another. The first, a normal five-bar pattern, typical of non-reproductive individuals, is frequently displayed in varying intensities during the morning hours. A second, the "white belly," also exhibited earlier in the day, is a noticeably blanched version of the first where the faded sidebars disappear as they spread onto the all-white belly. Individuals in the "dark phase" are believed to be females because they lead spawning rises. Their entire bodies and fins turn so dark that only faint outlines of their body bars remain. The "bicolor" is by far the most dramatic pattern. Although exhibited by a few individuals throughout the day, it becomes more prevalent as spawning nears. By evening, nearly 95 percent of the fish in large aggregations display the unmistakable two-tone wardrobe that divides their bodies longitudinally. The upper half of the body, from the eye to the tail base, intensifies to black, while the lower portion, including the pectoral, ventral, anal and tail fins, lightens to snow-white. A white bar running above each eye from the lips to the dorsal fin accentuates the striking presentation. The bicolor scheme, worn at times by both males and females, vanishes in a matter of seconds if the fish are disturbed. The same pattern is flashed by the smaller of two Nassau Grouper who encounter one another on their home reefs. The display is believed to be a sign of submission, possibly intended to decrease confrontations between members of the territorial species.

Groupers & Sea Basses

Spawning takes place ten to 20 minutes before sunset and continues until dark. As late afternoon approaches, the fish, which have been milling just above the bottom, rise 30 or 40 feet and move toward deeper water where they occasionally form towering columns. At this stage, nearly all the fish are in the bicolor or dark phase. Those in the bicolor, believed to include both males and females, hover well off the bottom, while a few dark-phase females remain below. Courtship begins when subgroups of bicolors begin to chase dark females across the sea floor. Suddenly females break toward the surface followed by three to 25 presumed males. The groups, occasionally spiraling as they rise, attract nearby fish who dash in and join the ascending packs. Thirty to 40 feet above the bottom, large, visible gamete clouds are shed as the fish sail apart in a starburst maneuver. A few trailing fish arch over the release area, apparently shedding their gametes. During a single spawning rush, a one- to two-foot female is believed to release between 400,000 and 600,000 eggs.

A smaller aggregation, made up of fewer than 100 fish, was observed to exhibit a slightly different courtship and spawning behavior. The individuals were more lethargic than those in the larger groups, and less than half the assembled fish displayed the bicolored pattern. Most showed either the normal or white-belly pattern and only a few changed into the dark phase. At sunset, bicolored fish followed a few barred individuals who, after a short run, retreated to the bottom and sought refuge. The small aggregation's rather unenthusiastic behavior might indicate that large gatherings are necessary for extensive spawning to occur.

Nassau Grouper rising into the water column just before forming subgroups.

Many questions remain unanswered concerning the Nassau Grouper's reproductive habits. It is still not known if the species pair-spawns, either at, or away from, aggregations. A number of adult Nassau Grouper do not leave their home ranges during the two monthly spawning periods. Dissection revealed one such male with swollen testes, indicating his ability to mate. This might indicate that pair spawning occurs outside aggregations. It is also uncertain whether the same individuals participate in only one, or both, monthly spawning events. Because all studies to date involved aggregations in the process of being harvested, it is unclear how, when or if grouper return to their home ranges after mating.

After fertilization, the positively buoyant one-millimeter eggs rise to the surface in three to five hours and hatch 23 to 40 hours later. Two days after hatching, the pigmented eyes of two-millimeter larvae are visible. With their yolk fat dwindling, larvae begin feeding within 60 hours. In the beginning they filter-feed on microscopic unicellular plants sieved from the water by a sticky network of mucous filaments secreted from glands in their gill arches. Later they dine on shrimplike mysids, copepods and, with growth, fish larvae as large as nine-millimeters. Their ability to capture such comparatively large food items is made possible by the extension of an upper jaw, which nearly doubles the width of their gape. Twenty-five days into their pelagic voyage, the translucent, seven-millimeter grouper are trimmed with foredorsal and anal fin spines over half the length of their bodies. During the last week of their 35- to 40-day pelagic existence, they transform into juveniles nearly an inch in length and, along with thousands of their cohorts, are carried by cross-shelf winds and currents through tidal cuts, where they settle in shallow inshore habitats. DNA analysis has been unable to disclose if these settling fish are recruits from local populations or the products of distant spawning sites.

One group of researchers discovered the recently settled fish hiding exclusively within algae-shrouded colonies of Finger Coral, *Porites porites*, scattered about a shallow, mangrove-lined bay. In different regions, similar habitats may also serve as nursery sites. At one-and-a-half inches the barred pattern appears and, except for size, the little fish resemble adults. During the next four or five months the secretive juveniles hide within algal masses while growing nearly a half-inch each month. In June, when they are three to four inches long, increasing demands for food force them to relocate to nearby breaks in the bottom. By summer's end the fish, having grown to nearly six inches, find homes in abandoned conch shells and coral patches in shallow grass beds where they reside until ready for life on the reef. The fish continue to grow rapidly until they reach sexual maturity in four to seven years at between 16 and 20 inches.Young fish from seven to 12 inches grow approximately 4.5 millimeters per month, while those measuring 13 to 17 inches slow to a growth rate of 1.9 millimeters each month. Fifty percent of the fish harvested from a spawning aggregation in the Cayman Islands were six to seven years old, and one large individual was 28 years.

With maturity juveniles switch from eating tiny crustaceans and begin to hunt for larger prey, including fishes, lobsters and mollusks. Wrasses, parrotfishes, grunts and snappers are the most frequently eaten fishes, while

Groupers & Sea Basses

crabs, mantis shrimps, octopuses, squids, shrimps and hermit crabs head a long list of favorite invertebrate foods. A 23-inch grouper was found with an intact 25-inch moray eel inside its stomach. The soft bodies of Queen Conchs, *Strombus gigas*, are also consumed, but it is not known how the fish remove the animals from their thick shells. Hunting occurs throughout the day, with increased activity during the low-light periods of early morning and dusk.

The species tends to be somewhat territorial, often living within a home range for a number of years. Tagging studies indicate a strong homing instinct, believed to be based on visual clues. Although primarily a solitary species, small groups are occasionally found together inside caves or under ledge overhangs. Members of the species spend a large amount of time at cleaning stations. Individuals raised in captivity without the services of cleaning organisms have been sighted at cleaning stations within an hour of their release. When startled by divers, especially near dusk, large individuals sometimes react with a loud, disconcerting boom produced by a violent contraction of muscles surrounding the air bladder.

Even though many factors such as spearfishing, trapping and intense, year-round fishing have taken heavy tolls on Nassau Grouper populations, nothing has devastated the stock more than the concentrated harvesting of spawning aggregations. More than 50 Nassau Grouper breeding grounds have been documented across the Bahamas and Caribbean Basin. Some of these sites were regularly fished for 80 years before ever-growing exploitation finally removed so many fish that the aggregations completely collapsed and have failed to recover. Spawning grounds in Belize, Bermuda, Cuba, the Dominican Republic, Puerto Rico, St. Croix and St. Thomas have completely disappeared. In the Bahamas, at a site that has been fished since 1900, the annual gathering has declined from thousands to only 100 fish in 1992. Not only has the number of fishing boats working breeding grounds increased substantially, but unscrupulous harvesting methods such as dynamiting and gill-netting also have added to the problem.

Imposing a closed season for Nassau Grouper harvesting during their brief reproductive periods seems to be an obvious answer; however, this strategy will create problems in many areas. For instance, in 1992 over 40 percent of the entire grouper harvest in the Bahamas occurred during breeding periods. Closed seasons would certainly deal a blow to the local fishing industry, but the alternative is a collapsed fishery. A few tentative steps are being taken: Cuba placed a quota on Nassau Grouper in 1985; the Bahamas now have a minimum size limit and closed one spawning aggregation in eastern Andros in 1999; Mexico has banned spearfishing along its Caribbean coastline; and the Cayman Islands have limited fishing on aggregations to hook-and-line by local fishers. Only Bermuda currently prohibits fishing on all grouper aggregations.

For the past decade, an effort has been made to spawn and raise Nassau Grouper in captivity. Although difficult, the project experienced some early successes. Hatchery-raised juveniles were released to test the possibility of restocking reef systems, and after nine months a few of the tagged fish were still alive.

Tiger Grouper customarily flush red when attending cleaning stations.

Spawning pattern of Tiger Grouper.

Tiger Grouper
Mycteroperca tigris

Tiger Grouper are the most impressively patterned grouper in the Caribbean. These piscivores can grow to over three feet, but are generally less than two feet in length. Juveniles are bright yellow with a dusky mid-body streak. As they mature, a series of from nine to 11 diagonal body bars develops. Young adults display contrasting black and white bars or tan bars over yellow. Adults exhibit brown, black or red bars that can rapidly lighten or darken. Individuals attending cleaning stations often flush red.

Groupers & Sea Basses

Male Tiger Grouper become aggressive as the spawning period approaches.

The species has been reported to spawn for a weeklong period beginning two days after each of the full moons falling between late January and April. A small number of individuals also intermingle with Nassau Grouper, *Epinephelus striatus*, aggregations. One aggregation of several hundred Tiger Grouper, in 110 to 120 feet of water off Puerto Rico, was studied for a number of days by researchers in 1992. During the afternoon hours the largest individuals, presumed to be males, displayed yellowish bronze heads and a large whitish patch covering the rear of their abdomens. The biggest fish were active and

Courting Tiger Grouper.

assertive, aggressively chasing away other males. As evening settled the same fish began to defend territories, intensify their spawning colors and become even more aggressive. Within minutes of sunset, the big males rose three or four feet off the sea floor and waited for females, also displaying white abdominal patches, to join them. When approached, the males moved toward the females and together, the pairs made quick vertical spawning rushes of a few feet, releasing a cloud of gametes at the peak of their ascent. During the short time the fish were observed, one male was seen mating twice, once with each of two females, within a 30-second period. Later, a second male streaked in and shed his gametes at the same time as the spawning pair.

Typical color pattern of Red Hind.

Red Hind
Epinephelus guttatus

Red Hind are moderate-sized grouper reported to reach over two feet in length, but generally averaging less than a foot. The solitary hunters, with attractive coats of reddish brown spots spread over a whitish undercoat, live near the bottom close to the protection of the reef's structure. They have little fear of divers and customarily allow a cautious observer to approach within two or three feet before slowly easing away. Crabs are the most common item on their menu, while fishes, such as Bluehead Wrasse, *Thalassoma bifasciatum*; Boga, *Inermia vittata*; goatfishes and small morays, follow close behind. Mantis shrimps comprise over 15 percent of their diet, with shrimps and octopuses rounding out their preferred foods.

Estimates of the species' sex ratio, made from specimens harvested at spawning aggregations, have varied widely although females were always found to outnumber males significantly. Females, who cannot be distinguished from males outside of reproductive periods, occupy broad home ranges that overlap with those of one to 18 other females. They live on reefs of shallow to moderate depths, well within safe diving limits, while larger males inhabit much deeper waters. Even though the fish live in close proximity to each other, there appears to be little social interaction, with most preferring to spend much

247

of their time alone, partially hidden in a favorite location. Not much is known about the species' early life stages. On rare occasions shy one- to two-inch juveniles, with widely spaced red body spots on a bright-white background, are sighted sneaking about near cover on patch reefs in moderate depths. Although most adults live for ten or 11 years, one 18-year-old specimen has been documented.

Red Hind are protogynous hermaphrodites, changing from females to males at some point in their life cycle. What triggers sex change is unknown, but individuals in transitional stages are found year-round. Spawning aggregations in Puerto Rico have been studied for more than a decade. There the fish gather in or near traditional spawning grounds along sections of the insular shelf during a single one- to two-week period associated with the lunar cycles of January or February. In 1992, token spawning occurred in a Puerto Rican aggregation in the latter part of January, while peak activity took place just prior to, and continued for a week after, the full moon of February. One tagged Red Hind traveled more than ten miles, at one point crossing water over 600 feet deep and bypassing other aggregations, to spawn at a particular site.

Aggregation areas studied to date are all quite large, typically encompassing over a square mile of patch reef sea floor, in depths beginning at 60 feet. These extensive tracts normally accommodate multiple congregations of fish, spaced 300 to 400 feet apart. One site was estimated to contain nearly 3,000 fish when at peak density on the day of the full moon. The females average nine inches and males 11 inches. For the first two days individuals are widely scattered, but, as the full moon approaches, the fish begin to gather in isolated groups of two to six females accompanied by a lone male. A few groups do not have a male, but none contains more than one. It appears that females establish clusters, and males affiliate with one or more of the gatherings. It is believed that individuals stay with the same group and remain at the spawning site throughout the entire aggregation period.

Because of their pallid complexions and distinctly swollen abdomens, females are easily distinguished from males. When courting, males typically exhibit dusky, mottled patterns with two or three dark one- to two-inch bars above the anal fin and pale heads with dark areas on the sides of their lips. While the females rest near bottom shelter, the males swim a few feet higher within approximately 50 feet of their females. Now and then, the suitors settle to the bottom and remain stationary for a few minutes. Approaching divers easily disturb the males, causing them to swim a short distance away until the observers leave. The males patrol their territories and occasionally engage in border confrontations with neighboring males. During the brief encounters the rivals raise their dorsal fins and rush each other with open mouths.

A male will sometimes execute a series of short, slow arching rises or hover just off the bottom in a head-up position in what are believed to be courtship displays. Actual spawns, which have been observed rarely, are rather uneventful. A single female lifts a foot or two off the bottom, where a male promptly joins her. Together, the pair rises slightly and releases a cloud of gametes before settling back to the sea floor. From inspection of gonadal tissue, it has been determined that females spawn more than once during each annual gathering.

As much as 20 percent of a Red Hind spawning aggregation can be made up of Rock Hind, *Epinephelus adscencionis*. The females of the modest-sized sea bass are also obviously full of eggs, while the males display black blotches over a white background. The spawning behavior for this species has yet to be reported.

Graysby
Epinephelus cruentatus

Graysby are normally the most common grouper, inhabiting shallow, high-profile reef systems from Bermuda to the northern shores of South America and throughout the Caribbean and Gulf of Mexico. The ill-tempered little sea bass, which can grow to just over one foot, live within limited territories often located among the nooks and crannies of star and lettuce corals. Although occasionally found at depths to 90 feet, the rather reclusive fish generally haunt the shadowy edges of overhangs or crevices at depths from 20 to 30 feet. Their bodies and fins, ranging from light brown to deep chocolate, are evenly spread with dark spots. Three to five distinctive white spots, spaced along each side of the dorsal fin base, change from white to black when Graysby become disturbed. Larger individuals occasionally display an indistinct pattern of body bars.

The tenacious predators hunt throughout the day, with distinct peaks at dawn and dusk. Fish, particularly Brown Chromis, *Chromis multilineata*, who move to and from the reef at sunrise and sunset – the Graysby's favorite dining time – make up the bulk of their diet. The stomach of one specimen contained four Brown Chromis, all in the same state of digestion, suggesting that they were consumed within a narrow time frame. Other small fishes, including Cherubfish, *Centropyge argi*; cardinalfishes; Bicolor Damselfish, *Stegastes partitus*; Blue Chromis, *Chromis cyanea*, and Yellow Goatfish, *Mulloidichthys martinicus*, are also common prey. Shrimps, crabs, mantis shrimps and a few other crustaceans make up the remaining 20 percent of their food. Most invertebrates are taken just after sunset as they emerge from their daytime hiding places. During the day Graysby often hunt with roving Goldentail Moray, *Gymnothorax miliaris*, and Spotted Moray, *G. moringa*, as the eels slip from crevice to crevice in pursuit of concealed prey. The hunters stay close, hoping the morays' surprise attacks will flush a fish into the open. As many as four Graysby accompany a single eel. The fish routinely fight among themselves to gain an advantageous position near the opening where the eel is foraging. During the prolonged hunts, the typically shy fish are so intent on their business that they can easily be approached by observers.

A single dominant male and several females share a territory, averaging 200 square feet, where resources and mates are aggressively defended. Ritualistic, but vicious, turf wars occasionally break out between two similar-sized individuals, possibly territorial males. We watched a 15-minute scrap between two ten-inch Graysby late one afternoon. When first observed, the pair was glaring at one another across a white sand shelf. Without warning, both simultaneously attacked with open mouths, crashing together so hard they spun in a complete turn, causing one to retreat a foot or two and pause, facing in the opposite direction. We thought the battle was over, but, in less than ten seconds

Groupers & Sea Basses

The beginning of a territorial dispute between two equally sized Graysby starts with a lengthy face-to-face standoff.

the retreating fish turned and cautiously began inching toward its rival until the pair's heads, from snouts to gill covers, touched. The fish imperceptibly pushed against its opponent until both were lying on their sides. They abruptly broke, pivoted and paralleled one another, facing the same direction. Within seconds, they were racing together back and forth through four sharp turns before stopping, as suddenly as they started, in a second extended face-off. In little more than a minute they attacked each other again. This time the power of their rush was so forceful that the fish, with jaws locked, sent up a storm of sand as they tumbled over the bottom. The series of events was repeated several more times before one fish, finally losing heart, disappeared inside a reef pocket.

Attacks are frequent and vicious.

The fish lie unmoving for several seconds with their heads pressed together.

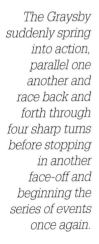

One fish pushes ever so slowly against the forebody of his rival until both lie flat.

The Graysby suddenly spring into action, parallel one another and race back and forth through four sharp turns before stopping in another face-off and beginning the series of events once again.

Groupers & Sea Basses

Graysby are protogynous hermaphrodites who generally change from females to males during their fourth or fifth years at a length of about eight inches. The transition, which usually occurs after the species' annual spawning season, is followed by a quick growth spurt. There is no visible sexual dimorphism in the species; but virtually all individuals over ten inches are males. Most females mature sexually during their third year, at a length of six inches, and by their fifth year all females have changed into males.

Not much is understood about the Graysbys' reproductive habits. The species pair spawns within territories. The reproductive season in the southern Caribbean occurs sometime between May and September but has been reported to take place during other months elsewhere. The sex ratio in an unfished population of Graysby is approximately two-and-a-half females for each male; but on one heavily fished reef system, the ratio was six females for every male.

Juvenile Graysby are extremely shy. They are distinguished by a yellowish wash covering the upper head and back and a conspicuous white band running from the lower lip to the leading edge of their dorsal fin. One- to two-inch youngsters often find sanctuary in the convoluted outer surface of Giant Barrel Sponges, *Xestospongia muta*. With growth, they seek shelter beneath low ledges, away from high-profile reef structures. The skittish juveniles appear in the open only when making short dashes between nearby hiding places. Juveniles, shorter than five inches, feed almost exclusively on shrimps, but occasionally consume tiny fishes. Young Graysby grow about two inches each year, slowing to less than an inch after six years.

A juvenile Graysby hides inside a tube sponge.

An adult Coney displaying a common reddish brown color pattern.

Coney
Epinephelus fulvus

Unlike the closely related and similar-sized Graysby, *Epinephelus cruentatus*, who live in complex coral structures, Coney prefer isolated patch reefs surrounded by sand in depths between 15 and 60 feet. Adults spend 95 percent of their time within a 15-foot radius of a central coral patch, where they live in harems composed of a male and three to four females. The number of cleaning stations in an area appears to have a direct bearing on choice of home sites. Adults reach a maximum length of 16 inches, but individuals over ten inches are rare in heavily fished waters. This common species occurs in the tropical western Atlantic from Bermuda to Brazil, including the Gulf of Mexico.

Adult and juvenile Coney display one of two distinct color patterns, both highlighted with a sprinkle of bright blue dots. The most common pattern, a solid tan to reddish brown body coat, can quickly change into a bicolor pattern that leaves the back dark while the lower body and tail turn white. The bicolor pattern tends to be displayed more in early morning and late afternoon, and possibly when the fish is excited or hunting. A blotched resting pattern occasionally appears when the fish settles on the bottom for an extended period or perches inside a vase sponge – a common daytime behavior that is not yet understood. A few Coney, both juveniles and adults, are golden except for small blue dots. Golden adults, believed to be the product of a single recessive gene, generally reside in the deeper end of the species' depth range.

The Coneys' diet is equally divided between small fishes and crustaceans, typically shrimps, crabs and mantis shrimps. These bottom hunters occasionally stalk prey in pairs and are relentless once in pursuit of a victim. They frequently shadow-feed with morays and octopuses. The protogynous hermaphrodites reach sexual maturity just over six inches, and become males between six and ten inches. The species is believed to live for at least nine years.

In Bimini, Bahamas, seven days after the full moon of May, we observed two adjacent harems of Coney courting and spawning during the last hour before sunset. Their activities were centered on two coral mounds 20 feet apart, probably the core sites of each harem's territory. The white bellies of the five

Groupers & Sea Basses

The courtship display of male Coney.

bicolored females – two with one harem and three with the other – were dramatically distended with eggs. When the two slightly larger males were on the move or near their females, both displayed a distinct spawning pattern. Their brown backs, from snout to just past the foredorsal, were lightly blotched, and a tan streak ran from tail to pectoral fins.

The females shuttled their bulging bellies about the coral mounds or rested heavily on the bottom, often near one another. When stationary, their bicolored bodies blotched. The males rapidly swam about the area just off the bottom, now and again settling next to a low-profile structure or inside a vase sponge and

Females with swollen abdomens hover above a coral head while waiting to spawn.

Within seconds of returning to his harem, the male positions next to a female and the pair dash side-by-side several feet into the water column where they release gametes.

developing a blotched pattern. Once swimming again, their spawning colors instantly returned. These jaunts, which took them 30 to 60 feet from their territories, kept them apart from the females most of the time, but once back, the males courted with enthusiasm. Returning males swam up to females, twitched repeatedly, performed two or three short upward dashes and even wedged their snouts beneath the females' bellies, attempting to coax them off the bottom. Occasionally their persistence caused the females to take flight, with the males in close pursuit.

At 7:15 PM, 45 minutes before sunset, the first observed spawn occurred. A female rose above a coral mound and paused. In an instant, a male dashed up from below, brushing against her abdomen as he passed, looped back sharply and positioned himself next to her side. Wildly thrashing tails carried the pair straight up eight to ten feet, where they released a thick cloud of gametes. Waiting Yellowtail Snapper, *Ocyurus chrysurus*, swarmed the dispersing eggs. Ten minutes later, we watched the same male spawn with the second of his two females. Through the dim light we spotted two other swirling aggregations of feeding Yellowtails, probably marking the sites of other Coney spawns.

Groupers & Sea Basses

On the following evening during the same time period, members of the two harems courted and spawned once again. This time, however, the two neighboring males engaged in a skirmish on a sand patch midway between their territories. The altercation began with a two-minute face-off and ended with a violent attack. During the third evening both males showed their spawning patterns, but we did not see any ripe females or observe courtship or spawning activities.

Hamlets
Genus *Hypoplectrus*

At first glance, the slim, deep-bodied hamlets look more like members of the damselfish family than the typically more muscular sea basses. However, on closer inspection the three- to five-inch carnivores' swimming style, large mouths and triangular pupils verify their family status. For decades debate among marine taxonomists has swirled around the species status of the many hamlets that make up the genus *Hypoplectrus.*

At the heart of the controversy is the essence of taxonomy: What defines a species? The intriguing dilemma centers on the small, brightly colored fishes' almost complete lack of anatomical differences and similar breeding habits; yet, for an unexplained reason, the otherwise identical fish display a variety of different color patterns. At least 11 distinct and regularly occurring color morphs have been documented. Adding even more spice to hamlet soup is the smorgasbord of hybrid color variations that occur in nature.

The stately little solitary hunters move about just above the bottom within home ranges that are defended against other hamlets. Their day is spent in a never-ending search for a quick meal of shrimps, crabs, fishes, or an occasional mantis shrimp. They tend to prefer complex reef structures in moderate depths. The genus is unique to the waters of the tropical western Atlantic. The Barred Hamlet, *Hypoplectrus puella*; Butter Hamlet, *H. unicolor*; and Black Hamlet, *H. nigricans*, are the most common and widely distributed of the 11 color morphs. The three are well represented throughout the entire region, with the Barred extending into the Gulf of Mexico and up to Bermuda. The distribution of the eight remaining morphs is more restricted, with several radiating out from distinct population centers, which indicates historic geographic isolation, a situation that possibly allowed the color morphs to differentiate. For example, the Blue Hamlet, *H. gemma*, is almost exclusively found in South Florida and the Keys; while the rare Golden Hamlet, *H. gummigutta*, and Masked Hamlet, *Hypoplectrus* sp., primarily inhabit the submerged banks between Central America and the Greater Antilles.

Like several other small sea basses, hamlets are simultaneous hermaphrodites that take turns releasing eggs and milt each evening of the year – a behavior known as egg trading. Fortunately for fish watchers, the little basses are so preoccupied with each other during courtship that neither seems disturbed by a diver's presence, allowing discreet observers to move within three or four feet. As early as an hour before sunset, mature hamlets begin acting giddy. At some point they swim rapidly out of their territories in search of mates for the evening.

256

These trips can take them over 100 yards from their permanent territories. It is speculated that because the fish are site-oriented, they are well aware of neighboring hamlets. On their way to spawning sites, hamlets occasionally happen upon other courting pairs. If they are the same color morph, the cruising hamlets might try to break in, but are generally driven away. When their regular mates are found extended courtship begins. For up to an hour before the first spawn occurs, the frisky pairs chase about the bottom, occasionally stopping to feed, all the while keeping a lookout for interfering rivals.

Finally, one of the hamlets assumes the female role and acts the aggressor. She strikes a rigid snout-up pose with fins flared while intermittently snapping her head sharply from side to side. The interim male, whose color is distinctly blanched, mills nervously about the bottom a few feet away. Gradually the two make their way to the top of a prominent coral head or gorgonian bush. Suddenly, the female darts to within inches of the male and pauses. Faster than a blink, the lovers clasp tightly together in what appears

Barred Hamlet – a common species.

Butter Hamlet – a common species.

Masked Hamlet – a rare genus member.

Golden Hamlet – a rare genus member.

Groupers & Sea Basses

to be unbridled passion. The acting male's body – head pointed directly down, mouth opened in an oval, ventral and dorsal fins spread and belly puckered – is enveloped by the arching body of its mate. One one-thousand, two one-thousand, three one-thousand and the fish pop apart. With color renewed, the male darts a short distance away with its mate in chase. The dramatic three-second spawning clasps generally begin ten to 15 minutes before sunset and reoccur every few minutes until the last light fades, with partners changing sexual roles between each bout. The number of clasps per spawning pairs we have observed varied from as few as three to a record ten by a robust pair of Indigo Hamlets, *H. indigo*. The affair ends when one of the spent partners discreetly vanishes into the night. The planktonic larvae settle back to the reef 22 days after spawning.

Fertile hybrids, the product of crosses between color morphs, have long been

Courtship between a Shy Hamlet (on the bottom) and a hybrid resulted in four spawning clasps.

used as evidence against granting separate species status to the members of the genus. The argument goes that if the different color morphs are indeed individual species, then there should be extremely limited intermorph spawning. Of the 28 spawns we witnessed during a two-week period, all but one occurred between like hamlets. The one exception was a brownish colored hybrid (the area's most common hybrid coloration) spawning with a Shy Hamlet, *H. guttavarius*. Hamlets use sight to choose a mate and, if given a choice, nearly always choose a like color pattern. During our dive, when the cross-spawn was observed, we didn't see any other Shy or brown hybrids in the vicinity.

Aquarium breeding research has documented that if a fish is given no option other than to spawn with a different morph, it will do so nearly 50 percent of the time. Field data recorded only seven of 189 pairings between unlike color morphs. Although limited, this is still a surprising amount of interbreeding between species.

Left: *The three-second spawning embrace of Barred Hamlet.*

Groupers & Sea Basses

In 1980, protein gel electrophoresis performed on nine different color morphs detected virtually no interspecific differences. However, this evidence, which relies on negative data, is considered inconclusive by many. One interesting conclusion that can be drawn from this work is that *Hypoplectrus* has differentiated recently. The genus may not have evolved until after the closing of the Isthmus of Panama, approximately 3.8 million years ago. This date might seem ancient, but, on an evolutionary time scale, hamlets are the new kids on the block. The different color morphs may have been segregated later into population centers by the rise and fall of sea level.

Further muddling the matter is the enticing hypothesis that aggressive mimicry is the mechanism driving speciation in *Hypoplectrus*. Morphs with color patterns resembling non-predatory reef fishes have a distinct advantage procuring food. For example: the Blue Hamlet closely resembles the plankton-feeding Blue Chromis, *Chromis cyanea*; the Butter Hamlet is much like the Foureye Butterflyfish, *Chaetodon capistratus*, that dines on Christmas Tree

The Black Hamlet, a carnivore, is a possible mimic of the Dusky Damselfish.

Dusky Damselfish – a herbivore.

The Blue Hamlet is a possible mimic of the Blue Chromis.

Blue Chromis – a planktivore.

Worms, *Spirobranchus giganteus*, and feather duster tentacles, and the Black Hamlet mimics the algae-eating Dusky Damselfish, *Stegastes fuscus*. In theory, functioning mimics should not only look like their models but should also be less abundant and evolve similar behavior characteristics. Hamlets meet the first two criteria, but the mentioned morphs display none of the behavior traits of those they mimic. Possibly the short evolutionary history of hamlets has not yet allowed them to develop complete mimicry. On the other hand, the similarities could well be nothing more than coincidence.

All this pushed the hamlet question to the point where it became necessary to interbreed color morphs in captivity before re-evaluating their taxonomic status. A laboratory breeding project did just that in the early 1990s. The research established that crosses between color morphs (in this case Blue Hamlets and Butter Hamlets) produced hybrids intermediate to both parents in color and markings. The research also found that self-fertilization of a Shy Hamlet resulted in offspring that resembled the parent species. This confirmed that color pattern is genetically determinate in *Hypoplectrus*. These new findings, combined with field observations verifying a low frequency of hybrid hamlets, have tilted the debate in the direction of granting full species rank to the regularly occurring color morphs.

Of course, everyone's opinion pivots on a preferred definition of species, and there seem to be as many as there are taxonomists. In fact, entire graduate-level courses are devoted to this one perplexing question. Michael L. Domeier, the researcher who interbred hamlets writes, "That there is no agreement of the precise nature of the species is a reflection of the nature of the dynamic process at work and thus we should not anticipate future agreement." His thoughts share good company. After discovering astounding differences in every genus of barnacles he studied, Darwin wrote, "After describing a set of forms as distinct species, tearing up my MS. and making them one species, tearing that up and making them separate, and then making them one again, I have gnashed my teeth, cursed species, and asked what sin I had committed to be so punished."

Hybrid hamlet – possible cross between a Yellowbelly Hamlet and a Shy Hamlet.

Hybrid hamlet – possible cross between a Blue Hamlet and an Indigo Hamlet.

Groupers & Sea Basses

Harlequin Bass
Serranus tigrinus

Monogamy is not a widely practiced mating strategy on the reef; however, the common Harlequin Bass not only share eggs exclusively with permanent partners, but also remain with them throughout the day, hunting cooperatively and defending jointly held territories for feeding, spawning and sleeping. Pairs generally inhabit one of several large, adjoining territories

Harlequin Bass hover briefly before spawning.

spread across rubble fields bordering reef structures. Territories held by mated pairs average 600 square feet, while those of solitary adults are only half as large. Juveniles, relegated to territorial outskirts, stay close to their hiding holes in small, weakly defended areas. Occasionally, Harlequin Bass are chased by larger food competitors, such as Graysby, *Epinephelus cruentatus*, and Coney, *E. fulvus*. In turn, they attack hamlets and other small, gleaning carnivores that encroach on their turf. When Harlequins confront neighbors at boundaries, the two momentarily pause and face one another with outspread dorsal and ventral fins. At times, one will lean to the side with its dorsal spines aimed in the direction of the adversary. On other occasions, the fish cautiously circle each other before ending the encounter with a rapid back-and-forth chase accented by an occasional nip.

Throughout the day pairs move about together, just off the bottom within their territories, feeding primarily on shrimps, with a few fishes, mantis shrimps and crabs rounding out the diet. Frequently, one of the hunters veers off from the other to poke around a crevice, but the pair seldom remains apart for long and generally keeps in eye contact. Abrupt feeding strikes are directed at the bottom. The species is unique among pair-bonded fish for its cooperative stalking behavior. The two hunters approach concealed prey from opposite sides of a crevice and attack simultaneously, driving their startled victim toward one mouth or the other.

Pairs of the two-and-a-half to four-inch adults are usually closely size-related in order to profit from maximum egg productivity. If given the opportunity, however, mates will abandon smaller partners to form new pair associations with larger solitary individuals. Before venturing into a new territory, a visitor must be signaled by an extended fin display from the resident. If welcomed, the guest follows the occupant around its territory. The following day, the newly formed pair actively patrols, hunts and spawns together. If a paired fish disappears, its partner makes courtship overtures the same evening and usually forms long-term bonds with a similar-sized solitary neighbor by the next day. The two live together within their joint territories, unless a portion is confiscated by a bordering pair during the changeover.

The simultaneous hermaphroditic Harlequins mate throughout the year, with increased activity during the week before and after the full moon. Spawning episodes begin 20 minutes before sunset and can last until ten minutes after the sun goes down. As with other small egg-trading sea basses, the goal is to spawn as males. The partner taking the female role controls the tempo of reproduction. Courtship starts with the pairs blanching slightly as the acting females lead their mates on a series of short runs interspersed with feeding. Now and then, the females raise their heads and twitch. Finally, the females swim to the top of prominent features in their territories and signal readiness by flexing their bodies. Acting males move near and, for a brief moment, the pairs hover inches apart. Without warning and faster than the eye can follow, the duos dart straight up several inches, spawn and return separately to the bottom. In the single spawn, each acting female releases her entire payload of eggs. On many evenings, especially those close to the full moon, the partners immediately reverse sexual roles and spawn a second time about two minutes later. However, spawning is not always so egalitarian. Encounters often end with only a single spawn. On other evenings a series of false starts may occur without spawning taking place. At times, both partners simultaneously present the curved-body pose or, in a few instances, neither signals before spawning.

In their quest to fertilize eggs, members of permanent pairs regularly go outside their territories to spawn as males with neighboring solitary adults, but never with members of other established pairs. These encounters are not reciprocal, indicating the secondary social status of loners. This is probably the reason single adults quickly replace missing partners. When pair members spawn with solitary individuals, the encounters occur prior to egg-trading with their partners. In some instances, both partners take part in simultaneous spawning rushes with solitary neighbors. However, things don't go so smoothly if a partner, after spawning as a male, heads for the neighbor's territory without trading eggs with its mate. The spurned companion attempts to block its partner's route, but often relents and joins the tryst.

Lantern Bass
Serranus baldwini

Lantern Bass spend their days scooting about coral rubble and sand bottoms hunting for tiny bits of animal matter. Now and then, the one-and-one-half to two-inch, blennylike sea bass dart up into the water column to snag floating specks of plankton. Populations are separated into harems consisting of from one to seven small simultaneous hermaphrodites living within small, overlapping ranges inside the patrolled territorial boundaries of single large dominant males. In the animal kingdom, this social system is unique to Lantern

Groupers & Sea Basses

Bass and a second genus member, *Serranus fasciatus*, from the Eastern Pacific. The smaller hermaphrodites have functioning ovarian and testicular tissue with separate ducts for the transfer of eggs and sperm; their visually identical harem-masters are sex-changed males who have lost their ovaries.

The males boldly move around their territories, guarding against the intrusion of neighboring males and chasing subservient hermaphrodites who are much more passive, seldom venturing far from a restricted area and often remaining hidden. Although hermaphrodites occasionally have altercations among themselves, it remains unclear if such conflicts are meant to protect territories or to maintain an individual's position in a hierarchical social system. Lantern Bass frequently survey their surroundings while perched on rocks or hovering in a head-up position just off the bottom.

Courting Lantern Bass.

During the last hour and a half of daylight, when courtship and spawning occur, the hermaphrodites become more settled while males pick up the pace of chasing, surveying and patrolling. Unlike other genus members, males control reproduction, spawning once each evening with their harems of hermaphrodites. Smaller harem members rarely spawn with one another or streak in and mix their sperm with a spawning pair. Courtship begins with a male approaching a hermaphrodite and signaling his intentions by jerking forward in a series of short, rapid movements or bobbing up and down from a horizontal hovering position. The male approaches from behind and rests his head on the rear of his partner's body or nudges its side repeatedly. If uninterested, the hermaphrodite scampers away and is either chased or ignored by the male. When responsive, the hermaphrodite lifts off the bottom, raises its head and bends laterally into an S-curve. The fish dart up one or two feet and spawn before returning separately to the bottom, where they dodge under cover. At times a hermaphrodite performs the S-curve without being courted, which immediately brings the male flying to its side.

Interesting questions remain unanswered concerning the curious mating behavior of Lantern Bass. It is still a mystery why hermaphrodites have both sexual functions if they spawn only as females; and what mechanism keeps the hermaphrodites from spawning among themselves? And why do males lose their female capabilities, which, if left in place, would greatly increase their productivity? Possibly, pure males have evolved only recently in the species, and there has not been sufficient time for the hermaphrodites to lose their testicular tissue.

Tobaccofish
Serranus tabacarius

Solitary three- to seven-inch Tobaccofish hunt throughout the day for small fishes and shrimps within their home ranges, which encompass between 40 to 500 square yards of sandy, low-lying rock and patch reef plains. Several weakly defended territories broadly overlap one another.

During one-hour periods between midafternoon and dusk, the simultaneous hermaphrodites seek out partners at locations within their hunting grounds and engage in entertaining courtship and spawning displays. The prolific egg traders typically spawn over a dozen times each afternoon, with from one to nine different partners. The number of matings and mates varies greatly each day, with a tendency for increased activity around the time of the full moon. Individuals change spawning partners every ten minutes on average, with reciprocal spawns between partners occurring approximately a minute apart.

Courtship usually begins when one or both partners rise a few feet off the bottom, arch their tails upward and lift their heads. Often one of the fish, generally the larger, chases the other briskly across the bottom. When ready to mate, the first to assume the male's role develops a distinctive black mask, collapses his fins and settles flat and still on the sand. The temporary female, wearing a pale blotched pattern, flexes laterally and fidgets nearby while repeatedly fluttering her rear dorsal and ventral fins. With an arched body, she begins swimming back and forth, brushing the vent on her white belly across her mate's darkened head. After a few passes the female swims up and away, with the male tagging close behind. As the pair rises several feet above the bottom, the acting male may repeatedly flick his dorsal fin and move to her side in a faltering start-and-stop-motion. But more often he slips up from below and bumps her vent with a partially open mouth. The female abruptly turns, to face her partner, and the pair immediately dashes up together, leaving a gamete cloud a foot above their starting point. Possibly, because home ranges are large and the pairs spawn in random locations, streaking rarely occurs in the species.

Larger Tobaccofish seem to attain a preferred status. They control more extensive home ranges, are seldom chased, typically spawn first and last in the male role and frequently refuse to reciprocate or mate consecutively as females. However, they never develop sufficient dominance to function exclusively as males.

Courting Tobaccofish display blotched backs and black masks.

Groupers & Sea Basses

Plankton-picking Chalk Bass hover above open bottom.

Chalk Bass
Serranus tortugarum

Unlike their brawny relatives that constantly probe the bottom for crustaceans, dainty, baby blue Chalk Bass gather in loose groups and pick plankton, just above rock piles on sandy sea floors. Juveniles, who look identical to adults, and sexually mature individuals, over one-and-a-quarter inches, inhabit the shallower end of the species' 30- to 300-foot depth range. Larger adults, which can grow to three inches, generally reside below 100 feet.

Late in the day, the egg traders leave their feeding areas and travel to an area containing a cluster of small spawning territories, where they hover a foot or two above the bottom with a customary partner of similar-size. Unpaired loners patrol the peripheries. Courtship displays are subtle, and with good reason: Chalk Bass are accomplished sneakers that keep a keen eye on nearby pairs, waiting for a chance to dart in at the last moment and add their sperm to the pair's gamete clouds.

The first partner to take the female role glides in front of her mate, cautiously lifts her dorsal fin, and, in slow motion, rises an inch or two. While the pair pauses, members of neighboring couples and loners inch in their direction. When approached too closely, the couple drives the intruders away. If the spawning rush continues, it is short, quick, and frequently joined by one to five streakers shedding sperm. Often, in an effort to disguise their timing, neither partner signals in any way before their rush; or the couples make false starts, which bring freeloaders flying in their direction. Mates usually spawn more than a dozen times during an evening, with the partners trading eggs 80 percent of the time.

Courting pairs located more than five feet from other spawners or isolated by bottom structures can afford to display more conspicuously. In these situations a partner might bob forward and down slightly once or twice. Occasionally her mate answers with a similar signal just before spawning. The same signal is also given when individuals leave protective cover or while heading for night shelter. A fear of predation is added reason for courting Chalk Bass to be cautious – lizardfishes often station themselves near active spawning territories to take advantage of preoccupied courters.

Cave Dwelling Basses
Genus *Liopropoma*

Sighting any of the four small, reclusive species forming the Caribbean contingent of *Liopropoma* is a worthy challenge for advanced fish watchers. The beautiful two- to four-inch, red-orange-black-and-yellow-striped, torpedo-shaped fish with electric blue highlights typically inhabit coral caves and dark reef pockets below 80 feet. However, the most prevalent of the four, the Peppermint Bass, *Liopropoma rubre*, is occasionally found in water as shallow as 20 feet, especially on slopes with shingled layers of plate corals. An underwater light helps to locate the solitary fish deep within the narrow crevices formed by the coral strata. The light beam is also necessary to bring out the exquisite colors of the lovely little fish. At times the shy loners can be seen hovering at the edge of ambient light. Once aware of divers, they slowly retreat into the shadows, but frequently return a few seconds later for a quick peek.

The three remaining species, the Candy Basslet, *L. carmabi*; Cave Bass, *L. mowbrayi*; and Wrasse Bass, *L. eukrines*, tend to dwell deeper and are believed to be common on walls below safe diving limits. Unstriped, salmon-colored Cave Bass prefer small individual cave pockets only a foot or two across rather than long ledge overhangs. Smaller and rarer, Candy Basslett are seldom sighted above 100 feet. While these three species range widely across the region, the slightly larger Wrasse Bass appears to be restricted to deeper areas off the U.S. east coast from Florida to North Carolina and to the Gulf of Mexico.

Even though widespread and fairly common, little is known about the group. The genus has been placed in the sea bass family, but debate continues about the proper classification. The species appear to be more closely allied with soapfishes than with other sea basses. Both groups share flat, sloping heads, comparable

A two-inch Candy Basslet.

A three-inch Wrasse Bass.

dorsal fins and vertebrate alignment, and have similar-appearing larvae that sport long, streaming foredorsal fins. Unlike hermaphroditic sea basses, *Liopropoma* are born, and remain, males or females. Because of their solitary nature the fish are assumed to be territorial, although aggression between individuals has never been recorded. Even their diet has yet to be substantiated; but the small predators are believed to subsist on crustaceans and small fishes.

We had the good fortune to observe a pair of Peppermint Bass spawning just after sunset eight days following the full moon of September. Two similar-sized individuals appeared from a colony of Finger Coral, *Porites porites*, but immediately vanished when illuminated by a light beam. A minute later the pair returned and remained near one another and only an inch or two above the coral. One had its head elevated and both twitched once or twice before moving together until the sides of their heads touched and pointed up. With their bodies angled apart 45 degrees, they rose slowly for a body length before rapidly jetting up and apart in an apparent spawning rush. The couple instantly disappeared back into the coral and failed to reappear.

Soapfishes
Subfamily Grammistinae

Soapfishes are rather strange and probably very recent descendants of the sea bass family whose exact classification is still in question. The group's common name comes from a coating of mucus, known as grammistin, secreted from body pores. When caught or handled, the fish excrete a lather resembling soapsuds. The substance, containing a protein toxin that irritates bare skin, is believed to protect the species from predation and fishes kept in captivity with a secreting soapfish often die from the poisonous lather. Soapfishes have yet to be found in the stomachs of predators, but the mucus seems to have little or no effect on cleaning organisms who readily pick parasites off soapfishes.

The group is represented by two genera in the Caribbean: *Rypticus*, with four species, and *Pseudogramma*, which includes only a single small, reclusive species. Greater Soapfish, *Rypticus saponaceus*, the species most frequently sighted by divers, behave oddly. During the day, the fish lie on their sides or lean next to a coral head, as if sick or dead. When approached closely, they promptly right themselves and skulk away to other protected locations. They have been reported to bury themselves partially in sand or mud. The eight- to 12-inch white and gray mottled fish, with large mouths and projecting lower jaws, regularly inhabit patch reefs in depths from ten to 60 feet. Soapfishes primarily feed at night on small fishes, shrimps, crabs and mantis shrimps. On one occasion we watched a Greater Soapfish slink about the bottom after dark, engulfing one cardinalfish after the other. In the Gulf of Mexico, adults of the five- to eight-inch Whitespotted Soapfish, *R. maculatus*, have been observed cleaning Jewfish. Members of both genera are known to be hermaphroditic. A single published observation of spawning reported the Greater Soapfish mating a half-hour before sunset in a spawning clasp similar to *Hypoplectrus* spp.

Left: *The cheek-to-cheek spawning rise of Peppermint Bass.*

Jawfishes
Family Opistognathidae

A male Yellowhead Jawfish churns his mouthful of eggs.

Yellowhead Jawfish
Opistognathus aurifrons

Passionate courtship displays, male mouthbrooding and burrow-building are a few of the delightful behaviors that make jawfishes so fascinating to observe. Typically, the rather small, elongate, blunt-headed fishes with great bulging eyes and large mouths inhabit sand plains, where they construct rock-lined burrows in the seafloor.

Of the eight species that inhabit the region's waters, the Yellowhead Jawfish is by far the most commonly sighted. These pearly, three- to four-inch fairylike fish with bluish fins and yellowish heads spend nearly all of their day plucking zooplankton from the current just above their burrow entrances. Colonies, which normally consist of two to ten individuals, are found on sand aprons encircling coral and rock reefs at depths from five to more than 150 feet. The association with reef structures insures an abundance of coral, rock and shell rubble essential for the construction of their masterfully built burrows.

Yellowheads usually allow divers to approach within five or six feet before dropping close to their burrow entrances or slipping inside tail first. Most reappear within a minute or two and cautiously begin feeding once again. If you

Right: *Males mouthbrood clutches of eggs for five to seven days.*

Jawfishes

The passionate courtship ballet of Yellowhead Jawfish.

remain motionless, a colony will become used to your presence and entertain you for an entire dive.

From early spring to fall, males incubate clutches of eggs inside their mouths. For fishes, oral brooding is considered an advanced parental behavior. It occurs in eight fish families, the majority from fresh water. In the western Atlantic only two families, jawfishes (all members) and cardinalfishes (seven species) are known to care for their eggs in this manner.

When searching for brooding males, look for fishes with distended cheeks. These fellows are quite wary, usually backing into their burrows when you are ten or more feet away. Every few minutes uneasy males will stick their heads above the sand to check your whereabouts before slipping out of sight once again. At times they briefly leave the egg masses inside the protection of their burrows before having a look around. In many cases brooders refuse to surface at all with divers nearby, while others reappear with bulging jaws after only a few minutes. Occasionally a slow, cautious approach will take you to within a few feet of a brooding male. If you have the time and patience, it is worth the wait to watch the ol' boys churning their mouthfuls of eggs.

Churning, as it is known to scientists, occurs when the clutch is partially spit out of the mouth and quickly sucked back in. This action removes waste, aerates the eggs and allows the embryos to mix, so all will have a chance to develop equally. The behavior serves much the same function as fin-fanning of external egg patches by benthic egg-layers. The mass might be agitated two, three or four times in rapid succession. Churning can occur as often as every minute, but at times, especially if you remain close, some males stubbornly choose to keep the batches tucked inside their distended cheeks.

The appearance of Yellowhead clutches is not directly synchronized with lunar periods, but 70 percent appear between the full and new moon. Incubation lasts between five and seven days. The age of a batch can be roughly estimated by noting the color of the eggs. When freshly laid and heavy with yolk they are yellow, gradually turning dark orange during days two and three. As the yolk is exhausted the eggs become silver. During the final day, it is possible to make out the pigmented eyes of each embryo. It has yet to be reported exactly how or when the hatchlings are cast into the currents as planktonic larvae. Most mature Yellowhead males incubate two clutches per month, on rare occasions three. A mouthful of eggs greatly limits feeding, and this in turn probably limits spawning.

Of course, romance leads to clutches, which leads us to the splendid courting ballet of Yellowheads. The monogamous couples, which live only a foot or two apart and share a third burrow as a honeymoon suite, are artists of passion. Courtship, which usually takes place in the early morning or late afternoon, can be identified by a pair unusually close together or sharing the same burrow. Unlike the brief, near-panic spawns of many reef fishes, the Yellowheads' sensuous display can last for the better part of a dive. If you delight in a good romance, calmly settle on the sand nearby and enjoy the spectacle.

The male will suddenly approach the female in a series of swoops. Once close, he arches his back, flares his beautiful pastel fins and opens his great mouth, as if singing a silent aria. The sweethearts may then separate for minutes at a time or drop out of sight in the third burrow for a few seconds of privacy. This charming ritual is repeated many times before spawning is completed and the fish resume their normal feeding behavior.

A courting male Yellowhead Jawfish displays to his partner.

Jawfishes

Digging a large hole by mouth is only the beginning of a seven-hour burrow building project.

Yellowheads are not only lovers but also marvelous engineers. Their well-built burrows are tributes to industry. Although it is common to see a Yellowhead busily maintaining its present home by removing mouthfuls of sand and carrying rocks in its jaws, the construction of a new burrow is observed less frequently.

The spirited building project, which takes nearly eight hours to complete, starts with the excavation of a funnel-shaped pit about eight inches in diameter and six inches deep. Next, rocks, shells and coral fragments are placed in the bottom on an underpinning of larger buried rocks. Building materials are positioned with the skill of Mayan artisans. The fitted-stone construction, which leaves room for a circular entranceway, continues until a tunnel is flush with the surface sand. With a framework in place, a lower chamber is excavated. It is usually tunneled under a buried stone that serves as support. The room's final size and shape are dictated by the position of immovable rocks encountered during the dig. Chambers can be up to ten inches long and three inches high. A sand blanket spread over the stonework's surface serves as a finishing touch – a mighty feat for a four-inch fish.

In the late afternoon, colony members become more conscious of burrowkeeping as they prepare for the night. Loose sand, pebbles and shell are brought up in their jaws and blown clear. Within minutes of sunset a nearby

A six-inch deep pit is dug by mouth.

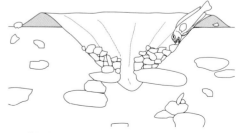

Shell, rock and coral are positioned.

Sand and stone are excavated a mouthful at a time.

rock, shell or tuft of algae is pulled over each entranceway to seal the burrow for the night. At sunrise the jawfish emerge and begin feeding within minutes.

There is good reason for Yellowheads to be wary; sand plains are hunting grounds for several large piscivores. The gravity of nearby danger can be gauged by the little jawfishes' reactions, which range from slowly moving closer to their burrows to wild headfirst dives inside. When large prowling predators, such as Hogfish, *Lachnolaimus maximus*; Yellowtail Snapper, *Ocyurus chrysurus*; Margate, *Haemulon album*, or Southern Stingray, *Dasyatis americana*, pass nearby, Yellowheads waste no time taking cover. Occasionally, when directly threatened, they even cap the openings with rocks. Smaller, less menacing sand flat-hunters, such as Yellowhead Wrasse, *Halichoeres garnoti*, and Slippery Dick, *H. bivittatus*, usually provoke mild aggression rather than flight. When smaller fishes like Hovering Goby, *Ioglossus helenae*, or Bridled Goby, *Coryphopterus glaucofraenum*, approach, they are energetically driven away by a hostile show of flared fins, open jaws or, occasionally, mouthfuls of sand spit in their direction.

Yellowhead Jawfish regularly feud with neighboring Sand Tilefish, *Malacanthus plumieri*, another common burrow-builder that lives on sand flats.

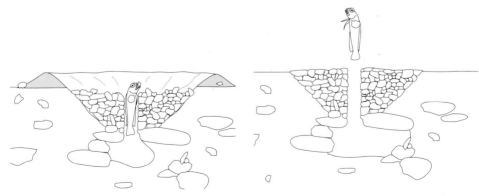

A chamber is excavated below the pit.   *A blanket of sand covers the stonework.*

Jawfishes

Wormfish temporarily share the burrow of a Yellowhead.

For an unknown reason, a Yellowhead flicks its tail under its gill cover.

Small tilefish are readily chased away, but the approach of larger individuals sends Yellowheads diving. Sand Tilefish have been observed circling an occupied burrow and aggressively darting toward a Yellowhead if it emerges and, in a few cases, actually thrusting their snouts into the opening and removing stones for their own burrow pile.

Even though small intruders are not tolerated near a burrow, adult Slippery Dick have been seen entering both occupied and unoccupied burrows and remaining for several minutes. And then there is the rather strange association with the Pugjaw Wormfish, *Cerdale floridana*, a rarely sighted three- to four-inch eel-like fish that burrows in soft sand. One afternoon we watched three wormfish move freely in and out of two adjacent burrows with no apparent concern from the resident Yellowhead. In fact, the jawfish moved aside to allow the little fish to slip in and out. At one point two wormfish and the Yellowhead perched side-by-side for several seconds with their heads projecting from the same burrow. After almost an hour, the wormfish swam off, one at a time, in different directions.

Banded Jawfish
Opistognathus macrognathus

Banded Jawfish share several family traits with Yellowhead Jawfish, including male mouthbrooding, but they are quite different in size, color and feeding behavior. These five- to eight-inch brownish mottled adults feed on bottom-dwelling invertebrates instead of drifting plankton. So, instead of flitting high above their burrows all day, they spend their time poised at the rims of their holes, with just their heads showing above the mound of rock and shell encircling their burrow entrances.

Banded Jawfish inhabit sand bottoms near patch reefs in three to 35 feet of water. Because of their low profiles and camouflage markings they blend like ghosts with the bottom. When one is discovered, look around carefully and you will probably see a few others nearby, staring intently in your direction.

A male Banded Jawfish churns its clutch of eggs.

Although they are wary of your presence, a slow, calculated approach can take you to within a few feet without the fish withdrawing into their burrows. Occasionally, an individual might even venture out and busy itself rearranging rocks or spitting sand.

Banded Jawfish.

Colonies typically vary between three to 11 individuals. Within the colony, mating groups, consisting of a single male and one or, occasionally two females live in close proximity to one another. Males, slightly larger than females, receive two to four clutches each month. Even though males might be incubating eggs at any time, the peak for receiving clutches is closely synchronized with the full moon. Males hold the egg masses for five days before releasing them into the pelagic environment as larvae that settle 18

Jawfishes

Digging a new burrow.

An overflowing mouthful of sand.

days later. Tiny juveniles, less than an inch long, immediately build miniature burrow holes for protection and for a period feed primarily on zooplankton. Other than their small size, a prominent foredorsal fin spot is the only distinguishable difference from adults.

Late one afternoon we discovered a female Banded Jawfish building a new burrow. The busy fish bolted at our approach, but was quickly harassed back to task by a Sand Tilefish, *Malacanthus plumieri*, who, it appeared, had laid claim to the jawfish's previous domain. During her brief absence, we quickly measured the construction. It was five inches wide, seven inches deep and just over a foot in length. The vertical walls of the rectangular hole were so smooth and hard that we surmised that she had selected the new site because of an advantageous break in the substrate.

Soon instinct kicked in. Ignoring our presence, the little engineer began digging with the energy and intensity of one possessed. Great mouthfuls of sand were scooped repeatedly from the bottom and blown clear of the hole, while coral and rock were wedged together to create a roof. Persistence rather than precision seemed to rule the enterprise. If, after several attempts, a rock refused to remain where placed, she abandoned the effort and returned to sand-blowing. Moments later she would again take up the cause of the fallen rock, as if the laws of physics had been altered during the interval. In this hit-or-miss manner, an overhead support slowly but surely began to take shape.

When large predators pass nearby, Bandeds rotate like periscopes inside their holes as they follow every move of the troublemaker. Like Yellowheads, they also experience ongoing altercations with neighboring Sand Tilefish, who seem to enjoy bullying the Bandeds and making off with their burrow rocks. Slippery Dick, *Halichoeres bivittatus*, which frequently move through the colonies, are belligerently shown an open mouth but are otherwise ignored. For some reason small Blue Goby, *Ioglossus calliurus*, and Hovering Goby, *I. helenae*, choose to build their tiny sand burrows in association with Banded Jawfish colonies, but we have never witnessed interaction among these species.

A Yellowhead confronts a Banded Jawfish digging a burrow too close to its territory.

One afternoon we watched a lengthy confrontation between two Yellowhead Jawfish and a small Banded Jawfish that, by the evidence of freshly disturbed sand, had recently built its home within two feet of the Yellowheads' burrows. Every few minutes one of the two Yellowheads would swoop toward the unwelcome neighbor with its fins spread and mouth wide. The Banded Jawfish responded to each incursion with an open-mouthed lunge. Two days later, when we revisited the site, the Banded Jawfish was nowhere to be found, while the Yellowheads gracefully danced above their burrows picking plankton.

Dusky Jawfish
Opistognathus whitehursti

The three- to four-inch Dusky Jawfish are cryptically colored and marked to match the shallow, four- to ten-foot, sandy rubble and Turtle Grass, *Thalassia testudinum*, bottoms where they build their burrows. Individuals of both sexes live in random clusters within large, widely scattered colonies. These small, active burrow-builders move their residences much more frequently than other jawfishes. They have been known to construct new burrows more than 25 feet from their original homes. If you move rocks a few inches away from their entrances, Dusky Jawfish are not shy about leaving the burrows' protection to retrieve the misplaced stones.

Males seem to be sexually promiscuous, incubating eggs for eight- to nine-day periods once or twice each month from spring to late fall. They accept clutches randomly throughout the lunar cycle, with a slight peak during the days following the full moon.

Dusky Jawfish.

Parrotfishes
Family Scaridae

A terminal phase Blue Parrotfish eliminates a chalky plume of excavated waste.

Virtually every reef in the tropical western Atlantic is home to a bustling community of parrotfishes. These robust assemblies are typified by foraging herds of nondescript, two- to six-inch females, and large, solitary, brightly colored males methodically taking bite after bite from the bottom. Parrotfishes share many traits with their forerunners, the wrasses. Members of both families swim primarily with their pectoral fins, change sex from females to males (protogynous hermaphroditism), generally exhibit two or more color patterns within the same species (dichromatism), and have complex social and mating systems. However, unlike most wrasses, which use conspicuous canines to capture hard-shelled crustaceans, the teeth of parrotfishes have fused into powerful beaks capable of rasping algae from the porous skeletons of dead coral. In the process, large quantities of the reef's structure – calcium carbonate – are routinely consumed. On average, nearly 75 percent of the gut content of parrotfishes is composed of inorganic sediment. Broad, bony teeth plates, known as the pharyngeal mill, grind the grit into tiny bits, and a specialized alimentary tract extracts food, leaving the remains with nowhere to go but back to the reef as sand. In fact, many divers first notice parrotfishes because of their rather unpleasant habit of voiding long plumes of excavated waste as they swim. The family's copious processing system

Right: *When feeding on algae covered rock, Parrotfishes excavate large amounts of calcium carbonate, which is returned to the reef as sand.*

Parrotfishes

generates much of the sand associated with tropical reefs and beaches. Caribbean parrotfishes seldom eat living coral, even though a small number of polyps are inadvertently consumed during their relentless foraging. However, two species, Stoplight Parrotfish, *Sparisoma viride*, and Queen Parrotfish, *Scarus vetula*, have been found to regularly take gouging bites from living coral, especially from the lobes of Boulder Star Coral, *Montastraea annularis*. Besides filamentous algae, the average parrotfish diet includes the tender, uncalcified tips of algal bushes, sea grass blades, occasional crustaceans and, now and again, a bite or two of sponge. Contrary to the territorial nature of many reef fishes, who partition and defend limited food supplies, parrotfishes specialize in specific segments of a plentiful and rapidly renewable plant food, allowing several species to share overlapping feeding grounds harmoniously.

The region's 14 species, from the worldwide catalog of 79, vary in size from the three-inch Bucktooth Parrotfish, *Sparisoma radians*, to the massive four-foot Rainbow Parrotfish, *Scarus guacamaia*. A typical population includes a few large, flamboyantly colored dominant males, known as terminal phase males; numerous small, rather drab, mostly female members in the initial phase, and sexually immature juveniles.

The origins of the western Atlantic's two primary parrotfish genera, *Scarus* and *Sparisoma*, have been traced to two primitive wrasselike species: the Emerald Parrotfish, *Nicholsina usta*, a rarely sighted inhabitant of northern Gulf of Mexico grass beds, and the Bluelip Parrotfish, *Cryptotomus roseus*, a slender, tropical grass bed-dweller. Both of these transitional species, the only representatives of their genera, have fused beaks with serrated edges – remnants of individual wrasselike teeth.

Of the 58 species in the genus *Scarus*, six make their home in the Caribbean. Genus members can be identified visually by upper beaks that overlap their lower. *Scarus* share a complex life history – all females who live long enough eventually change sex and color patterns. The genus has two types of males: primary males, those born male, and secondary males, those that were once females. If this sounds complicated, brace yourself for the even more perplexing social organization of the genus *Sparisoma*. Males are all secondary and occasionally remain in the initial phase instead of making the more conventional transformation into the terminal phase. At least three *Sparisoma* species including the Stoplight Parrotfish develop testes from ovaries without first functioning as females. The females of some *Sparisoma* are often as large or larger than males in either phase and, adding to the muddle, in some species, many females do not change sex at all. This odd little genus of six, with upper beaks that slip inside the lower, is restricted to the waters of the tropical western Atlantic. Members of these two genera have distinct grazing behaviors. *Scarus* species scrape filamentous algae from the surface at a bite rate two- to four-times more frequent than *Sparisoma* species that excavate into the rock leaving visible grazing scars.

Strict, size-related hierarchies that allow only the largest individuals in the initial phase to transform into terminal males govern many species of parrotfishes. These two- to three-week metamorphoses, usually occurring after the disappearance of dominant terminal males, reorder the gonads from ovaries to testes and confer a bright new coat on the recently transformed males. The colors and markings differentiating the phases do not always remain stable. Bright terminal male Bucktooth Parrotfish and Bluelip Parrotfish, both inhabitants of seagrass meadows, fire up their brightest colors when courting but tone down markedly when traveling outside the safety of their normal habitat. Initial phase Redband Parrotfish, *Sparisoma aurofrenatum*, alter color patterns to camouflage with their surroundings. Occasionally subordinates in the terminal phase signal submission to a dominant territorial male by suppressing their colors and markings. Two of the large *Scarus*, the Midnight Parrotfish, *S. coelestinus*, and Blue Parrotfish, *S. coeruleus*, exhibit the same basic color schemes throughout life.

A Queen Parrotfish sleeps cloaked in a mucous nightgown secreted from the mouth.

At night, family members utilize a variety of sleeping strategies. Most small parrotfishes seek safe haven deep inside reef pockets. Bluelip Parrotfish, like many wrasses, bury themselves under sand. Each evening at dusk, large Rainbow Parrotfish and Midnight Parrotfish return from distant feeding grounds to sleep inside a customary cave or overhang. A few parrotfishes bed down on open sand or next to a coral structure and change into outlandish night colors. The sleeping fish are often in such deep trances that they can be lifted while still slumbering. However, this is not recommended; in many cases, a disturbed fish suddenly awakens and may bolt blindly into the reef. Without question, the award for the most unusual sleeping habits goes to a few species of *Scarus*, notably the Queen Parrotfish who cloak themselves in mucous nightgowns secreted from their mouths. The transparent cocoons are believed to mask their scent from night-prowling predators such as morays, who rely on smell to locate food.

Parrotfishes

Parrotfishes are broadcast-spawners, releasing their gametes with single or multiple mates in open water. Most species become reproductively active for an hour either in the morning or the afternoon throughout the year. For a few species, including Redband Parrotfish and the Greenblotch Parrotfish, *Sparisoma atomarium*, terminal males control permanent territorial harems that include from two to seven females, with which they pair spawn exclusively. The terminal males of other species, such as Yellowtail Parrotfish, *S. rubripinne*, and Redtail Parrotfish, *Sparisoma chrysopterum*, defend spawning sites only during reproductive periods. Spawning sites are usually near prominent structures on the downcurrent outer edge of reefs, where egg-laden females arrive at an appointed hour.

Mixed aggregations of juvenile parrotfishes commonly forage together.

Pair-spawning parrotfishes all participate in a similar courtship and mating routine. Females, obviously swollen with hydrated eggs, gather at traditional sites and calmly forage while excited males, with fins collapsed and tails arched upward, zip in and out of the area. When ready to mate, females slowly rise several feet off the bottom, where they pause with fins extended. Returning males temporarily slow, spread their fins, jerk their bodies and often eliminate streams of waste as they assess the status of their partners. When one of the females begins to rise at an upward angle, the males dart in, positioning themselves next to the females' bodies and, with tail fins providing the thrust, blast up at a steep angle with their partners. Eggs released at the apex are immediately enveloped in clouds of sperm. The speed and height of spawning rushes are dictated by a species' size. Large species rise slower and higher than smaller species which are more prone to predation. Rival males venturing into spawning grounds are vigorously chased. With fins erect, the competing fish zigzag across the bottom at breakneck speed. The challengers must often be chased repeatedly before they relent.

A few species, with numerous initial phase males, such as the Striped Parrotfish, *Scarus croicensis*, and Yellowtail Parrotfish, pair spawn and group spawn. On reefs with large populations, initial phase Striped Parrotfish migrate every afternoon along established routes from their shallow inshore feeding grounds to customary group-spawning sites on outside reef shelves. There, dozens, or even hundreds, of individuals mill about the bottom before forming into small spawning units composed of multiple males and a single female. The subgroups dart back and forth in parallel formations before shooting up to spawn. These spawning rushes are often contagious; as soon as one group makes its move, other groups follow in rapid succession. Occasionally, these same initial phase males become streakers skulking around the spawning sites of terminal males constantly watching for opportunities to dart in and add their sperm to a pair's gamete clouds. Young interlopers, known as sneakers, mate with females waiting to spawn with territorial males.

Fertilized eggs drift with the currents for about 25 hours before hatching into tiny yolk-sac larvae. After three days, with their onboard supply of fat depleted, the bits of life must fend for themselves or starve. Settlement back to the reef occurs a few weeks later and, in most cases, many miles from their point of origin. The solitary juveniles begin their benthic existence hiding among algae, where they forage for tiny protein-rich crustaceans and single-celled plants, called diatoms.

Striped Parrotfish
Scarus croicensis

Loosely organized feeding herds of small, two- to five-inch, initial phase Striped Parrotfish are common in most rock bottom and reef habitats from three to nearly 100 feet. The constantly foraging herbivores primarily scrape filamentous algae from rock and dead coral pavement, and also browse on thin mats of olive-brown organic matter that collect in the bottoms of shallow sand depressions. Both the black-and white-striped initial phase and seven- to eight-inch greenish blue terminal males resemble the closely related and similar-sized Princess Parrotfish, *Scarus taeniopterus*.

Although females predominate, the initial phase also includes a substantial percentage of young primary males. Those in the colorful, all-male terminal phase are derived from initial phase males or initial phase females who change sex. Depending on the local environment and population size, those in the initial phase join a defended feeding territory, a nonterritorial stationary herd or large roving herds.

Groups living in defended feeding territories, averaging 150 square yards of sea floor, are common in regions with large populations. Territories occur most frequently in areas of sparse coral cover in 30 to 35 feet. On heavily

Parrotfishes

Initial phase Striped Parrotfish feeding at the reef's fringes.

populated reefs the entire bottom may be occupied by defended territories, forcing surplus fish to join roving bands. Territorial groups are composed of a single dominant female and from two to eight smaller subservient females that actively defend their personal feeding grounds from territorial neighbors and roving bands of initial phase trespassers. Territorial females are distinguished by yellow ventral fins extended during confrontational displays. Defense is strictly size-related, with females chasing only initial phase intruders of equal or smaller size. From time to time dominant females engage in border disputes with neighboring matriarchs. These brief tiffs begin when one of the females feeds or hovers near a common boundary. The neighboring dominant promptly approaches to within a foot and extends her yellow ventral fins. The challenged female either swims away or abruptly turns toward her adversary and strikes the same defiant pose. Face-to-face and with mouths agape, the rivals charge repeatedly but in nearly every case stop just short of contact.

Terminal males generally associate with one or several adjoining territories. They aggressively defend their turf from smaller, usually nonterritorial terminal males, but ignore larger males. Occasionally large initial phase males also defend territories. Most of the territorial males' day is spent swimming energetically about their domains, with brief pauses to forage with groups of females.

It has been documented that the species' system of shared territorial defense allows larger group members to feed at a faster and steadier rate than solitary foraging individuals or members of roving groups. On small reefs, where population levels are too low to support roving groups, nearly all feeding areas are controlled by either damselfishes or territorial parrotfishes. In these situations small, non-territorial individuals feed at a much slower rate, making group-living, even at the cost of subservience, advantageous. However, on large heavily populated reefs, small territorial females harvest less than their similar-sized counterparts living outside territories. An underling's contribution to group defense gives larger females the opportunity to mature at an accelerated rate, which, in turn, allows the smaller members to advance more rapidly through the group's hierarchy. Most females spend approximately two years as members of a feeding territory before sex reversal, which takes approximately ten days to complete.

As light levels fall each evening, Striped Parrotfish, except for dominant females who sleep in their territories, migrate along traditional routes that follow protective reef structure to deeper water. Initial phase fish leave first, followed by terminal males. Night is spent deep within reef crevices. Although it has not been observed in the wild, individuals in aquariums occasionally sleep within mucous bubbles. At daybreak the procession reverses, with terminal males taking the lead back along the same path to feeding areas. On arrival, females present themselves submissively before dominant females by extending blanched ventral fins and listing to their sides, exposing white bellies.

At many reef sites, roving bands comprised of initial and terminal phase males and a few initial phase females swim randomly about just above the bottom, descending together at intervals to rasp algae from rocks. These groups, often numbering in the dozens and regularly including a scattering of Doctorfish, *Acanthurus chirurgus*, Blue Tang, *A. coeruleus*, and goatfishes, remain stable over a period of months. The third type of social organization, nonterritorial stationary groups, consists of both primary and secondary males and small females.

Several male Striped Parrotfish break away from the main spawning aggregation to follow a single ripe female.

Parrotfishes

Both pair and group spawning occur every afternoon throughout the year. Reproduction has been reported to be more intense in the winter in some areas of the Caribbean and during the summer at others. Territorial terminal males pair spawn with members of their feeding groups and occasionally with stray females. Within territory boundaries males, with fins erect, repeatedly visit ripe females feeding on the bottom before rapidly swimming out of the area. Eventually one, or more females rise up to ten feet off the sea floor and calmly awaits the males' return. Once back, the males circle their hovering females, often jerking and occasionally discharging plumes of waste. When the females begin to rise males quickly join them. The pairs, with the males stationed against the females' lower backs, rapidly ascend several feet before releasing visible gamete clouds. Often males spawn in rapid succession with several partners before jetting off in a great circle that eventually brings them back to their territories and more waiting females.

Group spawning involving hundreds of initial phase fish occurs in regions with large populations. At midafternoon, roving bands migrate to a traditional site in deeper water near an outer reef shelf. Fish arriving over an extended period join groups already feeding on the bottom. After a period, tightly knit groups of 20 to 30 individuals rise about ten feet off the bottom and dart about before splinter groups suddenly break away and release spawn several feet above the others. The first group to spawn appears to spur others into action. A researcher observing a large spawning aggregation counted 35 spawning rushes within one minute.

Princess Parrotfish
Scarus taeniopterus

The body shape, size and markings of the Princess Parrotfish are confusingly similar to those of the Striped Parrotfish, *Scarus croicensis*. The two species can be differentiated by a solid upper and lower margin on the tails of both phases of the Princess Parrotfish. This marking is absent on the Striped Parrotfish. Princess Parrotfish typically inhabit areas of heavy coral growth in depths from 15 to 50 feet. Few primary males occur in the initial phase, and only a scattering of primary males have been documented to transform into terminal phase males.

Most terminal males dominate from three to five initial phase females who forage together as groups within the boundaries of permanent territories varying from 100 to nearly 500 square yards. Populations also include wandering bands of initial phase fish. These groups swim together a few feet off the bottom before dispersing as they descend to feed on filamentous algae. After a flurry of bites the groups reform and are off again to new locations. The species has also been reported to consume the mucous covering of sponges and the thin, greenish brown layers of detritus and diatoms that accumulate in bottom depressions. Although terminal males are generally solitary foragers, they occasionally join groups of feeding females. Most territorial males defend their borders from other males and spend a great amount of energy chasing both harem members and wanderers.

As daylight begins to fade, Princess Parrotfish assume a novel head-up stance for up to five minutes. Positioned with their tails on the bottom, the fish darken across their backs, rotate slowly in a circle and rapidly open and close their mouths. The posture is quite similar to that of fishes being cleaned, although no cleaning organisms are in the vicinity. This interesting behavior has yet to be explained.

Possibly because safe sleeping sanctuaries are limited within the species' low-profile feeding grounds, only a few adults remain to sleep in their territories while the others migrate, often up to 300 yards, each evening to find night refuge in complex reef structure. Once situated within protective pockets, mucous bubbles are extruded from their mouths to cloak the fish's scent. At first light they return along routes followed the evening before. Upon arrival at their feeding grounds, terminal males often find their territories occupied by other males, who are quickly chased away.

Although Princess Parrotfish and Striped Parrotfish are similar in social organization, spawning strategies, size, habitat, colors and markings, hybrids between the species have never been reported. Striped Parrotfish spawn during mid-to-late afternoon, while Princess Parrotfish become reproductively active from early to midmorning. This difference between spawning periods appears to be the main variable keeping the genes of the two species from mixing.

Terminal males court and spawn year-round within their territories in typical parrotfish fashion. The males swim rapidly around their territories with fins compressed for an average of 20 minutes before mating. From three to nine females change from a striped to a solid pale brown and rise six or seven feet off the bottom, indicating their readiness to spawn. Males wearing subdued colors circle the hovering females before darting to their sides. Together, the pairs make quick spawning rushes of only a few feet before shedding gametes and parting. No streaking or sneaking has been observed by terminal or initial phase males.

Queen Parrotfish
Scarus vetula

One- to two-foot Queen Parrotfish feed by scraping algae from the surface of dead coral skeletons within large shallow-water territories typified by high-profile coral structures. A survey taken in Puerto Rico found three fish in the initial phase for every terminal phase male. Although rare, there are a few primary males in both the initial and terminal phases, but no sex-changed secondary males in the initial phase.

Queen Parrotfish typically join harems consisting of three or four initial phase females and a single terminal male. Unattached Queens are vigorously chased away from jointly defended grazing territories that often encompass over 1,000 square yards of reef. Individuals tend to feed separately within territory boundaries, but, occasionally, two to three initial phase fish forage in close proximity. This species is one of the few parrotfishes that sleeps in the open inside mucous envelopes.

Pair spawning occurs within territorial boundaries during a two-hour midmorning period. The spawning rush is spectacular, carrying the pairs over ten feet into the water column before gametes are released in large visible

Parrotfishes

clouds. Researchers in Puerto Rico observed a spawning assembly on an outer reef in 65 feet of water during the mornings of cooler winter months. Terminal phase males, outnumbering those in the initial phase six to one, milled about the bottom within small defended territories. Excited males courted females passing through their areas but with little success. Only 12 of 50 courtship attempts ended in a spawning rush and, of these, four were joined by a nearby male.

Blue Parrotfish
Scarus coeruleus

Midnight Parrotfish
Scarus coelestinus

Rainbow Parrotfish
Scarus guacamaia

Little is known about the three largest members of the genus *Scarus*, and there has yet to be a published observation of their spawning behaviors. Blue Parrotfish are solitary feeders that frequently graze over the open sand surrounding reef structures. Although reported to reach four feet in length, we seldom observe members of the species larger than two feet. The species is monochromatic, with both initial and terminal phase individuals displaying a similar powder-blue wash; however, larger individuals, presumably terminal males, develop conspicuous squared-off snouts. Juvenile Blue Parrotfish inhabit shallow, protected reef habitats. Smaller juveniles are light blue to grayish with a yellow wash extending from snout to dorsal fin. The wash slowly disappears as the fish mature.

Although Midnight Parrotfish and Rainbow Parrotfish are obviously different in both color and size, they were once considered to be the same species because of significant anatomical similarities. The Midnight Parrotfish is the only family member in the western Atlantic exhibiting a single color pattern throughout life. This adaptation may be due to the species' habit of foraging with swarming schools of similarly colored Blue Tang, *Acanthurus coeruleus*. Both species share a diet of filamentous algae scraped from reef rock. By force of numbers these feeding aggregations overwhelm the defenses of damselfishes who have no trouble protecting their personal algal gardens from solitary herbivores, but have little chance fending off a swarm of feeding fishes.

In Key Largo, Florida, fish surveyors for the Reef Environmental Education Foundation (REEF) observed a large group of Midnight Parrotfish streaming down the side of a coral ridge and entering overhangs at the formation's base. Close observation revealed distinct white bite marks on several egg patches of Sergeant Major, *Abudeduf saxatilis*. The moving group repeated the same behavior further down the reef line.

Rainbows, the largest parrotfish in the Caribbean, are quite wary and usually swim away or enter caves when divers are about. A gut content analysis found Manatee Grass, *Syringodium filiforme*, and algae scraped from coral pavement

Midnight and Rainbow Parrotfishes converged at dusk. The large fishes reduced visibility considerably as they paraded past, high in the water column, eliminating clouds of waste.

to be a major component of their diet. Juveniles and greenish blue initial phase adults primarily inhabit shallow habitats and mangrove forest. It is believed that the great herbivores migrate to shallow feeding grounds during the day and return to the reef late each evening for shelter.

At dusk on three consecutive evenings in June, we observed 50 or more large Rainbows and Midnights suddenly converge on a reef site with an abundance of large caverns and ledges near Bimini, Bahamas. The fishes arrived in mixed groups that paraded past, high in the water column, excreting great streams of fecal matter. Within minutes water visibility dropped substantially from the suspended silt. Their processions were dramatic and, to all appearances, ritualistic. Most of the fish displayed erect fins. Shortly after their arrival, the largest individuals of both species aggressively charged oncoming fishes with their mouths opened so wide that their snouts flared back, although we never saw contact. The fish repeatedly dived to the bottom and disappeared inside deep undercuts for several seconds before flying out and rejoining the processions. Often five or six individuals entered the same undercut. When observed with a hand light most were restlessly moving about, while others were wedged far back under the overhangs.

Parrotfishes

A territorial confrontation between two terminal phase Redband Parrotfish.

Redband Parrotfish
Sparisoma aurofrenatum

Redband Parrotfish inhabit the lower slopes and sand halos of reefs with substantial living coral structures from the shallows to over 70 feet. All males are secondary, having changed from females. Most transform into the terminal phase, but a few retain their initial phase markings. The colorful five- to twelve-inch terminal males are solitary browsers that roam widely inside their large territories. Terminal males vigorously defend their sections of the reef and pair

A large male Redband Parrotfish follows a ripe female into the water column to spawn.

spawn with a single or possibly multiple harems of initial phase females. The three- to six-inch females display various color patterns, including green bodies highlighted with bright red fins, lackluster black and white stripes, and a mottled appearance. As the unassuming little initial phase fish move slowly about the bottom taking deliberate bites, they often switch to camouflage coats matching their surroundings. Fortunately for identification purposes, a small white saddle blotch on the tail base is always present on members of the initial phase.

Of all the Caribbean parrotfish species, Redbands have the most varied diet, including not only sea grasses, leaf and filamentous algae, but surprisingly, sponges, crabs, brittle stars and urchins. Individuals do not migrate to night shelter; instead, they bed down next to sponges or in shallow depressions inside their territories.

Pair spawning occurs daily for one-hour periods in late afternoon. Courtship begins when terminal males, with fins spread, busily cajole harem members as they feed on the bottom. Between visits, the males swim rapidly out of the area for several minutes at a time. Eventually females rise several feet into the water column, where they wait patiently for the males' return. Females ascending at the same time tend to remain relatively close together. If males are slow to reappear, the females occasionally drop back to the bottom and continue feeding. The males generally return along sweeping circular routes as if scrutinizing the situation from a distance before approaching. Once near, they spread their fins, twitch, rapidly beat their tails from side to side and excrete plumes of waste. Females often respond by voiding fecal matter before initiating the spawning rush by slowly ascending. Males quickly position themselves behind the rising females. Pairs, propelled by the males' thrashing tails, climb several feet at a steep angle before releasing gametes.

Stoplight Parrotfish
Sparisoma viride

One- to two-foot Stoplight Parrotfish, in both the reddish brown initial phase and bright green terminal phase, are among the most common and noticeable members of the Caribbean reef community. Recent studies in Belize, Grand Turk, and Bonaire determined that the protogynous hermaphrodites have an extremely flexible social structure much like the Striped Parrotfish, *Scarus croicensis*. An extensive five-year research project conducted in Bonaire concluded that Stoplights adapt their feeding, mating and social behavior to take advantage of local environments and food supplies. This in turn points to the likelihood that a population's size is not totally dependent on the random fluctuations of larval recruits.

At sites with abundant, fast-growing shallow-water algal crops supporting dense herbivore populations, most terminal phase males and initial phase females live together in stationary, nonterritorial groups in less than ten feet of water. Just offshore on the deeper reefs a much smaller number of Stoplights controls three-quarters of the inhabited reef as territorial harems. Roving groups of terminal phase males and separate groups of initial phase individuals occasional traverse these heavily populated areas as they range several hundred yards up and down the shoreline. However, on reefs with limited food resources, Stoplights live only in territorial harems composed of a single terminal male and from one to 14 initial phase females.

Ratios between the female dominated initial phase and the all-male terminal phase were found to range from nearly two-to-one to over four-to-one, indicating a significant variation across the Caribbean and from reef to reef. Initial phase males are generally rare and have not made up more than 10 percent of any populations studied. Females reach sexual maturity between six and seven inches but do not usually produce ripe eggs until sometime later, which indicates a period of rapid growth between maturity and reproduction. The change from the initial phase to the terminal phase occurs over a wide range of ages and sizes. Stoplights pair spawn during 90-minute periods each day throughout the year.

Parrotfishes

Stoplights settle to the reef as three-eighths-inch immature females. The juveniles typically inhabit complex bottom structures in depths from 12 to 38 feet. When young females reach sexual maturity on reefs with large populations, they either join shallow-water groups or become members of harems. Territorial males spawn with members of their harems and with additional females from the shallow-water groups. In Bonaire, Stoplights spawned at a different time at each of the three sites studied; but most become reproductively active between 7:00 AM and 9:30 AM. Unlike many protogynous species, the largest female living in a harem does not change sex when the dominant male disappears. Instead, initial phase females leave their harems at unpredictable times and join nonterritorial groups where they make the three-week sexual transition into terminal phase males.

Even though group terminal phase males are, on average, larger than territorial males, most are not sexually active, choosing instead to accelerate growth by concentrating their energies on food gathering. Spawning never occurs inside shallow feeding areas. A few group males spawn each day in deeper water with females from their groups and, occasionally, group males band together and overrun harems where the large individuals mate with territorial females. Smaller group terminal males replace dominant territorial males who disappear from their harems. A few of the largest group males, known as supermales, migrate below 90 feet each morning where they fiercely defend temporary territories and pair spawn with large females who arrive separately and, often, in such numbers that they must wait their turn to mate. One supermale was observed spawning 16 times within a ten-minute period. Most large group and territorial females spawn twice a day, first with a supermale and then with their usual mates. After the reproductive period, the supermales return to the shallows to feed.

A second Bonaire study site, with different offshore typography, supports a much smaller Stoplight population. The area's surge-swept bare-rock shallows unfit for heavy grazing, limit competition allowing terminal males to control the entire population within territorial boundaries. Few juveniles inhabit the southern site, possibly because of the area's lack of branching corals, which provide shelter essential

An initial phase Stoplight Parrotfish takes a bite of living coral.

In a recently documented behavior, Stoplight Parrotfish take repeated bites from living coral tissue. It has been speculated that the conspicuous white scars might serve as territorial markers.

for survival. However, the area hosts numerous initial phase males, made evident by a 14 percent occurrence of streak spawning – an alternate reproductive strategy almost nonexistent among the larger population at the northern study site. Young males, which look identical to females, are able to get away with their deviant behavior by hiding in the area's heavy gorgonian cover that grows inside the territories of terminal males.

Instead of scraping algae from the surface of dead corals and reef pavement, Stoplights use powerful jaws to gouge out the algae growing below the structure's surface. Like other member of genus S*parisoma*, Stoplights prefer concave rather than flat surfaces and typically take most of their bites from rubble and the dead bases of coral mounds. This excavating method of feeding causes a five time greater consumption of inorganic sediment than that taken in by similar-sized Queen Parrotfish, *Scarus vetula*, who ordinarily consume only surface growth. Stoplight Parrotfish generally forage on upper and lower reef slopes in depths from five to 75 feet. Groups feed inshore even though these individuals spend more time, bites and energy penetrating the dense matrix typical of shallow-water coral rubble. Deep-water territorial populations have a much easier time excavating the more porous skeletons of corals that more commonly grow below 15 feet. However, deep-water algae are limited, slow growing and must be regularly guarded from trespassing Stoplights. As a result, territorial terminal males spend nearly a fifth of their time high in the water column patrolling their high-yield algal crops. Inside the deeper territories the thick algal gardens of damselfishes cover much of the reef. The protective little gardeners, who attack other approaching herbivores with impunity, for some unknown reason allow resident Stoplights to take a bite or two from their prized crops before driving them away.

In Bonaire, St. Croix and Puerto Rico researchers have observed both terminal males and initial phase Stoplights taking repeated bites from the living tissue of Boulder Star Coral, *Montastrea annularis*, and Boulder Brain Coral, *Colpophyllia*

Parrotfishes

natans, leaving conspicuous white scars on the coral. The same fish return to the heads at two to 15 minute intervals, removing polyps and skeletal material along the edges of preexisting scars. Seventeen bites were taken from one coral head in just over an hour. After removing all the tissue from a lobe of star coral one group of Stoplights began grazing on an adjacent, previously undisturbed lobe. The majority of damaged colonies were located on reefs with large populations of territorial Stoplight Parrotfish leading to the speculation that the white lesions might serve as territorial markers. After patrolling boundaries or chasing a terminal male, territorial terminal males were observed taking one to three bites from deeply scarred star coral inside their territories. Each territorial initial phase female then took bites from the same head in order of descending size.

Yellowtail Parrotfish
Sparisoma rubripinne

A combination of the Yellowtail Parrotfish's lackluster colors, scattered populations and preference for shallow-water surge zones makes the species one of the least-noticed family members in the Caribbean. Yellowtail Parrotfish in both phases feed in scattered groups of up to 40 individuals. The species primarily scrapes filamentous algae from dead corals in the shallows, but it also consumes algal bushes from reef slopes and seagrass blades. Males in both phases are sex-changed females. The size of both sexes in the initial phase often equals or surpasses that of individuals in the terminal phase. Because a large number of males are in the initial phase, the sex ratio for the species is nearly equal; but there are roughly four times more Yellowtails in the initial phase.

Even though the species does not establish or defend permanent territories, we have seen Yellowtails involved in a great deal of chasing throughout the day. This constant aggression is possibly due to the high percentage of males in the initial phase. Pair spawning, beginning early to midafternoon, occurs at customary sites on the reef's outer shelf. The species follows the typical parrotfish pair-spawning scenario. Pairs slowly spiral upward before releasing a cloud of gametes high in the water column. Yellowtail Snapper, *Ocyurus chrysurus*, closely follow their progress and immediately swarm released eggs. Like other large parrotfishes, close observation may cause delayed spawning or force the groups to move down the reef line.

As might be expected with so many young males, initial phase group spawning also takes place. Researchers have observed group spawns on numerous occasions along the seaward edge of a fringing reef in Puerto Rico. Beginning just before noon and continuing over the next hour, hundreds of initial phase Yellowtails arrived from shallow inshore feeding areas. The assembled fish, approximately 80 percent males, milled about the bottom for about a half-hour before small groups, ranging from four to 13 individuals, formed into subunits that rose together in the water column and began bouts of rapid, erratic parallel swimming. Just before a spawning rush, the group paused briefly with heads pointed upward, then shot up about ten feet, releasing gametes at the peak of their rise.

Redtail Parrotfish
Sparisoma chrysopterum

Redtail Parrotfish in both the initial and terminal phase feed together in small to large groups over seagrass meadows bordering reefs, along lower reef slopes and in rocky shallows. Populations consist of equal numbers of both phases. Those in the initial phase can be males (generally the smaller individuals) or females that are often as large or larger than males in the terminal phase. Males in both phases are secondary, having changed from females. During midafternoon, brightly colored terminal males defend temporary territories where they display to, and pair spawn with, females passing through their areas. No group spawning, sneaking or streaking by initial phase males has been reported for the species.

Greenblotch Parrotfish
Sparisoma atomarium

Three- to four-inch Greenblotch Parrotfish typically inhabit coral-encrusted slopes below 50 feet; but we occasionally encounter the species on reefs as shallow as 35 feet and in grass beds less than 20 feet deep. Because of their small size, divers seldom notice these striking little fish. Both color phases are distinct and easily identified. The larger males sport multicolored coats of reds, yellows, greens, blues and tan that intensify during reproductive activity. Large females can turn bright red with yellowish anal fins; but they generally display a dull yellowish brown mottled pattern. Smaller one- to two-inch females have reddish brown backs and white bellies with a series of thin brown stripes.

Those in the initial phase outnumber terminal males nearly seven to one. The few males in the initial phase and all terminals are reported to be secondary, having changed from females. On the edge of reef slopes, feisty terminal males aggressively protect small harems from rival males. Rapid spawning rushes that carry the pairs only a foot or two above the bottom take place in midafternoon throughout the year.

A terminal male Greenblotch Parrotfish (upper fish) displays to his harem during the afternoon courtship period.

Parrotfishes

Bucktooth Parrotfish
Sparisoma radians

Averaging just over three inches in length, Bucktooth Parrotfish are the smallest genus members and one the smallest herbivorous fish. Individuals in both color phases are the same general size and share similar drab, nondescript color patterns except during courtship and spawning when terminal males switch on a few bright red and blue markings around their heads and acquire broad black margins on their tails. Members of both phases can quickly alter their body patterns to blend with their surroundings. The few males in the initial phase and those in the terminal phase are secondary, having changed from females.

Populations almost exclusively reside within thick tangles of Turtle Grass, *Thalassia testudinum*, or Manatee Grass, *Syringodium filiforme*, where the little parrotfish feed from dawn to dusk on the grass and clusters of tiny epiphytes clinging to the blades. Many grass meadows are alive with large populations numbering in the hundreds. When piscivores such as Bar Jack, *Caranx ruber*, prowl, we have observed large groups of Bucktooth Parrotfish rise in unison, seemingly from nowhere, and flee across the top of the grass en masse. If directly threatened, individuals dive deep in the blades, where they instantly change into their camouflage coats. Random groups occasionally forage in fields of benthic *Sargassum* surrounding grass meadows, where they nibble on leaf algae, *Halimeda* spp., or bristle brush algae, *Penicillus* spp. At night Bucktooths sleep on the bottom, nestled deep within the grass cover.

Many terminal males defend territories containing harems with up to 11 females who mate once each day. During 30 to 60 minute afternoon spawning periods, the excited little territorial terminal males buzz back and forth above the grass tops like attack helicopters, scouting aggregations of females foraging below. When females are sighted, the males swoop down displaying spread

A terminal male Bucktooth Parrotfish (left) circles a roving band of feeding females.

fins and their brightest colors. Nonterritorial terminal and initial phase males roam across the territories often following bands of unattached females, with whom they pair spawn and occasionally group spawn. But their favorite trick is to hide out in the thick grass waiting for a chance to streak spawn with territorial terminal males and their mates. Turn-about is fair play – territorial males regularly participate in group spawns with nonterritorial individuals, and readily interfere with the mating attempts of neighboring territorial terminal males. Males discharge more sperm when spawning with large females, who release more eggs than small females. Large females also have the highest spawning rises and attract more streakers.

Bluelip Parrotfish
Cryptotomus roseus

Because of their shape, the slender, cigar-shaped, one- to three-and-a-half-inch Bluelip Parrotfish, look more like a wrasse than a parrotfish, and with good reason. The species, the only representative of its genus and one of the least common parrotfishes in the western Atlantic, is believed to be a primitive link between the two closely related families. Males in both phases are secondary, having changed from females.

The active fish almost exclusively inhabit grass beds in depths from ten to over 60 feet, where small groups including both phases feed together within the forest of blades. Fishes

A terminal male Bluelip Parrotfish flashes his brightest colors during courtship.

in the somber brown-to-reddish-striped initial phase are primarily females and outnumber those in the terminal phase seven-to-one. Although terminal males are generally larger and have distinctly bulbous heads, they otherwise closely resemble individuals in the initial phase except during courtship, when terminal males intermittently display one of the most brilliant color patterns of any fish in the Caribbean. During courtship the larger terminal males swim rapidly over broad areas, periodically flashing their neon-intense yellow, red, blue and green colors to impress prospective mates. Only pair spawning between bright males and smaller initial phase females has been reported. The ability to switch on and off vibrant colors allows the fish to remain less conspicuous to predators for much of the day. At night, like several wrasse species, Bluelips bury in the sand and have been reported to secrete protective mucous envelopes.

Sharks & Rays
Shark Families Carcharhinidae, Sphyrnidae, Rhincodontidae
Stingray Family Dasyatidae

A Blacktip Shark rips a fish loose from a "chumsicle".

Unfortunately, divers in the Bahamas and Caribbean seldom encounter sharks in the wild. Although not uncommon, the primarily nocturnal predators seldom prowl the reefs during the day, and at night sharks are too wary to approach noisy, light-toting underwater visitors. Only Nurse Shark, *Ginglymostoma cirratum*, usually seen resting on the bottom under a reef overhang, are sighted on a regular basis. However, shark action, and plenty of it, is guaranteed at several locations in the Bahamas. At Walker's Cay, New Providence Island (Nassau), Grand Bahamas Island (Freeport) and the northern end of Long Island, enterprising dive operators, who have been feeding their local shark populations for years, take visitors to regularly scheduled daytime shark encounters. The sharks have become so accustomed to the handouts that little more than the arrival of a dive boat is sufficient to summon dozens of the dynamos to the dinner table. At Walker's Cay, a frozen block of fish scraps, known as a "chumsicle," attracts 50 or more sharks, mainly Blacktip Shark, *Carcharhinus limbatus*, Reef Shark, *C. perezi*, and Nurse Shark. Large jacks, groupers and dozens of small reef fishes compete for the easy pickings. Occasionally Lemon Shark, *Negaprion brevirostris*, Scalloped Hammerhead, *Sphyrna lewini*, and Bull Shark, *C. leucas*, also join the frenzied feast that continues nonstop during the 45-minute dives.

For those brought up in the wake of *Jaws*-mania, it is a sobering experience to watch the large predators ripping mouth-sized chunks of fish flesh from bait balls a short distance from where they kneel on the sand. As these encounters demonstrate, the likelihood of reef sharks attacking divers has been greatly exaggerated. In fact, in the clear waters of the Caribbean region, we have never heard of a shark biting a diver, other than the few instances when individuals foolishly grabbed the tails of resting Nurse Shark or when spearfishing or hand-feeding were involved. Typically, Caribbean reef sharks turn tail and flee at the first sight of divers. This is not to say that sharks cannot be dangerous. Whenever sharks are in the vicinity, they should always be watched closely. If their presence makes you uncomfortable or if a shark makes repeated passes, circles closely or acts aggressive, it would be wise to calmly leave the water. The Great White Shark, *Carcharodon carcharias*, Tiger Shark, *Galeocerdo cuvier*, and Bull Shark are believed to be the most dangerous species in the region. Fortunately, Great Whites and Tigers seldom, if ever, venture over coral reefs, and Bull Shark are rarely sighted in most locations.

While humans are seldom at risk from shark attacks, many species of the magnificent apex predators are under serious threat from humans. As stocks of traditional market fishes continue to decline, shark fishing has increased substantially to fill the void. Adding to the slaughter, shark fins, considered an aphrodisiac in many parts of Asia and traditionally used for making soup in China, bring top prices. Often fishermen remove nothing more than the fins, dumping the carcasses overboard to rot on the seafloor. In the late 1990s, more than 50 of the sharks which had been entertaining divers for years at Walker Cay were slaughtered within a few days by a single long-line fishing vessel. The incident prompted the Bahamian government to establish no-harvest zones around the economically valuable feeding sites, which attract thousands of tourists annually.

More than 50 sharks at a time are attracted to a feeding site.

A Great Hammerhead devouring a Southern Stingray.

Witnessing natural predation by sharks is rare. In 1988 researchers studying stingray biology near a submerged barge resting in 18 feet of water seven miles east of Bimini, Bahamas, had the opportunity to observe a Great Hammerhead, *Sphyrna mokarran*, capture and devour a Southern Stingray, *Dasyatis americana*. At mid-morning, when researchers first entered the water, three stingrays were lying in the sand near the wreck. An hour later, two more stingrays were noticed speeding toward the barge from the surrounding grass flat. Within minutes a stream of apparently panicked rays followed. Uncharacteristically, seven of the 15 assembled rays entered the wreckage, while others swam rapidly in tight circles and figure 8s near the hull. Minutes later, a ten-foot Great Hammerhead, followed closely by a five-foot Blacktip Shark, sailed into visibility, paralleled the barge and quickly disappeared from view. Both sharks soon reappeared and made a second pass before leaving the area.

Eight hours later, two researchers snorkeling over the grass flat 300 yards from the wreck site noticed a lone stingray with a three-foot wingspan sprinting across the bottom in the direction of the barge, followed by a Great Hammerhead swimming on the surface. As it passed the snorklers the shark accelerated, caught up with the ray and hammered its head into the fleeing ray's back from above with such force that it was slammed to the bottom. Braking with extended pectoral fins, the predator turned sharply and plowed into its victim a second time, forcing it to the sand, where the prey was held firmly in place by the shark's flattened head. Still in control, the shark pivoted and with a quick shake removed a crescent-

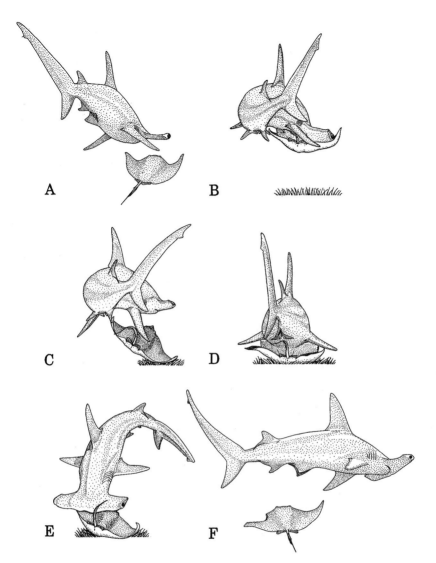

A. *The Great Hammerhead approaches quickly.* **B.** *Using its head, the shark strikes the Southern Stingray hard from above.* **C.** *The ray bounces off the bottom as the shark brakes overhead.* **D.** *A second blow forces the ray back to the bottom where it is held in place by the shark's flattened head.* **E.** *The shark pivots and takes the first bite.* **F.** *The shark circles before making a second attack.*

shaped bite from the ray's left front pectoral fin margin. As the shark circled, the crippled ray once again fled for the wreck. Unhurried, the shark followed. Thirty feet from the hull it attacked again, striking the ray hard and driving it to the bottom, where the shark pivoted and took a bite from the right rear pectoral fin. Surprisingly, the Southern Stingray did not attempt to use its venomous tail spine for defense during its struggle. With both wings damaged, the stunned stingray lay motionless, except for occasionally curling its wing tips. The shark, probably

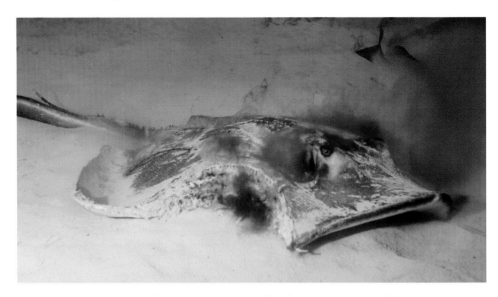

A Southern Stingray immobilized by bites to its pectoral fins.

distracted by the onlookers, circled a short distance away, while Sharksucker, *Echeneis* sp., Gray Snapper, *Lutjanus griseus*, Bar Jack, *Caranx ruber*, and Yellowtail Snapper, *Ocyurus chrysurus*, freely scavenged bits of the torn flesh. Twenty minutes passed before the hammerhead grabbed the limp ray by the head and swam 75 feet from the wreck, where it stopped and shook the large carcass until the rostrum severed and the lifeless body fell to the bottom. The same pattern of grabbing, shaking and circling continued until the Blacktip arrived. While the larger shark circled, it darted in and grabbed a scrap of meat. Before the Blacktip could turn to make a second pass, the hammerhead charged with open jaws,

The wing-shaped head of a Scalloped Hammerhead.

sending the Blacktip in retreat. The hammerhead immediately picked up the wingless ray and gulped down the remains headfirst, leaving the long tail dangling from its mouth as it vanished across the grass flat just before a second Blacktip and three Atlantic Sharpnose Shark, *Rhizoprionodon terraenovae*, arrived at the scene.

There has been much conjecture about the function of the dramatic wing-shaped heads of the eight species of hammerhead sharks in family Sphyrnidae, four of which inhabit the waters of the western Atlantic. Hypotheses range from improved visual, chemical and electrical reception to refined hydrodynamics. The Great Hammerhead's unusual capture technique observed in Bimini has opened the possibility that their oddly-shaped heads provide an adaptive benefit for

A male Nurse Shark bites the pectoral fin of a female during copulation.

A mixture of sperm, seminal fluid and sea water...

ramming and holding stingrays against the bottom – a behavior that would be impractical for pointed-nose sharks. Although other species of sharks feed on stingrays, batoids represent only a small portion of their diets. However, the large number of stingray spines found in the stomachs of the Great Hammerhead and Smooth Hammerhead, *Sphyrna zygaena*, (Ninety-six stingray spines were found inside a single Great Hammerhead.) indicates the importance of rays in the diets of both species.

Observations of the reproductive behavior of sharks are quite rare. For five weeks each summer, adult Nurse Shark gather in shallow, inshore breeding

overflows from the cloaca of an impregnated female.

grounds at traditional locations across the region. In 1992, researchers monitored a mating congregation of approximately 20 individuals in the Florida Keys. Females, not in the least cooperative, fought off repeated advances of eager males by thrashing wildly when approached. To avoid the smaller suitors, females occasionally moved into water too shallow to mate, where they rolled on their sides and dug their pectoral fins into the sand. Determined males engulfed the females' pectoral fins in their mouths and, with great effort, attempted to drag the struggling females toward deeper water. Six small males were observed working as a tag-team, taking turns biting and wrestling with a

A two-foot Lemon Shark emerges tailfirst at birth.

reluctant female, who arched and twisted to keep her fins free. Less than ten percent of mating attempts end in copulation, with only the largest and most tenacious males successful. While the combative courtship sometimes lasts for hours, copulation takes only a minute or two to complete. To mate successfully, a male must cling fiercely to a female's fin with his mouth, roll her over, wedge his tail under her body for leverage and twist like a contortionist to insert an erect clasper into her cloaca. Prior to insertion, water is drawn into a siphon sac associated with the male's reproductive organs and, along with sperm and seminal fluid, ejected in an overflowing stream through a skin fold in the clasper. After mating, the male collapses to the bottom in fatigue. Months later eggs hatch inside the mother, who gives birth to 20 to 30 pups.

In the shallow waters of the Bimini Lagoon, shark researchers witnessed the first live birth of a shark in its natural habitat when an eight-and-a-half-foot Lemon Shark tethered to their boat gave birth. Each of the ten two-foot pups emerged tail-first, trailing afterbirth that was quickly devoured by remora. The youngsters spent their first months at the fringes of the shallow mangrove-lined lagoon before migrating to open water.

Mating Southern Stingrays also put on quite a show. In one encounter observed at Stingray City at Grand Cayman Island, seven or eight considerably smaller males vigorously pursued and attempted to pin a lone female to the bottom. One of the males, gripping her wing margin firmly in his mouth, flipped upside-down beneath her body and inserted a clasper. During the five-minute copulation period, the writhing female was partially restrained by the other males, who pressed down on her body as she swam over the sand. When the first male finished, a second male flipped into place and successfully mated with the same female. After he finished the group dispersed.

Numerous smaller male Southern Stingrays attempt to pin a female to the bottom.

Gripping the rear margin of a female's dorsal fin in his mouth, a smaller male flips upside-down and underneath to insert a clasper.

A video sequence of mating Yellow Stingray, *Urolophus jamaicensis*, shows a lone male, similar in size to his mate, mounted head-to-head on her back and twisted awkwardly to insert a clasper. While mounted, the female swam rapidly across the bottom.

Surgeonfishes
Family Acanthuridae

A feeding aggregation of Blue Tang.

Each of the three members of the surgeonfish family inhabiting the tropical Western Atlantic – Blue Tang, *Acanthurus coeruleus*; Ocean Surgeonfish, *A. bahianus*, and Doctorfish, *A. chirurgus* – are common inhabitants of Caribbean reef fish communities. Surgeonfishes can be identified by the presence of a scalpel-like spine encased in a groove on each side of the tail base. Blue Tang are easily distinguished by their flat, oval-shaped, powdery blue to dark purple bodies and yellow or white spine grooves. Differentiating between the similar-appearing Ocean Surgeonfish and Doctorfish is a bit trickier. Both species range from bluish gray to dark brown and can pale or darken dramatically, but most are silvery gray. Doctorfish can be recognized by 10 to twelve thin body bars that are often quite faint. At times, both species display pale bands at the base of their tail fins.

Surgeonfishes, which feed continually throughout the day on a wide variety of plants, play a key role inhibiting the growth of filamentous and fleshy turf algae on the reef and contributing large amounts of detritus to the habitat. Blue Tang are specialized algae-browsers that feed without ingesting sediment and have the long intestines and thin-walled stomachs characteristic of herbivores. On the other hand, Ocean Surgeonfish and Doctorfish, both generalized grazers, have long intestines and thick-walled, gizzardlike stomachs for handling the large volume of detritus and sediment (up to 40 percent) ingested as they forage. Because these materials contain a significant number of microinvertebrates, mainly copepods and hydroids, both species can be considered omnivores. Unlike Blue Tang and Doctorfish, which forage on the reef's structure, Ocean Surgeonfish customarily graze over sand and seagrass beds up to 50 feet from the reef's fringes.

Where large populations occur, Blue Tang spend much of their day feeding in aggregations that can number over a hundred. These swarming assemblies, which regularly include other surgeonfishes and a scattering of Midnight Parrotfish, *Scarus coelestinus*, allow the herbivores to breach the defenses of algae-farming damselfishes. (Interestingly, Midnights, who share the same blue coloration, also associate with Blue Tang outside feeding aggregations, even traveling with them to mass spawning events.) The feeding throngs swim along the reef line, descending periodically onto a damselfish garden which they ravish for 10 to 15 seconds with a flurry of bites before moving a short distance to their next plunder. The nipping attacks of the four- to five-inch damselfishes, which easily repel solitary foragers, are no match for a horde of invaders. Blue Tang living in small populations, without the advantage of group feeding, spend significantly more time foraging in the water column than their more numerous counterparts.

Large populations of Blue Tang reproduce in pairs and in resident spawning aggregations. Only pair spawning occurs in small populations. In Bimini, Bahamas, we observed Blue Tang pair spawning from May through August. Late each afternoon, two to five large males defended personal areas of the water column above an isolated rock reef. Trespassing males were aggressively chased. When approached by smaller, rapidly swimming females, the courting males attempted to position themselves next to their sides. During these brief encounters, the heads and forebodies of the males lightened markedly. After lengthy courtship, pairs completed a few rapid ten- to 15-foot spawning rushes that left visible gamete clouds a few feet below the surface.

Ocean Surgeonfish often feed over sand.

We observed the resident group spawning activities of what we estimated to be 1,000 Blue Tang and Ocean Surgeonfish for three consecutive afternoons beginning the seventh day after the full moon of March. The spawning area, which

Doctorfish lighten and darken dramatically.

Surgeonfishes

covered approximately 5,000 square yards of coral and sand bottom in 45 feet of water, was just inside a dropoff paralleling the seaward shoreline of Turneffe Atoll, Belize. Prior to the gathering, large aggregations of Blue Tang swam rapidly along the dropoff. An hour before sunset several aggregations converged at the spawning grounds, accompanied by their entourages of Midnight Parrotfish. The fish milled about just above the bottom for five to ten minutes before forming into three to five compact schools, each numbering in the hundreds. The dark clouds of fish repeatedly ascended high into the water column, dropped back to the bottom, briefly dispersed, reassembled and ascended again. Subgroups of from five to 25 individuals, many displaying white tails (presumably males pursuing single females), periodically broke from the main group and zig-zagged about erratically. Eventually a single subgroup dashed toward the surface and expelled gametes, prompting a dozen or more groups to follow suit. After spawning, subgroups rejoined one of the constantly moving aggregations before breaking free, chasing and spawning once again. The water was a haze of gametes by the time group-spawning ceased, approximately 20 minutes before sunset. Isolated pair spawning continued until dark.

As the reproductive frenzy of the Blue Tang reached a fevered pitch, several hundred Doctorfish arrived at the scene and spread across the seafloor in a loose group. When the Blue Tang reproductive activities subsided, the Doctorfish joined into small subgroups and began to spawn in groups and pairs in a manner similar to the Blue Tang. Possibly because there were fewer participants, the Doctorfish never formed into compact clouds.

We have observed Ocean Surgeonfish pair spawning during the late afternoon in Bimini. Males encroaching into defended territories near the bottom often were chased in tight circles, as if the adversaries were attempting to use their sharp tail spines as weapons. Occasionally, territory holders and intruders swam rapidly side-by-side across the bottom or briefly positioned themselves next to one another in a nose-down posture.

A spawning aggregation of Doctorfish gathers below the spawning Blue Tang.

Blue Tang gather at a traditional spawning site an hour before sunset.

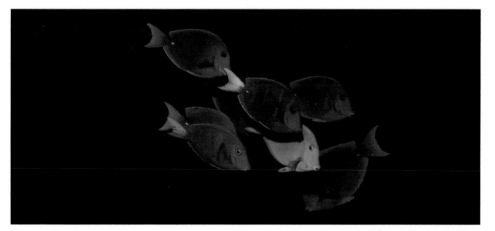

Subgroups consisting of a female and several males break away from the gathering.

Subgroups spawn high in the water column.

Surgeonfishes

A territorial confrontation …   *between Ocean Surgeonfish at dusk.*

For nearly a year, researchers in Puerto Rico documented the behavior of a resident spawning aggregation estimated to include more than 20,000 Ocean Surgeonfish and 6,000 Blue Tang at its zenith. The fishes assembled in the late afternoons during 21-day periods each month from December until March, beginning the day before the full moon until five days after the new moon. Peak activity occurred three to eight days after the full moon in the coolest winter months. From April through November the aggregations were smaller and less intense and spawned only from the third to the ninth day after the full moon. At the height of activity, researchers counted nearly 50 group spawning rushes in less than one minute. Even though the two surgeonfish species spawn in the same locations at approximately the same times, only one possible hybrid has been reported. Large, ripe male and female Doctorfish were in the vicinity of the Puerto Rico spawning site in the winter months, but were never observed spawning.

The surgeonfishes' tail-base spines, formed by modified scales and attached posteriorly by ligament to the spinal column, cannot be voluntarily erected. The forward-pointing tip on the convex surface slips slightly from the groove each time the tail flexes. If the exposed point happens to snag into something passing by, the spine extends at a right angle from the body. Although reported to carry toxins, a laboratory experiment using the spines of Ocean Surgeonfish to inflict wounds on various reef fishes proved negative.

Under laboratory conditions, the spherical eggs of Ocean Surgeonfish (0.67 mm in diameter) hatch in 28 hours. Settlement peaks during the darkened nights of the new moon, when the large, inch-and-a-quarter, transparent and silvery larvae drop to the seafloor. Blue Tang tend to settle onto hard reef structures while the Ocean Surgeonfish and Doctorfish choose low-profile rock and coral patches often in shallow back-reef habitats and in grassbeds near reefs. The vulnerable youngsters immediately seek shelter where they metamorphose into juveniles. Larval Ocean Surgeonfish are believed to use chemical cues to select advantageous settlement sites. Recruits have been

Pair spawning male Blue Tang wear a white-face pattern.

documented to settle primarily near established juveniles of their species and to avoid sites occupied by Beaugregory, *Stegastes leucostictus*, a small, territorially aggressive damselfish.

The smallest juvenile Ocean Surgeonfish, already resembling adults in body shape and color, feed in small groups within a confined area. With growth they become aggressive toward one another, especially at dusk, when defending sleeping sites. For a time they forage with schools of juvenile parrotfishes. When they grow to nearly three inches, they once again feed in small schools. Individuals become sexually mature and join adult schools after approximately two years, at a length of five to six inches. It is estimated that surgeonfishes can live up to 10 years.

To the contrary, bright yellow juvenile Blue Tang, strikingly different from blue adults, are highly territorial. As they grow, and the youngsters' bodies turn powder blue, except for yellow tails, they begin to mix with small foraging fishes. By the time they are four inches and completely blue they form small groups with their own species. Later, after developing their final dull blue coloration, they join large foraging aggregations of adults.

Post-larval surgeonfish.

Intermediate juvenile Blue Tang.

Tilefishes
Family Malacanthidae

Sand Tilefish spend much of the day maintaining their burrows.

Sand Tilefish
Malacanthus plumieri

   Widely spaced rock, coral and shell mounds marking the homes of Sand Tilefish are common fixtures on sand plains fronting Caribbean coral reefs. The two- to six-foot diameter piles, which add structure to an otherwise barren seascape, also provide sanctuary for numerous crustaceans and small fishes, including Bicolor Damselfish, *Stegastes partitus*, cardinalfishes, gobies and, in deeper water, harems of Cherubfish, *Centropyge argi*. The torpedo-shaped, one- to two-foot Sand Tilefish move about just above the bottom in a start-and-stop fashion. While hovering, their long dorsal and anal fins undulate in graceful waves. Sensing danger, tilefish cautiously move toward their mounds and, if threatened, dive into the single tunnel leading down at a ten- to 20-degree slope to an excavated chamber below. The fish spend considerable energy keeping their burrows in good repair. Pieces of rubble from the surrounding sand are carried periodically by mouth and added to the pile, and existing fragments are regularly shifted and rearranged. If building materials are in short supply, tilefish have been known to steal rocks from jawfishes and neighboring tilefish. The rubble roofs provide a barrier against large predators, such as Mutton Snapper, *Lutjanus analis*, and several species of sharks, which have been found with tilefish remains in their stomachs. To expedite hasty escapes, the sand chutes leading to the entranceway are picked free of debris and regularly loosened by a rapidly fluttering body. When researchers experimentally destroyed a burrow, the homeless female built a temporary refuge a few feet away. During the next two to four days, she constructed a permanent residence at the old site.

Each female maintains an individual burrow within a home range that generally lies adjacent to and overlaps slightly with those of other females. These defended feeding areas cover from 40 to nearly 300 square yards and average 150 square yards in size. The territories of from one to six females are encompassed within the territory of a single male, who appears similar to the females except for his larger size and tail streamers. Males spawn almost exclusively with the females living within their territorial boundaries but otherwise maintain little contact and seldom attempt to dominate partners physically. Even though all males are protogynous hermaphrodites derived from sex-changed females, there does not appear to be a size-related social hierarchy in tilefish harems. Unlike many protogynous species that live in harems, when male tilefish are experimentally removed, the largest female does not automatically change sex and dominate the group.

Females defend their personal feeding territories from other females regardless of the trespasser's size, but the dominant male is allowed free access. In rare instances, females displace neighbors. Territorial females confront female intruders just inside their borders and either chase or escort them out of their area. If, while

Loose rocks are continually added to the burrow pile.

Stealing burrow rocks from a jawfish.

Tilefishes

pursuing an intruder, the fish cross into the trespasser's turf, the tables are turned and the aggressor is chased back into her own territory. Although most confrontations end without further incident, feuding females will occasionally spread fins, make threatening upward jumps, bite, or closely circle each other with their mouths open and gill covers flared. Prolonged spats are settled by territorial males, whose sudden appearance causes the bickering pairs to flee or lower their heads in submission and swim cautiously away, passing under the approaching male.

Tilefish forage throughout the day within their territorial boundaries for an assortment of small bottom-dwelling invertebrates and fishes. Brittle stars, crabs, mantis shrimps, plumed worms, chitons, small wrasses and sand eels make up the bulk of their diet. Females protect their territories' food supplies by aggressively challenging neighboring females and other gleaning carnivores that enter their personal feeding grounds.

Males' territories can include as much as 900 square yards of sandy plain, but the sizes are not correlated to the occupants' body size. As with the home ranges of females, males' territories often overlap slightly. Males occasionally make extended excursions, crossing the territories of one or two neighboring males. The trespassers, either swimming rapidly or creeping slowly near the bottom, are challenged by both territorial males and females. A difference in size does not seem to matter in these exchanges.

When territorial males disappear, neighboring males begin to feud and encroach into the vacated area within an hour. By the second day, things are settled as a male gains control of the abandoned burrow or incorporates part or all of the adjoining territory into his personal domain. Within hours, the new male begins to make courtship overtures to the annexed harem members. Occasionally, vacated areas are divided among neighboring males. A few males live in territories without mates, but there do not seem to be any adult females without spawning partners. Because females seldom relocate to improve their spawning possibilities, bachelor males must either establish their territories close to females or be patient and wait for recently matured females to set up housekeeping within their boundaries. Mate-stealing is rare, but when it occurs a rather nasty confrontation ensues.

Reproductive activities occur each evening beginning an hour before, and lasting until ten minutes after, sunset. A female mates nearly 80 percent of evenings, usually once but occasionally two or three times. Males might spawn ten times during an evening depending on the number of females inside their territories. As the light begins to fade, females remain close to their burrows. Courting males visit each in turn, flaring pelvic fins as they approach in a conspicuous series of long, slow, arching dips. Females not yet prepared to spawn generally shun the early advances by swimming away. Later, as females become more receptive, pairs rub against each other, cross bodies and swim parallel to one another across the sea floor. Variations of the courtship dance continue for minutes before the first spawning rise. When ready to release their eggs, females hover three or four feet above the bottom and arch their bellies downward, dramatically accentuating the profile of their egg-swollen abdomens.

*The sand chute leading to a burrow's entranceway
is regularly loosened with a fluttering body.*

Feeding with a Smooth Trunkfish.

Juvenile Sand Tilefish.

Burrows are never completed. Building materials are constantly shifted and added.

Tilefishes

The arched back of a female (foreground) indicates her readiness to spawn.

The smaller female initiates the slow spawning rise.

Positioned side-to-side and with the female slightly in the lead, the pair slowly ascends at a 60-degree angle. Early rises are typically aborted without release of gametes. At this point the male might swim off to court elsewhere, but usually the two fish go through the entire routine once or twice more before finally rising six to 12 feet and, with a quiver, simultaneously release a cloud of spawn. They immediately part and swim rapidly to the bottom in opposite directions, where the female occasionally rubs her abdomen across the sand. From start to finish, the entire affair takes from one to eight minutes. As darkness approaches the females become more receptive and the males less formal, with partners often spawning as soon as the males arrive.

On six successive days, we watched the same male spawn with his five harem mates. The male followed a different sequence between mates each evening, always spending extra time with the most willing partners. When we approached too closely, the tilefish curtailed courtship. When we remained at

The pair release gametes at the peak of their spawning rise.

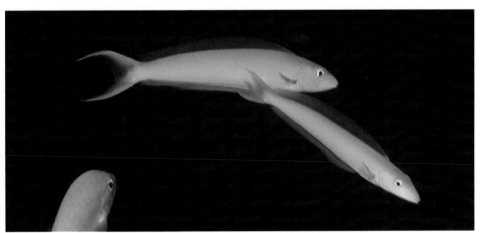

As the pair break apart after spawning,
a Yellowtail Snapper dashes toward the gamete cloud.

least ten feet away, however, the couples went about their business as usual. On two occasions, three Yellowtail Snapper, *Ocyurus chrysurus*, escorted the male from female to female. The notorious egg-predators hovered menacingly just inches away from the courting couples. Each time a pair began to rise the Yellowtails followed closely, often causing the tilefish to break apart prematurely. After several disrupted attempts, the harried pairs finally spawned in frustration, leaving their precious cargoes at the mercy of the Yellowtails, who crisscrossed through the clouds with open mouths before dashing off after the male as he dipped his way in the direction of another partner.

Wrasses
Family Labridae

Yellowhead Wrasse attempting to settle a territorial dispute.

Possibly because wrasses are generally small, continuously on the go and so common, they tend to be ignored. However, those divers and snorkelers who take the time to observe these energetic fish closely will find their behavior fascinating and their color patterns quite beautiful. Of the over 500 species worldwide, 18 make their homes in the tropical western Atlantic. The typical Caribbean wrasse is a colorful, three- to six-inch cigar-shaped fish that buzzes about endlessly just above the bottom in a small, loosely knit feeding aggregation known as a herd. However, there are considerable variations in size, body shape and behavior in the family. The variable wrasse family ranges from three-inch, plankton-feeding razorfishes, genus *Xyrichtys*, with hatchet-shaped heads designed for diving into the sand, to mollusk-crushing Hogfish, *Lachnolaimus maximus*, that approach three feet in length. Adding further confusion to identification, many wrasses have three distinct color phases, and a few species display as many as five color and marking patterns during their life cycles.

Like the closely related parrotfishes, wrasses have large, noticeable scales, swim primarily with their pectoral fins, are often quite colorful and change their sex from female to male when certain age, growth or social criteria are met. But unlike parrotfishes, which scrape algae from rocks with fused beaks, most wrasses feed on hard-shelled invertebrates including crabs, shrimps, brittle stars and small gastropods. When discovered, the delicacies are seized or scissored free with prominent sets of protruding canines and crushed with powerful pharyngeal teeth.

A few species – Creole Wrasse, *Clepticus parrae*; Rainbow Wrasse, *Halichoeres pictus*; Rosy Razorfish, *X. martinicensis*; and adult Bluehead Wrasse, *Thalassoma bifasciatum* – primarily rely on diets of zooplankton plucked from the currents. Juvenile Spanish Hogfish, *Bodianus rufus*, and Bluehead Wrasse obtain a portion of their diets by picking ectoparasites from a variety of fishes.

Wrasses inhabit a wide range of habitats, from shallow inshore grass beds to deep coral-encrusted outer banks. Except for the open water plankton-feeding Creole Wrasse, all occupy permanent territories in association with other members of their species. Also like parrotfishes, wrasses are protogynous hermaphrodites – females have the ability to change into terminal males, the pinnacle of reproductive prosperity. Understanding the species' social organization is, to say the least, challenging. For starters, the majority of wrasses have three distinct color phases representing their social status: the juvenile phase consists of sexually immature youngsters that nearly always live separately from adults; the initial phase includes sexually mature adults that in the majority of species are exclusively females but can be both males or females, and terminal males, nearly always the largest, brightest, most aggressive and least numerous individuals.

Females have a strong tendency to select the largest and most ornate males for mating. Unfortunately, eye-catching colors not only attract mates but also predators. For this reason, the conspicuous terminal males of species living around coral

Initial phase Bluehead Wrasse.

A two-inch male Rosy Razorfish.

A two-foot terminal male Hogfish.

Wrasses

habitats with the benefit of many accessible hiding places, show the brightest and most permanent dichromatism. Terminal males of species inhabiting sand flats, seagrass beds or hard bottom, without ready access to shelter, exhibit their most striking colors only briefly when courting or engaged in aggressive behavior.

The size of territories varies considerably among species. The small Rosy Razorfish require only a few feet of bare sand, while large Hogfish lay claim to areas the size of football fields. The terminal males of many wrasse species patrol and defend territories superimposed over the home ranges of three to six initial phase herds, each made up of three to eight fish. Dominant males visit groups periodically throughout the day zooming in with great fanfare before briefly foraging alongside the roving bands. Border disputes periodically take place between neighboring territory holders. Rather than resorting to physical clashes, ritualistic behavior settles disputes. Rankled males either assume defiant head-down stances, rapidly swim parallel to each other up and down their common borders or engage in head-to-head standoffs with their mouths opened wide. This common behavior, known as gaping, also occurs between younger members of a social group to establish or sustain their social ranking.

Most wrasses belong to a rigid size-related hierarchy that allows only the largest individuals in the initial phase to become terminal males. Sex-changed males are known as secondary males. Primary males, the few individuals born male, cannot change sex, but, with adequate size may one day develop into the terminal phase. The transformation from an initial phase female to terminal phase male is predictable, rapid and irreversible. Within hours after researchers experimentally removed the terminal males from a small Bluehead population, the largest initial phase female, who had spawned as a female the day before, began behaving aggressively, developed a slightly darkened head while courting and attempted to spawn as a male. Intermediate color changes were evident by the second day and distinct in four days. Eight days after the initiation of sex change it is physiologically possible for an individual to produce sperm. Within several weeks the full color transition is complete.

All wrasses are broadcast spawners that, as a rule, pair spawn daily at established locations within their permanent feeding territories. However, the terminal males of the ubiquitous Bluehead Wrasse do not defend feeding grounds or females; instead, they travel each afternoon to the downcurrent end of a reef line and take temporary control of a prominent structure, such as a large coral head, as a spawning site. Initial phase females soon follow, migrating from their home ranges along established routes.

The different species of cigar-shaped wrasses court and spawn in a similar fashion. With fins spread and displaying their brightest colors, terminal males repeatedly dive toward gatherings of females as they mill about the bottom. Suitors signal their readiness to spawn by executing a series of rapid vertical jumps. Egg-laden females rising in midwater are joined by males. Side by side, the pairs rocket up two or three feet where they snap apart, simultaneously releasing gametes.

Dominant males have no intention of sharing their many females. Young initial phase males, in their quixotic quest to reproduce, rely on stealth to penetrate the terminal males' defenses. Because their color patterns mimic those of females, young males, known as sneakers, are able to hang out undetected near spawning sites and, when the terminal males are temporarily occupied, sneak a quick spawn with waiting females. Streakers, on the other hand, lurk close by and dash in, at just the precise moment, to mix their sperm at the apex of a paired spawning rush. Occasionally, spurious young sneakers carry their masquerade to extremes by pretending to spawn with dominant males. Terminal males must resort to inspecting the vents of initial phase individuals to weed out the impostors who, when discovered, are aggressively chased from the site. These fast-paced pursuits, which often take the rivals 20 to 30 feet from the spawning site, are common occurrences during reproductive periods.

Terminal males have little problem dominating reproductive activity at isolated reef sites where populations are limited; but on large reefs the ratio of initial phase males increases substantially for several species of wrasses. On these reefs the young males congregate upcurrent from the preferred mating sites and mass spawn with passing females. Of course, their highly competitive hit-and-miss tactics have significant disadvantages. During group spawns, an individual's chance of successfully fertilizing eggs is reduced by the number of competing males. Initial phase males also have difficulty recognizing the sex of their look-alike cohorts. It is estimated that nearly half of group spawns do not even involve the release of eggs. To increase their odds, younger males have greater gonad mass and can release more sperm in proportion to body size than pair-spawning terminal males.

At dusk, some species seek night shelter inside nooks and crannies while others, including the Slippery Dick, *Halichoeres bivittatus*; Yellowhead Wrasse, *H. garnoti*; Rainbow Wrasse and Clown Wrasse, *H. maculipinna*, dive beneath the sand where they remain until the first light of dawn. Razorfishes have taken this behavior a step further by diving under the sand's surface, not only at night but also when threatened. The larger, plankton-feeding Creole Wrasse find refuge deep within tube sponges or crevices.

Like nearly all reef fishes, wrasses begin life as pelagic larvae that settle to a reef environment after an extended period. Researchers are able to establish the age and date of settlement for most reef fishes by counting concentric markings on three sets of tiny bones, known as otoliths, at the base of the braincase. These markings are especially clear in wrasses. Wide settlement bands indicate that most family members spend, on average, 24 days in the in the open ocean. Razorfishes, however, remain adrift for up to three months. Newly settled wrasses are believed to bury in the sand while they metamorphose into juveniles.

A terminal male Bluehead Wrasse courts a female.

Bluehead Wrasse
Thalassoma bifasciatum

From reef to reef, Blueheads are the most common fish in the tropical western Atlantic. Throughout daylight hours countless initial phase herds forage for small crustaceans on reefs, rubble beds and gorgonian fields, from depths of three to 80 feet. The relentless, ever-present hunting packs are the scourge of benthic egg layers. By sheer force of numbers they regularly breach the defenses of a nest's guardian and ravenously plunder eggs for minutes at a time before they can be driven away. When currents flow, the same herds switch feeding strategies and move up in the water column to pick plankton or pluck ectoparasites from hovering fish. After maturing into terminal phase males, individuals feed almost exclusively on benthic invertebrates. Unlike most wrasse species, Blueheads do not defend territorial feeding grounds or females; instead, herds roam freely in broad overlapping home ranges, where they are periodically visited by displaying terminal males throughout the day.

Blueheads are protogynous hermaphrodites, able to change from females to males. The initial phase is made up of females, non-sex-changing primary males and secondary males that have changed from large females. When terminal males disappear from a reef area, the largest initial phase individuals in the area go though a succession of intermediate color and marking changes while developing, over several weeks, into conspicuous blue-headed terminal males.

Spawning strategies, the number of fish in each color phase and sex ratios vary dramatically between small and large Bluehead populations. On small isolated reefs with fewer than 200 individuals, pair-spawning terminal males control all the preferred downcurrent spawning sites and nearly all mating activities. On these reefs terminal males make up about ten percent of the population, and the initial phase consists almost entirely of females. When populations hover between 200 and 500, terminal males still occupy the better sites but can no longer expend the energy necessary to exclusively dominate mating. In these populations, group spawning between an aggregation of initial phase males and single females takes place just upcurrent from the spawning sites of terminal males. As populations on larger reefs grow to more than 1,000, less than one percent of individuals are in the terminal phase, while nearly 50 percent of the initial phase is made up of males. In these situations, those individuals in the terminal phase still spawn in pairs, but the competition from initial phase males is so great that their mating activities are relegated to less desirable sites at the perimeter of the reef. Even there, young male sneakers and streakers continue to exert competitive pressure. On the largest reefs with over 10,000 fish, initial phase herds, including both males and females, migrate in steady streams from feeding areas as far as a mile away to spawn in large aggregations, while pair-spawning terminal males are virtually non-existent.

On small to medium reefs, during daily, two-hour afternoon spawning periods, terminal males occupy customary sites where they wait for females to arrive from their feeding grounds. To draw attention to themselves or possibly to demonstrate that their spawning site is safe from predators, males perform a series of short vertical dashes in rapid succession, known as signal jumps. When females approach, the males excitedly swim in tight circles, occasionally spiraling upward. When ready to spawn, one, or in some cases multiple, females rise from below. The males slow, allowing their temporary mates to pass just ahead. Side-by-side and almost touching, they swiftly ascend at a

Initial phase Bluehead Wrasse break through the defenses of a Sergeant Major and swarm its nest full of eggs.

Wrasses

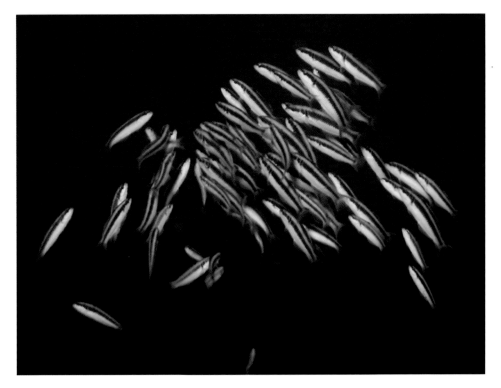

*Up to 50 initial phase male Bluehead Wrasse dash
into the water column in pursuit of a single, ripe female.*

sharp upward angle. In an instant the swollen females turn on their sides, positioning their ventral slits close to the males and release eggs which are immediately enveloped by a cloud of sperm. On medium to small reefs, terminal males controlling the prime sites pair spawn as many as 25 times each afternoon, while females, strapped by energy-expensive egg production, spawn once every other day for up to two years of their reproductive life cycles.

Despite the terminal male's bright coloration, his striking markings appear to have little or no effect on a female's mate selection. When terminal males were experimentally removed from traditional spawning sites, females remained faithful to their original sites that were occupied within two days by new terminal males from nearby sites. The new males were not followed by their previous spawning partners. Possibly females, always vulnerable to predation, prefer accustomed migration routes and spawning areas, where they are familiar with the location of shelter holes. Further research also has documented that spawning sites, used continually for generations, were not intentionally chosen to confer dispersal advantages to offspring. After removing all the Blueheads from a small isolated patch reef, researchers introduced a fresh population captured miles away. Within days the new residents were engaging in reproductive activities, but they adopted different spawning sites from those used by their predecessors. This study also indicates that migration to a particular site is probably a learned behavior.

On large reefs where initial phase Blueheads spawn in groups, their frenzied behavior easily attracts the diver's eye. These high-energy episodes take place along the reef's seaward edge, at traditional spawning sites. Look for several hundred individuals excitedly moving about the substrate in loose aggregations. Every few minutes, from five to 50 small males form tightly knit groups rapidly swimming several feet off the bottom in parallel formations. If you look closely a single female, swollen with eggs, can be seen leading the dodging and darting pack as it rises four or five feet above the substrate. In a split second, several members break free, rush upward, form into a tight ball and in unison shed a visible cloud of spawn. On large reefs when action is intense, spawning balls form one after the other. Even though large terminal males are believed to be 20 to 50 times more reproductively successful than small initial phase males, it is estimated that, because of their commanding numbers, nearly 75 percent of fertilized eggs are produced by spawning groups.

Blueheads spend their first six to ten weeks of life as pelagic larvae before settling to shallow water habitat in unpredictable mass recruitment waves. They immediately bury in the sand where they remain for several day while metamorphosing into juveniles. The bright yellow youngsters gather in restricted pockets of the reef or at the edge of seagrass beds where they remain until sexually mature. The few able to survive this perilous period develop a dark midbody stripe and join a local herd as initial phase Blueheads. Individuals do not leave the area where they settle, and remain faithful to the herd they initially join. At dusk, each fish takes refuge inside a personal reef pocket that is fervently defended from cohorts.

Clown Wrasse
Halichoeres maculipinna

Although the small, cigar-shaped Clown Wrasse are seldom noticed, they are usually quite common around the sandy fringes of patch reefs at moderate depth. Initial phase herds, numbering from three to three dozen individuals, often mix with juvenile surgeonfishes, young parrotfishes and other wrasse species. A single, brightly colored terminal phase male controls a permanent territory where he dominates as many as 30 initial phase fish that group into three to six herds. One to three subordinate terminal phase males round out the species' territorial society.

Initial phase Clown Wrasse can be females or primary or secondary sex changed males. Each retains vestiges of his bold gold, black and white-striped juvenile markings. Herds, composed primarily of females, remain stable, moving about and feeding together inside limited home ranges. Within these feeding groups, there is a rigid size-based pecking order with larger members frequently forcing smaller colleagues aside at food sources. Constantly moving herds spend their day rooting about the bottom for worms and other invertebrates hidden just beneath the sand. Even though they do not wander far, feeding grounds often overlap those of their neighbors. When paths cross, the herds intermingle briefly without incident.

Wrasses

Subordinate terminal males can be primary or secondary males. Unlike dominant males, they seldom display intense colors, never patrol territories in the water column and do not court or spawn. When briefly chased by a dominant male, which frequently happens, they collapse fins, turn tail and flee. However, subordinates systematically visit each initial phase herd within their territories.

Socially superior territorial males can be recognized by their intense colors and a dark mid-body blotch prominently displayed as they patrol a few feet off the bottom, confront neighboring dominants, chase subordinates, inspect herds, court and spawn. When not engaged in these behaviors their colors fade, and it is difficult to distinguish them from subordinates. As in most wrasse species, when a dominant male disappears, an extended power struggle ensues to gain control of his territory. Not only do local subordinates compete, but neighboring subordinates and dominants cross boundaries to vie for the vacant position. After several hours of spirited chasing and displaying, one of the challengers establishes supremacy and immediately begins displaying to his initial phase herds and patrolling boundaries while proudly showing off his flashy coat of bright colors.

The large territories of Clown Wrasse, ranging between 500 and 1,200 square yards and contiguous to other territories, are vigilantly patrolled and defended by both types of terminal phase males. When males in adjacent territories confront one another, they intensify markings, face off with their mouths open and canines exposed or, abreast, race back and forth, only inches apart, each fish prudently remaining just inside his own area. Such encounters are the only instances when subordinates intensify colors.

Clown Wrasse pair spawn year-round for short periods from late morning to midafternoon. Dominant males court during the day by streaking toward a foraging herd with fins flared and colors bright. As spawning episodes begin at various locations within their territories, dominant males increase displays and pursue subordinate males with heightened vigor. When ready to spawn, they advertise their intent with a sequence of quick signal jumps. Ripe females rising slightly off the bottom are joined by males in short spawning rushes. In some Clown Wrasse populations, possibly those with a large number of initial phase males, one or two small males sometimes streak in from the periphery and shed their sperm with the spawning pairs. In these same large populations, isolated initial phase pair spawning and group spawning also take place. Subordinate males, evidently celibate, have yet to be observed participating in reproductive activities. It is believed that vigilant dominant males easily detect subordinate males attempting to mate because they no longer resemble females,.

Yellowhead Wrasse
Halichoeres garnoti

Contrary to the social tendencies of cigar-shaped wrasses, Yellowhead Wrasse are less gregarious. Solitary terminal males and small groups in the initial phase feed within large, broadly overlapping home ranges with little conflict. Their ranges normally encompass hard coral habitats on deeper portions of the reef. Even the tiny yellow juveniles with electric blue streaks hang out alone or in twos or threes near small coral pockets or along the fringes of seagrass beds.

Instead of constantly searching sand flats for food, individual Yellowheads spend the majority of their feeding time poking inside narrow crevices and under rocks for a variety of invertebrates, such as crabs and brittle stars. These opportunistic feeders frequently join loose feeding aggregations consisting of other wrasses; porgies; Yellowtail Snapper, *Ocyurus chrysurus*; Bar Jack, *Caranx ruber*; and Spotted Goatfish, *Pseudupeneus maculatus*. It is generally believed that Yellowhead Wrasse do not defend feeding territories because their food supply is too widely distributed to favor group foraging.

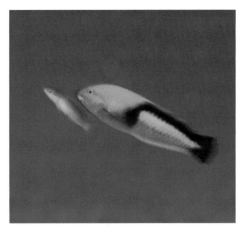

Pair spawning Yellowhead Wrasse.

It would be logistically impractical for males to keep tabs on groups of females constantly moving about such large areas.

A typical population consists of slightly more females than males and slightly more initial phase than terminal phase individuals. Though unproved, it appears that all males are secondary sex-changed females, whether in the terminal or initial phase. Many individuals in a population exhibit a variety of intermediate color patterns between the initial and terminal phases. It has yet to be determined if these Yellowheads are in the initial, terminal or a transitional phase, or even if they are all actually males. Complicating the matter further, large Yellowhead Wrasse can brighten dramatically, fade to white and temporarily lose their prominent black midbody bar.

For three successive afternoons we watched the same Yellowhead terminal male shuttle back and forth along a low reef line between three initial phase groups about 40 feet apart. The largest gathering consisted of approximately a

A terminal male Yellowhead Wrasse displays his brightest colors.

While inside the spawning territory of another male, a terminal male Yellowhead Wrasse blanches white.

Wrasses

A late-afternoon gathering of terminal male Yellowhead Wrasse.

A terminal male visits his sleeping site,

dozen females. The groups moved calmly about the bottom, occasionally feeding while the male was out of the vicinity. When the male approached, he performed one or two high signal jumps that carried him at least five feet from his starting point. In response, several females would rise together five or six feet off the sea floor and pause. When a single female began to rise again the male darted to a position with his belly next to her back and his head even with her pectoral fins. Together they shot up in a blur and released gametes several feet above the starting point. After one or two pair spawns, the male typically returned to the bottom and rapidly swam out of the area. Once we watched a male mate with ten females in succession with only seconds between each spawn.

noses around for ten minutes

Approximately an hour before sunset up to a dozen terminal phase Yellowheads, displaying bright colors, gather together and begin their nightly bedding routine by moving as groups across broad areas of the bottom. The individuals do not feed and show no aggression toward one another. After

and dives below the sand for the night.

a short period the big males break into smaller bands that are joined by a few Yellowheads in the initial phase. Together they nose about sand patches, repeatedly going back and forth between several spots. The large individuals begin to show preferences for particular locations by returning to the same areas repeatedly. Ten to 15 minutes later one of the bright males suddenly dives into the patch of sand he has been frequenting and drives his body below the surface by rapidly beating his tail. The others nose about where their colleague disappeared, possibly hoping to discover bits of uncovered food. Minutes later a second terminal male disappears in the same manner. Well before sunset all have buried for the night in different locations. Preferred sleeping areas tend to be in loose pockets of sand next to low-profile rock ledges.

We have observed the same terminal male bury himself at the same site on successive evenings. When we shoveled our hands into the sand where a fish disappeared, it came flying out and immediately began nosing about once more invariably choosing the same site to dive back into five or ten minutes later.

Slippery Dick
Halichoeres bivittatus

All sizes and color phases of cigar-shaped Slippery Dicks feed much of the day in small, loosely knit, opportunistic hunting packs. Together, they alertly patrol the bottom for a wide variety of animal matter. When a diver's fin disturbs the sand or a rock is overturned, exposing brittle stars, crabs or shrimps, these tenacious herds are first on the scene. Often, even before a horrified diver can reposition the rock, its hidden fauna are picked clean. Although herds occasionally forage about reefs, they are most common on the sand aprons surrounding widely scattered patch corals and on hard bottom in less than 15 feet of water.

Small initial phase primary males and females dominate population numbers. There are also quite a few primary males in the terminal phase. The colors of Slippery Dicks change dramatically to blend with their habitat. Those feeding over sand pale to white with only a dark mid-body stripe extending from snouts to the base of their tails; individuals inhabiting dark algae-covered bottoms display a reddish brown coloration.

Even though there is a distinct difference between initial and terminal phase color patterns, the species is considered only partially dichromatic because random females occasionally display terminal colors. However, individuals with the most pronounced terminal patterns are invariably males. Terminal color patterns are intensified to their full splendor only during courtship and spawning; otherwise they fade, often blurring the visual distinction between the sexes.

It is believed that terminal males do not form harems or maintain permanent feeding territories, but each day they temporarily defend specific spawning sites along the outside edge of shallow reefs near their feeding grounds. Reproductive periods, beginning in late morning and extending into early afternoon, coincide with those of Clown Wrasse, *H. maculipinna*, and Yellowhead Wrasse, *H. garnoti*, indicating that all three species are reacting to a similar set of environmental cues. Much like Bluehead Wrasse, *Thalassoma bifasciatum*, pair spawning occurs at these temporary sites, with occasional initial phase streaking and sneaking. Typical of their hyperactive nature, terminal males jet about just off the bottom between clusters of females during enthusiastic courtship episodes. Adding to the fast-paced action, smaller males are constantly chased. Often terminal males leave the area for several minutes at a time. When they return, one to three egg-swollen females rise off the bottom. The approaching terminal males dash into the group and, in a blur, pair spawn with one waiting female after another before zooming off once again. Although we have never observed this species spawning in initial phase groups, this behavior has been reported.

A terminal male Rainbow Wrasse courts with fins spread and colors blasting.

Rainbow Wrasse
Halichoeres pictus

Rainbow Wrasse, the smallest of the eight cigar-shaped species, feed on zooplankton in the water column on the outer slopes of shallow patch reefs and gorgonian thickets. Loosely structured herds of 20 to 40 fish regularly mix with equal numbers of similarly colored initial phase Bluehead Wrasse, *Thalassoma bifasciatum*. Because of their close similarity to the prolific Blueheads, these constantly moving two- to four-inch fish are frequently overlooked. The species is distinctly dichromatic, with terminal phase males bearing a striking blue, green and yellow coat that radiates brightly during their frequent courtship displays. As the lively males streak back and forth between herds their color fades, only to intensify each time they approach a group of females. A large dark blotch on each side of the tail base becomes prominent during these encounters. To date, only pair spawning has been reported for this species. At dusk terminal males dive beneath the sand for the night.

Both color phases include primary and secondary males, with secondary males more abundant in the terminal phase. A typical population contains

A pair of transitional phase Rainbow Wrasse attempt to establish dominance with a mouth-to-mouth confrontation, known as gaping.

slightly more females than males. Small groups of tiny, one-inch golden juveniles with black-and-white-striped heads typically inhabit deep walls, where they often mix with Masked Gobies, *Coryphopterus personatus*.

Creole Wrasse
Clepticus parrae

After watching the smaller, cigar-shaped wrasses going through their bottom-oriented routines, it is difficult to imagine that the robust-bodied, semi-pelagic Creole Wrasse are even remotely related. Although this abundant species has gone through considerable modification to adapt successfully to life as an open water plankton picker, it still relies on the reef structure for cleaning stations, spawning sites and night sanctuary. In mid to late afternoon, rapidly moving columns, often numbering in the hundreds, sweep along the outer reef, propelled by wildly beating pectoral fins. As they fly by, small groups of a dozen or more peel off and assume stationary, snout-up or snout-down positions at cleaning stations. On the outer reefs this species is, by far, the cleaners' best customer.

Juvenile Creole Wrasse settle on reef habitats, where the tiny one-inch lavender fish gather in small groups near the tops of coralheads. The initial phase is made up exclusively of females, who change into terminal males when they reach a length of six to seven inches. As they alter sex, their anal and dorsal fins develop elongate filaments, and the anterior half of their purplish bodies gradually transforms into an artist's palette of yellows, oranges and magenta.

Creole Wrasse visit a cleaning station.

Wrasses

The fast-paced courtship of Creole Wrasse is quite a performance. Spawning occurs year-round in mid to late afternoon but, although frequent, does not take place daily. There seems to be no territory defense or streaking, but larger males regularly and aggressively displace smaller males attempting to solicit a mate. A population's courtship, often lasting for hours, tends to occur in waves of ten to 20 fish that pair off at random locations within customary spawning areas. The show begins with males shadowing females from above, while the females cut and dive erratically in an attempt to lose their single-minded suitors. During these prolonged chases that can last for 15 minutes, the males intensify colors, extend their white mouth membranes into pronounced puckers and spread their dorsal and anal fins. Pairs are so preoccupied that they regularly rocket past divers without notice. Once in the throes of passion, males become so determined to spawn that they may attempt to mate with juveniles or even with other species.

A school of Creole Wrasse streams along the outer reef line in late afternoon.

When finally ready to comply, the females swim to the bottom and slow their pace, allowing the males to position beneath them. With the backs of their heads, the males begin to push their partners toward the surface. At this point the females often have a change of heart and attempt to flee forcing the males to scramble wildly to maintain position. When errant females are pacified, the males press their snouts against the listing females' flared gill covers and, with rapidly beating tails, slowly push their mates upward for several feet before the females release eggs. The males immediately move through the cloud, releasing sperm before setting out to court new partners.

A courting pair of Creole Wrasse (male above).

Rosy Razorfish
Xyrichtys martinicensis

Three wrasse species in the genus *Xyrichtys*, commonly known as razorfish, inhabit open sand flats in the tropical western Atlantic. When viewed head-on, the fishes' razor-thin bodies explain the group's name. Their bony, hatchet-shaped heads allow the small two- to six-inch fishes to dive into the sandy bottom when threatened. Without their ability to hide beneath the sand it would be impossible for the little fishes to survive on the barren sand plains where they make their homes. Rosy Razorfish live in harems grouped together in tightly packed colonies. Each harem consists of at least one dominant male and from three to 30 initial phase females that occupy a sandy patch only a few feet in diameter. From time to time entire colonies relocate to new feeding grounds.

Rosy Razorfish go through the initial phase as females. The protogynous hermaphrodites' transformation into terminal males is initiated by the loss of dominant males or when specific size or age requirements are met. On the same day that a researcher noted the absence of a male from a harem of two males and seven females, the largest female segregated herself at the outskirts of the territory. The remaining male spawned that evening with all the females except the isolated female, who was attacked. By day two the large female showed the beginnings of color change. Nine days later her color transformation was complete. Twenty-five days after the male's disappearance the new, sex-changed male spawned with one of the harem's original females.

When currents flow, colony members rise off the bottom to pick plankton, their major source of food. At other times they forage for benthic invertebrates within their restricted home range or tidy their grounds by picking rocks and other bits of

The transparent abdomen of female Rosy Razorfish allow the males to assess the condition of their eggs.

debris from the sand. Both males and females are extremely territorial and aggressively guard their sand patches from neighbors. Females charge and nip smaller neighboring females that venture too close to the harem's perimeter. If both females are the same size, they momentarily parallel each other and display by bending their bodies before launching an attack. When necessary, males repulse encroaching males. If competitive carnivores such as crustacean-eating goatfishes or Yellowfin Mojarra, *Gerres cinereus*, feed nearby, male razorfishes, although much smaller, do not hesitate to defend their feeding grounds.

Tightly bunched colonies offer the advantage of many eyes to keep tabs on the numerous predators that hunt on the flats. Throughout the day approaching Bar Jack, *Caranx ruber*, lizardfishes and other predators elicit a fright reaction that instantly spreads throughout a colony. Those closest to the danger drop to the sand, list to one side, and take on a blotched pattern, while keeping a sharp eye on the danger. If the predator continues to approach, they flex laterally and, with a powerful thrust, drive their bodies into the sand. Once buried, an individual occasionally remains hidden for up to an hour or tunnels away for some distance, but most fish pop their heads out after a few minutes at the exact spot where they disappeared. At dusk the fish bury in the sand for the night. Although razorfishes are completely buried, a few large piscivores – rays, dolphins and hammerhead sharks – have the ability to detect their hiding places. Random, cone-shaped depressions pock the bottom where dolphins hunt for buried razorfishes.

Courtship and pair spawning occur daily in the late afternoon. Males average just over three spawns per evening, while females mate only once. Dominant males

A male Rosy Razorfish ...

flexes laterally and, with ...

intensify colors and display spread fins when passing females throughout the day. This behavior increases during courtship. Males occasionally perform high signal jumps. Beginning three feet above their territories and powered by a thrashing tail, the fish rise vertically three to six feet. The males also assume stationary head-up or head-down positions a few inches above the bottom for three to five seconds. In a courtship behavior unique to Rosy Razorfish, males pass just beneath females. Researchers believe that the maneuver allows males to assess the state of eggs through a transparent window on females' abdomens. Females initiate spawning by lifting slowly two to three

Green Razorfish emerges from the sand.

feet off the bottom. Males dart in positioning themselves at the sides of the rising females. The species' comparatively slow spawning rushes last for two to four seconds before culminating in a release of gametes.

Interestingly, at the end of 40 percent of the spawning rushes of Rosy Razorfish and Green Razorfish, *X. splendens*, the males immediately turn on the cloud of eggs and appear to take several bites before darting back to the bottom. Video analysis revealed that the male razorfishes modify their normal spawning rush when they consume eggs. Just before egg release the males curve their bodies, allowing them to turn quickly into the cloud. This led the researcher to the hypothesis that a male anticipates cannibalizing the nutrient-rich eggs of its mate during a particular rush and probably does not release sperm. This behavior has not been observed for any other pelagic-spawning reef fish in the Caribbean, although it has been reported for *Anthias squamipinnis*, a small, plankton-feeding sea bass from the Red Sea. Pearly Razorfish, *X. novacula*, the Caribbean's third member of the genus and benthic carnivores, do not feed on their mates' eggs.

a rapidly beating tail, ...

power dives beneath the sand.

A male Spanish Hogfish displays a prominent set of incisors used to capture and crush crusteaceans and gastropods.

Spanish Hogfish
Bodianus rufus

From juveniles to the terminal phase, Spanish Hogfish exhibit the same distinctive purple and golden color pattern and basic body shape. Juveniles from less than one inch to just over three inches are active cleaners that busily swim about coral structures in ones, twos or threes. Client fishes swim near and pause, waiting to have ectoparasites picked from their bodies and occasionally from inside their opened mouths and flared gill covers. At about four inches, when the fish become sexually mature females, they join a harem and switch to a diet that includes a broad assortment of invertebrate life. Their favorite foods include crabs, brittle stars, sea urchins and a variety of gastropods. When females reach six to seven inches, they make a final transformation into secondary terminal phase males that grow to over a foot in length and eventually dominate harems of their own.

Courtship and pair spawning between females and their terminal male harem-masters occur late each afternoon throughout the year, beginning approximately an hour before sunset. Preceding the actual spawning, loosely organized groups of three to four females mill about inside their territories. For

Signaling her readiness to spawn, a female curves into an S-shape.

brief periods the small groups disappear inside the reef structure before suddenly reappearing and moving with other harem members to traditional spawning sites nearby. The large terminal males, who usually have been elsewhere, return and make passes near the females, prompting one or two to rise above the reef and signal their willingness to spawn by curving their bodies into an S-shape. The males swim slowly to the sides of hovering females and together the pairs calmly rise three or four feet before shedding gametes and returning to the reef. After one or two spawns the males swim away, only to return several minutes later to spawn with other waiting females. This pattern is usually repeated several times over a ten- to 15-minute period before mating is complete.

The slow spawning rise of Spanish Hogfish.

A male Hogfish changes colors, lists to his side and opens his mouth while visiting a cleaning stationed manned by Pederson Cleaner Shrimp.

Hogfish
Lachnolaimus maximus

Male Hogfish, capable of reaching three feet in length, are the largest wrasses in the region. These big fellows, with their elongate, concave snouts and reddish brown masks, all start life as females. The smaller females, usually less than half the size of males, reach sexual maturity at about eight inches. Both sexes frequently display a dramatic reddish mottled pattern when feeding near the bottom or settling next to cleaning stations. Unfortunately, this highly desired food fish has little fear of divers and has been overharvested by spearfishing in many areas.

A Hogfish spawning rise.

Males establish and patrol long, narrow territories, just over 300 feet in length, occupied by harems of ten to 15 females. During the day little interaction occurs among harem members as they independently root about the sand for mollusks, including snails, bivalves and occasionally crabs. Powerful jaws crush the hard-shelled invertebrates.

Courtship and pair spawning take place daily in the cooler winter months, during the last hour and a half before sunset. Males begin courtship by patrolling their territories at an accelerated pace. When prospective mates are sighted, they extend their long foredorsal spines and dive toward the females. If rebuffed, the males continue on to the next potential partner. When ready to spawn, females lift off the bottom and swim slowly upward at an angle. Males, approaching from behind, pick up speed as they switch from pectoral fin sculling to powerful strokes of their wide tails. Side-by-side and streaking toward the surface, the pairs roll to their sides with the males above and release gametes 20 to 30 feet above the bottom. Splitting apart and looping, they dive toward the bottom. As their paths cross, the males briefly extend their dorsal spines. A single male may take part in dozens of paired spawning rushes in an afternoon, while females are believed to spawn only once. The larvae hatch in 24 hours, begin taking food two days later and settle in shallow water habitats two to three weeks later.

Index Legend: photos - bold, photos and text - bold italic, species accounts - hyphenated

Index Legend: photos - bold, photos and text - bold italic, species accounts - hyphenated

References

REPRODUCTION 8-31

Appeldoorn, R.S., D.A. Hensley and D.Y. Shapiro. 1994. Egg dispersal in a Caribbean coral reef fish, *Thalassoma bifasciatum*. II. Dispersal off the reef platform. Bull. Mar. Sci. 54: 271-280.

Barlow, G.W. 1981. Patterns of parental investment, dispersal and size among coral reef-fishes. Env. Biol. Fish. 6: 65-85.

Bauer, J.A. and S.E. Bauer. 1981. Reproductive biology of pigmy angelfishes of the genus *Centropyge* (Pomacanthidae). Bull. Mar. Sci. 31(3): 495-513.

Burnett-Herkes, J. 1975. Contribution to the biology of the red hind, *Epinephelus guttatus*, a commercially important serranid fish from the tropical western Atlantic. Ph.D. Dissertation. Univ. Miami, Coral Gables.

Carter, J. and D. Perrine. 1994. A spawning aggregation of dog snapper, *Lutjanus jocu* (Pisces: Lutjanidae), in Belize, Central America. Bull. Mar. Sci. 55: 228-234.

Colin P.L. 1992. Reproduction of the Nassau Grouper, *Epinephelus striatus*, (Pisces: Serranidae) and its relationship to environmental conditions. Env. Biol. Fish. 34: 357-377.

Colin P.L. 1995. Surface currents in Exuma Sound, Bahamas and adjacent areas with reference to potential larval transport. Bull. Mar. Sci. 56(1): 48-57.

Colin, P.L. 1996. Longevity of some coral reef fish spawning aggregations. Copeia 1996: 189-192.

Colin, P.L. and I.E. Clavijo. 1988. Spawning activity of fishes producing pelagic eggs on a shelf edge coral reef, southwestern Puerto Rico. Bull. Mar. Sci. 43(2): 249-279.

Doherty, P.J., D.M. Williams and P.F. Sale. 1985. The adaptive significance of larval dispersal in coral reef fishes. Env. Biol. Fish. 12: 81-90.

Domeier, M.L. and M.E Clarke. 1992. A laboratory produced hybrid between *Lutjanus synagris* and *Ocyurus Chrysurus* and a probable hybrid between *L. griseus* and *O. chrysurus* (Perciformes: Lutjanidae). Bull. Mar. Sci. 50(3): 501-507.

Domeier, M.L. and P.L. Colin. 1997. Tropical reef fish spawning aggregations: defined and reviewed. Bull. Mar. Sci. 60(3): 698-726.

Hoffman, S.G. and D.R. Robertson. 1983. Foraging and reproduction of two Caribbean reef toadfishes (Batrachoididae). Bull. Mar. Sci. 33: 919-927.

Hoffman, S.G., M.P. Schildhauer and R.R. Warner. 1985. The costs of changing sex and the ontogeny of males under contest competition for mates. Evolution 39: 915-927.

Hourigan T.F. and C.D. Kelley. 1985. Histology of the gonads and observations on the social behavior of the Caribbean angelfish *Holacanthus tricolor*. Marine Biol. 88: 311-322.

Hubb, C.L. 1955. Hybridization between fish species in nature. Syst. Zool. 4(1): 1-20.

Johannes, R.E. 1978. Reproductive strategies of coastal marine fishes in the tropics. Env. Biol. Fish. 3: 65-84.

Leonard, J.L. 1993. Sexual conflict in simultaneous hermaphrodites: evidence from serranid fishes. Env. Biol. Fish. 36: 135-148.

Lobel, P.S. 1980. Nesting, eggs and larvae of triggerfishes (Balistidae). Envir. Biol. Fish. 5: 251-252.

Randall J.E. and H.A. Randall. 1963. The spawning and early development of the Atlantic parrotfish, *Sparisoma rubripinne*, with notes on other scarid and labrid fishes. Zoologica 48: 49-60.

Robertson, D.R., C.W. Petersen and J.D. Brawn. 1990. Lunar reproductive cycles of benthic-brooding reef fishes: reflections of larval biology or adult biology? Ecol. Monog. 60(3): 311-329.

Ross, R.M. 1990. The evolution of sex-change mechanisms in fishes. Env. Biol. Fish. 29: 81-93.

Shapiro, D.Y., D.A. Hensley and R.S. Appeldoorn. 1988. Pelagic spawning and egg transport in coral-reef fishes: skeptical overview. Env. Biol. Fish. 22: 3-14.

Thresher, R.E. 1984. "Reproduction in Reef Fishes" Neptune City, NJ: T.F.H. Publications.

Turner, G.F. 1993. Teleost mating behaviour. "Behaviour of Teleost Fishes" 2nd (T.J. Pitcher, ed.) Chapman & Hall.

Warner, R.R. 1987. Female choice of sites versus mates in coral reef fish, *Thalassoma bifasciatum*. Anim. Behav. 35: 1470-1478.

Warner, R.R. 1988a. Traditionality of mating-site preferences in coral reef fish. Nature 335: 719-721.

Warner, R.R. 1988b. Sex change in fishes: hypotheses, evidence, and objections. Env. Biol. Fish. 22(2): 81-90.

Warner, R.R. 1990. Resource assessment versus tradition in mating-site determination. Am. Nat. 135: 205-217.

Warner, R.R. 1995. Large mating aggregations and daily long-distance spawning migrations in the Bluehead Wrasse, *Thalassoma bifasciatum*. Env. Biol. Fish. 44: 337-345.

Warner, R.R. and D.S. Ross. 1978. Sexual patterns in the labroid fishes of the western Caribbean, I. The wrasses (Labridae). Smithsonian Contrib. Zool. 254: 1-27.

Warner, R.R. and S.G. Hoffman 1980. Local population size as a determinant of mating system and sexual composition in two tropical marine fishes (*Thalassoma* spp.). Evolution 34(3): 508-518.

Warner, R.R. and S.E. Swearer. 1991. Social control of sex change in the bluehead wrasse, *Thalassoma bifasciatum* (Pisces: Labridae). Biol. Bull. 181: 199-204.

LIFE CYCLE AND REEF FISH COMMUNITIES 32 - 43

Appeldoorn, R.S., D.A. Hensley and D.Y. Shapiro. 1994. Egg dispersal in a Caribbean coral reef fish, *Thalassoma bifasciatum*. II. Dispersal off the reef platform. Bull Mar. Sci. 54: 271-280.

Bakun, A. 1986. Local retention of planktonic early life stages in tropical reef/bank demersal systems: the role of vertically-structured hydrodynamic processes. " IOC/FAO Workshop on Recruitment in Tropical Coastal Demersal Communities," (D. Pauly and A. Yanez-Arancibia, eds.), IOC Workshop Rep 44 (suppl.), UNESCO, Paris: 15-32.

References

Bauer, J.A. Jr. and S.E. Bauer. 1981. Reproductive biology of pigmy angelfishes of the genus *Centropyge* (Pomacanthidae). Bull. Mar. Sci. 31(3): 495-513.

Bohnsack, J.A. 1982. Effects of piscivorous predator removal on coral reef fish community structure. "Gutshop '81: Fish Food Habits Studies" (G.M. Cailliet and C.A. Simenstad, eds.). Seattle: Washington Sea Grant Publ. 258-267.

Booth, D.A. and D.M. Broshan. 1995. The role of recruitment dynamics in rocky shore and coral reef fish communities. "Advances in Ecological Research" (M. Begon and A.H. Fitter, eds.) Academic Press Inc. San Diego, CA. 25: 309-385.

Castro, P. and M.E. Huber. 1992. "Marine Biology" Wm. C. Brown Communications, Dubuque, IA.

Colin, P.L. 1995. Surface currents in Exuma Sound, Bahamas and adjacent areas with reference to potential larval transport. Bull. Mar. Sci. 56(1): 48-57.

Doherty, P.J. 1983. Tropical territorial damselfishes: is density limited by aggression or recruitment? Ecology 64: 176-190.

Doherty, P.J. 1985. Predation on juvenile coral reef fishes: an exclusion experiment. Coral Reefs 4: 225-234.

Doherty, P.J. 1991. Spatial and temporal patterns in recruitment. "The Ecology of Fishes on Coral Reefs." (P.F. Sale, ed.) Academic Press, San Diego, CA: 261-293.

Doherty, P.J. and D. McB. Williams. 1988. The replenishment of coral reef fish populations. Oceanogr. Mar. Biol. Annu. Rev. 26: 487-551.

Hunte, W and I.M. Cote. 1989. Recruitment in the redlip blenny, *Ophioblennius atlanticus:* is space limiting? Coral Reefs 8: 45-50.

Hunter, J.R. 1981. Feeding ecology and predation of marine fish larvae. "Marine Fish Larvae: Morphology, Ecology and Relation to Fisheries" (R. Lasker, ed.) Seattle: Univ. of Washington Press. 33-77.

Johannes, R.E. 1978. Reproductive strategies of coastal marine fishes in the tropics. Environ. Biol. Fishes 3: 65-84.

Jones, G.P. 1991. Postrecruitment processes in the ecology of coral reef fish populations: a multifactorial perspective. "The Ecology of Fishes on Coral Reefs." (P.F. Sale, ed.) San Diego: Academic Press. 294-328.

Kelley, S. 1995. Preliminary guide to the identification of the early life history stages of Pomacanthid fishes of the Western Central Atlantic and Gulf of Mexico. NOAA Tech. Mem. NMFS-SEFSC-375.

Kingsford, M.J., E. Wolanski and J.H. Choat. 1991. Influence of tidally-induced fronts and langmuir circulations on the distribution and movement of presettlement fishes around a coral reef. Mar. Biol. 109: 167-180.

Lasker, R. 1981. The role of a stable ocean in larval fish survival and subsequent recruitment. "Marine Fish Larvae Morphology, Ecology and Relation to Fisheries" (R. Lasker, ed.) Seattle: Univ. of Washington Press. 80-87.

Leis, J.M. 1991. The pelagic stage of reef fishes: the larval biology of coral reef fishes. "The Ecology of Fishes on Coral Reefs" (P.F. Sale, ed.) San Diego: Academic Press. 183-230.

Lindeman, K.L. 1986. Development of larvae of the French grunt, *Haemulon flavolineatum*, and comparative development of twelve species of western Atlantic *Haemulon* (Percoidei, Haemulidae). Bull, Mar. Sci. 39(3): 673-716.

Mannoch, C.S. 1987. Age and growth of snappers and groupers. "Tropical Snappers and Groupers - Biology and Fisheries Management." (J.J. Polovina and S. Ralston, eds.) Boulder, CO: Westview Press. 329-373.

Morse, A.N.C. 1991. How do planktonic larvae know where to settle? American Scientist 79: 154-167.

Moser, H.G. 1981. Morphological and functional aspects of marine fish larvae. "Marine Fish Larvae: Morphology, Ecology and Relation to Fisheries" (R. Lasker, ed.) Seattle: Univ. of Washington Press. 30-88.

Panella, G. 1971. Fish otoliths daily growth layers and periodical patterns. Science 173: 1124-1127.

Panella, G. 1980. Growth patterns in fish sagittae. "Skeletal Growth of Aquatic Organisms: Biological Records of Environmental Change" (D.E. Rhoads and R.A. Lutz, eds.) New York: Plenum. 519-560.

Randall, J.E. 1961. A contribution to the biology of the convict surgeonfish of the Hawaiian Islands, *Acanthurus triostegus sandvicensis*. Pac. Sci 15: 215-272.

Richards, W.L. and K.C. Lindeman. 1987. Recruitment dynamics of reef fishes: planktonic processes, settlement and demersal ecologies, and fishery analysis. Bull. Mar. Sci. 41: 392-410.

Robertson D.R. 1988. Extreme variation in settlement of the Caribbean triggerfish *Balistes vetula* in Panama. Copeia: 698-703.

Robertson, D.R., D.G. Green and B.C. Victor. 1988. Temporal coupling of production and recruitment of larvaē of a Caribbean reef fish. Ecology. 69(2): 370-381.

Robertson, D.R., C.W. Petersen and J.D. Brawn. 1990. Lunar reproductive cycles of benthic-brooding reef fishes: reflections of larval biology or adult biology? Ecol. Monog. 60(3): 311-329.

Roughgarden, J. 1986. Dynamics of a metapopulation with space-limited subpopulations. Theor. Pop. Biol. 5: 163-186.

Sale, P.F. 1980. The ecology of fishes on coral reefs. Oceanogr. Mar. Biol. 18: 367-421.

Seong, S.C., M.F. McGowan and W. J. Richards. 1994. Vertical distribution of fish larvae off the Florida Keys, 26 May-5 June 1989. Bull. Mar. Sci. 54(3): 828-842.

Shulman, M.J. and J.C. Ogden. 1987. What controls tropical reef fish populations: recruitment or benthic mortality? An example in the Caribbean reef fish *Haemulon flavolineatum*. Mar. Ecol. Prog. Ser. 39: 233-242.

Sweatman, H.P.A. 1988. Field evidence that settling coral reef fish larvae detect resident fishes using dissolved chemical cues. J. Exp. Mar. Biol. Ecol. 124: 163-174.

References

Thresher, R.E. and E.B. Brothers. 1989. Evidence of intra- and inter-oceanic regional differences
   in the early life history of reef-associated fishes. Mar. Ecol. Prog. Ser. 57: 187-205.

Victor, B.C. 1982. Daily otolith increments and recruitment in two coral-reef wrasses, *Thalassoma bifasciatum*
   and *Halichoeres bivittatus*. Marine Biol. 71: 203-208.

Victor, B.C. 1983. Recruitment and population dynamics of a coral reef fish. Science 219: 419-420.

Victor, B.C. 1986. Larval settlement and juvenile mortality in a recruitment-limited coral reef fish population.
   Ecol. Monog. 56(2): 145-160.

Victor, B.C. 1986. Duration of the planktonic larval stage of one hundred species of Pacific and Atlantic wrasse
   (family Labridae). Mar. Biol 90: 317-326.

Victor, B.C. 1991. Settlement strategies and biogeography of reef fishes. "The Ecology of Fishes on Coral Reefs."
   (P.F. Sale, ed.) San Diego: Academic Press. 231-260.

Williams, D. McB. 1980. Dynamics of the pomacentrid community on small patch reefs in One Tree Lagoon
   (Great Barrier Reef). Bull. Mar. Sci. 30: 159-170.

FEEDING 44 - 85

Adey, W.H. and R.S. Steneck. 1985. Highly productive eastern Caribbean reefs: synergistic effects of biological,
   chemical, physical and geological factors. "The Ecology of Coral Reefs" (M.L. Reaka, ed.)
   NOAA Symp. Ser. Undersea Res. Natl. Oceanic Atmos. Adm., Rockville, MD. 3: 163-188.

Aronson, R.B. 1983. Foraging behavior of the West Atlantic Trumpetfish, *Aulostomus maculatus*: use of large,
   herbivorous reef fishes as camouflage. Bull. Mar. Sci. 33: 166-171.

Aronson, R.B. and S.L. Sanderson. 1987. Benefits of heterospecfic foraging by the Caribbean wrasse,
   Halichoeres garnoti (Pisces: Labridae). Env. Biol. Fish. 47: 129-141.

Bruckner A.W. and R.J. Bruckner. 1998. Rapid-wasting disease: pathogen or predator. Science. 279: 2023-2025.

Bythell J.C., E.H. Gladfelter and M. Bythell. 1993. Chronic and catastrophic natural mortality
   of three common Caribbean reef corals. Coral Reefs 12: 143-152.

Carpenter, R.C. 1986. Partitioning herbivory and its effects on coral reef algal communities.
   Ecol. Monogr. 56: 345-363.

Carpenter, R.C. 1990a. Mass mortality of *Diadema antillarum*. I. Long-term effects of sea urchin
   population-dynamics and coral reef algal communities. Mar. Biol. 104: 67-77.

Carpenter, R.C. 1990b. Mass mortality of *Diadema antillarum*. II. Effects on population densities
   and grazing intensity of parrotfishes and surgeonfishes. Mar. Biol. 104: 79-86.

Choat, J.H. 1991. The biology of herbivorous fishes on coral reefs. "The Ecology of Fishes on Coral Reefs"
   (P.F. Sale, ed.). San Diego: Academic Press. 120-153.

Davis, W.P. and R.S. Birdsong. 1973. Coral reef fishes which forage in the water column.
   Helgol. Wiss. Meeresunters. 24: 292-306.

Emery, A.R. 1968. Preliminary observations on coral reef plankton. Limnol. Oceanogr. 13: 293-303.

Gerking, S.D. 1994. "Feeding Ecology of Fish." San Diego: Academic Press.

Hay, M.E. 1991. Fish - seaweed interactions on coral reefs: effects of herbivorous fishes and adaptations
   of their prey. "The Ecology of Fishes on Coral Reefs." (P.F. Sale, ed.) San Diego: Academic Press. 96-118.

Hay, M.E., V.J. Paul, S.M. Lewis, K. Gustafson, J. Tucker and R.N. Trindell. 1988. Can tropical seaweeds
   reduce herbivory by growing at night? Diel patterns of growth, nitrogen content, herbivory, and chemical
   versus morphological defenses. Oecologia. 75: 233-245.

Helfman, G.S 1989. Threat-sensitive predator avoidance in damselfish-trumpetfish interactions.
   Behav. Ecol. and Sociobiol. 24: 47-58.

Helfman, G.S. 1993. Fish behaviour by day, night and twilight. "Behaviour of Teleost Fishes"
   2nd (T.J. Pitcher, ed.) London: Chapman & Hall. 479-512.

Helfman, G.S., J.L. Meyer and W.N. McFarland. 1982. The ontogeny of twilight migration patterns in grunts
   (Pisces: Haemulidae). Anim.Behav. 30: 317-326.

Hobson, E.S. 1973. Diel feeding migrations of tropical reef fishes. Helgol. Wiss. Meeresunters. 24: 361-370.

Hobson, E.S. 1991. Tropic relationships of fishes specialized to feed on zooplankters above coral reefs.
   "The Ecology of Fishes on Coral Reefs" (P.F. Sale, ed.) San Diego: Academic Press. 69-93.

Horn, M. 1989. Biology of marine herbivorous fishes. Oceanogr. Mar. Biol. Annu. Rev. 27: 167-272.

Hughes, T.P., D.C. Reed and M.J. Boyle. 1987. Herbivory on coral reefs: community structure
   following mass mortalities of sea urchins. J. Exp. Mar. Biol. Ecol. 113: 39-59.

Irvine, G.V. 1982. The importance of behavior in plant-herbivore interactions: a case study.
   "Fish Food Studies" (G.M. Caillet and C.A. Simenstad, eds.) Washington Sea Grant Program.
   Seattle: Univ. of Washington Press. 240-248.

Karplus, I. 1971. A feeding association between the grouper *Epinephelus fasciatus* and the moray eel
   Gymnothorax griseus. Copeia. 3: 164.

Kaufman, L. 1976. Feeding behavior and functional coloration of the Atlantic trumpetfish, *Aulostomus maculatus*.
   Copeia. 2: 377-378.

Lewis, S.M. 1986. The role of herbivorous fishes in the organization of a Caribbean reef community.
   Ecol. Mongr. 56: 183-200.

Lewis, S.M., J.N. Norris and R.B. Searles. 1987. The regulation of morphological plasticity in tropical reef algae by herbivory. Ecology. 68: 636-641.

Lobel, P.S. 1980. Herbivory by damselfishes and their role in coral reef community ecology. Bull. Mar. Sci. 30 (Spec. Issue): 273-289.

McFarland, W.N., J.C. Ogden and J.N. Lythgoe. 1979. The influence of light on the twilight migrations of grunts. Env. Biol. Fishes. 4: 9-22.

Nursall, J.R. 1982. Behavioral interactions between Caribbean reef fish and eels (Muraenidae and Ophichthidae). Copeia. 1: 229-232.

Paul, V.J. and K.L. Van Alstyne. 1988. Chemical defense and chemical variation in some tropical Pacific species of *Halimeda* (Halimedaceae,Chlorophyta). Coral Reefs. 6: 263-270.

Pressley, P.H. 1981. Pair formation and joint territoriality in a simultaneous hermaphrodite: the coral reef fish *Serranus tigrinus*. Z. Tierpsychol. 56: 33-46.

Randall, J.E. 1961. Overgrazing of algae by herbivorous marine fishes. Ecology. 42: 812.

Randall, J.E. 1967. Food habits of reef fishes of the West Indies. Stud. Trop. Ocean. 5: 665-847.

Randall, J.E. and W.D. Hartman. 1968. Sponge-feeding fishes of the West Indies. Mar. Biol. 1: 216-225.

Robertson, D.R. 1987. Responses of two coral reef toadfishes (Batrachoididae) to the demise of their primary prey, the sea urchin *Diadema antillarum*. Copeia. 3: 637-642.

Russ, G.R. and J. St. John. 1988. Diets, growth rates and secondary production of herbivorous coral reef fishes. Proc. Int. Coral Reef Symp. 6th 2: 37-43.

Schmitt, E.F. 1997. The influence of herbivorous fishes on coral reef communities with low sea urchin abundance: a study among reef community types and seasons in the Florida Keys. Ph.D. Dissertation. Univ. of Miami. Coral Gables, FL.

Steneck, R.S. 1983. Escalating herbivory and resulting adaptive trends in calcareous algal crust. Paleobiology. 9: 44-91.

Steneck, R.S. 1988. Herbivory on coral reef: a synthesis. Proc. Int. Coral Reef Symp. 6th 1: 37-49.

Wulff, J.L. 1997. Parrotfish predation on cryptic sponges of Caribbean coral reefs. Mar. Biol. 129: 41-52.

Zaret, T.M. 1980. "Predation and Freshwater Communities" New Haven, CT: Yale Univ. Press.

COLORS & CAMOUFLAGE 86 - 95

Lorenz, K. 1962. The function of colour in coral reef fishes. Proc. Roy. Inst. Gr. Brit. 39: 282-296.

Lorenz, K. 1966. "On Aggression." New York: Harcourt, Brace & World. Inc.

Nemtzov, S.C. 1993. Diel color phase changes in the coney, *Epinephelus fulvus* (Teleostie, Serranidae). Copeia. 3: 883-885.

Neudecker, S. 1989. Eye camouflage and false eyespots: chaetodontid responses to predators. Env. Biol. Fish. 25: 143-157.

Randall, J.E. and H.A. Randall. 1960. Examples of mimicry and protective resemblance in tropical marine fishes. Bull. Mar. Sci., Gulf Carib. 10: 444-480.

SYMBIOSIS 96 - 121

Bohlke, J.E. and C.C.G. Chaplin. 1993. "Fishes of the Bahamas and Adjacent Tropical Waters" 2nd edition. Austin: Univ. of Texas Press.

Brockmann, H.J. and J.P. Hailman. 1976. Fish cleaning symbiosis: notes on juvenile angelfishes (Pomacanthus, Chaetodontidae) and comparisons with other species. Z. Tierpsychol. 42: 129-138.

Darcy, G.E., E. Maisel, and J.C. Ogden. 1974. Cleaning preferences of the gobies Gobiosoma evelynae and *G. prochilos* and the juvenile wrasse *Thalassoma bifasciatum*. Copeia. 1974: 375-379.

Feddern, H.A. 1965. The spawning, growth, and general behavior of the bluehead wrasse, *Thalassoma bifasciatum* (Pisces: Labridae). Bull. Mar. Sci. 15:896-941.

Foster, S.A. 1985. Wound healing: a possible role of cleaning stations. Copeia. 1985(4): 875-880.

Gorlick, D.L., P.D. Atkins and G.S. Losey. 1978. Cleaning stations as water holes, garbage dumps, and sites for the evolution of reciprocal altruism? Am. Nat. 112: 341-353.

Johnson, W.S. and R. Ruben. 1988. Cleaning behavior of *Bodianus rufus, Thalassoma bifasciatum, Gobiosoma evelynae,* and *Perclimenes pedersoni* along a depth gradient at Salt River Submarine Canyon, St. Croix. Env. Biol. Fish. 23(3): 225-232.

Levy, J.M. 1994. Taxonomic review of ectoparasites of Epinepheline groupers in the Exuma Cays, Bahamas. Unpublished.

Levy, J.M., K.M. Sullivan and M. de Garine-Wichatitsky. 1994. Account of ectoparasites of Epinepheline groupers in the Exuma Cays, Bahamas. Proc. Gulf Carib. Fish. Inst. 43.

Limbaugh, C. 1961. Cleaning symbiosis. Sci. Am. 205: 42-49.

Limbaugh, C., H. Pederson and F.A. Chance Jr. 1961. Shrimps that clean fishes. Bull. Mar. Sci. Gulf & Carib. 11: 237-257.

Losey, G.S. Jr. 1972. The ecological importance of cleaning symbiosis. Copeia. 820-833.

Losey, G.S. Jr. 1987. Cleaning symbiosis. Symbiosis. 4: 229-256.

Losey, G.S. Jr. and L. Margules. 1974. Cleaning symbiosis provides a positive reinforcer for fish. Science. 184: 179-180.

Pagan-Font, F.A. 1967. The study of the commensal relationship between the conchfish, *Astrapogon stellatus,* and the queen conch, *Strombus gigas,* in southwestern Puerto Rico. Masters Thesis, Univ. of Puerto Rico.

References

Poulin, R. and A.S. Grutter. 1996. Cleaning symbioses: proximate and adaptive explanations. What evolutionary pressures led to the evolution of cleaning symbioses? BioScience. 46(7): 512-517.

Randall, J.E. and H.A. Randall. 1960. Examples of mimicry and protective resemblance in tropical marine fishes. Bull. Mar. Sci. 10(4): 444-480.

Sikkel, P.C. 1992. Interspecific feeding associations between the goatfish *Mulloides martinicus* (Mullidae) and a possible aggressive mimic the snapper *Ocyurus chrysurus* (Lutjanidae). Copeia. 3: 914-917.

Sluka, R. and K.M. Sullivan. 1996. Daily activity patterns of groupers in the Exuma Cays Land and Sea Park, Central Bahamas. Bahamas J. of Sci. 2: 17-22.

Snyder, D.B. In press. Mimicry of initial-phase bluehead wrasse, *Thalassoma bifasciatum* (Labridae) by juvenile tiger grouper, *Mycteroperca tigris* (Serranidae). Revue Francoise d' Aquariologie.

Thresher, R.E. 1977. Pseudo-cleaning behavior of Florida reef fishes. Copeia. 4: 768-769.

Thresher, R.E. 1979. Possible mucophagy by juvenile *Holacanthus tricolor* (Pisces: Pomacanthidae). Copeia. 1979(1): 160-162.

Wicksten, M.K. 1995a. Associations of fishes and their cleaners on coral reefs of Bonaire, Netherlands Antilles. Copeia. 1995: 477-481.

Wicksten, M.K. 1995b. Behaviour of cleaners and their client fishes at Bonaire, Netherlands Antilles. J. of Natural History. 32: 13-30.

Williams, E.H. and L.B. Williams. 1980. Four new species of *Renocila* (Isopoda: Cymothoidae), The first reported from the New World. Proc. Biol. Soc. Wash. 93(3): 573-592.

Williams, L.B. and E.H. Williams. 1981. Nine new species of *Anilocra* (Crustacea: Isopoda: Cymothoidae) external parasites of West Indian coral reef fishes. Proc. Biol. Soc. Wash. 94(4): 1005-1047.

Williams, E.H., L.B. Williams, R.E. Waldner and J.J. Kimmel. 1982. Predisposition of a Pomacentrid fish, *Chromis multilineatus* (Guichenot) to parasitism by a Cymothoid Isopod, *Anilocra chromis*. J. Parasito. 68(5): 942-945.

Williams, E.H. and L.B. Williams. 1985. Brood pouch release of *Anilocra chromis* (Isopods, Cymothoidae) a parasite of brown chromis, *Chromis multilineatus* (Guichenot) in the Caribbean. Crustaceana 49(1): 92-95.

Williams, L.B. and E.H. Williams. 1989. Hangers-on. Natural History 1: 40.

SENSES & SOUND COMMUNICATIONS 122 - 127

Hawkins, A.D. 1981. The hearing ability of fish. "Hearing and Sound Communication in Fishes" (W.N. Tavolga, A.N. Popper and R.R. Fay, eds.) Springer - Verlag.

Kenyon, T.N. 1994. The significance of sound interception to males of the bicolor damselfish, *Pomacentrus partitus*, during courtship. Env. Biol. Fish. 40: 391-405.

Myberg, A.A. 1981. Sound communication and interception in fishes. "Hearing and Sound Communication in Fishes" (W.N. Tavolga, A.N. Popper and R.R. Fay, eds.) Springer - Verlag.

Partridge, B.L. 1981. Lateral line function and the internal dynamics of fish schools. "Hearing and Sound Communication in Fishes" (W.N. Tavolga, A.N. Popper and R.R. Fay, eds.) Springer - Verlag.

Platt, C. and A.N. Popper. 1981. Fine structure and function of the ear. "Hearing and Sound Communication in Fishes" (W.N. Tavolga, A.N. Popper and R.R. Fay, eds.) Springer - Verlag.

MARINE LIFE MANAGEMENT 128 - 137

Alcala, A.C. and E.D. Gomez. 1987. Dynamiting coral reefs; a resource destructive fishing method. "Human Impact on Coral Reefs: Facts and Recommendations" (B. Salvat, ed.) Antenne Museum E.P.H.E., French Polynesia. 51-60.

Ballantine, W.J. 1997. Design principles for systems of "no-take" marine reserves. Paper for workshop on: the design and monitoring of marine reserves. Fisheries Center, Univ. of British Columbia, Vancouver.

Bohnsack, J.A. 1994. How marine fishery reserves can improve reef fisheries. Proc. Gulf Carib. Fish. Inst. 43: 217-241.

Bohnsack, J.A., A. Eklund and A.M. Szmant. 1997. Artificial reef research: Is there more than the attraction-production issue? Fisheries. 22: 14-16.

Coleman, F.C., C.C. Koenig and L.A. Collins. 1996. Reproductive styles of shallow-water grouper (Pisces: Serranidae) in the eastern Gulf of Mexico and the consequences of fishing spawning aggregations. Env. Biol. Fish. 47: 129-141.

Gilmore, R.G., and R.S. Jones. 1992. Color variation and associated behavior in the epinepheline groupers *Mycteroperca microlepis* (Goode and Bean) and *M. phenax* (Jordan and Swain). Bull. Mar. Sci. 51: 83-103.

Hixon, M.A. and J.P. Beets. 1993. Predation, prey refuges, and the structure of coral-reef fish assemblages. Ecol Monogr. 63: 77-101.

Huntsman, G.R. and W.E. Schaaf. 1994. Simulation of the impact of fishing on reproduction of a protogynous grouper, the graysby. N. Amer. J. of Fish. Management. 14: 41-52.

Jennings, S. and N.V.C. Polunin. 1996. Impacts of fishing on tropical reef ecosystems. Ambio. 25: 44-49.

Lindberg, W.J. and J.L. Loftin. 1998. Effects of artificial reef characteristics and fishing mortality on gag (*Mycteroperca microlepis*) productivity and reef fish community structure. Florida Dept. of Environmental Protection.

Manooch, C.S. III. 1987. Age and growth of snappers and groupers. "Tropical Snappers and Groupers: Biology and Fisheries Management." (J.J. Polovina and S. Ralston, eds.) Boulder, CO: Westview Press.

McClanahan,T.R. 1988. Coexistence in a sea urchin guild and its implications to coral reef diversity and degradation. Oecolgia. 77: 210-218.

McClanahan, T.R. 1992. Resource utilization, competition and predation: a model and example from coral reef grazers. Ecol. Model. 61: 195-215.

McClanahan, T.R. and N.A. Muthiga. 1988. Changes in Kenyan coral reef community structure and function due to exploitation. Hydrobiology. 166: 269-276.

Ogden, J. C. 1997. Marine managers look upstream for connections. Science. 278: 1414-1415.

Pauly, D., V. Christensen, J. Dalsgaard, R. Froese, and T. Francisco. 1998. Fishing down marine food webs. Science. 279: 860-863.

Polovina, J.J. and I. Sakai. 1989. Impacts of artificial reefs on fishery production in Shimarmaki, Japan. Bull Mar. Sci. 44: 997-1,003.

Roberts, C.M. 1997. Connectivity and management of Caribbean coral reefs. Science. 278: 1454-1456.

Russ, G.R. and A.C. Alcala. 1998. Natural fishing experiments in marine reserves 1983-1993: community and trophic responses. Coral Reefs. 17: 383-397.

Russ, G.R. and A.C. Alcala. 1998. Natural fishing experiments in marine reserves 1983-1993: roles of life history and fishing intensity in family response. Coral Reef. 17: 399-416.

Sadovy, Y. 1994a. Summary of papers presented at the grouper symposium of the 43rd annual meeting of the Gulf and Caribbean Fisheries Institute in Miami, Florida (Nov. 1990). Proc. Gulf Carib. Fish. Inst. 43: 482-484.

Sadovy, Y. 1994b. Grouper stocks of the western central Atlantic: the need for management and management needs. Proc. Gulf Carib. Fish. Inst. 43: 43-64.

Sadovy, Y. and A. Eklund. In press. Synopsis of biological information on *Epinephelus striatus* (Bloch, 1792), the Nassau grouper and *E. Itajara* (Lichtenstein, 1822) the jewfish. NOAA Tech. Rep. Ser.

Sluka, R., M. Chiappone, K.M. Sullivan and R. Wright. 1996. Habitat and life in the Exuma Cays, the Bahamas: the status of grouper and coral reefs in the northern cays. The Nature Conservancy, Florida and Caribbean Marine Conservation Science Center. Nassau, Bahamas: Media Publishing Ltd.,

Williams, N. 1998. Overfishing disrupts entire ecosystems. Science. 279: 809.

ANGELFISHES 138 - 151

Blasiola, G.C. 1976. *Centropyge aurantonotus* Burgess, 1974 (Pisces: Chaetodontidae): range, extension, and redescription. Bull. Mar. Sci. 26: 564-568.

Bruce, R.W. 1980. Protogynous hermaphroditism in two marine angelfishes. Copeia. 2: 353-355.

Clarke, R.D. 1977. Habitat distribution and species diversity of Chaetodontid and Pomacentrid fishes near Bimini, Bahamas. Mar. Biol. 40: 277-289.

Hourigan, T.F. and C.D. Kelley. 1985. Histology of the gonads and observations on the social behavior of the Caribbean angelfish *Holacanthus tricolor*. Mar. Biol. 88: 311-322.

Hourigan, T.F., F.G. Stanton, P.J. Motta, C.D. Kelley and B. Carlson. 1989. The feeding ecology of three species of Caribbean angelfishes (family Pomacanthidae). Env. Biol. of Fish. 24: 105-116.

Moyer, J.T., R.E. Thresher and P.L. Colin. 1983. Courtship, spawning and inferred social organization of American angelfishes (Genera *Pomacnathus, Holacanthus and Centropyge;* Pomacanthidae). Env Biol. of Fishes. 9: 25-39.

Neudecker, S. and P.S. Lobel. 1981. Mating systems of Chaetodintid and Pomacanthid fishes at St. Croix. Z. Tierpsychol. 59: 299-318.

Randall, J.E. 1967. Food habits of reef fishes of the West Indies. Stud. Trop. Ocean. 5: 665-847.

Thresher, R.E. 1984. "Reproduction in Reef Fishes" Neptune City, NJ: T.F.H. Publications.

BASSLETS 152 - 155

Asoh, K. and T. Yoshikawa. 1996. Nesting behavior, male parental care, and embryonic development in the fairy basslet, *Gramma loreto*. Copeia. 1-8.

Asoh, K. and D.Y. Shapiro. 1997. Bisexual juvenile gonad and gonochorism in the fairy basslet, *Gramma loreto*. Copeia. 22-31.

Freeman S. and W. Alevizon. 1983. Aspects of territorial behavior and habitat distribution of the fairy basslet, *Gramma loreto*. Copeia. 3: 829-832.

Thresher, R.E. 1980. "Reef fish: behavior and ecology on the reef and in the aquarium." St. Petersburg, FL: Palmetto Publ.Co.

BLENNIES 156 - 175

Buchheim, J.R. and M.A. Hixon. 1992. Competition for shelter holes in the coral-reef fish *Acanthemblemaria spinosa* Metzelaar. J. Exp. Mar. Biol. Ecol. 164: 45-54.

Clarke, R.D. 1994. Habitat partitioning by chaenopsid blennies in Belize and the Virgin Islands. Copeia. 2: 398-405.

Colin, P.L. and M.R. Gomon. 1973. Notes on the behavior, ecology and distribution of *Lucayablennius zingaro* (Pisces: Clinidae). Carib. J. Sci. 13: 56-61.

Cote, I.M. and W. Hunte. 1989. Male and female mate choice in the redlip blenny: why bigger is better. Anim. Behav. 38: 78-88.

Greenfield, D.W. and T.A. Greenfield. 1982. Habitat and resource partitioning between two species of *Acanthemblemaria* (Pisces: Chaenopsidae), with comments on the chaos hypothesis. Smithsonian Cont. Mar. Sci. 12: 499-507.

Greenfield, D.W. and R.K. Johnson. 1981. The blennioid fishes of Belize and Honduras, Central America, with comments on their systematics, ecology and distribution (Blenniidae, Chaenopsidae, Clinidae, Tripterygiidae).

References

Fieldiana, Zool. N.S. 8: 1-106.

Greenfield D.W. and R.K. Johnson. 1990. Community structure of western Caribbean blennioid fishes. Copeia. 2: 433-438.

Hunte W. and I.M. Cote. 1989. Recruitment in the redlip blenny, *Ophioblennius atlanticus*: is space limited? Coral Reefs. 8: 45-50.

Labelle, M. and J.R. Nursall. 1985. Some aspects of the early life history of the redlip blenny, *Ophioblennius atlanticus* (Teleostei: Blenniidae). Copeia. 1: 39-49.

Marraro, C.H. 1978. Some aspects of the life history and behavioral ecology of the redlip blenny (*Ophioblennius atlanticus*) (Pisces: Blenniidae). Master's Thesis, Dept. Zoology, Univ. Alberta, Edmonton, Canada. Unpublished

Marraro, C.H. and J.R. Nursall. 1983. The reproductive periodicity and behaviour of *Ophioblennius atlanticus* (Pisces: Blenniidae) at Barbados. Can. J. Zool. 61: 317-325.

Nursall, J.R. 1977. Territoriality in redlip blennies (*Ophioblennius atlanticus* - Pisces: Blenniidae).J. Zool. (London). 182: 205-223.

Robins, C.R. and J.E. Randall. 1965. Three new western Atlantic fishes of the Blennioid genus *Chaenopsis*, with notes on the related *Lucayablennius zingaro*. Proc. Acad. Nat. Sci. Philadelphia. 117(6): 213-237.

Smith-Vaniz, W.F. and F.J. Palacio. 1974. Atlantic fishes of the genus *Acanthemblemaria,* with descriptions of three new species and comments on Pacific species (Clinidae: Chaenopsidae). Proc. Acad. Natl. Sci. Philadelphia. 125: 197-224.

Stephens, J.S. Jr., E.S. Hobson and R.K. Johnson. 1966. Notes on distribution, behavior and morphological variation in some chaenopsid fishes from the tropical eastern Pacific, with descriptions of two new species, *Acanthemblemaria castroi* and *Corallozetus springeri*. Copeia. 424-438.

BUTTERFLYFISHES 176 - 179

Birkeland, C. and S. Neudecker. 1981. Foraging behavior of two Caribbean Chaetondontids: *Chaetodon capistratus* and *C. aculeatus*. Copeia 1981: 169-178.

Clavijo, I.E. 1985. A probable hybrid butterflyfish from the western Atlantic. Copeia. 1985: 235-238.

Colin, P.L. 1989. Aspects of the spawning of western Atlantic butterflyfishes (Pisces: Chaetodontidae). Env. Biol. Fishes. 25: 131-141.

Colin, P.L. and I.E. Clavijo. 1988. Spawning activity of fishes producing pelagic eggs on a shelf edge coral reef, southwestern Puerto Rico. Bull. Mar. Sci. 43: 249-279.

Fricke, H.A. 1986. Pair swimming and mutual partner guarding in monogamous butterflyfish (Pisces, Chaetodontidae): a joint advertisement for territory. Ethology 73: 307-333.

Gore, M.A. 1982. The effect of a flexible spacing system on the social organization of coral reef fish, *Chaetodon capistratus*. Behaviour 85: 118-148.

Lasker, H.R. 1985. Prey preferences and browsing pressure of the butterflyfish *Chaetodon capistratus* on Caribbean gorgonians. Mar. Ecol. Prog. Ser. 21: 213-220.

Neudecker, S. and P.S. Lobel. 1982. Mating systems of chaetodontid and pomacanthid fishes at St. Croix. Z. Tierpsychol. 59: 299-318.

Pitts, P.A. 1991. Comparative use of food and space by three Bahamian butterflyfishes. Bull. Mar. Sci. 48(3): 749-756.

Randall, J.E. 1967. Food habits of reef fishes of the West Indies. Stud. Trop. Ocean. 5: 665-847.

Reese, E.S. 1989. Orientation behavior of butterflyfishes (family Chaetodontidae) on coral reefs: spatial learning of route specific landmarks and cognitive maps. Env. Biol. Fishes. 25: 79-86.

Thresher, R. E. 1984. "Reproduction in Reef Fishes" Neptune City, NJ: T.F.H. Publications.

DAMSELFISHES 180 - 207

Albrecht, H. 1969. Behaviour of four species of Atlantic damselfishes from Colombia, South America (*Abudefduf saxatilis, A. taurus, Chromis multilineata, C. Cyanea*; Pisces, Pomacentridae). Z. Tierpsychol. 26: 662-676.

Cummings, W.C. 1968. Reproduction habits of the sergeant major, *Abudefduf saxatilis* (Pisces, Pomacentridae), with comparative notes on four other damselfishes in the Bahama Islands. Ph.D. Dissertation Univ. of Miami, Miami, FL.

de Boer, B.A. 1978. Factors influencing the distribution of the damselfish *Chromis cyanea* (Poey), Pomacentridae, on a reef at Curacao, Netherlands Antilles. Bull. Mar. Sci. 28: 550-565.

Draud, M., D.E. Itzkowitz and M. Itzkowitz. 1990. Co-defense of territory space by two species of coral reef fishes. Bull. Mar. Sci. 47: 721-724.

Gronell, Ann. 1980. Space utilization by the cocoa damselfish, *Eupomacentrus variabilis* (Pisces: Pomacentridae). Bull. Mar. Sci. 30: 237-251.

Itzkowitz, M. 1977. Group organization of a territorial damselfish, *Eupomacentrus planifrons*. Behaviour 10: 125-137.

Itzkowitz, M. 1985. Aspects of the population dynamics and reproductive success in the permanently territorial beaugregory damselfish. Mar. Behav. Physiol. 12: 57-69.

Itzkowitz, M. and T. Koch. 1991. Relationship between damselfish egg loss and brittlestars. Bull. Mar. Sci. 48: 164-167.

Knapp, R.A. 1993. The influence of egg survivorship on the subsequent nest fidelity of female bicolour damselfish, *Stegastes partitus*. Anim. Behav. 46: 111-121.

Knapp, R.A. and R.R. Warner 1991. Male parental care and female choice in the bicolor damselfish, *Stegastes partitus*: bigger is not always better. Anim. Behav. 41: 747-756.

Knapp, R.A., P.C. Sikkel and V.T. Vredenburg. 1995. Age of clutches in nests and the within-nest spawning-site preferences of three damselfish species (Pomacentridae). Copeia. 78-88.

Lobel, P.S. 1980. Herbivory by damselfishes and their role in coral reef community ecology. Bull. Mar. Sci. 30: 273-289.

Mahoney B.M. 1981. An examination of interspecific territoriality in the dusky damselfish, *Eupomacentrus dorsopunicans* Poey. Bull. Mar. Sci. 31: 141-146.

McDonald G.D. 1993. Reproductive behavior and social dynamics of the yellowtail damselfish, *Microspathodon chrysurus*. Master's Thesis, Univ. of Puerto Rico.

Myrberg, A.A. 1972. Ethnology of the bicolor damselfish *Eupomacentrus partitus*: a comparative analysis of laboratory and field behaviour. Anim. Behav. Monogr. 5: 197-283.

Myrberg, A.A. 1972. Social dominance and territoriality in the bicolor damselfish, *Eupomacentrus partitus*. Behaviour. 4: 207-231.

Myrberg, A.A., B.D. Brahy and A.R. Emery. 1967. Field observations on reproduction of the damselfish, *Chromis multilineata* (Pomacentridae), with additional notes on general behavior. Copeia. 4: 819-827.

Myrberg, A.A., M. Mohler and J.D. Catala. 1986. Sound production by males of a coral reef fish (*Pomacentrus partitus*): its significance to females. Anim. Behav. 34: 913-923.

Peterson, C.W. 1990. The occurrence and dynamics of clutch loss and filial cannibalism in two Caribbean damselfishes. J. Exp. Mar. Biol. Ecol. 1990: 117-133.

Petersen, C.W. and H.C. Hess. 1991. The adaptive significance of spawning synchronization in the Caribbean damselfish, *Stegastes dorsopunicans* (Poey). J. Exp. Mar. Biol. Ecol. 151: 155-167.

Pressley, P.H. 1980. Lunar periodicity in the spawning of yellowtail damselfish, *Microspathodon chrysurus*. Env. Biol. Fish. 5: 153-159.

Robertson, D.R. 1984. Cohabitation of competing territorial damselfishes on a Caribbean coral reef. Ecology. 65: 1121-1135.

Robertson, D.R., C.W. Petersen and J.D. Brawn. Lunar reproductive cycles of benthic-brooding reef fishes: reflections of larval biology or adult biology? Ecol. Soc. Of America. 60: 311-329.

Schmale, M.C. 1981. Sexual selection and reproductive success in male of the bicolor damselfish, *Eupomacentrus partitus* (Pisces: Pomacentridae). Anim. Behav. 29: 1172-1184.

Thresher, R.E. 1984. "Reproduction in Reef Fishes" Neptune City, NJ: T.F.H. Publications.

Waldner, R.E. and D.R. Robertson. 1980. Patterns of habitat partitioning by eight species of territorial Caribbean damselfishes (Pisces: Pomacentridae). Bull. Mar. Sci. 30: 171-186.

Wellington G.M. and B.C. Victor. 1989. Planktonic larval duration of one hundred species of Pacific and Atlantic damselfishes (Pomacentiedae). Mar. Biol. 101: 557-567.

Williams, A.H. 1978. Ecology of threespot damselfish: social organization, age structure, and population stability. J. Exp. Mar. Biol. Ecol. 34: 197-213.

DRAGONETS 208 - 211

FLOUNDERS 212 -217

Konstantinou H. and D.C. Shen. 1995. The social and reproductive behavior of the eyed flounder, *Bothus ocelltus*, with notes on the spawning of *Bothus lunatus* and *Bothus ellipticus*. Env. Biol. Fish. 44: 311-324.

Moyle, P.B. and J.J.Cech, Jr. 1996. Fishes — An Introduction to Ichthyology. 3rd Ed. New Jersey: Prentice Hall.

Norman, J.R. 1934. A systematic monograph of the flatfishes (Heterosomata). London: Trustees of the British Museum. 459.

Ramachandran, V.S., C.W. Tyler, R.L. Gregory, D. Rogers-Ramachandran, S. Duensing, C. Pillsbury and C. Ramachandran. 1996. Rapid adaptive camouflage in tropical flounders. Nature. 379: 815-818.

FROGFISHES 218 - 227

Michael, S.W. 1998. "Reef Fishes Vol. I" Shelburne, VT: Microcosm Ltd.

Theodore W.P. and D.B. Grobeeker. 1987. "Frogfishes of the World." Stanford, CA: Stanford Univ. Press.

Theodore W.P. and D.B. Grobeeker. 1990. Frogfishes. Scien. Amer. June: 96-103.

GROUPERS & SEA BASSES 228 -269

Aguilar-Perera, A. 1994. Preliminary observations of the spawning aggregation of Nassau grouper, *Epinephelus striatus*, at Majahual, Quintana Roo, Mexico. Proc. Gulf Carib. Fish. Inst. 43: 112-122.

Aguilar-Perera, A. and W. Aguilar-Dávila. 1996. A spawning aggregation of Nassau grouper, *Epinephelus striatus* (Pisces: Serranidae) in the Mexican Caribbean. Env. Biol. Fish. 45: 351-361.

Bannerot, S., W.W. Fox, Jr., and J.E. Powers. 1987. Reproductive strategies and the management of snappers and groupers in the Gulf of Mexico and Caribbean. "Tropical snappers and groupers: biology and fisheries management." (J.J. Polovina and S. Ralston, eds.) Boulder, CO: Westview Press. 561-603.

Barlow, G.W. 1975. On the sociobiology of some hermaphroditic serranid fishes, the hamlets, in Puerto Rico. Mar. Biol. 33: 295-300.

Beets J. and A. Friedlander. 1992. Stock analysis and management strategies for red hind, *Epinephelus guttatus*, in the U.S. Virgin Islands. Proc. Gulf Carib. Fish. Inst. 42: 66-80.

References

Bohnsack, J.A. 1994. How marine fishery reserves can improve reef fisheries. Proc. Gulf Carib. Fish. Inst. 43: 217-241.

Carter, J., G.J. Marrow and V. Pryor. 1994. Aspects of the ecology and reproduction of Nassau grouper (*Epinephelus striatus*) off the coast of Belize, Central America. Proc. Gulf Carib. Fish. Inst. 43: 65-111.

Clark, J.A., W.E. Farrell and W.R. Peltier. 1978. Global changes in postglacial sea level: a numerical calculation. Quat. Res. 9: 265-278.

Colin, P.L. 1992. Reproduction of the Nassau grouper, *Epinephelus striatus* (Pisces: Serranidae) and its relationship to environmental conditions. Env. Biol. Fish. 34: 357-377.

Colin, P.L. 1994. Preliminary investigations of reproductive activity of the jewfish, *Epinephelus itajara*. (Pisces: Serranidae). Proc. Gulf Carib. Fish. Inst. 43: 138-147.

Colin, P.L., D.Y. Shapiro and D. Weiler. 1987. Aspects of the reproduction of two species of grouper, *Epinephelus guttatus* and *E. striatus*, in the West Indies. Bull. Mar. Sci. 40: 220-230.

Domeier, M.L. 1994. Speciation in the serranid fish *Hypoplectrus*. Bull. Mar. Sci. 54(1): 103-141.

Domeier, M.L. and P.L. Colin. 1997. Tropical reef fish spawning aggregations: defined and reviewed. Bull. Mar. Sci. 60(3): 698-726.

Eggleston, D.B. 1995. Recruitment in Nassau grouper, *Epinephelus striatus*: post-settlement abundance, microhabitat features, and ontogenetic habitat shifts. Mar. Ecol. Prog. Ser. 124: 9-22.

Fine, J.C. 1990. Groupers in love: spawning aggregations of Nassau groupers in Honduras. Sea Frontiers 36: 42-45.

Fischer, E.A. 1980a. The relationship between mating system and simultaneous hermaphroditism in the coral reef fish, *Hypoplectrus nigricans* (Serranidae). Anim. Behav. 28: 620-633.

Fischer, E.A. 1980b. Speciation in the hamlet (*Hypoplectrus*: Serranidae) - A continuing enigma. Copeia 4: 649-659.

Fischer, E.A. 1981. Sexual allocation in a simultaneously hermaphroditic reef fish, *Hypoplectrus nigricans*. Amer. Nat. 117: 64-82.

Fischer, E.A. 1984a. Egg trading in the chalk bass, *Serranus tortugarum*, a simultaneous hermaphrodite. Z. Tierpsychol. 66: 143-151.

Fischer, E.A. 1984b. Local mate competition and sex allocation in simultaneous hermaphrodites. Am. Nat. 124: 590-596.

Fischer, E.A. and C.W. Petersen. 1986. Social behavior of males and simultaneous hermaphrodites in the lantern bass. Ethnology 73: 235-246.

Fischer, E.A. and C.W. Petersen. 1987. The evolution of sexual patterns in the seabasses. BioScience. 37: 482-489

Grace, M., K.R. Rademacher and M. Russell. 1994. Pictorial guide to the groupers (Teleostei: Serranidae) of the Western North Atlantic. NOAA Tech. Report NMFS 118.

García-Moliner, G.E. 1986. Aspects of the social spacing, reproduction and sex reversal in the red hind, *Epinephelus guttatus*. Master's Thesis, Univ. of Puerto Rico, Mayaguez.

Gilmore, R.G., and R.S. Jones. 1992. Color variation and associated behavior in the epinepheline groupers *Mycteroperca microlepis* (Goode and Bean) and *M. phenax* (Jordan and Swain). Bull. Mar. Sci. 51: 83-103.

Graves, J.E. and R.H. Rosenblatt. 1980. Genetic relationships of the color morphs of the serranid fish *Hypoplectrus unicolor*. Evolution 34: 240-245.

Grover, J.J. 1993. Trophic ecology of pelagic early-juvenile Nassau grouper, *Epinephelus striatus*, during and early phase of recruitment into demersal habitats. Bull. Mar. Sci. 53(3): 1117-1125.

Huntsman, G.R. and W.E. Schaaf. 1994. Simulation of the impact of fishing on reproduction of a protogynous grouper, the graysby. N. Amer. J. of Fish. Management 14: 41-52.

Johnson, A.G., and L.A. Collins. 1994. Age-size structure of red grouper (*Epinephelus morio*), from the eastern Gulf of Mexico. Northeast Gulf of Mexico. Northeast Gulf Science 13(2): 101-106.

Koenig, C., F. Coleman and A. Eklund. 1998. Studies of the jewfish (*Epinephelus itajara*) in the eastern Gulf of Mexico. Report to The Curtis and Edith Munson Foundation.

Leonard, J.L. 1993. Sexual conflict in simultaneous hermaphrodites: Evidence from serranid fishes. Env. Biol. Fish. 36: 135-148.

Lobel, P.S. 1992. Sounds produced by spawning fishes. Env. Biol. Fish. 33: 351-358.

Manooch, C.S. III. 1987. Age and growth of snappers and groupers. "Tropical Snappers and Groupers: Biology and Fisheries Management." (J.J. Polovina and S. Ralston, eds.) Boulder, CO: Westview Press. 329-373.

Moe, M.A. 1969. Biology of the red grouper, *Epinephelus morio* (Valenciennes) from the eastern Gulf of Mexico. Florida Dept. Nat. Res., Res. Lab. Prof. Pap. Ser. 10: 1-95.

Mullaney, M.D. Jr. 1994. Ontogenetic shifts in the diet of gag, *Mycteroperca microlepis* (Pisces: Serranidae). Proc. Gulf Carib. Fish. Inst. 43: 432-445.

Nagelkerken, W.P. 1979. Biology of the graysby, *Epinephelus cruentatus*, of the coral reef of Curacao and other Caribbean islands. Stud. of the Fauna of Curacao and Other Caribbean Islands. 61:1-118.

Nemtzov, S.C., S.M. Kajiura and C.A. Lompart. 1993. Diel color phase changes in the coney, *Epinephelus fulvus* (Teleostei, Serranidae). Copeia 3: 883-885.

Petersen, C.W. 1995. Reproductive behavior, egg trading, and correlates of male mating success in the simultaneous hermaphrodite, *Serranus tabacarius*. Env. Biol. Fish. 43: 351-361.

Petersen, C.W. and E.A. Fischer. 1986. Mating system of the hermaphroditic coral-reef fish *Serranus baldwini*. Behav. Ecol. Sociobiol. 19: 171-178.

Powell, A.B. and J.W. Tucker. 1992. Egg and larval development of laboratory-reared Nassau grouper, *Epinephelus striatus* (Pisces, Serranidae). Bull. Mar. Sci. 50: 171-185.

References

Pressley, P.H. 1981. Pair formation and joint territoriality in a simultaneous hermaphrodite: the coral reef fish *Serranus tigrinus*. Z. Tierpsychol. 56: 33-46.

Randall, J.E. 1967. Food habits of reef fishes of the West Indies. Stud. Trop. Ocean. 5: 665-847.

Sadovy, Y. 1994a. Summary of papers presented at the grouper symposium of the 43rd annual meeting of the Gulf and Caribbean Fisheries Institute in Miami, Florida (Nov. 1990). Proc. Gulf Carib. Fish. Inst. 43: 482-484.

Sadovy, Y. 1994b. Grouper stocks of the western central Atlantic: the need for management and management needs. Proc. Gulf Carib. Fish. Inst. 43: 43-64.

Sadovy, Y., M. Figuerola and A. Román. 1992. Age and growth of red hind *Epinephelus guttatus*, in Puerto Rico and St. Thomas. Fish. Bull. 90: 516-528.

Sadovy, Y., P.L. Colin, and M.L. Domeier. 1994. Aggregation and spawning in the tiger grouper, *Mycteroperca tigris* (Pisces: Serranidae). Copeia. 2: 511-516.

Sadovy, Y., A. Rosario and A Román. 1994. Reproduction in an aggregating grouper, the red hind, *Epinephelus guttatus*. Env. Biol. Fish. 41: 269-286.

Sadovy, Y. and A. Eklund. In press. Synopsis of biological information on *Epinephelus striatus* (Bloch, 1792), the Nassau grouper and *E. Itajara* (Lichtenstein, 1822), the jewfish. NOAA Tech. Rep. Ser.

Scott, D. 1962. Effect of food quality on fecundity in rainbow trout *Salmo gairdneri*. J. Fish. Res. Boars Can. 19: 715-731.

Shapiro, D.Y., Y. Sadovy, and M.A. McGehee. 1993a. Size, composition, and spatial structure of the annual spawning aggregation of the red hind *Epinephelus guttatus* (Pisces: Serranidae). Copeia. 1993: 367-374.

Shapiro, D.Y., Y. Sadovy and M.A. McGehee. 1993b. Periodicity of sex change and reproduction in the red hind, *Epinephelus guttatus*, a protogynous grouper. Bull. Mar. Sci. 53: 399-406.

Shapiro, D.Y., G. Garcia-Moliner and Y. Sadovy. 1994. Social system of an inshore stock of the red hind grouper, *Epinephelus guttatus* (Pisces: Serranidae). Env. Biol. Fish. 41: 415-422.

Shenker, J.M., E.D. Maddox, E. Wishinski, A. Pearl, S.R. Thorrold and N. Smith. 1993. Onshore transport of settlement-stage Nassau grouper, *Epinephelus striatus*, and other fishes in Exuma Sound, Bahamas. Mar. Ecol. Prog. Ser. 98: 31-43.

Sluka, R., M. Chiappone, K.M. Sullivan and R. Wright. 1996. Habitat and life in the Exuma Cays, the Bahamas: The status of grouper and coral reefs in the northern cays. The Nature Conservancy, Florida and Caribbean Marine Conservation Science Center. Nassau, Bahamas: Media Publishing Ltd.

Smith, E.L. 1972. A spawning aggregation of Nassau grouper, *Epinephelus striatus* (Bloch). Trans. Amer. Fish. Soc. 101: 257-261.

Sullivan, K.M. 1994. Energetics of juvenile *Epinephelus* grouper: impact of summer temperatures and activity patterns on growth rates. Proc. Gulf Carib. Fish. Inst. 43: 148-167.

Thompson R. and J.L. Munro. 1978. Aspects of the biology and ecology of Caribbean reef fishes: Serranidae (hinds and groupers). J. Fish Biol. 12: 115-146.

Thresher, R.E. 1978. Polymorphism, mimicry, and the evolution of the hamlets. Bull. Mar. Sci. 28: 345-353.

Tucker, J.W., P.G. Bush and S.T. Slaybaugh. 1993. Reproductive patterns of Cayman Islands Nassau grouper (*Epinephelus striatus*) populations. Bull. Mar. Sci. 52(3): 961-969.

JAWFISHES 270 - 279

Colin, P.L. 1971. Interspecific relationships of the yellowhead jawfish, *Opistognathus aurifrons* (Pisces, Opistognathidae). Copeia. 3: 469-473.

Colin, P.L. 1972. Daily activity patterns and effects of environmental conditions on the behavior of the yellowhead jawfish, *Opistognathus aurifrons*, with notes on its ecology. Zoologica 57: 137-164.

Colin, P.L. 1973. Burrowing behavior of the yellowhead jawfish, *Opistognathus aurifrons*. Copeia. 1: 84-90.

Hess, H.C. 1993. Male mouthbrooding in jawfishes (Opistognathidae): constraints on polygamy. Bull. Mar. Sci. 52: 806-818.

Leong, D. 1967. Breeding and territorial behavior in *Opistognathus aurifrons* (Opistogathidae). Naturwissenschaften. 54: 97.

PARROTFISHES 280 - 299

Barlow. G.W. 1975. On the sociobiology of four Puerto Rican parrotfishes (Scaridae). Mar. Biol. 33: 281-293.

Bellwood, D.R. and J.H. Choat. 1990. A functional analysis of grazing in parrotfishes (family Scaridae): the ecological implications. Env. Biol. Fish. 28: 189-214.

Bruckner, A.W. and R.J. Bruckner. 1998a. Destruction of coral by *Sparisoma viride*. Coral Reefs 17: 350.

Bruckner A.W. and R.J. Bruckner. 1998b. Rapid-wasting disease: pathogen or predator? Science. 279: 2023-2025.

Bruggemann, J.H., M.W.M. Kuyper and A.M. Breeman. 1994. Comparative analysis of foraging and habitat use by the sympatric Caribbean parrotfish *Scarus vetula* and *Sparisoma viride* (Scaridae). Mar. Ecol. Prog. Ser. 112: 51-66.

Bruggemann, J.H., M.J.H. van Oppen and A.M. Breeman. 1994a. Foraging by the stoplight parrotfish *Sparisoma viride*. I. Food selection in different, socially determined habitats. Mar. Ecol. Prog. Ser. 106: 41-55.

Bruggemann, J.H., M.J.H. van Oppen and A.M. Breeman. 1994b. Foraging by the stoplight parrotfish *Sparisoma viride*. II intake and assimilation of food, protein and energy. Mar. Ecol. Prog. Ser. 106: 57-71.

References

Bruggemann, J.H., A.M. van Kessel, J.M. van Rooij, and A.M. Breeman. 1996. Bioerosion and sediment ingestion by the Caribbean parrotfish *Scarus vetula* and *Sparisoma viride*: implications of fish size, feeding mode and habitat use. Mar. Ecol. Prog. Ser. 134: 59-71.

Buckman N.S. and J.C. Ogden. 1972. Territorial behavior of the striped parrotfish *Scarus croicensis*. Bloch (Scaridae). Ecology. 54: 1377-1383.

Bythell, J.C. and E.H. Gladfelter. 1992. Ecological studies of Buck Island Reef National Monument, St. Croix, U.S. Virgin Islands. U.S. Dept. of the Interior, Nat. Park Serv. II: 40-61.

Bythell, J.C., E.H. Gladfelter and M. Bythell. 1993. Chronic and catastrophic natural mortality of three common Caribbean reef corals. Coral Reefs. 12: 143-152.

Cardwell, J.K. 1989. Behavioural endocrinology of the stoplight parrotfish, *Sparisoma viride*, a protogynous coral reef fish. Ph.D. Thesis, Univ. of British Columbia, Vancouver.

Choat, J.H. 1991. The biology of herbivorous fishes on coral reefs. "The Ecology of Fishes on Coral Reefs" (P.F. Sale, ed.) San Diego: Academic Press. 120-153.

Clavijo, I.E. 1983. Pair spawning and formation of a lek-like mating system in the parrotfish *Scarus vetula*. Copeia. 1: 253-256.

Clifton, K.E. 1989. Territory sharing by the Caribbean striped parrotfish, *Scarus iserti*: patterns of resource abundance, group size and behaviour. Anim. Behav. 37: 90-103.

Colin P.L. 1978. Daily and summer-winter variation in mass spawning of the striped parrotfish, *Scarus croicensis*. Fish. Bull. 76: 117-124.

Dubin, R.E. 1981. Pair spawning in the princess parrotfish, *Scarus taeniopterus*. Copeia. 2: 475-477.

Dubin, R.E. and J.D. Baker. 1982. Two types of cover-seeking behavior at sunset by the princess parrotfish, *Scarus taeniopterus*, at Barbados, West Indies. Bull. Mar. Sci. 32: 572-583.

Farm, B.P. 1993. Territory dynamics in the bucktooth parrotfish (Sparisoma radian). Ph.D. Dissertation, Univ. of Minnesota.

Koltes, K.H. 1993. Aspects of the reproductive biology and social structure of the stoplight parrotfish, *Sparisoma viride,* at Grand Turk, Turks and Caicos Islands, B.W.I. Bull. Mar. Sci. 52: 792-805.

Lobel, P.S. and J.C. Ogden. Foraging by the herbivorous parrotfish *Sparisoma radians*. Mar. Biol. 64: 173-183.

Marconato, A. and D.Y. Shapiro. 1996. Sperm allocation, sperm production and fertilization rates in the bucktooth parrotfish. Anim. Behav. 52: 971-980.

McAfee, S.T. and S.G. Morgan. 1996. Resource use by five sympatric parrotfishes in the San Blas Archipelago, Panama. Mar. Biol. 125: 427-437.

Ogden J.C. and N.S. Buckman. 1973. Movements, foraging groups, and diurnal migrations of the striped parrotfish *Scarus croicensis* Bloch (Scaridae). Ecology. 54: 589-596.

Randall, J.E. 1967. Food habits of reef fishes of the West Indies. Stud. Trop. Ocean. 5: 665-847.

Randall, J.E. and H.A. Randall. 1963. The spawning and early development of the Atlantic parrot fish *Sparisoma rubripinne*, with notes on other Scarid and Labrid fishes. Zoologica. 48: 49-58.

Robertson, D.R. and R.R. Warner. 1978. Sexual patterns in the labroid fishes of the Western Caribbean, II: The parrotfishes (Scaridae). Smiths. Contr. Zool. 155: 1-26.

Schmitt, E.F. 1997. The influence of herbivorous fishes on coral reef communities with low sea urchin abundance: A study among reef community types and seasons in the Florida Keys. Ph.D. Dissertation, Univ. of Miami, Coral Gables, FL.

Shapiro, D.Y. 1991. Intraspecific variability in social systems of coral reef fishes. "The Ecology of Fishes on Coral Reefs" (P.F. Sale, ed.) London: Academic Press. 331-355.

Thresher, R.E. 1984."Reproduction in Reef Fishes" Neptune City, NJ: TFH Publications.

Van Rooij, J.M., E. de Jong, F. Vaandrager and J.J. Videler. 1996. Resource and habitat sharing by the stoplight parrotfish, *Sparisoma viride*, a Caribbean reef herbivore. Env. Biol. Fish. 47: 81-91.

Van Rooij, J.M., J.P. Kok and J.J. Videler. 1996. Local variability in population structure and density of the protogynous reef herbivore *Sparisoma viride*. Env. Biol. Fish. 47: 65-80.

Van Rooij, J.M., F.J. Kroon and J.J. Videler. 1996. The social and mating system of the herbivorous reef fish *Sparisoma viride:* one-male versus multi-male groups. Env. Biol. Fish. 47: 353-378.

SHARKS 300 - 309

Pratt, H.L. and J.C.C. Carrier. 1995. Wild mating of the nurse shark. Nat. Geo. 187: 44-53.

Strong, W.R. 1990. Hammerhead shark predation on stingrays: an observation of prey handling by *Sphyrna mokarran*. Copeia. 3: 836-840.

SURGEONFISHES 310 - 315

Alevizon, W.S. 1976. Mixed schooling and its possible significance in a tropical western Atlantic parrotfish and surgeonfish. Copeia. 4: 796-798.

Bardach, J.E. 1958. On the movements of certain Bermuda reef fishes.Ecology 39: 139-146.

Colin, P.L. 1985. Spawning of western Atlantic surgeonfishes. Natl. Geo.Soc. Rpts. 18: 243-250.

Colin, P.L. and I.E. Clavijo. 1988. Spawning activity of fishes producing pelagic eggs on a shelf edge coral reef, southwestern Puerto Rico. Bull. Mar. Sci.43: 249-279.

Clavijo, I.E. 1974. A contribution on feeding habits of three species of Acanthurids (pisces) from the West Indies. Master's Thesis. Florida Atlantic Univ. Boca Raton, FL.

Debrot, A.O. and A.A. Myrberg, Jr. 1988. Intraspecific avoidance as aproximate cause for mixed-species shoaling by juveniles of a western Atlantic surgeonfish, *Acanthurus bahianus*. Bull. Mar. Sci. 104-106.

Foster, S.A. 1985. Group foraging by a coral reef fish: a mechanism forgaining access to defended sources. Anim. Behav. 33: 782-792.

Risk, A. 1998. The effects of interactions with reef residents on the settlement and subsequent persistence of ocean surgeonfish, *Acanthurus bahianus*. Env. Biol. Fish. 51: 377-389.

Robertson, D.R. 1988. Abundances of surgeonfishes on patch-reefs inCaribbean Panama: due to settlement, or post-settlement events? Mar.Biol. 97: 495-501.

Robertson, D.R. 1991. Increase in surgeonfish populations after mass mortality of the sea urchin *Diadema antillarum* in Panama indicate food limitation. Mar. Biol. 111: 437-444.

Winterbottom, R. 1971. Movement of the caudal spine of some surgeonfishes (Acanthiurdae, Perciformes). Copeia. 3: 562-566.

TILEFISHES 316 - 321

Baird, T.A. 1988. Female and male territoriality and mating system of the sand tilefish, *Malacanthus plumieri*. Env. Biol. Fish. 22: 101-116.

Baird. T.A. and N.R. Liley. 1989. The evolutionary significance of harem polygamy in the sand tilefish, *Malacanthus plumieri:* resource of female defence? Anim. Behav. 38: 817-829.

Clark, E., J.S. Rabin and S. Holderman. 1988. Reproductive behavior and social organization in the sand tilefish, *Malacanthus plumieri*. Env. Biol. Fish. 22: 273-286.

WRASSES 322 - 343

Colin, P.L. 1982. Spawning and larval development of the hogfish *Lachnolaimus maximus* (Pisces: Labridae). Fish. Bull. 80: 853-862.

Marconato, A., D.Y. Shapiro, C.W. Petersen, R.R. Warner, and T. Yoshikawa. 1997. Methodological analysis of fertilization rate in the bluehead wrasse *Thalassoma bifasciatum:* pair versus group spawns. Mar. Ecol. Prog. Ser. 161: 61-70.

Nemtzov, S.C. 1992. Intraspecific variation in the social and mating behavior of Caribbean razorfishes. (Teleostei, Labridae) Ph.D. Dissertation. State Univ. of New York, Stony Brook.

Randall, J.E. and G.L. Warmke. 1967. The food habits of the hogfish (*Lachnolaimus maximus*), a labrid fish from the western Atlantic. Carib. JSci. 7: 141-143.

Reinboth, R. 1973. Dualistic reproductive behavior in the protogynous wrasse *Thalassoma bifasciatum* and some observations on its day-night changeover. Helgolander Wiss. Meersunters. 24: 174-191.

Robertson D.R. and S.G. Hoffman. 1977. The roles of female mate choice and predation in the mating systems of some tropical Labroid fishes. Z. Tierpsychol. 45: 298-320.

Shapiro, D.Y., A. Marconato and T. Yoshikawa. 1994. Sperm economy in a coral reef fish, *Thalassoma bifasciatum*. Ecology. 75: 1334-1344.

Thresher, R.E. 1979. Social behavior and ecology of two sympatic wrasses (Labridae: *Halichoeres* spp.) off the coast of Florida. Mar. Biol. 53: 161-172.

Victor, B.C. 1986. Duration of the planktonic larval stage of one hundred species of Pacific and Atlantic wrasses (family Labridae). Mar. Biol. 90:317-326.

Victor, B.C. 1987. The mating system of the Caribbean rosy razorfish, *Xyrichtys martinicensis.* Bull. Mar. Sci. 40: 152-160.

Warner, R.R. and E.T. Schultz. 1992. Sexual selection and male characteristics in the bluehead wrasse, *Thalassoma bifasciatum:* mating site acquisition, mating site defense, and female choice. Evol. 46: 1421-1442.

THE REEF SET

by
Paul Humann

REEF FISH IDENTIFICATION FLORIDA-CARIBBEAN-BAHAMAS
The book that revolutionized fish watching! Enlarged, 2nd edition.
428 pp., over 500 color plates, plastic covers, comb binding. $39.95

REEF CREATURE IDENTIFICATION FLORIDA-CARIBBEAN-BAHAMAS
More than 30 marine life scientists from eight nations collaborated with the author to compile the most comprehensive and accurate visual identification guide of reef invertebrates ever published for the region.
344 pp., 478 color plates, plastic covers, comb binding. $37.95

REEF CORAL IDENTIFICATION FLORIDA-CARIBBEAN-BAHAMAS
252 pp., 475 color plates, plastic covers, comb binding. $32.95

Shelf Case for the three volume REEF SET $10.00
Three volume REEF SET with Shelf Case $115.00

REEF FISH IDENTIFICATION CD-ROM FLORIDA-CARIBBEAN-BAHAMAS
More than 1,600 images at your fingertips. Digital book. A series of comprehensive, programmable interactive learning games plus many additional features. $39.95

REEF CREATURE AND CORAL CD-ROM FLORIDA-CARIBBEAN-BAHAMAS
2,000 Images. Six programmable, interactive learning games. $39.95

REEF FISH IDENTIFICATION – GALAPAGOS $34.95
COASTAL FISH IDENTIFICATION – CALIFORNIA TO ALASKA $32.95

Fish-In-A-Pocket Plastic, waterproof mini-books that go underwater with you!
4 3/4" X 6", 24 pages, 132 photographs. $9.95 each
REEF FISH In-A-Pocket FLORIDA-CARIBBEAN-BAHAMAS
REEF CREATURE In-A-Pocket FLORIDA-CARIBBEAN-BAHAMAS
REEF FISH In-A-Pocket INDO-PACIFIC

You may purchase any of the above products at your dive retailer or contact:
NEW WORLD PUBLICATIONS INC.
1861 Cornell Rd. Jacksonville, FL 32207
1-800-737-6558 www.fishid.com

Glossary

benthic – Relating to the bottom of a body of water.

carnivore – A species that preys on animals. Page 45

chromatophores – Irregular-shaped cells in the skin of fishes that darken or lighten to modify colors. Page 86

claspers – Organs modified from the inner edge of each pelvic fin of male sharks and rays. Sperm is transferred through a groove in the clasper into a female's cloaca. Page 29

cleaners – Certain species of shrimps or young fishes that prey on tiny crustaceans infesting fishes. Page 96

cleaning station – A location continuously inhabited by cleaner fishes and, or shrimps. Page 96

cloaca – Ventral opening of sharks and rays used for reproduction and excretion. Page 29

clutch – A cluster of eggs. Page 27

filamentous or turf algae – Prolific, fast-growing hair-like algae that is the primary food source of many herbivores. Page 85

gametes – Eggs and sperm. Page 8

generalist – A species that feeds on a variety of foods without a specific preference for one type. Page 47

gonochorist – An individual remaining the same sex for life. Page 18

harem – A group of two or more females and a single dominate male living together as a stable group within a defended territory.

herbivore – An animal that feeds primarily on plants. Page 45

home range – An area frequented but not defended by an individual. Page 48

initial phase – In sex-changing species, numerous, typically young, drab sexually mature individuals. Depending on the species, may include both males and females but generally females. Page 11

juvenile – The developmental stage preceding sexual maturity.

metapopulation – Widely separated populations of the same species that are isolated from one another by open sea or bottom unsuitable for larval settlement. Page 41

monogamy – Mating exclusively with a single partner. Page 18

nuclear hunting – Different species of carnivores or piscivores feeding in association with eels or octopuses. Page 67

otolith – One of three tiny calcium carbonate ear stones used for balance and sound detection, located within the semicircular canals at the base of the braincase in all bony fishes. Page 34

ontogenetic shift – Habitat change during the growth of young fishes – often due to dietary needs. Page 42

opportunist – A species that willingly eats food not included in its normal diet. Page 47

pelagic – Oceanic.